PRINCIPLES OF REAL ESTATE ANALYSIS:

Law Finance Appraisal and Investment

MICHAEL J. CREAN, D.B.A.
University of Denver

D. VAN NOSTRAND COMPANY
New York Cincinnati Toronto London Melbourne

D. Van Nostrand Company Regional Offices:
New York Cincinnati

D. Van Nostrand Company International Offices:
London Toronto Melbourne

Library of Congress Catalog Card Number: 78-62189
ISBN: 0-442-21249-6

Published by D. Van Nostrand Company
135 West 50th Street, New York, N.Y. 10020

10 9 8 7 6 5 4 3 2 1

Preface

PRINCIPLES OF REAL ESTATE ANALYSIS: LAW, FINANCE, APPRAISAL, AND INVESTMENT deals with the basics of real estate and prepares for state licensing exams. The book also goes beyond the basics to cover, in greater detail, the four functional areas of real estate—law, finance, appraisal, and investment. It develops advanced topics such as internal rate of return and mortgage-equity analysis to motivate the student for further study and research.

A unique aspect of the book is that, while it includes fewer topics than other similar texts, it presents these in greater depth. The author has, therefore, concentrated on the four functional areas of real estate: law, finance, appraisal, and investment. These four areas represent, in the author's judgment, the most important areas in preparing to become a real estate analyst. In fact, many states have passed laws requiring evidence of formal schooling in these areas to maintain or acquire a real estate broker's license. Competence in these four areas may qualify the student for many different employment opportunities in the field of real estate.

This book is divided into five parts. Part I presents an overview of the real estate industry and its markets. Chapter 1 traces the history and development of the real estate industry and provides an understanding of the vast scope of opportunities available in it. Chapter 2 explains why real estate markets are seldom in equilibrium. Only with a solid understanding of the various real estate markets and urban growth patterns can a real estate entrepreneur be successful.

Part II explores the legal and practical side of real estate required for passing state licensing exams.

Part III provides an introduction to real estate finance. The various types of financing—primary and secondary mortgage markets and loan-underwriting processes for both residential and commercial real estate—are thoroughly explained.

Part IV presents both the theories and practical applications of real estate valuation. Valuation principles, economic analysis, and the three approaches to value are covered. Explanations of the income approach to value range from direct capitalization with an overall rate to simplified mortgage-equity analysis and the Ellwood Method.

Part V is unique for a real estate principles text because it includes four chapters on real estate investment. Such topics as real estate investment characteristics and investor objectives, real estate investment risks, measurement of real estate investment returns, and the tax factors of real estate investments are included. The investment section completes the presentation of the basic framework of real estate analysis.

Several appendixes supplement the text. Appendix A, Legal Descriptions of Real Property, supplements Chapter 5, and includes tables of land measurements and their metric system equivalents. The National Association of Realtors (NAR) Code of Ethics is given in Appendix B and an explanation of the nine affiliated institutes, societies, and councils of the NAR is included in Appendix C. Appendix D, which supplements Chapter 8, gives sample real estate contracts. To supplement the appraisal chapters, a replacement cost example is given in Appendix E, the FNMA-FHLMC appraisal report and guidelines for its use in Appendix F, and Ellwood tables are included in Appendix G. Finally, an extensive glossary of real estate terms provides a reference to the nomenclature required for studying the principles of real estate analysis.

An Instructor's Manual is available to accompany the text.

Acknowledgments

I took my first real estate class while attending the Wharton School of Finance and Commerce at the University of Pennsylvania. This principles course was taught by a local real estate broker, Mr. Carroll. It was his course and the practical approach he used in teaching the course that "turned me on" to real estate. I thank Mr. Carroll and hope he is still exciting other Wharton students about real estate.

I'd like to thank Professors Steve Messner, Byrl Boyce, and Bill Kinnard of the University of Connecticut, three of the best people in the country from which to learn about the field of real estate. Thanks also go to Bob Harvey, former dean at the University of Connecticut, now at Southern Methodist University, for contributing to the learning environment at Connecticut.

Professors Clyde Richey and Lee Fusilier, of the University of Colorado, are due thanks for having created a meaningful and flexible doctoral program in real estate and for having given me my first opportunities to publish. Mike Palmer, of the University of Colorado, is due special thanks; without his personal guidance and friendship I probably would never have completed my doctoral program.

Rick Porter, now an independent broker in Los Angeles, has been my constant counselor and reviewer. Rick's guidance and opinions have been invaluable to the completion of this book. We have been personal friends for a long time and now share a professional relationship.

Last, but not least, I thank my wife, Peggy, for all her consideration during the development of the text. Many social engagements and other matters were sacrificed to complete the book. Peggy also did most of the work on the glossary.

This book is dedicated to my mother, Marion J. Crean, because I want the world to know how grateful I am to her. Upon the death of my father, my mother was left with the responsibility of four sons aged 8 to 17. Single-handedly she raised and educated the four of us, the last of whom recently graduated from the University of Denver as a real estate major. Curiously enough, my other two brothers are also involved with real estate with a large insurance company. I know that Marty, Terry, and Kevin join me in saying thanks to that special lady to whom we all owe so much.

Contents

PART I

Overview

CHAPTER 1

Real Estate Industry

KEY TERMS

Realtor® A copyrighted trade name that can be used only by members of the National Association of Realtors®, formerly the National Association of Real Estate Boards
National Association of Realtors® The oldest and largest trade organization in the real estate industry, formed in 1908
Affiliates Suborganizations or specialized trade groups within the National Association of Realtors®
Developer One who organizes, coordinates, and supervises the acquisition of land, construction of improvements, financing, sales, and management of a complete real estate project
Subdivider One who legally separates land into separate parcels for disposition or development
Real estate appraiser One who estimates the value of real property for a fee
General contractor One who constructs buildings and supervises the several building trades required to complete a real estate project
Real estate broker An intermediary agent who earns a fee or commission for negotiating sales and/or leases of real property between two or more parties
Real estate salesperson A subagent of and one working for a real estate broker
Real property manager An agent of a real property owner hired to maintain the physical features, investment, and income of the owner's real estate assets

"Under all is the land."[1] If one ponders this statement, one will soon realize that real estate and its related businesses and professions encompass a very large industry, if not the largest of all industries in human history. After all, it has been estimated that approximately two-thirds of

1. National Association of Realtors®, *Code of Ethics* (Chicago: National Association of Realtors, 1974), p. 1.

the total wealth of the United States economy consists of real estate. *Fortune* magazine once ran an article about the success stories of millionaires under 25 years of age; the majority of these entrepreneurs had accumulated their wealth in the real estate industry.

When people think of the real estate industry, probably many first think of the real estate *salesperson* or *broker*, who is engaged in the *marketing* and *sale* of real property. However, when one considers that the real estate must first be *produced* and, most probably, *financed* before a *sale* can take place, a treasure chest of other, related occupations begins to open. Other people who work in the real estate industry include land speculators, subdividers, developers, surveyors, engineers, architects, land planners, site planners, city planners, lawyers, contractors, subcontractors, tradesmen, laborers, material suppliers, lenders, appraisers, consultants, educators, researchers, property managers, investors, interior designers, and innumerable government agencies, to name just a few. There are millions of people employed in the real estate industry. Later in this chapter more will be said of the roles of and interrelationships among the participants in this vast industry.

HISTORY AND DEVELOPMENT OF THE REAL ESTATE INDUSTRY

Before America

One can go back as far as the third century B.C. and study stone tablets containing records of the transfer of real property. One need only read the Bible to find many references to the ownership of real estate.

One can trace the ownership of real estate in the United States back to ownership by a sovereign power who had acquired title by discovery, conquest, treaty, or purchase. Most land in the United States was at one time owned by the federal government, which had acquired title through treaties and purchases. Although much of this land is now privately owned, the federal government is still the largest landowner in the country.

Colonial Times

The 13 original colonies had acquired title to the land from England through charters or grants to trading companies or proprietors. These lands came into private ownership through grants to people of wealth, who would settle immigrant workers in this country, and through sales to private individuals. In 1774 the British government terminated land grants and initiated the sale of surveyed lands at public auction. After the American Revolutionary War the central government created by the Articles of Confederation and later by the Constitution handled disputes among the states regarding the public domain.

The Public Domain

The states of Ohio, Indiana, Illinois, Michigan, and Wisconsin and parts of Minnesota were carved out of cessions to the federal government by the original colonies right after the Revolutionary War. The state of Tennessee was ceded to the United States government by North Carolina in 1790; most of Alabama and Mississippi was ceded to the United States government by Georgia in 1802.

The Louisiana Purchase of 1803 added all of Arkansas, Missouri, Nebraska, and Iowa, most of Louisiana, Oklahoma, Kansas, Wyoming, Montana, North Dakota, South Dakota, and Minnesota, part of Colorado, and the rest of Mississippi and Alabama to the public domain. The Red River Basin, which covered the rest of the Dakotas and Minnesota, was acquired through the Convention of 1818 from England. The treaty with Spain in 1819 added all of Florida, part of Colorado, and the rest of Louisiana.

In 1845 the United States annexed Texas, which had established its independence from Mexico in 1836. Parts of this annexation later (1850) became parts of the states of Colorado, New Mexico, and Wyoming and the rest of Kansas and Oklahoma. The Oregon Compromise in 1846 acquired from England the states of Oregon, Washington, and Idaho and the rest of Montana. In 1848 Mexico sold to the United States the land currently consisting of California, Nevada, Utah, most of Arizona, the rest of Colorado, and parts of New Mexico and Wyoming. The Gadsen Purchase of 1853 from Mexico added the rest of Arizona and New Mexico and completed the present continental United States.

The territories of Alaska, Hawaii, Puerto Rico, the Philippines, Guam, Samoa, and other smaller Pacific islands were the last additions to the United States public domain. Of course, Alaska and Hawaii became the 49th and 50th states in 1959 and 1960, respectively.

Private Ownership of the Public Domain

There were many private claims to land within the public domain. Congress had to decide thousands of these private claims through many acts, and the federal courts had to decide those claims not satisfied through congressional actions. With the aid of the rectangular survey system devised by Thomas Jefferson in 1785, the United States government began to sell land within the public domain at public auctions to private individuals.

In the 1800s private individuals acquired title to government lands through squatter and homestead acts by (1) paying minimal prices, (2) inhabiting and improving the land, (3) erecting a dwelling, and (4) living there for a minimum number of years.

Another very interesting way in which government land became privately owned was through grants to men for enlisting in the military to fight in Revolutionary, Civil, and Spanish-American wars. Other grants were made to states for schools, transportation routes, and reclamation of swamplands. The largest and most growth-producing grants were those made to the railroads, which gave great impetus to the westward expansion of the country.

The United States federal government, through its auctions and sales of the public domain to pay its vast debts, was really the founder of the real estate brokerage business. Furthermore, through its huge land grants to the railroads, the federal government gave a great impetus to the brokerage business because the railroads formed land sales offices to sell their grants to farmers and settlers. Also, many homesteaders sold their rights to their lands and thus became land speculators or brokers.

The Twentieth Century

It has often been said that real estate has been an industry of the twentieth century. The real estate industry of the nineteenth century was mostly one of land speculation for westward expansion, agriculture, and livestock. By the twentieth century, the emphasis within the industry shifted to land for cities, as America began to urbanize at a frantic pace. The cities offered the conveniences of modern technology, economic opportunity, and a more exciting and more cosmopolitan way of life than was available in rural America. Vast hordes of European immigrants also flocked to the cities of America, in hopes of finding new opportunities and a better way of life.

The real estate industry, in short, grew and flourished as America (both urban and rural) grew and flourished. As has been the case in most industries, people occupied within the industry found that there was power in numbers. Hence, it was to their advantage to organize themselves formally. Local and state *real estate boards* were formed as trade organizations for the purposes of (1) gaining public recognition, (2) providing self-regulation, (3) lobbying in state legislatures, and (4) educating the membership to upgrade and professionalize the industry.

By 1908 there were over 40 of these real estate boards, and in that year they formed a national organization called the National Association of Real Estate Boards. In 1913 this trade organization adopted a Code of Ethics (see Appendix A), which has been amended 10 times, most recently in 1974. The trademark Realtor® was coined in 1916 as the title for members of this organization. The name of the organization was changed in 1972. This change was made effective as of January 1, 1974; the new name is the National Association of Realtors® (NAR).

As the real estate industry grew and became more complex, many people began to specialize in one of the various areas within the industry. To meet the organizational needs of these specialists, NAR has formed a number of suborganizations or institutes, known as the Affiliates, to include the following groups:

1. Realtors® National Marketing Institute
2. Society of Industrial Realtors®
3. Women's Council of Realtors®
4. Institute of Real Estate Management
5. International Real Estate Federation
6. Real Estate Securities and Syndication Institute
7. American Institute of Real Estate Appraisers
8. Farm and Land Institute
9. American Society of Real Estate Counselors

These specialized groups offer educational courses that, when coupled with experience requirements, can earn a member a professional designation. These are similar to the CPA designation in the field of accounting. Although the various real estate designations are not as well known to the general public as is the CPA designation, they are well known within the industry as true marks of professionalism.[2]

SCOPE OF THE REAL ESTATE INDUSTRY

One way to portray the vast scope of the real estate industry is to follow a rough chronological ordering of the series of events and activities that must take place to convert an idea or dream of a real estate development into a reality. This process begins with the concept in the mind of a *developer* and ends with the real estate product being sold or leased to the ultimate real estate consumer, who occupies, maintains, and/or manages the purchase.

The Real Estate Developer

There are many different types of real estate developers. Usually a developer is identified by the type of land use in which he or she specializes. One might specialize in residential (single-or multifamily), retail commercial (stores and shopping centers), office, industrial, transient commercial (hotels and motels), or multiuse (buildings, projects, or new towns) land uses.

Consultants and Researchers

Before even buying the land, a developer may hire real estate *consultants* and/or *research firms* to analyze and study the market or markets in which

2. See Appendix C for a detailed discussion of the various affiliates of NAR.

the project may be built. These specialists will do market studies to determine the market area, the market demand, the competition, and the potential market capture. This information, coupled with financial data and construction cost, will form a feasibility study from which the developer can decide whether or not and how to proceed with his or her project.

Obtaining the Land

Upon determining the feasibility of the project, the developer will seek to purchase or lease the required land. Normally the purchase or lease of the land will be contingent upon obtaining financing, proper zoning, utility connections, and all necessary approvals to build from a myriad of government agencies. *Attorneys* are used by the developer throughout the development process for legal advice and for the drawing of the many legal documents and contracts required for purchases, financing, construction, consultants, and government agencies.

The land might be obtained from a farmer or other owner or from a *land speculator*, a *subdivider*, or a *land developer*. Each of these can be a separate occupation within the real estate industry. Before the purchase of the land is consummated, a *surveyor* may be hired to clearly delineate the property boundaries and a *soil engineer* may be retained to determine if the ground is suitable for the intended development. An *environmental engineer* might also be used to prepare an environmental-impact study for local, state, and/or federal agency approval.

Financing

To obtain financing, the developer will need an estimate of value for the project from a professional real estate *appraiser*, since the loan amount will be a function of the property value upon completion. A real estate developer might obtain equity capital from his or her own coffers and establish a *sole proprietorship* or may obtain money from friends, relatives and/or investors by forming a *partnership*, a *corporation*, a *real estate investment trust* (REIT), a *joint venture*, or a *syndicate*. Each of these legal forms of ownership plays an important role in the real estate industry.

Borrowed capital, or debt financing, may be obtained from a variety of sources, including *life insurance companies, savings and loan associations, mutual savings banks, commercial banks, pension funds, REITs, mortgage bankers and brokers, individual investors*, and even *state and federal governments*. Many thousands of the employees working for these lenders, therefore, are either directly or indirectly associated with the real estate industry.

Planners and Designers

Coincident with obtaining the financing (and sometimes required to obtain the financing) the developer must implement the talents of a *land planner* to allocate the subject site to various land uses and a *site planner* to do the detailed planning of a specific building site. Next an *architect* must design a building, to be built within the constraints set by the planners. A *landscape architect* will design the exterior grounds, and an *interior designer* will choose the interior decor of the structure. Of course, a whole variety of *engineers* will work closely with the architects, planners, and designers throughout the entire planning and design stages of the development process.

Construction

Once the developer has obtained a commitment for financing and the appropriate approvals from the zoning department and other governmental entities, the developer can proceed with the architectural working drawings and material specifications, from which construction cost estimates can be finalized and contracts can be executed to construct the building. The job of the *general contractor* consists of coordinating materials, labor, subcontractors, and equipment on a specific site to produce a completed building.

A list of *material suppliers* for the construction of a building would fill volumes if one considers all the different types of construction and all the various types of materials, components, and equipment necessary to complete a structure. An equally long list of *tradesmen* and *laborers* evolves when one considers that the construction process includes site clearing and excavation; footings and foundations; floor, wall, and roof construction; roofing, gutters, and flashing; masonry; heating and air conditioning; plumbing, electrical, and insulation systems; interior and exterior painting and trim; carpeting; appliances and other hardware; and landscaping and paving.

Merchandising

During and upon completion of the construction process, the next step for the developer is to advertise, market, and sell his or her product. This may be done by developing a sales force consisting of internal *salespeople* or by hiring and/or soliciting *independent brokers and salespeople* to sell the project. *Advertising, public relations*, and *promotional consultants* may be retained to aid in the merchandising process. The use of newspaper, radio, and television advertising and promotional aids such as signs and brochures may be recommended by *marketing consultants* who specialize in real estate. A sales compound consisting of show models and sales offices may also be recommended by these people of the real estate industry.

Property Management

If the product of the real estate developer is leased to tenants, it will be necessary to hire a professional *property manager* to keep the records of operating the property, collect rents, pay expenses, secure new tenants, and insure and maintain the property.

Related Industries

In addition to the many real estate–related occupations discussed above, there are numerous other industries that depend on real estate for the sale of their products. Such industries include furniture; carpeting; draperies; kitchen appliances; stereo, radio, and television appliances; outdoor recreation equipment; lawn care equipment, etc. One need only walk through a large department store to realize that the volume of its business, employment, and income is closely tied to the volume of activity in the real estate industry.

Mention should be made of the many real estate *educators* who teach in license preparation schools, two-year and four-year colleges, and universities. Today one cannot only earn an associate's or a bachelor's degree, but also a master's degree and even a doctoral degree in real estate. Finally, a myriad of *government* employees work in areas related to real estate. State real estate licensing officials, city planners, zoning officials, environmental bodies, and state and federal housing and financial assistance administrators, to mention only a few, would be included in this governmental category.

SUMMARY AND CONCLUSION

"Under all is the land" is the first sentence of the Preamble to the National Association of Realtors® Code of Ethics. A truer statement was never uttered. Since the beginning of time, land or real estate has served as the basis of wealth. This was true in the third century B.C. and is still true today. The history of the settlement of America shows real estate to have always been at the root of expansion, progress, and prosperity.

Real estate may be called a twentieth century industry in its present sophisticated form, but it has been around as an industry ever since human beings evolved, and it has been around as a resource long before then. For example, the oil we drill today exists only because real estate was here long before people. Real estate as an industry today is so vast that it is virtually impossible to think of a person or entity that does not either use, occupy, own, or lease real estate. Think about it!

CHAPTER 2

Real Estate and Its Markets

KEY TERMS

Real estate or realty A tangible commodity or physical product consisting of land and improvements on and to the land

Real property Intangible interests, benefits, and rights inherent in the ownership of the tangible commodity or physical product of real estate or realty

Land The surface of the earth; the minerals, natural resources, and substances below the surface of the earth; and the airspace and natural resources and herbage above the surface of the earth

Improvements on the land Structures such as buildings, fences, and walls which have been permanently affixed on a site for its use

Improvements to the land Such things as curbs, sidewalks, streets, and utility lines which have been added to make the land and structures more usable

Personal property Anything that is not real property

Concentric circle theory Theory of land-use development patterns that concludes that land uses tend to develop in concentric circles out from the central business district, circled by a mixed commercial and industrial area, circled by a low-income housing area, circled by a middle-income housing arca, circled by a commuters' suburban area

Axial theory Theory of land-use development patterns that concludes that land uses tend to develop along and relative to time-cost functions of transportation axes that radiate out from the central business district

Sector theory Theory of land-use development patterns that concludes that land uses tend to develop along transportation corridors, with those uses that can pay the highest price (high-income housing) developing along the most preferred transportation corridor in a pie-shaped sector form

Multiple-nuclei theory Theory of land-use development patterns that concludes that the automobile has allowed land uses to tend to develop around a variety of economic focal points and that the type of land-use patterns that evolve are a function of the type of land use contained in each economic focal point

REAL ESTATE DEFINED

When one purchases a product in a real estate market, one obtains the ownership of much more than the tangible commodity itself. In addition, one acquires certain intangibles, known as "interests," "benefits," and "rights," inherent in the ownership of the tangible or physical product of *real estate* or *realty*. This intangible "bundle of rights" includes the rights of possession, use, enjoyment, control, and disposition and is referred to as *real property*. In other words, the ownership of the physical product of *real estate* is also endowed with the ownership of the rights of *real property*. Although the meanings of the words "real estate" (or "realty") and "real property" differ technically, these terms are most commonly used synonymously. In fact, in some states they have been made officially synonymous by state law.

Real estate (or *real property*) can be defined as land and improvement on and to the land.[1] *Land* includes the surface of the earth; the minerals, natural resources, and substances below the surface of the earth; and the airspace and natural resources and herbage above the surface of the earth.[2] *Improvements on the land* include structures, such as buildings, fences, and walls, which have been permanently affixed on a site for its use. *Improvements to the land* include such things as curbs, sidewalks, streets, and utility lines, which have been added to make the land and structures more usable.

Real estate possesses a variety of distinguishing physical and economic qualities or characteristics that cause it to be quite a unique good or commodity. Furthermore, the ownership of real estate is limited by a variety of public and private restrictions.

Physical Characteristics

Physical characteristics of real estate are as follows:

1. *Fixity of Physical Location.* The geographic location of land is rigidly fixed. Even though soils, minerals, and even improvements (at great expense) can be moved, the physical location of a parcel of land remains. It is this immobility of physical location that causes real estate markets to be quite local in nature.
2. *Nonhomogeneity.* Real estate is heterogeneous; each parcel is unlike any other parcel. When purchasing a share of common stock across a national stock exchange, it does not matter which particular share one gets since each is identical within each class of stock. However, in real estate no two parcels are exactly alike, and it can

1. *Personal property* can be defined as anything that is not real property.
2. The theoretical ownership of infinite airspace above the earth's surface has been restricted by congressional legislation to air travel.

matter greatly to a purchaser which parcel is acquired. Because of this characteristic, courts of law will enforce the remedy of specific performance (see Chapter 8) for contracts involving the transfer of real estate.

3. *Permanence.* Land is virtually indestructible in that its physical location will remain no matter what happens to it. Improvements usually have been constructed such as to have very long lives and are considered relatively permanent. It is this quality that allows an owner to obtain "permanent" (long-term) financing on real estate, because it provides strong collateral to secure the loan.
4. *Fixity of Supply.* The physical supply of land is limited by the finite size of the earth. No purely physical shortage has ever been experienced, and such is not likely for a long time to come. However, there is always a limited supply at a given location with a required amount of access and convenience.

Economic Characteristics

Real estate has certain economic characteristics, as follows:

1. *Fixity of Economic Location.* It has often been said that the three most important things in real estate are (1) location, (2) location, and (3) location. The importance and impact of physical location were discussed above. Here the term *situs* is used to describe the fact that in real estate more income can be produced at certain locations than at others; for example, a fast food restaurant is better situated on the corner of a busy intersection in a commercial area than at the corner of one of two intersecting streets where it dead-ends in an affluent residential area.
2. *Fixity of Investment.* In real estate, the product cannot follow the market as well as in many other types of business. Once a property has been developed, its economic success is dependent on its ability to draw the market's dollars to where its investments of land, labor, and capital are fixed. Furthermore, most real estate investments are relatively nonliquid; in other words, it is not very easy to quickly convert real estate into cash without a loss, in order to move the investment to the market.
3. *Modification or Improvement.* An economic characteristic unique to real estate is that any modification to, or improvement on, one property generally has a positive impact on the value of another property; for example, the value of a home in a rural area will increase when (1) the surrounding roads are paved and city utilities are provided (modification) and (2) higher-priced homes and new schools are built nearby (improvement).

4. *Ample Supply.* Although technically there is a physical limit to the supply of land, the economic limits to the supply of real estate are less restrictive, provided one has enough money. With modern construction methods and materials, the density and efficiency of land use and, therefore, the supply of real estate can be increased. A block of 20 single-family residences can easily be transformed into hundreds of high-rise apartment or condominium residences.
5. *Large Economic Units.* The amounts of land, labor, capital, and management that go into the production of a real estate project are massive. Coordination with the businesses and professions of construction, finance, marketing, law, engineering, architecture, etc., is very complex. The discussion of the real estate industry in Chapter 1 made this point very clearly. Even the purchase of a house is usually one of the largest economic and financial transactions ever made in the lives of many people.
6. *Dependence on the Public Sector.* No parcel of real estate can be useful without interplay with public roads, utilities, and other community services. As an area grows and urbanizes, its dependence on public alleys, roads, highways, parks, water supply, sewers, utilities, police and fire protection, health and welfare services, etc., becomes more important and more complex.

Public Land-Use Restrictions

As areas grow and the dependence on the public sector becomes more apparent, a variety of public or governmental restrictions also become more apparent. Public or governmental land-use controls include the following:

1. *Public Ownership.* The ownership of roads, parks, government buildings, and other facilities allows the various governments to restrict or prohibit the use of these properties.
2. *Property Taxation.* The owners of real estate are subject to a perpetual claim or lien on their properties for the collection of *ad valorem* (according to value) taxes that are used to pay for the costs of government administration and services.
3. *Eminent Domain.* Condemnation through the power of eminent domain allows governmental bodies to acquire private property by paying just compensation at fair market value. The property acquired can then be transferred into public use, or even private use, as long as the public benefits from such use.[3]
4. *Police Power.* This is the right of government to limit property

3. A 1968 Supreme Court decision allowed private use with public benefit.

rights, without compensation, in order to protect the health, welfare, safety, and morals of the public. The authorities of health, fire, safety, building, zoning, sanitary, traffic, and environmental codes and regulations are all derived from the police power.

5. *Escheat.* If a property owner dies with no heirs and with no last will and testament (intestate), the rights to the property will transfer to the state upon the passing of any required statutory period.

Private Land-Use Restrictions

In addition to the various public land-use restrictions (over which property owners have little or no say), there exist a variety of private controls that property owners can determine and/or agree to accept. These limitations include the following:

1. *Deed Restrictions or Covenants.* A developer may include a variety of restrictions in the deed used to transfer ownership of a parcel of real estate within a project; for example, minimum land and/or building size restrictions might be used to maintain property values within the project.
2. *Liens.* A lien is the right or claim of a creditor to satisfy the debt of a debtor by selling the debtor's property. Liens might be *involuntary*, as with the perpetual lien of property taxes, or *voluntary*, as in the case of a mortgage lien used as security for a loan.
3. *Leases.* A lease suspends the owner's (landlord's) rights of ownership during the term of the agreement in return for an income stream in the form of rent.
4. *Easements.* An easement is the nonpossessory right of one party to partially use the property of another for a specific purpose. Hence, the rights of ownership are limited to the extent of the easement agreement. For example, one's next-door neighbor might have an easement to use one's driveway to gain access to his or her garage.

REAL ESTATE MARKETS

Real estate markets are the course of commerce that facilitates the transfer of real property rights in our free enterprise system. Real estate markets also set or determine mutually advantageous prices, allocate space among the different types of land uses, determine the pattern of land use and urban growth, and adjust supply to meet demand. Theoretically, an efficient or perfect market is one in which there are many competitive and well-informed buyers and sellers who have freedom of entry and exit to and from the market and who are trading standardized products. In such a market, an equilibrium of the forces of supply and demand is a natural tendency.

Imperfect Markets

Unfortunately, real estate markets are quite imperfect. In fact, at the national level, supply and demand are rarely, if ever, in equilibrium, and the disparities often last for years. Buyers and sellers on the whole are poorly informed as to the products and the markets; real estate products are not at all standardized; and freedom in and out of the markets is often complicated by external reasons for buying or selling, such that it is common to have "buyers' markets" or "sellers' markets," rather than equilibrium. Furthermore, because of fixity of location, most real estate markets are very *local* in nature, with no central exchange, such that geographically scattered and individualized transactions take place at many prices rather than at a single one.

Because real estate is nonstandardized and immobile, production responds slowly to market conditions. Since the product cannot be removed from the market or quickly liquidated and transferred to another market, it is easy for oversupply to result. On the other hand, since the time from conception to completion for the development and construction of a real estate project is considerable, it is easy for undersupply to result. In other words, because of the nature of the construction process, the forces of supply and demand may never coincide.

Supply of Real Estate

Because of the long physical and economic life of real estate, the supply of real properties, especially in the short run, is relatively fixed. Furthermore, because of the length of the construction process, the supply of real estate is very inflexible and is slow to react to a change in the market demand for space. In fact, the wide variations common in real estate activity can be explained largely in terms of this relative inflexibility in the market supply of space.

The factors of supply of real estate can be analyzed at both the national or regional level and the local level. Such supply factors include the following:

1. *Land*. Although there has never been a physical shortage of land at the national level, land may be one of the dearest commodities at the local level. This is often the case in large cities, such as on Manhattan Island in New York City, where natural barriers limit the supply of well-located urban land. Barriers causing land to be in short supply might also be man-made, such as railroads, airports, highways, etc. Land that is *developable* can be in short supply if utilities such as water, electricity, gas, etc., are unavailable because

of moratoriums or the lack of sufficient municipal funding. Finally, governmental institutions may limit the supply of land by enforcement of planning, zoning, and building codes, environmental controls, or *ad valorem* and sales tax policies.

2. *Labor*. A second factor that impacts on the supply of real estate is the cost and availability of construction labor. Historically the construction industry has been subject to wide cyclical variations as a result of overbuilding and underbuilding. The cyclical phenomenon, when coupled with fluctuations due to the seasons of the year, have traditionally caused the construction industry to experience very unstable employment, with many periods of high unemployment. Finally, since employers of the building industry tend to be small, independent, and fragmented, the unstable employment conditions are intensified even more. However, to offset these volatile employment conditions, national trade and labor unions were formed. The power of the unions has been strong enough to raise pay scales significantly, to restrict entry in order to limit the labor supply, to sponsor building codes that require much labor-intensive practices, to limit the scope of each trade, and to resist capital-intensive tools and materials that would limit the need for labor. At the local level, the supply of labor is usually a function of the national unions. The cost of labor at the local level is usually a function of the presence and strength of the local unions.
3. *Materials*. Building materials are generally classified as (1) wood and wood products, (2) concrete and concrete products, and (3) steel and steel products. From time to time short-term shortages and bottlenecks have occurred, sending prices skyrocketing within these three materials industries. It is the wide variations in the construction industry's demands for these products, due to the cyclical nature of the industry, that cause these problems. On the other hand, over the years, modern technology and innovation have continued to increase the efficiency of construction materials and methods, thus lowering costs.
4. *Capital*. The supply of real estate capital is a function of the net savings of individuals, business firms, and governments and can be in the form of either equity capital (ownership) or debt capital in the form of a loan secured by the real estate as collateral (mortgage or deed of trust). The mortgage markets are part of the overall money and capital markets that channel savings to borrowers. However, mortgage borrowers are usually at the bottom of the money and capital market "totem poles" of borrowers. Mortgage borrowers must compete for funds with the federal government, which borrows to meet its fiscal policy expenditures when they exceed the amount of taxes collected. Since the federal government can afford almost

any price for these borrowed funds, it is at the top of the borrowing totem pole. Businesses can increase the price of their products if interest rates increase on the funds that they borrow, so they are next on the totem pole. This all leaves the mortgagor, as the "residual" borrower at the bottom of the totem pole, terribly subject to changes in monetary and fiscal policies, interest rates, savings, politics, and any other factors that affect the supply and demand for money.

Local supply of real estate capital usually varies greatly from area to area. Some parts of the country (the East) generally have more savings than other parts (the West and Southwest), where growth is taking place such that there is a greater borrowing demand to finance the expansion than there are dollars being saved. It is the role of mortgage brokers, mortgage bankers, and the financial institutions, such as banks and savings and loan associations, through the secondary mortgage market to serve as intermediaries to channel the funds from the areas where capital is in ample supply to areas where there exist capital shortages.

5. *Entrepreneurship*. As indicated above, the building industry is very fragmented. Therefore at the national level there are really no firms or individuals that can claim to be truly national entrepreneurs. Some, however, such as John Portman and Trammell Crow and a few housing firms such as Levitt or U.S. Homes, have come close. Generally, though, a few individuals provide the creative impetus to local real estate development.
6. *Existing Inventories*. Supply factors that are most relevant from local area to local area, rather than on a national basis, are the volume and quality of existing building inventories. The volume is a function of the *vacancies* or *vacancy rates* for each type of property. When vacancy rates fall, rents rise, which after a while induces more construction that after a while increases the local supply of real estate. The quality of existing inventories is a function of the degree of *functional obsolescence* possessed by the existing structures. Such a loss or impairment of the functional efficiency or adequacy of a property can be caused by changes in tastes of market participants or by introduction of modern construction materials and methods that make newer properties more desirable.
7. *Government Actions*. The local, state, and national governments are a pervasive force impacting on the supply of real estate as to the quantity and especially as to the quality of real estate. Land-use controls, building and zoning codes, rent controls, and tax policies at the local level; such things as monetary and fiscal policies; and governmental institutions such as the Federal Housing Administration, the Veterans Administration, the Department of Housing and

Urban Development, etc., all play important roles within real estate markets. Each of the listed items and many others affect how much and what type of real estate is supplied to the market.

Demand for Real Estate

Since the supply of real estate is relatively fixed, *demand* is the most important factor (especially in the short run) in determining prices and rents in the various real estate markets (see Figure 2-1). In addition to the fact that the supply of real estate is inflexible, it is also true that the demand for real estate can be quite volatile. Socioeconomic forces can change rather rapidly within our society, and the demand for real estate

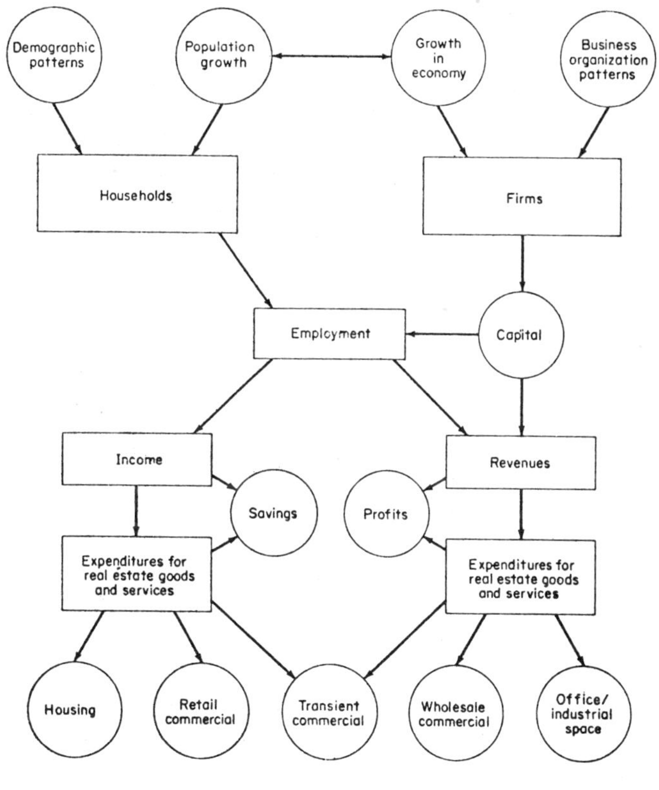

Figure 2-1 National Demand Patterns for Real Estate Goods and Services in the Private Sector

Source: John McMahan, *Property Development* (New York: McGraw-Hill Book Co., 1976), p. 85.

can vary just as quickly and in coincidence with reaction to the socioeconomic changes. As was true in the analysis of the supply factors in real estate markets, the demand factors can be analyzed from both the national and local levels. Of course, all the factors observed at the national level eventually filter down to and are brought to bear on the local real estate markets. These demand factors are many and include the following:

1. *Population Growth.* The growth of population is a function of the existing level or *base* of population and the annual *rate* at which the base grows. National population growth rates are a function of births (*fertility*) versus deaths (*mortality*) and *immigration* into the country versus *emigration* out of the country. Local population growth rates are a function of these same factors plus *migration patterns* within the country. Migration patterns may be either (1) *regional*, such as a shift of the population to the West; (2) *rural-urban*, such as a shift from the farms to the cities; (3) *urban-suburban*, such as a shift from central cities to the suburbs;[4] or (4) any combination of these three types of migration patterns. The migration patterns of businesses and industries to new locations as well as the migration of households also have an impact on the demand for real estate.
2. *Demographics.* Real estate markets must mirror socioeconomic changes to meet market demands. The type of population that exists in real estate markets can be determined by the study of *demographics*, including the sizes and age distribution of the population; the sizes, types, and timings of household formations; marriage and divorce rates; and ethnic makeup and concentration. The demand for certain types of real estate is affected by changes and trends in the demographics of the population; for example, a marriage may create a need for a housing unit while a divorce may create a need for two housing units. The age level of the World War II "war babies" is now causing a terrific demand for housing. Early retirements and higher incomes and savings of older people have created a demand for retirement communities. High incomes and later marriages have caused a demand for condominium projects that appeal to young singles.
3. *Employment.* Some of the most important factors creating demand in real estate markets are the economic activities and the jobs created by these activities within the market area. *Economic-base theory* divides the economic activities of a community into *basic* or *primary* activities and *service* or *secondary* activities. The basic activities

4. Some recent information has indicated that there might be some *suburban-urban* shifts due to the energy crisis and the nostalgia of buying and rehabilitating older homes in the central cities. See Gordon E. Von Stroh, Michael J. Crean, and Darl Bien, *Denver Metropolitan Area Residential Migration Study* (Denver: Denver Urban Observatory, 1975).

cause the community to exist (a college in a college town, or a mill in a mill town, for example) and provide jobs the incomes of which are paid with dollars that come from without the community to purchase the products *exported* by the basic economic activity. The service activities (the butcher, the baker, . . .) exist only to support the existence of the basic activities and their employees. The incomes of the service jobs are paid with dollars that merely circulate within the community (borrow from Peter to pay Paul).

Since it is the people and their incomes that demand real estate, it is important to know the future trends of the basic economic employers. If they grow as a group by internal expansion or by external business migration, so, too, will the service activities grow, and hence the demand for real estate will increase greatly. If basic industries and employees diminish, so, too, will the demand for real estate.

4. *Urban Growth Patterns.* The direction and patterns of growth within a community or local market area are important to the real estate developer in locating market demand. Traditionally, those who have studied urban growth have offered four different theories of land-use development patterns as follows (see Figure 2-2 also). The *concentric circle theory*, offered by Ernest W. Burgess in 1925, concludes that land uses tend to develop in concentric circles spreading out from the central business district, which is circled by a mixed commercial and industrial area, circled by a low-income housing area, circled by a middle-income housing area, circled by a commuters' suburban area. The *axial theory*, offered by F. M. Babcock in 1932, concludes that land uses tend to develop along and relative to time-cost functions of transportation axes that radiate out from the central business district. The *sector theory*, offered by Homer Hoyt in 1939, concludes that land uses tend to develop along transportation corridors, with those uses that can pay the highest price (high-income housing) developing along the most preferred transportation corridor in a pie-shaped sector form. The *multiple nuclei theory*, offered by C. P. Harris and E. L. Ullman in 1945, concludes that the automobile has allowed land uses to tend to develop around a variety of economic focal points and that the types of land-use patterns that evolve are a function of the type of land use contained in each economic focal point.

No one of these theories will likely fully explain where the developer within a particular local market area will find the market demand for his or her product. However, it is usually the case that a little of each theory applies, and a knowledge and understanding of these theories can aid the real estate developer in determining market demand.

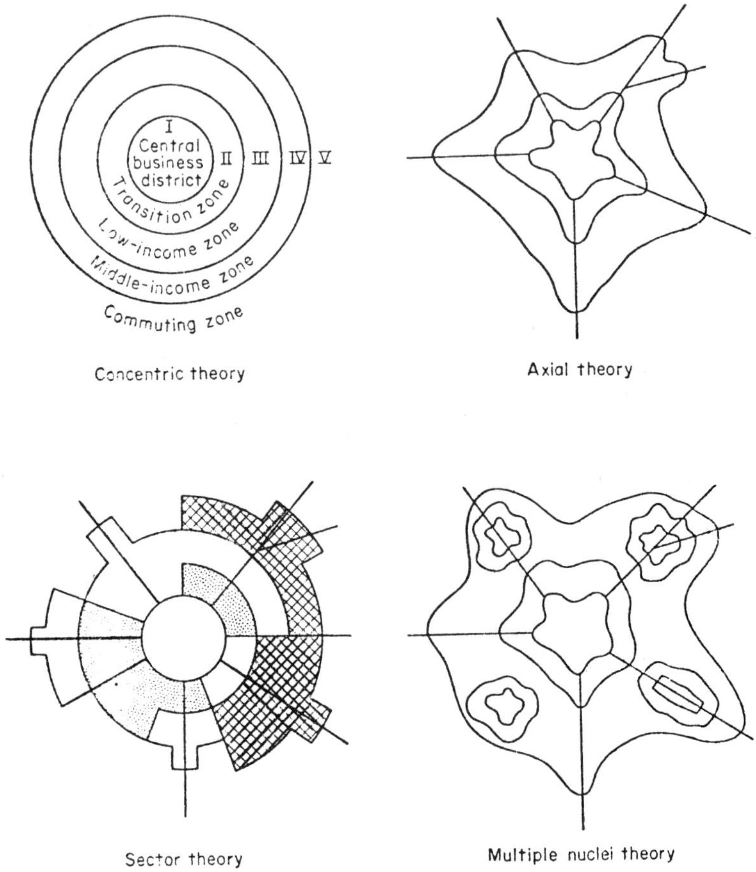

Figure 2-2 Theories of Land-Use Development Patterns

Source: John McMahan, *Property Development* (New York: McGraw-Hill Book Co., 1976), p. 110.

5. *Income and Spending Patterns*. For demand to be *effective*, it must be backed by income sufficient to make the *desired* purchase. Growing population and employment opportunities create the need and desire for more real estate. These forces, coupled with an ample force of income, will increase real estate development. The type of development that is created is a function of the spending patterns of real estate and other consumers. Consumer confidence and expectations for the future economy also have an impact on spending patterns.

   The spending of households influences the real estate markets of housing, retail commercial (stores and shopping centers), and transient commercial (hotels and motels) because households are consumers in these markets. The spending of businesses has an impact on the real estate markets of office and industrial space, wholesale commercial (warehouses), and transient commercial because businesses are consumers in these markets. Finally, the spending of the *public sector* influences all the real estate markets listed here because it is the remaining part of consumption in these markets.

SUMMARY AND CONCLUSION

Real estate is truly a unique commodity, traded daily within our economy within a very ill-defined set of markets, none of which has a fixed place of exchange. One might say there is no one location where "locations" are bought and sold. The quantity of restrictions, controls, and regulations placed on the owners of real property is almost beyond belief for a free-enterprise system. The supply and demand of real estate markets are seldom, if ever, in equilibrium simply because of the nature of the beast. However, only with a proper understanding of and an appropriate perspective regarding the various real estate markets and urban growth patterns can a real estate entrepreneur be successful.

PART II

Law

CHAPTER 3

Property and Property Rights, Interests, and Estates

KEY TERMS

Doctrine of tenures Doctrine that defined how land was *held* within the person-to-person relationships under the feudal system of property ownership

Doctrine of estates Doctrine that defined how long (timewise as opposed to tenancywise) the relationship between the *person and the land* would last under the allodial system of property ownership

Fixture An article that was once personal property and has been installed in or attached to real estate so that it is now regarded as part of the real estate

Freehold estates Interests in property for an indeterminable period of time or duration, "free" of a tenancy or lease

Leasehold estates Interests in property for a determinable period of time or duration, as determined by and "not free" of a tenancy or lease; usually considered personal property

Concurrent estates Interests in real property held simultaneously by more than one person

Estates in severalty Interests in property held by only one person to the exclusion or "severance" of all other persons

Encumbrance Any right or interest in real property that affects or limits the fee simple title to the real property by either impairing its marketability or diminishing its value; includes easements, encroachments, deed restrictions, and liens

Easement A nonpossessory right or interest held by one person in the land of another person such that the nonpossessing person is allowed partial use of the land for a specifically named purpose

Encroachment A trespass upon the property of another, such as the eave of a building that invades the airspace of a contiguous property

Lien An encumbrance that gives the right to one person or legal entity to satisfy a debt, claim, or charge out of the property of another person or legal entity

History and Development of Property Law

One can study the works of Cicero, Rousseau, Adam Smith, Jeremy Bentham, and others for early formal statements concerning the concepts of property. However, the various concepts evolved long before these famous writers had made their commentaries. The nomadic prepastoral and preagricultural tribes of hunters recognized the first "ownership of things" (a definition of property) by claiming that their weapons, clubs, spears, etc., could belong solely to individuals. The herders of pastoral tribes recognized tribal and individual ownership of their cattle.[1] The tillers of agricultural tribes recognized tribal or common ownership of the lands they had cultivated. As agriculture and society in general advanced and as the specialization of labor concept evolved, farmers recognized individual ownership of land. This ownership of immovable things (land) was "total," as was the ownership of movable things (chattels). Hence the system of ownership has been called "allodial" from the Old German *al* ("all") and *od* ("property").

The allodial system came to an end in 1066 A.D., when William the Conqueror defeated King Harold of England at the Battle of Hastings. Land was no longer owned in absolute independence by individuals (allodial), but rather the king was vested in title to all the land. Hence, William the Conqueror established the feudal system.

Under the feudal system a *doctrine of tenures* existed whereby the king would grant tenures to lords or barons and they to lower vassals called villeins, who would actually fight in the armies and till the soil in return for various services and obligations. A lord with a *tenure* (from the Latin, "to hold") did not own his land but rather *held* it of the king. Owed to the king were military, personal, and religious services and the obligations of good faith, loyalty, crops, and money.

This *doctrine of tenures* defined "how" land was *held* within the *person-to-person* relationships of the feudal system. Near the end of the medieval feudal period, frictions between lord and tenant mounted. During the thirteenth century a variety of legal enactments, such as the Magna Carta in 1215, eventually removed the feudal system and its *doctrine of tenures* and a new doctrine of ownership, the *doctrine of estates*, evolved. This new doctrine defined "how long" (timewise as opposed to tenancywise) the relationship between *the person and the land* would last. The king therefore no longer owned all the land. Once again the land could be held in absolute independence by the individual. Hence the allodial system of ownership was restored to the common law of England. It was this system and the *doctrine of estates* that were established in America.

1. "Chattel," which means "personal property," is a derivation of the Old French word *chatel*, which meant "cattle."

Property: Real and Personal

The terms "real property," or "realty," and "personal property," or "personalty," were derived from the Latin and French words used by the courts to describe the actions of legal remedy available to persons who had been deprived of their property. Since chattels could be moved, one would sue the person *in personam* (Latin for "person") for relief and restoration of the monetary value of one's property. However, since real property or land could not be moved, one would sue for the thing itself *in rem* (Latin for "thing"). The Old French for "thing" was *real*. Hence, the derivations of "real" and "personal" property are made clear.[2]

In Chapter 2 a technical distinction was made between *real estate* as a physical thing or commodity and *real property* as a set of rights in the thing (real estate) itself or as relationships that can exist between persons and the thing. Legally, the terms *corporeal* and *tangible* refer to *things* of real property and personal property, respectively. The terms *incorporeal* and *intangible* refer to rights or relationships of real property and personal property, respectively (see Figure 3-1). Incorporeal rights or relationships in real property include easements, licenses, emblements, profits, and liens. Intangible rights or relationships in personal property include patents, trademarks, copyrights, and royalties. Also in Chapter 2, the statement was made in a footnote that *personal property* could be defined as anything that is *not real property*. The laws that deal with real and personal property differ greatly. Some of these differences are as follows:

1. According to the *Statute of Frauds*, ownership of real estate *must* be transferred and evidenced by a written document called a "deed"; conveyance of personal property is accomplished through delivery of the object and *may* be evidenced by a bill of sale.
2. The legal estates of the surviving spouse, to include dower, curtesy, and homestead, apply to real but not to personal property.
3. The rules governing the disposition at death of real property differ from those governing personal property.
4. The lien laws that grant rights to creditors to satisfy debts out of the property of the debtor differ between real and personal property.
5. Real property is governed by the law of the state in which the real estate is located; personal property is governed by the law of the state in which the owner lives or is domiciled.

2. Paul T. O'Donnell and Eugene L. Maleady, *Principles of Real Estate*, (Philadelphia: W. B. Saunders, 1975), pp. 101–102.

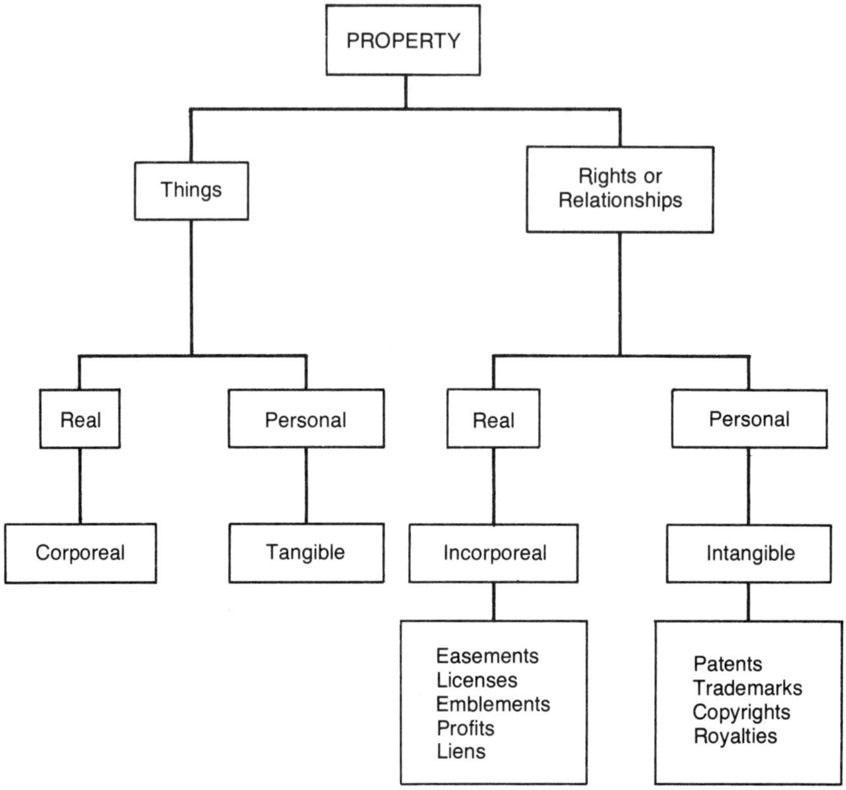

Figure 3-1 Property

6. Real property is subject to the public and private land-use restrictions discussed in Chapter 2, and personal property is not subject to these restrictions.[3]

FIXTURES

A fixture may be defined as "an article that was once personal property, but that has been installed in or attached to land or a building in some more or less permanent manner, so that such article is regarded in law as a part of the real estate."[4] A dishwasher on the showroom floor of an appliance store is personal property. Once this dishwasher is installed in a house, it becomes a fixture and is regarded in law as part of the real estate. It is not uncommon for controversies to arise over whether or not

3. William M. Shenkel, *The Real Estate Professional* (Homewood, Ill.: Dow Jones–Irwin, 1976), pp. 6–7.
4. Robert Kratovil, *Real Estate Law*, 6th ed. (Englewood Cliffs, N.J.: Prentice-Hall, 1974), p. 11.

a piece of property is a fixture. Such controversies usually pit a real property owner against either the owner's tenant, a purchaser of his or her property, or the mortgage lender.

To settle such controversies, courts of law generally apply the following five tests to determine whether or not a piece of property is a fixture:

1. *The Intent of the Parties.* This is determined by their actions and not by their statements. Intent can also be established through application of the other four tests.
2. *The Method of Attachment.* Conservative courts place most weight on this test in making the decisions of determination. If the item cannot be removed from the premises without substantial damage to the premises, it is usually determined to be a fixture.
3. *The Degree of Specialization or Degree to Which It Was Custom-Adapted to the Premises.* The more specialized or custom-adapted to the premises, the more likely it will be held to be a fixture.
4. *The Relationship between the Parties.* Buyers, tenants, and mortgage borrowers are usually favored by the courts on the grounds that their adversaries should have known enough to not let fixture controversies arise.
5. *The Existence of an Agreement between the Parties.* In a sales contract, for example, there may be an agreement as to whether or not an article should be considered a fixture. *Chattel fixtures*, or *tenant's fixtures*, are considered personal property, and such articles are removable from the premises by the tenants.

There are three classes of chattel fixtures as follows:

1. *Trade fixtures* are articles added by a tenant which are absolutely necessary for the conduction of the tenant's business, trade, or manufacture.
2. *Agricultural fixtures* are articles added by a tenant which are necessary for the cultivation of a crop.
3. *Domestic fixtures* are articles added by a tenant which are necessary for additional comfort or ornamentation within his or her domicile.

ESTATES IN LAND

The law pertaining to estates in land is very complex. The discussion of estates is limited here to the major types the real estate practitioner is likely to encounter in the normal course of day-to-day business affairs or on the licensing examination (see Figure 3-2). Specialized real estate law texts may be utilized for a more detailed analysis of this topic.

An *estate in land* can be defined as the degree, nature, or extent of

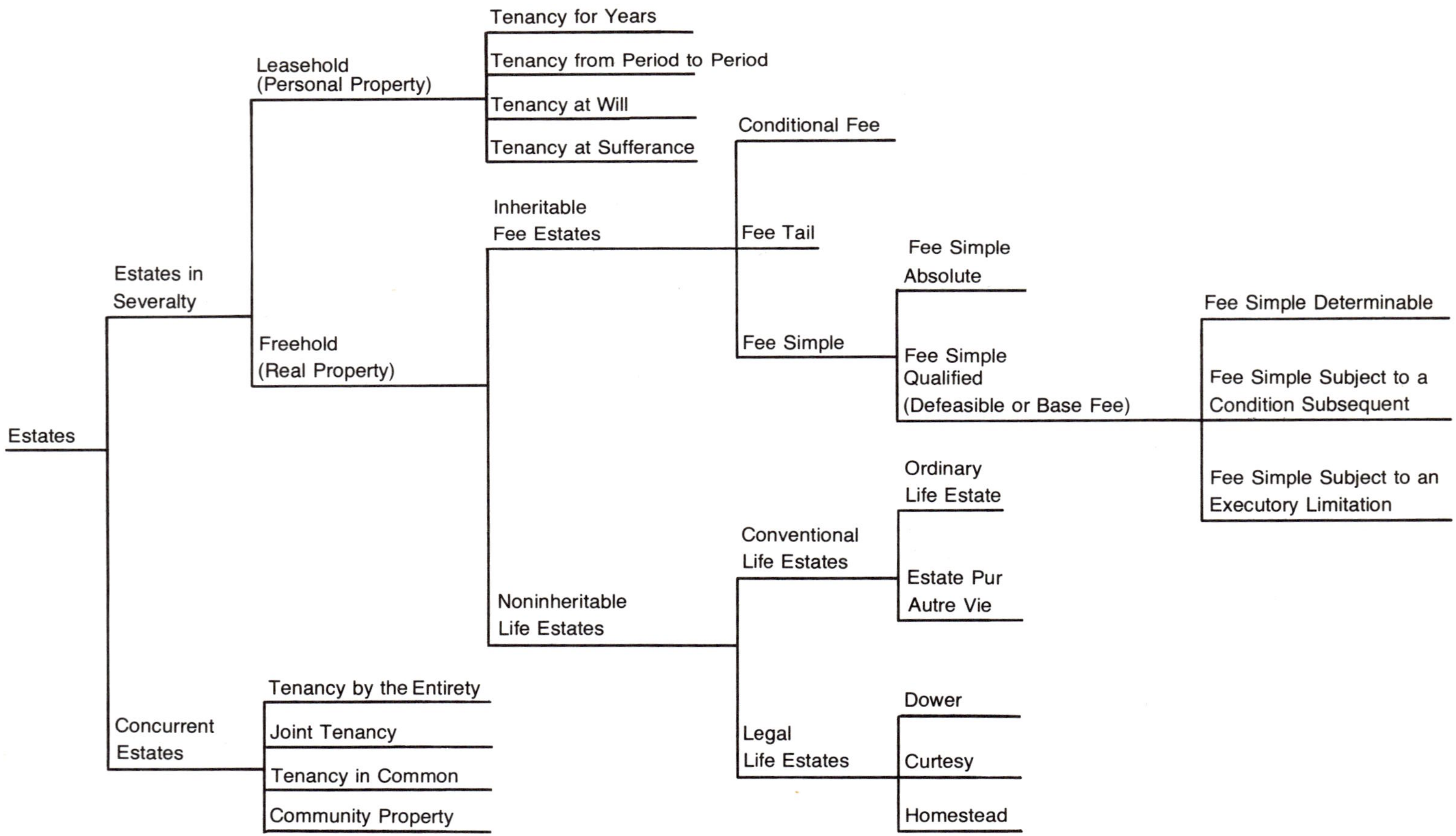

Figure 3-2 Estates

interest that a person has in the land. Estates in land are generally classified as either nonfreehold or freehold. *Nonfreehold estates* are for a determinable period of time or duration. The nomenclature is derived from the doctrine of tenures, which defined the relationship between a person (vassal) and another person (lord or king) regarding land that was *not free* of a tenancy from the king. In American law, nonfreehold estates, which are also called *leasehold estates*, are deemed personal property. The four leasehold estates are (1) tenancy for years, (2) tenancy from period to period, (3) tenancy at will, and (4) tenancy at sufferance.

A *tenancy for years* (also called an estate for years) is a leasehold for a definite period of time, be it an hour, day, year, or some other stated time period. A *tenancy from period to period* (periodic tenancy) is a leasehold with a definite rental period but no definite termination date. Proper notice as required by state law must be given in order to terminate such an agreement. A tenancy for years automatically terminates at the end of the stated time period, but a *tenancy at will* is a leasehold for an indefinite time period and is terminable at the will of either party. A *tenancy at sufferance* arises when a tenant holds over beyond the termination of a lease. The landlord has a choice of evicting the tenant or holding the tenant liable for the renewal of the original leasehold agreement.

Freehold Estates

Freehold estates are for an indeterminable period of time or duration. The nomenclature is derived from the doctrine of estates, which defined the relationship between a person and land *free* of a tenancy from the king. In American law, freehold estates are deemed real property and can be either *inheritable fee estates* or *noninheritable life estates*.

Inheritable Fee Estates. Fee simple, conditional fee, and fee tail are the three types of fee estates. A *fee* is an inheritable estate in real property.

Fee Simple. An estate that has no limitations as to any particular class of heirs and is not subject to any restrictions other than the usual public and private land-use restrictions is a *fee simple*. A fee simple estate may be either absolute or qualified. A *fee simple absolute* is the largest and most complete estate known to the law. It contains the total bundle of rights. Unless the seller of a property specifically indicates that he or she is transferring a lesser estate, the law presumes a fee simple absolute to be conveyed.

A *fee simple qualified* can be terminated by the occurrence or nonoccurrence of some event specified in the written document creating the estate. Since this type of estate may be terminated or defeated, it is sometimes called a *defeasible fee* or *base fee*. There are three kinds of fee simple qualified estates as follows:

1. *Fee simple determinable* is a fee simple qualified estate that *automatically* reverts to the grantor or the grantor's heirs upon the occurrence or nonoccurrence of a specified event. For example, some land was granted to the University of Denver "so long as" no alcoholic beverages were served on the premises.
2. *Fee simple subject to a condition subsequent* is a fee simple qualified estate that *can* revert to the grantor or the grantor's heirs upon the occurrence of nonoccurrence of a specified event only if they *reenter* and exercise their *power of termination* or *right of entry for condition broken*. For example, the land could have been granted to the University of Denver "on the condition that" if alcoholic beverages were served on the premises the grantor or heirs "may reenter and repossess the premises."
3. *Fee simple subject to an executory limitation* is a fee simple qualified estate that *automatically* passes to a *third person and that person's heirs* (not the grantor or the grantor's heirs) upon the occurrence or nonoccurrence of a specified event. For example, the land could have been granted to the University of Denver "so long as" no alcoholic beverages were served on the premises, "then to" Professor Crean and his heirs.

Conditional Fee. An estate having the limitation that upon death of the grantee it descends to "the heirs of his [or her] body" is a *conditional fee* (not to be confused with a fee simple subject to a condition subsequent or the conditional fee of early English law). The creation of such an estate was intended for the use of the landed gentry to allow their lineal descendants to maintain their landed gentry status. If the line of descent became extinct, the land would revert to the grantor. However, the objective for creating this estate could be foiled because, once an heir was born to the grantee, the grantee's estate became fee simple and was therefore freely transferable. This type of estate is recognized only in the states of South Carolina, Iowa, and Oregon.[5]

Fee Tail. An estate, which in England abolished the conditional fee and was created in 1285 by the Statute De Donis Conditionaibus, is a *fee tail*. This type of estate never ripened to fee simple, and therefore its landed gentry intent could not be foiled. Currently all states have either abolished this estate or modified it such that fee simple absolute can be obtained by deed (Delaware, Maine, Massachusetts, and Rhode Island) or by inheritance at the death of the first grantee (Colorado and Illinois).[6]

5. O'Donnell and Maleady, *Real Estate*, pp. 125–26.
6. Ibid., pp. 126–27.

Noninheritable Life Estates. A *life estate* is a noninheritable estate in real property which is held for the duration of the life of some specified person (see Figure 3-2). Upon the death of the specified person, a fee simple estate (absolute or qualified) is conveyed to either the original grantor or the grantor's heirs in the form of a *reversion* or to a third person (known as the "remainderman") and this person's heirs in the form of a *remainder*. If the remainderman is known at the time the life estate is granted, this person's interest is "choate" and is called a "vested" interest. If the remainderman is unknown or not yet even born at the time the life estate is granted, the interest is "inchoate" and is called a "contingent" interest. Life estates may be created *conventionally* through acts of the parties with a deed or will, or they may be created *legally* through operation of law or statute. Finally, a life tenant may not take or damage any part of the real estate during his or her tenure without the stated permission of the grantor. If, for example, a life tenant were to remove minerals or destroy a building on the property, he or she would be said to have committed *waste* and would be liable to the grantor or the remainderman.

Conventional Life Estates. There are two types of conventional life estates. An *ordinary life estate* is one measured by the life of the grantee. An *estate pur autre vie* (for the life of another) is one measured by the life or lives other than that of the grantee. The duration of an estate *pur autre vie* may be measured by more than one life.

Legal Life Estates. A variety of legal life estates (also known as *marital property*) evolved from the marital relationship in the laws of England. Two of these estates, *dower* and *curtesy*, and a third one unique to American law, *homestead*, exist in a few states in order to provide for the support of the surviving spouse and children by giving certain rights to each spouse, as a consequence of marriage, in the inheritable freehold property of the other.

Dower is a legal life estate in part of the real estate of a deceased husband given by law to his surviving wife. Prior to the husband's death, the wife would have to join her husband in any conveyance of the property for said conveyance to be valid and for her dower rights to be extinguished or waived.

Curtesy is a legal life estate in all of the real estate of a deceased wife given by law to her surviving husband provided a live child was born from their marriage. Prior to the wife's death, the husband would have to join his wife in any conveyance of the property for said conveyance to be valid and for his curtesy rights to be extinguished or waived.

Homestead is a legal life estate that provides for an exemption of a property, occupied by the surviving spouse of a family, from attachment by the creditors of the deceased spouse or from forced sale of the property to satisfy the general debts of the deceased. This life estate is not to be confused with the federal homestead acts discussed in Chapter 1.

The laws of the 50 states vary greatly regarding legal life estates. Some have abolished them; others have modified them. One is well advised to consult local legal counsel in order to be properly informed on the myriad of these variations.

CONCURRENT ESTATES

Common law recognizes that two or more persons may simultaneously or concurrently have an interest or estate in the same property at the same time. Such interests are called *concurrent estates*. An *estate in severalty* is an interest or ownership held by *one* person to the exclusion or *severance* of all other persons. In the United States four concurrent estates are recognized. Two of the four, tenancy by the entirety and community property, can exist only between husband and wife. The other two, joint tenancy and tenancy in common, can exist between or among any two or more persons.

Tenancy by the Entirety

Tenancy by the entirety is based on the concept that husband and wife are one person or entirety and that *collectively* as spouses they own the *entire* property interest, which neither as an *individual* owns separately. Furthermore, during the marriage the husband has control of the property, and upon the death of either spouse, the surviving spouse owns the entire property interest according to the *right of survivorship* even to the exclusion of the decedent's heirs. Hence, tenancy by the entirety may never be created by descent, but rather it is created by a deed or a will and said deed or will must be signed by *both* spouses. Finally, a divorce terminates this type of estate and causes the divorced persons to then hold the property as tenants in common.

Joint Tenancy

Joint tenancy may be between husband and wife, but it may also be between or among any two or more persons. Such an estate confers ownership of the entire property as well as an *equal* and *indivisible* portion to each person, who may convey his or her indivisible part or interest at any time during life. Said conveyance causes any new person to be a tenant in common with the other joint tenants. As with a tenancy by the entirety, the right of survivorship exists and therefore a joint tenancy may not be created by descent, but rather only by deed or will. Furthermore, said deed or will must have a granting clause that clearly states that the conveyance is in joint tenancy and not in tenancy in common. Without such a statement, the grantees are presumed by law to be tenants in common. Corporations, though they are legal "persons," may not hold property in joint tenancy, since they have perpetual life and therefore right of survivorship does not apply.

Tenancy in Common

Tenancy in common involves *any* two or more persons holding *indivisible* interests (that need not be equal) in the entire property. Since there is *no right of survivorship*, this type of estate may be created by descent as well as by deed or will. Hence, upon the death of a tenant in common, the heirs may receive title as tenants in common with the surviving persons.

Community Property

Community property did not evolve from the common law of England, as did the other concurrent estates, but rather from French and Spanish civil law. This type of ownership exists in eight states in lieu of the marital life estates of dower and curtesy.[7] In community property states, husband and wife are considered equal owners of all real and personal property that was acquired through their joint efforts during their marriage. Conversely, each may own and control property separately from the other spouse if it was acquired *before* the marriage or *separately* by gift, will, or descent *during* the marriage. Furthermore, any income, rents, royalties, profits, etc., earned by said separate property during the marriage is owned separately. Either spouse may will to anyone one-half of the community (nonseparate) property, while the other half, upon death, is vested in the surviving spouse. Regarding death without a will, the laws of the eight states vary greatly. In fact, there are a variety of subtle differences among the laws of the community property states, and one is therefore well advised to consult local legal counsel concerning these matters.

INCORPOREAL RIGHTS

A person occupying or possessing the tangible physical thing of real estate may convey out of his or her bundle of rights certain intangible, nonpossessory, or *incorporeal* rights to a nonoccupant person. Such rights include easements, licenses, emblements, profits, and liens.

Easements

An easement is a nonpossessory right or interest held by one person in the land of another person such that the nonpossessing person is allowed partial use of said land for a specifically named purpose. The fee owner of the land has the *servient tenement*, of which the rights of ownership are restricted by the rights of the holder of the easement, who has the *dominant tenement*. Easements may be appurtenant or in gross.

An *easement appurtenant* exists for the benefit of the dominant parcel of

7. Arizona, California, Idaho, Louisiana, Nevada, New Mexico, Texas, and Washington.

land, owned by one person, which *usually* adjoins (although it need not adjoin) the servient parcel of land, owned by a second person. Such an easement is regarded as being so closely connected to the dominant parcel that upon the sale of the dominant parcel, the easement is also conveyed even though the deed may *not* mention it. An easement appurtenant, therefore, is said to *run with the land* and such cannot be sold separate from the land; furthermore, it is irrevocable. An example of an easement appurtenant would be the right to drive across another's land for ingress (entrance) and egress (exist) to and from one's land.

An *easement in gross* exists for the benefit of a person or individual who *usually* does *not* own adjoining land, and therefore it does not run with the land but rather *runs to an individual person*. It cannot be sold; it, too, is irrevocable; and it dies with the death of the individual. If an easement in gross is held by a *corporation*, such as a utility company, it is called a *commercial easement in gross* and it may be sold and/or mortgaged.

An example of an easement in gross would be the right of a motel owner to place a sign, indicating the distance to the motel, on the property of a farmer that one would pass while heading toward the motel. An example of a commercial easement in gross would be the right of a telephone company to maintain lines that ran either over or under the land of the grantor.

Creation of Easements. Easements may be created by either expressed or implied grant or reservation, by mutual agreement, by necessity, by prescription, or by condemnation.[8] A separate deed or the same deed that conveys a dominant parcel of real estate may be used to *expressly* convey an easement *by grant*. If one conveys a parcel of land by deed and *reserves* specific rights, an easement *by reservation* is created, making the sold parcel servient. If the actions of two landholders would lead one to *reasonably* believe that an easement had been granted or reserved, an *implied* easement is created. A *party wall agreement* to share the expense and utilization of a common wall built on the boundary line of two properties is an example of the creation of an easement *by agreement*. If a landowner sells a parcel that has no outlet to a public road such that the parcel conveyed is "landlocked," the purchaser of said parcel acquires a right-of-way easement *by necessity*.

An easement is created *by prescription* if a person openly, visibly,

8. See Kratovil, *Real Estate Law*, pp. 18–34, for a complete discussion of the law of easements. It is interesting to note that the purchaser of a cemetery lot does not become the absolute owner of the lot. He or she merely obtains an *easement right of burial*, which also grants the right to enter the cemetery to care for and visit the graves subject to the reasonable regulations adopted by the cemetery company. See also Thomas H. Hall, III, MAI, "Easement Valuation," *The Appraisal Journal*, April 1971, pp. 245–55, for another in-depth listing and discussion of easements.

notoriously, continually, and exclusively uses a part of another's land for a certain period of time. Said time varies from state to state and ranges from 5 to 30 years. Prescription of an easement should not be confused with the acquisition of title through adverse possession (defined in Chapter 4); one does *not* acquire full title, but rather only an easement, through prescription.

In some states the power of eminent domain allows governmental authorities to acquire title through condemnation. In other states, however, condemnation grants only an easement to the property taken. Hence, it is possible for title to remain in the original owner subject to the easement even though full fair market value has been paid by the condemning authority. If for some reason the easement is extinguished, it is possible for the original owner or the owner's heirs to reacquire total use of the property without payment.

Termination of Easements. An easement may be extinguished in any of the following ways:

1. The owner of the dominant tenement may *convey* or *release* his or her rights to the owner of the servient tenement by deed or contract.
2. An easement is extinguished *by merger* if the owner of the dominant parcel purchases the servient parcel.
3. The owner of the dominant tenement may extinguish the easement *by abandoning* and no longer using the easement.
4. An easement is extinguished *by end of necessity*, if the purpose for which the easement was created ceases.
5. If a property (servient or dominant) is condemned through the power of *eminent domain*, any existing easements are automatically terminated by operation of law.
6. If an easement was granted for a specified time period, it is automatically extinguished at the *expiration of the time period* unless a renewal of a time period has been granted or purchased through negotiation between the owners of the servient and dominant estates.

Licenses

A license is a right or privilege granted to an individual person giving permission to enter and use the land of another for a particular purpose. The use of another's land without permission is called a *trespass* and causes the trespasser to be liable to the owner for any damages resulting from such an unauthorized use. Examples of licenses include those for hunting or fishing, admission tickets to performances such as a movie or ball game, and authorization to graze cattle on government lands.

A license may be distinguished from an easement as follows:

1. A license is a personal property right of a temporary nature; an easement is a real property right of a more or less permanent nature.
2. A license is revocable, is not transferable, and does not run with the land; an easement is irrevocable and is transferable, since when the land is sold it does run with the land.
3. Although both licenses and easements *may* be created orally, a license is often created orally and an easement is usually created by a written instrument.

Emblements

Emblements are the rights to the "fruits of the soil," which are crops that are planted annually and cultivated. Such crops are called *fructus industriales* and are dependent on human effort or industry for their annual growth. Vegetables, wheat, barley, etc., are examples of these crops. They are treated as personal property not conveyed in the sale of the land unless so stated in the deed of conveyance. Furthermore, the owner of emblements, who may or may not be the owner of the land, cannot be evicted upon sale of the land and has the right to continue to cultivate and harvest the already planted crops after a sale of the land.

"Fruits of the soil by nature" are called *frutus naturales* and do not require annual planting and cultivation. Such plants may have been originally planted by humans, but once planted they are perennial, or grow continuously at all seasons of the year naturally. Trees, bushes, wild plants and fruits, grass and other natural herbage are examples of these perennial plants. They are treated as real property conveyed in the sale of the land, unless excluded in the deed of conveyance. Timber, however, may be considered personal property if severed from the land or sold as personal property prior to having been severed. It should be noted that *ripened* fruit not yet picked is considered personal property, while *unripened* fruit not yet picked is considered real property.

Profits

A profit is the personal right to remove soil or minerals from the land of another; for example, the rights to take coal, oil, gas, water, or diamonds from the lands of other people are profits. Profits may be assigned, conveyed, or inherited; however, they are usually granted in favor of an individual person holding the dominant estate.

LIENS

An *encumbrance* is defined as any right or interest in real property that affects or limits the fee simple title to real property by either impairing its marketability or diminishing its value. Encumbrances include easements, encroachments, deed restrictions, and liens. Easements and encroachments are defined and discussed in this chapter; deed restrictions or covenants are defined and discussed in Chapter 2 as an example of a private land-use restriction. Liens are also listed as an example of a private land-use restriction in Chapter 2 and as an example of an incorporeal right in real property here in this chapter.

A *lien* is an encumbrance that gives the right to one person or legal entity to satisfy a debt, claim, or charge out of the property of another person or legal entity. Said satisfaction is usually obtained through foreclosure and public sale of the property so encumbered. The various liens discussed in this chapter include mortgages; deeds of trust; property taxes and special assessments; mechanics' liens; vendor's and vendee's liens; attachments; judgments at a court of law; surety bail bond liens; federal and state income, gift, inheritance and corporate franchise tax liens; and decedent's debts liens. However, before discussing each of these various liens, it is appropriate to first classify liens by type.

Classification of Liens

Liens may be classified as general or specific and as voluntary or involuntary. *General liens* encumber all of a person's property, both real and personal. General liens include judgment liens *in personam* ("against a person"), federal and state tax liens, and decedent's debts liens. *Specific liens* encumber only a particular piece or pieces of a person's property. Specific liens include judgment liens *in rem* ("against a thing"), mortgages, deeds of trust, property taxes and special assessments, mechanics' liens, vendor's and vendee's liens, attachments, and surety bail bond liens.

Voluntary or contractual liens arise out of agreements made between two or more parties. The encumbrance is voluntarily given by one party to another party in return for something. For example, a mortgage or deed of trust given by a borrower (mortgagor) to a lender (mortgagee) as security for a loan is a voluntary or contractual lien. A surety bail bond lien is also a specific voluntary lien.

Involuntary liens arise out of the operation of the law, either common law, civil or statutory law, or the law of equity. A *common law lien* is based upon a legal precedent set by a previous court decision and is best exemplified by the right of a hotel to retain the luggage of one of its guests until the guest pays his or her bill. A *statutory lien* is created or defined by a statute or civil code of law. Examples include mechanics' liens, attachments, judgments, property taxes and special assessments, federal and state tax liens, and decedent's debts liens. An *equitable lien* is declared so by a court to prevent injustice, especially in situations not encompassed by common law precedent, statute, or civil code. The best examples are the vendor's and vendee's liens.

Specific Liens

Since it has been stated that liens can be classified as either general or specific and as either voluntary or involuntary, it is now appropriate to discuss in detail each different lien.

Mortgages and Deeds of Trust. A mortgage or a deed of trust is given by a borrower to a lender (mortgage) or to a third-party trustee for the benefit of a lender (deed of trust) as security for a loan that is evidenced by a promissory note or a bond. The mortgage or deed of trust is a legal document by which a borrower pledges, or hypothecates,[9] certain real property or collateral as guarantee for the repayment of the loan. Such legal instruments or contracts create a voluntary or contractual specific lien or claim against the particular property pledged as security for the loan. Such a lien becomes null and void upon repayment of the debt. Upon any default of the loan agreement, however, the lienor-lender may employ his or her lien rights by instituting foreclosure proceedings to cause a public sale of the pledged property to satisfy the debt. Mortgages, deeds of trust, and foreclosure proceedings are discussed more fully in Chapter 10.

Property Taxes and Special Assessments. Property taxes are levied by various taxing bodies to raise revenue needed to provide various public services. Municipalities, school districts, water, sewer and drainage districts, rapid transit districts, etc., have the power to levy taxes upon the people and property within their respective jurisdictional boundaries in order to pay for the services which they provide.

There are two basic theories of taxation: (1) the *benefit-received* theory and (2) the *ability-to-pay* theory. The benefit-received theory argues that each citizen should pay his or her fair share for public services individually utilized each year. Since the benefit-received theory is usually very impractical, because the *poorest* people in a community often require the *most* public services, the ability-to-pay theory provides the basis for *ad valorem* ("according to value") property taxation. The thinking or logic applied here is that the ownership of valuable property evidences wealth and, hence, the ability to pay taxes.

Although the laws governing property taxation vary greatly among the states, some broad generalizations may be made, none of which may be true in all jurisdictions. Each taxing body must (1) *establish an annual budget of needed funds*, (2) *appropriate* or assign said funds to particular purposes or uses, (3) *levy* or impose a tax rate (usually called a "mill levy")[10] as determined by a ratio of the total dollars budgeted divided by

9. "Hypothecate" means to give a thing as security without having to give up possession of it.

10. A mill is a unit of monetary value equal to $.001.

the total value of property in the jurisdiction, (4) *assess* or appraise the value of each property on a uniform basis,[11] (5) *compute the tax* by multiplying the mill levy or tax rate times the assessed value of the property, and (6) *collect the tax* either through voluntary compliance by the taxpayers or through the exercise of rights of foreclosure and public sale granted by the tax law. Such a lien is usually *perpetual*, or prior and superior to all other liens, both those liens that come before and those that come after the date of the tax lien.

Usually exempt from property taxes are various types of properties, such as public property and cemeteries and property owned by religious, nonprofit, or charitable organizations. The Soldiers' and Sailors' Civil Relief Act provides that property owned by military personnel and occupied by their dependents or employees cannot be sold for nonpayment of property taxes or for special assessments without court permission. Normally the court will postpone a sale until six months after the termination of military service.

Payment of property tax extinguishes the tax lien. Nonpayment of property tax usually results in the giving of notice, often by publication, to the delinquent taxpayer that tax sale proceedings are under way to enforce payment. Unless the taxpayer offers a defense, a judgment *in rem* will be rendered for the amount of the tax and penalties due. Said judgment orders the property to be sold. Proper notice of the coming sale is published according to state law. The purchaser at the public sale, by paying the delinquent taxes, penalties, and costs of sale, receives a certificate of purchase that entitles the purchaser to a tax or treasurer's deed if the property is not redeemed during a statutory period of redemption. In some states, a foreclosure similar to a mortgage foreclosure (discussed in Chapter 10) is used in lieu of a tax sale ordered by a judgment *in rem*.

If taxpayers believe that they have not been treated uniformly or fairly, they can appeal to a board of review or board of assessment appeals and eventually to their district court. Most states also have a state board of equalization to raise or lower assessed values in various counties and in the tax authority districts to ensure equalization of assessed values at the percentage of fair market value prescribed by law.

Special assessments, like property taxes, are perpetual liens having priority over all liens except property tax liens. The major distinction between property taxes and special assessments is that property taxes are levied to pay for public improvements or services that *benefit the entire community* while special assessments are levied to pay for local improvements or services that *benefit only particular parcels of real estate*. Assessments, unlike property taxes, do not occur every year. Assessments are levied according to the benefits received and not according to the

11. Assessed value may be equal to or less than fair market value. In most states it is some percentage of fair market value.

value (*ad valorem*) of the property, such as is the case with property taxes. Examples of such improvements include paving and guttering streets and the installation of storm sewers, sidewalks, or street lights.

Payment of special assessments varies among the states and municipalities. If large, the assessments are often paid on an installment basis plus interest. Nonpayment or default on an installment payment plan is usually handled in the same manner as nonpayment of property taxes.

Mechanics' Liens. Builders, contractors, subcontractors, material suppliers, and laborers who supply labor and/or material in the construction, alteration, or repair of improvements on land are called "mechanics" and may acquire liens to encumber said land and improvements to ensure payment for their services. The effect of mechanics' liens resembles that of mortgages or deeds of trust, and in many states mechanics' liens are foreclosed like mortages or deeds of trust, to satisfy debts. Mechanics' liens are involuntary, statutory, specific liens. Since the mechanics' lien statutes vary among the states, only broad generalizations are presented here; local legal counsel should always be sought when dealing with a mechanics' lien problem.

Contract-statutes versus consent-statutes. In *contract-statute states* the mechanic must show that he or she was hired by the property owner or the owner's agent to furnish the labor and/or material for which the lien is claimed. The thinking or logic in these states is to protect the property owners from liens placed against their properties for work requested by others, such as tenants. In *consent-statute states* it is enough for the lien claimant to show that the property owner had knowledge of and consented to the work performed to improve the property even if such work was requested by another person, such as a tenant. In some states (such as Colorado and California), property owners are deemed to have approved and consented to work requested by others unless they conspicuously post a notice of nonresponsibility on the premises within a statutory period of time of becoming knowledgeable of said work. Such a notice may have to be recorded to be valid in some states.

If a co-owner of a property orders or consents to work performed on co-owned property and such work is not consented to by the other co-owners, there is no lien claim upon the shares of the nonconsenting co-owners. However, if the co-owners are married, the work ordered by one spouse may or may not ripen into a lien binding on the other spouse, depending on the laws of the particular state.

Lien inception and priority. The laws of the states vary as to the particular time when a mechanics' lien encumbers a property. Kratovil has presented a comprehensive listing of the various state laws regarding this matter:

1. The lien of any particular mechanic encumbers when the work of that particular mechanic begins.
2. All mechanics' liens begin on the first day of construction, even though the work of a particular mechanic did not commence until a later date.
3. All mechanics' liens begin on the day of the construction contract was signed, which of course would be before the first day of construction.
4. A mechanics' lien does not encumber against a mortgagee until it is recorded in the proper public office.
5. A mechanics' lien recorded after a mortgagee's lien that encumbers the land shall have priority over the mortgage as to the building but not as to the land.
6. Mechanics' liens have equal priority with the construction mortgage.
7. Mechanics' liens have senior priority over the construction loan regardless of the time work began.
8. Generally among mechanics' liens, subcontractors and materials suppliers have priority over contractors, and laborers have priority over contractors, subcontractors, and materials suppliers.[12]

Lien establishment. The proper steps to take to establish a lien are provided for in the various state statutes. Normally a lien claimant must prepare a notice of mechanics' lien that is then filed in the proper legal office. Said office then normally sends a copy of such notice to the property owner by registered or certified mail. The time in which a mechanic must file a lien claim also varies from state to state. Said time period is usually some number of days or months *after* completion of the work. Furthermore, the time period in which to file may also vary relative to the type of mechanic. For example, in Colorado laborers must file within two months of completion of their work while subcontractors, suppliers, and contractors are allowed a four-month period.

New York System versus Pennsylvania System. The lien rights of contractors and subcontractors, suppliers, or laborers relative to the property owner's responsibility for payment generally fall under the rules of the New York System or the Pennsylvania System. Under the *New York System* the property owner's responsibility for payment to subcontractors, suppliers, and laborers *ceases* when said owner has made full payment to the contractor, unless the subcontractor has given notice to the owner of the monies that will be due him or her from the contractor. If such notice is given, the owner may withhold the appropriate sum from the contractor.

12. Kratovil, *Real Estate Law*, pp. 227–28.

Under the *Pennsylvania System* the property owner's responsibility for payment to subcontractors, suppliers, and laborers *does not cease* when said owner has made full payment to the contractor. If the subcontractors, suppliers, or laborers are not paid by the contractor, they may, under this system, file valid mechanics' liens encumbering the property owner's title and forcing the owner to *pay twice* for some work to satisfy these valid liens.

Protection against mechanics' liens. Both property owners and mortgage lenders can protect their respective positions from mechanics' liens. For example, before paying a contractor the final payment or before disbursing mortgage funds, the property owner or the mortgagee, respectively, may obtain a *waiver of liens* from the contractor or property owner, respectively. Lien waivers may be partial or final. A *partial lien waiver* covers work and materials furnished up to the date of the partial waiver and does not cover work or materials yet to be furnished. A *final lien waiver* covers both work and materials furnished and to be furnished.

A property owner or mortgagee may employ the use of a *completion or performance bond* to be obtained by the contractor. Any and all lien claims of subcontractors, suppliers, or laborers are satisfied out of the bond.

A property owner or mortgagee may also employ the use of *holdbacks* of the last 5 to 10 percent owed the contractor until after the period for filing mechanics' liens has passed. The period for foreclosing a mechanics' lien varies from state to state, ranging from six months to six years after completion of all construction, with the majority of states falling in the six-to twelve-months range. Foreclosure of a mechanics' lien is handled much like a mortgage or property tax foreclosure.

Release versus discharge. When a lien claim has been paid or satisfied, a *release of mechanics' lien* form is filed in the proper public office to remove the lien claim from the public record. When the time period for foreclosure of a mechanics' lien has passed, an order of the court to *discharge* the lien for failure to prosecute is used to remove the lien claim from the public record. Discharge may also be effected by either filing a bond approved by the court or depositing money with the court sufficient to cover a successful claim. These actions are called "discharge by bond" and "discharge by payment," respectively.

Vendor's and Vendee's Liens. Vendor's and vendee's liens are involuntary, equitable, specific liens. In a real estate sales transaction the seller is called a "vendor" and the buyer a "vendee." If the seller-vendor conveys the property to the buyer and the buyer defaults by not making full payment, the seller-vendor has a *vendor's lien* against the property for said unpaid balance. Likewise, if the seller defaults by not conveying the property, the buyer-vendee has a *vendee's lien* against the property for the return of all money paid under the terms of the sales contract.

Surety Bail Bond Liens. When persons are arrested on criminal charges, they may offer their equities held in real property as bail in lieu of cash or bonds posted by professional bail bondspersons. When notices of such actions are filed in the proper public offices, they constitute *surety bail bond liens* against the properties. Such liens are removed from the public records by certificates of discharge granted by district attorneys when the persons are discharged from bail.

Attachments. Attachments are involuntary, statutory, specific liens filed by plaintiffs in a lawsuit to prevent defendants from disposing of their real property prior to a judgment being decreed by the court. Generally the court requires the plaintiffs to post a bond with the court to indemnify the defendants for any injuries they may suffer from the attachment if the plaintiffs lose the case.

Somewhat similar to an attachment is a *lis pendens*. Although technically not a lien, a *lis pendens* is a public notice, filed against specific real property, that an action at law is pending that may affect the title to the specific real property. Such a notice informs a prospective buyer, mortgagee, or other claimant that a case at court is pending and that title can be taken only subject to the outcome of the lawsuit.

General Liens

It was stated earlier in this chapter that general liens encumber *all* of a person's property, both real and personal. General liens include judgment liens *in personam*, federal and state tax liens, and decedent's debts liens.

Judgments in Personam. Most judgments rendered by a court of law to settle a lawsuit are judgments *in personam*, which means they are against a particular person. Generally, a judgment must be recorded or docketed, depending on state law, before it becomes an involuntary, statutory, general lien against all property that a defendant now owns or may acquire afterwards during the life of the judgment (usually 6 to 10 years). If a judgment for dollar damages is not paid by the judgment debtor, the judgment creditor will apply for a *writ of execution* that directs the sheriff or other proper public official to seize and sell the property of the judgment debtor to satisfy the payment of the judgment lien. In some states, the sheriff must first seize and sell all the judgment debtor's personal property before seizing and selling any of the judgment debtor's real property in order to satisfy the claim.

The sheriff's sale is a public auction held after proper notice has been published. The highest bidder is often the judgment creditor. Most states have a statutory redemption period (as with mortgage foreclosures), which is usually one year, during which time the judgment debtor may pay the claim plus interest and costs, thereby redeeming the auctioned property. Once the redemption period passes without a redemption having been made, a sheriff's deed is issued to the purchaser of the auctioned property. If a judgment is paid or redeemed, the judgment creditor must file a formal discharge of judgment, usually called a "satisfaction."

Federal Tax Liens. Federal tax liens are involuntary, statutory, general liens. When the federal government files a tax warrant against the property of a delinquent taxpayer, the warrant becomes a lien. A taxpayer may be delinquent in payments for income taxes, gift taxes, or inheritance or estate taxes. Such liens are subordinate to prior liens and encumbrances and have 10-year lives. Federal gift tax liens encumber only the gift property.

State Tax Liens. State tax liens are also involuntary statutory general liens. They, too, may arise from delinquencies in payments for income, gift, or estate taxes as well as corporate franchise taxes. Such liens are subordinate to prior liens and encumbrances and have lives according to the various state laws.

Decedent's Debts Liens. Decedent's debts liens are also involuntary statutory, general liens. Debts against a person's estate are paid first out of nonbequeathed personal property, then out of bequeathed personal property, and finally out of real property sold through foreclosure and public sale.

Summary of Liens

A lien is an encumbrance that gives the right to one person or legal entity to satisfy a debt, claim, or charge out of the property of another person or legal entity. *General liens* encumber all of a person's property, both real and personal; *specific liens* encumber only a particular piece or pieces of a person's property. *Voluntary* or *contractual* liens arise out of agreements made between two or more parties; *involuntary liens* arise out of the operation of the law (common, statutory, or equitable law). A *common law lien* is based upon a legal precedent set by a previous court decision. A *statutory* (civil) *lien* is created or defined by a statute or civil code of law. An *equitable lien* is declared so by a court of law to prevent injustice, especially in situations not encompassed by common law precedent or statute or civil code.

Table 3-1 properly classifies and categorizes the various kinds of liens discussed in this chapter.

Table 3-1. Liens

Specific Liens		General Liens	
Voluntary	*Involuntary*	*Voluntary*	*Involuntary*
Mortgages	Mechanics' liens		Judgments *in Personam*
Deeds of trust	Property taxes		Federal income, gift, or inheritance taxes
Surety bail bond liens	Special assessments		State income, gift, inheritance, or corporate franchise taxes
	Attachments		Decedent's debts liens
	Judgments *in Rem*		
	Vendor's liens		
	Vendee's liens		

MISCELLANEOUS RIGHTS

Appurtenances

An appurtenance is an incidental right, privilege, or improvement that has been permanently added to and belongs to another right in real property and is transferred along with that other right when it is conveyed or sold. An appurtenance usually has been adapted to the use of the real property to which it is connected. Since an appurtenance belongs to the property and not to the tenant-occupant, it is considered real property. Examples of appurtenances include the incorporeal rights (easements, licenses, emblements, profits, and liens); buildings and other improvements; and air, water, and mineral rights.

Air Rights

As noted in Chapter 2, the theoretical ownership of infinite airspace above the earth's surface has been restricted by federal laws for freely navigable air travel. Furthermore, various state and local ordinances restrict the ownership of airspace to permit the development of condominiums and to prohibit the development of tall buildings in order to preserve scenic views and air or light flows to adjacent properties. However, to the extent that a landowner does enjoy ownership and control of the airspace above a property, the owner may sell or lease it and still retain the ownership of the land's surface, subsurface, and airspace below the airspace sold or leased.

The limitations of space in large metropolitan areas today have greatly enhanced the value of urban air rights. For example, Park Avenue in New York City was developed after World War II by leasing the air rights over the Penn Central Railroad's tracks leading north from Grand Central Station. In 1969 the Illinois Center, a joint venture between Metropolitan Structures and Prudential Life Insurance, was developed on an 83-acre air rights parcel over the tracks of the Illinois Central Railroad in downtown Chicago. In Boston, the Prudential Tower is built over the Massachusetts Turnpike. The purchase or lease of such air rights also usually requires the purchase or lease of easements for supporting columns and some ground-level space for access.

"Horizontal subdividing" of airspace is also very common these days for the development of condominiums. The condominium owner is usually granted fee simple ownership to the airspace contained in his or her unit and tenancy in common ownership to the improvements and land.

Encroachments versus Encumbrances

An encroachment is a trespass upon the property of another. Many times an encroachment exists when the airspace of one property is invaded or encroached upon by the property of an adjacent parcel. For example, the branches of trees located on one property may hang into the airspace of another property, the eave of a building may invade the airspace of a contiguous property, or a stone wall may lie partially on the property next door. An example of a subsurface encroachment would be the extension and intrusion of a building's footings into and beneath the ground of an adjacent property.

An encroachment may or may not affect the marketability of the title or the value of the property. If the marketability or value of a property is affected by an encroachment, an encumbrance is said to exist. An encumbrance is defined as any right or interest in real property that affects or limits the fee simple title to real property by either impairing its marketability or diminishing its value. Encumbrances include easements, liens, deed restrictions, and encroachments.

Water Rights

In some states water rights are appurtenant to the land and therefore are conveyed along with the land; in other states water rights are conveyed separately from the land. Water rights may be classified as either (1) waters flowing naturally over the lands of another, (2) waters flowing in defined streams or watercourses, or (3) underground water.

When water flows naturally over the contours of one's land, it is legal for that water to flow off the land of one person (upper landowner) onto and over the land of another person (lower landowner). However, the upper landowner does not have the absolute right to artificially divert or concentrate the natural flow upon the lower landowner's property. Reasonable and noninjurious artificial diversion or concentration, however, is allowed in most states.

When water flows in defined streams or watercourses naturally, one may not obstruct or divert such a water flow without proper authorization from the appropriate local water or flood district or agency. If such flows overflow the defined channel, creating "flood waters," one may take any action necessary to protect one's property even if such action causes the flood waters to cross another person's land.

Rights to water that flows in defined streams or watercourses are classified as either (1) riparian rights or (2) prior appropriation rights. Prior appropriation exists in 17 arid and semiarid western states[13] and in Alaska and Mississippi. Some states have both classifications.[14]

Riparian Rights. Owners of land that borders on defined streams or watercourses are said to own *riparian land* and have *riparian rights*, which are equal rights to the use of the water. Riparian rights grant *unlimited use* of the water for domestic purposes and *reasonable use* of the water for nondomestic purposes, such as agriculture or manufacturing. The owner of riparian land does not have title to the water, but rather has use of the water.

If the lake or stream is unnavigable, the riparian landowner has title to the soil to the middle of the watercourse. If the watercourse is navigable, the riparian landowner has title to the soil to the banks of the watercourse or to the edge of the water at high tide in tidal areas. If the water is navigable, the riparian landowner cannot interfere with public rights and must obtain permission from proper authorities to build a pier or alter the coastline in any manner.

Prior Appropriation Rights. According to the *doctrine of prior appropriation*, the person who first diverts water to his or her own use has the right to continue that use, even if the person uses all of the water available from the entire watercourse. In other words, the right of a prior appropriator is senior to all other appropriators, both upstream and downstream. In times of water scarcity, there is no rationing of the total supply; the junior appropriators bear all the risks and consequences of a water shortage.

When water flows underground in a defined stream or channel, it is subject to the same laws as water that flows in defined streams or channels on the surface of the land. On the other hand, when underground water

13. Arizona, California, Colorado, Idaho, Kansas, Montana, Nebraska, New Mexico, North Dakota, Oklahoma, Oregon, South Dakota, Texas, Utah, Washington, and Wyoming.

14. California, Kansas, Mississippi, Nebraska, North Dakota, Oklahoma, Oregon, South Dakota, Texas, and Washington.

is not confined to a defined stream or channel, the laws may not be the same as those pertaining to unconfined waters on the surface of the land.

Unconfined underground waters are called *percolating waters* and in some states[15] are considered part of the land in which they are located, which grants the landowner *unlimited use* of such waters. However, the majority of states apply the rule of *reasonable use* to percolating waters.

Mineral Rights. Mineral rights may be subdivided into two categories: (1) minerals-in-place and (2) oil and gas. Minerals-in-place include gold, silver, coal, etc., and they are transferred with the sale of the land unless otherwise excluded. If they are excluded, they may be sold separately; unless otherwise stated, a sale of mineral rights also conveys the right of entry to mine and remove the minerals from the land.

Oil and gas rights differ from minerals-in-place because of their migratory character. When a reservoir of oil or gas is tapped, oil or gas may be drained from portions of the reservoir that underlie adjacent lands. In a few states,[16] called *ownership states*, oil and gas can be absolutely owned as real property by a landowner, subject to the *right of capture* by adjacent landowners; in other words, adjacent landowners may drill on their property and drain oil and gas from beneath an adjacent property.

In *nonownership states*, no person owns oil and gas while it is still in the ground but each landowner has the exclusive right to drill on his or her property and to extract all oil and gas that may be drained from beneath this property or adjacent lands. Once the oil or gas has been *captured*, it becomes the personal property of the one who has done the capturing. It should be evident that, because of the right of capture, there is only a subtle difference between ownership and nonownership states relative to oil and gas rights. In ownership states, oil and gas rights pass as part of the real property; in nonownership states, they pass as an appurtenance to the land. Finally, in all states, it is most common for landowners to lease their oil and gas rights to drilling and petroleum companies for a fee or for a royalty percentage of the dollar value of all oil or gas extracted from the wells on their land.

SUMMARY AND CONCLUSION

The history and development of property law is a most interesting area of study. It is interesting to note that the allodial system of ownership existed before as well as after the feudal system. The doctrine of tenures and the doctrine of estates were the precursors of today's leasehold and

15. Alabama, Connecticut, Illinois, Maine, Massachusetts, Montana, Ohio, South Dakota, Texas, and Vermont.

16. Alabama, Arkansas, Colorado, Kansas, Michigan, Mississippi, Montana, Ohio, Pennsylvania, Texas, and West Virginia.

freehold estates. There are corporeal and incorporeal rights in real property; there are tangible and intangible rights in personal property. The differences between real and personal property were discussed. A fixture is something that was once personal property but has become real property. The freehold estates include the inheritable fee estates of (1) fee simple absolute, (2) fee simple qualified, (3) conditional fee, and (4) fee tail. Freehold estates also include the noninheritable life estates of (1) conventional life estates and (2) legal life estates. Concurrent estates include (1) tenancy by the entirety, (2) community property, (3) joint tenancy, and (4) tenancy in common.

The incorporeal rights in real property include (1) easements, (2) licenses, (3) emblements, (4) profits, and (5) liens. The miscellaneous rights in real property discussed in this chapter were (1) appurtenances, (2) air rights, (3) encroachments, (4) encumbrances, (5) water rights, and (6) mineral rights.

It should be concluded from this chapter that property rights, interests, and estates are a very complex and legally technical area of study. The real estate student and practitioner must master this area of study, however, in order to successfully proceed with studies in real estate.

CHAPTER 4

Acquisition, Examination, and Protection of Title

KEY TERMS

Title A *legal concept* that confers the rights of ownership
Deed A formally written *legal instrument* that conveys and evidences title
Statute of Frauds A law that holds that certain contracts are unenforceable unless they or a note or memorandum thereof are in writing and are signed by the party to be charged or by a duly authorized agent
Adverse possession Acquisition of title to the real property of another by the hostile, actual, exclusive, open, notorious, and continuous possession and occupation under an evident claim or right or title for the appropriate statutory time period
Prescription The right to an easement acquired through the open, visible, notorious, exclusive, continuous, and adverse use of a part of another's real property for the appropriate statutory time period
Alienation The transfer of property ownership from one person to another
Merchantable or marketable title Title free of any major defects or clouds or color of title such that it is readily transferable to a prudent purchaser and/or is quite capable of being pledged as collateral to a lender
Abstract and opinion A method of title protection that includes a history of title as shown by a summary or abstract of all recorded instruments that have ever affected the title and an opinion of the condition of the title rendered by an attorney upon examination of the abstract
Certificate of title An opinion of the condition of title made from the examination of the "original" records affecting title rather than from an examination of an abstract
Title insurance A contract that guarantees title and indemnifies the insured (subject to certain exceptions) against financial loss resulting from claims, arising out of defects in title to real property, that were existent but undisclosed at the time the policy was issued
Torrens system A system of real property title registration used to verify the ownership and establish the status of title without the necessity of recurrent title searches and/or title insurance premiums

TITLE DEFINED AND DISTINGUISHED FROM DEED

Title to real property is a *legal concept* that confers the rights of ownership, namely, the rights of possession, use, enjoyment, control, and disposition. A *deed* to real property is a formally written *legal instrument* that, when properly executed, delivered, and accepted, conveys *title* to an interest in real property. A deed also evidences the ownership of title to real property. Prior to the seventeenth century, ownership of title to real property was evidenced or proven by possession and the power to defend. Original acquisition of title in these early times was generally achieved through either conquest or discovery. Conveyance, or transfer of title, was executed by the simple surrender or transfer of possession.

Between the end of the feudal period and 1677, when the Statute of Frauds was adopted in England, transfer of real property took place in a very symbolic manner called "livery of seisin", from the French words meaning "to deliver legal possession." The seller and purchaser would go upon the land with friends and witnesses. The seller or grantor would literally hand a clump of earth called a "feoffment" (or a twig of a tree when the earth was frozen or snow covered) to the purchaser or grantee. While handing the soil or branch to the grantee, the grantor would say in the presence of all that by this act he or she was putting the grantee into possession of the property. In some cases, it has been reported that the youngest of the witnesses would be severely beaten to strongly impress the fact that a transfer of property took place, lest the young person be forgetful and serve as a poor witness.[1]

This method of evidencing transfer of title was not only barbaric, but also was quite inadequate. Transfer by delivery and possession with no written document of proof gave rise to many disputes and frauds. Hence, in England in 1677, the Statute of Frauds was adopted into the common law and later was embodied into the statutes of all the states in the United States. The Statute of Frauds holds that certain contracts are unenforceable unless they, or a note or memorandum thereof, are *in writing and signed* by the party to be charged or by his or her duly authorized agent. A complete discussion of the more technical ramifications of the statute is presented in Chapter 6.

ACQUISITION OF TITLE

In America today there are many ways by which title may be acquired. These various methods can be classified into five general categories to include (1) will, (2) descent, (3) accession, (4) occupancy, and (5) transfer.

1. See Edna L. Hebard and Gerald S. Meisel, *Principles of Real Estate Law* (New York: Simmons-Boardman Publishing Corp., 1964), p. 218.

Title by Will

A *will* or *last will and testament* is a gift (usually a written instrument) by which a person may dispose of property to others *upon and only upon* death. The laws of wills vary from state to state. Most states impose certain limitations, such as that a surviving spouse may not be completely disinherited. Since the technicalities of wills can be quite complex, one should always consult legal counsel to be sure a will is properly drawn and in conformance with state statutes.

One who has died is called a *decedent*. One who dies leaving a will is said to have died *testate*. The person making a will is called a *testator* if male or a *testatrix* if female. A gift by will of real property is a *devise*, and the receiver of the real property is called a *devisee*. A gift by will of personal property is a *bequest*; the receiver is a *bequestee*. A gift by will of money is a *legacy*; the receiver is a *legatee*. A will may be revoked at any time prior to death and therefore is called an *ambulatory instrument*. A will may be changed at any time prior to death by the making of a new will or of a formal *codicil*, which is a supplement to a will made subsequent to the making of the will and must be signed and witnessed, like the will itself. The person charged with the responsibility of carrying out the provisions of a will is called an *executor* if male or an *executrix* if female.

There are three generally recognized types of wills as follows: (1) formally witnessed, (2) holographic, and (3) noncupative. A *formally witnessed will* is a written legal instrument drawn by a lawyer and signed by the testator and one or more witnesses in the presence of one another. A *holographic will* is totally written, dated, and signed in the handwriting of the testator *without* the presence or signatures of witnesses; this type of will is recognized in a minority of the states. A *noncupative will* is an *oral* will made by a person wounded in the armed forces or injured in an accident and who is in a state of the contemplation of death. Such wills can convey only personal property up to a certain value; they must be made in the presence of witnesses, one of whom must reduce the will to writing and offer it to the probate court within a stated time period (usually six months).

Title by Descent

Title by descent is also called *title by succession*. One who dies *without* leaving a will is said to have died *intestate*. When a decedent leaves no will, state statutes, called the *statutes of descent and distribution*, provide for the distribution of the decedent's property by descent, through an action called *intestate succession*. One who acquires title to real property in this manner is called an *heir*. One who acquires personal property in this manner is called a *next of kin*. Both heirs and next of kin are called *distributees*.

The laws of descent or succession vary from state to state. Usually the surviving spouse is entitled to one-third or one-half of the decedent's property, with the remainder going to the decedent's children. If there is no spouse or children, the order of succession might then be to the decedent's parents, brothers and sisters, descendants of the brothers and sisters, then to the grandparents, aunts and uncles, and cousins in that order. If there are no descendants, the property will ultimately escheat to the state. In community property states an intestate decedent's property automatically transfers to the surviving spouse. Any property held in joint tenancy, of course, passes to the surviving joint tenants, since such property can never be disposed by will, because of the right of survivorship.

Title by Accession

The right of a property owner to any increase in the property due to nature or to human action is called *accession*. Accession may occur through (1) accretion or (2) the addition of fixtures.

Accretion. An owner of riparian land can gain land gradually through *accretion* by the action of the water adjacent to the property. Accretion can happen in one of three ways.

Alluvion. Alluvion is soil that has been washed up and deposited on the banks of the water, producing additional firm ground. The loss of this soil is called "erosion," and the land may not be reclaimed by the original owner.

Reliction. Reliction, also called *dereliction*, is the increase in land caused when water recedes permanently below the normal water level.

Avulsion. Avulsion is the increase in land caused when water violently tears away land from one place and deposits it in another. Land lost through avulsion is reclaimable by the original owner if he or she acts within a certain time period (usually one year).

Addition of Fixtures. When a tenant, *without permission* for later removal, affixes personal property to the landlord's property such that it becomes a permanent fixture, said attached property is acquired by the landlord. A detailed discussion of fixtures, and disputes thereof was presented in Chapter 3.

Title by Occupancy

The three ways by which one can acquire title by occupancy include (1) adverse possession, (2) prescription, and (3) abandonment.

Adverse Possession. Title to the real property of another may be acquired by *hostile, actual, exclusive, open, notorious*, and *continuous* possession and occupation under an evident *claim of right or title* for the appropriate *statutory time period*. Said time period varies from state to state and can be as short as 5 years (Idaho, Montana, Nevada) or as long as 30 years (Louisiana), with most states using 20 years. The public purpose behind the concept of adverse possession is that it encourages the use of land.

The adverse possession must be obvious to the real owner and any neighbors. The adverse occupant must exercise dominion over the property, such as farming the land, building a house, or fencing the boundaries. The occupant must also exercise an actual claim of ownership to the exclusion of all other persons. Some states also require the payment of all real property taxes and assessments by the adverse possessor for the continuous statutory period of occupancy. The continuous occupancy for the statutory period may involve more than a single occupancy by one adverse possessor. In other words, the time period of one adverse possessor may be "tacked on" to that of another, as long as they are continuous.

Once all the requirements for acquisition of title by adverse possession have been fulfilled, the adverse possessor automatically obtains valid title without a deed and can compel a subsequent purchaser to accept a deed from him or her. However, some states require a court decree to "quiet title" before title can be considered marketable or insurable.

Possession under a color of title is *not* necessary to acquire title by adverse possession. *Color of title* exists when a person takes possession under a defective or void instrument. When both adverse possession and color of title exist together, however, the adverse possessor acquires title to *all* the property described in the defective or void instrument even if *only part* of it has been occupied.

Prescription. As discussed in Chapter 3, the right to an easement may be acquired through the open, visible, notorious, exclusive, and continuous use of a part of another's land for the statutory period of time. In some states one acquires only an easement by prescription if one complies with all the requisites of adverse possession but does not pay the real property taxes.

Abandonment. A landlord may reacquire a property from a tenant through abandonment if the tenant permanently leaves the premises prior to expiration of the lease.

Title by Transfer

Whenever title is conveyed from one person to another, either by the acts of the parties or by the operation of law, title by transfer exists. The transfer of property from one person to another is called *alienation*. The acquisition of title by transfer can be categorized as either by voluntary alienation or by involuntary alienation.

Voluntary Alienation. Voluntary alienation includes transfer of title by (1) private grant or sale, (2) public grant, or (3) gift.

Private Grant. A sale of real property between a purchaser and a buyer, with the purchaser paying a sale price for the property, is a private grant. A deed (discussed in Chapter 5) is the legal instrument used to voluntarily transfer the ownership for the price paid.

Public Grant. As discussed in Chapter 1, the United States government made many public land grants to individuals (Homestead Acts) for farming, to groups for the establishment of cities and towns, to railroads for westward expansion, and to educational institutions for the establishment of land grant colleges. The acquisition of title from the United States government is called a *patent*.

Gift. A gift may be *to a private person*, in which case it is identical to a private grant, with the exception that no money or consideration is tendered by the purchaser. A gift may be to the public and is called a *dedication*. A dedication may be one of the following three types:

1. *Common law dedication* results when an owner wishes to give some land for public use, such as a road in a subdivision. The owner must execute a deed, and the public may accept the property by local ordinance or by public use.
2. *Statutory dedication* results when a recorded map that expressly indicates dedicated areas, such as streets and parks, is approved by local government officials.
3. *Dedication by deed* results when a land developer specifically wishes to grant fee simple title in the land which might otherwise be considered to be an easement for public use. A common law dedication may be considered by the courts as only an easement.

Involuntary Alienation. Involuntary alienation is the transfer of title whether the owner wishes it or not (against the owner's will or volition) by operation of law or court action and includes (1) partition action, (2) quiet title action, (3) foreclosure action, (4) declaratory relief action, (5) execution or sheriff's sale, (6) forfeiture, (7) bankruptcy, (8) marriage, (9) escheat, (10) eminent domain and condemnation, (11) confiscation, (12) equitable estoppel, and (13) probate or estate sale.

Partition Action. When a co-owner sues the other co-owner(s) in order to have property interests severed or partitioned from the interests of the other co-owner(s), the judicial proceeding is called a partition action. If the property cannot be divided, the court will order a sale and divide the money proceeds of sale.

Quiet Title Action. The judicial proceeding used to clear a title from a disputed claim or color of title to make it marketable or insurable is called a quiet title action or suit. Such an action may be used by an adverse possessor to perfect his or her title.

Foreclosure Action. The judicial proceeding used by a lien holder to satisfy a debt through a forced sale of property that has been offered as security for the debt of the property owner is called a foreclosure action. A foreclosure suit may be filed by any lien holder, such as the holder of mortgages, deeds of trust, property tax or assessments liens, mechanics liens, etc.

Declaratory Relief Action. Whenever a controversy exists between two or more parties relative to their interests in a parcel of real property, either party may institute a declaratory relief or *equity action* to allow the court to settle the dispute. The court decides in whom title should be vested.

Execution or Sheriff's Sale. When one wins a money judgment at court against another person, the court will order the sheriff or other officer to satisfy the judgment out of a public sale or auction of the debtor's property.

Forfeiture. If a property is held in a *fee simple qualified estate*, there is the possibility that such an estate may be terminated by the occurrence or nonoccurrence of some specified event (see Chapter 3). When such a termination happens, a forfeiture is said to exist.

Bankruptcy. A person may voluntarily or involuntarily enter into bankruptcy. In such a case, the court will order the sale of the debtor's property to satisfy creditors.

Marriage. Marital property is any non–separately owned property acquired during marriage in community property states. In non–community property states, marital property may be acquired through dower, curtesy, or homestead rights.

Escheat. The legal proceedings that cause the property of an intestate decedent with no heirs to revert to the state is called escheat.

Eminent Domain and Condemnation. The legal proceedings of condemnation through the power of eminent domain allow governmental bodies to acquire title to private property by paying just compensation at fair market value (see Chapter 2).

Confiscation. This is the right of a country to take the property of its enemies in time of war. Confiscation can be likened to the old method of acquiring title known as "conquest."

Equitable Estoppel. A court of equity is often charged with having to transfer title in order to protect innocent parties to a fraudulent transaction. For example, if a property of A is fraudulently conveyed to B by C and A is aware of the fraud, A is *estopped* by the court from reclaiming ownership from C.

Probate or Estate Sale. In order to settle an estate, a probate court will often order a sale of the decedent's real property to pay for the administration of liquidating the estate, to pay creditors, and to make disposition of property to heirs or devisees. Sometimes this legal proceeding is called a *court sale* rather than a probate sale or an estate sale.

EXAMINATION OF TITLE

The purchaser of real property needs to be certain that the seller, at the time of sale, does indeed hold merchantable (marketable) title. Merchantable title need not be perfect. For example, the title to a property on which a garage eave encroaches onto an adjacent property is not perfect; however, it most likely could be freely sold in the market without fear of the title being assailed. In other words, marketable title is free of any major defects or clouds or color of title. It is readily transferable to a prudent purchaser and is quite capable of being mortgaged to a lending institution.

To ascertain the condition of the seller's title, an examination or search of title must be made. The responsibility of the examination of title in most states rests on the purchaser, who must notify the seller, within a reasonable time period, of any defects discovered so that the seller might cure said defects if possible. In other states, it is the responsibility and the expense of the seller to examine and report the condition of the title.

Two things must be done to ascertain the condition of title: (1) investigation of the parties in possession of the property and (2) investigation of all recorded documents or instruments that affect title to the property.

Possession: Actual Notice

The rights of the parties in possession of a property do not have to be entered in the public records. Leases, for example, are not usually recorded, but a tenant's rights cannot be defeated by a sale of the property. Everyone is presumed to have *actual notice* of all the rights and claims of any persons in possession of a property. Hence, a visitation to the property and a discussion with the occupants, if any, is required to properly ascertain the condition of title.

Recording: Constructive Notice

Every state provides for the recording, in a public office, of all instruments or legal documents that have an effect on a parcel of real estate. Unrecorded documents are valid between the parties to the instrument. However, unless or until such instruments are recorded, they are void and of no effect relative to the protection of innocent parties who have acted in ignorance of these documents. Once an instrument has been recorded, everyone is considered to have been given *legal* or *constructive notice* of the rights and claims so recorded. In other words, the law presumes that all parties have equal knowledge of all properly recorded instruments as if they had actually read them themselves. The public purpose behind recording laws is that the ownership of real property should be disclosed by the public records and that purchasers of real property should be able to rely on these records for protection against secret and unrecorded instruments.

The public office in which one records an instrument affecting real property is usually the office of the county clerk and recorder of the county in which the real property is located. The public official charged with the responsibility of recording may be the recorder of deeds, register of deeds, registrar of deeds, county clerk, county recorder, or county clerk and recorder, depending on the particular state. The recorder's job is most important, since the effectiveness of a recording system depends greatly on the completeness and accuracy of the records and on a meticulous indexing system.

The two most commonly used indexing systems include (1) *the grantor-grantee index system* and (2) *the tract index system*. A county might have a single grantor-grantee index or it might have many, one for each type of instrument. Such indexes list the grantor names alphabetically and chronologically. Hence, if one finds the record of the instrument by which one acquired title, only the records after the date of acquisition need be searched to discover what happen to the property during that person's tenure. Searching the recorded history of all documents affecting a title is called *running the chain of title*. The tract index system requires a separate index page for each parcel of real property in the county. Listed on these pages are recordings of all the instruments that, over time, have had an effect on each parcel.

PROTECTION OF TITLE

There are four ways by which a purchaser can protect himself or herself against acquiring an invalid, defective, or nonmerchantable title. The four methods offer varying amounts of protection and include the following: (1) *abstract and opinion* (common in farm areas), (2) certificate of title (common in eastern and some southern states), (3) *title insurance* (most widely used method), and (4) *Torrens certificate* (used mostly in Boston, Chicago, Duluth, Minneapolis–St. Paul, and New York City).

Abstract and Opinion

An *abstract of title* is a written summary of the running of the chain of title or the history of title as shown by all recorded instruments that have ever affected title. The material facts of all recorded instruments, such as deeds, wills, mortgages, and other liens, are summarized to show the continuity of ownership, interests, claims, and rights in a property over time. Abstracts may be prepared by public officials, attorneys, and abstract companies. Most abstracts are prepared by licensed, and often bonded, professional abstractors who have had the required amount of legal education and training to be so qualified.

An abstractor cannot guarantee or offer an opinion as to the condition of title. Abstractors can only certify that they are knowledgeable and competent experts. They may be held liable only for their proven negligence in the preparation of the abstract. If such negligence is charged, the charging party must sue in court to satisfy such a claim.

An abstract itself is of no protective value without an *opinion* as to the condition of title made by a competent attorney upon examination of the abstract. However, not even the attorneys can guarantee the validity of a title. They, too, can only certify that they are knowledgeable and competent experts. They may be held liable only for their negligence or mistakes made in interpreting the recorded instruments. For example, if there is a forged deed recorded, attorneys cannot be expected to know that, and therefore, cannot be held liable. Negligence or mistake, if any, must be proven in court.

Certificate of Title

In small communities, where the demand necessary to support an abstract company does not exist, it is common to have a lawyer's or conveyancer's certificate of title rather than an abstract and opinion. A certificate of title is an opinion of the condition of title made from the examination of the *original* records affecting title, rather than from an examination of an abstract or summary of these records. If there are no attorneys in a small community, a knowledgeable person or *conveyancer* will examine the original records and prepare a certificate of title. As with an abstract and opinion, there is no guarantee of title.

Title Insurance

Title insurance is a contract that insures title and indemnifies the insured (subject to certain exceptions) against financial loss resulting from claims arising out of defects in title to real property that were existent but undisclosed at the time the policy was issued. Only defects and claims prior to the policy date are covered. In other words, title insurance offers coverage into the past as opposed to coverage into the future, as automobile or life insurance offer. The insurance premium is a one-time fee, and an *owner's* (purchaser's) *title policy* is nontransferable. In other words, upon sale of the property, a new policy must be purchased. However, a *mortgagee's title policy* is transferable. Such a policy protects the lender against any loss he or she might suffer because of a defective title to a property against which he or she holds a loan security interest.

A list of the advantages of title insurance over an abstract and opinion has been distributed by the Transamerica Title Insurance Company as follows:

1. Title insurance provides protection, not obtained through abstracts, against hidden defects, some examples of which are:
   Forgery
   Lack of delivery
   Incapacity of a party
   Fraud
   Unprobated or lost wills
   Afterborn children
   Implied reciprocal easements
   Negative reciprocal covenants
   Irregular marriages
   Irregularity of tax sales
   Lack of service in legal proceedings
   Defect in power of attorney
2. A title company's liability is absolute. Also, a title company bears the cost of the insured's defense, when necessary.
3. Customers can be confident of the ability to pay claims should they arise, because corporate responsibility exists, rather than personal warranty.
4. Title insurance allows more real estate sales by:
   a. Guaranteeing purchaser that title is marketable.
   b. Facilitating a continuing flow of mortgage money by making local mortgages salable to large investors.
   c. Title companies will often insure against title defects that would otherwise defeat sales.
5. Title insurance shortens selling or buying process because:
   a. Title commitments go directly to buyer or agent and chosen lender, allowing processing to begin immediately.
   b. Title commitments can be issued faster with less detail for buyers, sellers, and agents.

   c. Specific requirements are set forth in clear, easy-to-follow form.
6. Title insurance makes escrow service available.

Some title risks that are *not* usually covered by the standard owner's title policy include:

1. Matters not disclosed by public record
2. Matters which an accurate survey would show
3. Taxes and assessments not yet due or payable
4. Zoning restrictions
5. Water and mineral rights
6. Defects known to insured

For an additional fee, most any exclusion can be removed. For example, the American Land Title Association has adopted an extended-coverage policy that insures the following additional risks:

1. Unrecorded mechanics liens
2. Unrecorded physical easements
3. Facts an accurate survey would show
4. Water and mineral rights
5. Rights of parties in possession

Finally, to save the time and expense of a title search back to the beginning of time, most states have passed laws that set a time limit (30 to 40 years usually) on real property claims. Title need not be searched beyond the statutory time period. Such laws also enhance the marketability of title and, therefore, are in the public interest.

Torrens System

The Torrens system of title registration was developed by Sir Robert Torrens in Australia in 1857, when he introduced a bill providing for the registration of land in the manner in which ships were registered at that time. Ship registrations then, like most automobile registrations today, listed all liens and claims against the named property. Such a list gave a brief and simple chain or condition of title. The Torrens system became law in South Australia in 1858. Illinois was the first state to enact a Torrens system in 1895 and then amended it in 1897 and 1907 to remove certain constitutional objections. Today the Torrens system is used mostly in only five metropolitan areas of the country.

To register title under the Torrens system one must essentially file a suit to quiet title. The court will order an official title examination; notice of the suit will then be sent to all parties who have an interest in the property according to the examination of title; public notice of the judicial proceeding is also published in the newspaper. Upon the holding of a court hearing at which all claims are heard, the court then issues its decree of confirmation of title and registration.

The court's decree is then filed with the *registrar of titles* (who might be the county clerk and recorder), who then makes an original certificate of title that sets forth the court's findings of the condition of title. The registrar then issues a copy of the original certificate, called an *owner's duplicate certificate of ownership*, to the property owner as his or her protection of title. Upon the passing of a statutory time period beyond the date of the court's decree (usually 90 days), if no one has made a claim against the property, the owner is presumed by law to have title decreed.

To transfer property under this system, one must surrender one's owner's duplicate to the registrar, who cancels it and its original and makes a new original and issues a new duplicate to the new owner. The new duplicate will list all outstanding claims against the property.

Title does not pass by deed alone under the Torrens system. Both the deed and owner's duplicate certificate of registration are taken to the registrar. The registrar keeps the deed and issues a new owner's duplicate. Hence, it is said that under the Torrens system "title passes by registration, not by deed."

The disadvantages of the Torrens system include the following:

1. Unlike with a title insurance policy, the expense of litigation attacking the title is borne by the property owner.
2. A rightful owner, if not capable of making the claim within the statutory time period, might be deprived of his or her property without due process of law.
3. Indemnity funds created to protect rightful owners from loss of property are often quite inadequately funded.

SUMMARY AND CONCLUSION

Title is a *legal concept* that confers the rights of ownership. Title is usually transferred by a *legal instrument* called a *deed*. Transfer may be voluntary or involuntary. Other than *by transfer*, title may also be acquired *by will, by descent, by accession* caused by nature or by human action, or *by occupancy* through adverse possession, prescription, or abandonment. The examination of the chain of title is an important prerequisite to the protection of title by (1) an *abstract and opinion*, (2) a *certificate of title*, (3) *title insurance*, or (4) *Torrens system*.

It may be concluded that title may not only be acquired in a variety of ways, but it may also be protected in a variety of ways. Regardless of how one acquires and protects title to *one's own* real property, the real estate student or practitioner needs to be knowledgeable of the myriad of other possibilities available.

CHAPTER 5

Deeds

KEY TERMS

Grantor The seller who conveys title by deed
Grantee The purchaser to whom a deed conveys title
Premises One of the three major parts of a deed; contains the terms and propositions upon which the transfer of title is to be made
Habendum One of the three major parts of a deed; defines the quantity of interest or the duration of ownership being conveyed to the grantee
Testimonium One of the three major parts of a deed; includes the covenants of warranty (if any), the execution, and the acknowledgment
Quitclaim deed A deed that does not imply that the grantor has good title or even any title at all; it conveys the grantor's present interest in the property such that if he or she has title, everything is conveyed and if he or she has no title, nothing is conveyed
Bargain and sale deed A deed that recites the consideration given and conveys the present and "after-acquired" title to real property without giving any warranties of title; also called a *deed without covenants*
General warranty deed A deed that conveys present and after-acquired title and contains three present and three future covenants or warranties of title with these warranties applying during and before the grantor's tenure of ownership
Special warranty deed A deed that conveys present and after-acquired title and contains fewer than the six usual present and future covenants or warranties of title; these warranties apply *only* to the grantor's tenure of ownership
Grant deed A deed used in California and other states in lieu of general or special warranty deeds; contains *only* the three present covenants applying *only* to the grantor's tenure of ownership

DEED: CONTRACT OR CONVEYANCE

A *deed* is a formally written legal instrument that, when properly executed, delivered, and accepted, conveys title to an interest in real property. A deed also evidences ownership of title to real property. The seller, who conveys property by deed, is called the *grantor*. The purchaser, to whom a deed conveys property, is called the *grantee*. A deed is a *conveyance, not* a contract; however, a deed is normally given in performance of a contract. A deed *may* be a contract if it states a consideration, however, the law is quite clear in that a deed need not be based on any consideration whatsoever in order to transfer title.[1] Once a deed is duly executed, delivered, and accepted, it supersedes the contract of sale. Since a deed *can be* a contract, all the laws and requirements pertinent to contracts (discussed in Chapter 6) *may* apply.

A deed usually begins with the words "this indenture" because of the old custom whereby two copies of the conveyance would be written upon a sheet of sheepskin that was then torn in half, supplying a copy to each party to the transaction. Proof of a valid transaction could be made by matching the *indentures* or indentations that had been made by tearing the sheepskin in half to provide both grantor and grantee with a copy of the deed instrument.

ELEMENTS OF A DEED

In order to transfer title, a deed need *not* contain any technical or formal wording. Some states do require a formal *seal* (discussed later) for a deed to be valid. The *manifested intent* of the parties to the transaction is the controlling and effective force that causes title to be transferred. As discussed in Chapter 4, according to the Statute of Frauds a deed must be written. In addition to being a written document, to be valid a deed must contain six or seven (depending on the state) essential elements. Some states do not require a recital of consideration, in which case the deed is not a contract. Depending on how one groups them, a deed also usually includes six or seven nonessential elements. All the elements are contained in one of the three major parts of a deed, which are (1) the premises, (2) the habendum, and (3) the testimonium.

The Premises

The premises of a deed contains the terms and propositions upon which the transfer of title is to be made. The elements usually contained in the premises include (1) the date, (2) the designation of the grantor and grantee, (3) the recital of consideration, (4) the words of conveyance, (5) the legal description of the property, and (6) the exceptions and restrictions.

The Date. Although *not necessary* for a valid deed, the date should be included because it might prevent any future question or controversy regarding the time of transfer of title.

1. See *American Jurisprudence 2d*, Vol. 23, pp. 118–19.

The Designation of the Grantor and Grantee. To be valid it *is necessary* for a deed to clearly name and identify a competent grantor and grantee so as to know from whom and to whom the title is being transferred.

The Recital of Consideration. Most states require a statement of *some* price paid; other states require that the *actual* amount paid be stated. Where such statements are required, the recital of consideration (actual or nominal) *is necessary* for a deed to be valid. When a deed recites consideration, the burden of proving a lack thereof is on the one who attacks the deed.

The Words of Conveyance. These are the operative words of a deed which manifest the intention of the grantor to convey title to the grantee. These words must be carefully chosen, for they reflect the type of deed being used. These words are also commonly called the *granting clause* and *are necessary* for a deed to be valid.

The Legal Description of the Property. Another element that *is necessary* for a deed to be valid is an unquestionable identification of the property (see Appendix A for a summary of Legal Descriptions). To avoid confusion, discrepancies, and perhaps litigation, it is advisable to use the same legal and technical description contained in the previous deeds used to convey title to the property. Following the legal description there may also be a *recital clause* that will state all or part of the chain of title, to show how the grantor had originally acquired title.

The Exceptions and Restrictions. The conveyance of title to real estate is assumed to be made free and clear of all encumbrances and restrictions except those expressly stated. The words that are used to expressly state any encumbrances (such as easements, encroachments, mortgages, deeds of trust, and any other liens) or any deed restrictions or restrictive covenants created by a previous grantor or developer are contained in what is called the "under and subject clause." This clause *is not necessary* for a deed to be valid.

The Habendum

The habendum part of a deed defines the quantity of interest or the duration of ownership being conveyed to the grantee. The habendum usually begins with the words "to have and to hold" and then describes the estate (fee simple, life, etc.) being transferred. Within the body of the habendum is the *appurtenance clause*, which defines all the additional rights that are necessary to the proper use and enjoyment of the property and all the improvements (buildings, fences, etc.) that exist on the property. Both the additional rights and improvements, by law, run with the land as appurtenances, and therefore a listing of such *is not necessary* for a deed to be valid. However, if included, the habendum should be consistent with the granting clause in the premises. If there is an inconsistency between the granting clause and the habendum or appurtenance clauses, the granting clause will usually prevail.

The Testimonium

The testimonium portion of a deed includes the covenants of warranty (if any), the execution, and the acknowledgment.

The Covenants of Warranty. It *is not necessary* for a deed to contain any guarantees from the grantor to be valid. The grantor may convey with no warranties, such as in a quitclaim deed, or may convey with certain warranties, such as in a special warranty deed or a general warranty deed. Said warranties will be explained in the discussion of types of deeds.

The Execution. In order for a deed to be properly executed it must be signed, sealed (in some states), and delivered. The signatures or marks (if they cannot write) of the grantors are necessary for a deed to be valid. In most states, a signature by grantor's mark [John (X his mark) Grantee] must be witnessed. Some states require the signatures of grantors to be witnessed by one or more persons; other states require no witnesses. Many states require witnessing in order for a deed to be recorded. Yet in some of these states, a deed need not be witnessed or recorded to be valid. A deed might also be executed via a power of attorney, which is a written instrument authorizing a person, the attorney-in-fact, to act as the agent on behalf of the grantor to the extent indicated in the instrument.

Some states require that the marital status of the grantors be stated, and if married, require the spouse's signature in order to release any dower, curtesy, or homestead rights. Still other states require the grantors' names to be typewritten beneath their signatures.

In some states, it *is necessary* for a deed to bear a seal to be valid. Historically, a seal was accepted as conclusive evidence of consideration. Most states have abolished the power of a seal; yet in some states, a sealed instrument has a longer statute of limitations than one with no seal. Most states do require a corporate seal if a corporation is the grantor. Such a seal evidences that the proper corporate officer, with the power to convey and with control of the corporate seal, has duly executed the deed.

It *is necessary* for a deed to be delivered to be valid. Delivery is a question of intent by the grantor and must be made during the life of the grantor. However, the grantor, during his or her lifetime, may insert a clause that states that the deed takes effect only *upon* his or her death because the *intent* is to deliver *now* the right to the property upon death. Delivery may be to a third person, in trust for the grantee, if the grantor surrenders all rights to control or recover the deed. In some states, delivery is presumed to have been made and accepted once the deed has been acknowledged and recorded.

Acceptance of delivery by the grantee *is also necessary* for a deed to be valid. However, very few disputes arise regarding acceptance. Most courts presume acceptance unless there exists great evidence and proof of rejection.

An *acknowledgment* is a formal declaration, before a duly authorized officer (usually a notary public), by a person who has executed an instrument (the grantor, in the case of a deed) that such execution is one's own free and voluntary act. In other words, an acknowledgment affirms the authenticity of the grantor's signature on the deed. In some states it *is necessary* for a deed to be acknowledged to be valid. In some states a deed must be acknowledged to be recorded. In some states, even though acknowledgment is not required for validity, an acknowledged deed may be offered in court as prima facie evidence of conveyance, whereas an unacknowledged deed may have to have been recorded for 10 or more years or may have to meet other court rules of evidence to be accepted as evidence of conveyance.

In most states, it *is not necessary* to record a deed for it to be valid. If a deed is unrecorded, and a third person innocently purchases from a grantor who has already sold the property to a grantee who has neither recorded the deed (constructive notice) nor taken possession (actual notice), the third person may acquire title to the exclusion of the grantee. Some states require that the third person record his or her interest first (ahead of the grantee) to acquire title. Other states give the grantee a grace period to record, during which time the grantee's rights are superior to a third party's but after which they are not. To be safe, one should always have a deed acknowledged and recorded.

Prior to 1968 there existed a federal tax for the transfer of real estate called the federal revenue stamp tax. Stamps costing $.55 each had to be purchased and pasted to deeds for every $500 of purchase price or for every $500 of purchase price above any liens against the property. Upon the repeal of this law, most states maintained the system or adopted a similar one. Some states call the real-estate-transfer tax a *documentary fee* and use it to aid county assessors in their determination of property values for property tax purposes. Table 5-1 lists the system of real-estate-transfer tax for each state.

ESSENTIALS OF A VALID DEED

From the previous discussion, a summary of the essential elements of a valid deed may be presented as follows:

1. Written
2. Designation of grantor and grantee

Table 5-1. REAL-ESTATE-TRANSFER TAX RATES
Note: Consult specific state law for details.

State	Rate	State	Rate
ALABAMA	$.50 per $500 or fraction thereof	MONTANA	None
ALASKA	None	NEBRASKA	$.55 per $500 or fraction thereof
ARIZONA	None	NEVADA	$.55 per $500 or fraction thereof
ARKANSAS	$1.10 per $1,000 or fraction thereof	NEW HAMPSHIRE	$.15 per $100 or fraction thereof
CALIFORNIA	$.55 per $500 or fraction thereof	NEW JERSEY	$.50 per $500 or fraction thereof
COLORADO	$.01 per $100 in excess of $500	NEW MEXICO	None
CONNECTICUT	$.55 per $500 or fraction thereof	NEW YORK	$.55 per $500 or fraction thereof
DELAWARE	2% of property value	NORTH CAROLINA	$.50 per $500 or fraction thereof
FLORIDA	$.30 per $100 plus $.55 per $500 or fraction thereof	NORTH DAKOTA	None
GEORGIA	$1.00 per first $1000, $.10 for each additional $100	OHIO	$.30 per $100 and/or $1.00, or $.10 per $100 whichever is greater
HAWAII	$.05 per $100	OKLAHOMA	$.55 per $500 or fraction thereof
IDAHO	None	OREGON	None
ILLINOIS	$.50 per $500 or fraction thereof	PENNSYLVANIA	1% of value
INDIANA	None	RHODE ISLAND	$.55 per $500 or fraction thereof
IOWA	$.55 per $500 in excess of $500	SOUTH CAROLINA	$1.00 per $100 to $500; $1.00 additional for each $500
KANSAS	None	SOUTH DAKOTA	$.50 per $500 or fraction thereof
KENTUCKY	$.50 per $500 or fraction thereof	TENNESSEE	$.26 per $100
LOUISIANA	None	TEXAS	None
MAINE	$.55 per $500 or fraction thereof	UTAH	None
MARYLAND	$.55 per $500 or fraction thereof	VERMONT	½ of 1% of sales price
MASSACHUSETTS	$1.14 per $500 or fraction thereof	VIRGINIA	$.15 per $100; $.50 per $500 or fraction thereof
MICHIGAN	$.55 per $500 or fraction thereof	WASHINGTON	$.50 per $500 plus 1% of sales price
MINNESOTA	$2.20 per first $1,000; $1.10 per each additional $500	WEST VIRGINIA	$1.65 per $500 or fraction thereof
MISSISSIPPI	None	WISCONSIN	$.10 per $100
MISSOURI	None	WYOMING	None

Source: Paul T. O'Donnell and Eugene L. Maleady. *Principles of Real Estate* (Philadelphia: W.B. Saunders, Co., 1975), p. 441.

3. Recital of consideration (in most states)
4. Words of conveyance
5. Legal description
6. Signature of grantor
7. Witnessed (in some states)
8. Sealed (in some states)
9. Delivery and acceptance
10. Acknowledged (in some states)
11. Recorded (in some states)

Six of the eleven items listed above *are necessary* in *all* states for a deed to be valid. Since five of the eleven *are necessary* in *some* states, it is advisable to consult local legal counsel.

TYPES OF DEEDS BY DEGREE OF GUARANTEE

Deeds may be classified in a variety of ways. However, perhaps the best way is that used by Kratovil.[2] Kratovil classifies deeds by the degree of protection of guarantee of title offered by the grantor to the grantee. In so doing, three general types of deeds may be listed as follows: (1) quitclaim deed, (2) bargain and sale deed, and (3) warranty deed. No one of these three can convey a greater or better title than any of the others; each is totally sufficient to convey title. The differences lie in the amount of assurance or guarantee by the grantor that the title conveyed is good and merchantable.

Quitclaim Deed

A quitclaim deed does not actually convey the property, but rather conveys all the *grantor's present interest in the property*, if any. Such a deed does *not* imply that the grantor has good title or even any title at all. In other words, if the grantor has no title, nothing is conveyed; if he or she has title, everything is conveyed. For example, if the grantor holds a fee simple and uses a quitclaim deed, then a fee simple is conveyed; without any guarantees, however.

Quitclaim deeds are used when there is really no need for the grantor to guarantee title and/or when no consideration is given by the grantee. For example, a residential developer may use a quitclaim deed to give a gift of land within a housing project to the city to be used as an elementary school site. A lender or a public trustee may use a quitclaim deed to

2. Robert Kratovil, *Real Estate Law*, 6th ed. (Englewood Cliffs, N.J.: Prentice · Hall, 1974), Chap. 7.

release a mortgage or deed of trust interest in a property when the borrower pays off the loan. Since such an interest is only a lien or a title representing a lien, the lender has no reason to guarantee title to property he or she never really owned. Finally, quitclaim deeds are often used in quiet title suits to clear up any disputes or technical defects in the chain of title which may be impairing or clouding the title.

Bargain and Sale Deed

A bargain and sale deed actually conveys the property and *not* merely the grantor's present interest in the property, if any. Since such a deed does convey the property, it is not a quitclaim deed. However, since such a deed does not give any warranties of title, it is not a warranty deed and is also called a *deed without covenants*. Bargain and sale deeds emphasize the recital of consideration given or price paid by the grantee.

To further distinguish a bargain and sale deed from a quitclaim deed, it can be noted that a bargain and sale deed conveys any "after-acquired" title while a quitclaim deed does not. For example, if the grantor conveys property *not currently* owned and later acquires title to this property, it is automatically conveyed then to the grantee. Such would not be the case with a quitclaim deed, for that conveys only the grantor's *present* interest, if any.

To further distinguish a bargain and sale deed from a warranty deed, it can be noted that a bargain and sale deed, which does not contain any warranties of title, may contain a warranty as to the acts of the grantor. For example, the grantor may warrant that while he or she held title, the grantor did nothing to impair or encumber the title. Grantors who have held legal title only, such as guardians, trustees, or executors, may grant such a personal warranty to the grantees to which they convey title. This type of personal warranty is only to the first grantee and does not run with the land.

Warranty Deeds

If a warranty deed contains the six usual covenants or warranties of title, it is a general warranty deed. If a warranty deed contains less than the six usual covenants or warranties of title, it is a special warranty deed.

General Warranty Deed. The covenants of a general warranty deed cover the time periods of *both* before and during the grantor's ownership. The six usual covenants or warranties of title include three present covenants and three future covenants. Present covenants, if breached, are breached at the moment the deed is delivered and accepted. The present covenants are as follows:

1. *Covenant of seisin* guarantees that the grantor has absolute, perfect, full, and indefeasible title subject only to named encumbrances. This covenant is personal to the grantee and, therefore, does *not* run with the land.
2. *Covenant of right to convey* guarantees that the grantor, because of his or her seisin, has full rights to sell the property. This covenant is usually cited with the covenant of seisin, and it also does *not* run with the land.
3. *Covenant against encumbrances* guarantees that there exist no claims or encumbrances against the property *other* than the ones specifically named in the under and subject clause of the deed. The grantee purchases the property subject to the named encumbrances. This covenant is also personal to the grantee and does *not* run with the land.

Future covenants can be breached only at some future date. The three future covenants are as follows:

1. *Covenant of further assurance* guarantees that the grantor will voluntarily execute, procure, and deliver to the grantee, or to any future grantee, any instruments or conveyances that subsequently become necessary to vest good title in the grantee. This covenant is considered *real* and does run with the land, meaning that *any* subsequent grantee can sue for its breach.
2. *Covenant of quiet enjoyment* guarantees that the grantee will not be disturbed in possession or be evicted by someone holding a superior title. To sue for breach of this covenant, the grantee must prove actual eviction. This covenant is real and therefore runs with the land.
3. *Covenant of warranty forever* guarantees title and possession to be absolute and guarantees that the grantor will protect and defend the grantee against anyone who may attack the title. This covenant is very similar, if not identical, to the covenant of quiet enjoyment, and it, too, runs with the land.

Special Warranty Deed. A special warranty deed guarantees only against the lawful claims of all persons claiming by, through, or under the grantor, or under the grantor's heirs or administrators. In other words, if the grantor has in no way encumbered the title, he or she is *not* liable for an outstanding claim or title maintained by a third person. Sometimes a grantor of a special warranty deed will include the covenant against encumbrances for any encumbrances that may have been created during his or her period of ownership.

OTHER TYPES OF DEEDS

There exist a wide variety of deeds that are used for very specific purposes. These deeds may be quitclaim, bargain and sale, or even warranty in nature as well as specific in purpose. A list and brief description of these special deeds is as follows:

1. *Grant deeds* are used in California and a few other states in lieu of a general or special warranty deed. However, a grant deed contains only the three present covenants, and they apply only during the grantor's possession.
2. *Administrator's deeds* are used by the person charged with the responsibility of distributing an *intestate* estate.
3. *Executor's deeds* are used by the person charged with the responsibility of distributing a *testate* estate.
4. *Deeds of trust* are used to convey title to a third-party public or private trustee to serve as a security instrument for a real estate loan.
5. *Deeds in trust* are used to create secret ownerships in land trusts in states where such trusts are legal.
6. *Correction deeds* are used to correct minor mechanical errors (such as the spelling of a name) in another deed and are also called *confirmation deeds*.
7. *Sheriff's deeds* are used to convey property after the passing of the redemption period following a foreclosure.
8. *Deeds in lieu of foreclosure* are used by borrowers who wish to avoid foreclosure by directly conveying the encumbered property to the lender.
9. *Committee's deeds* are used by court appointed committees to transfer the property (with court approval) of an insane or otherwise legally incapacitated person.
10. *Guardian deeds* are used by court-appointed guardians to transfer the property (with court approval) of an infant or minor.
11. *Reconveyance deeds* are used by trustees to reconvey legal title to a borrower when the borrower has settled the debt with the lender.
12. *Partition deeds* are used by concurrent owners (such as joint tenants or tenants in common) to divide their property into individually owned parcels.
13. *Deeds of release* are used to release property from a blanket mortgage or deed of trust that encumbers more than one property.
14. *Support deeds* are used to convey property (usually to a younger family member) in return for the promise of the grantee to financially support the grantor for the rest of his or her life.

15. *Statutory deeds* are short-form or condensed deeds that state legislatures have deemed as substitutable for the full-length, bulky, and legal-jargon-filled deeds.

DEEDS SUMMARY AND CONCLUSION

A deed conveys and evidences title. It may or may not be a contract. In either case, however, a deed is given in performance of and supersedes a contract of sale. According to the Statute of Frauds a deed must be in writing. The three major portions of a deed include (1) the premises, (2) the habendum, and (3) the testimonium.

The laws of the states vary greatly as to what elements are essential for a deed to be valid. In all states, however, a deed must (1) be written, (2) designate the grantor and the grantee, (3) contain words of conveyance, (4) include a legal description of the property, (5) be signed by the grantor, and (6) be delivered and accepted.

Deeds may be categorized in many ways. Classification according to the degree of title guarantee includes (1) quitclaim deeds, (2) bargain and sale deeds, and (3) warranty deeds. There are six possible warranties or covenants that might be contained in a deed. The three covenants that apply to the *present* are considered personal in nature and do not run with the land; they include (1) the covenant of seisin, (2) the covenant of right to convey, and (3) the covenant against encumbrances. The three covenants that apply to the *future* are considered real in nature and do run with the land; they include (1) the covenant of further assurance, (2) the covenant of quiet enjoyment, and (3) the covenant of warranty forever.

There exists a wide variety of deeds that are used for very specific purposes and may carry all, some, or none of the six covenants of warranty. It may be concluded from the reading of this section that the topic of deeds and their use is very complex and legally technical. Therefore, it is most advisable to consult with local legal counsel for advice concerning the proper type of deed to use to convey property and to be sure that one follows the laws of one's state regarding deeds.

Legal Descriptions of Real Property

One of the elements that is necessary for a deed to be valid is an unquestionable identification of the property. This requirement is usually accomplished by including a legal description of the real property to be transferred in the deed. Appendix A (p. 353), presents a variety of methods of legally describing real estate, including: (1) the U.S. Governmental Survey System, often referred to as the "rectangular survey system," (2) metes and bounds, (3) recorded plat, and (4) Colorado Coordinate System. This information is given as an appendix so that the reader can easily access this reference material.

CHAPTER 6

Contracts

KEY TERMS

Instrument A formal legal document
Contract A deliberate agreement made between two or more legally competent persons, upon some legal (good or valuable) consideration, to do or not to do some legal act
Competent party An individual who is of legal age (not an infant or a minor), not insane, not drunk, not a convict, not a spendthrift, or not an aged person with an appointed guadian; one of the four essentials of a valid contract
Mutual assent Also called the meeting of the minds, the reality of consent or mutual consent, or the offer and acceptance; exists when the parties to a contract agree on all the terms and conditions of the contract; one of the four essentials of a valid contract
Legal consideration A promise of one party bargained and exchanged for the promise of another party, whereby each party is obligated to do or not to do some legal act; one of the four essentials of a valid contract
Legal purpose One of the four essentials of a valid contract, which holds that a contract's purpose and means of performance must not violate any laws or public policy
Valid contract A contract that contains the four essential elements of a contract and is without defects, is legally sufficient and authorized by law, and therefore is legally binding and enforceable in court.
Void contract A contract that lacks one or more of the four essential elements of a contract and therefore is *not* legally binding and enforceable in court
Voidable contract A contract that is valid and enforceable in court but can be made void and unenforceable at the option of one or more of the parties
Unenforceable contract A contract that was valid when made but cannot be proved or, that for some legal reason, the courts cannot protect the obligations to perform (enforce)

CONTRACT DEFINED

Formal legal documents are called *instruments*. A variety of instruments are used in the field of real estate. Many of these instruments take the form of a contract. A *contract* is a deliberate agreement made between two or more legally competent persons, upon some legal (good or valuable) consideration, to do or not do some legal act. A contract might also be defined as "an agreement between two or more persons consisting of a promise or mutual promises which the law will enforce, or the performance of which the law will recognize as a duty."[1]

The more common contracts used in the field of real estate include the listing agreement, the contract of sale, the lease, the option, the installment contract, the mortgage, the escrow instructions, and possibly the deed. (see Chapter 5). The writing of contracts is considered the practice of law, which is usually reserved for duly authorized or licensed attorneys at law. However, a real estate agent is allowed to write contracts or, more specifically, to fill in the blanks of statutorily approved contract forms and, therefore, "practice law" if he or she does so for no fee and if such action is incidental to the performance of his or her licensed business as a real estate agent. Some states, however, only allow the real estate agent to prepare preliminary sales agreements, also called *binders*, which oblige the purchaser and seller to enter at some future time into a formal contract of sale, prepared by an attorney.

PURPOSE OF A SALES CONTRACT

It should be noted that it is not technically essential to have a sales contract to transfer the ownership of real property. A legal transfer may be made using only a deed if it is properly executed and delivered as discussed in Chapter 5. However, since it takes quite a bit of time to actually close a real estate transaction, it is in the better interests of all parties involved to reduce to writing all the things upon which they have agreed in order to transfer title. Furthermore, time is needed to prove ownership of title (title search or title insurance), to arrange financing (loan application and approval), and to prepare all the information and documentation required at closing (escrow instructions). The contract, therefore, can serve as a blueprint for all the duties that must be performed and for all the other instruments (mortgage, deed, etc.) which are required to complete the transaction.

CONTRACT TERMINOLOGY

Several adjectives are commonly used to describe and distinguish different types of contracts. A clear and definite understanding of the following

1. B. E. Tsagris, *Real Estate License Examination Study Manual* (Sacramento: State of California Department of Real Estate, 1974), p. 22.

terms is very important to the real estate agent or any person involved in a contract.

Formal versus Informal

A formal contract is written and *under seal* whereby the seal itself represents the existence of consideration, even if none is expressed. Negotiable instruments, such as a check or promissory note, are also formal contracts. It is the seal or the wording of the contract which makes it formal and, thereby, enforceable in some situations where informal contracts are unenforceable. An informal or *simple* contract may be oral or written, or partly oral and partly written, and in any case is *not under seal*. It is the nature of the transaction and not the wording that makes a contract informal. Oral contracts are as valid as written contracts (except where the Statute of Frauds applies), however, they may be more difficult to prove and enforce.

Expressed versus Implied

In an expressed contract, the parties declare the terms and manifest their intentions by specifically stating them either orally or in writing. In an implied contract the parties do not specifically state the terms or their intentions, but rather manifest or show them without words by their actions or conduct.

Unilateral versus Bilateral

In a unilateral contract, the pro[illegible] given to another party to induce that person to act. The [illegible] not bound to act, but if he or she does act, the former [illegible] keep his or her promise. For example, a real estate listing [illegible] states) is a unilateral promise by the seller to pay a [illegible] the agent if he or she acts by making a sale to a purchaser. [illegible] agent acts and brings in an acceptable purchaser, the seller [illegible] her promise to pay a commission.

In a bilateral contract, the [illegible] is given in exchange for the promise of another party. [illegible] act. In some states, for example, a real estate listing [illegible] because the seller's promise to pay a commission [illegible] agent's promise to act with "due diligence" to sell the [illegible]

Executory versus Executed

An executory contract has not [illegible] still remains something to be done by one or more [illegible] executed contract has been completed; all parties [illegible] their respective contractual obligations.

Valid versus Void

A valid contract contains the four essential elements of a contract (discussed below and is legally binding and enforceable in court; a court will protect the obligations to perform. A void contract lacks one or more of the four essential elements of a contract and is *not* legally binding and enforceable in court. A void contract is not a contract at all; it is a nullity with no legal force or effect; it is invalid.

Voidable versus Unenforceable

A voidable contract is valid and enforceable but can be made void and unenforceable at the option of one or more of the parties. In other words, a voidable contract can be accepted (ratified) or rejected by one or more of the parties. Until such a choice is made, the contract is valid. For example, a contract with an infant (minor) is valid until, upon the majority of the infant, he or she elects to ratify (keep valid) or reject (make void) the contract. Contracts made under fraud, misrepresentation, undue influence, or with a legally incompetent person such as a minor, a convict, or an intoxicated or mentally unsound person are also voidable by the legally incompetent person.

An unenforceable contract is valid but, for some legal reason, the courts cannot protect the obligations to perform. In other words, although the contract is valid, one cannot seek judgment to prove validity and obtain performance of the contract through judicial proceedings. The obligation to perform still exists but cannot be enforced. In a voidable contract the obligation to perform can be extinguished or destroyed, which makes enforcement moot or of no practical significance. Examples of unenforceable contracts are those that have been barred by the statute of limitations or have not met the requirements of the Statute of Frauds. These contracts may contain the four essential elements of a valid contract, but are unenforceable for some other reason.

THE FOUR ESSENTIALS OF A VALID CONTRACT

As implied in the definition of a contract, there are four requisites or essentials for a contract to be valid; they are (1) competent parties, (2) mutual assent, (3) legal consideration, and (4) legal purpose. A detailed discussion of each of these requirements is quite necessary to the needs of the real estate student or practitioner.

Competent Parties

In order to be legally competent an individual must *not* be an infant (or minor), insane, drunk, a convict, or a spendthrift or aged person with an appointed guardian. The age of majority in most states has been lowered from 21 to 18 years old. Some states provide that a 17-year-old male person, if married, is an adult; others provide that married women are adults, regardless of age. Contracts of infants are *voidable* by the infant and enforceable upon the adult unless the infant disaffirms the contract. An infant's contract for the necessities of life (food, drink, clothing, etc.) are also voidable by the infant, but the infant is liable for the fair market value of whatever was received.

Contracts with an insane person under guardianship or with a spendthrift or aged person under guardianship are *void*, while those with an insane person not under guardianship are *voidable*. If a contract is made while the insane person is lucid, he or she is liable for the fair market value of whatever was received.

Finally, there is the possibility of *constructive fraud*, where one party uses superior knowledge to take surreptitious advantage of the mental weakness or necessity of another person to draw a contract which, under normal circumstances, would not otherwise have been made. Such contracts are *void*.

Intoxication must be present to the degree that one cannot comprehend the ramifications of his or her actions in order for a contract with a drunkard to be *voidable*. Furthermore, if an innocent third party would be injured by the drunkard's disaffirmation, such is not allowed. Like infants, drunkards may be held liable for the fair market value of the necessities of life.

Convicts, in some states, are considered civilly dead if they have been imprisoned for a felony. However, such a person may have a court-appointed committee which can contract for the convict.

When a party to a contract is a corporation, a partnership, a nonprofit organization, an executor (or executrix) of a testate estate, or an administrator (or administratrix) of an intestate estate, care must be taken to be sure that the person signing the contract truly has the official power to do so.

Mutual Assent

In order for a valid contract to exist, the parties to the contract must mutually agree on all of the terms and conditions stated in the contract. This mutual assent is also called the *meeting of the minds*, *the reality of consent*, *the reality of mutual consent*, or *the offer and acceptance*. The offer and acceptance actually evidence the mutual assent, which must be real or genuine; it must be free from fraud, misrepresentation, duress, menace, undue influence, or mistake. Otherwise, the contract is *void* or *voidable*.

Fraud may be actual or constructive. *Actual fraud* includes causing or tending to cause injury to another by stating known or unknown falsehoods, suppressing truths, making promises with no intention to perform them, or acting with the intention to deceive. *Constructive fraud* includes taking advantage of another to his or her detriment without actually deceiving him or her. *Misrepresentation* includes an unknowing or innocent misstatement of fact with no intention to deceive or injure the other party. If fraud or misrepresentation exist, a contract is *voidable* by the injured innocent party who might also, in some cases, recover damages suffered.

Duress is the use of force or restraint to compel someone against his or her free will or volition to enter a contract. *Menace* is the threat to commit duress or the threat to inflict personal injury to the body or character of an individual to induce him or her to enter a contract. *Undue influence* is the taking advantage of a confidential fiduciary relationship or a position of authority to induce one to enter a contract. Contracts made under duress, menace, or undue influence are *voidable* by the aggrieved party.

Mistakes may be mutual, of fact, or of law, and the effects upon contractual obligations vary with the type of mistake made. A *mutual mistake*, such as one involving the identity or existence of the subject matter or party, causes a contract to be *void*. *Mistakes of fact* are errors which misstate the conditions of a contract and, if curable and not caused by neglect of a legal duty or by ignorance of the law, cause a contract to be *voidable*. A *mistake of law* is made with full knowledge of the facts but with ignorance of the legal effects of these known facts. Such an erroneous conclusion itself does not make the contract void unless the contract itself or one of the acts it calls for is illegal.

The offer. As stated earlier, the offer and acceptance actually evidence the mutual assent. An offer is a proposal by one party (offeror) to act in a certain manner on the condition that the other party (offeree) will act in a certain requested manner. To be effective, an offer must be: (1) *intentional*, (2) *definite and certain in its terms*, and (3) *communicated to the offeree* by a means chosen by the offeror. If an offer is terminated before it is accepted, no contract exists.

An offer may be terminated by:

1. *Rejection* by the offeree
2. *Counteroffer* (or qualified acceptance) by the offeree (any change in terms or conditions of the original offer by the offeree constitutes a rejection of the original offer and a proposal of a new offer which, of course, reverses the roles of the parties)
3. *Failure* of the offeree to comply with a condition of the offer or to accept in the manner prescribed by the offeror
4. *Revocation* by the offeror before acceptance and even before the end of the time that the offeror said the offer was to be open (however, if an option, which is a promise to hold an offer open in return for some legal consideration, exists, it is irrevocable)

5. *Lapse of time* specified by the offeror as a deadline for acceptance
6. *Operation of law* because of either the death, insanity, or bankruptcy of the offeror or offeree, or the destruction of the subject matter, or a change in the law making the offer illegal

The acceptance. An acceptance is the indication by some word or act that the offeree is willing to be bound by the terms and conditions of an offer. Silence is generally not interpreted to constitute acceptance, unless the circumstances or previous course of dealing with an offeree places the offeree under a duty to act or to be bound by the terms and conditions of the offer. An offer may be accepted only by the person to whom the offer was made (the offeree); offers are not assignable. To be effective, an acceptance must be (1) *definite* and *unambiguous*, (2) *unqualified* and *absolute*, (3) *expressed* or *communicated* to the offeror, and (4) *made in the manner prescribed* by the offeror, if any (otherwise any reasonable or customary manner of acceptance will suffice).

Legal Consideration

Consideration may be defined as an act or promise of one party bargained and exchanged for the act or promise of another party, whereby each obligates himself or herself to do or not to do something that he or she was not otherwise obligated to do or not to do. Usually both parties have an obligation, called a *legal detriment*, and receive something, called a *legal benefit*. If each party suffers a detriment and receives a benefit, consideration is present.

In the early days of English common law, consideration for the validity of formal contracts was evidenced by the mere presence on the contract of a *seal*, usually made by an impression from a signet ring or other device on wax on the contract or on the paper of the contract. The seal itself gave the required formal authority to the contract and was offered as the guarantee of the contract's fulfillment. Most states have modified their laws relative to sealed contracts. If required at all (as on governmental or corporate contracts), the word "seal," or the initials "L.S." for *locus sigilli* ("the place of the seal"), or some other material attached to the contract may serve as a seal.

Although consideration must have *some value*, there is no law that requires that the two considerations being exchanged for one another be of equal value. For example, a nominally stated consideration, such as $10 or even $1, is sufficient consideration for a $100 million contract to be valid. The only time the law requires adequate consideration is when two sums of money are being exchanged simultaneously. However, the adequacy of consideration is important if one seeks the remedy of specific performance upon the alleged breach of contract. In such a case, sufficient and reasonable consideration, with respect to the nature of the transaction, must be evident. Otherwise, the remedy will be denied because of the appearance of fraud, misrepresentation, duress, menace, undue influence, or mistake.

Finally, consideration may be either valuable or good. *Valuable* consideration is money, property, or a right or benefit with value. *Good* consideration is love, affection, or friendship, and is also called *moral* or *meritorious*. Good consideration is sufficient to validate an executed contract. However, good consideration is not sufficient to *enforce* and validate an executory contract in court, because the offeree gives no consideration in return.

Legal Purpose

For a contract to be valid, its purpose and means of performance must not violate any laws or public policy. All illegal contracts are *void* and, if they are in operation despite the laws (such as a wager), neither party can enforce them nor seek a remedy at law for a contract breach. In some states, contracts executed or performed on a Sunday are illegal.

THE STATUTE OF FRAUDS

A contract need not be in writing to be valid unless it is made under seal. Furthermore, a contract need not be in writing to be enforceable unless it falls under the Statute of Frauds. However, oral contracts are often difficult to prove and great misunderstandings often arise as to what was actually said and agreed upon orally. Hence, if a contract is at all important, it should be reduced to writing so that it may be easily enforceable under the law. Furthermore, if a contract is reduced to writing, its terms, conditions, or wording cannot be changed later by oral (parol) evidence. The so-called *Parol Evidence Rule* makes inadmissible all oral or other extrinsic (outside the contract) information or evidence which would change the terms, conditions, or wording of a written contract. Furthermore, due to the *Doctrine of Promissory Estoppel*, a written contract supersedes and estoppes all prior negotiations and conversations where it is intended that the contract be reduced to writing or be an integration of all prior discussions. It is also worthy of note that if handwritten portions and printed portions of a contract contradict one another, the handwritten portions prevail.

In order to avoid perjuries and frauds committed by claims of oral agreements, a law was enacted in England under the reign of King Charles II in 1677, called the Act for Prevention of Frauds and Perjuries. This law, commonly called the *Statute of Frauds*, has been adopted, in a more or less altered form, in every state within the Uniform Commercial Code.

The chief characteristic of the Statute of Frauds is that certain contracts are *unenforceable* unless they or some note or memorandum are in writing and signed by the party (or the party's agent) to be charged or bound. Furthermore, the parties, the subject matter, and the price, terms, and conditions of the contract must be described in the written contract, note, or memorandum. The note or memorandum need not be of any particular or required form and may be made at any time, even *after* the contract has been orally made.

It is important to note that the Statute of Frauds relates only to the *remedy* of the contract, and not to the validity of the contract. A contract which fails to comply with the statute is not void, but rather is unenforceable at law in court. The contracts that fall under the purview of the Statute of Frauds are:

1. Contracts for the sale of real property or interests therein
2. Contracts not to be performed within one year, such as real estate leases for more than one year
3. Contracts for the sale of goods or personal property for $500 or more
4. Contracts where one person promises to answer for the debt, default, or miscarriage of another
5. Contracts made upon a promise of marriage when the promise received in return is not a promise of marriage

DISCHARGE AND PERFORMANCE OF CONTRACTS

A contract is discharged or terminated by performance, by another agreement or arrangement, or by the operation of law.

Performance

There are many types of performance that may discharge or terminate a contract:

1. *Full* or *complete performance* means *all* the terms and conditions of the contract have been met by all parties.
2. *Part performance* means only *some* of the terms and conditions of the contract have been met, yet all parties accept the contract as discharged.
3. *Timely performance* relates to the importance of the clause "time is of the essence," which means that legally strict adherence to the contractual time provisions is required. However, this clause may be waived by the person entitled to enforce it by accepting a later performance.
4. *Substantial performance* means a party has acted in good faith but has failed to do totally or exactly as the contract requires. Such performance justifies enforcement of the contract with a monetary

adjustment being made to equalize the positions of the contractual parties.

5. *Satisfactory performance* means one has agreed to perform to the satisfaction of another, at which time the contract is discharged and terminated.
6. *Impossibility of performance* involves an act of God or a change in the laws which causes the performance of the contract to be no longer feasible or illegal; hence, the contract is discharged.

Another Agreement or Arrangement

There are some situations where one or both parties to a contract may wish to withdraw from or change a contract without totally terminating it. Examples of these situations include:

1. *Assignment* is the transfer of one's *rights* in a contract to another person. *Duties* may also be assigned or delegated if they are *not*, personal to the obligee, such as the duty of personal performance of a real estate agent in a listing contract. Such a personal obligation may not be assigned. However, obligations such as rent or mortgage payments may be assigned. Unless specifically released by the obligee, the assignor remains *secondarily* liable for the duties assigned.
2. *Novation* is the substitution of the original party or parties and/or the original agreement with a *new* party, parties, or agreement without changing any of the original obligations. A novation extinguishes or discharges the original contract and does not include any secondary liabilities for the original party or parties that have been substituted.
3. *Agreements* between the parties may discharge a contract at any time whether or not there has been any performance.
4. *Accord and satisfaction* is when a new contract has been agreed upon (accord) to replace the original one and its terms and conditions are completed (satisfaction). Unless stated otherwise, both the accord and the satisfaction must take place before the original contract is discharged.
5. *Alteration* of a material portion of a contract (such as date or price) made with a fraudulent intent discharges the duty of the other party to perform.
6. *Release* of all obligations of an unperformed executory contract may be made at any time by mutual agreement. However, if one party has fully performed, a release must be in writing, with or without consideration. Such would be the case between a debtor and a creditor.

Operation of Law

Contracts may also be automatically discharged by the operation of law:

1. *The Statute of Limitations* sets a maximum time limit within which a lawsuit must be filed, either after the consummation of a contract or after the reason for the lawsuit arises. If action is not initiated within the statutory period, the contractual obligations are discharged. The time periods vary from state to state and whether the contract is oral, written, or written and sealed.
2. *Bankruptcy* of either party to a contract discharges the contract.

BREACH OF CONTRACTS

A contract is breached when one of the parties fails to perform (in whole or in part) the terms or conditions of the contract. Upon a breach of contract, the nonbreaching party has the following, legal rights available: (1) recision, (2) damages, (3) liquidated damages, (4) forfeiture, and (5) specific performance.

Recision

Recision may be bilateral or unilateral. With *bilateral recision* both parties agree to rescind the contract and to restore one another to their original positions. Such restoration might involve the return of possession of property for the return of any monies paid. *Unilateral recision* is accomplished solely by the aggrieved person, who has not breached the contract. The rescinding party must do so promptly upon discovering the breach and must restore or offer to restore the breaching party to his or her original position, upon condition that the breaching party shall do likewise for the aggrieved party. Unilateral recision may also take place where a contract has been entered under fraud, misrepresentation, duress, menace, undue influence, or mistake, or if the contract is or becomes illegal. If one of the parties is a minor or incompetent, he or she may unilaterally rescind the contract.

Damages

When a party to a contract has suffered a detriment due to a breach of contract, he or she may seek to recover compensation thereof in money or dollars. Such action is called *action for dollar damages*, or just *damages*. The nonbreaching party must first offer to perform and then sue for the actual damages suffered by the other party's breach. The lawsuit may also seek the cost of all expenses incurred and a reasonable rate of interest on the actual damages and the expenses.

Liquidated Damages

The parties to a contract in anticipation of a breach may insert a clause in the contract itself which specifies the amount of damages to be paid in the event of a breach. Such a provision is called *liquidated* or *stipulated damages*. The courts will enforce such a provision provided the dollar amount is not excessive, or if it is impractical or impossible to determine an amount for actual damages.

Forfeiture

Some contracts, upon breach by the purchaser, provide for the forfeiture of the purchaser's consideration, which is usually an earnest money deposit. This procedure may simply be a way of stating and providing for liquidated damages.

Specific Performance

When dollar damages cannot provide an adequate remedy for a contract breach, the aggrieved nonbreaching party may initiate court action to force the breaching party to comply with the terms of the contract. This remedy is called *specific performance* and is often quite applicable with real estate contracts because of the uniqueness of each parcel of real property. Specific performance must be mutual; both parties must fully comply with the terms and conditions of the contract. This remedy is available only where it can be shown that such specific performance is just and reasonable upon the breaching party. Specific performance is not an available remedy to enforce a contract where only *good* consideration (love and affection) or *inadequate* consideration (less than a reasonable price, or personal services) has been received by the breaching party. Finally, specific performance cannot be used against a person whose consent to the contract was obtained through fraud, misrepresentation, duress, menace, undue influence, or mistake.

EXCUSES FOR NONPERFORMANCE OF CONTRACTS

Normally, nonperformance of a contract results in an action for one of the remedies (discussed above) available to an aggrieved nonbreaching party. However, in some instances under unforeseen circumstances, the courts or the law may allow for the nullification or recision of a contract whereby all parties are excused from performance and relieved of all liabilities. Six examples of these so-called *excuses for nonperformance* are (1) destruction of the subject matter, (2) death or illness, (3) mistake, (4) hardship, (5) prevention, and (6) frustration of purpose.

Destruction of the Subject Matter

If anything essential to the completion of a contract is destroyed, it is possible for all parties to be relieved of their contractual obligations and the contract to be rescinded. In real estate contracts, it is customary to have the property properly insured against such destruction. However, there are certain events—like acts of war—that may not be insurable.

Death or Illness

Normally death or illness does not rescind a contract. However, if personal services have been contracted for, death or illness may be an acceptable excuse for nonperformance.

Mistake

Only when mutual mistake causes there to be no meeting of the minds may mistake be an acceptable excuse for nonperformance.

Hardship

Only when potential hardships are specifically stated in the contract as valid excuses for nonperformance may such be effective.

Prevention

It is implied in every contract that if one party takes action to prevent the other party from performing, the party being prevented from performing may rescind and sue for damages. In other words, one is excused from performance if prevented from so doing by the other party to the contract.

Frustration of Purpose

If the purpose for which a contract was made becomes illegal or impossible to accomplish for reasons beyond the control of the parties to the contract, both parties are excused from performance of the contract.

SUMMARY AND CONCLUSION

A contract is a deliberate agreement made between two or more legally competent persons, upon some legal (good or valuable) consideration, to do or to not do some legal act. The purpose of a real estate sales contract is to reduce to writing all agreements and obligations relative to the transfer of title in order to avoid any possible disputes due to the relatively long time period necessary to close a real estate transaction. A clear understanding of all contract terminology is a requisite to the study of the law and the ramifications of contracts.

In order for a contract to be valid, the following four essentials must be present: (1) competent parties, (2) mutual assent, (3) legal consideration, and (4) legal purpose. A complete understanding of these four concepts is essential to the needs of the real estate student or practitioner. The Statute of Frauds requires that certain contracts be in writing and be signed in order to be enforceable by a court of law.

A contract may be discharged or terminated by performance, by another agreement or arrangement, or by the operation of law. If a contract is breached, the remedies available to the aggrieved party include (1) recision, (2) damages, (3) liquidated damages, (4) forfeiture, and (5) specific performance. In unusual situations one may be excused for nonperformance of a contract because of (1) destruction of the subject matter, (2) death or illness, (3) mistake, (4) hardship, (5) prevention, or (6) frustration of purpose.

In addition to the importance of the study of the law and the ramification of contracts to the real estate student or practitioner presented here, this chapter sets the stage for the proper understanding of the next two chapters—Agency and Real Estate Contracts. The real estate agent should consider himself or herself privileged to be able to "practice law" by playing a role in the drawing of real estate contracts. It cannot be overemphasized that this privilege carries with it heavy and serious fiduciary and public responsibilities. The material on contracts contained in this chapter (and in the following chapters) must be mastered in order to meet the responsibilities inherent in the practice of real estate.

CHAPTER 7

Agency

KEY TERMS

Agent A person who is employed by and acts for, on behalf of, or in the place of another person (principal) in dealing with yet another person (third party)
Principal The employer of an agent
Third party The person an agent deals with for a principal
Independent contractor An employee who agrees to perform for an employer but whose time and efforts are not regulated by the employer and who has no authority to deal with third parties for the employer
Factor Generally a commission merchant who usually sells personal property
General agent An agent with wide authority to conduct a series of transactions of a continuous nature for and on behalf of the principal
Special agent An agent with limited authority to conduct a single transaction or a specified set of transactions for or on behalf of the principal
Actual authority Authority given to the agent by the principal in either an expressed or an implied manner
Expressed authority Authority given the agent by the principal either in writing, orally, or by the conduct of the principal
Implied authority That authority which the agent reasonably needs to perform the expressed authority
Apparent authority Authority created when the words or conduct of the principal have led third parties to believe that an agency relationship exists; also called "ostensible authority."

THE LAW OF AGENCY

The law of agency governs the legal relationships which exist when one person (agent) acts for and on behalf of or in place of another person (principal) in dealing with yet another person (third party). In other words, an agent interacts with the third party for and on the behalf of the principal. For example, when a homeowner (principal) arranges to have his or her home sold by a real estate broker (agent) to someone (third party) in the market, an agency relationship exists between the seller and the broker. The law of agency permeates this relationship and recognizes certain duties and responsibilities owed by each of the parties (including the third party) to each of the other two parties.

Before proceeding with an in-depth discussion of agency, it is necessary to differentiate some other forms of employment. An understanding of these other relationships will aid in the understanding of the agency relationship. These other forms of employment include the independent contractor, the master-servant relationship, and the principal acting on his or her own behalf. A real estate broker may act as both a principal and an agent if he or she fully discloses this fact to all parties to the transaction. The objective of the broker or principal acting on his or her own behalf is to make a profit. A person or agent should not be deprived of profit opportunities simply because he or she is a broker or salesperson.

An *independent contractor* is one who "contracts to render an agreed performance for another, called an employer, does not act on his employer's behalf, has no authority to deal with third persons or to affect the employer's contractual relations with third persons, and whose manner of performance is not subject to any right of control by the employer."[1] Furthermore, the recipient of an independent contractor's services is usually *not* responsible to third parties for the independent contractor's torts or contract actions. An example of this relationship may be a homeowner's hiring a plumber to fix a leaky faucet. Note, however, that some real estate brokers hire salespeople as independent contractors. Also note that while a *real estate broker* may establish an office and operate independently as an agent for others in any of the various areas of real estate, a *real estate salesperson* must work for and under the supervision of a licensed real estate broker, even if an independent contractor relationship exists between the broker and the salesperson.

One other distinction needs to be made, regarding the differences between a broker and a factor. Both are agents subject to the law of agency. However, a *factor* is generally a commission merchant who usually sells personal property. The factor receives, takes possession, controls, and sells the goods of another to earn a commission. The factor usually has the right to sell the goods *in his or her own name,* as opposed to the usual broker arrangement in which the broker may act only *in the name of his or her principal*.

Creation of Agency

The relationship whereby one acts for and on behalf of another in dealings with a third party (the agency relationship) may be created by either (1) agreement, (2) estoppel, (3) ratification, or (4) operation of law.

1. Joseph L. Frascona, *C.P.A. Law Review*, 3rd ed. (Homewood, Ill.: Richard D. Irwin, Inc., 1966), p. 641.

Agency by Agreement. The agency relationship is most usually created by an expressed (oral or written) employment agreement between the principal and the agent. In real estate, such an agreement is commonly called a *listing contract* (see Chapter 8). Some states, including California, require that the listing contract be in writing,[2] on the theory known as the *equal dignities rule*. According to this rule, since a real estate broker is authorized by the listing contract to execute real estate contracts that are required by the Statute of Frauds to be in writing to be enforceable, so too should the agreement granting this authority be in writing. Whether required or not, the real estate broker is better protected by reducing to writing the employment or listing agreement.

Agency by Estoppel (Ostensible Agency). Agency may be created by estoppel when one leads others (by action or words) to believe that some one is his or her agent, or when a third party acts in belief that one is another's agent. In either case the parties are estopped from denying the supposed agency relationship.

Agency by Ratification. If one falsely poses as the agent of another and interacts with a third party, and if the supposed principal, after the fact, *consents* to the agreement or action made by the supposed agent with the third party, an agency relationship is created by the principal's consent or *ratification* of the act. If a duly authorized agent performs an unauthorized act or agreement with a third party for and on behalf of his or her principal, and if this principal later consents to this action, agency is created by ratification.

Agency by Operation of Law (by Necessity). If an agent is in an unusual or unforeseen set of circumstances, such as an emergency situation, and acts outside the scope of his or her authority but in the best interests of his or her principal, an apparent agency relationship may be created by operation of law. For example, if a flood warning has been received when a building owner is not available to direct the employees, they may act to protect the building, even though they have no authority to do so. In such an emergency situation, agency is created by operation of law, also called *by necessity*.

Types of Principals

A principal may be (1) disclosed, (2) undisclosed, or (3) partially disclosed. A *disclosed* principal's identity and the existence of the agency relationship are made known to third persons. An *undisclosed* principal's identity and the existence of the agency relationship are *not* made known to third

2. The other states which require written listing contracts are Arizona, Idaho, Indiana, Michigan, Montana, Nebraska, New Mexico, Oklahoma, Oregon, Texas, and Utah.

persons. Hence, the agent appears to be working for himself or herself. A *partially disclosed* principal's identity is not made known, but the existence of the agency relationship is made known. The rights, duties, and responsibilities of a principal to his or her agent or to third parties vary with the type of principal. Anyone legally competent to act for oneself may be a principal and may appoint an agent to act for and on behalf of himself or herself.

Types of Agents

An agent may be general or special. A *general agent* has wide authority to conduct a series of transactions of a continuous nature for and on behalf of his or her principal. A store manager, with authority to buy and sell goods, to hire and fire employees, and to do whatever else is necessary for the proper operation and management of the store, is an example of a general agent.

A *special agent* has limited authority to conduct a single transaction or a specified set of transactions for and on behalf or his or her principal. Attorneys at law and real estate brokers are usually special agents. Anyone may be an agent, whether one is legally competent or not. However, great care must be taken by a principal in appointing someone who is not legally competent as his or her agent, since the acts of the agent are deemed to be those of the principal. In other words, the principal may be held ultimately responsible for the acts of his or her agent.

Types of Agent Authority

The agent's authority to act for and on behalf of his or her principal is granted by the terms of the agency agreement. The authority of the agent may be actual or apparent.

Actual authority is that given by the principal in either an expressed or implied manner. *Expressed actual authority* is that authority given to the agent either in writing, or orally, or by the conduct of the principal. *Implied actual authority* is that authority which the agent reasonably needs to perform his or her expressed actual authority. For example, if a real estate broker has a listing contract granting the expressed authority to sell his or her principal's property, the broker may also reasonably have the implied authority to aid the prospective purchaser in finding suitable financing necessary to consummate the sale. Or, for example, the same real estate broker may have the implied actual authority to delegate authority to salespeople or subagents. Normally, since the agency relationship is a personal one, the agent does not have the authority to appoint subagents. However, in this real estate example the implied actual authority arises out of custom and general usage or accepted business practice. To avoid any controversy it is suggested that the listing contract expressly grant the authority to appoint and delegate duties to subagents. The standard listing contract forms of many states do specifically grant such authority.

Apparent authority, also called *ostensible authority*, arises or is created when the words or conduct of the principal have led other persons (third parties) to believe that an agency relationship exists. As stated earlier, agency is created by estoppel in these situations and the principal is held liable for the acts of the apparent agent. If a third party acts in belief that one is the agent of another, apparent authority exists and the third party is estopped or denied the privilege of ignoring the apparent authority and agency.

Duties and Liabilities: Agent to Principal

The cornerstone of the agency relationship is the fiduciary duty that the agent owes his or her principal. As a fiduciary, the agent is bound to exercise the utmost obedience, good faith, loyalty, honesty, prudence, and skill in executing the duties of his or her agency. Some authors[3] identify the following four basic duties that the agent owes to his or her principal: (1) to perform the agency agreements, (2) to be loyal to the principal, (3) to use reasonable care in the performance, and (4) to account for all money and property received.

The real estate agent must abide by the terms of the listing or employment contract. He or she must obey the reasonable instructions of his or her principal. If the agent does not perform—for example, if he or she does not put out a "for sale" sign, or fails to advertise the sale, or does not bring prospects to see the property, of if the agent breaches the contract in any way— he or she may be held liable for any resulting loss to the principal.

The real estate agent must be loyal and worthy of the principal's trust. The agent must not make secret profits or act for more than one party to the transaction without complete and full disclosure to all parties to the transaction. The agent must also disclose any personal interest he or she may have or come by from the transaction. The agent must keep the principal informed of any and all material facts which may have a bearing on the value of the principal's property or which may influence the principal's decision concerning the transaction.

The real estate agent must act with such care as to not lead anyone to believe any untruths. The real estate agent is deemed to be an *expert* in the eyes of the public and by the courts. Erroneous impressions regarding the listed property can arise from (1) expressions of opinion, called "puffing," made by the agent ("the best deal in town"), (2) falsehoods made in good faith and contained in the purchase or lease contract (such can

3. H. Lee Fusilier, *Real Estate Fundamentals* (Boulder, CO: Division of Continuing Education, University of Colorado, 1973), p. 7-5; *State of Colorado Real Estate Manual* (Denver: The Colorado Real Estate Commission, 1976), pp. 2-2, 2-3.

void the contract), (3) mutual mistake (voids the contract), (4) statements intended and understood as representations of fact which later prove to be false, and (5) nondisclosure of material facts by silence. Litigation usually occurs with items (4) and (5).

Statements intended and understood as representations of fact, but which later prove false, are of three kinds:

1. *Innocent misrepresentations* are statements not known to be false but which, in fact, are false. They usually permit recision of the contract without liability against the real estate agent.
2. *Negligent misrepresentations* are statements believed to be true, but which are made without reasonable grounds for such belief and are, in fact, false. They usually are considered a form of deceit, and the real estate agent is held liable for both a civil action for damages by the injured party and a disciplinary action to suspend or revoke the agent's license by the state real estate commission.
3. *Fraudulent misrepresentations* are material statements made at a time when the agent knows the statements to be false and are clearly fraud, subjecting the real estate agent to civil, disciplinary, and possibly criminal actions.

Nondisclosure of material facts by the real estate agent when he or she has knowledge of facts that affect the property to the transaction and also knows that the prospective purchaser or seller is not aware of these material facts, results in the real estate agent being liable. The real estate agent is held to be an expert. Any facts or information that an expert should reasonably be aware of are held to be known by the agent, and he or she can be held liable for not disclosing such information even if he or she did not know it or did not know it to be false. The agent is also liable if the false information was supplied by the principal and if, as an expert, he or she should have known or suspected the information to be false.

The fourth and final duty of the agent to the principal is to account for all money and property received in the course of the agency. Accurate records and accounts must be kept. The real estate agent must not *commingle* the money or property received with his or her own money or property. The best, and in some states the required, method of keeping the principal's money and property separated from that of the agent is for the real estate broker to maintain an escrow or trust account for money and property received for and on behalf of the principal. Furthermore, state laws usually require real estate salespeople to turn over to the broker all money and property they receive as soon as possible.

Duties and Liabilities: Principal to Agent

The duties owed by the principal to the agent are (1) to perform the agency contract, (2) to compensate the agent, (3) to reimburse the agent for expenses, and (4) to indemnify the agent for losses incurred due to the agency relationship.[4]

The principal must abide by the terms of the listing or employment contract. The principal must not interfere with or hamper the efforts of the agent to fulfill his or her obligations to the agency relationship. Since the agency relationship is a personal one, requiring personal service, either party may terminate the relationship by revocation at any time for any reason, provided reasonable notice has been given. The exception to this general rule is when the real estate agent has been given the exclusive right to sell the principal's property for a specified period of time. In such a situation, the real estate broker may be entitled to a commission if the property is subsequently sold within the specified time period, or to liquidated damages for his expenses if no sale subsequently takes place.

The most important duty owed the agent by the principal, from the agent's point of view, is that the agent be paid the appropriate compensation for his or her performance of the listing or employment contract. Performance is measured by the *successful completion* of the transaction and *not* by time spent on completing the transaction. If no amount or rate of compensation was specified in the listing contract, the customary fee or commission must be paid.

Normally, it is customary for the expenses of a real estate agent to be paid by the agent out of his or her commission (if any). In most other agency relationships, however, the principal pays all the agent's expenses.

Finally, if the agent incurs a loss due to the actions of the principal—for example, a misrepresentation made by the principal and innocently passed on to a third party by the agent, or any other improper yet innocent conduct of the agent ordered by the principal—the principal may be required to indemnify or insure and repay the agent for such a loss.

Duties and Liabilities: Agent and Third Party

If the agent has *disclosed* his or her principal to the third party, he or she assumes no liability regarding the contractual obligations between the principal and the third party as long as the agent has acted within the scope of his or her authority. In a real estate transaction, the agent or broker does not usually have the authority to sign a contract for the principal. The authority is usually limited to the finding of a ready, willing, and able buyer to purchase on terms acceptable to the seller (principal). If after having found such a third party–buyer, the principal-seller fails or refuses to perform, the agent-broker is not liable to the third party. However, the third party–buyer may sue the principal-seller for specific performance or actual or liquidated damages. Furthermore, the principal-seller will be liable to the agent-broker for the commission.

4. Ibid.

However, if the agent has *not disclosed* his or her principal or the existence of an agency relationship to the third party, he or she can be held personally liable by the third party for the performance of the contract. Furthermore, if the agent incurs a loss when forced to perform the contract, he or she is entitled to indemnification by the principal. Since in the case of the undisclosed principal the agent is liable for performance to the third party, so too is the third party liable for performance to the agent.

Both the agent and the third party are liable to one another for their own torts (civil wrongs) upon each other. For example, if the agent-broker is guilty of misrepresentation or fraud, whether with or without the knowledge and consent of his or her principal, the agent is personally liable to the third party. Of course the third party, in turn, is liable for his or her torts against the agent. If the agent commits a tort with the principal's knowledge and consent or within the scope of his or her authority, the third party has the choice of suing the agent or the principal.

When an agent acts with a third party, he or she implicitly warrants to the third party that he or she has the authority to do so. An agent does *not* implicitly warrant the principal's legal competency and capacity to contract. However, if the agent warrants that the principal is legally competent and is, therefore, capable of being bound, said agent is liable. The agent can be held liable by the third party for breaching either of these implied or expressed warranties or guarantees unless it can be proven that the agent honestly thought he or she had the proper authority to act for the principal, or that he or she was innocent of the knowledge of the principal's legal incompetency.

Duties and Liabilities: Principal and Third Party

Since the agent acts for and on behalf of or in place of the principal, the principal is liable to the third party for performing contracts made by his or her agent, whether such agency was created by agreement, estoppel, ratification, or operation of law, provided, however, that the agent has acted within the scope of his or her actual or apparent authority. The third party, in turn, is liable to the principal for performing contracts made with the principal's duly authorized agent acting within the scope of his or her authority. In most real estate transactions, since both principal and third party usually sign the contract, the question of the agent's contractual liability is moot. However, when an agent acts beyond the scope of his or her actual authority, a determination must be made as to whether or not the words or actions of the principal could have granted the agent the apparent authority to so act.

The principal is personally liable for his or her agent's torts, if the principal authorized the agent to commit the tort or if such action was taken within the scope of the agent's employment. For example, if the agent-broker, with the knowledge and consent of the principal, fraudulently misrepresents a material fact regarding the principal's property to induce the sale of said property to a third party, the principal-seller is liable to the third party–purchaser. The real estate broker should thoroughly investigate any property that he or she lists to sell for a principal to avoid having his or her business reputation tarnished by any innocent or fraudulent misrepresentation. To take all that the seller-principal says at his or her word may not be sufficient protection. Both the principal and the third party are liable to one another for their own torts upon each other. The principal is not liable for his or her agent's willful or intentional torts against a third party, unless the agent was seeking to further the principal's interests. Finally, the principal usually is not liable for his or her agent's crimes unless he or she aids or participates in the commission thereof. The exceptions, in some states, to this general rule are for such things as the sale of liquor to a minor by the principal's agent-bartender.

Termination of Agency

The agency relationship may be terminated either (1) by the acts (rightful or wrongful) of the parties or (2) by operation of law due to an event which makes the relationship impractical or impossible.

Termination by Acts of the Parties. The four ways by which the acts of the parties may cancel an agency relationship are:

1. *Mutual agreement* at any time for any reason.
2. *Terms of the agency* (or listing) contract, whether it be performance of the contract or expiration of the contract time limit.
3. *Revocation* or discharge of the agent by the principal at any time, since a contract to *render services* cannot be specifically enforced. If the agency is coupled with an interest of the agent, the principal is then guilty of breach of contract and may be held liable by the agent for damages, but the agency is still terminated. If a definite time limit has been set for the agency relationship, the principal may be held liable for a commission if the agent-broker accomplishes the task of the agency contract before the contract expiration date, despite the revocation. In any case, all third parties who have had dealings with the agent should be notified of any revocation in order to assure that not even apparent authority remains with the agent. Finally, if the agency was created by a recorded instrument, then an instrument recorded in the same place must be used to revoke the agency relationship.
4. *Renunciation* or breach by the agent, since the agent may simply quit. One cannot be forced to work against his or her will. However, if such termination is wrongful or the agent cannot show good reason for his or her renunciation, the agent may be guilty of breach of

contract and may be held liable to the principal for damages, despite the renunciation.

Termination by Operation of Law. The five ways by which the operation of law may automatically cancel an agency relationship are:

1. *Death* of agent or principal, with no notice of death to the other party required
2. *Insanity* of agent or principal, with no notice of insanity to the other party required
3. *Bankruptcy* of agent or principal, with no notice of bankruptcy to the other party required
4. *Change in the law*, such that the object or purpose of the agency relationship becomes illegal
5. *Destruction or loss of the subject matter* of the agency, such as the listed house burning to the ground

SUMMARY AND CONCLUSION

The law of agency governs the legal relationships that exist between the principal and the agent, the principal and the third party, and the agent and the third party. An agent works for and on behalf of or in place of his or her principal in dealing with third persons. The employee (or servant) and the independent contractor work for and not on behalf of their respective employers. A real estate broker and his or her subagent-salesperson are usually agents acting for principals who own real property. However, they may, in some situations, be employed by another broker as independent contractors.

Agency may be created by agreement, estoppel, ratification, or operation of law. In real estate the usually written listing contract or agreement is the most common instrument used to create the agency relationship between the broker and the property owner. The real estate agent is a special agent with limited authority to conduct a single transaction or a specified set of transactions, as opposed to being a general agent with wide authority to conduct a series of transactions of a continuous nature.

The authority of the real estate agent may be actual or apparent. Actual authority may be expressed orally, in writing, or by the conduct of the principal. Implied actual authority is that authority which the agent reasonably needs to perform his or her expressed actual authority. Apparent or ostensible authority exists when the words or conduct of the principal have led third parties to believe that an agency relationship exists.

The four basic duties owed by the agent to the principal are (1) to perform the agency agreements, (2) to be loyal to the principal, (3) to use reasonable care in the performance, and (4) to account for all money and property received. The four basic duties owed by the principal to the agent are: (1) to perform the agency contract, (2) to compensate the agent, (3) to reimburse the agent for expenses, and (4) to indemnify the agent for losses incurred due to the agency relationship.

If the agent has disclosed his or her principal and has acted within the scope of his or her authority, the agent assumes no contractual liability. However, if the principal is undisclosed, the agent can be held to the contract by the third party; and the third party may likewise be held by the agent. Both the agent and the third party are liable for their own torts. The third party may sue either the agent or the principal if the agent commits a tort with the knowledge and consent of the principal or if the agent has acted within the scope of his or her authority. Finally, an agent implicitly warrants to the third part that he or she has the proper authority, but an agent does *not* implicitly warrant the principal's legal competency and capacity to contract.

The principal is liable to the third party for performing contracts made by his or her agent, provided that the agent acted within the scope of his or her actual or apparent authority. The third party, likewise, is liable to the principal for performing such contracts. The principal is liable for his or her agent's torts unless they were committed willfully, intentionally, and outside the scope of the agent's employment. The principal normally is not liable for his or her agent's crimes. Finally, both the principal and the third party are liable to one another for their own torts upon each other.

Agency may be terminated by the acts of the parties either by mutual agreement, by the performance or expiration of the terms of the agency contract, by revocation by the principal, or by renunciation by the agent. Agency may be terminated by operation of law either by the death, insanity, or bankruptcy of either the principal or the agent, by a change in the law, or by the destruction or loss of the subject matter of the agency.

The real estate agent must be quite knowledgeable regarding the law of agency. The fiduciary relationship which the broker has with the principal must be respected and guarded at all times. The liabilities and duties of the agency relationship are numerous and complex. To serve the public and to protect himself or herself, the real estate broker must never violate or take advantage of the agency relationship.

CHAPTER 8

Listing, Sales, and Other Real Estate Contracts

KEY TERMS

Listing contract The employment agreement that establishes the agency relationship between the real estate agent and the principal, who is usually the owner of a property to be sold, leased, or exchanged

Equal dignities rule Rule stating that since the Statute of Frauds requires contracts for the sale of real property to be in writing, so, too, should listing contracts, which grant the authority to act as agent in such transactions, be in writing

Net listing A listing for a "net" price acceptable to the seller that is specified, the commission (if any) is the difference between the net price and the actual or "gross" price at which the broker is able to sell or lease the property

Open listing A listing for a set sales price, at a set commission percentage, for an unspecified time period, made with (open to) more than one broker, each of whom has an equal opportunity to earn a commission, with the reservation that if the property owner sells the property no one earns a commission; also called a general, simple, "pocket," or nonexclusive listing.

Exclusive agency listing A listing for a set price, at a set commission percentage, for a specified time period, with only one broker, with the reservation that the owner may sell the property and pay no commission

Exclusive right-to-sell listing A listing for a set price, at a set commission percentage, for a specified time period, with only one broker, with *no* reservation that the owner may sell the property to save paying the commission

Multiple-listing service A cooperative sales arrangement whereby brokers agree to pool their listings into the multiple list of a central listing bureau; when a broker works on the listing of another broker, he or she works as a subagent, and when a sale is consummated the commission is shared

Option listing A variation of the exclusive right-to-sell listing which gives the broker an option to purchase the property at the listed or some lower price

Certified listing A variation of the exclusive right-to-sell listing which requires the seller to pay a deposit ($75 to $150) to cover the cost of a market data appraisal of the listed property; if the seller lists at the appraised value, the deposit is deducted from the commission at closing; if the seller does not list, the deposit is forfeited.

Binder A preliminary informal contract that says that the purchaser and seller agree to contract in a formal manner within a short period of time in the future and that, until such time, the informal contract will *bind* the two parties to contract with one another

LISTING CONTRACTS

As discussed in Chapter 7, the *listing contract* in real estate is the employment agreement which establishes the agency relationship between the real estate broker-agent (and with his or her salespeople-subagents) and the principal, who is usually the owner of a property to be sold, leased, or exchanged. Sometimes, however, the principal may be a purchaser or tenant who has hired a real estate broker to find the property desired. In such cases said property is usually one of a very special or unique type, and a particular expertise is required to analyze the property for and in the interests of the principal. When the real estate broker is representing the principal in a purchase, sale, lease, or exchange, he or she has the authority of a special agent. On occasion, however, the broker may be employed as a general agent, as is the case when he or she is hired as a property manager with the authority to lease space, collect rents, hire professional and manual workers, contract for services and repairs, etc.

Although *oral listing contracts* are legal in most states, the real estate broker is better protected by the use of a *written listing contract* signed by both the principal and the broker-agent. The signature of the broker's salesperson is acceptable, provided it follows the name of the broker or his or her firm. It is simply sound business practice to use written listing agreements to avoid any possible misunderstandings or litigation that may arise regarding the listing or the exact terms thereof. The broker must prove the existence and status of his or her employment to earn a commission. With a written contract, the broker may avoid, for example, the situation wherein he or she has been the procuring cause of a transaction between a property owner and a buyer, lessee, or trader who have "gone around the broker" to consummate the deal and avoid paying a commission. After the fact, it is most difficult for the broker to prove the existence of an oral listing or one implied by the words or actions of the property owner. Even if such words or actions exist, the intent or meaning thereof is usually most difficult to establish and prove. The law will not protect "volunteer" agents, so the prudent broker should be sure that the agency relationship is established in writing.

Types of Listing Contracts

The four basic types of listing contracts are (1) net listing, (2) open listing, (3) exclusive agency listing, and (4) the exclusive right-to-sell listing. Three variations on these four basic types include: (1) multiple listing, (2) option listing, and (3) certified listing. These are most commonly variations on the exclusive right-to-sell listing contract.

Net Listing. In a net listing the commission is not specified, but rather a net price that the seller will accept is specified. Hence, the commission (if any) is the difference between the net price and the actual or gross price at which the broker is able to sell or lease the property.

This type of contract has been the subject of much criticism for the following reasons:

1. Since the broker must present all offers, there may be no commission earned. Hence, if there is a chance of no commission, the chances of the broker using his or her best efforts for the principal may be quite slim.
2. Since the broker is deemed to have real estate knowledge and ability superior to that of the principal, a net listing may provide an easy opportunity for fraud, misrepresentation, and/or double dealing for the dishonest or unscrupulous real estate broker-agent. The classic example of this criticism is the case of the uninformed person who purchased a house 40 years ago for $5,000 and would be delighted to settle for a net sales price of $20,000 when the broker knows he or she can sell it for $40,000 and, therefore, earn an inordinate commission of $20,000. It should be quite clear that such a situation is a flagrant violation of the agent's fiduciary responsibility and the duty to fully disclose to the principal all material facts relative to the property and its value.

Because of the potential problems and unfairness that may result from the use of net listings, some state legislatures have made them illegal (New York and New Jersey for example), and in other states, state regulatory agencies, such as state real estate commissions, have made them illegal or have at least publicly discouraged their use.

In the states where net listings are legal, it is usually required that (1) the contract state whether or not the net price is before or after the deduction of selling cost, and (2) the broker reveal the exact gross selling price to buyer and seller. When the gross price and, therefore, the commission have been revealed, the courts still may set aside any "inordinate" commission amount and award only a "reasonable" commission, or the courts may find the broker guilty of fraud or some other tort.

Generally speaking, the use of net listings is being discontinued in the sale of developed or improved property. The most common usage seems to appear with speculative land sales. In such cases the net listing is usually also open to more than one broker. However, when such is the case, another problem arises. It is possible for two or three brokers to offer the *same* property for sale at two or three *different* prices. Such practice can only damage the reputation for integrity and honesty of the real estate business in the public's eyes.

Open Listing. Open listings are also known as general, simple, "pocket," or nonexclusive listings. Regardless of the nomenclature, such a listing is usually for a set price, at a set commission percentage, for an unspecified time period, and made with (open to) *more than one* broker, each of whom has an equal opportunity to earn a commission, with the reservation that, if the property owner sells the property himself or herself, no one earns a commission. In other words, whoever (including the owner) consummates a contract of sale first, earns the commission.

The advantage of an open listing is that a property owner may list his or her property with all his or her real estate broker friends without offending or antagonizing any of them by listing with just one of them. This situation may be common in small, close-knit communities, where the seller-principal knows all or nearly all the brokers in town. The disadvantage of an open listing is that the individual brokers have no strong incentive to spend time and, especially, money for advertising or promotion to work on a "best efforts" basis for the seller, since at any time all their efforts may be for nil if one of the other brokers (or the owner) makes the deal.

Exclusive Agency Listing. An exclusive agency listing is for a set price, at a set commission percentage, for a specified time period, and with *only one* broker to whom the commission will be paid, with the reservation that, if the property owner sells the property himself or herself, no one earns a commission. Since this listing contract is made with only one broker, he or she has some incentive to spend time and money for marketing the property on a "best efforts" basis. Hence, the seller is better served than with an open listing. If other brokers have interested clients, they must work through the broker with the exclusive agency listing. In such a case the two brokers may establish a *cooperative sales agreement* to consummate the deal with the second broker's prospective buyer and to share the commission paid to the broker with the exclusive agency listing. The listing broker is under no obligation to cooperate but, if he or she does not do so, he or she may be open to just criticism from the seller if cooperation best serves the seller's interests.

Exclusive Right-to-Sell Listing. An exclusive right-to-sell listing (also known as an exclusive authorization and right-to-sell listing) is for a set price, at a set commission percentage, for a specified time period, and with only one broker to whom the commission will be paid, *without* the reservation that, if the property owner sells the property himself or herself, no one earns a commission. In other words, even if the owner sells the property, the broker will be paid the full commission. Because of this, the broker has the strongest incentive to spend time and money for marketing the property on a "best efforts" basis. Hence, the seller is best served. If other brokers have interested clients, they usually work through the broker with the exclusive right-to-sell listing by means of a *multiple listing service* (MLS). Under an MLS arrangement, brokers pool their listings through the facilities of a central listing bureau. In some states, the MLS is organized by the Realtors® and one must be a Realtor® to use the service. In some areas, members of the MLS are required to submit all their listings to the service; in other areas submittal is optional. Any member of an MLS who chooses to work on another broker's listing works as that broker's subagent; when a sale is procured from such work the commission will be shared between the two brokers, with a small fee paid to the MLS.

Another provision common to the exclusive right-to-sell listing contract is the so-called *safety clause*. This clause provides that if the property is sold, within a stated time period after the listing's expiration, to any party with whom the listing broker had negotiated and whose name was revealed in writing to the property owner by the broker, then the owner is liable to the broker for the full commission.

Option Listing. A variation of the exclusive right-to-sell listing, called an option listing, gives the broker an option to purchase the property himself or herself at the listed or some lower price. Such an arrangement is often used in connection with a *guaranteed trade-in program*, where the broker agrees to offer the property for sale for a specified time period at the end of which, at the seller's option, the broker will purchase the property at a price less than the listed price by an amount equal to the commission plus estimated carrying and closing costs to be incurred by the broker. This price "discount" may amount to 10 to 15 percent of the original listed price. This may appear to be a severe discount, but such an arrangement guarantees the seller a sale and allows him or her the capability and flexibility to negotiate and enter a contract for the purchase of another property. In some markets such an option may be quite valuable to a seller and quite comforting to his or her peace of mind.

In an option listing the broker still remains in a fiduciary position and must make full disclosure of all outstanding offers to purchase and any other information pertinent to the seller's interests. An option listing can be a situation ripe for fraud, misrepresentation, and/or double dealing. The seller needs to be protected from the possibility that the broker will exercise his or her option and then sell to a willing and able buyer which he or she knew about during the listing period. Most states, therefore, require the broker to disclose fully any profit made on such a transaction and to obtain written permission from the seller-principal for the earning of the profit.

Certified Listing. Another variation of the exclusive right-to-sell listing contract is the so-called certified listing, which requires the seller-principal to pay a deposit ($75 to $150) to cover the cost of a market-data appraisal of the listed property. The broker certifies that said appraisal is a fair estimate of market value and provides the basis for the listing price. If the seller agrees to list his or her property with the broker who has made the appraisal, the deposit is deducted from the commission paid at closing. If the seller chooses not to list, he or she forfeits the deposit and receives the appraisal report.

If the property is listed, the certified appraisal may be used as a marketing tool in procuring the sale of the property. Furthermore, the use of this listing technique or device may instill the buyer and seller with a confidence in the broker's professionalism by removing some of the mystique of determining a fair market price.

Listing Broker's Responsibilities and Compensation

The listing broker, as the agent of the seller-principal, owes the principal the four basic duties (discussed in Chapter 7) of performance, loyalty, reasonable care, and accountability. In addition to fulfilling these agency duties, in order to earn and have a valid claim for a real estate commission as his or her compensation, the broker must also (1) hold a valid real estate license according to and required by the law of the state in which the property is located (see Chapter 10), (2) be duly authorized (preferably by a written listing) to act as the principal's agent, (3) produce a ready, willing, and able purchaser or tenant, and (4) be the "procuring cause" of the offer to purchase, lease, or exchange.

A *ready* purchaser is one who is *presently* capable of closing the sale of the property; a *willing* purchaser *desires* to buy; and an *able* purchaser has the *financial backing* and *contractual authority* to complete the sale. If the seller-principal refuses to complete the sale with a ready, willing, and able purchaser presented by the broker-agent, the broker is still entitled to the commission.

If the sale is defeated by a defect in the title which the owner refuses to correct, the broker is still entitled to the commission *if* he or she has used a contract form which includes a clause binding the purchaser to complete the transaction upon the correction of such defect within a reasonable time.

If the purchase contract itself provides for a contingency, such as available and acceptable financing, and said contingency cannot be met, the principal will not be liable for the commission. However, if the performance of a contingency is prevented by fraud, misrepresentation, or double dealing by the principal, or by the principal in collusion with other parties, the broker is entitled to the full commission.

If the purchaser–third party wrongfully defeats or refuses to consummate the sale, the broker usually receives part of the earnest money deposit that was paid by the purchaser upon signing the contract. The purchase contract usually covers this situation in two separate clauses. One clause states that the earnest money will be forfeited as liquidated damages if the purchaser fails to complete the contract; another clause usually states that said liquidated damages will be equally divided between the seller-principal and the broker-agent, except that the broker may not receive more than what the full commission would have been had the sale been completed. Hence, to fully protect himself or herself, the broker should attempt to secure an earnest money deposit equal to twice the amount of the commission.

To be considered the *procuring cause* of a sale, the broker must be the cause which originates a series of continual events which results in the presentation of the ready, willing, and able purchaser to buy in accordance with the terms and conditions stated in the listing contract, or any other set of terms and conditions acceptable to the seller as evidenced by his or her signature on the offer to purchase. If the negotiations of one broker fail to secure an offer to purchase, but later the efforts of another broker induce the same purchaser to buy the same property, even at the same price and terms originally offered by the first broker, the first broker is *not* the procuring cause and is not therefore, entitled to a commission. However, a broker is entitled to the commission if he or she can show that it was his or her efforts that brought a meeting of the minds of the seller and purchaser, even if the contract to purchase is drawn by an intervening broker.

The issue of who is the procuring cause can become quite complex. The courts often have to make the final decisions. These decisions have awarded the commission to the broker *through whose instrumentality the sale was effected* or who was *the predominating effective cause of the sale*.

There are other aspects inherent in a listing arrangement that can result in litigation or in ethical problems. For example, a broker should not take an obviously overpriced listing and just "sit on it," making no effort to market it until the seller, in apparent desperation, lowers the price to a reasonable figure. The broker, as agent, owes it to the seller to indicate a fair listing price based on recent sales of comparable properties.

Regarding loyalty and trust, the broker cannot serve two masters. If the broker's personal interests conflict with the principal's interests—as in the case of the broker's buying the property—a full disclosure must be made. If the broker represents both purchaser and seller in a transaction, full disclosure must be made to all parties. If such is the case, as in an exchange or trade, the broker may even collect a commission from both parties.

The most common violation of the broker's loyalty and obedience as agent occurs when he or she informs the buyer or other agents that the seller-principal will accept a price less than the listing price. Even though the seller may confide to his broker-agent that the bottom price may be somewhat lower than the listed price, such confidence should never be revealed to the purchaser.

Another ethical problem often arises when a property is listed with one broker (listing broker) and the contract for purchase is presented by another broker (selling broker), who is technically a subagent of the listing broker, but practically considers himself or herself as the purchaser's agent and acts accordingly. The purchaser also most often feels that the selling broker is working for his or her interests. Hence, it is common for a very awkward conflict of interests to exist for the selling broker, not to mention the selling broker's own interest in receiving a commission from the sale. This commission is almost always paid by the seller to the listing broker, who shares it with his subagent, the selling broker.

Some real estate brokerage firms offer services as purchasing brokers with a purchaser-paid fee or commission. The idea is to avoid the inherent conflict of interests discussed above. Such arrangements are uncommon and, although there may be a trend in this direction, the practice is not at all widespread at the present time.

SALES CONTRACTS

As stated in Chapter 6, real estate brokers in most states are privileged to "practice law" by drawing contracts for the sale, lease, option, and exchange of real property by filling in the blanks on standard and approved forms. The laws of the different states vary as to which contracts may be drawn by real estate agents and as to how much latitude the agent may exercise in making any changes, additions, and/or deletions to the standard and approved forms.

State laws also vary as to what type of real estate contract or contracts are most commonly used to consummate a transaction involving the transfer of real property rights or interests. For example, some states use a preliminary informal contract, often called a *binder*, to initiate a transaction to be followed, a few days later, by a formal contract of sale. The informal contract essentially says that the purchaser and seller agree to contract in a formal manner within a short period of time and, until such time, the informal contract will *bind* the two parties to contract with one another. In some states the real estate broker is allowed to draw only the informal binder; the drawing of the formal contract is reserved only for duly licensed attorneys.

Even the type of formal contract commonly used varies from state to state or even among localities within the same state. For example, in some areas of the country, agents use nothing for the sale of real estate but *specific performance contracts*; in other areas, agents use primarily *receipt and option contracts*; and in some areas, agents use either of these two types, depending on the type of transaction or type of property involved.

Receipt and Option versus Specific Performance

A receipt and option contract is both a receipt by the broker for the earnest money he or she has collected from the purchaser and a contract granting the purchaser an option to buy the seller's property. In effect, the seller agrees to hold the property off the market during the option period. A sale takes place upon the exercise of the option. If the purchaser does not exercise the option, the seller (not the broker) may declare a forfeiture of the earnest money as liquidated damages and usually will share it with the broker. In other words, even though the purchaser can compel the seller to sell by exercising the option, the seller cannot compel the purchaser to buy. Only the liquidated damages become available.

On the other hand, a specific performance contract compels *both* parties to perform according to the specific terms and conditions of the contract. However, if one party refuses to perform, court action is necessary to force compliance with the contract. Such litigation usually takes a long time, during which the property may not be offered for sale to anyone else. For these reasons a specific performance contract may not necessarily best serve the interests of the seller of the average home. The specific performance contract is better suited for the sale of a very unique residence, or one that would appeal to a very thin market of purchasers. In commercial, industrial, agricultural, farm, and ranch sales the specific performance type contract is quite appropriate because of the uniqueness and dollar magnitude of the typical transaction.

In some states, variants of the receipt and option and specific performance contracts are commonly used. For example, in California a *real estate purchase contract and receipt for deposit* has been approved by the California Association of Realtors® (CAR). In this contract the buyer and seller may initial a clause which states that the "Buyer and Seller agree it would be impractical or extremely difficult to fix actual damages in case of Buyer's default, that the amount of the deposit is a reasonable estimate of damages, and that Seller shall retain the deposit as his sole right to damages." Otherwise, if this clause is not initialed, upon the buyer's default "Seller shall be released from his obligation to sell the property to Buyer and may proceed against Buyer upon any claim or remedy which he may have in law or equity."

The CAR contract form was revised in 1967 to read as quoted above, eliminating the phrase *deposit receipt*, which appeared to automatically allow *(without express agreement)* the seller to retain as damages any of the buyer's deposit money if the buyer decided not to go through with the transaction through no fault of the seller. However, the California courts have held that while a seller has a right to compensation upon a buyer's default, problems arise in determining the extent and amount of actual damages incurred. Many a California seller has become embroiled in lengthy and costly litigation in solving this problem. Hence, the new CAR contract wording solves this problem by expressly incorporating an agreement as to what "a reasonable estimate of damages" is, and by determining that the seller may retain the deposit amount as his or her sole right to damages.

Even today both the old and new CAR forms are used in different parts of California. Across the nation there are not only many different state laws relating to real estate sales contracts but also innumerable legal jurisdictions and varying local customs. Such a state of affairs makes it impossible for one text to relate all possible contract situations. Suffice it to say that one should consult his or her local real estate board or state real estate commission for guidance in the selection and use of the proper real estate sales contract form.

Importance of the Sales Contract

The sales contract, regardless of type is perhaps the most important legal document (*instrument*) used in a real estate transaction. The sales contract determines the kind and quantity of title to be conveyed, the type of deed used to transfer title, the liens and encumbrances (if any) that will or will not be assumed, the type of financing (if any) to be employed to make payment, and the time for closing and possession.

As a more detailed example of the importance of the sales contract, consider the following legal ramifications. Since the deed, as an executed contract, supersedes the sales contract, which is an executory contract, it is important that the sales contract provide for the appropriate type of deed. In other words, the sales contract is *merged in the deed*. In fact, in most states, unless otherwise provided for in the sales contract, any provisions contained in the sales contract which are not included in the deed become unenforceable once the purchaser has accepted the deed.

Provisions of the Sales Contract

An explanation of the various contract provisions may best be presented by following through, line by line, the example of the Colorado standard approved receipt and option contract, Exhibit 8-1.

Receipt of Purchaser's Earnest Money. Item #1 is the *date* on which the offer to purchase is made by the buyer. This date may be quite important if the contract contains time limitations for the seller's acceptance of the contract. The purchaser(s) is (are) identified by items #2 and #3. Full legal names should be used. In Colorado it is customary for husband and wife to take title as joint tenants unless otherwise stated. For example, a "single person" is one who has never been married; an "unmarried

The printed portion of this form approved by the Colorado Real Estate Commission (SC 20-10-75)

RECEIPT AND OPTION CONTRACT
(RESIDENTIAL)

#1 ____________, 19____

RECEIVED FROM #2 ____________,
Purchaser (as joint tenants #3), the sum of $ #4 ______, in the form of #5 ______
to be held by #6 ______, broker, in his escrow or trustee account, as earnest money and part payment for the following described real estate situate in the #7 ______
County of #8 ______, Colorado, to wit: #9

with all improvements thereon and all fixtures of a permanent nature currently on the premises except as hereinafter provided, in their present condition, ordinary wear and tear excepted, known as No. #10 ______
______,

which property purchaser agrees to buy upon the following terms and conditions, for the purchase price of $ #11 ______, payable as follows: $ #12 ______ hereby receipted for, $ #13 ______

1. If a note and trust deed or mortgage is to be assumed, the purchaser agrees to pay a loan transfer fee not to exceed $ #14 ______ and it is a condition of this contract that the purchaser may assume such encumbrance without change in its terms or conditions except #15 ______
______.

2. Price to include any of the following items currently on the premises: Lighting, heating and plumbing fixtures; all outdoor plants, window and porch shades, venetian blinds, storm windows, storm doors, screens, curtain rods, drapery rods, central air conditioning, ventilating fixtures, attached TV antennas, attached mirrors, linoleum, awnings, water softener (if owned by seller), fireplace screen and grate, built-in kitchen appliances, wall to wall carpeting ______ #16
______,
all in their present condition, free and clear of all taxes, liens and encumbrances except as provided in paragraph 4; provided, however, that the following fixtures of a permanent nature are excluded from this sale: #17 ______
______.

3. An abstract of title to said property, certified to date, or a current commitment for title insurance policy in an amount equal to the purchase price, at seller's option and expense, shall be furnished the purchaser on or before #18 ______, 19____. If seller elects to furnish said title insurance commitment, seller will deliver the title insurance policy to purchaser after closing and pay the premium thereon.

4. Title shall be merchantable in the seller. Subject to payment or tender as above provided and compliance with the other terms and conditions hereunder by purchaser, the seller shall execute and deliver a good and sufficient #19 ______, warranty deed to said purchaser on #20 ______, 19____, or, by mutual agreement, at an earlier date, conveying said property free and clear of all taxes, except the general taxes for 19 #21, payable January 1, 19 #22, and except #23 ______
______
______,
free and clear of all liens for special improvements now installed, whether assessed or not; free and clear of all liens and encumbrances except easements for telephone, electricity, water and sanitary sewer, and except #24 ______
______
______,
and subject to building and zoning regulations, and restrictive covenants of record. Any encumbrance required to be paid may be paid from the proceeds of this transaction.

5. General taxes for 19 #25 shall be apportioned to date of delivery of deed based on the most recent levy and the most recent assessment. Prepaid rents, water rents, sewer rents, FHA mortgage insurance premiums and interest on encumbrances, if any, and #26 ______
______
shall be apportioned to date of delivery of deed.

No. SC 20-10-75. Receipt and Option Contract (Residential) — Bradford Publishing Co., 1824-46 Stout Street, Denver, Colorado — 10-75

EXHIBIT 8-1

6. The hour and place of closing shall be as designated by ______#27______.

7. Possession of premises shall be delivered to purchaser on ______#28______

subject to the following leases or tenancies: #29

If the seller fails to deliver possession on the date herein specified, the seller shall be subject to eviction and shall be liable for a daily rental of $______#30______until possession is delivered.

8. In the event the premises shall be damaged by fire or other casualty prior to time of closing, in an amount of not more than ten per cent of the total purchase price, the seller shall be obligated to repair the same before the date herein provided for delivery of deed. In the event such damage cannot be repaired within said time or if such damage shall exceed such sum, this contract may be cancelled at option of purchaser. Should the purchaser elect to carry out this agreement despite such damage, such purchaser shall be entitled to all the credit for the insurance proceeds resulting from such damage, not exceeding, however, the total purchase price. Should any fixtures or services fail between the date of this agreement and the date of possession or the date of delivery of deed, whichever shall be earlier, then the seller shall be responsible for the repair or replacement of such fixtures or services with a unit of similar size, age and quality or an equivalent credit.

9. Time is of the essence hereof, and if any payment or any other condition hereof is not made, tendered or performed as herein provided, there shall be the following remedies. In the event a payment or any other condition hereof is not made, tendered or performed by the purchaser, then this contract shall be null and void and of no effect, and both parties hereto released from all obligations hereunder, and all payments made hereon shall be retained on behalf of the seller as liquidated damages. In the event that the seller fails to perform any condition hereof as provided herein, then the purchaser may, at his election, treat the contract as terminated, and all payments made hereunder shall be returned to the purchaser: provided, however, that the purchaser may, at his election, treat this contract as being in full force and effect with the right to an action for specific performance and damages.

10. In the event the seller fails to approve this instrument in writing on or before______#31______ 19______, or if title is not merchantable and written notice of defects is given to the seller or agent within the time herein provided for delivery of deed and shall not be rendered merchantable within 30 days after such written notice, then this contract, at purchaser's option, shall be void and of no effect and each party hereto shall be released from all obligations hereunder and the payments made hereunder shall be returned forthwith to purchaser upon return of the abstract, if any, to seller; provided, however, that in lieu of correcting such defects, seller may, within said 30 days, obtain a commitment for Owner's Title Insurance Policy in the amount of the purchase price showing the title to be free from such defects and seller shall pay full premium for such Title Insurance Policy.

11. Additonal Provisions: #32

12. Upon approval hereof by the seller, this agreement shall become a contract between seller and purchaser and shall inure to the benefit of the heirs, successors and assigns of said parties.

______#33______ Agent ______#34______
Purchaser Date

______________________ By: ______#35______
Purchaser Date

Seller approves the above contract this______#36______day of ______#37______, 19______ and agrees to pay a commission of ______#38______% of the gross sales price for services in this transaction, and agrees that, in the event of forfeiture of payments made by purchaser, such payments shall be divided between the seller's broker and the seller, one-half thereof to said broker, but not to exceed the commission, and the balance to the seller.

______________________ #39 ______________________
Seller Seller

Purchaser's Address ______#40______

Seller's Address ______#41______

person'' is one who has been legally divorced and has not remarried; a ''widow'' or ''widower'' is one whose spouse is deceased. Hence, if something other than ''joint tenants'' is appropriate, that phrase would be deleted and the appropriate set of words added in space #2.

Incidentally, the proper manner by which to delete a printed portion of a standard approved form is to draw one line through that portion so that it may still be read. The printed portion should never be totally obliterated. The logic here is that by using only one line it is not only clear that the portion is to be deleted, but it is also quite clear (since the portion remains legible) exactly what the parties agreed to delete or exclude from the contract. Furthermore, if a discrepancy exists between a printed portion of the standard approved form and a portion which has been typed or handwritten, the portion done by hand takes precedence over the printed portion.

The amount of *earnest money* is inserted in space #4, while its form (cash, check, note) is inserted in space #5. The amount of earnest money is usually a matter of local custom and a function of the property value, with 2 to 10 percent of the offered purchase price being a reasonable amount. The earnest money is usually held by the listing broker, as agent for the seller, in a separate escrow or trustee account until the closing or transfer of title, or by an escrow agent or title company in those states (such as California) where title is transferred by means of an escrow arrangement. The listing broker's name and/or firm name is entered in space #6. If the sale is consummated, the earnest money is applied against the purchase price; otherwise it becomes liquidated damages to be divided between the seller and the listing broker-agent.

Property Description. Items #7 to #10 are used to state the city, county, legal description, and street address, respectively, of the property. The legal description should be stated identically to the description in the seller's deed. The buildings, fences, sidewalks, and other improvements need not be separately and distinctly described, since they are appurtenances to the land and are automatically transferred, unless otherwise excluded.

Purchase Price and Form of Payment. Item # 11 states the purchase price offered by the seller; item #12 reiterates that the earnest money is to be applied against the purchase price; and item #13 relates how the remainder of the purchase price is to be met. The rest of the purchase price may be paid in a variety of ways:

1. All cash (or certified or cashier's check) at closing
2. Part cash at closing plus a new first loan from a third-party institutional lender

3. Part cash plus a new first loan "carried-back" (purchase-money loan) by the seller
4. Part cash plus a new first loan and a new second loan from third parties
5. Part cash plus a new third-party first loan and a new second loan "carried-back" (purchase-money loan) by the seller
6. Part cash plus the assumption of an old loan or set of loans already encumbering the property
7. Part cash plus assumption of old loans plus new purchase-money or third-party loans
8. No cash and all loans of any of the above listed combinations.

If a loan is to be assumed, clause 1, containing items #14 and #15, states how much of a loan transfer fee the buyer is willing to pay and what changes (if any) in the assumable loans are acceptable to the buyer.

Fixtures and Personal Property. The fixtures and/or personal property normally included in the sale of real property is a matter of local custom. Clause 2 lists what is customarily included in Colorado and allows space (#16) to add and space (#17) to delete any fixtures or personal property whose disposition may vary from what is customary. In some state contract forms a large blank space is given to list and describe (1) terms (how price is to be paid), and (2) conditions (what other property is included or excluded). In such contracts the conditions portion may also contain other agreements, which are usually listed under the additional provisions portion of the contract presented here.

Good and Merchantable Title. In some states, it is the seller's duty to prove good and merchantable title by means of an abstract and opinion or a title insurance policy. In other states, the seller owes no such duty and the buyer must protect himself or herself against an invalid or clouded title. Clause 3 in Exhibit 8-1 states that the seller must provide evidence of title on or before the date inserted in item #18. This date is usually two or three weeks prior to the day of closing, which date is stated in space #20. The type of deed used to convey title is stipulated in space #19.

Liens and Encumbrances. Since the property taxes for the current year (#21) are not payable until the following year (#22), the property cannot be transferred free and clear. If there are any exceptions to this general rule, such should be noted in space #23. Any special improvements—such as sidewalks, presently installed, whether assessed or not—are usually the seller's responsibility. If such improvements have been assessed but not yet installed, they too are usually the seller's responsibility, unless otherwise agreed. Any other liens or encumbrances, unless excepted in clause 4 or space #24, are the seller's responsibility and may be paid, if necessary, from the proceeds of the sale. However, the purchaser does have to buy the property "subject to building and zoning regulations, and restrictive covenants of record," since the seller has no control over or responsibility for these items.

The property taxes excepted in clause 4 are apportioned or prorated, in clause 5, between purchaser and seller to the date of closing, with the buyer usually paying for the day of closing itself. Any other charges that need to be prorated are designated in the remainder of clause 5 and in space #26.

Closing and Possession. The hour and place of closing (#27) is designated by the listing broker. However, in practice, it is usually designated by the lender. (Those with the gold make the rules.) Possession of the premises (#28) may be before or after the closing, depending on the particular circumstances of the parties and/or local custom. For example, in Colorado possession is usually three days after closing, to allow the sellers time to move out. Even though the purchasers are the owners of the property during these three days, usually no rental is paid. However, if the sellers wish to remain more than three days after closing, for whatever reason, a daily rental is normally negotiated for this period, including the three days.

Sometimes the property is vacant long before closing and the purchasers may wish to move in prior to closing. In such cases, a rental is agreed upon, to be paid by the purchasers up to the day of closing.

The sale of a property does not terminate any lease or tenancies presently in force on the property. Hence, it is possible to have to state (#29) that possession is subject to said leases. In other words, title and ownership may transfer at closing, but possession will not be transferred until the present lease expires or until such tenants agree to vacate the premises.

Finally, as an extra inducement to get the seller to remove himself or herself from the premises and deliver possession on the specified date, it is customary (in Colorado) to subject him or her to eviction and some exorbitant daily-rental penalty (space #30) until possession is delivered. This penalty is usually at least three times as great as a normal rental.

Risk of Loss. If the premises are damaged or destroyed between the time the contract of sale was executed and the day of closing, most states, unless otherwise agreed, place the risk of loss on the purchaser, because he or she is deemed the holder of *equitable title* upon the signing of the contract, and as such can force the seller, who holds *legal title*, to convey that legal title. Some courts have ruled that it is unfair for the risk of loss to fall on the purchaser, who does not have possession and control of protection of the property. In these jurisdictions the seller bears the risk of loss until closing. Other states have adopted the Uniform Vendor and Purchaser Risk Act, which states that the seller cannot enforce a sales contract when neither legal title nor possession have been delivered to the purchaser.

Clause 8 of the Colorado form provides a set of agreements and options relative to the problem of damage or destruction to the premises or any of its fixtures or services. Essentially, if such damage is less than 10 percent of the purchase price, the seller must repair the damage. If the damage exceeds the 10 percent or the repairs cannot be made by the day of closing, the purchaser has the option to cancel the contract or to collect the insurance proceeds and complete the contract performance.

Remedies upon Default. The "time is of the essence" phrase allows either party to declare a contract default if any of the terms, conditions, or provisions of the contract are not met by or within the specified time periods. The clause which contains the remedies upon default (clause 9 in Exhibit 8-1) usually contains the words which indicate whether the contract is a receipt-and-option type or a specific-performance type. Here the respective rights of the parties upon the default of the other party are listed and explained. For example, the agreed-upon liquidated damages, if any, are stated here. Whether or not specific performance is a remedy is also stated in this clause.

Acceptance by Seller. In clause 10 the purchaser gives the seller a time (#31) by which he or she must sign and accept the purchaser's offer; otherwise the offer is revoked and all monies receipted are to be returned. Furthermore, if title is not merchantable and cannot be made merchantable within a stated time period, the contract is void and of no effect, at the purchaser's option.

Additional Provisions. Space #32 is reserved for any other agreements the parties may make which have not been covered in any of the previous clauses. Any conditions or contingencies—termite inspection, appraisal, available financing, rental agreements, sale of purchaser's present home, etc.—may be inserted here and become part of the contract.

Death. The death of buyer or seller, unless otherwise agreed, does not terminate the sales contract. The surviving party can compel the heirs, successors, and assignees of the deceased party to perform the terms of the contract. This provision is covered in clause 12.

Signatures. Item #33 provides space for the purchaser's signature and the date, which evidence the validity of the offer to buy. The broker's name or firm name appears in space #34; space #35 is reserved for the broker's signature, or that of his subagent, broker associate, or salesperson. This signature evidences the receipt of earnest money.

Following the date of the seller's acceptances (spaces #36 and #37) of the offer to purchase, the amount of commission (#38), and the disposition of earnest money upon any default, is the space (#39) for the seller's signature, evidencing these acceptances. Finally, spaces are provided (#40 and #41) for the purchaser's and seller's addresses.

OTHER REAL ESTATE CONTRACTS

It is virtually impossible to present and discuss every other type of real estate contract. No two real estate transactions are ever identical in concept or form. However, a list of the most common types of real estate contracts may be offered. Such a list would consist of all the various standard and approved forms used in a particular state. Appendix D contains a copy of each of the standard and approved forms used in the state of Colorado. A few of the most frequently encountered contracts include (1) counteroffer or proposal, (2) option contract, (3) exchange contract, and (4) installment land contract.

Counteroffer

If a seller does not wish to accept the offer to purchase presented by a purchaser, he or she may wish to propose a counteroffer, which simply states that he or she accepts the original offer, subject to some changes or amendments.

A counteroffer may be made by actually crossing out items on the original offer and changing them and/or adding other provisions, terms, or conditions. Any such changes are initialed by the seller and then offered to the purchaser for initialing.

A better and, at least, neater way of making a counteroffer is to use either the back side of the original contract or a separate form specifically designed as a counteroffer. Such a form first references the original contract and then states that it is acceptable subject to the amendments listed on the counteroffer form. A place for the purchaser's signature is provided at the end of the counteroffer form. If signed by the purchaser, the original contract and the counteroffer merge as one single binding contract under the law.

Option Contract

An option contract is a contract to keep an offer to sell at a specified price open for a specified time period upon the consideration of the option fee paid by the prospective purchaser. If the purchaser and holder of the option exercises his or her option during the specified time period, the seller is compelled to consummate the transaction at the price specified in the option contract. Normally, the option fee is applied against the purchase price.

Exchange Contract

If two or more parties wish to liquidate some of their property holdings and acquire others elsewhere, it may be possible and advantageous for these parties to trade or exchange properties and still meet their objectives. A typical reason to trade rather than to sell and buy is to avoid capital-gains taxes payable on the sale portion of the transaction. Other reasons to make a trade include the lack of sufficient or reasonable financing or a desire to increase one's tax basis, to avoid a management type of property and procure a management-free type of property, or to trade a cash-flow type of property for a tax-shelter type of property.

Installment Land Contract

The installment land contract goes by many names, including land contract, land contract for deed, contract for deed, or (in California) agreement of sale. Regardless of the nomenclature used, such a contract provides that the buyer (vendee) will pay the seller (vendor) for the property in installment payments. The buyer will not receive the deed until all, or some agreed-upon portion, of the purchase price has been paid. Once the contract is signed, the purchaser becomes the holder of equitable title whether or not he or she takes possession, and the seller becomes the holder of legal title.

In the past, if the purchaser defaulted on the installment payments, he or she lost all rights to the payments made and to the property itself. However, more recent court cases have recognized that the defaulting purchaser should not be deprived of the equity accumulated from the installment payments. In such cases the courts have treated the installment land contract as a security device that must be foreclosed as a mortgage or deed of trust.

Such a foreclosure may be much like a strict foreclosure; there is no public sale, but rather a transfer of the property directly to the seller. The courts also usually hold that the choice of the foreclosure remedy causes a recision of the original contract which denies the foreclosing seller any rights to a deficiency judgment if the property at foreclosure is not worth what is owed to the seller. Furthermore, the court may allow the defaulting purchaser six months or more to redeem the property from foreclosure by making payment of the full purchase price remaining. Other jurisdictions allow the seller, upon the buyer's default, a choice between foreclosure and a suit for payments as each one falls due.

To protect the buyer's interests from the seller's death, from liens or encumbrances the seller placed on the property, or from similar problems that may not make conveyance of legal title free of any other claims, the original contract should be recorded and placed in escrow with instructions for conveyance of title and deed upon the meeting of the contract terms.

For example, many speculative land sales use installment land contracts. Purchasers in such transactions seldom take possession, and therefore, no public notice of sale is given. A public recording and an escrow arrangement would best protect everyone's interests.

The installment land contract can be a very involved and legally complex instrument. If not properly used, the seller and/or buyer may be injured. Whether this type of contract is used as a security device for financing a sale or purely as a conveyance instrument, it is highly advised that legal counsel be sought.

SUMMARY AND CONCLUSION

The listing contract is the employment agreement which establishes the agency relationship between the real estate broker and the principal, who is usually the owner of a property to be sold, leased, or exchanged. The real estate broker is usually a special agent. Oral listings are legal in most states; however, their use is ill-advised.

The four basic types of listing contracts are (1) net listing, (2) open listing, (3) exclusive agency listing, and (4) exclusive right to sell listing. Multiple, option, and certified listings are variations of the exclusive right to sell listing.

To earn a commission, a real estate broker must not only meet his or her agency obligations but also (1) hold a valid real estate license, (2) establish the employment arrangement with a listing contract, (3) produce a ready, willing, and able purchaser or tenant, and (4) be the "procuring cause" of the transaction. The transaction may be defeated, but the broker may still be entitled to a commission if he or she has done all these and the seller's actions or lack thereof defeated the deal. If the third party defeats the transaction, the broker and his or her principal may have to settle for liquidated damages (usually the earnest money divided equally between them). Hence, for full protection, the broker should attempt to secure an earnest money deposit equal to twice the amount of the commission.

A real estate broker should not take and/or "sit on" an obviously overpriced listing, but should suggest a fair market price supported by recent sales of comparable properties. If a broker represents both parties in a transaction, full disclosure must be made to both to avoid a conflict of interests.

A common violation of the broker's loyalty to his or her principal is when he or she informs prospective buyers and/or other agents that the seller will accept a price below the listing price. Another common conflict of interests often arises when a selling broker acts in the interests of the purchaser when in fact he or she is technically and legally the subagent of the listing broker and owes loyalty to the seller-principal. Some realty firms, in an effort to avoid this conflict of interests, specialize as purchasing agents employed and compensated by purchasers only.

The degree to which a real estate broker is allowed to "practice law" by drawing sales contracts varies among jurisdictions. Most states, however, allow real estate brokers to fill in the blanks on standard approved contract documents.

State laws also vary as to the type or types of sales contracts commonly used. Some states, for example, use a binder contract as a preliminary instrument until a formal contract of sale is executed. Some jurisdictions and areas use only receipt and option contracts or specific performance contracts; California uses a purchase contract and receipt for deposit contract, which has generally replaced the use of the deposit receipt.

The sales contract is thought by many to be the most important instrument used in a real estate transaction, since it sets the stage or provides the blueprint for the transaction and will eventually be merged in and superseded by the deed. Each of the many provisions of the sales contract has its own importance, and extreme care must be taken to insure a full understanding of the meaning of each clause.

Four other contracts which are quite frequently encountered in the field of real estate are (1) counteroffer, (2) option contract, (3) exchange contract, and (4) installment land contract. Regardless of the type of contract used in a real estate transaction, it is always good advice to seek legal counsel, advise, and opinion from a duly licensed attorney.

CHAPTER 9

Settlement of Title

KEY TERMS

Settlement of title The completion of the title transfer process

Closing A meeting of all parties to a real estate transaction to complete the title transfer process and to monetarily conclude or settle the transaction

Escrow An arrangement whereby either or both purchaser and seller are not present to complete the title transfer process and a disinterested third-party agent is hired and instructed to handle the closing and conclude the transaction

Truth In Lending Act (TIL) Title I of the National Consumer Credit Protection Act, which makes lenders responsible to disclose to certain consumer borrowers certain information regarding the financing of real property

Reg Z A Federal Reserve Board regulation issued to implement the Truth In Lending Act and enforced by the Federal Trade Commission

Finance charge The total of certain costs incurred by the borrower in obtaining a real estate loan, such as loan origination fee, discount points, finder's fees, mortgage insurance, and credit life insurance

Annual Percentage Rate (APR) The effective rate of interest paid on a real estate loan considering, in addition to the stated interest rate, all the financing charges

Uniform Consumer Credit Code (UCCC) A law that makes lenders responsible for certain disclosures similar to those required by Reg Z of TIL

Equal Credit Opportunity Act Regulation B of the Federal Reserve Board: outlines procedures lenders must follow in judging mortgage loan applicants and avoiding discrimination with respect to marital status, sex, age, race, color, religion (creed), national origin, or public assistance income or welfare support

Real Estate Settlement Procedures Act (RESPA) Congressional act that imposes requirements on lenders in regard to the closing of real estate transactions and other related matters involving real estate brokers.

Title may be acquired in a variety of ways other than through a normal sales transaction between willing and able buyers and sellers. As indicated earlier, title may be acquired by will, by descent, by accession, by occupancy, and by transfer through voluntary and involuntary alienation. The normal sales transaction (voluntary alienation) is by far the most common method of acquiring title to real property. The consummation of such a transaction and the passing of legal title from seller to buyer happens when the legal instrument of conveyance, such as a deed, has been properly executed, delivered, and accepted. The completion of the title-transfer process is called the *settlement of title*. Such a settlement may occur either through a *closing* or an *escrow*.

CLOSING

A *closing* is a meeting of all parties to the transaction, including buyers and sellers and their respective attorneys, lenders, and real estate brokers, as well as the person or representative of the firm that did the title search. At such a meeting all the appropriate documents and papers are passed around,[1] examined and signed by the proper persons in order to conclude or settle the transaction. The contract of sale should designate the day of closing; the clause "time is of the essence" (when included) means that, if closing does not take place on the designated date, the party causing the delay is in default and is usually subject to a monetary adjustment to compensate for the delay. The sales contract should also provide enough time between contract execution (signing) and closing to allow completion of title examination and protection, loan approval (if applicable), deed preparation, prorations of property taxes, and any other items or fees which need to be handled or paid before title is conveyed. At closing, therefore, the buyer pays the seller's purchase price and the seller delivers the buyer's deed for the property of the sales transaction. Actually, closing can be quite complicated; seller and buyer, real estate broker, closing agent (if applicable), and lender must be aware of their respective duties and responsibilities.

Seller's Responsibilities

The seller's and/or his or her attorney's prime responsibility at closing is to be prepared to transfer title in the manner stipulated in the contract of sale (seller should have this contract at closing). In other words, the proper type of deed must be fully prepared, signed, and ready for delivery to the buyer. Documents showing the removal of liens or other encumbrances not being assumed by the buyer must be presented. Normally the title search will denote such claims against the property. In most states the cost of the title examination and title protection is the responsibility of the buyer. In other states (Colorado, for example) it is the seller's duty,

1. In Massachusetts, a closing or the day of closing is often referred to as "the passing of papers" or as "the day to pass papers."

as stated in the standard contract of sale, to provide "good and merchantable title," which customarily makes the cost of title examination and protection the responsibility of the seller. Regardless of who must bear the expense of search and examination, the seller should have at closing an *affidavit of title*, which is a written statement of ownership signed and sworn to by the seller.

The seller may also be required to present the following documents at closing:

1. Property tax certificate showing current status of payment and liability (paid for by buyer in some states)
2. Property hazard insurance policy (if to be assumed)
3. Estoppel certificates showing current status of payment and liability of mortgage loans (if to be assumed)
4. Satisfaction pieces of liens, mortgages, or judgments to be paid at or prior to closing
5. Termite and wood-rot inspection report
6. Bill of sale for personal property to be transferred
7. Current receipts for utility bills
8. Current readings for utility meters
9. Appraisals or surveys, if required by contract
10. Assignment of leases, tenant and rent schedules, and tenant notification letters if property is income producing

Buyer's Responsibilities

The buyer, like the seller, should bring his or her copy of the contract of sale to the closing meeting to aid in clarification of any disputes or misunderstandings that may arise regarding settling the transaction. The buyer's prime responsibility at closing is to be prepared to tender payment, according to the contract terms. Such payment may involve cash to cover (1) the remainder of the down payment not covered by the earnest money that was paid upon signing the contract of sale, or (2) the remainder of the purchase price beyond the earnest money, if no loan is involved, and (3) all closing costs owed by the buyer. If the transaction is not an all-cash deal, then the down payment must be accompanied by either borrowed funds from a mortgage or deed-of-trust loan, or a purchase-money mortgage, or an installment contract for deed, or some other legal instrument evidencing some other creative financing technique. In the process of obtaining financing, it is the buyer's responsibility to provide the prospective lender with all the information (credit references, employment and income verifications, etc.) required to analyze or underwrite the real estate loan.

The buyer should also obtain at closing the documents, if applicable, listed earlier as the seller's responsibility. All these documents should be examined to the satisfaction of the buyer and his or her attorney.

Broker's Responsibilities

Technically, the broker's function ends when he or she has obtained the signatures of buyer and seller on the contract for sale.[2] However, the wise and professional broker makes it his or her added responsibility to do whatever is necessary to ensure a smooth and very professional closing. Usually there is considerable nervous tension at a real estate closing, since all parties meet face to face to handle a relatively large (and sometimes very large) financial transaction. The wise broker can avoid confusion, misunderstandings, and possible resentment toward himself or herself and his or her firm and profession by explaining in advance of closing all the closing costs likely to be incurred by buyer and/or seller. When the parties to the transaction are informed of what to expect at the closing, the closing should run smoothly and the transaction settlement should end on a high note of confidence, competency, and professionalism.

Many brokers use checklists, which include all the steps and items that are the responsibilities of either the buyer or the seller, to monitor the progress of events and duties which must be completed by the closing day. By putting himself or herself at the disposal of the buyer and/or seller to aid in meeting their responsibilities, the broker can foster a smooth closing, including the collection of the brokerage commission.

Closing Agent's Responsibilities

The closing agent may be the real estate broker, the lender, the title insurance company, a disinterested third-party accountant, or one or both of the attorneys of the buyer and the seller. Local custom and/or the nature of the transaction usually dictates who is to be the closing agent. In any case, the closing agent's prime responsibility is to prepare the closing or settlement statement. This statement provides a full accounting for both buyer and seller of all the prorations and costs of closing the transaction. The closing statement should be thought of as an accounting after the completion of the transaction rather than as a statement of funds due prior to the closing. In other words, even though the closing statement is prepared prior to the closing itself, it is actually an accounting of debits and credits for the buyer and seller as of the conclusion of the transaction. A full explanation of these debits and credits is provided in the closing example later in this chapter.

2. The act of acquiring buyer and seller signatures on a contract of sale is often referred to as "closing the sale" or as "the close of the sale." This terminology should not be confused with closing the transaction or the closing or settlement day discussed in this section.

The closing agent is in charge of the closing and is, therefore, responsible for making sure that everything necessary to consummate the transaction is completed in a timely fashion. Some other possible functions of the closing agent include:

1. Prepare and/or record necessary legal documents, and return them after recording
2. Collect and disburse funds at closing
3. Order a survey, appraisal, title search and title insurance, tax certificate, termite and wood-rot inspection and report, affidavit of title, or power of attorney
4. Calculate all prorations or apportionments between buyer and seller
5. Act as mediator to settle any misunderstandings or disputes that may arise

Lender's Responsibilities

Whether or not the lending institution also acts as the closing agent, there are specific duties imposed upon lenders by federal legislation. This legislation includes:

1. The Truth In Lending Act
2. The Uniform Consumer Credit Code
3. The Equal Credit Opportunity Act
4. The Real Estate Settlement Procedures Act

The Truth In Lending Act. Title I of the National Consumer Credit Protection Act, which became effective on July 1, 1969, is commonly known as the Truth In Lending Act (TIL). This act of Congress authorized the Federal Reserve Board of Governors to prescribe regulations pursuant to the act. Consequently, Regulation Z (Reg Z) was issued to implement the act. This regulation is enforced by the Federal Trade Commission (FTC).

Essentially, TIL makes lenders responsible to *disclose* to certain consumer borrowers information including, but not limited to, the following:

1. The *Finance Charge*, which is the total of costs incurred by the borrower in obtaining the real estate loan. These include interest, origination fee, discount points, finder's fees, mortgage insurance, and credit life insurance.
2. The *Annual Percentage Rate* (APR), which is the *effective* rate of interest paid on the loan considering, in addition to the stated interest rate, all the other costs that encompass the finance charge.
3. The borrower's *Right of Recision* within three business days follow-

ing the date of the loan or the date of delivery of required disclosures, except in certain cases.

Reg Z is far more encompassing and complex than this very brief discussion can convey. Further discussion and explanation are provided in Chapter 14. The point to be remembered here is that in making real estate loans and closing real estate transactions, lenders must be keenly aware of their responsibilities under Reg Z of the Truth In Lending Act.

The Uniform Consumer Credit Code. The Uniform Consumer Credit Code (UCCC) makes lenders responsible for certain disclosures similar to those required by Reg Z of TIL. The states that have adopted the UCCC may or may not be exempted from Reg Z. Hence, lenders in some states (Colorado, for example) may be responsible for disclosures under both laws. For example, under the UCCC, if a real estate loan provides for a *balloon payment* which is twice as large as the average of earlier scheduled payments, and the interest rate on that loan exceeds 12 percent, the lender must disclose that the borrower has the right to refinance the amount of payment at the time it is due, without penalty and on terms no less favorable than those of the original loan. The UCCC provisions are more fully explained in Chapter 14. Lenders closing transactions in UCCC states must be keenly aware of their responsibilities under this set of laws.

The Equal Credit Opportunity Act. Regulation B of the Federal Reserve Board outlines procedures that lenders must follow in judging mortgage loan applicants and avoiding discrimination with respect to marital status, sex, age, race, color, religion (creed), national origin, and public-assistance income or welfare support. In other words, the lending institution cannot take the presence, absence, or status of any of these items under consideration in determining the credit worthiness of any real estate loan applicant. Lenders subject to this act, therefore, must be fully informed of their duties to disclose borrower rights before, during, and after a closing under this law.

The Real Estate Settlement Procedures Act. In 1974 Congress enacted the Real Estate Settlement Procedures Act (RESPA), which imposed certain requirements on lenders in regard to the closings of real estate transactions and other related matters involving real estate brokers. Initially, RESPA generated so many complaints and criticisms regarding confusion, red-tape, and inconveniences suffered by lenders, brokers, and consumers that the law, which had only become effective on June 20, 1975, was significantly amended in 1975, effective June 30, 1976.

RESPA applies to sales or transfers of one-to-four-family residences (including cooperatives, condominiums, building lots, mobile homes, and mobile-home lots) financed by "federally related" first mortgages. *Federally related mortgages* include:

1. FHA, VA, or other government-sponsored loans
2. Loans from institutions with federally insured (FDIC, FSLIC) deposits
3. Loans eligible for purchase by federally related (FNMA, GNMA, FHLMC) secondary mortgage market participants
4. Loans from lenders with more than $1 million per year invested in residential loans

Hence, the act covers the vast majority of all loans made by most financial institutions on one-to-four-family residences. RESPA also applies to sales or transfers in which a loan is assumed or taken subject to, if the loan terms are modified or if the lender charges a fee of over $50 for the assumption.

RESPA does *not* apply to the following situations:

1. Refinancings, junior mortgages, consumer borrowings, and other situations in which no property transfer occurs
2. Loans on property in excess of 25 acres
3. Home improvement loans
4. Land acquisition and development loans
5. Construction loans
6. Loans assumed, except as noted above
7. Purchases by nonconsumers who hold the property for resale in their ordinary course of business

RESPA was not enacted to set the prices of settlement or closing costs. Rather, RESPA was enacted to provide more effective advance disclosure of closing costs (in the hope of taking some of the mystery out of the closing process), to allow buyers and sellers to shop for closing services, and to thereby aid in the making of informed decisions. RESPA does aim to lower the costs of closing by prohibiting certain kickback and referral-fee practices and by limiting the amounts placed in reserve or impound accounts held by lenders. Finally, the required use of RESPA's uniform settlement sheets is an attempt to reform, modernize, and standardize local record keeping of real property title transfer information. Violations of RESPA do not affect the validity or enforceability of any sale or loan.

RESPA *prohibits* the following practices:

1. The giving or accepting of any kickbacks, compensation, or referral fees in connection with any settlement services including, but not limited to, loan referral, title search, title examination, or title protection, legal services pertaining to closing, preparation of documents, surveys, appraisals, credit reports, pest-control services, processing and closing of title. Violation of this provision may result

in a $10,000 fine and one year's imprisonment via a criminal court, as well as liability of up to three times the value of the illegal compensation plus court costs and attorney fees via a civil court proceeding. Specifically exempted from the kickback provision, however, are cooperative brokerage or referral commission arrangements among real estate brokers and salespeople.

2. Sellers requiring, as a condition of sale, that a buyer purchase title protection from a particular title company, abstractor, or attorney. Violation of this provision subjects the seller to a liability to the buyer for an amount equal to three times the cost of the title protection. In states (such as Colorado) where it is customary for the seller to purchase the title protection, the seller may choose the source of title protection without fear of penalty. However, if mortgagee's title insurance is required to be purchased by the buyer, a problem may arise for the real estate broker who usually orders the owner's title insurance for the seller. Since the mortgagee's policy purchase by the buyer will be very inexpensive if purchased from the company issuing the owner's policy, the broker may be placed in the position of indirectly influencing the buyer's choice of title company. In such a situation the real estate broker is well advised to have the buyer designate in the written contract of sale the name of the chosen title company.
3. Lenders demanding of a borrower an advance reserve, impound, or escrow of money exceeding two months' worth of property taxes, hazard insurance, mortgage insurance, or condominium assessments.

RESPA *requires* the following practices:

1. The lender must, within three days of loan application, supply the buyer-borrower with a copy of a special RESPA information bulletin prepared or approved by the Department of Housing and Urban Development (HUD), which describes the closing process. The HUD booklet also contains information on the rights and remedies available under RESPA, alerts one to unfair or illegal settlement practices, and offers an item-by-item explanation of closing services and costs with sample forms and worksheets.
2. The lender must include with the HUD booklet a good-faith estimate of the amount or range of closing costs likely to be incurred on the day of closing. The law does not require estimates be made for the advance reserve, impound, or escrow monies. However, the lender may voluntarily add these items to the good-faith estimate form.
3. The lender must also supply the buyer-borrower with the actual closing costs "at or before" the closing. Borrowers may waive this requirement or they may demand a review of the actual closing costs at least one business day before the day of closing.

4. Finally, although the lending institution may use its own closing statement form for the advance disclosure described above, at the closing meeting the buyer must be supplied with a completed Uniform Settlement Statement prepared by HUD. The lender may make no charge for preparation of the HUD statement. If the borrower or his or her agent does not attend the closing or the closing agent does not require a meeting of the parties (as occurs with settlement by escrow), the settlement statement must be supplied "as soon as practicable after settlement." A copy of the HUD settlement statement must remain in the lender's files for two years.

The HUD Uniform Settlement Statement is thoroughly explained in the Settlement Problem section of this chapter. Before attacking the settlement problem, however, it is appropriate to discuss settlement through escrow and to compare it with settlement through closing.

ESCROW

Escrow Defined

The word *escrow* can mean different things to different people. To some, escrow or an escrow account is synonymous with *reserve* or *impound* account, which is money accumulated and held by a lender from which the lender pays property taxes, hazard insurance, mortgage insurance, etc., when these liabilities (and potential liens) fall due. In the context of settlement of title, escrow can have different but similar meanings.

Technically speaking, an escrow is a legal instrument (deed or grant) deposited by the grantor (seller) with and held by a disinterested third party (escrowee) until the happening of a contingency or performance of a condition, and then by him or her delivered to the grantee (buyer). While the document is deposited with the escrowee, it is *not*, strictly speaking, a deed, since it has not actually been delivered. Hence the instrument, while in this intermediate position, is more correctly referred to as an escrow.

An explanation of the *doctrine of relation back* allows a clearer understanding of why the conveyance instrument, while held by the third party, is not truly a deed. If the grantor has deposited the instrument with the escrowee and then dies, marries, goes bankrupt or insane, or otherwise changes his or her legal status, and thereafter the happening of the contingency takes place or the condition is performed, the instrument must be delivered passing title to the grantee (buyer) as of the date the instrument was delivered to the escrowee. In other words, the acquisition of title *relates back* to the date on which the instrument or escrow was deposited with the escrowee. If the condition or contingency does not come about, the instrument is not considered to have been delivered and title does not pass to the grantee-buyer; thus the escrow is not, and does not become, a deed.

Escrow or *closing in escrow* is also commonly used to describe the arrangement whereby either the buyer or the seller cannot be present at the closing meeting. In such a case, a disinterested third-party agent is selected to handle the closing and conclude the transaction. In California especially,[3] and in other western states, an escrow closing is used exclusively. In these states the *escrow agent*, *escrow holder*, *escrow officer*, or *escrowee* is a person, bank, title insurance company, or an independent licensed and bonded escrow corporation. The escrowee is chosen jointly by the buyer and seller.

The escrowee sees to it that the obligations and responsibilities of both buyer and seller necessary to close the transaction are completed as stipulated in a set of *escrow instructions* contained in the negotiated *escrow agreement*. This agreement is a legal contract requiring that the four essentials of a legal contract exist. It supplements the contract of sale and is *irrevocable* by either buyer or seller unless one of them has legal cause. Even so, the escrowee may refuse such a demand and may insist on an *action of interpleader* in court for an adjudication of the rights of the parties in order to settle the matter. The escrowee cannot act as a mediator, for he or she is considered a ''limited agent'' for both parties, limited specifically to the duties prescribed in the escrow instructions. The escrowee acts by virtue of his or her own powers and is responsible for his or her actions. While in escrow, the buyer holds equitable title (doctrine of relation back) and the seller holds legal title (as security); either interest in title is transferrable *subject to the contract of sale*.

Objectives of an Escrow

The principal objective of an escrow is to minimize the risks incident to the transfer of real property. These risks are chiefly due to the fact that a long time lapse (four to six weeks) usually exists between the execution of the contract of sale and the final consummation of the transaction. The time lapse is quite necessary to allow the title search, appraisal, credit report, loan approval, etc. to be completed. If any insoluble problems arise during the time lapse, the escrowee may return whatever has been deposited in escrow to both buyer and seller, thereby returning each to his or her original position prior to entering the transaction. Other advantages of or reasons for using an escrow include:

1. Avoidance of any personality conflicts that might arise in a face-to-face closing meeting

3. The importance of escrows in California is evidenced by the fact that the College of San Mateo offers a certificate program approved by the California Escrow Association, and an associate-in-arts degree program with an escrow specialization.

2. Provision of a custodian of legal documents and funds who can make simultaneous delivery thereof
3. Convenience of a clearing house to sort out the diverse mechanical considerations, including payment and prorations of liens and other settlement charges, especially in complex and multipartied transactions
4. Availability of the benefits of the doctrine of relating back
5. Relief of the real estate broker from the tedious responsibilities of closing the transaction (however, the broker should closely monitor the escrow process, be available to aid the escrowee, if necessary, and act as a constant communication link between and among buyer, seller, and escrowee)

Elements of a Valid Escrow

For an escrow to be valid, the following elements or items must exist:

1. A valid and enforceable written contract of sale between buyer and seller.
2. A truly impartial, disinterested third-party escrowee
3. Condition or contingency for delivery of deed to buyer stated in escrow agreement
4. An absolutely irrevocable delivery of a duly and validly executed deed to the escrowee

The Escrow Process

Basically, the escrowee performs all the functions of the buyer, seller, broker, and closing agent when settlement of title is accomplished through a closing. Once the contract of sale and escrow agreement have been negotiated, the following procedures are commonly performed in accomplishing a settlement of title through escrow:

1. Seller deposits deed with escrowee.
2. Buyer deposits earnest money with escrowee.
3. Escrowee orders preliminary title search and report.
4. Encumbrances found in title search are removed by seller or accepted by buyer.
5. Title protection is obtained.
6. Escrowee requests loan payoff statements and necessary mortgage releases for the seller.
7. New lenders are asked to order the appraisal, survey, credit report, pest-inspection report, etc., in order to gain loan approval for the buyer.

8. Hazard insurance, property taxes, interest, and other liabilities of settlement are adjusted and/or prorated between buyer, seller, and lenders.
9. Leases, rent schedules, tenant letters, etc. (if applicable) are deposited with escrowee.
10. Balance of down payment and settlement expenses are collected by escrowee.
11. Title is run to date as of the close of business on date set for close of escrow, and if no change of title is found, the deed, mortgage (deed of trust), and other documents are recorded on the next day, the moment the recorder's office opens.
12. On the day recording takes place, the escrowee disburses funds and delivers documents to the proper persons and presents completed RESPA settlement sheets to buyer and seller.
13. Sometime after the close of escrow, the title insurance policy, deed, mortgage release, new mortgage or deed of trust, and other recorded instruments are delivered (mailed) to the proper persons.

SETTLEMENT PROBLEM

Whether settlement of title is accomplished by means of a closing or an escrow, if RESPA applies to the settlement, the lender is required to supply the buyer-borrower with a completed copy of the HUD-approved Uniform Settlement Statement. An explanation of this required form is presented in the solution to the following settlement problem.

A Real Estate Transaction

Mr. Bob Buyer has consummated a contract to purchase the home of Ms. Sue Seller located at 123 Any Street, Hometown, U.S.A. Mr. Buyer had been searching for a home for two weeks with the aid of Mr. Selling Agent, broker of Atlantic Realty, Inc., when they found the property at 123 Any Street, which was listed for sale in the Multi-List Service by Ms. Listing Broker, Broker of Pacific Realty, Inc. The Multi-List Service cooperative sales commission agreement states the standard 6 percent brokerage commission be split 55 percent to the listing brokerage firm, 40 percent to the selling brokerage firm, and 5 percent to the Multi-List Service.

The terms of the contract and settlement information are as follows:

1. *Price*. \$50,000, payable by \$2,000 earnest money, \$45,000 FHA loan, \$3,000 plus closing costs at settlement.

2. *Settlement Date.* Tuesday, July 2, 1980 (a 366-day leap year), allowing an equal division of the year's days for proration purposes.
3. *Buyer's Mortgage Loan.* $45,000 at 8.5 percent interest rate plus .5 percent FHA insurance, computed to be $16 per month with a two-month reserve required by the lender; a loan origination fee of one point, and a loan discount of four points; first payment (totaling $452, including $346 principal and interest, $70 tax reserve, $20 insurance reserve, and $16 FHA insurance reserve) due 9-1-80.
4. *Seller's Deed of Trust Payoff.* $37,500, including prepayment penalty and return of tax and insurance reserve account balances.
5. *Title Insurance.* Owner's policy $150; mortgagee's policy $30.
6. *Recording Fees.* Release of deed of trust, $5; mortgage, $8; deed, $6.
7. *Property Taxes.* $840 a year; certificate of taxes due, $5; realty tax service, $15; two months' reserve required by lender.
8. *Hazard Insurance.* New policy requiring one year's premium of $240 payable in advance; two months' reserve required by lender.
9. *State Transfer Tax/Stamps.* State documentary fee of $.01 per $100 of sales price.
10. *Other Charges or Fees.* Appraisal, $100; survey $50; credit report, $20; buyer's attorney, $250; seller's attorney, $350; the water and sewer bill for July, $31, has been paid by Ms. Seller.

The settlement of the transaction between Mr. Bob Buyer and Ms. Sue Seller is presented in Exhibits 9-1 through 9-3. Exhibit 9-1 is page 1 of the HUD Uniform Settlement Statement, containing sections A through K. Exhibit 9-2 is page 2 of the HUD form, containing section L. Exhibit 9-3 is a Broker's Worksheet for Real Estate Settlement and contains the settlement accounting format used prior to the enactment of RESPA. This worksheet is presented for comparison purposes and because many brokers and lenders still use it for their own in-house accounting. The broker's portion of this worksheet, by itself, is called the "Broker's Reconciliation Statement." The seller's and buyer's portions of this worksheet, by themselves, are called the "Seller's Statement of Settlement" and the "Buyer's Statement of Settlement" respectively. These buyer's and seller's statements are often provided in lieu of the HUD form for transactions to which RESPA does not apply.

Form Explanation

Sections A through I of the HUD form contain information concerning the loan and parties to the settlement. Sections J and K contain a summary for both the buyer and the seller of the charges, receipts, and prorated adjustments which they are liable or due themselves, lenders, and pro-

HUD-1 REV. 5/76

A. U. S. DEPARTMENT OF HOUSING AND URBAN DEVELOPMENT — SETTLEMENT STATEMENT	B. TYPE OF LOAN: 1. ☒ FHA 2. ☐ FmHA 3. ☐ CONV. UNINS. 4. ☐ VA 5. ☐ CONV. INS.
	6. FILE NUMBER: 000 — 7. LOAN NUMBER: 0000
	8. MORTGAGE INSURANCE CASE NUMBER: 00000

C. NOTE: *This form is furnished to give you a statement of actual settlement costs. Amounts paid to and by the settlement agent are shown. Items marked "(p.o.c.)" were paid outside the closing; they are shown here for informational purposes and are not included in the totals.*

D. NAME OF BORROWER:	E. NAME OF SELLER:	F. NAME OF LENDER:
Bob Buyer	Sue Seller	U.S. Savings & Loan

G. PROPERTY LOCATION:	H. SETTLEMENT AGENT:	I. SETTLEMENT DATE:
123 Any Street Hometown, U.S.A.	Listing Broker PLACE OF SETTLEMENT: Hometown, U.S.A.	7-2-80

J. SUMMARY OF BORROWER'S TRANSACTION		K. SUMMARY OF SELLER'S TRANSACTION	
100. GROSS AMOUNT DUE FROM BORROWER:		400. GROSS AMOUNT DUE TO SELLER:	
101. Contract sales price (1)	$50,000.00	401. Contract sales price (1)	$50,000.00
102. Personal property		402. Personal property	
103. Settlement charges to borrower *(line 1400)*	1,704.50	403.	
104.		404.	
105.		405.	
Adjustments for items paid by seller in advance		*Adjustments for items paid by seller in advance*	
106. City/town taxes to		406. City/town taxes to	
107. County taxes to		407. County taxes to	
108. Assessments to		408. Assessments to	
109. Water and Sewer (32)	30.00	409. (32)	30.00
110.		410.	
111.		411.	
112.		412.	
120. GROSS AMOUNT DUE FROM BORROWER	$51,734.50	420. GROSS AMOUNT DUE TO SELLER	$50,030.00
200. AMOUNTS PAID BY OR IN BEHALF OF BORROWER:		500. REDUCTIONS IN AMOUNT DUE TO SELLER:	
201. Deposit or earnest money (2)	2,000.00	501. Excess deposit *(see instructions)*	
202. Principal amount of new loan(s) (3)	45,000.00	502. Settlement charges to seller *(line 1400)*	5,305.00
203. Existing loan(s) taken subject to		503. Existing loan(s) taken subject to	
204.		504. Payoff of first mortgage loan (5)	37,500.00
205.		505. Payoff of second mortgage loan	
206.		506.	
207.		507.	
208.		508.	
209.		509.	
Adjustments for items unpaid by seller		*Adjustments for items unpaid by seller*	
210. City/town taxes to		510. City/town taxes to	
211. County taxes to 7-2-80 (18)	420.00	511. County taxes to (18)	420.00
212. Assessments to		512. Assessments to	
213.		513.	
214.		514.	
215.		515.	
216.		516.	
217.		517.	
218.		518.	
219.		519.	
220. TOTAL PAID BY/FOR BORROWER	$47,420.00	520. TOTAL REDUCTION AMOUNT DUE SELLER	$43,225.00
300. CASH AT SETTLEMENT FROM/TO BORROWER		600. CASH AT SETTLEMENT TO/FROM SELLER	
301. Gross amount due from borrower *(line 120)*	51,734.50	601. Gross amount due to seller *(line 420)*	50,030.00
302. Less amounts paid by/for borrower *(line 220)*	47,420.00	602. Less reductions in amount due seller *(line 520)*	43,225.00
303. CASH (☒ FROM) (☐ TO) BORROWER	4,314.50	603. CASH (☒ TO) (☐ FROM) SELLER	6,805.00

EXHIBIT 9-1

L. SETTLEMENT CHARGES	PAID FROM BORROWER'S FUNDS AT SETTLEMENT	PAID FROM SELLER'S FUNDS AT SETTLEMENT
700. TOTAL SALES/BROKER'S COMMISSION based on price $ 50,000 @ 6 % =$3,000		
Division of Commission (line 700) as follows:		
701. $ 1,650.00 to Pacific Realty, Inc.		
702. $ 1,200.00 to Atlantic Realty, Inc.		
703. Commission paid at Settlement	(37)	$2,850.00
704. $ 150.00 to Multi-List Service	(37)	150.00
800. ITEMS PAYABLE IN CONNECTION WITH LOAN		
801. Loan Origination Fee 1%	(27) 450.00	
802. Loan Discount 4%	(28)	1,800.00
803. Appraisal Fee to Appraiser	(31) 100.00	
804. Credit Report to Credit Bureau	(38) 20.00	
805. Lender's Inspection Fee		
806. Mortgage Insurance Application Fee to		
807. Assumption Fee		
808.		
809.		
810.		
811.		
900. ITEMS REQUIRED BY LENDER TO BE PAID IN ADVANCE		
901. Interest from 7-2 to 8-1 @ $10.45 /day	(29) 313.50	
902. Mortgage Insurance Premium for months to		
903. Hazard Insurance Premium for 1 years to insurance company	(23) 240.00	
904. years to		
905.		
1000. RESERVES DEPOSITED WITH LENDER		
1001. Hazard insurance 2 months @ $ 20.00 per month	(24) 40.00	
1002. Mortgage insurance 2 months @ $ 16.00 per month	(26) 32.00	
1003. City property taxes months @ $ per month		
1004. County property taxes 2 months @ $ 70.00 per month	(19) 140.00	
1005. Annual assessments months @ $ per month		
1006. months @ $ per month		
1007. months @ $ per month		
1008. months @ $ per month		
1100. TITLE CHARGES		
1101. Settlement or closing fee to		
1102. Abstract or title search to		
1103. Title examination to		
1104. Title insurance binder to		
1105. Document preparation to		
1106. Notary fees to		
1107. Attorney's fees to		
(includes above items numbers;)		
1108. Title insurance to	(7) 30.00	(7) 150.00
(includes above items numbers;)		
1109. Lender's coverage $ 30.00		
1110. Owner's coverage $150.00		
1111. Seller's attorney		(21a) 350.00
1112.		
1113.		
1200. GOVERNMENT RECORDING AND TRANSFER CHARGES		
1201. Recording fees: Deed $6.00 ; Mortgage $8.00 ; Releases $5.00 (11)&(12)	14.00	(13) 5.00
1202. City/county tax/stamps: Deed $5.00 ; Mortgage $	(15) 5.00	
1203. State tax/stamps: Deed $; Mortgage $		
1204.		
1205.		
1300. ADDITIONAL SETTLEMENT CHARGES		
1301. Survey to surveying company	(30) 50.00	
1302. Pest inspection to		
1303. Certificate of taxes due	(16) 5.00	
1304. Realty tax service	(39) 15.00	
1305. Buyer's attorney	(40) 250.00	
1400. TOTAL SETTLEMENT CHARGES *(enter on lines 103, Section J and 502, Section K)*	$1,704.50	$5,305.00

HUD-1 REV. 5/76

EXHIBIT 9-2

BROKER'S WORKSHEET FOR REAL ESTATE SETTLEMENT

SELLER: Sue Seller PURCHASER: Bob Buyer

PROPERTY ADDRESS: 123 Any Street, Hometown, U.S.A.

SETTLEMENT DATE: July 2, 1980 DATE OF PRORATION: July 2, 1980

LEGAL DESCRIPTION: Lot 1, Block 1, Crean Acres, Hometown, U.S.A.

	SELLER		BUYER		BROKER	
	DEBIT	CREDIT	DEBIT	CREDIT	DEBIT	CREDIT
1. Selling Price		50,000 00	50,000 00			
2. Deposit, paid to				2,000 00	2,000 00	
3. Mortgage, payable to				45,000 00	45,000 00	
4. Trust Deed, payable to						
5. Trust Deed, payoff to	37,500 00					37,500 00
6. Interest on Loan Assumed						
7. Title Insurance Premium	150 00		30 00			180 00
8. Abstracting: Before Sale						
9. After Sale						
10. Title Examination by						
11. Recording: Deed			6 00			6 00
12. Mortgage			8 00			8 00
13. Release Deed of Trust	5 00					5 00
14. Other						
15. Documentary Fee			5 00			5 00
16. Certificate of Taxes Due			5 00			5 00
17. Taxes for Preceding Year(s)						
18. Taxes for Current Year	420 00			420 00		
19. Tax Reserve			140 00			140 00
20. Special Taxes						
21. Personal Property Taxes						
21.a. Seller's Attorney	350 00					350 00
22. Hazard Ins. Prem. Assumed						
23. Premium for New Insurance			240 00			240 00
24. Hazard Insurance Reserve			40 00			40 00
25. FHA Mortgage Ins. Assumed						
26. FHA Mortgage Ins. Reserve			32 00			32 00
27. Loan Service Fee (Buyer)			450 00			450 00
28. Loan Discount Fee (Seller)	1,800 00					,800 00
29. Interest on New Loan			313 50			313 50
30. Survey			50 00			50 00
31. Appraisal Fee			100 00			100 00
32. Water &/or Sewer		30 00	30 00			
33. Rents						
34. Security Deposits						
35. Loan Transfer Fee						
36. Loan Payment Due						
37. Broker's Fee	3,000 00					3,000 00
38. Credit Report			20 00			20 00
39. Realty Tax Service			15 00			15 00
40. Buyer's Attorney			250 00			250 00
Sub-Totals:	43,225 00	50,030 00	51,734 50	47,420 00	47,000 00	44,509 50
Balance Due to/from Seller	6,805 00					6,805 00
Balance Due to/from Buyer				4,314 50	4,314 50	
TOTALS:	50,030 00	50,030 00	51,734 50	51,734 50	51,314 50	51,314 50

EXHIBIT 9-3

viders of settlement services. The bottom-line figures of these sections indicate the net results of all charges, receipts, and prorated adjustments. In this example, the buyer to settle must pay $4,314.50 in addition to the $2,000 earnest money already paid; the seller will receive $6,805 total upon settlement, including any earnest money held by the listing broker or escrowee.

To arrive at the bottom-line figures in sections J and K, the total settlement charges (line 1400) of section L must be entered on line 103, section J, and line 502, section K. It is important to note this transposition, since it is one of the distinguishing characteristics which differentiates the HUD form from the Broker's Worksheet (Exhibit 9-3). Essentially, the HUD form segregates charges and receipts (debits and credits) into various categories, while the Broker's Worksheet does not categorize at all. However, both forms contain the same information. Another differentiating characteristic is that the Broker's Worksheet includes a broker's debit and credit to allow double-entry bookkeeping. Whenever a charge or receipt requires payment to or from a third party such as a lender or provider of settlement services (appraiser, attorneys, lenders, etc.), the broker's columns are credited or debited, respectively. The item-by-item explanation that follows clearly manifests the relationship between the entries of each form.

To facilitate explanation and comparison of the HUD form and the broker's form, the line numbers (1 to 40) of the broker's form appear in parentheses on the HUD form. Once the reader has understood an item as it appears on the HUD form, the numbers in parentheses may be used to observe the treatment of the same item in the double-entry bookkeeping system of the broker's form. The buyer and seller are debited on the broker's form for the items they are responsible to pay.

Section L—Settlement Charges. Section L of the HUD form is analyzed first, since its bottom-line results are contained in the summary sections J and K.

700–704. Sales/Broker's Commission or (37) Broker's Fee. The listing agreement provided for a 6 percent commission to be split according to the cooperative sales commission agreement of the Multi-List Service. Commissions are usually paid by the seller, with custom and/or the negotiated arrangement of the listing contract determining the amount or percentage. If the broker retains the earnest money deposit to apply toward the commission, then line 703 will show only the remainder to be paid at settlement. Sue Seller has been debited for the full $3,000 on the broker's form (line 37).

800. Items Payable in Connection with Loan. These are items charged by the lender to process, approve and fund the buyer's loan.

801. Loan Origination or (27) Loan Service Fee. Lenders usually tell the buyer that this fee is necessary to cover the lender's administrative cost in processing the loan. Regardless of such a statement, this fee increases the lender's effective yield or annual percentage rate on the loan, and is usually paid by the buyer to get the loan. Hence, Bob Buyer has been charged $450, since one point is 1 percent of the loan amount. Bob has also been debited for this charge on the broker's form (line 27). The fact that the Internal Revenue Service allows this fee as a tax-deductible interest charge shows that it is indeed interest and not a processing fee to cover overhead.

802. Loan Discount or (28) Loan Discount Fee. The loan discount, often called "points," is a one-time interest charge used to increase the lender's yield on below-market-interest-rate government-sponsored loans. The lender is induced to make the lower interest-rate loan, since the "points" increase the rate to the market rate obtainable on conventional loans. The buyer is prohibited by federal law from paying the loan discount. Since one point is equal to 1 percent of the loan amount, Sue Seller has been charged $1,800 on the HUD form (section L) or debited with $1,800 on the broker's form (line 28).

803. Appraisal Fee or (31) Appraisal Fee. The buyer's lender will require an estimate of value to determine the loan amount. Since obtaining the loan is to the buyer's benefit. Bob Buyer has been charged or debited with the $100 fee. It is possible, however, for the seller to order and pay for an appraisal to aid in setting a listing price or to aid in obtaining a firm loan commitment, which will aid in the marketing of the property to financially qualified buyers.

804. Credit Report or (38) Credit Report. The lender requires a credit report to determine the buyer's "willingness to pay" the loan as evidenced through an analysis of the buyer's past record of payment of other liabilities presented in the credit report. Hence, Bob Buyer has been charged (HUD form) and debited (broker's form) the $20 credit report fee.

805. Lender's Inspection Fee. This charge, not applicable here, covers inspections, often of newly constructed houses, made by the lender's staff or by an independent inspection service company.

806. Mortgage Insurance Application Fee. This charge covers processing the application for private mortgage insurance, which may be required on conventional loans. It could cover the appraisal fee as well. Since Bob Buyer has obtained an FHA-insured loan, this item does not apply in his case.

807. Assumption Fee or (35) Loan Transfer Fee. This charge, usually paid by the buyer, covers the processing of the paperwork involved in a loan assumption. This fee is much smaller than the normal loan origination fee charged on new loans.

900. Items Required by Lender to Be Paid in Advance.

901. Interest or (29) Interest on New Loan. Bob Buyer's first monthly mortgage payment is due 9-1-80 and covers interest in arrears for the month of August. The interest for the days from and including the settlement date (July 2, 1980) to and including the last day of the month of the settlement date (July 31, 1980) must be paid in advance of the settlement date. Hence, Bob Buyer has been charged or debited $313.50 for 30 days of interest in the month of July. Note that usually the buyer pays for the settlement day itself. The proration of $10.45 was calculated as follows:

$$
\begin{array}{rl}
\$45{,}000 & \text{loan amount} \\
\times\ .085 & \text{interest rate} \\
\hline
\$3{,}825 & \div\ 366 \text{ days in } 1980 = \quad \$10.45/\text{day} \\
 & \qquad\qquad\qquad\qquad\quad \times\ \ 30 \text{ days} \\
 & \qquad\qquad\qquad\qquad\quad \$313.50 \text{ interest}
\end{array}
$$

902. Mortgage Insurance Premium. Private mortgage insurance is required on conventional loans with a loan-to-value ratio in excess of 80 percent. This insurance protects the lender against loss due to default and foreclosure. If the lender requires payment of the premium in advance, it is charged in space 902 on section L of the HUD form, or on a space added to the broker's form. This insurance should not be confused with mortgage life and disability insurance. Such insurance pays off the mortgage balance upon death or makes the mortgage payments while a borrower is physically disabled.

903. Hazard Insurance Premium or (23) Premium for New Insurance. It is customary for the buyer, who benefits from this insurance, to pay one or more years premium in advance. Protection against fire, windstorm, and natural hazards, plus additional risks such as theft and personal liability, may be combined in a "homeowner's policy." Bob Buyer has been charged or debited $240 for one year's coverage. Usually loss caused by flooding is not covered by such a policy. Flood insurance may be purchased separately and may be required in certain flood-prone areas designated by HUD. Flood insurance in these areas may be purchased at low federally subsidized rates in participating communities under the National Flood Insurance Act.

1000. Reserves Deposited with Lender. Reserve accounts (also called escrow or impound accounts) are funds required by the lender to be held to assure the availability of funds to pay recurring items such as property taxes and hazard insurance. RESPA limits the amount of the original deposits to start these accounts to a maximum of one-sixth (two months) the estimated annual charge.

1001. Hazard Insurance or (24) Hazard Insurance Reserve. Bob Buyer's annual premium is $240 and he is, therefore, charged or debited with one-sixth or two months' worth ($40) of this total premium to create the reserve account.

1002. Mortgage Insurance or (26) FHA Mortgage Insurance Reserve. The same logic as above applies here, causing Bob Buyer to be charged or debited with $32 to start this reserve account. The case of an assumption of an FHA loan where the seller had paid into this account in advance would be handled as an adjustment in section J, line 104 and section K, line 403 on the HUD form, or by debiting the buyer and crediting the seller on the broker's form (line 25).

1003–1004. City/County Property Taxes or (19) Tax Reserve. Once again Bob Buyer must deposit another $140 of the annual taxes of $840, following the same logic as above.

1100. Title Charges. The fact that this section contains thirteen lines (1101–1113) indicates the variety of possible services available to settle and protect title. Who is liable to pay for these charges varies by custom and negotiation from area to area around the country.

1101. Settlement or Closing Fee. This charge is paid to the closing agent or escrowee for handling the settlement of title.

1102–1104. Abstract or Title Search, Title Examination, Title Insurance Binder or (8–10) Abstracting, Title Examination. These services are necessary to determine whether the seller can convey clear title to the property, and to disclose any matters on record that could adversely affect the buyer or the lender.

1105. Document Preparation. This charge covers preparation of the final legal papers, such as the mortgage or deed of trust, note, or deed. Such service may be included in other fees.

1106. Notary Fees. This charge is incurred to have an appointed or licensed person sign and affix a notary seal on various documents acknowledging and authenticating the execution of the documents by the parties.

1107 and 1111. Attorney's Fees or (21a) Seller's Attorney. It may be necessary to enlist the services of an attorney to examine title and to provide other legal advice. Line 1107 only allows this charge to be made to the buyer's account, since in most areas the buyer pays for the title charges. In the case of Sue Seller, it is customary in her area for the seller to pay these charges to fulfill the duty of providing good and merchantable title to the buyer. Therefore, Sue Seller has been charged and debited her attorney's total fee of $350 on line 1111 (HUD form) and on line 21a (broker's form).

1108–1110. Title Insurance or (7) Title Insurance Premiums. Two kinds of title insurance are handled here. The lender's policy, which protects the lender against loss due to title defects, is usually paid by the borrower-buyer. Hence, Bob Buyer has been charged and debited for this $30 cost. The owner's policy, which protects the buyer against loss due to title defects, is often paid by the buyer as well. However, in the example area the seller is responsible for this to provide good and merchantable title to the buyer. Hence, Sue Seller has been charged and debited with this $150 cost.

1200. Government Recording and Transfer Charges. The recording fees are usually paid by the person who benefits from having the particular document recorded. The transfer charges are almost always the buyer's responsibility.

1201. Recording Fees or (11–14) Recording. Bob Buyer is responsible for recording his deed ($6) and his mortgage ($8) for a total of $14. Sue Seller is responsible for recording her release of deed of trust ($5).

1202–1203. City/County/State Stamps or (15) Documentary Fee. Bob Buyer must pay $.01 per $100 of purchase price to the state as a transfer tax, called a documentary fee. This fee amounts to $5 for his $50,000 purchase, and he has been so charged and debited. In some states the seller pays this fee, also known as a "real estate transfer tax."

1300. Additional Settlement Charges.

1301. Survey or (30) Survey. Bob Buyer benefits by having a survey showing property lines, encroachments, etc. Therefore, Bob Buyer has been charged and debited for this fee of $50.

1302. Pest Inspection. The payment of this fee is negotiable and covers inspections for termite or other pest infestation of the house. Usually the seller pays for any corrective work required due to pests such as termites.

1303. Certificate of Taxes Due or (16). This certificate, usually secured from the county treasurer's office, is the buyer's future insurance that no taxes other than those stated on the certificate can be claimed after the date of the certificate. Hence, Bob Buyer has been charged and debited $5 for this service.

1304. Realty Tax Service or (39). This service is required by the lender and therefore payable by the borrower-buyer. This service keeps the lender informed of the property tax assessments and billings so that the lender can keep the taxes current to protect its mortgage lien claim. Bob Buyer has been charged and debited with this one-time $15 fee.

1305. Buyer's Attorney or (40). Bob Buyer has hired his own attorney to examine all settlement documents, to be present at closing, and to advise him when necessary. The price for this "peace-of-mind guarantee" is a charge and debit of $250.

1400. Total Settlement Charges. All the charges in the buyer's column (section L of the HUD form) entitled "Paid from Borrower's Funds at Settlement" are totaled and transferred to section J, line 103, "Settlement Charges to Borrower" on page 1 of the Uniform Settlement Statement. All the charges in the seller's column (section L of the HUD form) entitled "Paid from Seller's Funds at Settlement" are totaled and transferred to section K, line 502, "Settlement Charges to Seller" on page 1 of the HUD form. In the case of Bob Buyer and Sue Seller, these totals are $1,704.50 and $5,305.00, respectively.

The Broker's Worksheet Form does *not* total settlement charges as does the HUD form. Rather than segregate these costs and then integrate them as totals into summary forms (such as sections J and K), the broker's form integrates *all* charges on one page of double-entry bookkeeping.

Section J—Summary of Borrower's Transaction. The first page of the HUD form summarizes all actual costs and adjustments for the borrower-buyer and the seller, including total settlement charges, found on line 1400 of section L.

100. Gross Amount Due from Borrower.

101. Contract Sales Price or (1) Selling Price. This is the price of the house agreed to in the contract of sale. Bob Buyer and Sue Seller have agreed upon a price of $50,000; hence, Bob Buyer has been charged and debited (broker's form) with this amount.

102. Personal Property. If the price of personal property has also been negotiated in the sales contract, a separate accounting may be provided on this line. Otherwise, any and all personal property transferred will be contained in the contract sales price on line 101.

103. Settlement Charges to Borrower. The total charges listed in section L and totaled on line 1400 are entered here. For Bob Buyer these charges amount to $1,704.50.

104–105. Assumptions. This space is for listing any additional amounts owed the seller, such as reserve funds if the buyer is assuming the seller's loan and/or insurance policies. On the broker's form these entries would be accounted for by debiting the buyer and crediting the seller on lines 19, 20, 21, 22, 24, and 34, as appropriate.

106–112. Adjustments. Adjustments are necessary when the seller has paid a charge in advance beyond the settlement date. These costs are usually divided or prorated on a proportional basis, the seller being reimbursed for charges accruing on and after the date of title settlement and transfer.

For example, Sue Seller, on line 109, is being reimbursed for having paid the $31 water and sewer bill for the 31-day month of July. Sue is liable for only one day in July and must therefore be reimbursed $30. Line 32 on the broker's form handles this by debiting Bob Buyer and crediting Sue Seller.

120. Gross Amount Due From Borrower. The total of price, settlement charges to borrower, and adjustments for items paid by seller in advance (the total of lines 101 through 112) equals the "Gross Amount Due from Borrower." For Bob Buyer this number is $51,734.50; it also appears on the Broker's Worksheet as the "subtotal" of the buyer's debit column.

200. Amounts Paid by or on Behalf of Borrower.

201. Deposit or Earnest Money or (2) Deposit. This is the amount paid by the buyer against the sales price at the time the contract of sale was signed to show the seriousness of the buyer's intent to complete the purchase on the settlement day. Often, this money is held in the listing broker's trust account. Hence, the broker is liable for this amount and is debited on the broker's form, while the buyer is given a credit against the purchase price. Bob Buyer wrote a check for $2,000 to Pacific Realty, Inc., the listing broker for Sue Seller.

202. Principal Amount of New Loan or (3) Mortgage, Payable to. A new first loan will aid the buyer in meeting the purchase price. On the broker's form, therefore, Bob Buyer is credited on line 3 with the $45,000 FHA loan amount and the broker is debited, since he is responsible, as settlement agent, to collect these funds.

203. Existing Loan(s) Taken Subject to. If the buyer assumes the seller's loan, the balance assumed would be credited to the buyer's account, reducing his or her cash required at settlement. This situation would be handled on line 4 of the broker's form. Second or other loans which would further reduce the cash required at settlement could be accounted for on lines 204 through 209 of the HUD form or on line 4 of the broker's form.

210–219. Adjustments for Items Unpaid by Seller. Adjustments are necessary when the seller has *not* paid a charge which covers a period prior to the settlement. This charge will be paid either at settlement if due, or at some future time (including the seller's liability) by the buyer when it is due. The seller, therefore, must credit the buyer with the amount for which he or she is liable. Such a credit reduces the buyer's required amount of cash at settlement.

In the case of Bob and Sue, the 1980 taxes of $840 must be prorated, and Bob must receive a reduction in required cash to settle in an amount equal to Sue's liability for the 1980 property taxes. Since closing is July 2, each party is liable for 183 days, or exactly one-half the $840 tax bill. Hence, the entries of $420 on line 211 of the HUD form and line 18 of the broker's form.

220. Total Paid by/for Borrower. This is the sum total of lines 201 through 219, representing items which go against the gross amount due from the borrower in determining the cash needed to close the transaction. These very same items are found on the broker's form in the buyer's credit column (lines 3, 4, and 18 in the example). These items total $47,420 for Bob Buyer on line 220 of the HUD form and on the subtotal line in the buyer's credit column of the broker's form.

300–303. Cash ☐ from ☐ to Borrower or Balance Due to/from Buyer. The remaining lines of section J simply calculate the net result of subtracting the "amounts paid by/for borrower" (302) from the "gross amount due from borrower" (301) to obtain the amount of cash which the borrower will either receive or (more likely) have to pay to settle title. Bob Buyer must remit payment of $4,314.50 (line 303) to settle title. The same result is shown on the broker's form by netting the buyer's subtotals to obtain what is there called "balance due from buyer."

Section K—Summary of Seller's Transaction. The remaining half of page 1 of the Uniform Settlement Statement summarizes all actual costs and adjustments for the seller.

400. Gross Amount Due to Seller. With only one exception, this part of the HUD form (lines 401 through 420) is identical to section J's "Gross Amount Due from Borrower." The exception is the deletion of the settlement charges to the borrower. Since these charges are due various third parties, they are *not* due to the seller. Hence, lines 120 and 420 differ by line 103 or line 1400. Sue Seller is due $50,030, consisting of the contract sales price (line 401) and the water and sewer adjustment (line 409). On the broker's form, these same numbers are found on lines 1, 32, and subtotals in the seller's credit column.

500. Reductions in Amount Due to Seller. The gross amount due to the seller is reduced by his or her settlement charges (lines 502 and 1400), any loans assumed by the buyer or paid off by the seller (lines 503 through 505), and/or any adjustments for items unpaid by seller (lines 510 through 519). These same seller responsibilities (except that the settlement charges are itemized rather than totaled) appear as debits to the seller on the broker's form. For Sue Seller, the total settlement charges (line 502) are $5,305; her first trust deed payoff figure (line 504) is $37,500; and the adjustment for property taxes (line 511) is $420. The total of these reductions is $43,225, which appears on line 520 of the HUD form and as the subtotal of the seller's debit column on the broker's form.

600–603. Cash to/from Seller or Balance Due to/from Seller. The remaining lines of section K simply calculate the net result of subtracting the "Reductions in Amount Due Seller" from the "Gross Amount Due to Seller" to obtain the amount of cash which the seller will either have to pay or (more likely) receive to settle title. Sue Seller will receive $6,805 (line 603) to settle title. The same result is shown on the broker's form by netting the seller's subtotals to obtain what is there called "Balance Due to Seller."

It may be concluded from the above explanations and comparison of forms that both the HUD form and the broker's form present the same accounting of the settlement of title, but do so differently. Each uses a different format of presentation of the same information. Finally, the broker's debit and credit columns on the broker's form serve as an accounting check and therefore must balance. In fact, the broker's columns are separately called the "Broker's Reconciliation Statement."

SUMMARY AND CONCLUSION

The completion of the title transfer process is called the settlement of title. Settlement may occur through either a closing or an escrow. A closing is a face-to-face meeting of the parties to a transaction for the purpose of examining and signing the proper documents required to settle and transfer title. Sellers, buyers, brokers, closing agents, and lenders must be aware of their respective duties and responsibilities related to the settlement of title. For example, lenders have specific duties and responsibilities imposed upon them by such federal legislation as the Truth In Lending Act, the Uniform Consumer Credit Code, the Equal Credit Opportunity Act, and the Real Estate Settlement Procedures Act.

An escrow or closing in escrow is not a face-to-face meeting. Rather an escrow is an arrangement whereby a disinterested third party (escrowee) is jointly chosen by buyer and seller to follow a set of specific instructions (contained in negotiated escrow agreement) to accomplish the settlement and transfer of title. The escrowee, in other words, makes it his or her business to do all the things which the buyer and/or seller usually do in order to settle title. The escrow business is a very professional field, especially in states like California where settlement of title is accomplished exclusively through escrow. One can even earn an associate-in-arts degree with an escrow specialization.

Finally, the presentation of a settlement problem allowed an in-depth analysis, explanation, and comparison of both the HUD-approved Uniform Settlement Statement and the pre-RESPA Broker's Worksheet for Real Estate Settlement. It was concluded that both the HUD form and the broker's form present the same accounting of the settlement of title, but that they do so by using different formats of presentation of the same information.

CHAPTER 10

Legal Aspects of Real Estate Finance

KEY TERMS

Hypothecation The pledging of property as security or collateral for a debt without delivery of title or possession of the property to the lender

Mortgage A two-party hypothecation instrument that pledges property as security for a loan, thereby creating a lien or title interest against the property which must be foreclosed through court action

Mortgagor The borrower in a mortgage loan transaction

Mortgagee The lender in a mortgage loan transaction

Equitable right of redemption The legal common law right of a borrower to redeem property after a loan default and avoid foreclosure

Statutory right of redemption The right of a borrower under civil law in some states to redeem property *after* foreclosure

Deed of trust A three-party hypothecation instrument that pledges property as security for a loan, thereby creating a lien or title interest against the property which may be foreclosed (in some states) without court action; also called *trust deed*

Trustor The borrower in a deed-of-trust loan transaction

Trustee A disinterested third-party (public or private) who holds and usually records legal title of hypothecated property for the benefit and protection of a lender in a deed-of-trust loan transaction

Beneficiary The lender in a deed-of-trust loan transaction

Promissory note (bond) A legal instrument that creates and evidences the debt between borrower and lender and establishes an unconditional written promise of the borrower to repay the loan according to the stated terms

---

Today's financing of real estate provides the glue to keep together the agreement of sale between buyer and seller. Many a real estate transaction has failed to reach settlement and many a real estate brokerage commission has been lost because, for one reason or another, financing was unavailable or unattainable. It can be said that in the twentieth century, one usually needs to borrow money in order to own real estate. Such has not always been the case. There was a time when one usually needed to own real estate in order to borrow money, since early mortgages were deeds conveying title and possession to the lender. The history of mortgage law relates how this reversal took place, so that today lenders have only a lien on the property. This history is an endless battle between lenders and borrowers. Despite the saying "those with the gold make the rules," the borrowers appear to be winning the war.

HISTORICAL DEVELOPMENT OF MORTGAGE LAW

Early Mortgages

The Babylonians and the Egyptians under the Pharaohs were early users of mortgage instruments. The Romans developed a variety of mortgage instruments, including the *fiducia*, the *pignus*, and the *hypotheca*. Today, *hypothecation* means to pledge property as security or collateral for a debt without delivery of title or possession of the property to the lender. The fiducia actually transferred title and possession of the "mortgaged" property to the lender, and the pignus pledged title conditional upon nonpayment of the debt. Mortgages, therefore, have always been some sort of pledge to secure a debt. A Roman who defaulted on payment of the debt became the slave of the lender!

In early Anglo-Saxon common law there were two types of real property pledges: the "living pledge" (*vivum vadium*) and the "dead pledge" (*mortuum vadium*). The living pledge or *gage* (German for "pledge") required the lender to apply the rents and profits of the mortgaged property to the payment of the debt. The dead pledge allowed the lender to keep the rents and profits of the mortgaged property without applying them to the debt, making the property "dead" to the borrower. The derivation of the word *mortgage* is from the Latin *mort* ("dead") and the German *gage* "pledge." With either the living pledge or dead pledge the lender took possession and collected the rents and profits, because at that time a conveyance of real estate was not valid without possession and the Church did not allow its members to collect interest on loans.

From these early English mortgage forms evolved the so-called commonlaw mortgage of the fourteenth century. This instrument was a simple deed conveying title from the borrower (mortgagor) to the lender (mortgagee), subject to the following conditions: (1) the rents and profits were applied to the debt, resulting in the mortgagee's allowing the mortgagor to remain in possession; and (2) payment of the debt on the "law day" defeated the mortgage and extinguished the lender's title interest (defeasance clause). If payment were not made on the law day, the borrower's title interest was totally extinguished by the default clause. Furthermore, in addition to permanently losing ownership of the mortgaged (deeded) property, the borrower was still obligated to repay the debt. Although this penalty was not as severe as becoming a slave to a Roman lender, many felt it to be neither fair nor equitable.

Redemption versus Foreclosure

Eventually, borrowers who had suffered the apparent injustice of the default clause petitioned the king for relief, offering to pay the debt plus interest, if the king would order reconveyance of the property to the borrower. The king would hear the circumstances of the case and render an equitable solution, usually allowing the borrower the time required to make payment. By the seventeenth century (around 1625), King James I found this remedy so popular and time consuming that he appointed his churchman, or chancellor, to hear all such petitions. The chancellor would hear these cases in what came to be called the court of chancery or the court of equity. Originally the chancellor, like the king, would allow the borrower a fair amount of time to redeem the property only in cases of extreme hardship. However, this practice soon became so routine that rules and procedures for property redemption were published. What was originally a matter of grace eventually became a legally entrenched right of the borrower. This right was then, and is today, called the *equitable right of redemption* or *equity of redemption*.

The equitable right of redemption caused lenders problems, since the grace period for redemption could be many months and the lenders never knew when or if they would be paid. To counter the right of redemption, the lenders began inserting a mortgage clause, which recited that the borrower waived and surrendered his right of redemption. However, the courts soon held that such *waiver of right of redemption* clauses were void, saying "once a mortgage, always a mortgage" and ruling that a default could not convert a mortgage to a deed. Once again, lenders were in a difficult position, yet they were quite resilient and full of ideas to remedy the situation.

The next development in this confrontation was called *strict foreclosure*. Upon default, the lender would file a petition with the court, and the judge would enter a decree granting a specified time period (six months to a year) for the borrower to redeem. If the borrower did not redeem the property within the specified time limit, the equitable right of redemption was "forever barred and foreclosed" and the lender became the absolute owner of the property. The states of Connecticut, Vermont, and Illinois practice strict foreclosure today, but not to the extent whereby lenders can take unfair advantage of borrowers. For example, if the property's value were greatly in excess of the debt outstanding, the lender could profit exorbitantly by acquiring all the borrower's equity. If the lender, however, resold the property for less than the loan amount, he or she would lose by the amount of such a deficiency.

The next logical step, therefore, was the development of *foreclosure through public sale*. If the property sold for *more* than the debt outstanding, the excess (minus expenses and penalties, if any) would go to the borrower. If the property sold for *less* than the debt outstanding, the lender could sue for the deficit by means of a *deficiency judgment*, which could force the liquidation of other unsecured real or personal property belonging to the borrower. The lender today must sue on the promissory note or bond to obtain the deficiency judgment. This note or bond, which evidences and creates the liability to pay, today accompanies the mortgage or deed of trust, which secures the debt.

In the United States, some state legislatures have granted borrowers additional rights of redemption. The foreclosure sale extinguishes the equitable right of redemption, which, by definition, exists *before* foreclosure. Indeed, the purpose of a foreclosure suit is to terminate this right. However, some state legislatures have granted borrowers additional rights of redemption *after* foreclosure. Since these rights have been created by state statute, they are called *statutory rights of redemption* or *statutory redemption*. Under these laws, which vary from state to state, the borrower is allowed an additional, but final, period of time within which to redeem the property from the lender. State laws vary greatly regarding the time period allowed to redeem (from two months to two years), the rights of possession during this time, and the detailed procedures required to exercise these rights. Local legal counsel should be consulted regarding these matters. Table 10-1 offers a brief outline of the procedures in the various states.

Whether a state allows only equity of redemption or statutory redemption, foreclosure through public sale has been another victory for the borrower. It has set the stage for acceptance of the view that the mortgage is not really a deed conveying a title interest, but rather a lien or claim to satisfy a debt out of the liquidation of the debtor's property. Furthermore, where statutory redemption applies, the purchaser at foreclosure only acquires "nascent title" (title coming into being). Absolute title is acquired only after all rights of redemption have expired. Refer to Figure 10-1 for the sequence from default to absolute title.

Summary of Foreclosure Methods

Present-day mortgage law varies greatly across the 50 states. However, a general and very simplified summary of foreclosure methods is presented. It should be noted that the terminology is very inconsistent countrywide.

Strict Foreclosure. Strict foreclosure is a court proceeding upon default that allows the borrower a specified time period to pay off totally or satisfy the debt. If no redemption is made, the borrower is forever barred and

TABLE 10-1. Selected Aspects of Foreclosure Operations in the Various States

State	*Nature of Mortgage*	*Customary Instrument*	*Predominant Method*	*Statutory Redemption Period*	*Possession during Redemption*	*Average Time Involved*[a]
Alabama	Title	Mortgage	Power of sale	2 years	Purchaser	4–6 weeks
Alaska	Lien	Trust deed	Court action	1 year		4 months
Arizona	Lien	Mortgage	Court action	6 months	Mortgagor	3 months
Arkansas	Intermediate	Mortgage	Court action	2 years		2 months
California	Lien	Trust deed	Power of sale	None		5 months
Colorado	Lien	Trust deed	Power of sale	6 months	Mortgagor	4–6 weeks
Connecticut	Intermediate	Mortgage	Strict foreclosure	None		4 months
Delaware	Intermediate	Mortgage	Court action	None		7 months
Dist. of Columbia	Intermediate	Trust deed	Power of sale	None		4–6 weeks
Florida	Lien	Mortgage	Court action	None		45 days
Georgia	Title	Security deed	Power of sale	None		1 month
Hawaii	Lien	Mortgage	Court action	None		1 month
Idaho[b]	Lien	Trust deed	Power of sale	None		3 months
Illinois	Intermediate	Mortgage	Court action	1 year[c]		3 months
Indiana	Lien	Mortgage	Court action	6 months	Mortgagor	3 months
Iowa	Lien	Mortgage	Court action	1 year	Mortgagor	4–6 weeks
Kansas	Lien	Mortgage	Court action	18 months[d]	Mortgagor	3 months
Kentucky	Lien	Mortgage	Court action	1 year[e]	Mortgagor	3 months
Louisiana	Lien	Mortgage	Court action	None		3 months
Maine	Title	Mortgage	Public notice	1 year	Mortgagor	4–6 weeks
Maryland	Title	Mortgage	Power of sale[f]	None		4–6 weeks
Massachusetts	Intermediate	Mortgage	Power of sale	None		3 months
Michigan	Lien	Mortgage	Power of sale	1 year	Mortgagor	13 weeks
Minnesota	Lien	Mortgage	Power of sale	1 year	Mortgagor	6 weeks
Mississippi	Intermediate	Trust deed	Power of sale	None		4 weeks
Missouri	Intermediate	Trust deed	Power of sale	1 year[g]	Mortgagor	4–6 weeks
Montana	Lien	Mortgage	Court action	1 year	Mortgagor	3 months
Nebraska	Lien	Mortgage	Court action	6 months	Mortgagor	90 days
Nevada	Lien	Mortgage	Court action	1 year	Mortgagor	3 months

TABLE 10-1. (Continued)

State	*Nature of Mortgage*	*Customary Instrument*	*Predominant Method*	*Statutory Redemption Period*	*Possession during Redemption*	*Average Time Involved*[a]
New Hampshire	Title	Mortgage	Power of sale	None		4–6 weeks
New Jersey	Intermediate	Mortgage	Court action	None[h]		4 months
New Mexico	Lien	Mortgage	Court action	9 months[i]	Purchaser	4 months
New York	Lien	Mortgage	Court action	None		5 months
North Carolina	Intermediate	Trust deed	Power of sale	None		4–6 weeks
North Dakota	Lien	Mortgage	Court action	1 year	Mortgagor	3 months
Ohio	Intermediate	Mortgage	Court action	None		4 months
Oklahoma	Lien	Mortgage	Court action	6 months[j]	Mortgagor	3 months
Oregon	Lien	Mortgage	Court action	1 year	Purchaser	3 months
Pennsylvania	Title	Mortgage	Court action	None		3 months
Rhode Island	Title	Mortgage	Power of sale	None		4–6 weeks
South Carolina	Lien	Mortgage	Court action	None		3 months
South Dakota	Lien	Mortgage	Power of sale	1 year	Mortgagor	6 weeks
Tennessee	Title	Trust deed	Power of sale	None[k]		4–6 weeks
Texas	Lien	Trust deed	Power of sale	None		4–6 weeks
Utah	Lien	Mortgage	Court action	6 months	Mortgagor	3 months
Vermont	Intermediate	Mortgage	Strict foreclosure	1 year	Mortgagor	3 months
Virginia	Intermediate	Trust deed	Power of sale	None		6–8 weeks
Washington	Lien	Mortgage	Power of sale	6 months	Purchaser	6 months
West Virginia	Intermediate	Trust deed	Power of sale	None		2 months
Wisconsin[b]	Lien	Mortgage	Court action	6 months	Mortgagor	4–6 weeks
Wyoming	Lien	Mortgage	Power of sale	6 months	Mortgagor	6–8 weeks

Source: William Atteberry, Karl G. Pearson, and Michael P. Litka, *Real Estate Law*, 2nd ed. (Columbus, Ohio; Grid Publishing, 1974), pp. 216–17.

[a] Time computed is for completion of foreclosure.
[b] Listings for Idaho and Wisconsin contemplate certain mortgages on properties of 3 acres or less.
[c] Redemption period may be shortened under certain conditions. Receiver may be had for rents if authorized by security instrument.

[d] Redemption period is six months in cases of (1) abandoned property, (2) purchase money mortgages with less than one-third paid down.

[e] However, if sale brings two-thirds or more of appraised value (court appraiser), there is not redemption after sale.

[f] Except in Baltimore, where decree of equity court orders sale.

[g] Provided mortgagor has within ten days of sale given notice of intent to redeem, together with security for payment of taxes, interest, etc.; otherwise, no redemption.

[h] Provided no suit is instituted for deficiency.

[i] Nine months maximum, one month minimum, as court directs.

[j] The redemption period precedes sale in Indiana, Nebraska (court stays sale on borrower's request), and Wisconsin.

[k] Provided redemption rights have been waived expressly in the security instrument.

SOURCES: Russell and Bridewell, "Mortgage Law and Mortgage Lending," *Journal of Land and Public Utility Economics*, Vol. XIV, No. 3, August, 1938; Guiliani, "Some Legal Considerations—Methods of Foreclosure," *U.S. Investor*, Vol. 61, 1950, pp. 846, 849; Jones, *Mortgages*, Vol. 1, pp. 18–69, 1928; Russell, *Home Owner's Loan Corporation, Survey of Foreclosure Operations*, 1937; Sherman, *Mortgage and Real Estate Investment Guide*, 1957; and a private study of foreclosure costs and time elements by Melvin F. Lanphar and Co., mortgage bankers, published in 1954.

foreclosed, giving the lender absolute title without a public sale of the property. This method is used in Connecticut, Vermont, and Illinois.

Foreclosure by Entry and Possession. This method of foreclosure is a form of strict foreclosure. The only difference is that the lender takes *peaceful possession* of the property during the redemption period. This method is used in Maine, Massachusetts, New Hampshire, and Rhode Island.

Foreclosure by Writ of Entry. This foreclosure method is identical to foreclosure by entry and possession except that possession is not peaceful; the borrower refuses to surrender possession. This state of affairs forces the lender to obtain a court order, called a writ of entry, in order to take possession during the redemption period.

Foreclosure by Judicial Sale. This is the most common method, and involves filing suit with the court which will order the sale. This method of foreclosure is also called a *suit in equity*, *legal foreclosure*, or *action at law*.

Foreclosure by Power of Sale. In this method the courts need not get involved. Generally this method is used with a deed of trust, with the trustee having the power to sell the property. This method is also called *foreclosure by advertisement*.

Soldiers' and Sailors' Civil Relief Act. This act of Congress protects active-duty military persons from foreclosure if their inability to meet payments is impaired by reason of their military service. The lender cannot foreclose while such persons are on active duty, and duty time is not computed or included in any redemption period. Furthermore, the lender

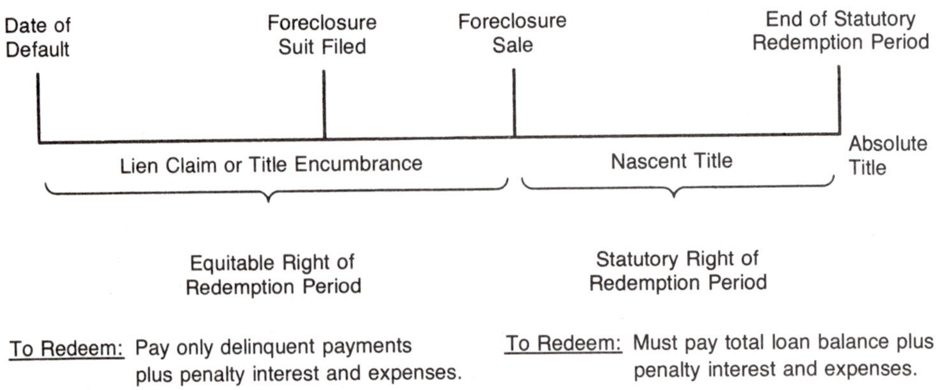

Figure 10-1 Events from Default to Absolute Title

may accrue interest during the military service at the rate of 6 percent. Career soldiers are not included in the protection offered by this act.

Other Lender Remedies

Foreclosure is the mortgage lender's very last resort upon default. Foreclosure is expensive and time consuming. Furthermore, the lender is in the business of making loans and collecting interest and not in the business of owning properties and collecting rents or sales proceeds. Hence, it is very likely that the lender may try some other remedy upon default to avoid the foreclosure process.

Management Agreement. The lender on an income property may feel that the payment problem could be solved by hiring a professional property manager who, presumably, could profitably operate the property. The borrower may well agree to this arrangement in order to avoid foreclosure.

Mortgagee in Possession. In this arrangement the borrower agrees to allow the lender to operate the property until the default has been cured through an *assignment of the rents* to the lender. The lender in possession has no greater title interest than under the mortgage, and possession must be returned to the borrower as soon as the default has been cured.

Deed in Lieu of Foreclosure. Another alternative to foreclosure is a voluntary transfer of title to the lender. In this situation, the lender takes title subject to junior liens, whereas foreclosure removes all junior liens if the lien holders do not redeem the property.

Lenders must be very careful in using this remedy, since the courts tend to favor borrowers. If a substantial equity in the property exists, the lender may have to purchase this equity from the borrower so that the borrower cannot later sue on the basis of duress or unfair advantage.

Extension of Mortgage. One final alternative would be for the lender to rewrite the note extending the repayment schedule. By so doing the payment would be reduced, in the hope of allowing the borrower to afford the payments.

Title Theory versus Lien Theory

Whether a mortgage is legally a lien, a title interest, or something in between differs across the fifty states. Today there are 32 "lien theory" states.[1] In these states a mortgage is considered to create a lien and not

1. Alaska, Arizona, California, Colorado, Delaware, Florida, Georgia, Hawaii, Idaho, Indiana, Iowa, Kansas, Kentucky, Louisiana, Michigan, Minnesota, Missouri, Montana, Nebraska, Nevada, New Mexico, New York, North Dakota, Oklahoma, Oregon, South Carolina, South Dakota, Texas, Utah, Washington, Wisconsin, and Wyoming.

to convey any title. Upon default, the mortgagor (borrower) usually maintains possession both before and after foreclosure until all rights of redemption have terminated. The mortgagee's (lender's) security interest is deemed a personal property right.

Fourteen states have adopted a modified version of the common-law title theory of mortgages.[2] In these "title theory" states, the mortgagee usually is deemed to hold legal title conveyed by the mortgagor, subject to defeat by payment of the debt by the mortgagor, who holds equitable title. Upon default, the mortgagor usually maintains possession only before foreclosure. The mortgagee's interest is deemed a real property right.

Five states, called "intermediate theory" states, have taken a position midway between title and lien theories.[3] Usually this means there is a transfer of legal title, but foreclosure is in the nature of a lien. In practice, the differences between title, lien, and intermediate theories are more technical than real.

METHODS OF HYPOTHECATION

Hypothecation is the pledging of a property to secure a loan without having to deliver title or possession. There are four basic methods of hypothecation available to the borrower-pledgor. The *regular* (standard) *mortgage* discussed above is the most common method and involves two parties: the mortgagor-borrower and the mortgagee-lender. The *deed of trust* or *trust deed* is a three-party arrangement involving the borrower-trustor, the neutral third-party public or private trustee, and the lender-beneficiary. In this arrangement the borrower-trustor hypothecates to the trustee, who holds only legal title for the benefit of the lender-beneficiary (see Figure 10-2a). If or when the debt is satisfied, the trustee reconveys legal title to the borrower-trustor (see Figure 10-2b). The major advantage of a deed of trust is that the trustee is authorized to foreclose by public sale without going through the courts, which is required with a mortgage foreclosure. Hence, the lender is saved both time and money by using the deed of trust. However, some states require a court foreclosure if the trustee is a private party rather than a public official. The option of a court foreclosure is also available to the beneficiary, if desired.

The states in which the trust deed is used nearly exclusively include California, the District of Columbia, Mississippi, Missouri, Tennessee, Texas, and West Virginia. The following states also use the trust deed to some degree: Alabama, Alaska, Colorado, Delaware, Illinois, Montana, Nevada, New Mexico, North Carolina, Oregon, Utah, Virginia, and Wash-

2. Alabama, Arkansas, Connecticut, Maine, Maryland, Massachusetts, New Hampshire, Pennsylvania, Rhode Island, Tennessee, Vermont, Virginia, West Virginia, and the District of Columbia.
3. Illinois, Mississippi, New Jersey, North Carolina, and Ohio.

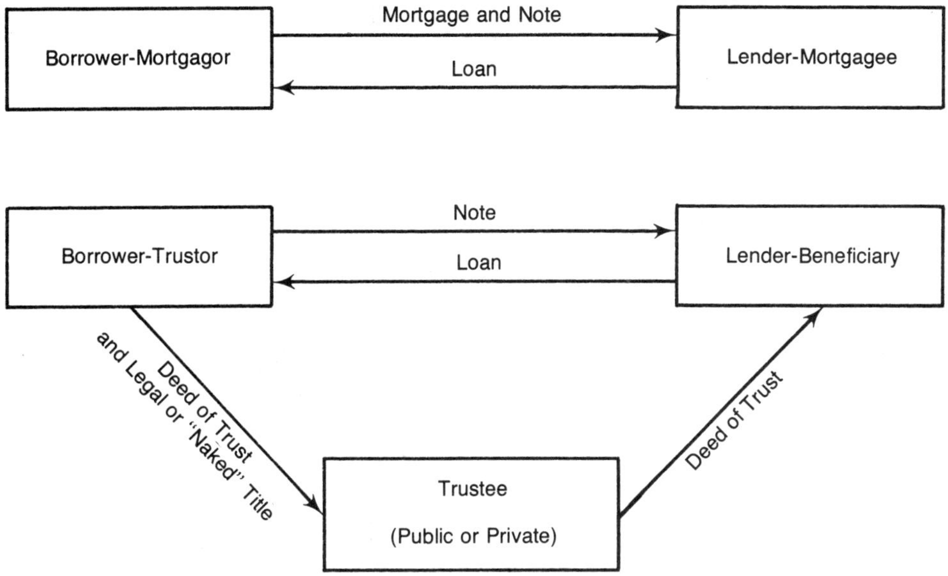

Figure 10-2a Mortgage versus Deed of Trust when loan is made

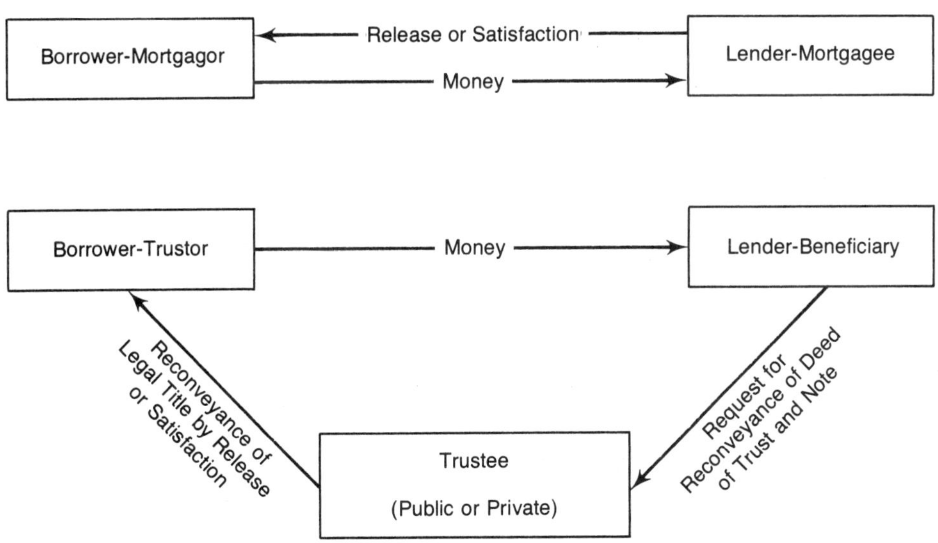

Figure 10-2b Mortgage versus Deed of Trust when loan is repaid

ington. The remaining states nearly exclusively use the mortgage for the hypothecation of real estate. Personal property may also be hypothecated in all states by using a *chattel mortgage*, as with an automobile loan, or a *crop mortgage* to a farmer on growing crops.

An *equitable mortgage* exists when the intent of any instrument is to hypothecate real property to secure a loan. For example, a promissory note which evidences a debt and also contains a recital that the note is secured by some properly described real property may be considered an equitable mortgage. Or a regular mortgage with a defect may also, because of intent, be ruled an equitable mortgage.

Finally an *absolute deed*, which appears to sell and convey title, may actually be only a hypothecation if it can be proven that the intention was to offer security for a loan. The tests of intention usually include (1) the adequacy of consideration given and received, (2) the prior negotiations between borrower and lender, and (3) the subsequent behavior of the parties. In other words, if it can be concluded from the analyses of these factors that an intent to hypothecate exists, then it may be deemed so by a court of law.

EVIDENCE OF THE DEBT: NOTE OR BOND

Regardless of the method of hypothecation used to secure the real estate loan, an additional legal instrument will accompany the security document—either a promissory note or a bond (used in a minority of states). The following discussion applies to both notes and bonds. The note or bond creates and evidences the debt between borrower and lender; it establishes an unconditional written promise of the borrower to repay the loan according to the stated terms. The note, therefore, makes the borrower *personally liable* for the debt regardless of the nature of the document used for hypothecation. Said personal liability is the mechanism that allows a lender (after foreclosure) to sue for a deficiency judgment (if necessary), which may allow the lender to garnishee the borrower's wages or have his or her other property sold to pay the balance remaining.

Assignment versus Assumption

The lender, who holds the note secured by the hypothecation instrument, may sell the note by merely endorsing (signing) it over to the purchaser. Such a transfer of a note from one lender to another lender is called an *assignment*. No assignment of the hypothecation instrument is *required*. However, where the note is secured by a mortgage or deed, the mortgage or deed *should* be assigned to the new note holder and the assignment recorded. There is no need to assign a deed of trust, since the trustee always holds legal title and will reconvey legal title to the borrower upon full payment, no matter who holds the note. With a mortgage, the mortgagee must execute the release or satisfaction piece upon full payment of the mortgage. Only the mortgagee shown in the public record is authorized to execute this release.

The assignment instrument includes a clause called the *covenant*, which recites the unpaid loan balance, the annual interest rate, and the date to which the interest payments are current. In return for including the covenant, the assignor (lender transferring the debt) will insist upon inclusion of a *no-recourse clause*, which effectively transfers the note or bond and mortgage without any further obligation on the part of the assignor. Since the covenant is binding only upon the assignor (note seller) and not upon the mortgagor-borrower, the assignee (note purchaser) will insist on a statement, called an *estoppel certificate*, from the mortgagor-borrower, which also attests to the unpaid loan balance, the annual interest rate, and the date to which interest is current.

Holder in Due Course Doctrine. Since a note and mortgage may be transferred, sold, or assigned many times, there is always the opportunity for a fraudulent transfer. If the holder of the note has purchased the instrument in good faith, for value, and *without* notice that it is overdue, dishonored, or that the maker (original borrower) has a defense against its collection, such a person is deemed a *holder in due course*. In such a situation the holder in due course doctrine may protect the purchaser from nonpayment of the note. In other words, the note remains collectable even though the maker may have a good defense against its collection. The Uniform Consumer Credit Code covers this doctrine of law. Local legal counsel should be consulted to see how this doctrine applies in any particular state.

As discussed above, an assignment of a note and mortgage involves a change in *lenders*, or receivers of the loan payments. An *assumption*, on the other hand, involves a change in *borrowers*, or payers of the loan payments. For example, when real estate is sold, the buyer and seller may wish to effect the title transfer with the existing loan remaining as a specific lien against the property. The buyer may purchase the property *subject to* the existing loan or the buyer may *assume and agree to pay* the existing loan. In the *subject to* arrangement the buyer does not accept personal liability for the debt, which means that the seller remains liable for it. In the *assume and agree to pay* arrangement the buyer agrees to be primarily liable for the debt. However, the lender may still seek payment from the seller if the buyer defaults and the debt cannot be satisfied. The seller should request a written release of liability from the lender to become totally removed and absolved from any future liability for the debt.

When an assumption is effected, the lender provides the buyer with a *certificate of reduction* (also called an *offset statement*) which indicates the unpaid balance, annual interest rate (which may escalate upon assumption), and periodic payment size and schedule. This certificate is akin to the covenant clause included in an assignment of note and mortgage.

USUAL ELEMENTS OF THE NOTE OR BOND

The promissory note or bond, which creates and evidences the debt and accompanies the mortgage or deed of trust, will usually contain the following elements:

1. Identification of the lender (obligee) and borrower (obligor)
2. Identification of the property and mortgage or deed of trust securing the note or bond
3. An unconditional promise to pay a certain sum of money to the holder of the note
4. A clear statement of the terms of payment, including the annual interest rate, the amount of the payments, and the time schedule of payments
5. Prepayment privileges (if any) and the cost (penalty) or ramifications thereof
6. *Acceleration clause*, which demands full payment of the debt upon default or the happening of some other specified event
7. *Alienation clause* (due-on-sale clause), which stipulates the rights of the lender upon sale and transfer of title of the hypothecated property[4]
8. *Assumption clause*, which stipulates the rights of the lender upon the taking over of the debt by another person (buyer)
9. *Escalation clause*, which allows the lender to raise the interest rate if the loan is assumed
10. The signature of the maker-borrower (which in some states must be acknowledged, and the note or bond recorded, to be valid).

USUAL ELEMENTS OF THE MORTGAGE OR DEED OF TRUST

Although a mortgage is a two-party arrangement and a deed of trust a three-party arrangement, they are both used as hypothecation documents to secure specified property for the benefit of the lender or note holder. Each is a contract and must therefore contain the four essential elements of a contract (competent parties, consideration, mutual assent, and a legal

4. Alienation or assumption may institute the acceleration clause and/or the escalation clause.

objective) in order to be legally valid. Although a competent real estate attorney should be consulted in each individual case, the normal elements found in a mortgage or deed of trust are as follows:

1. Identification of mortgagor and mortgagee or trustor, trustee, and beneficiary
2. Identification and pledge of the specific property offered as security for the loan
3. Amount of the debt (may or may not be stated)
4. Covenant to pay according to the note or bond
5. Covenant to pay property taxes, special assessments, and all lien claims
6. Covenants to insure, to maintain and not to remove or demolish improvements
7. Covenant to guarantee title to the lender
8. *Default clause*, which stipulates all the rights of the lender (acceleration, foreclosure, etc.) upon any default or breaking of any of the covenants (this clause may also impose financial penalties for late payments)
9. Covenants to assign rents, to appoint a receiver, and to determine the method of sale upon default
10. *Defeasance clause*, which stipulates that the lien or title claim is defeated upon payment in full of the debt
11. *Condemnation clause*, stating that any condemnation awards must be applied first to the debt outstanding
12. *Release mechanism* or *partial release clause* (if applicable) which allows part of the secured property (such as one lot in a subdivision) to be removed from hypothecation under a blanket mortgage (covering more than one property)
13. *Subordination clause* (if applicable), which reorders the priority of liens such that the mortgage or deed of trust first recorded becomes a second lien, as in the case of a land loan's moving to second priority to allow a construction loan to be first
14. The borrower's signature, with an acknowledgment (notarization)
15. Although not legally required to be valid, the security document may be recorded in the county in which the property is located. An unrecorded mortgage or trust deed is void as to subsequent purchasers, lenders, or creditors who are *ignorant* of its existence. The priority of successive claims or liens is often determined by priority of recording. Since foreclosure of a first lien extinguishes all second, third, etc. (junior) liens, the importance of prompt recording is clear.

SUMMARY AND CONCLUSION

The history and development of mortgage law is truly fascinating. Times have changed; at one time one had to own real estate to borrow money, and now most people have to borrow money to own real estate. At one time a borrower's default put him or her into slavery; today a borrower's default puts him or her into court. Even though the saying "Those with the gold make the rules" still applies today, it certainly does not apply to the degree that it did when, if a borrower missed payment on the "law day," he or she not only lost the mortgaged property but, in addition, still owed the debt. The legal history of real estate financing has been a long-term struggle between lender and borrower, each trying to gain an advantage over the other.

The gradual evolution of consumer rights has materialized from a situation of potential slavery, through double jeopardy of loss of property and liability of debt, through equitable and statutory rights of redemption, to legislation like the Truth in Lending Act, the Uniform Consumer Credit Code, and the Equal Credit Opportunity Act. Consumer advocates of real estate financing have been at work a very long time. Lenders today have to look to the interests of consumers at all times because of these developmental changes.

The legal instruments, be they mortgages or deeds of trust, notes or bonds, are full of legal jargon; good legal counsel should be consulted for advice and consultation to protect one's own interests. Some attorneys say: "Education is what you get from reading the fine print and experience is what you get from not reading the fine print." The thrust of this saying should be taken very seriously by both the student and practitioner of real estate. One should be keenly aware of the elements and fully understand the clauses and covenants of the legal documents necessary to the financing of real estate.

Finally, the importance of real estate financing should be noted. Credit is the basic economic energizer which stimulates, supports, and makes possible real estate construction and development. It is the lifeblood of the real estate market. Without real estate financing few real estate brokerage commissions would be earned, fewer projects would be available for appraisers to analyze, for investors to purchase, and for property managers to operate. So important is real estate credit to the American society and economy that one should understand the sources and markets from which real estate dollars are obtained. Chapter 12 will meet this objective, after the various possible mortgage or deed of trust arrangements are discussed in Chapter 11.

PART III

Finance

CHAPTER 11

Types of Mortgages

KEY TERMS

Interim financing Term that includes any and all types of real estate loans required during the time interval between "front-end" equity financing and long-term permanent financing; also used synonymously with construction financing

Take-out commitment A formal commitment by either a permanent or a standby lender to pay off (take out) the construction loan when a real estate project is "completed according to plans and specifications"

Floor-to-ceiling loan A two-staged take-out loan: the "floor" amount is funded when the project is completed; the remainder of the loan, or "ceiling" amount, is funded when a given percentage (70 to 85 percent) of the project has been leased (rental achievement clause)

Conventional loan A non-government-sponsored residential real estate loan

Equity The difference between a property's market value and the balance of any loans on the property

Purchase-money mortgage A type of mortgage used when a purchaser executes a promissory note and mortgage (deed of trust) in favor of the seller in lieu of cash or purchase money and the seller executes a deed to the purchaser

Installment contract for deed A financing technique employed to purchase real estate wherein the price plus interest is paid in installments, with the seller or third-party trustee holding title until a set percentage of the price has been tendered

Wraparound mortgage A loan that is subordinate to but acknowledges and encompasses one or more senior loans, such that the wraparound lender makes the payments on the senior liens out of the payments received on the wraparound loan

Equity kicker A real estate loan that, in addition to the interest rate, returns to the lender "a piece of the action," such as a percentage of the gross or net income, a portion of any resale or refinancing proceeds, or simply a share in the equity ownership of the project

In Chapter 10, mortgages—or more accurately, security documents—were classified according to the various methods of hypothecation as either mortgage, deed of trust, equitable mortgage, or absolute mortgage deed. Henceforth, the term *mortgage* will be used to refer to any or all of these loan instruments. Furthermore, the terms *borrower* and *lender* will be used rather than mortgagor and mortgagee, or trustor and beneficiary. The discussion of mortgage types and classification which follows is filled with mortgage terminology, but it should not be inferred that the individual terms are mutually exclusive. Any given mortgage arrangement may involve, and therefore be called, more than one of the different types. For purposes of discussion, mortgages may be differentiated by listing them in the following six categories: (1) stage of property development, (2) financing method, (3) type of collateral, (4) priority of lien, (5) method of payment, and (6) experimental mortgage proposals.

STAGE OF PROPERTY DEVELOPMENT

There exists a time sequence which begins with the idea of a real estate development in the mind of a real estate developer and ends with an occupied structure or set of structures ready to be managed and operated. The various stages of property development require different types of real estate financing.

Equity Financing

Usually the developer starts a project with his or her own cash as "front-end" or "seed" money. Money is needed at this stage to pay for land options, feasibility studies, architects, engineers, attorneys, and other professionals for planning and designing the project, debt financing, and overhead and any other expenses incurred in bringing the idea into reality. Equity financing may be hard cash from the developer's pocket, or it may (and often does) come from other sources. Seed money may be obtained by taking on wealthy partners in a general or limited partnership arrangement, by joint-venturing with a large institutional lender, by forming a syndicate, by selling real estate securities, or by having the professionals (attorneys, etc.) put in their time for a piece of the ownership ("sweat-equity" arrangement). Once the equity financing is secured and the project conceptualization is under way, the next step is to secure control of the land.

Land Financing

There are a variety of ways of gaining control or ownership of the land required for the real estate development. The developer or development team may have *purchased* the land long ago (perhaps through a *land syndication*) in anticipation of developing it some time in the future. If this were the case, the land itself would most likely have been offered as security for the initial equity financing. If the developer does not own the required land, he or she might joint-venture (as partners) the entire project with the owner of the desired land. Another alternative is to purchase an *option* to buy the land at a set price during some designated future time period. The use of a *ground lease* allows the developer control of the land with only a minimal financial commitment, namely paying rent rather than purchasing at the full sales price. Two other methods of obtaining control and/or ownership of developable land are the *deed and purchase money mortgage* and the *land contract for deed*. These two arrangements are discussed later in this chapter, in the section "Financing Method" (p. 172).

Interim Financing

Technically, *interim financing* includes any and all financing techniques used during the time interval between equity financing and permanent financing, or the long-term real estate mortgage loan. However, this term is also commonly used to mean construction financing, although this is only one type of interim financing. Land financing may also be considered a type of interim financing. However, since the land often serves as the equity in a real estate project, it has been discussed separately.

Land Development Loans. The next step in financing real estate developments might be the *land development loan*. Land development is the establishment of streets, greenbelts, and other land-uses, and the installation of curbs, gutters, sidewalks, street lights, and utilities (water, sewers, electricity, gas, and telephone). In other words, land development transforms raw subdivided land into buildable construction sites. The security hypothecated for a land development loan is typically the land itself.

Construction Loans. Construction financing is the next type of financing required in the development process. Construction loan dollars pay for the labor, materials, overhead, expenses, and interest incurred during the construction of the structures or improvements. They may also pay for the land development discussed above. Construction financing is unique in that a total dollar amount is committed by the lender, but the disbursement of funds takes place in stages as construction progresses, requiring bills to be due and payable. The individual disbursements of funds are called construction draws. The borrower is charged interest only on the amount that has been drawn or "taken down." Usually the interest is not paid periodically, but rather is accrued and added to the balance of the loan upon completion of construction. The construction lender is paid the principal borrowed and interest accrued from the proceeds of the long-term mortgage loan. It is said that the construction lender is "taken out" by the long-term lender. Construction loans are short term, since they mature when construction is completed. The construction period may run three to six months for residences and six months to three years for income properties.

It is quite common in the financing of a single-family residence for one lender to handle both the short-term construction loan and the long-term (20 to 30 years) permanent loan. Such a financing package minimizes the lender's risk since: (1) the construction process can be monitored to ensure quality is maintained and specifications are met, and (2) the construction lender will be taken out upon completion.

In commercial real estate the construction lender frequently does not handle the permanent financing. A commitment for permanent financing usually must be obtained before the construction loan will be funded. If there is no commitment for permanent financing, the *short-term* construction lender could very easily and unwillingly become a *long-term* lender. To avoid such an undesirable situation, a commitment for permanent financing to take out the construction lender should be a requirement of the construction loan.

Take-out Commitments. There are generally two kinds of take-out commitments: (1) permanent, and (2) standby. The *permanent* take-out commitment is a written contractual agreement which guarantees that the construction lender will be fully paid off upon completion of construction according to plans and specifications. Permanent take-out commitments are made by long-term lenders.

Standby take-out commitments are typically made by short-term lenders, since such loans, if funded at all, are usually paid off in a short period of time. A standby is typically used in one of the following situations:

1. Money is so tight that no lenders will make a permanent take-out commitment.
2. Interest rates are high and the developer thinks they will fall by the time construction is completed, yet the developer needs a commitment in order to have the construction loan funded.
3. The developer feels that the property will be of much greater value (and can therefore borrow much more money) after a "track record" or rental history has been established.

In each of these three situations the developer intends to pay off the standby (if funded) when more favorable conditions exist. If money loosens up and/or interest rates fall, there may be no need to use the standby. If the standby is funded to take out the construction lender, it may be prepaid in full *without penalty* at any time in order to obtain a permanent long-term mortgage loan.

Permanent Financing

Eventually, whether or not a standby commitment or loan is used, permanent financing will be obtained on the commercial real estate project. The interest rate, term, and method of repayments are always negotiable items; they are discussed later in this chapter and in Chapter 12. Permanent financing is long term and usually carries very stiff penalties for prepayment prior to the maturity date, or during a fairly lengthy period (at least the first 10 years) of the loan. It is often common for the payoff schedule or amortization period to be longer than the maturity date, which causes a balloon payment at maturity. Another common element of commercial loans is a rental achievement agreement, which may force the use of floor-to-ceiling loans and gap financing.

Floor-to-Ceiling Loans. In order to provide a very strong incentive for the developer to lease a project fully as soon as possible, a commercial real estate mortgage loan commitment is often made in two stages. When the project is completed, the first portion of the loan is funded. This minimum amount, called the *floor of the mortgage* (or simply the floor) is typically 70 to 85 percent of the total loan amount. The remaining portion of the loan will be funded once a certain *rent roll* has been *achieved*. The *rental achievement* may be stated as a dollar amount or as an occupancy rate, typically 50 to 80 percent of the net leasable space. This second funding brings the loan balance to the full amount of the commitment and is called the *ceiling*. A floor-to-ceiling commitment encourages the developer to maximize the leasing effort so that there will not be a shortage of funds (gap) to take out the construction lender.

Gap Financing. Whenever the preleasing campaign does not meet the required rental achievement, the gap between the floor and the ceiling amounts must be funded with yet another type of loan, called gap financing. A *gap loan* is intended as a short-term second mortgage used to complete the construction-loan take out. The gap loan will be repaid as soon as the required rental achievement is attained and the permanent lender disburses the ceiling loan amount. Since the gap loan interest rate is 2 to 3 percent more than the permanent loan rate, the developer is easily motivated to attain the rental achievement to pay off the gap loan. The payoff of the gap loan completes the list of possible interim financing options and ends the sequence of financing alternatives with the full funding of the permanent loan. It then becomes the responsibility of the property manager to maintain an occupancy level high enough to cover all operating expenses, debt service, and owner's profit. However, it is always possible for a whole new set of refinancing alternatives or other creative financing techniques to be considered at some future time. These possibilities are discussed later in this chapter.

FINANCING METHOD

Mortgages may be classified by financing methods of the following kind:

1. Federal Housing Administration (FHA)
2. Veterans Administration (VA)
3. Farmers Home Administration (FmHA)
4. Conventional (nongovernment sponsored)
5. Purchase money mortgage (owner will carry)
6. Installment contract (contract for deed)
7. Wraparound mortgage (all-inclusive deed of trust)
8. Equity participation (equity kickers)
9. Piggyback mortgage

FHA Loans

The Federal Housing Administration was established in 1934, not to make mortgage loans, but rather to insure them against loss upon default and foreclosure. An annual insurance premium of 1/2 percent of the average outstanding loan balance for each 12 months is paid by the borrower to protect the lender against any loss. The lender is not the FHA, but any traditional lending institution which has been approved by the FHA. The insurance is called Mutual Mortgage Insurance (MMI) and covers the total loan amount. The various FHA programs stress small down payments, long-term, fully amortized loans at below-market interest rates, and quality construction standards.

VA Loans

The VA or GI loan program was established in 1944 by the Veterans Administration. The VA, unlike FHA, does not insure mortgage loans (no insurance premium), but guarantees loans against loss upon default and foreclosure. The maximum coverage of the guarantee is 60 percent of the loan or $17,500 (as of 1978), whichever is less. As with FHA loans, VA loans are usually made by approved lenders. However, the VA will make a *direct loan* in areas where mortgage funds are not readily available. VA loans are obtainable with *no* down payment, and, like FHA, are typically long-term, fully amortized loans at below-market interest rates.

FmHA Loans

The Farmers Home Administration is an agency of the U.S. Department of Agriculture and was established to facilitate real estate lending in rural areas where the population does not exceed 10,000. FmHA insures loans made by institutional lenders at below-market interest rates which are directly subsidized by funds from Congress.

FmHA is involved in both farm ownership loans accompanied by technical management assistance, and rural housing loans, which is its largest program. The farm ownership loans are made only when funds are not obtainable from other lenders at reasonable rates and terms. The rural housing loan program emphasizes new construction of single-family housing, but also offers financial assistance for rental multifamily housing programs.

Conventional Loans

A conventional loan is any nongovernment-sponsored (insured or guaranteed) loan. The requirements to qualify for conventional loans are determined solely by the lender and vary greatly across the industry. The two most important determining factors are the borrower's ability to pay, as evidenced by income and net worth (assets and liabilities), and the borrower's willingness to pay, as evidenced by a credit report. Generally, the greater the risk of repayment as determined by the lender, the higher the interest rate, or the shorter the loan term, and/or the lower the loan amount as a percentage of value (requiring larger down payment). Conventional mortgage loan terms are also a function of the supply and demand conditions of both the money market and the real estate market.

The use of private mortgage insurance (PMI) with conventional loans reduces the lender's risk and allows a larger loan to be made. PMI is very similar to the FHA's MMI, except than it insures only the top 15 to 20 percent of the loan, rather than 100 percent of the loan. However, the top of the loan is the riskiest portion. Since PMI is partial insurance, its cost is less than MMI.

Purchase Money Mortgage

When a buyer gives a seller a mortgage in lieu of cash or purchase money, such a mortgage is called a *purchase money* mortgage. The seller conveys title by deed to the buyer, and the buyer executes a promissory note (bond) and mortgage (deed of trust) in favor of the seller. It is said that the seller "takes back" the mortgage or that the "owner will carry" the mortgage as part of the purchase price. The seller, therefore, is in fact a lender in such a transaction. However, instead of a third-party lender's conveying cash to the buyer-borrower (sometimes called a "hard money" mortgage), the seller-lender conveys the deed to the buyer-borrower. Most purchase money mortgages carried back by sellers are second mortgages behind a first mortgage loan made by a third-party lender.

For example, assume the following financing package on a $50,000 home:

Buyer's down payment (cash)	$ 5,000
Third-party lender first mortgage (cash)	40,000
Purchase money second mortgage (not cash)	5,000
TOTAL PRICE	$50,000

Although the example above is the more likely situation, it is possible for the purchase money mortgage to be a first mortgage in the amount of $45,000, with no third-party lender involved. In any case, *the buyer gets the deed* and gives the purchase money mortgage.

Installment Contract

Although the installment contract is not technically a mortgage, it is often treated as one by the courts. It is presented here for comparison with the purchase money mortgage. The distinguishing difference between the installment contract and the purchase money mortgage is that in the former arrangement the buyer does *not* get the deed upon sale, but rather gets only the rights to possess and use the property. The buyer has entered a contract to obtain the deed at a later date; hence the alternative name, *contract for deed*.

Numerical examples identical to the ones presented for the purchase money mortgage may be made, substituting an installment contract for the purchase money mortgage. The buyer makes periodic payments with interest to the seller; however, the seller does not convey the deed until an agreed-upon number of payments have been made by the buyer. To protect the deed and to maintain a clear title, the buyer should insist that the deed be held by a disinterested third-party trustee who will eventually convey the deed and transfer title to the buyer.

Wraparound Mortgage

Another example of involving the seller in the financing of a real estate transaction is the wraparound mortgage, or all-inclusive deed of trust. This financing technique is most effectively employed when the seller's equity is substantial and there is a sizable first mortgage bearing an interest rate much lower than the present market rate. The objectives of such a loan include (1) maintaining the advantage of the low interest rate first mortgage, and (2) minimizing the cash down payment requirement. In other words, the buyer does not desire or is incapable of assuming the first mortgage because of the large amount of equity required to do so. Yet the buyer does desire holding the advantage of the low interest rate of the first mortgage. Furthermore, the seller is interested in getting involved with the financing in order to make the sale. An example will best describe such a situation.

Assume an original property value and sales prices of $40,000. The original loan balance was $36,000 at 7 percent interest for 30 years, with a $240 monthly payment.[1] Ten years later the property has appreciated in value to $50,000 and the loan balance has been paid down to $30,000, resulting in $20,000 of equity. Further assume that the buyer has only $5,000 or is only willing to pay a $5,000 down payment. The present market interest rate for a $45,000 loan is 9.25 percent, requiring a $370 monthly payment over 30 years. The present market interest rate for a $15,000 second mortgage is 12.25 percent, requiring a $200 monthly payment over 12 years. The buyer's alternatives are as follows:

1. New $45,000 loan: $370 monthly payment

or

2. Assume $30,000 loan: $240 and $15,000 second loan: $200 } $440 monthly payment

Rather than choosing either financing alternative, a $45,000 wraparound mortgage and note (which acknowledges and includes the first mortgage in the total) can be offered by the seller at 8.25 percent interest for 30 years. The monthly payment would be $340 paid to the seller. The seller pays the $240 first mortgage payment, leaving the remaining $100 per month for 20 years plus, at the end of that time, a loan balance payoff of $27,720. This balance would most likely be paid off by the owner's refinancing the property at that time. If the $27,720 were financed over only 10 years at 9.25 percent, the monthly payment would still be only $355; at 20 years the payment would be only $254 per month.

In this example, the seller has effectively invested $15,000 of the $20,000 equity in return for $100 per month for 20 years and a payment of $27,720 at the end of 20 years. The yield to the seller on such an investment can be calculated to be 9.65 percent! Hence, it should be evident that with a wraparound mortgage (1) the buyer is able to purchase the property and have lower monthly payments, and (2) the seller is able to sell the property and earn an excellent return on the equity investment.

It should be noted that, for title purposes, a wraparound mortgage is treated as a second mortgage.

Equity Participation

The equity participation mortgage loan, also termed a *contingent interest* loan, is commonly used in commercial income property lending. The lender, in addition to collecting interest on the loan, participates in the

1. All numbers in this example have been rounded off to facilitate the explanation.

benefits that normally accrue only to the equity position. In other words, the lender gets "a piece of the action" called an "equity kicker." The kicker may be a set percentage of the gross or net income, a portion of any resale profits, a portion of any refinancing proceeds, or simply a share in the equity ownership of the project. In return for these benefits the lender will usually offer the borrower a below-market interest rate and hope that this low rate plus the kicker, which is contingent on the project's being successful, will eventually yield the lender an above-market return. This loan should not be confused with a *participation* or *trust mortgage*, which is used when two or more lenders pool funds to make a loan which is too large for any one lender to fund. Such a loan is common in large commercial real estate transactions.

Piggyback Mortgage

The piggyback mortgage is used in residential financing and involves two lenders sharing in a single loan (similar to a trust mortgage), resulting in a larger loan for the homeowner. Such a loan is an alternative to a second mortgage. For example, an institutional lender might originate a loan equal to 95 percent of the purchase price or value. This lender, however, funds only 80 percent and a second lender (institutional or private) funds the top 15 percent, which is insured by private mortgage insurance.

TYPE OF COLLATERAL

The collateral of a loan is the property which is hypothecated or pledged as security for payment of the loan. If there is a default, the collateral is sold to satisfy the debt. Another way of categorizing different types of mortgages is by the type of collateral offered to secure the loan.

Open-end Mortgage

Often the typical home loan will be an open-end mortgage, which allows the borrower at any time to reborrow part or all of the equity build-up obtained by paying off or amortizing the loan. In other words, as the loan balance declines through monthly payments, the borrower's equity increases. The borrower may reborrow the equity, increasing the loan amount (and loan payment) to a maximum equal to the original balance. The additional funds advanced are not treated as a second or junior mortgage, which may cause some concern to lenders in a subordinate position.

An open-end mortgage should not be confused with an *open mortgage*, which is one that is due but not yet paid (or, as in the case of a construction loan, not yet fully funded). A *closed mortgage* is the opposite of an open mortgage. It is either not due or in default, or, with a construction loan, fully funded.

Blanket Mortgage

A blanket mortgage covers or is secured by more than one parcel of real estate. Such a loan usually contains a *release mechanism* which allows parcels to be freed from the blanket mortgage claim upon payment of a designated amount. For example, a subdivider may have a blanket mortgage covering many lots which, when developed with roads, sewers, and other utilities, will be sold as developed buildable lots to builders. Or the subdivider may build the homes and sell them directly to the consumer.

In either case, the lots, at some point in time, must be released from under the claim of the blanket mortgage in order to resell them. Typically, the release clause will allow a lot to be freed and unencumbered upon payment of 100 to 120 percent of the proportional loan amount for that lot. Such a system, if more than a 100-percent payoff is required, pays off the total loan amount before all the lots are sold.

For example, assume there were six lots with a $60,000 blanket loan against them, and that the release clause called for a 120-percent payment for release. Since it would take a $12,000 payment to release each lot, the total loan ($60,000) would be paid off upon release of the fifth lot (5 × $12,000 = $60,000), leaving the subdivider or developer with one lot free and clear. The lender's logic is to minimize risk: since the most desirable lots tend to sell first, the lender is not left with the least desirable lot or lots as security for the loan.

Package Mortgage

A loan which includes personal property as security is termed a package mortgage. For example, a builder may offer in the price of a home a "package deal" to include all appliances, carpeting, and window coverings. If the mortgage is based on the total package price, then the personal property, as well as the real property, may be pledged to maximize the loan amount.

Spreading and Consolidation Agreements

A change in collateral may come about through either a spreading agreement or a consolidation agreement. A spreading agreement extends or spreads a mortgage lien over additional property or collateral. One may resort to such an arrangement in order to obtain more funds to maintain the investment viability of the first property. For example, a property may need to be remodeled to maintain its competitive position in the rental market. The owner may not wish to incur the high cost of a second mortgage, and instead obtains the needed funds from the first mortgagee by supplying another property as additional security or collateral. Hence, one mortgage is secured by two (or more) properties.

A consolidation agreement is the opposite of the spreading agreement.

In this situation two (or more) mortgages secured by one property are consolidated into one loan. For example, a second mortgage may be paid off by the first mortgagee and incorporated (consolidated) or added to the balance of the first loan. In such a situation the first lender no longer needs to worry about the second lender's foreclosing because of a default on the second or junior loan.

Leasehold Mortgage

A leasehold mortgage exists when a loan is obtained for a building located on leased land. Income to the property in such a situation is derived from (1) the ground rent paid by the developer who holds a *leasehold* (tenant) interest in the land, and (2) the rents paid to the developer by the tenants who occupy and use the building built by the leasehold developer. The loan obtained by the developer to build the building is called a leasehold mortgage because the builder's interest in the land, which is hypothecated to secure the building loan, is a leasehold interest, not a fee simple interest. If the developer defaults on the leasehold mortgage, the leasehold mortgagee may pay the ground rent and take over operation of the building.

In most cases, unless the landowner is willing to subordinate the ground lease to the leasehold mortgage, the leasehold mortgage loan amount will be much lower than a fee mortgage loan, since the lender's risk is greater. However, since the developer has not employed capital to buy the land, the leasehold mortgage amount may be sufficient to cover most or even all the developer's cost of construction.

Collateral Loans

When the buyer does not have enough cash for the down payment and the seller is unwilling to take back or carry a purchase money mortgage or make a wraparound loan, a collateral loan may be arranged. An agreement is made between the seller and the first mortgage lender (which must be a savings institution) whereby the seller agrees to open a savings account with the lender. The amount of this account is equal to the amount the buyer is short for the down payment, and is added to the buyer's first mortgage so the sale can be completed. The seller earns interest on the savings account, but cannot withdraw the funds until the buyer has paid down the loan balance by the amount of the savings account. The account, therefore, is held as additional collateral for the buyer's mortgage loan. If the buyer defaults, the lender has claim on the seller's savings or collateral account to satisfy the debt if the foreclosure proceeds do not completely pay off the outstanding loan balance plus penalty interest and expenses.

PRIORITY OF LIEN

The priority of a mortgage lien is typically determined by one or more of the following items:

1. Time of recording
2. State lien statutes
3. Subordination clauses or agreements

Recording and Lien Laws

Generally speaking, the mortgage recorded first is a *first mortgage*; the mortgage recorded second is a *second mortgage*; and so on. Recorded mortgages are termed by the order of recording. "First in time is first in line" is a common phrase used to describe this state of affairs. A *senior mortgage* is generally one that has been recorded before another; a *junior mortgage* is one that has been recorded after another. There are exceptions, however, to these generalizations.

For example, in most states if a mortgage is recorded with the knowledge of the existence of a prior unrecorded mortgage, it is junior to the prior unrecorded mortgage. In some states mechanic's liens have priority over all mortgages. Hence, a first mortgage may be senior to subsequent mortgages, but at the same time it may also be or become junior to prior and/or subsequent mechanic's liens. It is always highly advisable to seek competent legal counsel as to a particular state's lien laws. In all states, property taxes and special assessments are considered "perpetual" liens and always take precedence over the recording of any mortgage lien. This is why the lender requires the borrower to agree in the security document to pay these liens or be held in default.

Subordination

Because of subordination clauses or agreements, it is possible that a first mortgage could later become a second mortgage automatically or that the lien priorities could later be rearranged. For example, a land loan often contains a subordination clause which states that a later construction loan and/or permanent loan may have a lien ahead of the land loan. In other words, an otherwise senior land loan lien might automatically become a junior lien. The land loan lender is willing to agree to such a clause because land with improvements on it usually appreciates in value such that the second position is not that bad. Furthermore, the developer most likely would not agree to purchase the land without such a subordination clause. Hence, the landowner often becomes the land loan lender in order to sell the land.

It is possible for a need to arise for the maintenance of an existing lien order, or for the reordering of liens where there exists no prior subordination clause. For example, assume first and second loans exist on a property. Further assume that the owner desires to refinance the first mortgage. In order to refinance, the first loan would be paid off and the second would automatically move to first position, totally defeating the owner's objective of refinancing. To avoid this outcome, a subordination agreement may be drawn and implemented whereby the second mortgage will remain in second position.

Another example of the need for a subordination agreement may arise in the case of a mortgage spreading agreement, discussed earlier in this chapter. Assume a first mortgage exists on the property, to be added to the security of another first mortgage on another property. It would be necessary to the implementation of the spreading agreement to reorder the lien order on the added property. A subordination agreement may also be used in this case.

METHOD OF PAYMENT

Mortgages may also be classified according to the method of payment. Essentially there are five basic ways of repaying a mortgage loan, from which are derived the names of the following types of mortgages:

1. Term (straight) mortgage
2. Fully amortized mortgage
3. Partially amortized mortgage
4. Variable rate mortgage (VRM)
5. Graduated payment mortgage (GPM) or flexible payment mortgage (FPM)

Variations of payment plans within these five basic categories are presented below.

Term Mortgage

A term or straight mortgage is one that matures at the end of the term with the total loan amount due and payable. There is no payment of the principal amount of the loan during the term; there is no *amortization*. The periodic payments made on a term loan consist totally of interest; they are interest-only payments. Term mortgages today are usually second mortgages: either "hard money" seconds or purchase-money seconds. Term mortgages usually have a short maturity (three to five years), which makes them reminiscent of the home lending practices employed by lenders prior to 1934, when the Federal Housing Administration introduced the fully amortized mortgage loan.

Fully Amortized Mortgage

Amortization is the payment of principal during the term of the loan. A fully amortized loan is one whose payment schedule provides for the *complete* or *total* payment of the principal (amount borrowed) during the term of the loan. Upon the making of the last payment, the outstanding loan balance is zero. Two variations of the fully amortized loan are (1) constant payment loan and (2) the level payment loan.

Constant Payment Loan. The constant payment plan calls for equal amounts of the principal, plus the accrued interest, to be paid each period. Since the loan balance is constantly decreasing each period, so too is the accrued interest. Hence, the total periodic payment of principal (which is constant) and interest (which is declining) declines each period. The constant payment loan is also called the *installment mortgage* or the *straight amortization* loan. Regardless of nomenclature, the important point is that the total payment continually decreases.

Level Payment Loan. Unlike the constant payment loan, the level payment plan provides for the total principal and interest payment to be the same or level for the life of the loan. A nineteenth-century mathematician named William Inwood originally derived the complex formula that allows such a payment to be calculated.

The initial payments consist mostly of accrued interest, with a small amount of principal repayment or amortization. As the loan matures, the outstanding principal balance continues to be reduced through amortization, causing the accrued interest of each period's payment to decline. Since the total payment remains level, the portion of the total principal and interest payment that goes toward amortization increases each period, such that the last few payments consist mostly of principal repayment (amortization) with a small amount of accrued interest. In contrast to the constant payment loan, the total payment remains the same or level for the life of the loan.

Budget Mortgage. Most home loans today provide that the monthly payment to the lender include, in addition to principal and interest, one-twelfth of the annual property taxes and annual hazard insurance. These additional funds are held in a reserve account (also called an escrow account or impound account) by the lender, who will pay the taxes and insurance when due. Such a provision forces the borrower to *budget* his or her money for payment of these liabilities; hence the term *budget mortgage*. The lender does not presently pay interest to the borrower on the reserve accounts. However, it is soon likely to be common practice for lenders to pay interest on these accounts, since many consumer groups are presently urging such a goal.

Partially Amortized Mortgage

A partially amortized loan is one whose payment schedule provides for an *incomplete* or *limited* payment of the principal during the term of the loan. At the end of the loan term a portion of the principal remains due and payable. Since the remaining portion is usually a relatively large amount, this balance is satisfied with what is called a *balloon payment*. The terms *balloon mortgage* and *limited reduction mortgage* are also commonly used to describe this type of loan.

In commercial income property loans, balloon payments are typically the result of a payment schedule which is calculated on a long loan term (25 to 30 years, or more) coupled with a loan maturity and payoff calculated on a shorter loan term. For example, a $1 million loan at 9 percent interest for 30 years has a monthly principal and interest payment of $8,046.23. However, if this loan matures at the end of the 25th year, a loan balance of $387,614.04 will remain, which must be satisfied by a balloon payment of that amount. In other words, the loan at the end of the 25th year has been only partially amortized.

Partially amortized loans, and especially balloon payments, are generally discouraged for homeowner residential lending. The reasoning employed is to avoid the large balloon payments, which cause havoc with the typical homeowner's budget. Such loans are common, however, for residential second mortgages, especially with purchase-money seconds.

Furthermore, both the Truth In Lending Act (TIL) and the Uniform Consumer Credit Code (UCCC) provide some protection to consumers against balloon payments. Under TIL the lender must disclose and identify the amount of such payment as a "balloon payment" and must state the conditions, if any, under which that payment may be refinanced if not paid when due. Under UCCC, if the note bears an interest rate in excess of 12 percent, the lender must disclose to the borrower that he or she has the right to refinance a balloon payment at the time it is due, without penalty and on terms no less favorable than the original loan.

Variable Rate Mortgage (VRM)

A loan whose interest is tied to some market index, such as the prime rate or the rate of long-term government bonds, is called a variable rate mortgage or VRM. The interest rate on these loans rises and falls over the life of the loan, keeping pace with current changes in overall interest rates. California state savings and loan associations have been successfully using VRMs since early 1975. The intended benefits of VRMs are:

1. Consumers are encouraged to purchase homes even when interest rates are high, without their being locked in at the high rate; they can "ride the rate down" rather than postponing the purchase until rates go down. The idea is to remove some of the cyclical swings

in the real estate market and to stabilize the demand for money in the mortgage market.

2. Lenders are protected against inflation in that their overall portfolio interest return will rise with inflation; some proponents claim that if lenders do not have to suffer having old low-interest loans in their portfolios, then they can offer relatively lower rates to new borrowers than they would without VRMs.
3. Borrowers of VRMs are offered an initial interest rate that is below market, are relieved of prepayment penalties, and are charged a lower loan origination fee.

There are three possible ways of handling the result of a change in the interest rate:

1. Increase or decrease the monthly payment
2. Lengthen or shorten the term of the loan, keeping the payment constant
3. Raise or lower the principal balance owed, keeping the payment and term constant, resulting in either a balloon payment or refund at maturity of the loan

The first of these three methods is most common, with limits (once every six months) as to how often an adjustment might be made, and a maximum limit (usually 2 percent) that the interest rate could rise during the life of the loan.

The VRM concept is not yet universally accepted. Congress has voted down the idea of nationally chartered lending institutions two or three times. Many studies of this concept and of the limited experiences with VRMs have been made and will be made in the future before the final votes of lenders and consumers can be counted.

Graduated Payment Mortgage (GPM) or Flexible Payment Mortgage (FPM)

The graduated or flexible payment mortgage is aimed at making it possible for more consumers to qualify for the financing and ownership of a home. Such loans provide for a *divided amortization schedule,* with low monthly payments in the early years of the loan and gradually higher payments in later years. Proponents say this type of loan allows younger people to buy early while their incomes are low; then, as their incomes presumably increase over time, the larger payments in later years will also be affordable.

The possibilities for structuring the payment schedules of GPMs or FPMs are numerous. For example, such a payment plan could be "interest only" for five years and then amortized over 25 years thereafter; or the 30 years could be divided into six five-year amortization periods or three

10-year amortization periods. As these examples show, the total payment schedule is completely and precisely determined before any payments are made. The increases in payments are known in advance and can therefore be planned and prepared for in the homeowner's budget. Such is not the case with VRMs.

The FHA began to implement GPMs in early 1977. As with the VRMs, the GPM experience is too limited to draw any conclusions or to make any projections as to their future success or acceptance.

EXPERIMENTAL MORTGAGE PROPOSALS

The high cost of housing has recently turned the American dream of owning a home into a nightmare or mirage for a large portion of American families. The statisticians tell us that the vast majority of Americans cannot afford to buy the median-priced home of today. The two major rising cost items within the price of a home are inflation and mortgage financing. Some very unique and, perhaps, unusual experimental proposals for lowering mortgage payments are as follows:

1. Rollover mortgage
2. Shared-equity mortgage
3. Deferred interest mortgage
4. Reverse annuity mortgage

Some of these ideas may appear somewhat bizarre today, yet they may be quite common in the future.

Rollover Mortgage

The rollover mortgage is a proposed variation of a VRM, but the interest rate could only be adjusted at the end of a five-year time span. At that time, the borrower has a choice of (1) accepting the new rate offered by the lender, (2) shopping around for a new mortgage loan, and/or (3) paying off the balance of the loan. Such a proposal is reminiscent of the pre-FHA days of mortgage financing, when all mortgage loans were short term and continually rolled over and over until the Depression and the runs on banks caused lenders to stop refinancing. Millions of loans in the 1930s were foreclosed upon because of this short-term rollover feature.

Shared-Equity Mortgage

The shared-equity mortgage is quite similar to the equity participation loan or equity kicker discussed earlier in the context of commercial income property lending. Under this proposal the lender would charge a below-market interest rate; the borrower, in return, would promise the lender part of any capital gain or profit realized when the home was sold. In other words, the lender gets a piece of the action as protection against inflation.

Such a proposal may partially or totally eliminate one of the investment advantages purportedly offered by homeownership. However, by lowering the mortgage interest rate, it is hoped that more families could qualify or afford homeownership.

Deferred Interest Mortgage with Recapture

The deferred interest mortgage proposes that lenders charge below-market interest rates and the federal government pay the difference. In return, the homeowner would repay the government out of any capital gain or profit realized when the home was sold.

A particular example of the deferred interest mortgage that has been proposed by the National Association of Home Builders (NAHB) calls for the federal government to make a one-time, direct mortgage interest payment to the lender making the below-market rate loan on new construction. This one-time payment would function as a loan discount or points paid to the lender, which would increase the lender's yield (on the net amount effectively loaned out) to the market rate.

Furthermore, the federal payment to the lender would be secured by a non–interest-bearing second mortgage (deed of trust) in favor of the federal government. A prorated portion of this second mortgage would be assumed by all subsequent buyers of the home during the first 12 years of the loan, and the subsidy payment would be recaptured in full from the owner on any sale after 12 years.

For example, the federal government would pay the lender about $5,000 in a transaction that involved the sale of a home priced at $50,000, given a market interest rate of 9 percent and a preestablished below-market interest rate of 7.25 percent for a $46,000 loan over 30 years. The NAHB has estimated that an additional 100,000 new homes would be built per year if this program were implemented.

Interest Subsidy. The NAHB has also proposed two graduated interest rate subsidy programs, under which the below-market rate would be increased by .25 percent per year until the rate met the prevailing market interest rate. The two proposals differ only in that one calls for the subsidy to be a one-time, front-end payment and the other calls for annual subsidy payments until the market rate is reached, but not to exceed 12 years of subsidy payments.

Reverse Annuity Mortgage

A very novel idea which has been successfully implemented in France for many years is the reverse annuity mortgage. From the lender's point of view, a mortgage represents an annuity (or periodic payments) paid by the borrower. The reverse annuity mortgage reverses the flow of payments, from borrower-to-lender to lender-to-borrower. This proposal is intended for retired people who can no longer afford monthly payments. Upon retirement, the lender would agree to reverse the cash flow, in effect buying the homeowner's equity in the home, and paying for it by sending a monthly check to the retiree.

There are obvious drawbacks to this proposal. Upon full payment or death the lender owns the home, which must then be resold in order to liquidate the capital investment in the home. And the children of the retiree do not inherit the property, since it is owned by the lender. However, the reverse annuity works well in France. Perhaps some day it will be quite common in America as well.

SUMMARY AND CONCLUSIONS

In addition to the method of hypothecation or type of pledge made to secure a real estate loan, there are numerous other ways and techniques available for structuring such a loan. This chapter has categorized these different types of mortgages according to the following six categories: (1) stage of property development, (2) financing method, (3) type of collateral, (4) priority of lien, (5) method of payment, and (6) experimental mortgage proposals.

Nearly 50 different terms have been discussed and explained as different types of loans. The word *type* has been used rather loosely; each is not mutually exclusive of the others. For example, a permanent loan could also be floor-to-ceiling, open-ended and leasehold while also being partially amortized with a balloon payment, and include an equity kicker. With some creative thinking, one could form a list of far more than 50 "types" of mortgages by combining the various alternatives discussed in this chapter.

CHAPTER 12

Primary Mortgage Market Lenders

KEY TERMS

Primary mortgage market Lenders who deal face-to-face with mortgage borrowers in originating or underwriting loans, thereby serving as a direct source of mortgage funds

Secondary mortgage market Investors who deal through intermediaries in making mortgage investments, thereby serving as an indirect source of mortgage funds

Loan underwriting The investigation, analysis, and determination of the risks involved in the making of a mortgage loan

Mortgage banker A mortgage company that (1) originates or underwrites mortgage loans with its own funds or, more likely, with a warehousing line of credit; (2) sells these loans in packages to secondary mortgage market investors; and (3) maintains a servicing arrangement for these investors

Loan servicing Term that includes collecting monthly principal, interest, taxes, and insurance payments for the secondary mortgage market investor; maintaining records for each loan; and handling any payment problems, even to the extent of handling a foreclosure, as agent of the investor

Mortgage warehouse loan A short-term line of credit, obtained by a mortgage banker, used to originate loans prior to their sale in the secondary mortgage market; the loans prior to sale are the security or collateral for the warehouse loan

Demand deposits Checking account deposits at commercial banks

Debt service Periodic payment of principal and interest on a real estate loan

At this point the reader should be comfortably knowledgeable of the development of mortgage law from the earliest of mortgages, or hypothecation documents, through the continuing battle of borrower redemption rights versus foreclosure rights and other lender remedies, to the elements of modern mortgage or deed of trust and promissory note or bond instruments. Furthermore, the reader should be reasonably knowledgeable of a virtual plethora of mortgage types. The reader has been exposed to mortgages categorized by (1) stage of property development, (2) financing method, (3) type of collateral, (4) priority of lien, (5) method of payment, and even (6) experimental mortgage proposals.

Chapters 12, 13, and 14 complete the section of the book dedicated to real estate finance by covering the following topics: (1) primary mortgage market lenders (Chapter 12), (2) secondary mortgage market investors (Chapter 13), and (3) mortgage lending (Chapter 14).

PRIMARY MORTGAGE MARKET VERSUS SECONDARY MORTGAGE MARKET

Mortgage markets are generally classified as either primary or secondary. The *primary mortgage market* consists of *lenders* who deal face-to-face with *borrowers* in making mortgage loans. The *secondary mortgage market* consists of *investors* who deal through *intermediaries* in making mortgage investments. An individual or legal entity may operate in *both* markets, making both direct loans and indirect investments.

The primary mortgage market participant is a direct source of funds for the mortgage borrower by being a lender who *originates* or underwrites the mortgage loan. The *mortgage loan underwriting process* may be defined as the investigation, analysis, and determination of the risks involved in the making of a mortgage loan. (This process is discussed in detail in Chapter 14). The mortgage risk analysis determines whether or not a loan will be made, and if so, under what terms it will be made.

The secondary mortgage market participant is an indirect source of funds for the mortgage borrower by being an investor who seeks employment of capital to earn a rate of return commensurate with the risk of an investment. Secondary mortgage market investors treat mortgages as investments in competition with other securities, such as stocks and bonds. They do not originate or underwrite mortgage loans; rather, they buy and sell mortgages much like a bond investor buys and sells bonds.

Secondary mortgage market investors provide a mechanism for primary mortgage market lenders to sell or to liquidate (turn into cash quickly, without a loss) their mortgage loans. By serving as a means by which primary mortgage market lenders can adjust their mortgage portfolios, the secondary market has not only enhanced the liquidity of mortgages, but also has increased the attractiveness of home mortgages as investments. Furthermore, the secondary mortgage market has facilitated the flow of mortgage funds from capital-surplus areas of the country to capital-shortage areas, thereby contributing to the efficient allocation of credit in the housing market and in the economy.

For example, a savings and loan association in a nongrowth part of the country may have savings which far exceed loan demand: a capital surplus. These excess savings need to be *invested* to earn a return out of which interest is paid to the savers. A purchase of mortgages in the secondary mortgage market will meet this need. A commercial bank in a growth part of the country may have loan demand which far exceeds savings: a capital shortage. The excess loan demand needs to be met to satisfy borrowers and to allow growth to continue. A sale of mortgages in the secondary mortgage market will meet these needs.

The savings and loan association in the capital-surplus area and the commercial bank in the capital-shortage area are participants in the secondary mortgage market buying and selling, respectively. However, note that each operates in the primary mortgage market when originating local loans. In other words, even the savings and loan association will make some loans to local area borrowers on a "face-to-face" basis.

PRIMARY MORTGAGE MARKET LENDERS

Primary mortgage market lenders include the following:

1. Savings and loan associations (S&Ls)
2. Mutual savings banks (MSBs)
3. Commercial banks (CBs)
4. Life insurance companies (LICs)
5. Mortgage companies
6. Real estate investment trusts (REITs)
7. Pension funds
8. Credit unions
9. Individual lenders
10. Government credit agencies

Sometimes the first four, plus pension funds, credit unions, and government credit agencies, are called the fiduciary sources for real estate finance. Mortgage companies and REITs are sometimes referred to as semifiduciary sources, while nonfiduciary refers to individual lenders.

Savings and Loan Associations (S&Ls)

For home mortgages, S&Ls are by far the largest and most important source of funds. They typically originate about 50 percent and hold slightly more than 50 percent of all one-to-four-family residential mortgages. Originally S&Ls were formed expressly to accumulate capital for building houses by having members make regular mandatory payments to the S&L. When enough capital was accumulated to make a loan, members were given an opportunity to bid for the loan. Thus the original purpose of

S&Ls was to meet the needs of borrowers. Today S&Ls are located in all 50 states; they are called *homestead associations* and *cooperative banks* in Louisiana and Massachusetts, respectively. In addition to home loans, which make up about 80 percent of the typical S&L portfolio, S&Ls make multifamily residential loans (9 percent of portfolio), commercial real estate loans (9 percent of portfolio), as well as some mobile home, home improvement, and educational loans (2 percent of portfolio).

Although the first S&L was formed in Philadelphia in 1831, national regulation and supervision of the industry did not come about until 1932, when Congress created the Federal Home Loan Bank System (FHLB). Today all nationally chartered S&Ls are controlled by the FHLB, as are most state-chartered S&Ls. In 1934 Congress created the Federal Savings and Loan Insurance Corporation (FSLIC) to insure public deposits against any loss up to a set limit per account ($40,000 as of 1978). Nearly all S&Ls belong to the FSLIC, and thereby enjoy great depositor confidence because of the insurance coverage.

The FHLB regulates the S&L industry by:

1. Controlling the amount or percentage of funds S&Ls cannot loan out and must therefore hold on reserve
2. Controlling the interest rate charged S&Ls to borrow from the FHLB
3. Controlling loan-to-value ratios, maximum loan terms, and maximum loan amounts on single-family dwellings (see Table 12-1)

In addition to the conventional loans shown in Table 12-1, S&Ls make loans insured by the Federal Housing Administration (FHA) or guaranteed by the Veterans Administration (VA) and, in so doing, comply with the appropriate rules and regulations of these government agencies.

TABLE 12-1. FHLB Regulations: Maximum Loan and Terms

Property Type	*Maximum Loan*	*Maximum Term*
Single family	$60,000 on 95 percent LTVR	30 years
	$75,000 on 90 percent LTVR	30 years
	no limit on 80 percent LTVR	30 years
Two-to-four family	80 percent LTVR	30 years
Five or more dwelling units	75 percent LTVR	25 years
Commercial property	75 percent LTVR	25 years
Developed building lot	75 percent LTVR	Individual—5 years Builder—3 years
Mobile homes	New—100 percent Manufacturer's invoice price	12 years
	Used—100 percent Wholesale value	8 years
Construction loans		3 years

Mutual Savings Banks (MSBs)

MSBs were originally formed (the first in 1816) to meet the needs of savers, especially poor factory workers. Today MSBs are located mainly in the northeastern states (almost 90 percent in New York, Massachusetts, Connecticut, New Jersey, and Pennsylvania) and in Washington and Oregon. They typically originate about 5 to 6 percent and hold about 10 percent of all one-to-four-family residential mortgages. Statistics indicate that nearly half of the loans that MSBs hold are purchased in the secondary mortgage market, and most of these are FHA and VA loans. In other words, MSBs are *net purchasers* of mortgages in the secondary mortgage market.

MSBs are state chartered but may be members of both the FHLB and the FSLIC. The typical portfolio of an MSB looks much like that of the typical S&L. However, MSBs are generally much more conservative in the implementation of lending policies and underwriting guidelines than are S&Ls.

Commercial Banks (CBs)

CBs are either state chartered or nationally chartered. If nationally chartered, a CB must be a member of the Federal Reserve Bank System (the Fed) and the Federal Deposit Insurance Corporation (FDIC). If state chartered, a CB is regulated by a state banking commission, unless it is also a member of the Fed or the FDIC, in which case it is regulated by the Fed or the FDIC, respectively.

CBs have been nationally regulated only since 1913, when Congress created the Fed. Because of differing regional economic interests, prior attempts to form a national banking system, in 1791 and 1816, failed. Since the first commercial bank was founded in 1781, it took 132 years for the United States to form a lasting national banking and bank regulation system.

CBs typically originate about 20 to 22 percent and hold about 15 to 16 percent of all one-to-four-family residential mortgages. In other words, CBs are *net sellers* of mortgages in the secondary mortgage market.

CBs were not created with the mortgage borrower in mind. They are general purpose or commercial lenders, primarily providing short-term loans to businesses for operations, inventory, and expansion, and to consumers for automobiles and consumer goods. Most of a CB's funds come from checking accounts, called demand deposits, because they can be drawn, as checks, for payment upon demand. Furthermore, regulations limit holdings of mortgage loans to no more than 70 percent of savings or 100 percent of equity capital; hence, real estate loans make up only about 15 to 17 percent of a typical CB portfolio. Not counted in the real estate portion of a CB portfolio are large amounts of short-term construction and land development loans, which are crucial to the creation of new real estate resources, especially in growth areas of the country.

In rural areas, CBs may be the only source of long-term mortgage financing. In these areas, it is typical for a larger portion of a CB's assets to be in savings deposits, since the competition with savings institutions for savings dollars may not be keen or may not even exist. Hence, rural CBs can handle a larger proportion of long-term loans. And since CBs tend to be net sellers of mortgages in the secondary mortgage market, such rural CBs are able to originate more loans than they choose to hold.

Finally, many CBs make mortgage lending possible by providing a short-term line of credit to mortgage bankers who "warehouse" mortgage loans at a CB in order to obtain the line of credit. Mortgage bankers draw on their CB credit lines to originate mortgage loans and simultaneously pledge these same mortgages to secure the credit lines until such time as they can accumulate a large package of loans, which they sell to an investor in the secondary mortgage market and thereby repay the CB. Hence, CB mortgage warehousing provides a very valuable service to primary mortgage market borrowers and secondary mortgage market investors.

Life Insurance Companies (LICs)

LICs are state chartered and state regulated. Today LICs typically originate only about .5 percent and hold about 3 to 4 percent of all one-to-four-family residential mortgages. Hence, like MSBs, LICs are net purchasers of mortgages (mostly FHA or VA) in the secondary mortgage market. Prior to the mid-1960s, LICs used to originate and hold nearly 20 percent of the one-to-four-family residential mortgages. Since then LICs have shifted out of the residential mortgage market into the larger, higher-yielding, commercial income-producing real estate mortgage market.

In the late 1960s and early 1970s LICs found they could demand a "piece of the action" of the commercial real estate projects on which they were making loans. In order to get the loan, the real estate developer was required to give the LICs an "equity participation" or "equity kicker" in addition to the principal and interest payment (debt service) on the loan. These equity kickers were usually a percentage of the gross or net income produced by the project.

The fact that LICs collect premiums during the entire lives of their policy holders, combined with the mathematical accuracy of actuarial calculations of mortality data, make LIC cash inflows and outflows quite predictable, and therefore ideally suited for long-term investments like stocks, bonds, and especially fully amortized mortgages. Most LICs are legally constrained to a 75 percent maximum LTVR and a 25- to 28-year maximum term.

Large LICs have a great deal of flexibility and can make loans in all parts of the nation through company branch offices and/or independent mortgage correspondents to originate and service such loans. The large LICs have considerable amounts of funds to invest and therefore seek to underwrite large loans for large commercial real estate projects. The developer in need of millions of dollars to build a regional shopping center, a high-rise downtown office building, an industrial park, or a large apartment complex will likely seek mortgage funds from a large LIC. In the area of one-to-four-family residential mortgages, the large LICs will invest in large mortgage packages consisting of perhaps a hundred or more loans assembled by a mortgage company, which services them for the large LIC. Typically these residential loan packages consist of FHA and VA loans, although conventional loan packages with private mortgage insurance have become quite acceptable since the late 1970s.

Mortgage Companies

Mortgage company is a term used to describe either a mortgage banker or a mortgage broker or both. A *mortgage banker* originates mortgage loans for a fee by completing the entire loan underwriting process. The money used to fund these loans may be the mortgage company's own funds, but they are more likely borrowed at the prime rate through a warehousing arrangement with a commercial bank. After the mortgage banker has accumulated a package of loans through warehousing, the loan package is sold to an investor in the secondary mortgage market, such as a LIC, MSB, S&L, or one of several governmental or quasigovernmental agencies. The proceeds from the sale in the secondary market provide funds to repay the warehouse line of credit at the commercial bank and, it is hoped, provide some profit as well to the mortgage banker. Once the loans are sold, the mortgage banker, for a fee, *services* the loans for the secondary mortgage market investor.

Loan servicing includes collecting the monthly principal, interest, taxes, and insurance payments for the secondary market investor, maintaining records for each loan, and handling any payment problems, even to the extent of handling a foreclosure, if necessary, as the investor's agent. The mortgage banker, as a loan servicing agent, takes an annual fee of .25 to .50 percent of the outstanding loan balance out of the principal and interest portion of the payment and forwards the balance to the investor. The property tax and hazard and/or mortgage insurance portions of the periodic payments are held by the mortgage banker in an escrow account (also called impound or reserve account) to be available when taxes and insurance premiums fall due, at which time the mortgage banker tenders payment.

Implied in this description of mortgage banking are five sources of income for the mortgage banker:

1. The loan origination fee of 2 to 4 percent of the loan amount
2. A spread of possibly 1 to 3 percent between the prime rate, which

the mortgage banker *pays* for the warehousing line of credit, and the mortgage interest rate, which the mortgage banker *collects* on the mortgages while they are warehoused, before the sale of a mortgage package to an investor

3. The profit earned on the sale of the mortgage package, if sold at a premium; if sold at a discount the mortgage banker would lose on the sale (premiums are possible when the interest rate sought by the investor is lower than the interest rate on the mortgage package; discounts result when the opposite is the case)
4. The loan servicing fee of .25 to .50 percent
5. The interest earned on the property tax and hazard and/or mortgage insurance escrow or reserve accounts

A *mortgage broker* does not have all the possible sources of income available to a mortgage banker. A mortgage broker arranges (rather than originates) mortgage loans by bringing together borrower and lender, and collects a fee or commission for so doing. A mortgage broker does *not* make loans, either with his or her own funds or with borrowed funds. A mortgage broker does not service loans either; he or she is simply a commission-earning middleperson between borrower and lender. One can do both mortgage banking and mortgage brokering within the same company or firm. Hence, such a firm may be called a *mortgage company*; although one which does only mortgage banking or only mortgage brokering may also be described as a mortgage company.

Mortgage companies typically handle nearly 20 percent of all one-to-four-family loan originations, yet only hold about 1 percent of these loans. Obviously, mortgage companies are very much net sellers in the secondary mortgage market, providing investors with a huge supply of mortgage investments to purchase. Although mortgage companies hold only a very small portion of mortgage investments, they are a very important and crucial catalyst in the mortgage financing industry.

Real Estate Investment Trusts

Most of today's real estate investment trusts (REITs) are the result of a 1960 amendment to the Internal Revenue Code—Sections 856, 857, and 858—which provided REITs with certain tax advantages similar to those available to mutual funds since 1940. Essentially, if REITs follow strict financial and investment regulations, profits distributed to their shareholders are not taxed at the corporate level, and are therefore "passed through" directly to the shareholders, who pay tax on these profits at the individual level only. Thus a REIT is a tax conduit through which profits may pass to small investors. Basically, the investment regulations force REITs to invest most of their money in real estate equities and/or mortgages. In fact, those that specialize in owning buildings to collect rent are termed "equity REITs"; those that specialize in making mortgage loans to collect interest are termed "mortgage REITs"; and those that invest in both equities and mortgages are termed "hybrid REITs."

Through the sale of REIT shares in denominations as low as $1 to $10, REITs allow the small investor the opportunity to invest in large, professionally managed real estate projects. The "piece of the rock" theory is truly applied here. Like the mutual fund shareholder who obtains an interest in a large, fully diversified portfolio of stocks and bonds, the REIT shareholder obtains the benefits of diversification by owning a "piece of the rock" in the form of either buildings or loans secured by buildings. REITs are today a $20 billion dollar industry, with about 80 to 82 percent of their assets invested in mortgages and 18 to 20 percent in property ownership.

Pension Funds

Pension funds act as trustees for funds accumulated over the working lives of employees to provide income for their retirement. Historically, pension funds have been very conservative, investing most of their money in high-grade government securities and blue-chip corporate stocks and bonds. Although pension funds are not regulated at either the federal or state level, they have followed the so-called prudent-man rule, which means they must exercise the judgment and care in investment decision making which a reasonable and wise person would intelligently exercise in personal investment decisions and other personal affairs of monetary consequence.

However, since the early and mid-1970s there has been a trend toward placing more pension fund money into real estate loans. Poor stock market performance, rapid growth in pension fund capital, maximum investment flexibility, and aggressive mortgage bankers have combined to change the thinking of many pension fund managers. The specialized talents and services of mortgage bankers, the liquidity offered by the secondary mortgage market, and the mortgage-backed "pass-through" securities programs guaranteed by the U.S. government and large private institutions have all helped to overcome the reluctance of pension funds to participate in mortgage investments. All indications are that pension funds will likely become a major source of real estate financing in the future. Since their hold and control on assets is very long-term, similar to LICs, some experts are predicting their growth to approach the magnitude of the mortgage business presently done by LICs, roughly $300 billion.

Credit Unions

Credit unions have generally been founded in order to provide cheap credit and encourage savings among individuals sharing a common bond, such as employment. Depositors own a credit union by holding shares in proportion to their savings, and are paid dividends, rather than interest, as their share of the profits each year. Credit unions have traditionally specialized in consumer loans for automobile and household-appliance purchases by their depositors. However, since 1977 credit unions have begun to expand into traditional commercial banking areas. In April 1977 President Carter signed Public Law 95-22, which extends to credit unions such banking functions as long-term mortgage lending, savings certificates, credit cards, and even checking accounts that pay dividends. The checking account function was immediately attacked in the courts by the American Bankers Association, and the issue is yet to be resolved at the time of this writing (1978).

The new legislation applies to the 13,000 federally chartered credit unions; many of the 10,000 state-chartered credit unions already had much of the new flexibility. The National Credit Union Administration, a federal government agency, regulates the federally chartered credit unions and also provides deposit insurance of $40,000 per account. Most state-chartered credit unions are regulated by state banking commissions.

A special sort of credit union, spawned in the late 1960s as part of the Office of Economic Opportunity's war on poverty, are the so-called community development credit unions (CDCUs). CDCUs are chartered (both state and federal) in low-income urban and rural neighborhoods. Many religious and social organizations place large amounts of money in CDCUs. In some poor neighborhoods CDCUs have become the largest or primary mortgage lender. Public Law 95-22 allows mortgage loans in amounts up to 150 percent of the local area's median sale price of a home, with terms up to 30 years. The law also allows mobile home loans with terms up to 15 years.

Individual Lenders

Individual lender loans include loans made by friends and relatives, trustees of personal trusts and estates, managers of endowment and corporate funds, and fraternal and other not-for-profit organizations. Although individual lenders provide only a small minority of total mortgage funds, they are the largest source of junior mortgage loans. For example, many a seller will carry-back a purchase money mortgage in order to consummate a sale. Such lenders are called "unintentional investors," since it is not their prime activity to be active in the lending market. The great majority of individual lender mortgages are secured by one-to-four-family residences.

Individual lenders follow no particular or typical lending practices. They are virtually totally unregulated and as a result often take greater risks and charge higher interest rates than institutional lenders. However, individual lenders are not competitive with institutional lenders in securing prime mortgage loans, primarily because of the economies of scale enjoyed by the large institutional lenders.

Government Credit Agencies

The government, through a variety of agencies, affects real estate financing in the following six general ways:

1. Controlling money and credit through the Federal Reserve Bank System and the Federal Home Loan Bank System
2. Insuring deposits through the Federal Deposit Insurance Corporation and the Federal Savings and Loan Insurance Corporation
3. Insuring or guaranteeing mortgages through the Federal Housing Administration and the Veterans Administration
4. Operating in the secondary mortgage market through the Federal National Mortgage Association, the Government National Mortgage Association, and the Federal Home Loan Mortgage Corporation
5. Lending to farmers, ranchers, and rural homeowners through the Cooperative Farm Credit System and the Farmers Home Administration
6. Providing public housing through the Department of Housing and Urban Development

Items (1) and (2) have already been discussed in this chapter; items (3) and (4) were discussed in Chapter 11; and items (5) and (6) are discussed below.

Cooperative Farm Credit System. The Federal Farm Loan Act of 1916 created the Cooperative Farm Credit System, consisting of a nationwide system of 12 districts to serve the various financial needs of farmers, ranchers, rural homeowners, and some specified farm- and ranch-related businesses. The system is regulated by the Farm Credit Administration in Washington, D.C. Each of the 12 districts contains the following federal credit agencies:

1. Federal Land Bank
2. Federal Land Bank Associations
3. Federal Intermediate Credit Banks
4. Production Credit Associations
5. Banks for Cooperatives

The *Federal Land Bank System* was established in 1917 by Congress in a manner similar to the Federal Reserve Bank System and the Federal Home Loan Bank System (created by Congress in 1913 and 1932, respectively). This system makes loans through over 500 *Federal Land Bank Associations*, which own the 12 Federal Land Banks.

The types of loans made include mortgage loans (1) to purchase farms, nonfarm rural homes, farm land, machinery, equipment, and livestock; (2) for refinancing, (3) for construction and repair of farm buildings, and (4) for farm-related businesses. These loans have a maximum 85 percent LTVR, 5- to 40-year terms, variable interest rates, and payment plans especially tailored to each borrower's particular situation. Farmers and ranchers typically have unusual and erratic cash-flow positions because of weather and other natural forces which require maximum flexibility in financing arrangements.

The *Federal Intermediate Credit Banks* were created in 1923 to provide a secondary market for farm and ranch loans. These banks also make short-term (intermediate) loans to finance the seasonal, operational, production, and marketing activities of farming and ranching.

The Farm Credit Act of 1933 authorized farmers and ranchers to form local cooperative *Production Credit Associations* to make short and intermediate (a few months to seven years) direct loans to its members. These loans are for operations capital and other production needs and are either unsecured or secured by livestock, crops, and machinery. The loans are sold through a discounting process in the secondary market provided by the Federal Intermediate Credit Banks.

The *Banks for Cooperatives* is a 13-bank national system, one in each of the 12 Farm Credit districts, plus a central bank located in Denver, Colorado. Each district bank makes seasonal and short-term loans to marketing, supply, and business cooperatives for farmers and ranchers within its own district, and the central bank participates with the district banks in making very large loans to farm and ranch cooperatives.

The Farmers Home Administration. In 1946 the Farmers Home Administration (FmHA) was created to make and insure loans to farmers and ranchers unable to secure credit elsewhere. Regulated and supervised by the Farm Credit Administration, FmHA makes farm ownership loans accompanied by technical management assistance to farmers and ranchers who are or will become operators of family farms. The loans are either advanced by private lenders and insured by FmHA or made directly by FmHA with congressionally authorized funds.

When there are no available FHA 235 and 236 funds to finance low-rent housing in rural communities for eligible low- and moderate-income tenants, FmHA will provide grants to finance such housing facilities. The largest part of FmHA's activities involves making loans in rural areas to finance homes and building lots, with emphasis on new construction. A rural area is defined by FmHA to consist of not more than 10,000 people not closely associated with an urban area.

In addition, FmHA provides financing for rural improvement projects such as water- and waste-disposal systems, parks, and recreational areas for hiking, camping, fishing, and hunting. Finally, FmHA can make loans in disaster areas declared by state governors, the secretary of agriculture, or the president.

Department of Housing and Urban Development. The Department of Housing and Urban Development (HUD) was created in 1965 by combining several federal housing agencies. HUD's roots go back to the U.S. Housing Authority, created in 1937 to administer loans and grants to local housing agencies for slum clearance and neighborhood rehabilitation, with the objective of providing a decent home and suitable living environment for each American. Between 1937 and 1965 other agencies involved with public housing were absorbed by the U.S. Housing Authority. Today, as part of HUD, the Housing Assistance Administration, also referred to as the Public Housing Administration (PHA), administers public housing and other special subsidy programs. The PHA usually either provides loans to finance preliminary development or makes annual contributions to permit operation of projects at rent levels affordable by the tenants. Usually FHA insurance or other government guarantees are used to remove risk from such projects, in order to entice private developers to enter public housing ventures which can be both profitable and socially beneficial.

HUD also administers urban renewal and rehabilitation projects. HUD aid for these projects may be:

1. Funds for surveys and studies of a proposed project
2. Temporary loans for slum acquisition, clearance, and redevelopment
3. Grants to help cover cost differentials between acquisition and rehabilitation of land and the eventual sale to private investors for development

Funds for up to 50 percent of the costs to acquire, preserve, and develop land for parks, recreation, scenic and/or historic uses may be provided to communities through HUD's Open Space Land Grants. The HUD Model Cities Program, under the Demonstration Cities and Metropolitan Development Act of 1966, provides loans and grants to cities for the planning and development of special prototype improvement projects for analysis and possible use in other cities. Finally, under the New Communities Act of 1968, HUD makes government guarantees available on loans to developers of up to $50 million per project for the land acquisition, development, and construction of totally preplanned "new town" communities, which balance residential, commercial, industrial, and recreational development. Flower Mound, Texas; Soul City, North Carolina; Jonathon, Minnesota; and Shenandoah, Georgia are well-known examples of HUD-sponsored new towns.

State Credit Agencies. Some states have created agencies, much like HUD on the national level, to provide financial assistance for real estate development at the state level. Generally, such agencies are either industrial development organizations or local housing authorities.

The industrial development groups purchase and improve land for industrial and office parks used to entice new industries and corporations to locate in given areas. The state's bonding authority is used to issue revenue bonds to finance this activity. The obvious goal of such groups is to stimulate community growth and expand the economic base, employment opportunities, population, and commercial activity in the designated cities of a state.

The local housing authorities are usually created either as a requirement of, or to work in tandem with, the federal housing assistance programs. Some states, however, have created their own special real estate mortgage insurance programs and/or their own direct loan programs, some only for veterans and some for anyone meeting the loan qualifications.

SUMMARY AND CONCLUSION

There are many sources of mortgage money in the primary mortgage market. Sometimes the term "institutional lenders" is used to refer to S&Ls, MSBs, CBs, and LICs. The fiduciary sources for real estate finance include the four institutional lenders and pension funds, credit unions, and government credit agencies. Semi-fiduciary sources of mortgage money are mortgage companies and REITs. Non-fiduciary sources are individual lenders.

Government credit agencies also either supply or aid the supply of funds to the primary mortgage market in a variety of ways. The Cooperative Farm Credit System and the Farmers Home Administration serve the financial needs of farmers, ranchers, rural homeowners, and certain farm- and ranch-related businesses. The Department of Housing and Urban Development's programs are so vast, far reaching, and important that HUD has Cabinet-level status in the federal government. Many states have created real estate financing agencies to aid the expansion and growth of industrial, commercial, and residential development within their borders.

CHAPTER 13

Secondary Mortgage Market Investors and The Impact of Monetary and Fiscal Policies on the Mortgage Market

KEY TERMS

Money market The market for short-term borrowing and lending

Capital market The market for long-term borrowing and lending

Fiscal policy Policy that consists of the actions of the federal government, including the collection of funds by taxation and the spending of funds by the federal budget

Deficit budget The phenomenon that exists when the federal government spends more than it taxes

Monetary policy Policy that consists of the actions of the Board of Governors of the Federal Reserve Banking System to control, monitor, and change the supply and price of money and credit within the economy

Crowding-out effect Situation that occurs when the demand for loanable funds is high because of deficit budget financing and an expansionary economy and the mortgage borrower is often outbid or "crowded out" by the federal government and corporations for the available loanable funds in tight money and capital markets

Disintermediation Condition that exists when the supply of loanable funds at financial intermediaries declines because savings are withdrawn to be invested directly in government securities, which offer high yields in order to attract the loanable funds required to finance deficit federal budgets

Monetization of the debt Situation that exists when deficit budgets are financed by the sale of government securities to the Federal Reserve Banking System, which "pays" for the securities with "new money" created by increasing the checking account balance of the Treasury at the Federal Reserve

"Printing press effect" Term for the creation of "new money" by monetization of the debt, an action that is purely inflationary

Inflation An increase in the volume of money and credit without a comparable increase in productivity and/or output, resulting in a rise in the general level of prices

HISTORICAL DEVELOPMENT OF THE SECONDARY MORTGAGE MARKET

As stated in Chapter 12, the secondary mortgage market consists of investors who deal through intermediaries in making mortgage investments, and in so doing are an indirect source of funds for the mortgage borrower. In addition, the secondary mortgage market is a mechanism which allows the transfer of mortgage funds from capital-surplus areas to capital-shortage areas by providing a national market for the purchase and sale of home mortgages by institutional investors. It is the liquidity of this market that has enhanced the attractiveness of mortgages as investments and has provided the housing industry a means of leveling out the peaks and valleys of available home financing through an efficient allocation of credit.

The "mortgage brokers" and "mortgage bankers" of the 1800s and early 1900s were the creators of the secondary mortgage market. The first mortgage brokers were lawyers and real estate brokers who arranged loans for their clients with interested investors in order to ensure the close of the real estate transactions in which they were involved. Eventually, these "loan arranger" lawyers and real estate brokers became known as the persons to see when money was needed for a real estate loan. For some, loan arranging became so time consuming that they started doing it full time for a fee. The first mortgage bankers were the mortgage brokers who started lending their own funds to borrowers and then either kept these loans in their own portfolios or sold them to interested investors.

This early secondary market was far from efficient and not truly national. It was not until President Roosevelt's New Deal of the 1930s that a truly national secondary mortgage market developed. During the Great Depression millions of mortgage loans were foreclosed, totally souring traditional primary mortgage market lenders on making any more mortgage loans. The New Deal's first action aimed at this foreclosure problem was taken in 1933, when the Home Owners Loan Corporation (HOLC) was formed to refinance the foreclosed loans with funds raised by issuing government-guaranteed bonds. Well over a million loans were refinanced by the HOLC.

The New Deal next created the Federal Housing Administration (1934), which offered governmental mutual mortgage insurance (MMI) on loans made by traditional lenders complying with FHA loan regulations. The idea was to remove the risks of mortgage lending, thereby enticing lenders back into the mortgage market. Furthermore, in 1935 the Reconstruction Finance Corporation (RFC) established the RFC Mortgage Company to aid in the establishment of a "national mortgage market." The RFC Mortgage Company was authorized to buy FHA-insured mortgage loans. However, lenders at that time did not accept the FHA-insured loan concept and resisted governmental intervention into their part of the private enterprise system.

The federal government was not about to give up, and the RFC created yet another entity to function as a secondary mortgage market, one that is most relevant today.

THE SECONDARY MORTGAGE MARKET OF TODAY

Federal National Mortgage Association

In 1938 the Federal National Mortgage Association (FNMA), popularly known as "Fannie Mae," was created by the RFC as a standby organization to give relief in time of emergency by buying FHA-insured (and since 1948, VA) loans. Traditional lenders, who were resisting the FHA concept, were thus offered a place to liquidate the government-sponsored loans they disliked so much. FNMA's functions were defined as "maintaining an active market for insured mortgages and a steady flow of mortgage money at relatively favorable interest rates and of providing an avenue of investment for individuals and institutions heretofore unable to benefit directly from the insured mortgage program."

The secondary mortgage market had arrived! Between FHA and FNMA, and in 1944 the Veterans Administration's Home Loan Guarantee Program, the secondary mortgage market blossomed. And since traditional lenders continued to shun governmental intervention and red tape, the opportunity was ripe for mortgage bankers to specialize in FHA and VA loans. The mortgage banking business was booming, especially after more than 5 million veterans returned home with VA benefits. The tremendous pent-up demand for housing, combined with the fact that life insurance companies were bursting at the seams with ready cash for mortgage loans, added to the boom. In fact, over 60 percent of today's mortgage companies were established since 1944.

During periods of tight credit FNMA would *purchase* blocks of mortgages from lenders, thus easing the tight credit situation by providing these lenders with additional funds to originate new mortgage loans. During periods of easy credit FNMA would *sell* blocks of mortgages to lenders, thus tightening the easy credit situation by absorbing excess funds that could lead to overbuilding in the various real estate markets.

In 1954, Congress rechartered FNMA with three separate operations, providing for (1) a secondary mortgage market for FHA and VA loans, (2) special assistance for housing financing programs, and (3) management and liquidation of the mortage portfolio existing from the previous charter.

During the 1950s and 1960s criticisms were levied at the policies and functions of FNMA. These criticisms included the following:

1. No provision for a secondary market for conventional mortgage loans
2. Too much emphasis on new construction

3. Purchases, sales volume, and timing politically, rather than economically, motivated
4. Too much emphasis on purchasing loans in risky areas and a tremendous lack of power to reject bad loans, causing FNMA to be too much of a subsidy operation

In order to meet some of these criticisms, but mostly to bolster the lagging housing industry in 1968, Congress ordered, by the Housing and Urban Development Act of 1968, FNMA to split into two separate entities: (1) FNMA, which would eventually be privately owned and (2) the Government National Mortgage Association (GNMA) popularly called "Ginnie Mae," which would remain government owned.

Of the three FNMA operations provided for in the 1954 charter, only the first, providing liquidity to the secondary mortgage market, was retained by FNMA in the 1968 split. GNMA took over the other two operations—special assistance for the federal housing programs and the management and liquidation of the FNMA portfolio. In 1972, FNMA began dealing in conventional loans insured by private mortgage insurance, as well as FHA and VA loans.

FNMA funds for operations come from the sale of preferred stock sold to the U.S. Treasury and from the sale of common stock and bonds to the public over the New York Stock Exchange and to lenders who sell loans to FNMA. Sellers of loans to FNMA are required to buy FNMA stock whenever they sell loans to FNMA.

FNMA also has a $2.5 billion line of credit with the U.S. Treasury if it ever needs to borrow more funds to operate efficiently in the secondary mortgage market. Hence, FNMA is not a totally private corporation; it is quasigovernmental. FNMA is a *private* corporation with a *public* purpose.

FNMA is the nation's largest single purchaser of residential mortgages. Biweekly announcements are made by FNMA informing all eligible sellers of the funds FNMA has available to purchase loans. These sellers bid for FNMA commitments to purchase loans by bidding an interest rate at which they would like to deliver loans to FNMA over a specified future time period. The results of the bidding at these so-called free market auctions provide one indication of mortgage interest rate trends.

Government National Mortgage Association

The Government National Mortgage Association (GNMA) took on the special assistance and mortgage portfolio operations of FNMA in 1968. Today GNMA subsidizes the financing of over twenty special assistance programs for military housing, low and middle-income housing, housing for the elderly, and other housing programs that have little appeal to private investors because of poor borrower credit, high mortgage risk locations, and/or the presence of adverse economic conditions.

One such subsidy program is the so-called tandem plan wherein GNMA works in tandem with FNMA. GNMA makes a commitment to a traditional lender to purchase below-market interest rate loans at par, or the full amount loaned, to induce the lender to make the loan at the low rate. GNMA then sells these loans to FNMA at the market price, which will be substantially lower than what GNMA paid for the loans. This discounted resale price results because of the interest rate differential between the below-market rate being paid by the borrower and the market rate return required by FNMA. This discount loss is absorbed (subsidized) by GNMA in order to provide low interest rate loans to certain borrowers.

Perhaps GNMA's greatest contribution to making mortgage credit available is provided by its *mortgage-backed securities program*. Under this program GNMA attracts capital to the mortgage market from institutional and individual investors by selling them securities which are backed or secured by blocks or pools of mortgages in the GNMA portfolio. Payment of interest *and principal* on these securities is guaranteed by GNMA and the full faith and credit of the United States government, since GNMA is part of HUD. Most of these securities, and therefore indirectly most of the GNMA mortgage portfolio, are owned by the private institutional and individual investors.

Federal Home Loan Mortgage Corporation

The Federal Home Loan Mortgage Corporation (FHLMC), popularly known as "Freddie Mac," was created in 1970 by the Federal Home Loan Bank Board as a wholly owned subsidiary of the Federal Home Loan Bank System. FHLMC's primary purpose was to create a secondary mortgage market for lender members of the FHLB system for conventional mortgage loans insured by private mortgage insurance. This market was to parallel the market for FHA-insured and VA-guaranteed mortgages which S&Ls traditionally have preferred not to originate. The FHLMC, however, deals in FHA and VA loans in the secondary mortgage market in addition to conventional loans.

The FHLMC *purchases* conventional home loans under two programs: (1) the Whole Loan Program and (2) the Class B Participation Program. In the first program, individual loans are purchased in \$100,000 to \$5 million packages; in the second program, undivided interests of 50 to 85 percent of a pool of loans are purchased in \$100,000 to \$5 million contracts. The FHLMC *sells* loans by means of mortgage participation certificates (PCs) and guaranteed mortgage certificates (GMCs). PCs represent an undivided interest in conventional mortgages individually underwritten and previously purchased by the FHLMC and are sold to thrift institutions, such as S&Ls. GMCs also represent an undivided interest in conventionals, but are sold through securities dealers to investors who traditionally do not invest in mortgages. The principal and interest payments to the investors are guaranteed by the FHLMC. The FHLMC finances its secondary mortgage market operations through the sale of stock to the 12 Federal Home Loan Banks and the sale of bonds and notes in the open market.

Private Mortgage Corporations

Mortgage Guaranty Insurance Corporation of Milwaukee, Wisconsin, the first private mortgage insurance corporation, also created the first private mortgage corporation (PMC) to buy and sell mortgages in the secondary mortgage market, adding yet another dimension of liquidity to this market. The name chosen for this first PMC was Mortgage Guarantee Mortgage Corporation (MGMC), better known as "Maggie Mae." MGMC and all other PMCs, as a group, are referred to as Maggie Mae. The purpose of the Maggie Mae market, like the other Maes, is to attract investors who might not otherwise invest in mortgage loans. The participants in the Maggie Mae market, however, are not governmental or even quasigovernmental; they are all members of the economy's private sector.

The private sector also entered the market of mortgage-backed pass-through securities and mortgage-backed bonds for the first time in 1977. The Bank of America in California, First Federal of Chicago, and other lenders successfully issued over $1 billion of such securities in 1977. These securities are not obligations of the issuer itself, but rather are secured by conventional mortgages insured by private mortgage insurance. Since the market for this new investment vehicle is backed by conventional loans, it has been dubbed the "Connie Mac" market. It has been determined by some experts that the capital raised through the Connie Mac market comes largely from new sources and is not, therefore, money that would have ended up in S&Ls and other thrift institutions. In 1977, 60 percent or more of this money came from pension funds, retirement funds, and life insurance companies. Private enterprise has provided yet another way of channeling investment capital into the secondary mortgage market, which adds even more liquidity and marketability to mortgage investments.

SUMMARY AND FUTURE OF THE SECONDARY MORTGAGE MARKET

To summarize, it can be noted that the secondary mortgage market can be grouped into the following three categories.

1. Federal agencies (FNMA, GNMA, and FHLMC) directly buying from loan originators and selling to investors
2. Federally sponsored and guaranteed pools which use pass-through mortgage-backed securities to attract investor capital
3. Private financial institutions, mortgage companies, and individual investors, who mainly consist of primary mortgage market participants

TABLE 13-1. Originations and Holdings

One-to-Four-Family Residential Mortgages 1970–1976

	Originations Yearly Average: 1970–1976		*Holdings December 31, 1976*	
Lender Group	*$ Billion*	*Percent*	*$ Billion*	*Percent*
Federal credit agencies	2.2	3.1	36.6	7.5
Federal-sponsored pools	0.0	0.0	41.9	8.6
Private sector:	69.8	96.9	411.4	84.0
Commercial banks	15.6	21.7	77.5	15.8
Mutual savings banks	4.5	6.2	52.4	10.7
Savings & loan associations	35.8	49.7	253.5	51.7
Life insurance companies	0.4	0.5	15.5	3.2
Mortgage companies	12.8	17.8	4.2	0.9
Others	0.7	1.0	8.4	1.7
Total	72.0	100.0	489.9	100.0

Source: Peggy Brockschmidt, "The Secondary Market for Home Mortgages," *Monthly Review*, Federal Reserve Bank of Kansas City (September–October 1977), p. 12.

Of these three groups, the federal credit agencies and pools tend to be net buyers in the secondary market, and the nonpool private sector tends to be a net seller. However, within the private sector, some institutions are almost always net buyers, while others are almost always net sellers. Those in the capital-surplus parts of the United States (Northeast and Southeast, usually) are generally the net buyers, and those in the capital-shortage areas (West and Southwest) are the net sellers. Study Table 13-1 to understand clearly these net positions.

Typically, the nonpool private sector is considered the most important group of participants on both sides of the market. On the buying side, the private sector accounts for almost half of the purchases, while the federal agencies and pools share equally in the other half. On the selling side, the private sector accounts for about 80 percent of total sales, while the federal agencies and pools account for about 18 percent and 2 percent, respectively.[1] The recent growth of all three sectors of the secondary mortgage market is portrayed in Table 13-2.

The four-year period from 1973 to 1976 shows a 90 percent increase in purchases. Two factors are primarily responsible for this rapid growth:

1. Peggy Brockschmidt, "The Secondary Market for Home Mortgages," *Monthly Review*, Federal Reserve Bank of Kansas City (September–October 1977), p. 13.

TABLE 13-2. Secondary Mortgage Market Purchases

One-to-Four-Family Residential Mortgages 1970–1976

	Total Purchases	Federal Credit Agencies		Federally Sponsored Pools		Private Sector	
Year	*$ Billion*	*$ Billion*	*Percent*	*$ Billion*	*Percent*	*$ Billion*	*Percent*
1970	13.4	5.4	40.1	1.8	13.7	6.2	46.2
1971	18.3	3.7	20.4	3.9	21.6	10.6	58.0
1972	25.1	5.0	19.9	4.8	19.0	15.3	61.1
1973	22.6	7.4	32.8	4.2	18.5	11.0	48.7
1974	23.0	8.8	38.2	6.3	27.4	7.9	34.5
1975	31.9	10.7	33.6	11.2	34.9	10.0	31.4
1976	42.8	9.6	22.3	16.4	38.4	16.8	39.3
Yearly average	25.3	7.2	28.6	6.9	27.5	11.1	44.0

Source: Peggy Brockschmidt, "The Secondary Market for Home Mortgages," *Monthly Review*, Federal Reserve Bank of Kansas City (September–October 1977), p. 13.

TABLE 13-3. Federal Agency Participation

One-to-Four-Family Secondary Mortgage Market 1970–1976

	Yearly Average: 1970–1976					
	Purchases		*Sales*		*Net Purchases (Sales)*	*December 31, 1976 Holdings*
Agency	*$ Billion*	*Percent of market*	*$ Billion*	*Percent of market*	*$ Billion*	*$ Billion*
FNMA	3.7	14.7	0.0	0.2	3.7	26.9
GNMA	1.9	7.7	1.9	7.8	0.0	2.0
FHLMC	1.1	4.4	0.4	1.8	0.7	3.9
FmHA	0.4	1.5	1.8	7.4	(1.5)	0.5
Total	7.2	28.6	4.5	18.3	2.7	36.6

Source: Peggy Brockschmidt, "The Secondary Market for Home Mortgages," *Monthly Review*, Federal Reserve Bank of Kansas City (September–October 1977), p. 15.

1. Federally sponsored mortgage pools, whose purchases went from \$1.8 billion in 1970 to \$16.4 billion in 1976[2]
2. Transactions involving conventional mortgages insured by private mortgage insurance (PMI), whose purchases went from \$2.8 billion in 1970 to \$20.1 billion in 1976, due primarily to the PMI and the authorization of federal agency purchases, which rose from \$0.1 billion in 1970 to \$7 billion in 1976.[3]

Tables 13-3 through 13-5 indicate the transaction magnitudes of the three categories of secondary mortgage market participants.

To summarize the recent growth and future potential of the secondary mortgage market, the following comments can be made. For the period 1970 to 1976, activity in the secondary mortgage market nearly tripled. Since 1973, the growth of this market has been double that of the primary market. The GNMA pass-through security has enabled mortgage investors to circumvent most of the administrative difficulties associated with mortgage originations, thereby opening up a new source of funds for FHA and VA loans. The FHLMC mortgage participation programs have done the same for conventional loans. The private sector's mortgage-backed securities programs have been and should continue to be successful in attracting more new money to the secondary mortgage market. PMI has been instrumental in the growth of the conventional loan side of the market. These innovative ideas, and ideas yet to come, should further stimulate the growth of the secondary mortgage market for many years.

TABLE 13-4. Federally Sponsored Pool Participation

One-to-Four-Family Secondary Mortgage Market
Yearly Average: 1970–1976

	Purchases		*Sales*		*Net Purchases (Sales)*
Pool	*\$ Billion*	*Percent of market*	*\$ Billion*	*Percent of market*	*\$ Billion*
GNMA	4.7	18.6	0.0	0.0	4.7
FHLMC	0.4	1.6	0.0	0.0	0.4
FmHA	1.8	7.2	0.4	1.5	1.5
Total	6.9	27.5	0.4	1.5	6.6

Source: Peggy Brockschmidt, "The Secondary Market for Home Mortgages," *Monthly Review*, Federal Reserve Bank of Kansas City (September–October 1977), p. 19.

2. Ibid., p. 14.
3. Ibid.

TABLE 13-5. Private Participation

One-to-Four-Family Secondary Mortgage Market
Yearly Average 1970–1976

Lender Group	*Purchases* $ Billion	*Purchases* Percent of market	*Sales* $ Billion	*Sales* Percent of market	*Net Purchases (Sales)* $ Billion
Commercial banks	0.7	2.8	2.3	9.3	(1.6)
Mutual savings banks	1.7	6,9	0.2	1.0	1.5
Savings & loan associations	6.9	27.4	3.4	13.6	3.6
Life insurance companies	0.2	0.7	0.0	0.0	0.2
Mortgage companies	1.0	4.0	13.7	55.5	(12.7)
Others	0.5	2.1	0.2	0.7	0.4
Total	11.1	44.0	19.8	80.2	(8.7)

Source: Peggy Brockschmidt, "The Secondary Market for Home Mortgages," *Monthly Review*, Federal Reserve Bank of Kansas City (September–October 1977), p. 19.

THE IMPACT OF MONETARY AND FISCAL POLICIES ON THE MORTGAGE MARKETS

As discussed in Chapter 10, today most people *must* borrow money in order to own real estate. As the United States' population grows and income levels rise, the demand for mortgage money increases continually. For example, in the nineteenth century, only about one-third of American families owned homes, whereas today more than two-thirds own or are buying their own homes. The demand for mortgage money or real estate credit is a subset of the total demand for funds in the money and capital markets.

The *money market* consists of *short-term* borrowing and lending, such as treasury bills of the United States government, state and local government short-term borrowing, the commercial paper market of private corporations, the federal funds market of commercial banks, consumer financing, and construction loans for real estate development. The *capital market* consists of *long-term* borrowing and lending such as treasury and state and local government bonds, corporate stocks and bonds, and permanent mortgage financing. Hence, mortgage borrowers and investors vigorously compete to get their share of the total loanable funds within the economic system. This competition can be quite fierce.

Loanable Funds Totem Pole

There exists what one might call the borrowing "totem pole" or "pecking order." The borrower who is willing to pay the highest price or interest rate is always at the top, making first claim on the available loanable funds. The United States government is generally conceded this top position, since the Treasury can borrow with virtually no limits on the interest rate. High interest rates can always be paid by either raising taxes or borrowing more money (selling yet more government securities). Large corporations usually hold second position on the borrowing totem pole because they generally can pass on the high interest costs by raising the prices of their products. Such is true as long as demand for the products is strong and the competition is in relatively the same economic and financial position. Furthermore, large corporations generate cash of their own through profits and depreciation allowances, they enjoy preferred access to banks loaning at the low prime rate, and they can even bypass the banks by borrowing from one another in the so-called commercial paper market.

Perhaps consumers appear as holding third position in the borrowing pecking order, since they are willing to pay a relatively high rate of interest in good times and bad, since their borrowing is usually short term and often based on the inflation psychology, which suggests buying now to beat the

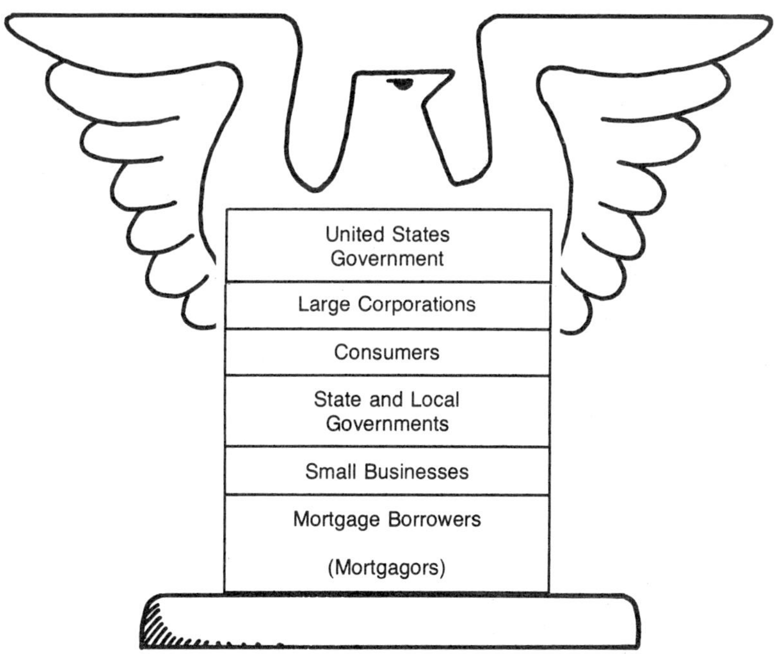

Figure 13-1. Borrowing Totem Pole

anticipated higher inflationary prices later. Fourth on the totem pole might be state and local governments, since the interest they pay is nontaxable or "tax-free" to the investor supplying these funds. This feature tends to attract loanable funds from investors in high tax brackets. Next in line may be small businesses with limited resources and weak lines of credit. At the very bottom of the totem pole sits the mortgage borrower, who is either unwilling or unable to pay a high interest rate.

In the residential owner-occupied sector of the mortgage market there is usually an interest rate that creates a psychological barrier which makes the potential homeowner *unwilling* to borrow and likely to postpone the home purchase to "when rates come down again." Whether or not rates ever do come down, this psychological phenomenon can cause erratic movements in the demand for mortgage money. For example, when the interest rate reaches this level (say 10 percent in the 1970s or as low as 7 or 8 percent in the early 1960s), demand for mortgage money all but disappears. If the rate stays high, more and more usual buyers hold off, waiting for the rate to drop. Then, when the rate does drop, there is a tremendous surge in mortgage money demand which has been "pent-up" during the high-rate period.

In the commercial income property sector of the mortgage market there is usually an interest rate that causes "the numbers not to work." In other words, the high interest rates cause the cost of borrowing to be so high that, given the rents obtainable in the market, there is not enough income to cover operating expenses and debt service, and still make a desirable profit. Potential investors are therefore *incapable* of paying the high interest rate. In this situation the demand for mortgage money all but disappears. Later, if and when either rates and/or expenses come down or rents go up, "the numbers work" and the demand for mortgage money increases.

Mortgage borrowers' unwillingness or inability to pay high interest rates is not their only problem. Since mortgage borrowers are at the bottom of the totem pole, they often suffer from the "crowding-out effect." When the supply of loanable funds is low and the demand high, the mortgage borrower is quite frequently outbid for the available loanable funds. The borrowers on the totem pole above the mortgage borrower (virtually all other borrowers) "buy" (borrow) all or most of the loanable funds, leaving no or few funds for the mortgage borrower. When the supply of funds dries up *because of high demand*, the mortgage borrowers who cannot obtain a loan because of it are said to have been crowded out of a tight money or capital market.

Fiscal Policy Impact

The federal government's demand for loanable funds from the borrowing totem pole is a function of the government's fiscal policy. *Fiscal policy*, very simply, is the collection of funds by taxation and the spending of funds by the federal budget. This two-sided fiscal policy is determined by the president and Congress. Some say the president proposes and Congress disposes. In any case, when the federal government spends more than it taxes, the result is called a deficit or deficit budget. This deficit is financed by the government's borrowing loanable funds through the sale of government securities (treasury bills, notes, and bonds).

The larger the deficit to be financed, the more securities must be sold, and thus the greater the crowding-out effect. Furthermore, since loanable funds are limited, the larger amount of securities to be sold causes the interest rates on the securities to rise. In order for the Treasury to successfully sell government securities to finance a deficit budget, an attractive yield or high interest rate must be offered on these securities to attract and induce investors with loanable funds to purchase them. High interest rates on government securities tend to cause savers to draw funds out of their savings accounts at financial intermediaries (such as commercial banks, savings banks, and savings and loan associations) and directly invest these savings in the high-yielding government securities. These financial intermediaries are the traditional mortgage lenders. The withdrawal of funds from these institutions is called *disintermediation,* and it causes these mortgage lenders to be short of dollars to loan to prospective homeowners and commercial property investors. This shortage of mortgage funds causes mortgage interest rates to rise. Hence, the mortgage borrower may find the supply and availability of funds decreased because of the crowding-out effect and the cost of funds increased because of disintermediation.

The impact of deficit budgets and governmental borrowing upon the mortgage market can be even more dramatic depending on who loans the money to the government. If the money is borrowed from private and banking sources, the impact may stop at crowding-out and disintermediation. However, if some of this deficit financing is arranged directly through a loan from the Federal Reserve Banking System (the Fed), the process is called *monetization of the debt* and is quite *inflationary*. The inflation results from the fact that the Fed makes the loan or purchases the government securities with "new money" created by simply increasing the checking account balance of the Treasury at the Federal Reserve. This new money creation is often called the "printing press effect,"[4] since the Fed effectively pumps more dollars into the economy out of thin air. Such an injection of credit into the economy is pure inflation, which may be defined as an increase in the volume of money and credit without a comparable

4. The Fed does not actually print more green dollar bills with which to purchase the government securities, but rather pushes a button on its computer to increase the Treasury account balance. The end result, however, is the same as if more green bills had been printed.

increase in productivity and/or output, resulting in a rise in the general level of prices.

Monetary Policy Impact

Inflation, whether caused by a monetization of the debt or other factors, is often the number-one target of monetary policy. *Monetary policy* consists of the actions taken by the Board of Governors of the Fed to control, monitor, and change the supply and price of money and credit within the economy. This board itself is also referred to as the Fed.

The Fed has three primary and two secondary tools of monetary policy as follows:

A. *Primary Tools*

1. *Open market operations*. The Fed can either buy government securities to inject money into the economy or sell government securities to eject money out of the economy.
2. *Reserve requirements*. This requirement determines what percentage of bank deposits can be lent and what percentage of bank deposits must be held as reserves. A decrease in the reserve requirement increases the supply of loanable funds in the borrowing totem pole; an increase in the reserve requirement decreases the supply of loanable funds
3. *Discount rate*. This is the interest rate the Fed charges commercial banks to borrow from it. A decrease in the discount rate lowers the cost for banks to borrow, which tends to cause banks to make more loans, thereby increasing the money or credit in the economy. An increase in the discount rate has the opposite effect, decreasing the money or credit in the economy.

B. *Secondary Tools*

1. *Direct or selective credit controls*. From time to time, the Fed issues regulations aimed at specific parts of the economy to either encourage or discourage an increase or decrease in the supply or cost of credit in that individual sector of the economy. For example, Regulation Q controls maximum interest rates payable to savers by financial institutions, and Regulations T and U control maximum amounts of credit available from stockbrokers for purchasing stocks and bonds.
2. *Moral suasion*. Also called "jawboning," this is the influence or persuasive powers the Fed has over bankers, politicians, economists, and consumers. Thus, the Fed chairperson may make announcements and/or statements to the national press in order to change or alter the economic behavior of various people.

Proper implementation of the tools of monetary policy can fight inflation by ejecting out or decreasing the supply of money and credit in the economy. On the other hand, injecting in or increasing the supply of money and credit in the economy may make it possible for more people to borrow mortgage funds at reasonable rates. The following two examples of monetary and fiscal policy decisions and effects are offered to show the impact of monetary policy on real estate and, it is hoped, to stimulate thought and discussion about a very complex subject.

Tight Money versus Easy Money. Real estate markets are hurt by high interest rates, since they increase the cost of mortgage debt. Real estate markets are hurt by inflation, since it increases the cost of real estate; higher costs lead to higher mortgage debt, regardless of the interest rate, since more money must be borrowed for the higher priced property. Thus the real estate industry faces a dilemma: If the Fed employs a tight monetary policy, interest rates rise, increasing the cost of mortgage debt; if the Fed employs an easy monetary policy, inflation results, which increases real estate prices and therefore the amount and cost of mortgage debt. Apparently, the real estate industry must make a choice: high interest rates or inflation.

The ramifications of a tight monetary policy to fight inflation might be as follows:

1. The Fed slows the growth of the money supply.
2. The lower supply of money growth causes the price of the money, the interest rates, to rise.
3. The government and corporate borrowers (at least initially) can afford the higher rates more easily than mortgage borrowers.
4. If governmental and corporate needs for funds increase (due to deficit budgets and economic expansion), the mortgage borrower can be crowded out of the tight money and capital markets.
5. If interest rates rise very high, savings at mortgage lending institutions can be attracted away (disintermediated) from these financial intermediaries, causing the availability and cost of mortgage credit to tighten even further.

The ramifications of an easy monetary policy to fight high interest rates might be as follows:

1. The Fed increases the growth of the money supply.
2. The larger supply of money growth causes the price of the money, the interest rates, to decline.
3. If the money supply grows faster than the economy, inflation results.
4. To speed up economic growth, the federal government increases spending and/or decreases taxes.

5. The result of increased spending and/or lower taxes is a deficit budget, which must be funded by the sale of government securities.
6. Deficit budgets funded by financial intermediaries cause the supply and availability of mortgage money to tighten by crowding out.
7. The funding of deficit budgets by the Fed—monetization of the debt—is very inflationary.
8. The increase in the demand of government borrowing to finance deficit budgets can lead to a rise in interest rates, which can cause disintermediation.
9. Disintermediation causes the availability and cost of mortgage credit to tighten.

One might conclude from the tight money versus easy money scenarios that a vicious circle of economic forces—money, interest rates, and inflation—affects the housing and other real estate markets. What shall it be: high interest rates or inflation? Choose your poison! However, choose carefully, so as not to end up with *both* high interest rates and inflation, especially since one might cause the other.

Inflation can cause high interest rates when lenders add an inflation hedge to the so-called real rate of interest to protect themselves from the expected future inflation. If the inflation becomes reality, the dollars paid back to lenders in the future are less valuable. Hence, to protect against being paid back with cheaper dollars, lenders charge higher rates. This situation may, in fact, be a self-fulfilling prophecy.

High interest rates can cause inflation, since the cost of money enters into almost every price in the economy. Nearly all manufacturers, farmers, public utilities, builders, wholesalers, and retailers must borrow money to buy equipment and supplies and to finance production and inventories. In other words, borrowing costs are a cost of doing business, and such costs are generally passed on to the purchasers or consumers through higher prices, thus leading to inflation.

CONCLUSION

In conclusion, it's no wonder that a Catch-22 might exist for real estate, since inflation can cause high interest rates and high interest rates can cause inflation. Hence, the proper implementation of both monetary and fiscal policies is crucial to the avoidance of a set of economic conditions that can quickly and easily destroy a viable and prosperous real estate market.

A good example of a coordinated program of monetary and fiscal policies is that which was offered in 1978 by the Chairman of the Federal Reserve Board, G. William Miller. Mr. Miller's eight-point program for returning the nation to full economic health was as follows:

1. A balanced budget by 1982
2. A reduction in federal expenditures over the next five years or so to 20 percent of the nation's output of goods and services from the current 22 percent
3. An annual reduction in the inflation rate of one-half to three-quarters of a percentage point
4. An increase in business investment over the next five years to 12 percent gross national product from 9 percent
5. An annual increase in housing starts of 75,000 to 100,000 units over five years
6. An increase in exports to 10 percent of gross national product from 7 percent
7. Tax reductions for businesses and individuals
8. Efforts to ease the drag of federal regulations on economic activity

This program is presented only as an example, showing the complexity of the implementation of monetary and fiscal policies.

CHAPTER 14

Mortgage Lending

KEY TERMS

LTVR Loan-to-value ratio; the loan amount as a percentage of the property value

Redlining Designation by lenders and/or appraisers of certain neighborhoods as high-risk loan areas, because of the racial or ethnic makeup, crime rates, and/or age of properties in the area

PITI Principal, interest, taxes, and insurance payments made periodically, usually monthly, to the lender who escrows the taxes and insurance amounts; also referred to as a "budget mortgage payment method"

Usury The act of charging an interest rate above the maximum rate of interest that can be legally charged to a borrower

Debt coverage factor A ratio of the net operating income over the debt service, which gives a lender an indication of the cushion for error allowed for over-optimistic income projections

Default ratio A ratio of operating expenses plus debt service over effective gross income, which indicates the cushion for error in projecting income, vacancies, and expenses

Expense ratio A ratio of operating expenses over effective gross income, used by lenders to check for underestimation of expenses

Gross rent multiplier A ratio of sales prices or values over effective gross incomes representative of a given market, which can be multiplied by income to obtain an estimate of value

Credit deal A real estate loan that has the borrower's income and/or credit rating as the prime security

Real estate deal A real estate loan that has the income from the property itself as the prime security

RESIDENTIAL LOAN ANALYSIS

As shown in Chapter 13, monetary and fiscal policies have a tremendous impact upon the supply-and-demand conditions of the money and capital markets, which in turn directly affect the cost and availability of mortgage credit. These macroeconomic factors play an important role in a loan underwriter's review and analysis of loan applications. However, there are also microeconomic factors which a lender must study and analyze to determine whether to make a loan and what set of mortgage terms to offer potential borrowers. This chapter discusses those factors which constitute the mortgage loan underwriting process.

The mortgage loan underwriting process is the investigation, analysis, and determination of the risks involved in making a mortgage loan. The mortgage risk analysis determines whether or not a loan will be made, and if so, under what terms it will be made. The terms under which a loan are made include the following:

1. Loan amount or loan-to-value ratio (LTVR)
2. Interest rate
3. Term to maturity
4. Payment plan
5. Mortgage insurance (if required)
6. Any and all finance charges and closing costs

Mortgage Lending Risks

In Chapter 10 it was noted that two legal instruments are used in making real estate loans: (1) a promissory note or bond, which legally pledges the personal promise of the borrower to repay the loan, and (2) a mortgage or deed of trust, which legally pledges the property as collateral security for the loan upon nonpayment by the borrower. Both legal documents are used because the two major risk factors in mortgage lending are the *borrower* and the *property*. Hence, both the borrower and the property must be investigated by mortgage lenders.

One can argue the order of importance of borrower credit and collateral value. Some lenders argue that the borrower's credit status and/or financial ability may change unpredictably with his or her attitude, health, and luck, and with economic, political, and social events beyond the borrower's control. Therefore, the ultimate and constant protection for the lender against default is the value of the real estate, which is secured by the mortgage or deed of trust.

Other lenders argue that real estate values are subject to considerable variation, especially the values of foreclosure properties. This suggests that the prime and most reliable protection for the lender is the financial position of the borrower, who must make the mortgage payments. Obviously, both the borrower's credit ability and the collateral's value are very important to mortgage lenders. All loan underwriters investigate the potential risks inherent in each.

Analyzing the Property

If a lender has to foreclose and obtain title to the real estate pledged or hypothecated as security for the loan, the lender's ultimate position will be determined by the value of the real estate. A real estate appraisal is an estimate or opinion of value. Lenders depend upon an appraisal and the loan-to-value ratio (LTVR) as their protection against making a loan that might be greater than the value, even upon foreclosure, of the real estate collateral.

Mortgage lenders loan a percentage (LTVR) of the appraised value or the price paid by the borrower, whichever is lower. The difference between the loan amount and the property value provides lenders with a cushion to protect against a loss upon foreclosure. Loan amortization and appreciation in value over the term of the loan increase the cushion of protection, the difference between the loan balance and the property value.

Real estate appraisal analysis and the three approaches for determining value are discussed in Chapters 15 and 16. The old adage that "the three most important factors in real estate are location, location, and location" is still the fundamental concern to real estate value and long-term lending. A residential real estate appraisal, therefore, very closely analyzes the city, neighborhood, and specific site of the subject property in order to investigate, analyze, and determine its locational risk. An appraisal also analyzes the physical condition and functional adequacy of the improvements in determining value. The usage of residential properties is also important to the mortgage lender. Four categories of usage are (1) owner occupied, (2) tenant occupied, (3) resort homes, and (4) second homes. Owner-occupied homes are considered best for lender security and will command the highest LTVR. Tenant-occupied homes fall into commercial property loan analysis. Resort and second homes are considered more risky, and therefore require larger down payments, shorter terms, and higher interest rates.

Redlining. In the past, appraisers have downgraded the value of certain properties located in racially or ethnically "transitional" neighborhoods. Lenders have been criticized for designating certain neighborhoods as high-risk areas because of their social or ethnic makeup, crime rates, and age of properties. Since such designations are purportedly done by circling these areas in red ink on a city map, the process has been named *redlining*.

In April 1976, the Department of Justice filed suit against the American Institute of Real Estate Appraisers (AIREA), the Society of Real Estate Appraisers (SREA), the Mortgage Bankers Association of America (MBA), and the United States League of Savings Associations (Savings League), charging violation of the Fair Housing Act of the Civil Rights Act of 1968. The suit claimed that the defendants maintained overtly discriminatory standards and practices, that they instructed their members that properties in racially integrated neighborhoods have a substantially lower value than similar properties in all-white neighborhoods, and that loans on properties located in such neighborhoods were less secure than loans on properties located in all-white neighborhoods. The AIREA settled its lawsuit in November 1977 by agreeing not to use a neighborhood's racial, ethnic, or religious makeup as a basis for determining value. As of early 1978 the suits against the SREA, MBA, and Savings League were still pending. The Federal Home Loan Bank Board had also proposed some new regulations to end redlining by member S&Ls and other member lenders.

Analyzing the Borrower

Prior to the 1930s there was little need to investigate the risk of the borrower's not making mortgage payments, since the borrower's down payment was typically 40 to 50 percent of the property price or value. Today, however, LTVRs of 90 to 95 percent or even 100 percent (VA) are not uncommon. The borrower's down payment or monetary interest in a property, therefore, may be very minimal or even nonexistent. Hence, emphasis on savings has been replaced by emphasis on income, which is required to support repayment of the mortgage debt.

The analysis of a mortgage borrower's capacity to support repayment of a mortgage loan can be divided into two categories: (1) ability to pay and (2) willingness to pay.

Ability to Pay. A borrower's financial capacity is determined by his or her income and his or her assets versus liabilities. Income is analyzed from two points of view, quality or type of income and quantity of income.

Quality of Income. A determination must be made as to the probable stability and tenure of income. The type of work performed and length of time on the job are analyzed to make this determination. For example, workers with salaried jobs in large companies, hourly wages with a union contract, and professional people such as doctors, nurses, lawyers, executive secretaries, government employees, and teachers or professors with tenure are considered the most secure. On the other hand, commission salespeople, entertainers, seasonal workers, clerical workers, models, and waiters are considered the most risky. Self-employed people might be considered risky unless they can show a track record of successful operations and a relatively stable income over time.

Most lenders look for some minimum term of employment, usually one to three years. "Job hopping" is considered risky and could cause an erratic income flow. However, a history of many job changes with noticeable career improvement or moves up the corporate ladder to positions of greater responsibility, income improvement, and/or growth potential is considered very favorably by mortgage lenders. In any case the lender will send an employment verification form to the borrower's employer in order to verify the employment and income claimed by the borrower when applying for the loan. Comments by the employer as to the past performance and future potential of the borrower sometimes weigh heavily in the lender's determination of the borrower's character, which is one of the important intangibles used in mortgage loan analysis.

Quantity of Income. In many families today there is more than one source of income; this can cause some difficulty in calculating "total effective income." *Effective income* is income which is regular, stable, calculable, and legal, and is therefore counted toward qualifying for a mortgage loan. According to HUD, effective income is the estimated amount of the borrower's earning capacity that is likely to prevail over the first five years of the mortgage term.

Some types of income are not counted by lenders unless a regular pattern can be established for several years or verified as guaranteed by the borrower's employer. For example, income from commissions, bonuses, overtime wages, a second job, part-time employment, interest and dividends, or child support and alimony may fall into this category and might not be considered in the calculation of effective income. Unreported income is never counted; income from children is rarely counted.

Under the Equal Credit Opportunity Act and its subsequent amendments, the calculation of effective income cannot discount income because of age, sex, marital status, race, color, religion, national origin, or the fact that all or part of the borrower's income is in the form of welfare or public assistance payments. A lender may ask to what extent a loan applicant's income is affected by obligations to make alimony, child support, or maintenance payments, or to what extent a loan applicant is relying on alimony, child support, or maintenance payments to repay the mortgage loan. However, the lender must inform the borrower that no such disclosure is necessary if the borrower does not need or wish such income to count for loan qualification purposes.

Income Ratios and Multipliers. Most lenders establish certain basic minimum standards to evaluate the quantity of a borrower's income. These minimum standards or rules of thumb are usually expressed as ratios or multipliers. Ratios state that the monthly mortgage payment must not exceed a certain percentage of monthly income. Multipliers state that monthly income must be at least a certain times as large as the monthly mortgage payment. The monthly mortgage payment includes principal, interest, tax escrow, and insurance escrow (PITI).

With conventional loans, for example, the following rules of thumb are the most common:

1. The monthly mortgage payment (PITI) must not exceed 25 percent of the monthly effective income.
2. The monthly effective income must be at least 4 times as large as the monthly mortgage payment (PITI).

These two rules of thumb are commonly known as the 25 percent rule and the 4:1 rule, respectively. Two other conventional-loan rules of thumb are as follows:

1. PITI plus monthly installment payments (car payment, credit card bills, life insurance charges, etc.) must not exceed 33 1/3 percent of monthly effective income.
2. The monthly effective income must be at least 3 times as large as the PITI plus monthly installment payments.

These rules of thumb are commonly known as the 33 1/3 percent rule and the 3:1 rule, respectively.

Still other conventional lenders like to employ "net effective income" in their loan analyses. *Net effective income* is equal to effective income less the estimated federal income tax based on Internal Revenue Service withholding tables. The typical rule of thumb used by these lenders is that PITI should not exceed 30 percent of net effective income.

The FHA employs yet another pair of income qualification rules of thumb:

1. Total monthly housing expense (PITI plus monthly utilities and maintenance estimates) should not exceed 35 percent of net effective income.
2. Total monthly obligations (total housing expense plus installment payment plus state income taxes plus social security payments) should not exceed 50 percent of net effective income.

The VA may employ some of the guidelines listed above, as well as a system referred to as "income available for family support." The VA lender will deduct from monthly effective income all the borrower's obligations to calculate the amount of income remaining to support (feed, clothe, and medically care for) the members of his or her family. A table showing annual income and number in family is then consulted to determine the minimum income required to support the given family. If the requirement is met, the loan is approved.

An example may make these rules of thumb more easily understood. Assume the following monthly information applies to a loan applicant:

1. Effective monthly income: $1200
2. Federal income tax withheld: $200
3. Car payment: $75

4. Life insurance: $25
5. Utilities: $35
6. Maintenance: $15
7. State tax: $75
8. Social security: $75

Applying the various rules of thumb indicates that a PITI of $300 is affordable.

1. Conventional 25 percent or 4:1 rule for effective income ($1200):
   —25 percent of $1200 is $300 (PITI)
   —$1200 is 4:1 of $300 (PITI)
2. Conventional 33 1/3 percent of 3:1 rule for effective income ($1200):
   —33 1/3 percent of $1200 is $400 (PITI plus installments)
   —$1200 is 3:1 of $400 (PITI plus installments)
3. Conventional 30 percent rule for net effective income ($1000):
   —30 percent of $1000 is $300 (PITI)
4. FHA 35 percent rule for net effective income ($1000):
   —35 percent of $1000 is $350 (total monthly housing expense)
5. FHA 50 percent rule for net effective income ($1000):
   —50 percent of $1000 is $500 (total monthly obligations)
6. VA income available for family support:
   —According to one VA table, $500 will support a family of four with an annual income of $14,000 to $15,000

Assets versus Liabilities. Income is not the only item of interest to the mortgage analyst in determining the borrower's ability to pay. The borrower's assets and liabilities must be investigated also. If *net worth*—assets minus liabilities—is not positive, a loan will most likely not be made. The borrower's cash assets are of prime importance. The cash assets, usually checking and savings accounts, must be sufficient to cover the down payment and the closing costs. The cash assets should exceed these two requirements such that the borrower will have a cash reserve to cover any unforeseen emergencies. The lender will send deposit verification forms to the borrower's banks and savings institutions in order to verify the existence of sufficient cash assets.

Other near-cash assets include stocks, bonds, and cash value of life insurance policies. These assets will strengthen any loan application, since they can usually be liquidated quickly should the need arise. Other real estate owned by the borrower, especially if it has a high equity value, may provide future opportunities for cash through refinancing and certainly would strengthen a loan application. Such assets as a business, auto, furniture, and household goods are also included in the analysis.

The importance of liabilities was clearly highlighted in the discussion of the rules of thumb. The mortgage lender wants to be sure that the borrower's other financial obligations will not hamper his or her ability to make the mortgage payments. Notes payable are considered a priority claim against cash assets, and are therefore of prime importance to the mortgage lender. Other installment payments are listed and worked into the various rules of thumb to determine if they are too burdensome on the borrower and thereby create too much risk for the mortgage lender. Refer to Exhibits 14-1 through 14-3 for copies of a Residential Loan Application, Employment Verification Form, and Deposit Verification Form.

Willingness to Pay. An analysis of a borrower's credit status or credit character is the lender's method of determining a borrower's willingness to pay. The single most tangible source of information concerning a potential borrower's track record of paying former financial obligations is a credit report provided by a credit bureau. Additional information may be obtained from public records regarding litigation, judgments, or criminal lawsuits that may have been filed against the potential borrower. An erratic credit history or one containing bankruptcy or foreclosure is usually sufficient reason for a lender to reject a mortgage loan application. Under the Fair Credit Reporting Act, an individual is given the right to examine (free of charge) a summary of the information on file with any credit reporting agency or bureau making reports on him or her. One may also demand correction of any erroneous information reported. The Federal Trade Commission is responsible for the administration of this act.

A credit report itself (See Exhibits 14-4 and 14-5) is an abbreviated or codified listing of the status of borrower accounts, both current and past. The abbreviated form will usually list by name the bank, credit card, or store at which an account has been maintained. It will also comment on the paying habits for each account, using the following terminology: pays as agreed, satisfactory, fair, slow, very slow, unsatisfactory, or too new. The codified form will usually list the same kind of information as the abbreviated form, but using a letter and number code, rather than naming each account and verbally describing the paying habits.

Letters are used to identify the bank (B), credit card (C), or store (D), and whether the account is open (O), revolving (R), or installment (I). Installment accounts also list the monthly payment. Numbers from 1 to 9 are typically used to describe payment habits, with 1 representing the best (pays as agreed) and 9 the worst (turned over to a collection agency). For example, I-$50-1 indicates a $50-a-month installment account paid as agreed.

A credit report also typically indicates the date that each account was opened, the highest credit, and current balance. The borrower's employment history, income, marital status and dependents, and court records (if any) might also be reported in the credit report.

MORTGAGE APPLIED FOR	☐ Conventional ☐ VA	☐ FHA ☐ ______	Amount $	Interest Rate ___%	No. of Months	Monthly Payment Principal & Interest $	Escrow/Impounds (to be collected monthly) ☐ Taxes ☐ Hazard Ins. ☐ Mtg. Ins. ☐ ______

Prepayment Option

SUBJECT PROPERTY

Property Street Address	City	County	State	Zip	No. Units

Legal Description (Attach description if necessary) — Year Built

Purpose of Loan: ☐ Purchase ☐ Construction-Permanent ☐ Construction ☐ Refinance ☐ Other (Explain)

Complete this line if Construction-Permanent or Construction Loan	Lot Value Data / Year Acquired	Original Cost $	Present Value (a) $	Cost of Imps. (b) $	Total (a + b) $	ENTER TOTAL AS PURCHASE PRICE IN DETAILS OF PURCHASE.

Complete this line if a Refinance Loan — Purpose of Refinance — Describe Improvements [ ] made [ ] to be made

Year Acquired | Original Cost $ | Amt. Existing Liens $ — Cost: $ ______

Title Will Be Held In What Name(s) — Manner In Which Title Will Be Held

Source of Down Payment and Settlement Charges

This application is designed to be completed by the borrower(s) with the lender's assistance. The Co-Borrower Section and all other Co-Borrower questions must be completed and the appropriate box(es) checked if ☐ another person will be jointly obligated with the Borrower on the loan, or ☐ the Borrower is relying on income from alimony, child support or separate maintenance or on the income or assets of another person as a basis for repayment of the loan, or ☐ the Borrower is married and resides, or the property is located, in a community property state.

BORROWER	CO-BORROWER
Name / Age / School Yrs ____	Name / Age / School Yrs ____
Present Address No. Years ____ ☐ Own ☐ Rent	Present Address No. Years ____ ☐ Own ☐ Rent
Street	Street
City/State/Zip	City/State/Zip
Former address if less than 2 years at present address	Former address if less than 2 years at present address
Street	Street
City/State/Zip	City/State/Zip
Years at former address ☐ Own ☐ Rent	Years at former address ☐ Own ☐ Rent
Marital Status ☐ Married ☐ Separated ☐ Unmarried (incl. single, divorced, widowed) — DEPENDENTS OTHER THAN LISTED BY CO-BORROWER: NO / AGES	Marital Status ☐ Married ☐ Separated ☐ Unmarried (incl. single, divorced, widowed) — DEPENDENTS OTHER THAN LISTED BY BORROWER: NO / AGES
Name and Address of Employer — Years employed in this line of work or profession? ____ years — Years on this job ____ — ☐ Self Employed*	Name and Address of Employer — Years employed in this line of work or profession? ____ years — Years on this job ____ — ☐ Self Employed*
Position/Title — Type of Business	Position/Title — Type of Business
Social Security Number*** — Home Phone — Business Phone	Social Security Number*** — Home Phone — Business Phone

GROSS MONTHLY INCOME

Item	Borrower	Co-Borrower	Total
Base Empl. Income	$	$	$
Overtime			
Bonuses			
Commissions			
Dividends/Interest			
Net Rental Income			
Other† (Before completing, see notice under Describe Other Income below.)			
Total	$	$	$

MONTHLY HOUSING EXPENSE**

	PRESENT	PROPOSED
Rent	$	
First Mortgage (P&I)		$
Other Financing (P&I)		
Hazard Insurance		
Real Estate Taxes		
Mortgage Insurance		
Homeowner Assn. Dues		
Other		
Total Monthly Pmt.	$	$
Utilities		
Total	$	$

DETAILS OF PURCHASE

a. Purchase Price	$
b. Total Closing Costs (Est.)	
c. Prepaid Escrows (Est.)	
d. Total (a + b + c)	$
e. Amount This Mortgage	( )
f. Other Financing	( )
g. Present Equity in Lot	( )
h. Amount of Cash Deposit	( )
i. Closing Costs Paid by Seller	( )
j. Cash Reqd. For Closing (Est.)	$

DESCRIBE OTHER INCOME

B—Borrower C—Co-Borrower	NOTICE: † Alimony, child support, or separate maintenance income need not be revealed if the Borrower or Co-Borrower does not choose to have it considered as a basis for repaying this loan.	Monthly Amount
		$

IF EMPLOYED IN CURRENT POSITION FOR LESS THAN TWO YEARS COMPLETE THE FOLLOWING

B/C	Previous Employer/School	City/State	Type of Business	Position/Title	Dates From/To	Monthly Income
						$

THESE QUESTIONS APPLY TO BOTH BORROWER AND CO-BORROWER

If a "yes" answer is given to a question in this column, explain on an attached sheet.	Borrower Yes or No	Co-Borrower Yes or No
Have you any outstanding judgments? In the last 14 years, have you been declared bankrupt?		
Have you had property foreclosed upon or given title or deed in lieu thereof?		
Are you a co-maker or endorser on a note?		
Are you a party in a law suit?		
Are you obligated to pay alimony, child support, or separate maintenance?		
Is any part of the down payment borrowed?		

	Borrower Yes or No	Co-Borrower Yes or No
Do you have health and accident insurance?		
Do you have major medical coverage?		
Do you intend to occupy this property?		
Will this property be your primary residence?		
Have you previously owned a home?		
Sales Price of previously owned home?	$	$

*FHLMC requires self employed to furnish signed copies of one or more most recent Federal Tax Returns or audited Profit and Loss Statements. FNMA requires business credit report, signed Federal Income Tax returns for last two years, and, if available, audited P/L plus balance sheet for same period.
**All Present Monthly Housing Expenses of Borrower and Co-Borrower should be listed on a combined basis.
***Neither FHLMC nor FNMA requires this information.

Rocky Mountain Bank Note 656

Exhibit 14-1 Residential Loan Application

This Statement and any applicable supporting schedules may be completed jointly by both married and unmarried co-borrowers if their assets and liabilities are sufficiently joined so that the Statement can be meaningfully and fairly presented on a combined basis; otherwise separate Statements and Schedules are required. If the co-borrower section was completed about a spouse, this statement and supporting schedules must be completed about that spouse also.

☐ Completed Jointly ☐ Not Completed Jointly

STATEMENT OF ASSETS AND LIABILITIES

ASSETS		LIABILITIES AND PLEDGED ASSETS			
		Indicate by (*) those liabilities or pledged assets which will be satisfied upon sale of real estate owned or upon refinancing of subject property.			
Description	Cash or Market Value	Creditors' Name, Address and Account Number	Acct. Name If Not Borrower's	Mo. Pmt. and Mos. left to pay	Unpaid Balance
Cash Deposit Toward Purchase Held By	$	Installment Debts (include "revolving" charge accts)		$ Pmt./Mos. /	$
Checking and Savings Accounts (Show Names of Institutions/Acct. Nos.)				/	
				/	
				/	
Stocks and Bonds (No./Description)				/	
				/	
				/	
Life Insurance Net Cash Value *Face Amount ($*		Automobile Loans		/	
SUBTOTAL LIQUID ASSETS	$				
Real Estate Owned *(Enter Market Value from Schedule of Real Estate Owned)*		Real Estate Loans		X	
Vested Interest in Retirement Fund				X	
Net Worth of Business Owned (ATTACH FINANCIAL STATEMENT)				X	
Automobiles (Make and Year)		Other Debts Including Stock Pledges		/	X
Furniture and Personal Property		Alimony, Child Support and Separate Maintenance Payments Owed To		/	X
Other Assets (Itemize)		TOTAL MONTHLY PAYMENTS		$	X
TOTAL ASSETS	A $	NET WORTH (A minus B) $		TOTAL LIABILITIES	B $

SCHEDULE OF REAL ESTATE OWNED (If Additional Properties Owned Attach Separate Schedule)

Address of Property (Indicate S if Sold, PS if Pending Sale or R if Rental being held for income)	▽	Type of Property	Present Market Value	Amount of Mortgages & Liens	Gross Rental Income	Mortgage Payments	Taxes, Ins. Maintenance and Misc.	Net Rental Income
			$	$	$	$	$	$
		TOTALS →	$	$	$	$	$	$

LIST PREVIOUS CREDIT REFERENCES

▽ B–Borrower C–Co-Borrower	Creditor's Name and Address	Account Number	Purpose	Highest Balance	Date Paid
				$	

List any additional names under which credit has previously been received ____________

AGREEMENT: The undersigned applies for the loan indicated in this application to be secured by a first mortgage or deed of trust on the property described herein, and represents that the property will not be used for any illegal or restricted purpose, and that all statements made in this application are true and are made for the purpose of obtaining the loan. Verification may be obtained from any source named in this application. The original or a copy of this application will be retained by the lender, even if the loan is not granted.

I/we fully understand that it is a federal crime punishable by fine or imprisonment, or both, to knowingly make any false statements concerning any of the above facts as applicable under the provisions of Title 18, United States Code, Section 1014.

____________ Date ________ ____________ Date ________
Borrower's Signature Co-Borrower's Signature

VOLUNTARY INFORMATION FOR GOVERNMENT MONITORING PURPOSES

If this loan is for purchase or construction of a home, the following information is requested by the Federal Government to monitor this lender's compliance with Equal Credit Opportunity and Fair Housing Laws. The law provides that a lender may neither discriminate on the basis of this information nor on whether or not it is furnished. Furnishing this information is optional. If you do not wish to furnish the following information, please initial below.

BORROWER: I do not wish to furnish this information (initials)________

RACE/ NATIONAL ORIGIN ☐ American Indian, Alaskan Native ☐ Asian, Pacific Islander ☐ Black ☐ Hispanic ☐ White ☐ Other (specify)____________

SEX ☐ Female ☐ Male

CO-BORROWER: I do not wish to furnish this information (initials)________

RACE/ NATIONAL ORIGIN ☐ American Indian, Alaskan Native ☐ Asian, Pacific Islander ☐ Black ☐ Hispanic ☐ White ☐ Other (specify)____________

SEX ☐ Female ☐ Male

FOR LENDER'S USE ONLY

(FNMA REQUIREMENT ONLY) This application was taken by ____________ (Interviewer), a full time employee of

____________ (Name of Lender), in a face to face interview with the prospective borrower.

Rocky Mountain Bank Note 656

REVERSE

REQUEST FOR VERIFICATION OF EMPLOYMENT

INSTRUCTIONS:

EMPLOYER — Please complete Items 9 thru 16 and return directly to

PART I — REQUEST

1. TO: (Name and Address of employer)

3. SIGNATURE OF LENDER	4. TITLE	5. DATE	6. LOAN NUMBER

I have applied for a mortgage loan and stated that I am employed by you. My signature below authorizes verification of this information.

7. NAME AND ADDRESS OF APPLICANT	8. SIGNATURE OF APPLICANT

PART II — VERIFICATION

EMPLOYMENT DATA	PAY DATA			
9A. IS APPLICANT NOW EMPLOYED BY YOU? ☐ YES ☐ NO (If "No," complete Items 9c and 9d.) 9B. HOW LONG HAS APPLICANT BEEN EMPLOYED BY YOU? (If Military, enter total service)	12A. BASE PAY (Enter amount and check period) ☐ ANNUAL ☐ HOURLY ☐ MONTHLY ☐ OTHER (Specify) $ ☐ WEEKLY		12C. TO BE COMPLETED FOR MILITARY PERSONNEL ONLY PAY GRADE	
	12B. EARNINGS LAST 12 MONTHS		TYPE	MONTHLY AMOUNT
9C. DATE APPLICANT LEFT	TYPE	AMOUNT	BASE PAY	$
9D REASON FOR LEAVING	BASE PAY	$	RATIONS	$
			FLIGHT OR HAZARD	$
10. PRESENT POSITION	OVERTIME	$	CLOTHING	$
	COMMISSIONS	$	QUARTERS	$
11. PROBABILITY OF CONTINUED EMPLOYMENT	BONUS	$	PRO PAY	$
			OVER SEAS OR COMBAT	$

13. REMARKS

The above information is provided in strict confidence in response to your request.

14. SIGNATURE OF EMPLOYER	15. TITLE	16. DATE

THE INFORMATION ON THIS FORM IS CONFIDENTIAL. IT IS TO BE TRANSMITTED DIRECTLY, WITHOUT PASSING THROUGH THE HANDS OF THE APPLICANT OR ANY OTHER PARTY.

Exhibit 14-2 Employment Verification Form

FNMA

Federal National Mortgage Association

REQUEST FOR VERIFICATION OF DEPOSIT

INSTRUCTIONS: LENDER - *Complete Items 1 thru 8. Have applicant(s) complete Item 9. Forward directly to depository named in Item 1.*
DEPOSITORY - *Please complete Items 10 thru 15 and return DIRECTLY to lender named in Item 2.*

PART I - REQUEST

1. TO *(Name and address of depository)*	2. FROM *(Name and address of lender)*

3. SIGNATURE OF LENDER	4. TITLE	5. DATE	6. LENDER'S NUMBER *(Optional)*

7. INFORMATION TO BE VERIFIED

TYPE OF ACCOUNT	ACCOUNT IN NAME OF	ACCOUNT NUMBER	BALANCE
			$
			$
			$
			$

TO DEPOSITORY: *I have applied for a mortgage loan and stated in my financial statement that the balance on deposit with you is as shown above. You are authorized to verify this information and to supply the lender identified above with the information requested in Items 10 thru 12. Your response is solely a matter of courtesy for which no responsibility is attached to your institution or any of your officers.*

8. NAME AND ADDRESS OF APPLICANT(s)	9. SIGNATURE OF APPLICANT(s)

TO BE COMPLETED BY DEPOSITORY

PART II - VERIFICATION OF DEPOSITORY

10. DEPOSIT ACCOUNTS OF APPLICANT(s)

TYPE OF ACCOUNT	ACCOUNT NUMBER	CURRENT BALANCE	AVERAGE BALANCE FOR PREVIOUS TWO MONTHS	DATE OPENED
		$	$	
		$	$	
		$	$	
		$	$	

11. LOANS OUTSTANDING TO APPLICANT(s)

LOAN NUMBER	DATE OF LOAN	ORIGINAL AMOUNT	CURRENT BALANCE	INSTALLMENTS *(Monthly/Quarterly)*	SECURED BY	NUMBER OF LATE PAYMENTS
		$	$	$ per		
		$	$	$ per		
		$	$	$ per		

12. ADDITIONAL INFORMATION WHICH MAY BE OF ASSISTANCE IN DETERMINATION OF CREDIT WORTHINESS:
(Please include information on loans paid-in-full as in Item 11 above)

Subject to the requirements of the Fair Credit Reporting Act, the information provided in Items 10 thru 12 is furnished to you in strict confidence in response to your request. The accuracy of such information is not guaranteed.

13. SIGNATURE OF DEPOSITORY	14. TITLE	15. DATE

This form is to be transmitted directly to the lender and is not to be transmitted through the applicant or any other party.

★ ★ ★ ★ THIS FORM MUST BE REPRODUCED BY LENDER ★ ★ ★ ★

FNMA Form 1006
Rev. Dec. 75

Exhibit 14-3 Deposit Verification Form

NAME: DOE, JOHN J. (MARY F.)
PHOENIX, ARIZONA

This report is given simply as an aid in determining the propriety of dealing with the subject or extending credit. It is based upon information obtained in good faith by this Agency from sources deemed reliable. The accuracy of same however is in no way guaranteed. The information thus communicated is strictly confidential for your exclusive use and benefit and shall never be revealed to the subjects reported nor to anyone else, and neither Credit Associates nor any of its representatives shall be responsible for violation of any of these conditions and by your acceptance of this report you specifically agree to the same.

DATE	ACCT. NO.	FHA NO.	BASE	CHARGE	NON-LOCAL	PREPARED FOR
	260					THE KISSELL COMPANY

1	A	YES	1–A. Do name and address agree with information shown on request?
	B	33	B. Approximate age of subject
	C	MARRIED 4(WIFE, 3 CHILDREN)	C. Marital status – Number of dependents
	D	6 1/2 YEARS (6-15-66)	D. Length of time married
	E	N/A	E. Did you learn of any separation or divorce?
2	A	UNION LOCAL #394	2–A. Name of employer
	B	CEMENT MASON	B. Position held?
	C	14 YEARS	C. Length of present employment
	D	NO	D. Has his employment status changed within the past two years?
	E	$15600	E. Annual earned income from his employment or business
	F	NONE	F. Approximate income, if any, from other sources
3	A	HOUSEWIFE	3–A. If wife is employed, name of her employer
	B	N/A	B. Position held?
	C	N/A	C. Length of present employment
	D	N/A	D. Has her employment status changed within the past two years?
	E	N/A	E. Annual earned income from her employment or business

CREDIT REPORT ORDER FROM FHA ☐ OR MORTGAGEE ☒
CREDIT REPORT ORDER RECEIVED BY CONTRACT AGENCY:
CREDIT REPORT MAILED: TO FHA ☐ OR MORTGAGEE ☒

REMARKS 1. Amplify his business history. (This report shall contain information as to the subject's previous employment status, location and salary, if there has been a change in employment status within the past two years.)

2. The reporting bureau certifies (a) ☒ public records have been checked for suits, judgments, foreclosures, garnishments, bankruptcies, and other legal actions involving the subject with the results indicated below, or (b) ☐ equivalent information has been obtained through use of a qualified public records reporting service with the results indicated below. (Give details.) (The records of real estate transfers which do not involve foreclosure may be excluded.)

3. The reporting bureau certifies that the subject's credit record in the payment of bills and other obligations has been checked, (a) ☒ through the credit accounts extended by the designated credit grantors under the Classes and Trades identified in the contract for the community in which the subject resides with the results indicated below, or (b) ☐ through accumulated credit records of such credit grantors of the community in which the subject resides with the results indicated below.

4. (No reference shall be made in this report to race, creed, color, or national origin.)

TRADE LINE	DATE OPENED	HIGHEST CREDIT	TERMS	BALANCE NOW	PAYING HABITS
LANDLORD	1-73	225	225	-0-	SATIS
VALLEY NATIONAL BANK	10-72	5403	150	4803	SLOW
	4-69	3000	N/A	CLOSED	VERY SLOW
*INTERSTATE SECURITIES	9-72	847	35	703	SLOW
PHYSICIAN	8-72	32	OPEN	32	UNSATIS
	7-71	106	OPEN	106	UNSATIS
JOHN C. LINCOLN HOSPITAL	11-72	2190	OPEN	26	AS AGREED
MARYVALE HOSPITAL	3-73	230	OPEN	230	TOO NEW
DENTIST	1972	70	OPEN	-0-	FAIR
LOMAS & NETTLETON	5-69	19000	195	CLOSED	FAIR
PRODUCERS FINANCE	5-68	1200	N/A	CLOSED	VERY SLOW
AVCO FINANCE	3-69	1200	N/A	CLOSED	VERY SLOW
MONTGOMERY WARDS	10-69	906	N/A	CLOSED	UNSATIS
ST. JOSEPHS HOSPITAL	3-70	218	N/A	CLOSED	UNSATIS
GOOD SAMARITAN HOSPITAL	10-69	500	N/A	CLOSED	UNSATIS
GOODYEAR TIRE & RUBBER	10-69	208	N/A	CLOSED	UNSATIS
WOOLCO	1968	154	N/A	CLOSED	UNSATIS

*SUBJECT HAD 2 PREVIOUS RATED UNSATIS.

PREVIOUS RESIDENCE: 1. 1601 WEST WILLOW - 2 1/2 YEARS

COLLECTIONS: 1. SUBJECT'S ACCOUNT WAS SUBMITTED TO COLLECTION IN 1966 FOR $105; DISMISSED IN BANKRUPTCY.

COURT RECORDS: 1. SUBJECT FILED BANKRUPTCY ON 7-24-70; SECURED $6,465; UNSECURED $3,151; TOTAL $9,796; EXEMPT $2,100; CLOSED 4-30-71.
2. SUBJECT FILED DECLARATION OF HOMESTEAD ON 4-30-71.

FORM NO. 100 FHA STANDARD FACTUAL DATA REPORT

Exhibit 14-4 Credit Report—Abbreviated Form

TYPE OF REPORT:

FACT DATA

BUREAU NO.	DATE RECEIVED	DATE MAILED
90--60207	4/20/76	04/28/76

DATE TRADE CLEARED	DATE EMP. VER. (MO.-YR.)	INCOME VERIFIED
SEE BELOW	3/74	YES ☐ NO ☒

This information is furnished in response to an inquiry for evaluating credit risks. It has been obtained from reliable sources, the accuracy of which is not guaranteed. The inquirer agrees to indemnify the reporting bureau for any damage arising from misuse of this information, and this report is furnished in reliance upon that indemnity. It must be held in strict confidence, and must not be revealed to the subject reported upon. If adverse action is taken based on this report, the subject reported on must be so advised and the reporting agency identified.

FILE SINCE (MO.-YR.)	COMPUTER I.D. NO.	SOCIAL SECURITY NO.
6/73	03-12352605	046-42-9974

REPORT ON (SURNAME): GIVEN NAME: CREAN, MR. MICHAEL J

SPOUSE'S NAME:

ADDRESS: 2664-B S XANADU WY, DENVER, CO 80232 S 1/74

COMPLETE TO HERE FOR TRADE REPORT AND SKIP TO CREDIT HISTORY

PRESENT EMPLOYER:	POSITION HELD:	SINCE: (MO.-YR.)	MONTHLY INCOME:
DENVER UNIVERSITY	PROF REAL EST	6/73	$

COMPLETE TO HERE FOR SHORT REPORT AND SUMMARY REPORT AND SKIP TO CREDIT HISTORY

DATE OF BIRTH: (MO.-YR.)	NUMBER OF DEPENDENTS INCLUDING SELF		
9/48	2	☒ OWNS OR BUYING HOME	☐ RENTS HOME

FORMER ADDRESS:	FROM: (MO.-YR.)	TO: (MO.-YR.)
2459 S YORK, DENVER, CO	-	1/74

FORMER EMPLOYER:	POSITION HELD:	FROM: (MO.-YR.)	TO: (MO.-YR.)	MONTHLY INCOME:
UNIVERSITY OF COLO	-	-/71	-/73	$ -

SPOUSE'S EMPLOYER:	POSITION HELD:	SINCE: (MO.-YR.)	MONTHLY INCOME:
--			$

CREDIT HISTORY *(Complete this section for all reports)*

REPORTING BUREAU CERTIFIES COMPLIANCE WITH CONTRACTUAL REQUIREMENTS GOVERNING CHECK OF PUBLIC RECORDS AS WELL AS CREDIT INFORMATION INVOLVING SUBJECT

KIND OF BUSINESS AND IDENTIFICATION	DATE REPORTED	DATE OPENED	DATE OF LAST SALE	HIGHEST CREDIT	BALANCE	AMOUNT PAST DUE	TERMS AND USUAL MANNER OF PAYMENT	REMARKS
03 B--1	4/76	11/73	-	938	167	00	R-1 B	
03 F--124	4/76	2/74	-	24250	23817	00	I$246-1 A	
03 B--34	3/74	7/73	-	1500	0	00	R-0	*SEE BELOW
03 C--1326	4/76	7/73	-	150	0	00	R-0	
03 B--421	4/76	12/73	4/76	293	264	00	R$10-1 C	
03 D--1906	4/76	3/74	4/74	42	00	00	R$10-1	
03 B--8	2/76	3/74	1/76	206	00	00	R-1 A	*SEE BELOW
03 D--716	4/76	11/74	-	-	0	00	R-1	
03 D--29	4/76	8/75	1/76	-	00	00	R-1	
03 C--40	4/76	11/73	12/75	340	0	00	O-1	
03 C--1051	4/76	2/75	-	200	0	00	R-1	
03 F--1172	4/76	2/75	-	3082	1340	00	I$57-1 D	
03 F--1172	4/76	2/75	-	1044	0	00	I$49-1	
03 B--1510	4/76	2/74	-	HIGH 3			CHECKING	
03 B--1510	4/76	4/75	-	MED 4			SAVINGS	

*AS OF REPORT DATE, FIRM HAS NOT REPORTED NEW STATUS. TO EXPEDITE THIS REPORT, PREVIOUSLY REPORTED INFORMATION IS GIVEN.

Exhibit 14-5 Credit Report—Codified Form

Credit standards analysis, in summary, should consider all aspects of the borrower's credit before approving or rejecting a mortgage loan application. The amount and type of income (both present and anticipated) and the asset versus liability (net worth position) should be related to the proposed mortgage credit obligation. This should not increase dramatically as compared with previous housing expenses. The borrower's motivation for homeownership or investment and demonstrated ability to manage financial affairs should be related to the proposed mortgage credit obligation. If the underwriting analysis indicates a likelihood that the borrower can conveniently repay the debt, the loan should be approved. If the analysis indicates that proper debt management is improbable, the loan should be rejected.

Most mortgage lenders make the final decision to make a loan through a loan committee. A loan committee usually consists of a group of senior officers, who analyze the loan applications that have been recommended to them by loan processors, who have compiled and analyzed the underwriting information including the borrower interview, appraisal report, and credit report. Loan applications before the loan committee compete against all other current applications for the lending institution's currently available loanable funds. It is therefore possible, because of a given supply-demand relationship of loanable funds, for a loan application to be rejected which might have been approved under different economic conditions or by another lender. Hence, if a borrower is turned down, it is not necessarily the end of the road. Persistence to proceed with another lender may very possibly result in getting the loan.

REGULATORY ASPECTS OF RESIDENTIAL LENDING

Federal legislation has impact on the mortgage lending industry in a variety of ways. Chapter 9 discussed the following four federal laws:

1. Truth In Lending Act (Reg Z)
2. Uniform Consumer Credit Code (UCCC)
3. Equal Credit Opportunity Act (ECOA)
4. Real Estate Settlement Procedures Act (RESPA)

RESPA was completely and thoroughly discussed in Chapter 9; the other three were only briefly introduced. This section will thoroughly discuss Reg Z, UCCC, and ECOA and will briefly discuss usury laws and the National Flood Insurance Act.

Truth In Lending Act (Reg Z)

Title I of the National Consumer Credit Protection Act, which became effective July 1, 1969, is commonly known as the Truth In Lending Act.

This act of Congress authorized the Federal Reserve Board of Governors to prescribe regulations pursuant to the act. Therefore, the Fed issued Regulation Z (Reg Z) to implement the act. Reg Z is enforced by the Federal Trade Commission. Real estate lenders must be keenly aware of their responsibilities under Reg Z. Both new loans and assumptions of existing loans come under the purview of Reg Z.

Essentially, Reg Z requires disclosure of certain information to a borrower, and it permits a borrower to rescind a credit transaction in certain instances. Reg Z applies only to an extension of *consumer* credit to a natural person and not to credit extended to corporations or other legal entities or to credit extended for business or commercial purposes, such as a construction loan to a builder. A residential property containing more than four housing units is considered a business or commercial property. Reg Z applies only if payment of the loan is to be made in more than four installments or if there is a finance charge.

Reg Z disclosures are required to be made by two types of persons:

1. "Creditors," who regularly extend credit in the ordinary course of business
2. "Arrangers of credit," who (a) are paid a fee or commission by a creditor to arrange the extension of credit or (b) have knowledge of the credit terms and assist in the preparation of the credit instruments as an agent of a creditor.

An owner-occupant selling his or her own home is not a creditor. Therefore, one could assist in the preparation of the credit instruments as an agent of such a seller and not be considered an arranger of credit under Reg Z. Therefore, a real estate broker can assist in the preparation of a purchase money mortgage or an installment contract for deed for such a seller and not be subject to Reg Z disclosure regulations.

Disclosure. Reg Z requires uniform disclosure of the terms of consumer loans so that consumers can intelligently compare credit terms. To meet this requirement, the creditor or arranger must provide the borrower with a disclosure statement prior to the creation of a contractual relationship between the borrower and the lender, irrespective of the time of disbursement of the borrowed funds. This disclosure statement must be printed on only one side of a single sheet of paper and must include disclosure of the following items:

1. *Finance charge*, which is the total of certain costs incurred by the borrower or by another party on behalf of the borrower to obtain the loan, including (a) interest, loan origination fee, discount points, finder's fees; (b) mortgage insurance and credit life insurance premiums, *unless* it is clearly stated in writing that such insurance is not a condition to obtaining the loan; and (c) hazard insurance

premiums, *unless* the creditor provides a cost statement of such insurance and a statement informing the borrower of his or her right to obtain such insurance elsewhere.

2. *Annual percentage rate* (APR), which is the *effective* rate of interest paid on the loan considering, in addition to the stated interest rate, all the other costs that encompass the finance charge. The APR must be computed to the nearest .25 percent; such a computation will vary with the term of the loan and the frequency of payments. The Fed publishes tables which may be used to calculate the APR.
3. Date on which the finance charge begins to accrue
4. Total loan amount, termed *amount financed*
5. Number, amount, due dates, and total of all loan payments. If any payment is more than twice the amount of any other payment, the creditor must identify this amount as a balloon payment and state the conditions, if any, under which the balloon payment may be refinanced if not paid when due.
6. Amount of any default or delinquency charges
7. Amount of prepayment penalty
8. Legal description of the property being secured
9. In the case of a purchase money mortgage or installment contract for deed, the cash price, total down payment, and unpaid balance of the cash price
10. Closing costs, such as fees for appraisals, title insurance, and credit reports, which are not included in the finance charge

In the case of a first loan to finance the construction or acquisition of a dwelling (or an assumption of such a first loan), the total of all loan payments and the composition of the finance charge need not be disclosed.

Real estate brokers often arrange credit for sellers without being considered an arranger under Reg Z, since the seller would rarely be a creditor. However, a real estate broker does have disclosure responsibilities in the following situations:

1. If the broker prepares a sales contract in which the seller is a creditor and extends credit
2. If the broker, with actual knowledge of the terms, assists in the preparation of the credit instruments for a lender who is a creditor
3. If the broker receives a fee, commission, or other consideration from a creditor lender for arranging the loan
4. If the broker is selling on his or her own account in the ordinary course of business and takes payment by way of a mortgage on the property

5. If the broker takes the sales commission by way of an installment note or note and mortgage (or deed of trust) on the property
6. If, as a part of the sales transaction, the broker arranges for the sale of the seller's contract or note and mortage (or deed of trust) to a third party and receives a commission for such sale

Recision. In addition to the disclosure requirements imposed on lenders to protect consumers, Reg Z gives the consumer the right to rescind a credit transaction if it results in a lien on the consumer's principal residence, with one exception. Reg Z's right of recision does *not* apply to a credit transaction involving a first mortgage (or deed of trust), the assumption thereof, or an installment contract for deed to finance the acquisition of a dwelling in which the consumer resides or expects to reside.

The consumer recision rights under Reg Z are undoubtedly intended to protect the homeowner from unscrupulous sellers of home improvements, appliances, furniture, encyclopedias, etc., who secure the credit to purchase these items by taking a second mortgage on the consumer's home. Many people, especially low-income families, have lost their homes through default on such second mortgages.

To protect the consumer from such practices, the creditor must give *Notice* to the consumer of his or her rights to rescind the transaction. The Notice must be printed in capitals or lower-case letters of not less than 12-point boldface type on only one side of a single sheet of paper which also contains a statement identifyng the transaction. Two copies of the Notice must be given to the consumer, one of which may be used to rescind the transaction. The consumer has the right to rescind the transaction until midnight of the third business day following the date of purchase or the date of delivery of the Notice of Recision, whichever is later.

If the regulations for disclosure are not followed or if the Notice of Recision is not given to the borrower, the borrower's right to rescind continues for three years after the date of consummation of the transaction. However, the right of recision expires upon resale of the property secured. When a consumer exercises the right of recision, he or she is not liable for any finance or other charge, and any lien becomes void upon recision. Furthermore, the creditor has 10 days after receipt of a notice of recision to return any and all consideration paid by the borrower as earnest money, down payment, or otherwise, and to release the lien claim on the consumer's property. If the creditor has delivered property to the borrower and upon recision does not take possession within 10 days after the borrower has offered the property back, ownership of the property vests in the borrower without obligation to pay.

Advertising. Reg Z does not prohibit the advertising of credit terms, but it does determine how credit terms may be advertised; therefore, all real estate brokers must comply when marketing their listings. Reg Z allows one to advertise, without restriction, only the cash price and the annual percentage rate (APR). No other credit terms may be advertised unless *all* the following information is provided as well:

1. Cash price or loan amount
2. Down payment
3. Number, amount, and due dates of all payments
4. APR

The total of payments over the term of the loan must also be provided in the advertisement *unless* the credit advertised refers to a sale of that dwelling or a first lien to finance the acquisition of that dwelling.

These advertising restrictions eliminate the advertising of down payments and other credit information on resale listings, since the financing terms are not usually known until a potential buyer has been approved for a loan on such properties. However, sellers of new homes may find it much easier to comply with Reg Z advertising regulations, since the financing of entire new home subdivisions is often prearranged and used as a marketing tool. Reg Z does not, however, prohibit advertising in such general terms as "Excellent Loan Assumption," "Reasonable Financing Available," or "FHA (VA-) approved project."

Uniform Consumer Credit Code (UCCC)

The Uniform Consumer Credit Code (UCCC) is a set of state-level consumer laws. In some states the UCCC makes lenders responsible for certain disclosures similar to those required by Reg Z. If a state's adopted UCCC is inconsistent with and less demanding than Reg Z, then Reg Z will control. In some states, however, the UCCC goes beyond or is more demanding than Reg Z. In such states, lenders are subject to both Reg Z and the UCCC.

For example, in Colorado the UCCC goes beyond Reg Z in the following areas:

1. If a loan involves a balloon payment and has an interest rate in excess of 12 percent, the borrower has the right to refinance the balloon payment and the lender must disclose this right,
2. Provisions in notes providing for judgment, called *cognovit notes*, are prohibited and void,
3. A court may refuse to enforce any "unconscionable" loan agreement,
4. Unlicensed lenders may charge only 12 percent interest per annum.

The UCCC is an extremely complex set of laws, and one should always consult local legal counsel for advice regarding such matters.

Equal Credit Opportunity Act (ECOA)

The Equal Credit Opportunity Act (ECOA) was discussed in the "Quantity of Income" section of this chapter as well as in Chapter 9. Some items not specifically mentioned in those discussions which also fall under the ECOA (also known as Reg B) include the following:

1. "Credit scoring" based on age, sex, marital status, race, color, religion, national origin, or public assistance or welfare income is strictly forbidden.
2. Upon request of a loan applicant, lenders must provide in writing the reasons for terminating or denying credit.
3. Lenders may not inquire about potential borrowers' birth-control or childbearing intentions, nor may lenders make presumptions based on a woman's age that her income may be interrupted due to the likelihood of having children.
4. Alimony, child support, or maintenance payments, if court ordered, must be counted toward income qualification if the borrower so desires.
5. After November 1, 1976, records of accounts usable by both spouses or for which both spouses are liable must be reported to credit bureaus in the name of each spouse. Hence, a subsequently divorced or separated person will have his or her own credit history and rating based on the track record of the joint accounts.

Usury Laws

Most states have a usury law which sets a maximum rate of interest that can be charged to a borrower. For a lender to charge interest above the maximum legal rate is to commit the crime of *usury*. The penalty for usury varies from state to state and may be any of the following:

1. The entire loan is void.
2. The lender forfeits all interest.
3. The lender forfeits only interest in excess of the maximum legal rate.
4. The borrower may sue the lender for some statutory penalty, such as double or triple the interest paid.

In most states, corporations may be legally charged and pay interest rates above the maximum for individuals. A lender may be committing usury if it forces an individual to incorporate in order to charge the usurious rate. The charging of discount points and/or points up front is employed by lenders in order to earn a *yield* above the usury rate of interest.

National Flood Insurance Act

The National Flood Insurance Act of 1968 and its subsequent amendments requires property owners in HUD-designated flood plains to obtain flood damage insurance on properties financed with loans obtained from federal agencies and federally insured or regulated lending institutions. Without such insurance, the loans will not be made.

COMMERCIAL LOAN ANALYSIS

Commercial loan analysis is synonymous with the loan underwriting process for income-producing real estate. As with residential loan analysis, commercial loan analysis involves the investigation, analysis, and determination of the risks involved in making a mortgage loan. If a loan is to be made, the risk analysis determines the set of mortgage terms to be offered to the loan applicant. Residential loan analysis involves analysis of both the credit and financial ability of the borrower and the value of the real estate offered as collateral to secure the mortgage loan. Although viewed from a different perspective, analysis of these same items is also of prime importance in commercial loan analysis.

Analyzing the Property

Upon foreclosure, a lender's ultimate position is a function of the collateralized real estate. The value of income-producing real estate is affected by many things that are not relevant to the value of owner-occupied properties. For example, location (as usual) can make or break an income property. However, it is not the esthetic location, which is critical to the value of a home, but the economic location or *situs* that is critical to the value of an office building or shopping center. Commercial properties must be located near or have easy access to the markets (income generators) which they aim to serve. Hence, an analysis of the market demand for a particular income property must be an integral part of commercial loan analysis.

Seldom is a commercial loan made without benefit of a feasibility study. Generally, a feasibility study determines the feasibility of a real estate project from the following three points of view:

1. *Market feasibility*. Is there demand for the property, and how much income can be produced for the property by this demand, given the competition and timing of the project?
2. *Physical feasibility*. Can the property demanded by the market be constructed at a reasonable cost, given the desired construction quality, design, and functional adequacy?
3. *Financial feasibility*. Do the numbers work? In other words, given

the income produced by the market demand and the costs of construction, is there enough income to pay operating expenses, loan debt service, and still provide a reasonable profit margin for the borrower-investor?

The value of income properties is ultimately determined by the bottom-line cash flow produced and available to cover expenses, debt service, and profit. Part IV of this book explains the income property appraisal analysis which converts income to value through capitalization. In addition to the appraised value, mortgage lenders typically use some rules of thumb to aid and simplify the commercial loan analysis process.

Rules of Thumb Analyses. The following is a sample of some of the rules of thumb used in commercial loan analysis:

1. *Debt coverage factor*. The ratio of net operating income over debt service should be some minimum number greater than 1.00 (such as 1.25), to provide a cushion of income above and beyond the loan payment requirement to offset the risk of overoptimistic income projections.
2. *Default ratio*. The ratio of operating expenses plus debt service over effective gross income should not exceed some maximum percentage (such as 85 percent), to provide a cushion against the risk of error in projecting income, vacancies, and expenses.
3. *Expense ratio*. The ratio of operating expenses over effective gross income should not exceed some maximum percentage (such as 45 percent) nor be less than some minimum percentage (such as 35 percent); otherwise a profit may not be feasible or expenses have most likely been underestimated in order to artificially increase the income and value.
4. *Mortgage multiplier*. The ratio of the loan amount over the effective gross income should not exceed some maximum number (such as 6) so as not to overextend the borrower with too large a loan.
5. *Gross rent multiplier*. The ratio of the sales price or value over the effective gross income should not exceed some maximum number (such as 7), otherwise the value may have been overestimated.
6. *Rate of return*. Some minimum rate of return may be required, since such a calculation is a measure of the profitability of a real estate project; a variety of methods for calculating rate of return are presented in the investment section of the book.

Analyzing the Borrower

The ability to pay commercial real estate loans is more a function of the property's cash flow than of the borrower's income. Certain commercial real estate loans, known as *credit deals*, do depend upon the borrower's income from other sources as the prime security for the loan. However, the more typical real estate deal depends upon the income from the property itself as the prime security for the loan. Hence, the analysis of ability to pay is usually contained in the analysis of the property.

Willingness to pay for commercial loans, as for residential loans, is investigated and analyzed in a credit report. Such a credit report may likely be a corporate rather than an individual report. An example of a corporate credit report is presented in Exhibit 14-6.

In addition to the credit report, commercial lenders will usually require audited financial statements by an independent accounting firm showing assets, liabilities, and actual income and expenses over a period of several years. A Dun and Bradstreet Report (D&B), which, in addition to reporting a firm's credit, gives a history of the company and comments on its future capabilities, might be required by some lenders.

Perhaps the most important part of an analysis of a commercial loan borrower is the track record of the developer, builder, or investor. The history of the borrower's other real estate projects is considered to be a good indicator of the potential success of proposed projects. A bit of a circularity exists in this area; one needs a track record to get a loan, but one needs a loan to get a track record.

Another problem with track-record analysis is the possibility of granting a loan in the wrong market or at the wrong time. For example, the fact that a developer has successfully completed a number of previous projects does not imply that his or her next project will succeed. Many developers have been led to believe that the very willingness of the lender to provide funds is more than adequate justification for a proposed project. However, supply may have caught up with demand, the competition might provide a better product, consumers' tastes may change, material shortages may be right over the horizon. While a developer's track record does merit close scrutiny, so do the current market conditions and other related factors.

SUMMARY AND CONCLUSIONS

In addition to macroeconomic factors—such as the impact of monetary and fiscal policies upon the supply and demand conditions of the money and capital markets, which directly affect the cost and availability of mortgage credit—certain microeconomic factors play an important role in a loan underwriter's analysis of real estate mortgage loan applications. The mortgage loan underwriting process involves the investigation, analysis, and determination of the risks involved in the funding of a mortgage loan. Both the credit rating of the borrower and the value of the collateral are very important to mortgage lenders, although lenders may argue the priority of importance of these two factors.

SEPTEMBER 27, 1973

SUBJECT: HUNSINGER CONSTRUCTION CO., INC.

I. DATE OF INCORPORATION: 2-68.

II. PRINCIPALS OF CORPORATION: JALMA W. HUNSINGER - PRESIDENT
CAROL HUNSINGER - VICE PRESIDENT/SECRETARY

III. PURPOSE OF CORPORATION: UNKNOWN

IV. PAID IN CAPITAL: UNKNOWN

V. NET WORTH: 7-30-72 - $300,000

VI. CREDIT REFERENCES AND OUTSTANDING LIABILITIES:

REFERENCES	DATE OPEN	HIGH CREDIT	TERMS	BALANCE	RATING
SUTTER TRUST COMPANY	1968	MED 6	NOTE	220000	AS AGREED
UNIVERSAL MORTGAGE COMPANY	1968	500000	OPEN	450000	AS AGREED
FIRST FEDERAL SAVINGS & LOAN	SUBJECT HAS $90,000 HIGH IN CURRENT CONSTRUCTION LOANS SINCE 1973; CURRENT AND AS AGREED.				
O'MALLEY LUMBER	1968	50000	30 DAY	30000	AS AGREED
TRI CITY READY MIX	1970	21000	30 DAY	3959	AS AGREED
DEARING PLUMBING	1968	MED 4	OPEN	CLOSED	AS AGREED
GOETTL BROTHERS	1968	50000	30 DAY	12000	AS AGREED
SMITH PIPE & STEEL	1969	LOW 4	30 DAY	CURRENT	AS AGREED
IDEAL ELECTRIC	1968	16556	30 DAY	2181	AS AGREED
MESA WHOLESALE SUPPLY	1968	LOW 4	30 DAY	CURRENT	AS AGREED
ROOFING WHOLESALE	9-68	19784	30 DAY	8714	AS AGREED
EDCO ELECTRIC DISTRIBUTORS	4-73	LOW 4	30 DAY	CURRENT	TOO NEW
ARIZONA SASH & DOOR	10-65	39534	30 DAY	27000	AS AGREED
RENCON	4-73	7000	30 DAY	CURRENT	TOO NEW
UNITED BANK	SUBJECT HAS HAD SEVERAL LOANS SINCE 1968 FOR A HIGH OF LOW 6 AND CURRENT BALANCE OF HIGH 5; RATED AS AGREED.				

VII. COURT RECORDS:

1. SUBJECT HAD SEVEN SUITS FILED AGAINST HIM BETWEEN 1-16-69 AND 9-28-70; ALL DISMISSED.
2. SUBJECT HAD SIX SUITS FILED AGAINST HIM BETWEEN 11-5-65 AND 10-23-70; ALL SATISFIED.

Exhibit 14-6 Corporate Credit Report

Lenders use the appraisal process to reach an estimate of value for loan purposes, and then lend only a percentage of the value to protect against the risk of a foreclosure sale's resulting in a price lower than this value. The fact that location is considered a prime determinant of value has caused some lenders to practice redlining, whereby they refuse to lend in certain neighborhoods which have been designated as "high-risk areas" due to racial or ethnic makeup, crime rates, and/or age and condition of properties. The federal government has sought legal redress to put an end to redlining.

Lenders analyze a potential borrower's ability to pay a loan by investigating the borrower's quantity and quality of income and his or her assets versus liabilities. Sufficient income quantity is determined by applying one or more income ratio or multiplier formulas to the borrower's reported income. The income quality is determined by an analysis of the borrower's job type and job stability. Assets should exceed liabilities, and there should not be an overwhelming amount of monthly debt payments, in order for a borrower to qualify for a residential mortgage loan. The credit report of a potential borrower manifests to the lender the borrower's credit rating and willingness to meet his or her financial obligations.

Residential mortgage lending is subject to much regulation. The Truth In Lending Act requires lenders to disclose the true costs of mortgage financing and allows the consumer to rescind lending transactions if proper disclosures are not made by the lender. In some states the Uniform Consumer Credit Code goes a step or two further than the Truth In Lending Act in protecting consumer borrowers. Local legal counsel should be consulted in such states. Additional credit-related regulations have been mandated by the Equal Credit Opportunity Act to avoid discrimination based upon age, sex, marital status, race, color, religion, national origin, or receipt of public assistance or welfare income. Most states have usury laws, which set maximum rates of interest. The National Flood Insurance Act may require borrowers to purchase flood insurance in certain situations in order for mortgage loans to be made.

Although viewed from a different perspective from that of a residential mortgage lender, commercial income-producing property mortgage lenders must analyze both the credit and financial ability of the borrower and the value of the property offered as collateral to secure a commercial real estate mortgage loan. Location, or more precisely situs (economic location) is of prime importance to commercial loan underwriters. There must also be evidence of strong market demand with easy access to the situs. Seldom is a commercial loan commitment made on a proposed real estate project without benefit of studies which indicate the market feasibility, the physical construction feasibility, and the financial feasibility of such a project.

The value of a commercial property is determined by the income productivity of the project converted to value by an appropriate method of capitalization. In addition to the capitalized value, commercial loan underwriters employ a variety of rules of thumb in their income property analyses. These rules of thumb or ratio analyses are used in conjunction with the analyses of the borrower's credit report and track record of development and/or investment to determine whether a loan should be granted. Lenders must be careful not to overemphasize any one item of analysis in commercial lending, but rather view all the information provided in a commercial loan application package.

PART IV

Appraisal

CHAPTER 15

Fundamentals of Real Estate Valuation

KEY TERMS

Value The quantity of one thing that can be obtained in exchange for another thing; the ratio of exchange of one commodity for another commodity
Price The amount of money paid, offered, or asked in a sale
Cost A price once paid in the past
Anticipation The principle of valuation that holds that the value of a property is determined by the present worth of all present and future benefits expected to be derived from the ownership and/or use of the real estate
Substitution The principle of valuation that holds that a property is not worth any more than the cost of a comparable property with the same utility and desirability
Regression Principle holding that among unlike properties, where a better or more valuable property is in the minority, the value of the better property will be adversely affected by the properties of lower value
Progression Principle holding that among unlike properties, where a worse or less valuable property is in the minority, the value of the worse property will be favorably affected by the properties of greater value
Appraisal process The orderly program or set of procedures followed to arrive at the solution to an appraisal problem
Highest and best use The land use that is most likely to return the greatest net present value in income or amenities

Before any real estate transaction can be consummated, a determination of value must be made by both parties. Such a determination is necessary so that each party to the transaction will feel he or she has made a fair exchange of money for property or property for property. Hence, *value* may be defined as "The quantity of one thing which can be obtained in exchange for another: the ratio of exchange of one commodity for another, . . . Money is the common denominator by which real property value is usually measured."[1] However, the meaning of value may not be as simple as the above explanation might suggest.

To understand why the meaning of value can be very complex and, perhaps, elusive, one need only refer to the following list of the different types of value.

1. Appraised value
2. Assessed value
3. Book value
4. Capitalized value
5. Cash value
6. Economic value
7. Exchange value
8. Expected value
9. Face value
10. Future value
11. Gross value
12. Intrinsic value
13. Insurable value
14. Just value
15. Liquidation value
16. Market value
17. Mortgage value
18. Net value
19. Nuisance value
20. Objective value
21. Potential value
22. Present value
23. Real value
24. Rental value
25. Sales value
26. Salvage value
27. Subjective value
28. Stable value
29. Tax value
30. Use value

It should come as no surprise that, as Justice Brandeis of the Supreme Court is often quoted to have said, "Value is a word of many meanings." Nor is it any wonder that another Supreme Court justice is often quoted as expressing the opinion that value "gathers its meaning in a particular situation from the purpose for which the valuation is being made."

ADAM SMITH'S CONCEPTS OF VALUE

In his *Wealth of Nations* (1776), Scottish economist Adam Smith observed that "the word 'value' has two different meanings, and sometimes expresses the utility of some particular object and sometimes the power of purchasing other goods which possession of that object conveys." The former concept is called "value in use"; the latter is called "value in exchange." It is interesting to note, however, that often the items which have the greatest value in use (such as air and water) have limited value in exchange, and often the items which have the greatest value in exchange (such as diamonds and pearls) have limited value in use. Value in use is

1. Byrl N. Boyce, *Real Estate Appraisal Terminology* (Cambridge, MA: Ballinger Publishing Company, 1975), p. 215.

usually considered synonymous with *subjective value*; and value in exchange is usually considered synonymous with *objective value* or *market value*.

CHARACTERISTICS OF VALUE

Regardless of the type of value one is discussing, there are four prime characteristics of value. All are essential in varying degrees depending on the type of value, and none alone suffices to create value. These four characteristics of value are (1) utility, (2) scarcity, (3) demand, and (4) transferability.

Utility

Utility can be defined as the capacity of an economic good to provide a service or to fill a desire or need. A piece of chalk may be of great value to an instructor teaching an appraisal class even though it may not have a great dollar value.

Scarcity

Scarcity refers to limitations on the availability of the supply of an economic good relative to the demand or desire for that good. The more scarce a good is, the greater its value. For example, if the appraisal instructor had only one piece of chalk in his classroom, its value would be so great that he might conserve its use by giving fewer blackboard examples.

Demand

In appraisal, the word "demand" usually refers to *effective demand*, which is the desire for an economic good coupled with the buying power or ability to pay for that good. If the appraisal instructor runs out of chalk in the middle of a class, his demand for more chalk may be so great that one of his students could charge him an exorbitant price for another piece. (This situation illustrates utility and scarcity as well as demand.)

Transferability

Transferability is a legal concept that must exist for a sale or exchange of an economic good to take place. If a good cannot be conveyed its value will be diminished. In real estate, it is possible for a property to be so encumbered by liens and other claims that, for all practical purposes, its title would not be marketable and the property could not be transferred.

VALUE VERSUS PRICE VERSUS COST

The general public frequently and incorrectly uses the terms value, price, and cost interchangeably. To the economist each has a very different meaning. The real estate student and practitioner should use these terms as properly defined.

Value is the present *worth* of benefits derived by present owners (value in use) or the future *worth* of future benefits capable of being derived by future owners (value in exchange). In other words, *value is worth*, whether present or future.

Price is the amount of money paid, asked, or offered in a sale. Price expresses an individual estimate of value in terms of money. Price may be more or less than value, and therefore not justified. Price will equal value only when the price is properly justified.

Cost is historical; it relates to a price that was paid in the *past*. What something cost in the past may have little or no bearing on its value or worth today. It may have an effect on the price asked by the seller, but it usually has no effect on the price offered by the buyer.

For example, if a person paid $30,000 for a house 10 years ago, the *cost* of the house to that person was $30,000. However, if this person put the house up for sale today for $42,000, that would be the asking *price*. If two parties agreed to consummate the sale at $40,000 and similar houses had recently sold at $40,000, this would be the market *value* of the house.

In other words, one might say that value is created in the minds of people; people's minds are influenced by a myriad of forces. The five general forces which influence value, coupled with the four characteristics of value discussed above, constitute the basic ingredients necessary to make the concept of value meaningful.

FORCES INFLUENCING VALUE

There are five general forces influencing value and one another that must be recognized by anyone preparing or utilizing an appraisal of real property.

Physical or Natural Forces

This category concerns factors which can create, modify, preserve, or destroy value. For example, in determining the value of land, the appraiser must consider location, size, shape, area, frontage, topsoil, drainage, contour, topography, accessibility, utilities, roads, climate, even the view. In improvements, the appraiser must consider material, workmanship, and wear and tear on the property (physical deterioration).

Economic Forces

Here one must consider income of the property, the earning power of the community, prevailing terms and availability of mortgage credit, secondary mortgage market activity, price levels, tax burdens, trends in real estate development and employment, and general business conditions at the local, state, and national levels.

Social Forces

The items in the social category that affect value include neighborhood character, population trends (marriage, birth, death and migration rates and patterns), family size and composition trends, urban renewal, civic attitudes, and attitudes toward architectural design and utility.

Political Forces

The government at the national and state level influences property values through price and rent controls, credit controls, national defense programs and installations, government-sponsored housing and loan programs, and monetary and fiscal policies. At the local government level, civic services, police and fire protection, school systems, and public recreational facilities influence property values.

Legal Forces

Here one must consider how value is influenced by such items as condition of title, easements, deed restrictions, liens, zoning codes, building codes, city planning ordinances, and environmental legislation.

The four characteristics of value and the five forces influencing value may be applied to any one of the many possible types of value. In real estate appraisal analysis, the type of value most often sought is market value.

MARKET VALUE

The American Institute of Real Estate Appraisers and the Society of Real Estate Appraisers, in their jointly sponsored text, *Real Estate Appraisal Terminology*, say:

> *Market Value*—The highest price in terms of money which a property will bring in a competitive and open market under all conditions requisite to a fair sale, the buyer and seller, each acting prudently, knowledgeably and assuming the price is not affected by undue stimulus.

Implicit in this definition is the consummation of a sale as of a specified date and the passing of title from seller to buyer under conditions whereby:

1. Buyer and seller are typically motivated.
2. Both parties are well informed or well advised, and each acting in what he considers his own best interest.
3. A reasonable time is allowed for exposure in the open market.
4. Payment is made in cash or its equivalent.
5. Financing, if any, is on terms generally available in the community at the specified date and typical for the property type in its locale.
6. The price represents a normal consideration for the property sold unaffected by special financing amounts and/or terms, services, fees, costs, or credits incurred in the transaction.[2]

This is a very lengthy and complex definition. One cannot be expected to memorize it, but by reading through it a few times, one will gain a general understanding of the meaning of market value. However, a greater understanding of market value, and of real estate appraisal in general, can come from studying several of the basic *principles* of valuation.

PRINCIPLES OF VALUATION

There are 10 principles of valuation generally accepted in real estate appraisal as underlying the various procedures of valuation. Comprehension of these principles is essential to the study of real estate appraising.

Anticipation

The principle of anticipation holds that the value of a property is determined by the present worth of all present and future benefits (income or amenities) *expected* to be derived from the ownership and/or use of the real estate. This principle is especially applicable to the income approach to value, in which future income is *estimated* and then capitalized to obtain value.

Substitution

The principle of substitution holds that a property is not worth any more than the cost of a comparable property with the same utility and desirability, assuming the other property can be obtained in the market-place without any undue delay. In other words, the rational buyer will not buy a particular property if he or she can buy another property equally suitable at a lower price.

2. Boyce, *Real Estate Appraisal Terminology*, p. 137.

Change

The principle of change holds that the real estate market is dynamic and forever changing because of the perpetual shifting that takes place in the five general forces that influence value. An example of change can be observed in the life cycle of a neighborhood: (1) *integration* (formation), (2) *equilibrium* (relatively static state), and (3) *disintegration* (decline or decay).

The principle of change encompasses the concepts of regression and progression. *Regression* holds that among unlike properties, where a better or more valuable property is in the minority, the value of the better property will be adversely affected by the properties of lower value. *Progression* holds conversely that among unlike properties, where a worse or less valuable property is in the minority, the value of the worse property will be favorably affected by the properties of greater value.

Competition

The principle of competition holds that profit breeds competition and excess profits breed potentially ruinous competition. In other words, the excess profits of one developer may attract so many other developers that they supply more real estate than the market will demand. The result is that some or even all the developers either make no profits or lose money.

Increasing and Decreasing Returns

This principle relates to the apportionment of the four agents or factors of production: labor, capital, management, and land. According to this principle, increasing the amount of one or more factors of production will increase value up to a certain point, known as the point of diminishing returns. Once this point is reached, any further increase in the factor(s) of production will have a negative effect; the resulting value increases will be less than the cost of the additional factor(s) of production.

Contribution

This principle relates to the principle of increasing and decreasing returns applied to a portion of a real property. The value of any individual factor of production is a function of how much it enhances the property value by its presence or how much it detracts from the property value by its absence.

Balance

The principle of balance holds that value is maximized when all the factors of production are present in proper proportions. Furthermore, value is maximized when there is equilibrium in the amount, character, and location of all the services and amenities required by the particular real property use.

Conformity

The principle of conformity holds that property value is maximized when there exists a "reasonable" degree of social, economic, and architectural homogeneity (which does not mean monotonous uniformity) within the neighborhood area. For example, dwellings in a residential neighborhood that conform in size, age, condition, and style tend to maximize property values.

Supply and Demand

This principle holds that value is created by a high effective demand and/or low supply of the particular type of real estate being analyzed. Demand must be backed by purchasing power to be effective; supply must be backed by utility and/or exchangeability to be desirable.

Highest and Best Use

The use which is most likely to return the greatest net present value (income or amenities) as of the date of the appraisal is the highest and best use. It can also be defined as that available use and program of future use which produces the highest present land value. If the land is already improved, its highest and best use may be different than if it were unimproved. It is possible that the existing use of improved property may not necessarily be the best use. However, the existing use will continue, unless and until the *land value* in its highest and best use exceeds the *total value* of the property in its existing use.

A complete understanding of these ten principles of value will aid the student and practitioner to comprehend fully the three approaches (cost, market, and income) used in the *appraisal process* to determine real property value.

THE APPRAISAL PROCESS

To appraise real property is to solve a problem. An appraisal report is the end-product presentation of the solution. The orderly program or set of procedures followed to arrive at the solution of the appraisal problem is called the *appraisal process*. Table 15-1 illustrates the appraisal process as a flow chart.

Definition of the Problem

At the outset the appraiser must identify the property to be appraised by both its mailing address and its legal description. The property rights (fee

TABLE 15-1. The Appraisal Process

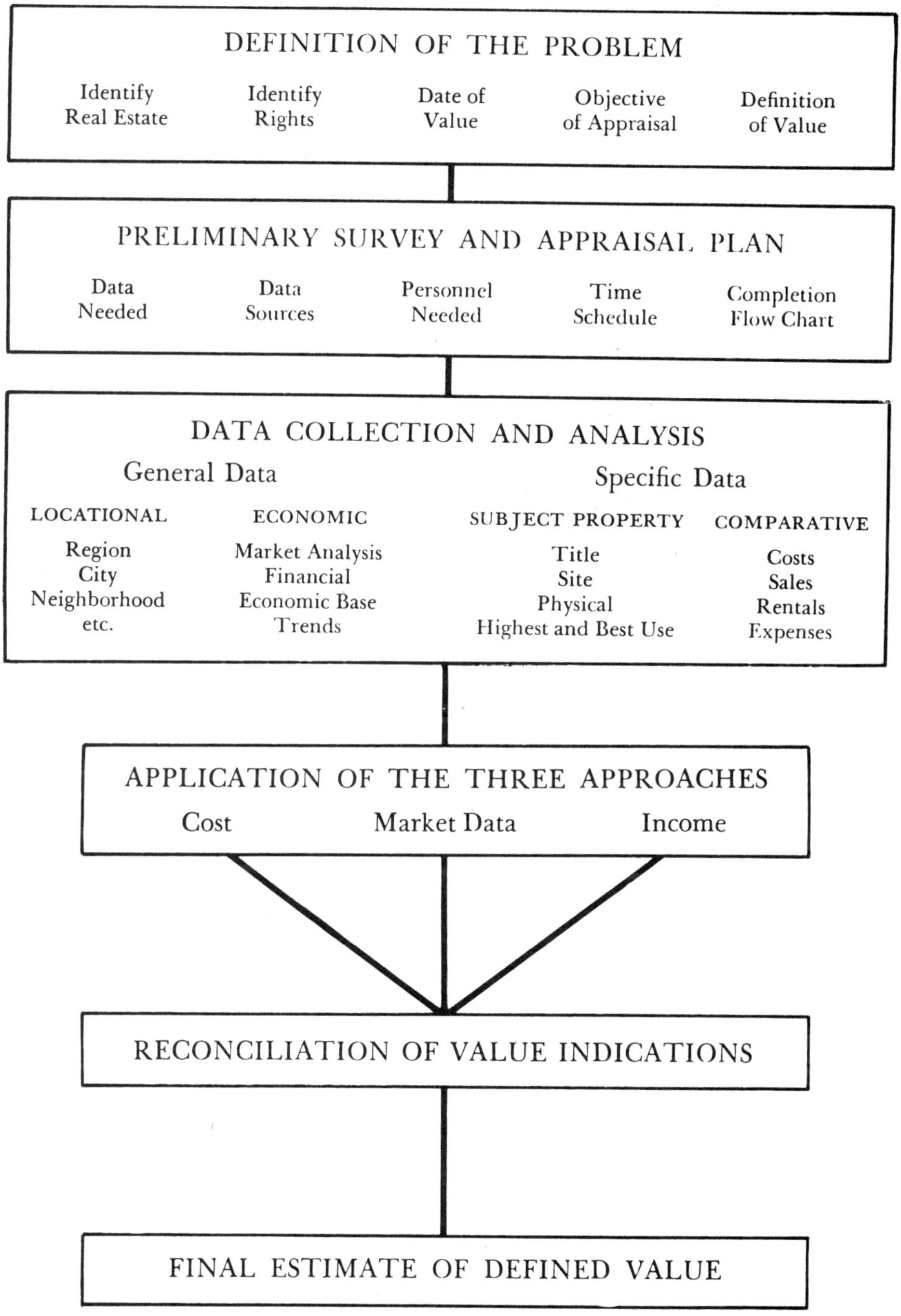

Source: *The Appraisal of Real Estate* (Chicago: American Institute of Real Estate Appraisers, 1973), pp. 50–51.

simple, leasehold, air rights, mineral rights, etc.) actually being appraised must be clearly indicated. The date, the objective or use of the appraisal, the determination of highest and best use, and the proper definition of value sought must also be clearly indicated to the client.

Preliminary Survey and Appraisal Plan

The preliminary survey should consist of an estimate of the time, labor, and expense involved in the appraisal assignment, accompanied with a written request for the appraisal and its fee. All data estimated to be required and their sources should be included in this step. The appraisal plan should include the assignment of work details by a flow chart and time schedule, and the means for proper assemblage of the required appraisal data.

Data Collection and Analysis

Before the three approaches to value are implemented into the analysis, the appraiser should conduct a study of the general economic, social, and political forces influencing value at the international, national, regional, state, metropolitan, city, and neighborhood levels. Study of specific physical and legal forces influencing the value of the site should also be made.

Application of the Three Approaches

In this step the appraiser analyzes the appraisal data and reaches a value conclusion under each of the following approaches to value: cost, market, and income. These approaches will be discussed in detail in Chapter 16.

Reconciliation of Value Indications

The last step in the appraisal process is to recheck all calculations and correlate the indication of value from each of the three approaches into a final estimate of the defined value. To correlate does *not* mean to calculate an arithmetic average. The correlation process involves recognizing which of the three approaches is most applicable to the particular appraisal problem at hand and placing the *most emphasis* on that approach's value indication. The appraiser must then call upon judgment and experience to choose a single estimate of value; the final figure must reflect, most of all, the single approach to value chosen as the most applicable. But it must also represent the other indications of value of the less applicable approaches.

Final Estimate of Defined Value

The final figure is a round number similar in size to the commonly quoted prices of comparable properties. It is an estimate and an opinion of value, not a precisely calculated digit.

The appraisal report is a formal written presentation. Such a report can be expected to include most, if not all, of the items in Table 15-2.

TABLE 15-2. Appraisal Report Outline

Part One—Introduction
- Title page. Frontispiece, if any, may face title page[§]
- Letter of transmittal. May include certification of value.
- Table of contents
- Summary of salient facts and important conclusions

Part Two—Descriptions, Analysis, and Conclusions
- Objective of the appraisal, and definition of value
- Identification of the property, legal description, also underlying assumptions (specific)
- Property rights appraised and date valuation applies
- City data, neighborhood and locational data, and trend
- Land or site data, zoning, utilities and taxes
- History
- Description of improvements
- Highest and best use analysis
- Development of an indication of value by
  - The cost approach
  - The market data approach
  - The income approach
- Reconciliation of value indications and conclusion of value
- Qualifying and limiting conditions. These include underlying assumptions (general).
- Certification of value if not combined with letter of transmittal
- Qualifications of appraiser

Part Three—Addenda
- Maps, plats, photographs[§]
- Detailed statistical data
- Detailed property data, if too lengthy to be included in Part Two
- Detailed market data, if too lengthy to be included in Part Two
- Leases or lease summaries.

This general outline is illustrative, and the arrangement set forth is flexible and adaptable to almost all appraisal assignments.

[§] A single photograph of the property or other exhibit may be used as a frontispiece or instead appear in Part Three.

Source: *The Appraisal of Real Estate* (Chicago: American Institute of Real Estate Appraisers, 1973), p. 488.

BACKGROUND ANALYSIS

Before implementing the three approaches to value, the appraiser must complete the third step in the appraisal process, data collection and analysis. As previously stated, this step consists of analyzing general social, economic, and political forces at all levels, as well as specific physical and legal forces that influence property value. The appraiser should attack the appraisal problem by starting with a general or background analysis and then moving to an analysis of the specific details of the market area, neighborhood, subject property, and comparable competitive properties.

Area Analysis

The market area pertinent to an appraisal depends on the type of property being appraised. Some properties compete in a worldwide market; others only compete in a small section of a neighborhood, or even a block. The market area is defined by the arena within which similar properties compete in the minds of the most probable purchasers or investors. The larger this arena, the greater the impact and importance of international, national, and regional economic, social, and political trends on the valuation of the property being appraised, the *subject property*.

At the international level, wars, energy sources, crop and raw-material shortages, and inflation in foreign countries may have an impact on the value of the subject property. At the national level, congressional decisions and laws, monetary and fiscal policies, and federal housing programs may affect the supply and demand for housing and mortgage credit and thus change property values. At the regional level, trends in business conditions, population migration, and location of new industries can influence local property values.

Perhaps the greatest impact on values takes place within the immediate market area. Population, climate, topography, employment, economic base, incomes, prices, mortgage interest rates, availability of mortgage credit, property taxes, municipal services, utilities, transportation, housing supply, new construction, vacancy rates, and buyer attitudes can all affect property values. It is the appraiser's job to collect all pertinent data, note trends, and judge the impact of these factors on present and future property values within the market area.

Neighborhood Analysis

The neighborhood, the immediate environment of the subject property, has a tremendous influence on value. Since people of similar social and economic status tend to live in the same type of environment, prices at which houses in that area have sold in recent years tend to fall within a definite range. In order to determine this price range, the appraiser makes a neighborhood analysis. Many factors studied in an area analysis are also important considerations in a neighborhood analysis, where the impact on value is more localized.

Items pertinent to neighborhood analyses that do not appear in area analyses include prestige, civic attitudes, police and fire protection, accessibility to schools, churches and shopping; ratio of owner-occupancy to tenant-occupancy, age distributions of buildings and their inhabitants, precentage of neighborhood that is developed, protection from adverse influences, freedom from hazards and nuisances, historical appeal, and improvements conformity. It is the appraiser's responsibility to collect all pertinent data, note trends, and judge the impact of these factors on present and future property values within the neighborhood.

Site Analysis

A *site* is more than just a parcel of land; it is land that has been improved so that it is ready to be used for the intended purpose. A site is land that has been cleared, graded, landscaped, improved for access, and linked to all necessary utilities. An analysis of the site itself is necessary because some valuation techniques require a separate valuation of the site.

The factors to be considered in site analysis include:

1. *Location* within its neighborhood, perhaps the most important factor in a site analysis
2. *Title data* such as legal description, easements, deed restrictions, zoning, building, and sanitation codes
3. *Physical data*, such as frontage, width, depth, shape, area, topography, soils, and landscaping
4. *Relation to land pattern*, abutting lots, corner influence, plottage, traffic patterns and controls, public transportation availability, convenience to employment, schools, shopping, and other related land uses
5. *Services and utilities*, including water, storm and sanitary sewers, street lighting, gas, electricity, telephone, garbage and trash collection, fire and police protection, and other civic services
6. *Highest and best use*, present and future

It is up to the appraiser to collect and analyze all appropriate site data, note any trends, and make judgments as to the impact of these factors on the value of the site.

Site Valuation

As stated above, a separate valuation of the site alone is sometimes necessary as an input to a valuation approach or technique. There are several methods available for site valuation; the market comparison method is by far preferred.

Market Comparison Method. This method calls for obtaining sales data of vacant sites that are similar to the subject site and which have recently been sold in the same market. Once it is verified that these comparable sales were *arm's-length transactions* (voluntary and bona fide), adjustments are made "from the comparable to the subject" for differences of time, location, and physical characteristics. In other words, adjustments are made to determine what the comparable sites would have sold for if they were exactly like the subject site and sold on the date of the appraisal. The adjusted values of the comparables are the indications of value for the subject, and these adjusted figures are correlated and rounded to a final estimate of value for the subject site.

Abstraction Method. To use this method, the appraiser must know the typical allocations of total property value between site and building. Given a typical ratio (percentage) of site value to total property value, he can obtain a value estimate of the site values of the comparable properties. This value results from multiplying the sales prices of improved properties within the subject site's market by the typical ratio. The Department of Commerce reports such ratios on a regional average basis.

Alternatively, if recent sales of improved comparable properties are available, if the buildings on these sites are the highest and best use, and if an estimate of the buildings can be determined, the appraiser, through abstraction, can subtract the building values from total values to obtain site values. Both of these abstraction techniques produce very dubious indications of site value, however.

Cost of Development Method. This method is normally justified for use only in the valuation of raw acreage ripe for development. To determine undeveloped land value by this method, one estimates what the total property value would be if the land were subdivided and sold as improved sites. The total of all development costs—including costs of streets, utilities, etc., and the costs of sale, overhead, carrying charges, and profit—are deducted from the estimated revenue from the sales of the improved sites. The result is the value of the undeveloped land.

This method is not justifiable for the valuation of an individual site, since it implicitly assumes the sales prices of fully developed sites are known. However, an appraiser would be justified in using this method to determine how much a developer could pay for raw acreage to be developed.

Land Residual Method. This method is applicable principally to sites of income properties and will be explained in Chapter 16 in the section on the income approach (p. 273). Briefly, this method converts a residual income imputable to the land into a land or site value estimate.

Ground Lease Method. This method is also applicable to income properties and will be discussed in Chapter 16 in the section on direct capitalization (p. 279). Briefly, the typical ground rent for similar sites is converted (through direct capitalization) into a land or site value estimate.

Improvements Analysis

Improvements analysis is synonymous with *structure analysis* and *building analysis* and consists of an on-site inspection and rating of pertinent aspects of the character, contents, condition, and functional adequacy of all structures and improvements on the subject property. Such an analysis is necessary to identify clearly all the *physical* characteristics of the real estate being appraised and is fundamental to the application of all three approaches (cost, market, and income) to value. Parallel logic may be observed in noting the necessity to identify clearly all the *legal* characteristics of the real property rights being appraised.

The appraiser's improvements analysis must be comprehensive and objective. The standards for rating structural quality, adequacy of function, and condition must be market standards determined by typical, informed purchasers. In the inspection, the appraiser should use a detailed checklist for identifying all components, their condition, and functional adequacy so that no item is overlooked and a second inspection will not be necessary. Functional adequacy is partially a function of structural quality.

Functional utility of the improvements is a prime essential in the analysis of their contribution to total property value. Such an analysis should include study of the architecture, design, layout, traffic pattern, room types and sizes, and the adequacy of any equipment in the buildings.

Two final important estimates which the appraiser must make in improvements analysis are (1) an estimate of the effective age and remaining economic life of the structures and (2) an accurate estimate of the square and/or cubic footage of the structures. These estimates are essential to value estimation in one or more of the three approaches to value.

SUMMARY AND CONCLUSION

An estimate or opinion of property value, called an appraisal, must be made to facilitate a fair and equitable real estate transaction. However, it must be remembered that "value" has many meanings and its meaning in a given situation is a function of the purpose for which the appraisal is being made. Value in use and value in exchange are the two most basic concepts of value; the former term is synonymous with subjective value, while the latter is synonymous with objective or market value. The four essential characteristics of value are utility, scarcity, demand, and transferability.

Value, price, and cost do not mean the same thing. Value is worth; price is the amount of money paid, asked, or offered in a sale and may be more or less than value; and cost is a historical price.

To better understand value, appaisers often use the so-called forces that influence value. These forces of value include the physical, economic, social, political, and legal variables that act upon and affect real property values. These forces are interpreted by an appraiser in determining the market value of a property at a specific point in time. Market value has been defined as the highest price a property will bring in a competitive and open market under all conditions requisite to a fair sale, assuming the buyer and seller each act prudently and knowledgeably and assuming the price is not affected by undue stimulus.

A greater understanding of market value may be obtained from study of the so-called principles of valuation. These principles are actually founded in the field of economics and include anticipation, substitution, change, progression, regression, competition, increasing and decreasing returns, contribution, balance, conformity, supply and demand, and highest and best use.

To appraise real property is to solve a problem. An appraisal report is the end-product presentation of the problem solution. The orderly program or set of procedures followed to arrive at the solution of the appraisal problem is called the appraisal process. The appraisal process includes (1) definition of the problem, (2) preliminary survey and appraisal plan, (3) data collection and analysis, (4) application of the three approaches, and (5) reconciliation of value indications to obtain a final estimate of the defined value.

Prior to implementing the three approaches to value, the appraiser should attack the appraisal problem by starting with a general or background analysis and then move to an analysis of the specific details of the market area, the neighborhood, the subject property, and the comparable competitive properties. To accomplish this task of background analysis, the real estate appraiser completes and includes in the appraisal report an area analysis, a neighborhood analysis, a site analysis, a site valuation (by either market comparison, abstraction, cost of development, land residual, or ground lease method), and an improvements analysis. Only upon completion of these important steps of the process can the real estate appraiser proceed to the application of the three approaches to value (cost, market, and income) that are the subjects of the next chapter.

CHAPTER 16

The Three Approaches to Value

KEY TERMS

Reproduction cost The cost of constructing, at current prices, an exact duplicate or replica using the same materials, construction standards, design, layout, and quality of workmanship and embodying all the deficiencies, superadequacies, and obsolescence of the subject building

Replacement cost The cost of constructing, at current prices, a building having utility equivalent to the building being appraised but built with modern construction materials and methods according to current standards, design, and layout

Accrued depreciation The difference between reproduction cost new or replacement cost new and the present worth of the improvements; also called "diminished utility"

Physical deterioration A loss in value due to wear and tear, decay, dry rot, cracks, encrustations, or structural defects

Functional obsolescence A loss in value arising from decreased utility, inadequacy, superadequacy, or changes of taste in architectural style or design inherent in the structure itself

Economic obsolescence A loss in value due to environmental forces existing outside the property itself; also called "locational diminished utility"

Capitalization The conversion of income to value

Capitalization rate The sum of the discount rate and the capital recapture (recovery) rate, used to convert net operating income to value

Discount rate An annual competitive rate of return "on" total invested capital necessary to compensate the investor for all the various risks inherent in a particular investment

Capital recapture (recovery) rate The return "of" total invested capital, expressed as an annual rate

COST APPROACH

In the execution of the three approaches to value—cost, market, and income—it is rational and efficient to begin with the cost approach, since this approach utilizes the physical data regarding site and improvements which should have been compiled by the appraiser in the site analysis and valuation and in the improvements inspection and analysis. The cost approach, which consists of adding site value to the depreciated reproduction cost of the building improvements, is particularly applicable in the following situations:

1. When there is no competitive market for the subject property, or when the level of market activity is insufficient to provide enough recent sales of comparable properties for use in a market approach
2. When the subject property is truly a unique, one-of-a-kind property (designed by Frank Lloyd Wright, for example) or is a special purpose property (a museum, for example), which indicates that comparable properties may not even exist
3. When appraising very new or proposed construction
4. When the subject property produces no income, such as a church or government building

Steps in the Cost Approach

There are five steps to be followed in executing the cost approach.

1. Estimate site value as if vacant and available to be utilized at its highest and best use.
2. Estimate reproduction cost new of the building improvements.
3. Estimate all accrued depreciation (also called diminished utility).
4. Subtract accrued depreciation from the reproduction cost new of the building improvements, the difference being the depreciated cost of the building improvements.
5. Add the site value to the depreciated cost of the building improvements to obtain the total property value.

Since the methods of site valuation have already been discussed, we need here discuss only the methods of estimating building cost and the methods of estimating accrued depreciation.

Reproduction Cost versus Replacement Cost

Before discussing the various methods of estimating building cost, it is necessary to distinguish clearly the differences between reproduction cost and replacement cost.

Reproduction cost is the cost of construction at current prices of an exact duplicate or replica using the same materials, construction standards, design, layout, and quality of workmanship, embodying all the deficiencies, superadequacies, and obsolescence of the subject building.

Replacement cost is the cost of construction at current prices of a building having utility equivalent to the building being appraised but built with modern materials and according to current standards, design, and layout. The use of this concept presumably eliminates all functional obsolescence, and the only depreciation to be measured is physical deterioration and economic obsolescence.[1]

Theoretically, replacement cost would seem to be the preferable cost to use in appraisal, since the typical purchaser or investor would seek the same utility rather than the same physical improvements. However, the functional obsolescence (implicitly eliminated in replacement cost) of the subject property must be inferred from prices of comparable property sales in a competitive market. Furthermore, if replacement cost is used, the estimation of physical deterioration must be made against a hypothetical replacement property rather than against the subject property. For these reasons reproduction cost is generally used in appraisal analysis. One exception would be the case of an investor choosing between buying an existing property or building a new one. In this situation replacement cost may be used as a guide to the upper limit the investor should pay for the existing property. Replacement cost might also apply to determining the feasibility of rehabilitation, modernization, or remodeling.

Methods of Estimating Reproduction Cost

The appraiser has the choice of processing a detailed cost analysis using one of the commonly accepted costing methods, or a short-cut method using one of the published construction cost services.

Cost Services. Published cost services approximate costs for typical structures. Such estimates are usually within reasonable ranges and do serve the needs of an appraisal. Often, reliance on these services is dictated by the need for speed and economy of appraisal assignments. Cost services are designed to translate the costs of various types of buildings to average costs per square or cubic foot. Some services are more detailed than others and include more complex cost breakdowns. Instructions are always given for adapting the average costs to fit variations from the standard prototype used in computing average costs. Also provided are a time index and local cost index modifiers for adjusting the average costs to the actual costs at a particular time in different locations in the country. Such indexes are usually updated monthly or quarterly.

Quantity Survey Method. This is the most complexly detailed, expensive, and time-consuming method available to the appraiser. A complete itemized inventory of prices for all materials, equipment, labor, overhead,

1. Byrl N. Boyce, *Real Estate Appraisal Terminology* (Cambridge, MA: Ballinger Publishing Company, 1975), p. 176.

fees, and profit required to currently reproduce the subject property are summed to a total building cost. Those using this method must have a special expertise that few appraisers have. And this method is usually prohibitively expensive for the typical appraisal assignment.

Unit in Place Method. This method involves the unit costing of materials and labor for each portion of a structure installed. For example, the cost of an interior wall in place would involve a summation of the costs per unit of materials and labor for framing, plumbing and electrical (if applicable), wallboard, and painting. This unit cost is then multiplied by the number of square, cubic, or lineal feet to derive the installed cost of the interior walls in place. The installed costs of all other component units are summed, and lump sums for equipment, overhead, and profit are added to derive the total building cost estimate.

Building Trade Segregated Breakdown Method. In this method of estimating reproduction cost, an installed unit cost, including overhead and profit for each major functional part of the building, is developed from the local market. Each major functional part (excavation, foundation, framing, electrical, plumbing, roofing, etc.) of the structure is usually bid on and constructed by a different subcontractor. The sum of all these bids will be the total building cost estimate. This method is sometimes called the *subcontract method*.

Comparative Unit Method. This method derives a standard cost per square or cubic foot, or a standard cost per unit of use (room, apartment, hospital bed, etc.). The comparative unit costs are derived by dividing the total *known* costs of similar structures by the appropriate comparative unit. The standard comparative unit cost is then multiplied by the number of comparative units contained in the subject to derive the total building cost estimate for the subject property.

The chief weakness of the costing methods discussed above stems from the fact that appraisers seek to determine value, not cost. At any point in time, abnormal market conditions may serve to modify costs as indications of value. Imbalance between costs and values is usually created by an imbalance in supply and demand factors and by the necessity of having to make allowances for accrued depreciation.

Accrued Depreciation (Diminished Utility)

Professional appraisers use the following definition:

Accrued Depreciation—The difference between reproduction cost new or replacement cost new of the improvements and the present worth of those improvements, both measured as of the date of the appraisal. In measuring accrued depreciation, the appraiser is interested in identifying and measuring the loss

> in utility experienced by the subject structure in its present condition, as compared to the utility it would have as a new improvement representing the highest and best use of the site. Accrued depreciation is sometimes referred to as diminished utility.[2]

Accrued depreciation consists of the following three basic elements: (1) physical deterioration, (2) functional obsolescence, and (3) economic obsolescence.

Physical deterioration is evidenced by wear and tear, decay, dry rot, cracks, encrustations, or structural defects. The effects of physical deterioration may be accelerated by lack of proper maintenance, the presence of adverse chemicals in the air, biological hazards such as termites, and any other special hazard or extraordinary condition surrounding the property. Physical deterioration can be further subdivided into curable and incurable types.

Curable physical deterioration is physical diminished utility which the wise purchaser would anticipate fixing upon buying the property. The cost to cure should be no more than the value of the anticipated addition to utility. Incurable physical deterioration is physical diminished utility which it is not feasible or economically justifiable to correct. In other words, the cost to cure is greater than the value of the anticipated addition to utility; hence, the wise buyer will not spend the money.

Functional obsolescence is the loss in value arising from decreased utility, inadequacy, superadequacy, or changes of taste in architectural style or design inherent in the structure or one of its component parts. Since functional obsolescence arises from conditions *inherent* in the improvements, corrections may be possible at some cost. Therefore, as with physical deterioration, functional obsolescence may be divided into curable and incurable, depending upon the trade-off between the costs to cure and the value of the anticipated addition to utility to be gained from the correction.

Economic obsolescence is also called locational diminished utility. This type of depreciation is a reduction in utility as a result of negative environmental forces existing *outside* the property. Because economic obsolescence is caused by *external* forces over which the owner has no control, it is always deemed, for practical purposes, incurable. Examples of outside forces include: change in character of a neighborhood; presence of a nuisance, such as a recently built factory; adverse legislation, such as a change in zoning; or a breakdown in public transportation.

Measures of Depreciation

There are five basic methods commonly used to estimate the dollar amounts to be charged for accrued depreciation: (1) capitalized income

2. Ibid., p. 3.

method, (2) market method, (3) straight-line (age-life) method, (4) engineering method, and (5) breakdown method.

The *capitalized income method* is a by-product of the income approach to value. In the income approach, depreciation is considered to reduce the amount, quality, and duration of the net income and is therefore reflected in the income-stream estimate (see p. 274).

The *market method* considers the differences in selling prices of two properties which are reasonably alike except that one is brand new and the other is old. These differences, often translated into percentages associated with building ages, are then used as clues to estimating depreciation in other properties.

The *straight-line method* provides for a constant percentage of value to be deducted for each year of structure age. This percentage is subtracted directly from the estimated reproduction cost without any consideration for individual variations.

The *engineering method* provides for reductions to be applied to the individual parts of the structure—foundations, walls, floors, roofs, etc. The reductions to be made are determined by making a detailed observation of the physical utility loss for each part of the structure. This method does not provide a way to account for depreciation due to obsolescence.

The *breakdown method* is a further refinement of the engineering method. Not only are the construction components analyzed, but the three basic elements of depreciation (physical deterioration, functional obsolescence, and economic obsolescence) are each analyzed in separate steps.

The estimation of all elements of accrued depreciation is the last data input required to estimate value by the cost approach. The appraiser then simply subtracts the accrued depreciation from the reproduction cost new to get the current depreciated reproduction cost. This is then added to the site value, and the sum is rounded to the final estimate of total property value.

MARKET APPROACH

The market approach to value is sometimes called by more descriptive names, including comparative sales approach, market comparison approach, market data approach, or sales comparison approach. Whichever name is used, the techniques of analysis and the principles and rationale applied are the same. There are five basic steps to this approach to value.

1. Analysis of the subject property
2. Selection of the comparable properties recently sold
3. Analysis of the comparable properties as to time of sale, location, physical characteristics, and terms of financing

4. Comparison between the subject property and the comparables, making adjustments for value differences from the comparables to the subject, the results of which are indications of value for the subject property
5. Correlation of the indications of value to a final value estimate or a final value range of what the subject property would sell for in the market as of the date of the appraisal

Rationale of the Market Approach

The purpose of any appraisal is to estimate value, most often market value. The market approach is based on the analysis of typical buyers and sellers in the given market of the subject property. The appraiser attempts to find out what properties of comparable type, location, and owner amenities have recently been sold for under the same market conditions. The reliability of this approach depends on the thoroughness with which the appraiser defines and analyzes the market. The appraiser must be sure that the comparable property transactions meet the following requirements: (1) there was no undue pressure on either buyer or seller to act, (2) the buyer and seller were well informed, (3) the parties acted with rational and prudent behavior based on market information, (4) the comparable properties were exposed to the market for a reasonable amount of time, and (5) the prices paid for comparables reflected current market terms and conditions.

The *principle of substitution* is the basic principle underlying the market approach. This principle states that the upper limit of value of a property is usually equal to the cost or price of an equally desirable substitute or comparable property. A wise and rational buyer should pay no more than the cost of acquiring such a similar property for sale in the same market. The substitution principle is used to choose comparable properties. Then a comparison is made between the subject property and the comparable properties as to time of sale, location, utility, physical characteristics of the improvements, conditions of sale, income-expense ratios, rental rates, and any other pertinent characteristics. The next step is to develop, through an appropriate adjustment process, indications of what the comparables would have sold for had they possessed all of the fundamental and pertinent physical and economic characteristics of the subject property. Finally, after all adjustments, the adjusted sale prices of the comparables (which are indications of value for the subject property) should all fall around one central figure which, when properly rounded, will provide an indication of the market value or value range of the subject property as of the date of the appraisal.

Market standards must be used for comparing the sales of similar properties with the subject property. To be applied properly and effectively, this approach requires sufficient quantities of good market data. The point of view taken by the appraiser should be that of a *typically informed buyer* acting prudently on the available market information.

The appraiser should focus the analysis on the *local market* in which the subject property exists. Area and neighborhood analyses are used to indicate the scope of the local market. A large area is apt to be more helpful than a small one. However, a larger area is of no use if it does not contain reasonably comparable properties.

The appraiser should also focus on *current market data*. It is obvious that sales made very near the date of the appraisal should be given the greatest weight in the comparative analysis. Sales dating back over a long period of time may include different levels of economic activity, and this may cause them to have doubtful application to current market conditions. Using recently sold comparables avoids the necessity of making time adjustments, which are subjective and difficult to substantiate.

Finally, in terms of market standards, rational behavior requires that the buyer will plan to use the subject property at its *highest and best use*. Hence, the appraiser should value the subject property in terms of this best use, which may vary with the degree of property improvement.

Elements of Comparison

The appraiser must analyze sales data to determine the degree of comparability that exists between the subject property and each of the comparables. Through analysis of the subject property, the appraiser will have identified the important characteristics of comparison. A similar identification must also be made for each comparable. Appropriate application of the market approach entails a knowledge of the standards of the local market, a detailed property inspection, and keen observation, as well as the ability to interpret structural quality. Finally, knowledge of typical buyer preferences, local price reactions, and the application of sound judgment is necessary to produce reliable results.

The comparisons must be made in terms of salient characteristics of both the subject and comparable properties, including the following items.[3]

1. Financial terms of sale
2. Conditions of sale
3. Date of sale
4. Character of tenancy
5. Style and layout
6. Size, rooms, functional adequacy
7. Structural type and quality

3. Sanders A. Kahn, Frederick E. Case, and Alfred Schimmel, *Real Estate Appraisal and Investment* (New York: Ronald Press Company, 1963), p. 91.

8. Improvements and accessory buildings
9. Income-expense ratio
10. Gross and net rentals
11. Condition of mechanical equipment
12. Functional utility
13. Age of buildings
14. Size, shape, and location of plot
15. Zoning
16. Neighborhood changes during period studied
17. Sale-included other assets, such as furniture or fixtures

Units of Comparison[4]

Units of comparison or units of analysis can be used to account for differences in size between the subject property and the comparable properties. The aim is to reduce a property to a per-unit basis to obtain a closer comparison. This method of analysis should be used only when the differences in size are small, otherwise properties which are really in separate markets might be compared.

Only units that reflect the thinking and behavior of those in the market should be used. In other words, the unit of analysis used must be one of common usage for the particular type of property being analyzed. For residential property appraisal, the common units of comparison include: price per square foot of living area, price per square foot of ground area covered, price per apartment, price per suite, and price per room. For commercial property, common units include: price per square foot of selling area, price per square or cubic foot, price per front foot, price per seat in a theater, and price per bed in a hospital. Industrial property units are usually per square or cubic foot, and agricultural property is usually quoted per acre.

Adjustment and Correlation Processes[5]

In the adjustment process the appraiser must adjust each of the comparable properties to an estimate of what the property would have sold for had it possessed all of the important characteristics of the subject property. The appraiser must be able to defend and justify with market data any and all adjustments made between the subject and the comparables. Among the factors that are adjusted, the appraiser should be sure to include the elements for which deductions are made in the subject property

4. William N. Kinnard, *An Introduction to Appraising Real Property* (Chicago: Society of Real Estate Appraisers, 1968), pp. 13-11 and 13-12.
5. Ibid., pp. 13-12 through 13-16.

in estimating accrued depreciation in the cost approach and in estimating rent differentials in gross income multiplier analysis (see below).

All adjustments are made *from* the comparable properties *to* the subject property. If a comparable property has some improvement (such as an extra bathroom) which the subject property does not have, then a downward adjustment in the sales price of the comparable property is required. The subject property is always considered the 100 percent standard; the comparables are always treated as deviations from this norm. The three most common adjustment techniques are (1) plus and minus dollar adjustments, (2) plus and minus percentage adjustments, and (3) cumulative percentage adjustments (this technique is not preferred; it is prone to error).

An adjusted sales price is derived for each of the comparable properties. These adjusted sales prices are then correlated to a final indication of the market value of the subject property, the greatest emphasis having been given to those comparables regarded as most similar to the subject property. This final estimate is then rounded to the market value estimate or value range for the subject property. (See Exhibit 16-1.)

Gross Income Multipliers Approach

The gross income multiplier is simply a rule-of-thumb method of calculating real estate value. It is used as a general indicator of market value and is calculated as the ratio of sale price to gross annual or monthly income. This approach is used in comparing different properties with the same general characteristics and use. For example, if the monthly gross income multipliers of comparable properties all fall between 110 and 130, a multiplier of 120 may be used to multiply the subject property's gross income to get a rough estimate of its market value.

This quick and easy method of calculating market value should be used only as a check on the other approaches to value, because it suffers from some important basic shortcomings. It does not allow for different operating ratios, different vacancy rates, different ages of property, different neighborhoods, or different qualities of income among the comparable properties.

Advantages of the Market Approach

Some of the advantages of the market approach to value are as follows:

1. It is the easiest of the three approaches to learn and to use.
2. It is particularly applicable to residential transactions, which make up a great portion of all real estate transactions.
3. It is the approach most easily understood by the nonprofessional.
4. It is the approach on which most courts have placed greatest reliance

RESIDENTIAL APPRAISAL REPORT

File No.

To be completed by Lender

Borrower/Client John M. Freeman & Rose B. Freeman — Census Tract 84-9 — Map Reference 15747614

Property Address 33 North Road

City Typicaltown — County Cook — State IL — Zip Code 60119

Legal Description SW Qu. Sec. 19 Township 41 N, Range 11 - 66' on North Rd & 132' deep

Sale Price $ 41,500 — Date of Sale 6/9/7- — Property Rights Appraised [X] Fee [ ] Leasehold [ ] DeMinimis PUD (FNMA only [ ] Condo [ ] PUD)

Actual Real Estate Taxes $ 642.21 (yr) Loan charges to be paid by seller $ — Other sales concessions —

Lender Typa-Savings & Loan Assn. — Lender's Address 1241 Harvard Ave, Typicaltown, IL

Occupant Owner — Appraiser Leslie E. Clinton — Instructions to Appraiser Call for appointment

NEIGHBORHOOD

Location [ ] Urban [X] Suburban [ ] Rural

Built Up [X] Over 75% [ ] 25% to 75% [ ] Under 25%

Growth Rate [ ] Fully Dev. [ ] Rapid [ ] Steady [X] Slow

Property Values [ ] Increasing [X] Stable [ ] Declining

Demand/Supply [ ] Shortage [X] In Balance [ ] Over Supply

Marketing Time [X] Under 3 Mos. [ ] 4–6 Mos. [ ] Over 6 Mos.

Present Land Use 75 % 1 Family 5 % 2–4 Family 5 % Apts. ___ % Condo 5 % Commercial 5 % Industrial 5 % Vacant ___ %

Change in Present Land Use [X] Not Likely [ ] Likely (*) [ ] Taking Place (*)

(*) From ______ To ______

Predominant Occupancy [X] Owner [ ] Tenant ___ % Vacant

Single Family Price Range $ 35,000 to $ 50,000 Predominant Value $ 40,000

Single Family Age 25 yrs to 50 yrs Predominant Age 25 yrs

	Good	Avg.	Fair	Poor
Employment Stability	[ ]	[X]	[ ]	[ ]
Convenience to Employment	[ ]	[X]	[ ]	[ ]
Convenience to Shopping	[ ]	[X]	[ ]	[ ]
Convenience to Schools	[ ]	[X]	[ ]	[ ]
Adequacy of Public Transportation	[ ]	[X]	[ ]	[ ]
Recreational Facilities	[ ]	[X]	[ ]	[ ]
Adequacy of Utilities	[ ]	[X]	[ ]	[ ]
Property Compatibility	[X]	[ ]	[ ]	[ ]
Protection from Detrimental Conditions	[ ]	[X]	[ ]	[ ]
Police and Fire Protection	[ ]	[X]	[ ]	[ ]
General Appearance of Properties	[ ]	[X]	[ ]	[ ]
Appeal to Market	[ ]	[X]	[ ]	[ ]

Note: FHLMC/FNMA do not consider the racial composition of the neighborhood to be a relevant factor and it must not be considered in the appraisal.

Comments including those factors, favorable or unfavorable, affecting marketability (e.g. public parks, schools, view, noise) Part of a subdivision of 254 houses built in 1954-55. All houses are same basic type. Income range: $11,000-$16,000. Typical resident is young family in first home. Typical sale is financed with 75% conventional mortgage. Quality of the schools is average.

SITE

Dimensions 66' on North Rd. x 132' deep = 8,712 Sq. Ft. or Acres [ ] Corner Lot

Zoning classification Residential — Present improvements [X] do [ ] do not conform to zoning regulations

Highest and best use: [X] Present use* [ ] Other (specify)

	Public	Other (Describe)
Elec.	[X]	
Gas	[X]	
Water	[X]	
San. Sewer	[X]	

[ ] Underground Elect. & Tel.

OFF SITE IMPROVEMENTS: Street Access: [X] Public [ ] Private — Surface Bituminous paving — Maintenance: [X] Public [ ] Private — [X] Storm Sewer [ ] Curb/Gutter — [X] Sidewalk [X] Street Lights

Topo Level — Size Typical of neighborhood — Shape Rectangular — View Typical — Drainage Typical - Good

Is the property located in a HUD Identified Special Flood Hazard Area? [X] No [ ] Yes

Comments (favorable or unfavorable including any apparent adverse easements, encroachments or other adverse conditions) * See notes on physical deterioration

IMPROVEMENTS

[X] Existing (approx. yr. blt.) 1953 [ ] Proposed [ ] Under Construction — No. Units 1 — No. Stories 1 — Type (det, duplex, semi/det, etc.) detached — Design (rambler, split level, etc.) ranch — Exterior Walls 5/8" redwood

Roof Material asphalt shingles — Gutters & Downspouts [ ] None galvanized sheet metal — Window (Type) double hung [ ] Storm Sash [ ] Screens [X] Combination — Insulation [ ] None [X] Floor [X] Ceiling [ ] Roof [X] Walls

Foundation Walls concrete — [ ] Crawl Space [X] Slab on Grade

BSMT: 0 % Basement [ ] Outside Entrance [ ] Concrete Floor — [ ] Floor Drain [ ] Sump Pump ___ % Finished — Finished Ceiling — Finished Walls — Finished Floor — Evidence of: [ ] Dampness [ ] Termites [ ] Settlement

Comments

ROOM LIST

Room List	Foyer	Living	Dining	Kitchen	Den	Family Rm.	Rec. Rm.	Bedrooms	No. Baths	Laundry	Other
Basement											
1st Level		1		1				3	1		
2nd Level											

Finished area above grade contains a total of 5 rooms 3 bedrooms 1 baths.

INTERIOR FINISH & EQUIPMENT

Kitchen Equipment: [ ] Refrigerator [ ] Range/Oven [ ] Disposal [ ] Dishwasher [ ] Fan/Hood [ ] Compactor [ ] Washer [ ] Dryer [ ]

HEAT: Type hot air Fuel gas Cond. good — AIR COND: [ ] Central [ ] Other [ ] Adequate [ ] Inadequate

Floors [X] Hardwood [ ] Carpet Over [ ]

Walls [X] Drywall [ ] Plaster [ ]

Trim/Finish [ ] Good [X] Average [ ] Fair [ ] Poor

Bath Floor [ ] Ceramic [X] asphalt tile

Bath Wainscot [ ] Ceramic [X] 4" plastic tile

Special Features (including fireplaces):

ATTIC: [ ] Yes [X] No [ ] Stairway [ ] Drop-stair [ ] Scuttle [ ] Floored [ ] Heated

Finished (Describe)

CAR STORAGE: [ ] Garage [ ] Built-in [X] Attached [ ] Detached [X] Car Port

No. Cars 1 [X] Adequate [ ] Inadequate Condition Average

PROPERTY RATING

	Good	Avg.	Fair	Poor
Quality of Construction (Materials & Finish)	[ ]	[X]	[ ]	[ ]
Condition of Improvements	[ ]	[X]	[ ]	[ ]
Rooms size and layout	[ ]	[X]	[ ]	[ ]
Closets and Storage	[ ]	[ ]	[X]	[ ]
Plumbing—adequacy and condition	[ ]	[X]	[ ]	[ ]
Electrical—adequacy and condition	[ ]	[X]	[ ]	[ ]
Kitchen Cabinets—adequacy and condition	[ ]	[X]	[ ]	[ ]
Compatibility to Neighborhood	[X]	[ ]	[ ]	[ ]
Overall Livability	[ ]	[X]	[ ]	[ ]
Appeal and Marketability	[ ]	[X]	[ ]	[ ]

Effective Age 20 Yrs. Est. Remaining Economic Life 40 Yrs.

PORCHES, PATIOS, POOL, FENCES, etc. (describe) 3.5' x 9' storage area in rear of carport

COMMENTS (including functional or physical inadequacies, repairs needed, modernization, etc.)
Kitchen & bathroom tiles need repair
Driveway has ruts & needs repair
Entrance into kitchen and kitchen in front of house accepted in this market

FHLMC Form 70 Rev. 7/77 — ATTACH DESCRIPTIVE PHOTOGRAPHS OF SUBJECT PROPERTY AND STREET SCENE — FNMA Form 1004 Rev. 7/77

Exhibit 16-1 Sample Appraisal

Source: George F. Bloom and Henry S. Harrison, *Appraising the Single Family Residence* (Chicago: American Institute of Real Estate Appraisers, 1978), pp. 390–91.

VALUATION SECTION

COST APPROACH

Purpose of Appraisal is to estimate Market Value as defined in Certification & Statement of Limiting Conditions (FHLMC Form 439/FNMA Form 1004B). If submitted for FNMA, the appraiser must attach (1) sketch or map showing location of subject, street names, distance from nearest intersection, and any detrimental conditions and (2) exterior building sketch of improvements showing dimensions.

Measurements	No. Stories	Sq. Ft.
24 x 44	x 1	= 1,056
x	x	=
x	x	=
x	x	=
x	x	=
x	x	=

Total Gross Living Area (List in Market Data Analysis below) 1,056

Comment on functional and economic obsolescence: Traffic on Stevenson Rd. causes economic obsolescence estimated to be $975.

Estimated physical incurable deterioration is $20,100.

ESTIMATED REPRODUCTION COST – NEW – OF IMPROVEMENTS:

Dwelling 1,056 Sq. Ft. @ $ 47.64	= $ 50,300
Sq. Ft. @ $	=
Extras	=
	=
	=
Porches, Patios, etc.	=
Garage/Car Port Sq. Ft. @ $	= 2,700
Site Improvements (driveway, landscaping, etc.)	= 1,000
Total Estimated Cost New	= $ 54,000
Less Depreciation: Physical $ 20,675; Functional $ –; Economic $ 975	= $ (21,650)
Depreciated value of improvements	= $ 32,350
ESTIMATED LAND VALUE (If leasehold, show only leasehold value)	= $ 9,000
INDICATED VALUE BY COST APPROACH	$ 41,400 (Rd.)

MARKET DATA ANALYSIS

The undersigned has recited three recent sales of properties most similar and proximate to subject and has considered these in the market analysis. The description includes a dollar adjustment, reflecting market reaction to those items of significant variation between the subject and comparable properties. If a significant item in the comparable property is superior to, or more favorable than, the subject property, a minus (-) adjustment is made, thus reducing the indicated value of subject; if a significant item in the comparable is inferior to, or less favorable than, the subject property, a plus (+) adjustment is made, thus increasing the indicated value of the subject.

ITEM	Subject Property	COMPARABLE NO. 1		COMPARABLE NO. 2		COMPARABLE NO. 3	
Address	33 North Road Typicaltown	65 North Road Typicaltown		38 Cottken Street Typicaltown		23 McKinley Street Typicaltown	
Proximity to Subj.		Same Street		1 Block north		1 Block south	
Sales Price	$ 41,500		$ 46,000		$ 42,300		$ 44,700
Price/Living area	$ 39.30 ⌀		$ 39.48 ⌀		$ 36.47 ⌀		$ 38.21 ⌀
Data Source	Lender	Grantee- Atwood		MLS		MLS	
	DESCRIPTION	DESCRIPTION	+(–)$ Adjustment	DESCRIPTION	+(–)$ Adjustment	DESCRIPTION	+(–)$ Adjustment
Date of Sale and Time Adjustment	6-8-7-	5-18-7-	–	11-14-7-	+4,500	10-28-7-	+4,150
Location	Average	Equal	–	Equal		Equal	
Site/View	Good/Good	Larger/Equal	-400	Larger/Equal	-1,500	Larger/Equal	-950
Design and Appeal	Average	Equal	–	Equal	–	Equal	–
Quality of Const.	Average	Equal	–	Equal	–	Equal	–
Age	20 yrs.	Equal	–	Equal	–	Equal	–
Condition	Average	Equal	–	Equal	–	Equal	–
Living Area Room Count and Total Gross Living Area	Total 5, B-rms 3, Baths 1; 1,056 Sq.Ft.	Total 6, B-rms 3, Baths 1; 1,165 Sq.Ft.	-4,300	Total 6, B-rms 3, Baths 1; 1,160 Sq.Ft.	-4,000	Total 5, B-rms 3, Baths 1; 1,170 Sq.Ft.	-4,150
Basement & Bsmt. Finished Rooms	Slab	Equal	–	Equal	–	Equal	–
Functional Utility	Average	Equal	–	Equal	–	Equal	–
Air Conditioning	None	Equal	–	Equal	–	Equal	–
Garage/Car Port	car port (1)	Equal	–	Equal	–	2-car det.	-2,450
Porches, Patio, Pools, etc.	None	Equal	–	Equal	–	Equal	–
Other (e.g. fire-places, kitchen equip., heating, remodeling)	No kitchen or laundry equipment	Equal	–	Equal	–	Equal	–
Sales or Financing Concessions	75% conv. No concessions	Equal	–	Equal	–	Equal	–
Net Adj. (Total)		☐ Plus; ☒ Minus	$ 4,700	☐ Plus; ☒ Minus	$ 1,000	☐ Plus; ☒ Minus	$ 3,400
Indicated Value of Subject			$ 41,300		$ 41,300		$ 41,300

Comments on Market Data: Equal weight given to each sale. Excellent market data

INDICATED VALUE BY MARKET DATA APPROACH $ 41,300

INDICATED VALUE BY INCOME APPROACH (If applicable) Economic Market Rent $ 315 /Mo. x Gross Rent Multiplier 130 = $ 40,950

This appraisal is made ☒ "as is" ☐ subject to the repairs, alterations, or conditions listed below ☐ completion per plans and specifications.

Comments and Conditions of Appraisal: Estimated cost of Kitchen and bathroom tile repair is $275. Estimated cost of driveway repair is $700.

Final Reconciliation: $41,300 indicated by market data approach is the best indication of the final value. It is well supported by the $41,400 indicated by the cost approach and the $40,950 indicated by the income approach.

This appraisal is based upon the above requirements, the certification, contingent and limiting conditions, and Market Value definition that are stated in

☐ FHLMC Form 439 (Rev. 9/75)/FNMA Form 1004B filed with client ______ 19____ ☒ attached.

If submitted for FNMA, the report has been prepared in compliance with FNMA form instructions.

I ESTIMATE THE MARKET VALUE, AS DEFINED, OF SUBJECT PROPERTY AS OF June 19 197- to be $ 41,300

Appraiser(s) Leslie E. Clinton   Review Appraiser (If applicable)

☐ Did ☐ Did Not Physically Inspect Property

FHLMC Form 70 Rev. 7/77   REVERSE   SAF (American Savings and Accounting Supply, Inc.) (12502-3)

Exhibit 16-1 (Continued)

and emphasis for reaching judgments as to market value for awarding just compensation.

5. The information developed through the market approach provides both a basis and support for judgments in the application of the cost and income approaches to value. For example, the basis for estimating depreciation in the cost approach is established in the market approach. The market approach also establishes standards for estimating the gross rent multiplier used in the income approach.

Disadvantages of the Market Approach

Some of the disadvantages of the market approach to value include the following:

1. Sales of comparables may not be frequent enough to establish a proper representative price.
2. The subject property may be so unique that no comparable properties exist.
3. Since comparable sales have taken place in the past, the appraiser must assume that the market behavior and forces of the past will continue in the future.
4. Even though properties may be comparable as to use and physical characteristics, the market conditions and terms of sale may be so different as to cause the properties not to be comparable.
5. There is always the possibility of some undue pressure having been placed upon either the buyer or the seller.

INCOME APPROACH

The income approach to value is based upon the *principle of anticipation*, which holds that value is created or equal to the present worth of all future benefits (both income and amenities) expected, estimated, forecasted, or anticipated to be derived from the ownership of any or all of the interests in real or personal property. In other words, income creates value. In order to know how much value is created by a particular income stream, the appraiser must implement a process which converts anticipated future periodic income to value. Such a process in real estate appraisal is known as capitalization. *Capitalization* is simply the conversion of income to value.

In order to convert income to value, the income approach to value utilizes the following five basic steps:

1. Estimate potential gross income.
2. Estimate effective gross income.

3. Estimate net operating income.
4. Estimate an appropriate capitalization rate.
5. Estimate or choose an appropriate capitalization method to convert income to value.

In real estate appraisal, the income which is converted to value is usually net operating income (NOI), also called net income or net income before capital recapture (or depreciation) and debt service (mortgage payments)[6]. Normally in real estate appraisal, income is capitalized on an annual basis. Usually such income represents an average or stabilized amount. The first three steps in the income approach to value are the procedures used to derive this number.

Potential Gross Income

Potential gross income is the income that a property will produce with 100 percent occupancy at the market rent. *Market rent* is the rental income most probably commanded by a property on the open market (as of the date of the appraisal) as indicated by current rentals paid for comparable space. Market rent is the terminology preferred over the often synonymously used term "economic rent."

Three basic income characteristics must be considered in the potential gross income estimation process.

1. *Quantity*. What *amount* of income could be expected to be produced by the property during the future period of ownership being analyzed? The amount of income to be expected is a function of past and present performance of the subject property, rentals being earned by comparable properties, and the amount of rent which present and prospective tenants are justified in paying.

2. *Quality*. What is the financial responsibility and condition of the tenant? The estimated future rental from a triple-A-rated, national-firm tenant may be of better quality and less risk than that of a local proprietorship tenant.

3. *Durability*. What is the timing of the rental income and how long can the owner expect to receive it? Durability is enhanced by a well-written lease. For example, a long-term lease with escalation clauses should provide a more durable income stream than a short or intermediate-term lease with no escalation clauses but rather "loophole" clauses, which make it easy for the tenant to break the lease. Other clauses, such as those dealing with graduated and/or percentage rentals, and the payment for expenses and collateral services also have an impact on durability as well as quantity of income estimates.

6. In mortgage-equity analysis, discussed later, NOI less debt service as well as another type of income called *net reversion* (net proceeds to the owner upon resale) are both converted to value.

Effective Gross Income

Effective gross income is the potential gross income *less* allowance for vacancy and rent loss *plus* other income. The *allowance for vacancy and rent loss* should reflect the effect of probable vacancy and turnover, or nonpayment of rent by tenants, as evidenced in the market of the subject property. This amount is commonly expressed as a percentage of potential gross income and is then converted to a dollar figure. The percentage of vacancy and rent loss is the complement of the paid occupancy ratio.

Other income may be derived from the rental of parking or storage space, the use of personal property (recreational and laundry facilities, for example), and profit from services supplied to the tenant (for example, electricity purchased at wholesale and sold at retail). Other income may prove to be irregular or short lived and must therefore be stabilized. The professional treatment of other income in appraising is not standardized, and variations in accounting for it may be observed in practice. In any case, this extraneous income must be specifically identified so that it may be included, eliminated, or separately treated as is appropriate for the individual appraisal problem.

Net Operating Income

Net operating income is the effective gross income *less* all expenses chargeable to the operation of the property.

Expense Categories. A typical classification of expenses would include the following:

1. *Fixed expenses*, such as property taxes and insurance, which change periodically but do not vary with occupancy
2. *Operating expenses*, which are necessary to maintain the production of income by the property and usually vary with occupancy, including utilities, cleaning, painting and decorating, alterations, supplies, garbage and trash removal, general payroll, and miscellaneous
3. *Management, maintenance, and repairs* are sometimes included under operating expenses because they do vary with occupancy, but are usually categorized separately because of their magnitude and importance.
4. *Replacement reserves*, which, in practice, are often not set aside but must be considered in appraisal analysis; should provide for replacing appliances, furniture, carpet, building components, machinery and equipment with limited lives (roof, storefront, elevators, boiler, etc.)

Excluded Items. Charges which are not included in the calculation of net operating income because they are charges against the owner and not against the property include:

1. *Reserves for future depreciation* (capital recapture or recovery)
2. *Financing costs* to include cost to originate a loan and costs of carrying the loan (debt service)
3. *Income taxes* (which vary with type of ownership)
4. *Special corporation costs* (franchise taxes, directors' fees, etc.)
5. *Business expenses* of the owner
6. *Additions to capital* or capital improvements (which tend to increase the income-producing potential and/or the economic life of the property)

Future Expenses. The appraiser must seek to forecast what the net operating income will be in the future, because it is the future anticipated income that is converted or capitalized to a present worth or value. The starting point for such an estimate is the recent past and present operating statements of the subject property and comparable properties. These historical and current expenses must be adjusted, stabilized, and forecast by the appraiser into a so-called reconstructed operating statement through careful application of the appraiser's experience, judgment, and opinion as to what the market will be in the future. The anticipated future expenses estimate is deducted from the anticipated future effective gross income estimate to derive the anticipated future net operating income estimate, which is converted or capitalized to a present value or present worth estimate.

Capitalization Rates

A capitalization rate is the sum of a *discount rate* and a *capital recapture (recovery) rate*. This term, often called the "cap rate," has traditionally been misused as synonymous with the overall rate. The *overall rate* is a ratio of the annual net operating income over the property value or (more often) the sales price.

Discount Rate. A *discount rate* is an annual competitive rate of return *on* total invested capital. This term should be distinguished from an *interest rate* on borrowed funds, which is the lender's discount rate or return *on* invested (loaned) capital. The discount rate is sometimes referred to as a *risk rate*, the rate of return necessary (in a market of competitive investments) to attract investment capital.

The discount rate is generally considered to be the rate necessary to compensate the investor for all the various risks inherent in the particular investment. The risk rate, therefore, would have to be greater than the so-called *riskless rate* or *safe rate*, the rate or return which an investor could earn on an investment considered to have minimum risk and maximum safety, such as an investment in Treasury securities or an insured savings or passbook account.

A theoretical explanation of why a discount rate used in the valuation of real property is greater than the riskless or safe rate may be seen in a summation or buildup of rates of return considered to compensate the investor for the risks inherent in a real estate investment. This summation has been incorrectly explained in the past as a technique for deriving a discount rate rather than as simply a theoretical justification for why a discount rate must be greater than the safe or riskless rate. Such a summation would be as follows:

	Percentage
Safe or riskless rate	x
Type of property (business) risk	i_1
Location risk	i_2
Nonliquidity risk	i_3
Management burden risk	i_4
Theoretical justification for discount rate being greater than the safe or riskless rate.	$x + i_1 + i_2 + i_3 + i_4$

A consideration of the risks inherent in a real estate investment explains the logic of the above summation. Each real property has a risk related to the type of business it is or contains. For example, a budget motel might be more risky than an apartment building. Properties of the same type may differ in risk simply because one is well located and the other is poorly located. All real estate investments are considered nonliquid (difficult to quickly turn into cash), some more so than others. And finally, compared with most other investments, real estate investments require the investor to "look after" the investment closely because of its complex nature.

Estimating the Discount Rate. One way to estimate a discount rate, using a "band of investment theory," calculates the weighted average of the most probable mortgage interest rates available in the market and the required rate of return *on* equity required in the market. Each of these rates is weighted by the respective portions of total value they represent, as follows:

	Rate		*Portion of Value*		*Product*
First mortgage	.09	×	.75	=	.0675
Second mortgage (if any)	.12	×	.15	=	.0180
Equity	.15	×	.10	=	.0150
					.1005
Discount rate					.10 or 10 percent

Another way to estimate the discount rate, called *abstraction*, calculates overall rates (NOI divided by sales price) of recently sold comparables and subtracts a percentage to provide for capital recapture. The results would be a group of discount rates from which a representative single discount rate could be correlated. A final and perhaps most common and easy way to estimate the discount rate is for the appraiser to make a survey of what typical investors are seeking for a return *on* total investment in the market as of the date of the appraisal.

Capital Recapture (Recovery) Rate. The capital recapture rate is the return *of* total invested capital, expressed as an annual rate. Capital recapture may occur in one of several ways. Consider the example of a savings account investment. Here the interest paid by the savings institution represents the investor's return *on* invested capital, while the amount of the originally invested capital (principal) withdrawn at the end of the investment holding period represents the investor's return *of* capital.

In real estate investments the proceeds upon resale, (also called *reversion*) may be equal to, more than, or less than the amount of the originally invested capital, depending on whether the property has maintained value, gained value (appreciated), or lost value (depreciated).

If the property is estimated to maintain value, then all of the recapture or return *of* capital is in the reversion (as in the savings account example), and none must come out of the net operating income (NOI), leaving all the NOI for the return *on* capital. If the property is estimated to appreciate, then all of the recapture or return *of* capital plus some of the return *on* capital is in the reversion, with the rest of the return *on* capital being all the NOI. If the property is estimated to depreciate, then only part of the recapture or return *of* capital is in the reversion, and the balance must come out of the NOI.

Once the manner in which recapture of capital will take place has been estimated, the appraiser must determine an appropriate annual rate at which the capital is to be recovered. This capital recapture rate added to the discount rate equals the capitalization rate. For example, assuming a discount rate of 10 percent and a capital recapture rate of 2 percent, the capitalization rate would be 12 percent:

Discount rate	10 percent or .10
Capital recapture rate	2 percent or .02
Capitalization rate	12 percent or .12

The capital recapture rate of 2 percent per year corresponds to a straight-line write-off of the depreciable property in 50 years with a commensurate decline in income during the write-off period. This assumed decline may or may not occur, but the appraiser may nevertheless require this rate surcharge to cover the risk of physical and functional losses as the property gets older. The capital recapture rate may be considered an allowance for future diminished utility and is not necessarily a prediction of remaining economic life.

It is important to note that there are several methods for deriving capital recapture rates and capitalization rates. The explanations of these methods and the theories and assumptions upon which they are based are beyond the scope of this text. To the interested student, however, the author highly suggests the courses taught by the American Institute of Real Estate Appraisers and the Society of Real Estate Appraisers, which cover capitalization theory and techniques and income property valuation. Since this area of study is so vast and complex, only a limited number of the current capitalization methods and techniques commonly applied to today's appraisal problems will be presented here.

Capitalization Methods

At the outset of any discussion of capitalization methods, it is imperative to state that there is no single and infallible "right way" to convert income to value. Each appraisal problem should be taken as a separate case. Each capitalization method has certain built-in assumptions. The "right way" to capitalize income is to use the method or techniques whose built-in assumptions fit those of the particular appraisal problem. Different types of income property investments have different groups of people that constitute the market for those investments. It is the appraiser's function to interpret the appropriate market. Furthermore, the appraiser must seek to understand the investment objectives and aspirations of the appropriate market participants.

Direct Capitalization with the Overall Rate. Assume that an 11 percent overall rate has been derived from the ratios of net operating incomes to sales prices of comparable properties. If the subject property's stabilized annual NOI has been estimated to be $10,000, its value would be estimated as follows:

$$V = I/R$$

$$V = \frac{\$10{,}000}{.11}$$

$$V = \$90{,}909.09$$

Property value say $91,000

In this method there is no inherent estimate as to the behavior of the income or the capital recapture period, since there is no assumption or statement of remaining economic life. Furthermore, this method of capitalization does not differentiate what portion of the investment is land and what portion is building. However, this method is certainly very simple and can be considered very convincing and appropriate where sufficient open market sales of comparable properties exist to prove that the overall rate is truly representative of the market.

Straight-Line Recapture with Building Residual Technique. This method assumes a declining annual NOI, estimates a remaining economic life, and differentiates between the building and land portions of the investment. Furthermore, this method assumes that (1) the land value can be estimated separately by a market comparison, (2) the discount rate is known or can be estimated, and (3) the capital recapture rate is the reciprocal of the remaining economic life. Assuming the following:

Land value	$15,000	
NOI	10,000	
Discount rate	.10	
Recapture rate	.02	(50 years remaining economic life)

Value would be calculated as follows:

NOI		$10,000
Less income attributable to land at the discount rate ($15,000 × .10)		− 1,500
Equals income attributable to building (building residual)		$ 8,500
Building value equals building residual divided by capitalization rate ($8,500 ÷ .12)		$70,833.33
Plus land value		+ 15,000.00
Equals property value		$85,833.33
Property value	say	$86,000

Straight-Line Recapture with Land Residual Technique. This method holds the same assumptions as the building residual technique. However, rather than the land value being known, the building value is estimated by the cost approach. Using the same assumptions as in the previous example and assuming a building value by the cost approach of $71,000, value would be calculated as follows:

NOI		$10,000
Less income attributable to the building at the capitalization rate ($71,000 × .12)		− 8,520
Equals income attributable to the land (land residual)		$1,480
Land value equals land residual divided by discount rate ($1,480 ÷ .10)		$14,800
Plus building value		+ 71,000
Equals property value		$85,800
Property value	say	$86,000

Annuity Recapture with Property Residual Technique. This method assumes an assured net income for a reasonably long period, which has a favorable impact on the quality and durability of the income stream.

Because of this assumption, a so-called Inwood factor from a present worth of an annuity table and a reversion factor from a present worth of a reversion table are used to calculate value.

Assume there are 20 years remaining on a net lease at $10,000 per year, and that at the expiration of the lease there will be a property value (reversion) remaining of $70,000, and the appropriate capitalization rate has been determined to be 11 percent. Value would be calculated as follows:

Factors from tables (11 percent, 20 years)	Inwood factor 7.9633
	Reversion factor .1240
Present worth of income stream ($10,000 × 7.9633)	$79,633
Plus present worth or reversion ($70,000 × .1240)	+ 8,680
Equals property value	$88,313
Property value	say $88,000

Investor's Cash Flow Method. In this technique (which is a simplified mortgage-equity method) the amount and terms of the mortgage which can be obtained determine the price that the investor will pay. The rates of return required to attract equity capital are a matter for the appraiser to observe and judge. The strength of this method is that it recognizes the realistic fact that most investors utilize mortgage capital in purchasing real estate investments. The weakness of this method is that the amount and terms of the mortgage obtainable may vary according to the identity of the investor-purchaser and the state of the economy and the mortgage market at a particular point in time.

Assume a stable annual NOI of $10,000, the availability of a 75 percent mortgage loan at 9 percent, 30 years, level monthly payments, and a rate of return necessary to attract equity capital of 13 percent. Value would be calculated as follows:

1. Reference to standard mortgage amortization tables reveals that cash flow required for annual debt service (principal and interest payments) on the available loan would be 9.66 percent of the principal amount borrowed.
2. The two cash flow rates can be combined into an overall rate, as follows:

	Rate		*Portion of Value*		*Product*
Mortgage	.0966	×	.75	=	.0725
Equity	.1300	×	.25	=	.0325
Overall rate					.1050

$$V = I/R$$

$$V = \frac{\$10{,}000}{.1050}$$

$$V = \$95{,}238$$

Property value say $95,000

Mortgage-Equity Method. This method calculates the so-called *cash throw-off to equity* as NOI *less* debt service on the available mortgage. The cash throw-off to equity is capitalized to an equity value, which when added to the amount of the available mortgage equals property value. The weakness of this method is that it requires knowing the dollar amount of the available mortgage, which is seldom known without first knowing the property value.[7] However, assume an $80,000 mortgage is available at 9 percent for 30 years with an annual debt service of $7,728, NOI of $10,000, and a 13 percent equity rate. Value would be calculated as follows:

NOI		$10,000
Less debt service		− 7,728
Equals cash throw-off to equity		$ 2,272
Capitalize cash throw-off to equity at 13 percent ($2,272 ÷ .13)		$17,477
Add mortgage		+ 80,000
Equals property value		$97,477
Property value	say	$97,000

Ellwood Method. This method is a refinement of the investor's cash flow method. Furthermore, it treats the income projection as a relatively short (5 to 15 years) investment holding period. The appraiser is required to make an additional judgment as to whether the property will depreciate or appreciate in the future. In other words, the equity may or may not increase in dollar amount as the amount of the mortgage is reduced. Prospects for appreciation, with its favorable capital gains tax treatment, represent an important real-world attraction to investors. This required adjustment for property appreciation or depreciation at the end of the investment holding period calls for skilled judgment, however; as in any reversion estimate, parallels usually can be found in the existing market which are comparable to what the subject property should be worth at the end of the investment holding period.

Assume an NOI of $10,000, a 75 percent mortgage at 9 percent for 30 years, and a required equity rate of 13 percent. In addition assume a 10-year investment holding period and an anticipated increase in total property value of 10 percent. Capitalize as follows, using the "Ellwood Tables" published by the American Institute of Real Estate Appraisers:

Construction of overall rate from tabular entries (p. 340):	
Basic rate	.100616
Less adjustment for appreciation (.1 × .05429)	− .005429
Equals capitalization rate	.095187

7. However, this approach may be most applicable in an appraisal problem in which the financing involves the assumption of an existing loan, since the dollar amount of the mortgage balance to be assumed can be calculated very easily.

$$V = I/R$$

$$V = \frac{\$10{,}000}{.095187}$$

$$V = \$105{,}056$$

Property value "say $105,000

The Ellwood method is an advanced treatment of the mortgage-equity and band of investment theory techniques. This method recognizes the real-world inputs of mortgage financing, required equity rates of return, and the prospects of appreciation as well as depreciation. The capitalization rate is available either in the precalculated tables (see Appendix B) or can be derived by the "Ellwood formula" in cases where the tables do not directly show the appropriate rate. These rates are also useful in a comparative analysis of capitalization rates obtained by other methods of capitalization.

It is important to note that the seven examples given above for estimating value are based upon different assumptions about quantity, quality, duration of income, appreciation or depreciation, and estimates (if any) of remaining economic life and provisions for capital recapture. The fact that (with the exception of the land and building residual techniques) no two estimates of value were the same pointedly demonstrates that the final value estimate must be consistent with the assumptions which are expressed or implied in the technique chosen by the appraiser. In the final analysis, the appraised value of a property is only as good as the experience, opinions, and judgment of the real estate appraiser.

SUMMARY AND CONCLUSION

In the execution of the three approaches to value, it is rational and efficient to begin with the cost approach, since this approach utilizes information from the background analysis, namely, the physical data regarding site and improvements which should have been compiled in the site analysis and valuation and in the improvements inspection and analysis. The cost approach includes the following five steps:

1. Estimate site value as if vacant and available to be utilized at its highest and best use.
2. Estimate reproduction cost new of the building improvements.
3. Estimate all accrued depreciation.
4. Subtract accrued depreciation (step 3) from the reproduction cost new (step 2) to obtain depreciated cost.
5. Add the site value (step 1) to the depreciated cost (step 4) to obtain the total property value.

There is an important distinction between reproduction cost and replacement cost. The former is the cost of an exact replica, while the latter is the cost of equivalent utility. The various methods of cost estimation discussed include (1) cost services, (2) quantity survey, (3) unit-in-place, (4) building trade segregated breakdown, and (5) comparative unit. An example of a cost estimation may be found in Appendix C.

Accrued depreciation may consist of three basic elements: (1) physical deterioration, (2) functional obsolescence, and (3) economic obsolescence. The dollar amount of accrued depreciation may be estimated by one of the following methods: (1) capitalized income, (2) market, (3) straight-line (age-life), (4) engineering, or (5) breakdown.

The market approach to value is also known as the "comparative-sales approach," the "market-comparison approach," the "market-data approach," or the "sales-comparison approach." Regardless of nomenclature, this approach includes the following five steps:

1. Analysis of the subject property
2. Selection of the comparable properties recently sold
3. Analysis of the comparables
4. Comparison between the subject and the comparables, making adjustment for value differences from the comparables to the subject to get indications of value for the subject
5. Correlation of the indications of value to a final value estimate.

A "rule of thumb" method of calculating market value, without the five-step approach outlined above, is the gross income multiplier approach. A multiplier obtained from the ratios of sales prices to gross incomes of comparable properties is multiplied by the subject property's gross income to get a rough estimate of its market value.

The income approach to value estimates property value by the capitalization process. Capitalization is the conversion of income to value. The income approach includes the following five steps:

1. Estimate potential gross income.
2. Estimate effective gross income.
3. Estimate net operating income.
4. Estimate an appropriate capitalization rate.
5. Estimate or choose an appropriate capitalization method to convert income to value.

Potential gross income is the income a property will produce with 100 percent occupancy at the market rent. Effective gross income is the potential gross income, less allowance for vacancy and rent loss, plus other income. Net operating income is the effective gross income less all operating expenses.

A capitalization rate is the sum of a discount rate (return "on" investment) and a capital recapture (recovery) rate (return "of" investment). The various capitalization methods discussed include (1) direct capitalization with the overall rate, (2) straight-line recapture with the building residual technique, (3) straight-line recapture with the land residual technique, (4) annuity recapture with the property residual technique, (5) investor's cash flow method, (6) mortgage-equity method, and (7) Ellwood method.

Finally, it is important to note that usually a different value estimate will be obtained by the income approach, depending upon the method or technique of capitalization utilized by the appraiser. Such is and should be the case, since each method is based upon a different set of assumptions, which are expressed or implied in the appropriate technique chosen by the appraiser. It is the job of the appraiser to properly match the right method of analysis and its inherent assumptions with the right appraisal problem. The final value estimate, therefore, is only as good as the experience, opinions, and judgment of the real estate appraiser.

PART V

Investment

CHAPTER 17

Real Estate Investment Characteristics and Investor Objectives

KEY TERMS

Broad market A market in which there are many buyers and sellers at the same time, such that a sudden but temporary surge in buyers and sellers can be handled without extreme price variations

Thin market A market in which there are few buyers and sellers and slow turnover, resulting in difficulty in obtaining comparable sales and in determining prices; prices are highly vulnerable to change if just a few more buyers and/or sellers enter the market

Leverage of capital The borrowing of other people's money by an investor to raise or to increase (lever) the total amount of capital committed to an investment and increase the rate of return to equity

Mortgaging-out The borrowing of 100 percent of the costs to develop and build a real estate project

Walking money Money borrowed in *excess* of 100 percent of the costs to develop and build a real estate project

Economic value The value of a real estate project as determined by the capitalization of the projected income rather than by the costs of development; economic value usually exceeds cost

Equity buildup The amortization or paying off of principal on a loan (increases the investor's equity position, assuming the property value does not decline)

Tax shelter The amount of write-offs against investment income allowed by the Internal Revenue Service

Tax saving The amount of income taxes avoided because of tax shelters

Tax-bracket The percentage paid in income taxes on the last dollar earned in a given year

INVESTMENT DEFINITION

An *investment* is a commitment or outlay of financial capital for the purpose of earning a financial return commensurate with the risks to which the outlay is subject during the time the commitment is maintained. The motivation for investment is future consumption; people save and invest in the present to provide possible future consumption. A wide variety of investment opportunities are available to individuals in a capitalist economy.

One possible outline of investment alternatives is as follows:[1]

I. Direct Investment Alternatives
   A. Fixed-principal investments
      1. Cash
      2. Savings accounts
      3. Marketable savings certificates
      4. Corporate bonds
      5. Government bonds
   B. Variable-principal securities
      1. Preferred stocks
      2. Common stocks
      3. Convertible securities
      4. Warrants
      5. Options
   C. Nonsecurity investments
      1. Real estate
      2. Mortgages
      3. Commodities
      4. Business ventures
      5. Art, antiques, and other valuables

II. Indirect Investment Alternatives
   A. Pension funds
   B. Insurance company portfolios
   C. Investment companies
   D. Trust funds

Such a list is not meant to be all-inclusive or complete. In fact, each item listed could be further subdivided to provide more details and specifics. However, this list should offer the reader an appreciation of the immense diversity of investment possibilities.

To emphasize further the immense diversity of investment possibilities, the following list is illustrative of the spectrum of income-producing real estate investments:[2]

1. Stephen D. Messner, Irving Schreiber, and Victor L. Lyon, *Marketing Investment Real Estate* (Chicago: Realtors National Marketing Institute, 1975), pp. 13–14.

2. Ibid., pp. 20–21

I. Residential income
   A. Apartment houses
      1. Garden
      2. High-rise
   B. Hotels
   C. Motels
   D. Rest homes
   E. Single-family and condominium rentals
II. Commercial
   A. Professional buildings
   B. Office buildings
   C. Shopping centers
      1. Local
      2. Community
      3. Regional
   D. Single-purpose buildings
      1. Theaters
      2. Bowling alleys
      3. Free-standing retail stores
      4. Service stations
III. Industrial
   A. Warehouses
   B. Industrial parks
   C. Manufacturing facilities
   D. Utility-company buildings
IV. Institutional
   A. Hospitals
   B. Government office buildings
   C. Churches
   D. Schools
V. Farms and Land
   A. Recreational land
   B. Subdivision land
   C. Residential multiunit land
   D. Commercially zoned land
   E. Industrially zoned land
   F. Raw acreage
   G. Farms
   H. Ranches

Even this list could be expanded to provide yet more detail and/or specialization of investment type. Just as there is a myriad of investment types, so too is there a myriad of investor types. Particular investors have different needs and desires concerning the different investments they make. It follows, therefore, that there are basic investment characteristics that must be matched with basic investor objectives.

INVESTMENT CHARACTERISTICS

The prudent investor will investigate the status of the following list of investment characteristics in judging whether or not any given investment meets his or her investment objectives.

Safety of Income

Safety is the opposite of risk. Certainty is a measure of safety; uncertainty is a measure of risk. The degree of certainty that an investment will return a periodic income stream to the investor is analyzed in terms of income quantity, quality, and durability.

Quantity of Income. The amount of income to be expected from an investment is a function of the marketplace. For a real estate investment, it is a function of past and present performance of the subject property, rentals earned by comparable properties, and the amount of rent which present and prospective tenants are justified in paying.

Quality of Income. The quality of rental income is a function of the type of tenant paying the rent and/or the type of business in which the tenant is involved. Income generated by a blue-chip tenant operating a viable and competitive business is likely to be a constant and dependable income stream. The income from a warehouse leased to Sears, Roebuck and Co., for example, would be considered high quality. Income generated by a rooming house for transients or by a "no-tell motel," however, might be variable and uncertain. Such income would be considered poor quality.

Durability of Income. The durability of income is a function of the length of time over which the projected quantity of rental income may reasonably be expected to last. Durability of income is enhanced by a well-written lease; a long-term lease which contains escalation, graduated, and/or percentage rent clauses should provide a more durable income stream than a short-term lease.

Generally speaking, real estate investments provide relatively good safety of income. The long economic life and permanence of the real estate product itself and the usual ability to convert the use of buildings from one type of income generator to another have made real estate an excellent and relatively safe long-term investment, in terms of both current and future income. Current income on many types of real estate investments compares quite favorably with alternative investment income. Some investors in high tax brackets, however, prefer future income. Real estate investments which require considerable capital outlay over 10 to 15 years before returning future income—such as fruit orchards, vineyards, or timberland—are often attractive to this type of investor. Similarly, investment in developable land in the apparent path of future urban growth would meet the needs of people who desire to invest for future income.

Safety of Capital

The degree of certainty that an investor's initial capital outlay will be returned is a very high priority item for all investors. Over the years real estate has been a safe place to invest capital, primarily because of the long life and durability of the product. In today's market, many foreign investors are purchasing real estate assets in the United States merely to protect their capital from the ramifications of unstable governments in their own countries. The United States is thought to have one of the most stable political systems in the world, and therefore real estate in the United States is very attractive to many foreign investors.

Quantity of Capital

The amount of the initial capital outlay is an investment characteristic that often determines who gets to "play the game." Investments requiring a large capital outlay often limit or exclude the participation of the small investor. Real estate investments generally require a relatively large initial capital outlay. Since real estate investments are usually large economic units, even considering high-ratio mortgage financing, 10 to 20 percent down payments are still measured in thousands and tens of thousands of dollars. Such dollar magnitudes preclude the involvement of many small investors.

The small-time real estate investor, like the small-time stock and bond investor who buys into a mutual fund, may buy into a real estate investment trust (REIT) in order to literally "own a piece of the rock." However, owning shares in a REIT is really not comparable to owning a building; investment in REIT stock is more like investment in other stocks and bonds.

Turnover of Capital

Capital turnover is a measure of the time it takes for investment income to equal or return the total amount of invested capital to the investor. Some assets, especially inventory merchandise which is continuously sold and restocked, have a very quick turnover. Supermarket assets, for example, may turn over once a week. Real estate, on the other hand, generally has a very slow capital turnover. Real estate investments are generally held for at least five to 10 years or more before being resold or before gross income equals the amount of invested capital.

Liquidity of Capital

Liquidity of capital is a measure of how quickly an investment can be converted into cash without a loss. The quicker the capability of an investment to be converted to cash (liquidated without a loss), the greater its liquidity. Liquidity is a very desirable investment characteristic. For example, the ability of an investor to almost instantaneously sell stocks and bonds over a national exchange, such as the New York Stock Exchange, is a very popular feature of such investments.

Perhaps the greatest disadvantage of real estate investments is their lack of liquidity. It is often said that the Achilles' heel of real estate investment is nonliquidity. One cannot simply pick up the phone and say "sell" to a real estate broker and obtain an almost instantaneous sale or investment liquidation.

The real estate market is not as formal, national, and automated as the stock market. Real estate brokers may require months, rather than moments, to liquidate a real estate investment. A real estate broker requires time to expose and advertise the sale of a property to a reasonable number of buyer-investors, arrange financing, obtain proper title investigation and protection, and attend to a myriad of legal details involved in contract negotiations. Finally, the real estate itself is a very heterogeneous product; no two properties (unlike two shares of stock in the same corporation) are alike. Time is required for the buyer-investor to visit, inspect, and determine his or her own estimate of investment value. The time required to come to a meeting of the minds on price and other terms of sale and the time to actually complete a real estate closing may cover many months. Thus, a quick conversion to income without loss is not an attribute common to real estate investments.

Marketability of Capital

Marketability or transferability of capital is a measure of how quickly an investment can be converted into cash regardless of loss. For example, a stock on the New York Exchange can almost always be sold at *some* price; a market exists to purchase even though the sales price may be well below the original capital investment. Such a stock may be very marketable but not very liquid. Note that the distinction between marketability and liquidity is a function of the sales price.

Since real estate is often sold in local markets and is a heterogeneous product, it is often considered not highly marketable relative to other types of investment. Some types of real estate are more marketable than others. For example, a single-family residence in suburbia might be more marketable than a resort condominium in the mountains, because a broader market usually exists for primary residences than for second homes. A *broad market* means that there are many buyers and sellers in the market at the same time and that a sudden but temporary surge in buyers and sellers can be handled without extreme price variations.

Some types of real estate are less marketable than other types because of a thin market. A *thin market* means that there are few buyers and sellers and slow turnover, which result in difficulty in obtaining comparable sales and in determining prices that are not highly vulnerable to change when just a few more buyers and/or sellers enter the market. For example, thin markets might exist for special or single-purpose properties such as manufacturing facilities, theaters, or bowling alleys. Or a thin market might exist for one-bedroom condominiums, since the family market would not be attracted to such a property type.

Appreciation of Capital

Capital appreciation is an increase or growth in the value of an investment. It is possible for either the dollar value or the real value of an investment to increase. The dollar value increase is simply a function of inflation; the real value increase is a true increase in value net of, or in addition to, inflation.

Bond and savings account investments usually do not have an appreciation factor potential. The face amount of the capital investment remains unchanged. In fact, such investments are subject to real value losses after deducting the effects of inflation. Other investments, like common stocks, oil, gas, cattle and real estate, typically enjoy great potential for capital appreciation because of inflation, market demand, and expectations of future income-generating ability.

Real estate investments in particular, especially during recent decades, have shown truly remarkable increases in value because of a variety of factors. These include:

1. *Population Growth*. Many studies by land economists have revealed an amazingly close relationship between the rise of land values and the increase of population. When a fixed supply of land is demanded by an ever-increasing number of people, economic theory states that the outcome of such a set of economic forces is an increase in the price of land.
2. *Construction Cost Inflation*. As the costs of new construction increase, the value of construction already in place rises. Hence, the owners of the construction-in-place investments enjoy appreciation, which to the new investor is simply a higher price.

3. *Increased Income.* The typical American family income rises as the employed members of the family achieve job maturity and tenure. With increased income comes a demand for a higher standard of living, which may include a home purchase or discretionary income available for investment in real estate.
4. *Leisure Time and Recreation.* Shortening of the average work week, combined with higher incomes, have provided a demand for second homes, golf courses, resorts, and other land-use types to accomodate the new leisure.
5. *Highway Growth.* New and improved transportation routes, especially the interstate highway system, have improved access to previously distant properties. One determinant of increase in land value is good access.
6. *Suburban Industrial Growth.* The improved access of the interstate highway system, coupled with the change from vertical to horizontal manufacturing production, have caused a trend toward suburban industrial growth. Such growth has caused certain suburban land values to increase dramatically.
7. *Urban Renewal.* The energy crisis and the public demand to clear blighted parts of urban America have caused a new wave of demand for central-city real estate. Urban renewal, housing rehabilitation, energy conservation, and even historical restoration have all revived interest in urban-core properties, causing the values of such properties to increase dramatically.
8. *Education and Public Awareness.* Many more people are learning about real estate investments. Seminars, radio talk shows, articles in the news media, and college courses concerning real estate are more prevalent than ever before. People are learning about the availability of mortgage financing, the income tax advantages of real estate, and how to get involved in real estate investments. These people are increasing the demand for real estate and are thereby continuing to increase its value.

Appreciation in value of an investment usually is not realized until the investment is sold or liquidated. However, with real estate investments, realization of the cash benefits of property appreciation may be enjoyed without the investor's having to sell the property. A common practice used by real estate investors who enjoy capital appreciation is to refinance the property based on the new property value. The cash difference between the larger new loan and the old loan (which is paid off or wrapped around) is pocketed by the investor and is not subject to income taxation until the property is sold.

Leverage of Capital

Leverage of capital allows an investor to raise or increase the size of the invested capital by borrowing other people's money. In other words, the use of borrowed capital is employed to purchase an investment with the anticipation that the investor will realize returns, not only on his or her own investment or equity position, but also on the borrowed funds.

If the return on the total capital investment (debt and equity positions) is greater than the cost of the borrowed capital, such excess return is added to the return on the investor's equity, thereby increasing or *levering* the rate of return to the investor's equity position. This financial device of using other people's money to increase the rate of return to the investor's equity position is often called "trading on the equity."

Stock market investors often employ this profit-making technique by borrowing from their stockbrokers on a so-called margin account. In this case, the descriptive terminology employed is "trading on the margin." The percentage which stock market investors may borrow is controlled by the Federal Reserve Board of Governors and usually varies between 50 and 75 percent.

Real estate investors generally enjoy high-ratio leverage financing. A loan-to-value ratio of 75 to 80 percent is considered a minimum percentage by most investors. It is not uncommon for real estate developers to be able to "mortgage out" or borrow 100 percent of the costs to develop and build a real estate project. Sometimes it is even possible to borrow in excess of 100 percent of development costs. Such excess funds are affectionately called "walking money," since these funds have a tendency to "walk away" from the real estate project into the hip pocket of the real estate developer.

It is possible to borrow 100 percent or more of costs when the economic value of the project, as determined by the capitalization of the projected income, greatly exceeds the development costs. For example, assume development costs of $750,000 and an economic value of $1 million. A 75 percent loan based on economic value (75 percent of $1 million is $750,000) equals 100 percent financing of costs. If the economic value in this example were greater than $1 million, the developer could borrow some walking money.

Many other benefits of leverage will be explained with numerical examples later in the text. However, two additional comments should be made at this point. The payments on the borrowed capital usually consist of both interest and principal amortization. The interest portion of these payments is a tax-deductible item for income tax purposes. The principal portion, by lowering the outstanding debt, increases or builds up the investor's equity position, assuming the property value is at least maintained. Equity buildup can be converted to a cash return if and/or when the investor sells or refinances the property.

Income Tax Benefits

As will be more fully explained in Chapter 20, Congress passes tax legislation in order to induce certain desired types of economic activity in the system. Such laws can make certain investments more attractive than others. Hence, investors must consider the impact of federal tax legislation in making investment choices.

Real estate investments enjoy the deductability of operating expenses (including property taxes) and mortgage interest expenses in calculating taxable income. However, since these deductions require a cash outlay by the investor, they do not increase after-tax cash flows to the investor. Depreciation deductions, on the other hand, do *not* require a cash outlay by the investor. Since the accounting measure of taxable rental income is reduced by depreciation deductions, such deductions *can* increase after-tax cash flows to the investor.

For example, if taxable real estate income, not considering depreciation deductions, was $100,000 and the investor was in the 50-percent tax bracket, after-tax cash flow would be $50,000. However, if a depreciation deduction of $100,000 were allowed, after-tax cash flow would be $100,000, as shown below:

	No Depreciation	versus	Depreciation
Real estate income	$100,000		$100,000
Depreciation	− 0		−100,000
Taxable income	$100,000		$ 0
Tax rate	× .50		× .50
Tax	$ 50,000		$ 0
Real estate income	$100,000		$100,000
Tax	−50,000		− 0
After-tax cash flow	$ 50,000		$100,000

In this example the depreciation has sheltered all of the real estate income, causing the after-tax cash flow to be increased by one-half of the depreciation deduction, or $50,000. If depreciation in this example were allowed (by Congress) to be greater than $100,000, the property would show a net loss. However, such a loss is only a "paper loss" and would have the effect of sheltering additional income from sources other than the real estate investment itself: perhaps, the investor's salary. Assume the same example, yet also assume (1) a $150,000 depreciation deduction is allowed by an accelerated depreciation method and (2) a salary of $100,000:

Real estate income	$100,000	
Depreciation	− 150,000	
Tax loss	$ 50,000	loss, hence zero tax

	No Tax Loss	versus	Tax Loss
Salary	$100,000		$100,000
Tax loss	− 0		−50,000
Taxable salary	$100,000		$ 50,000
Tax rate	× .50		× .50
Salary tax	$ 50,000		$ 25,000

Note: Tax savings of $50,000 minus $25,000 equals $25,000
Hence:

	No Depreciation	versus	Depreciation with no tax loss	versus	Depreciation with tax loss
Real estate income	$100,000		$100,000		$100,000
Tax	−50,000		− 0		− 0
Tax savings	+ 0		+ 0		+25,000
After-tax cash flow	$ 50,000		$100,000		$125,000

In summary, these examples have shown how the tax benefits of depreciation of $100,000 increased after-tax cash flow from $50,000 to $100,000 and how accelerated depreciation of $150,000 increased after-tax cash flow an additional $25,000 to a total of $125,000. The cash flow benefits of depreciation and accelerated depreciation, therefore, can be seen to be a most attractive and important investment characteristic. Such benefits can direct investment capital to where Congress thinks it ought to be invested. Congress has used accelerated depreciation methods to direct capital into real estate investments.

Chapter 20 will more fully explain the different methods of depreciation and the applicability of these methods to the various types of real estate investment. It will also explain the tax benefits available to real estate investors regarding tax treatment of capital gains, tax-deferred exchanges, installment sales, and other related topics. Upon study of the tax chapter, the reader should conclude that tax-benefit characteristics of real estate investments are among the best available to the many different types of investment.

INVESTOR OBJECTIVES

Thus far, this chapter has contained a listing of investment types and a discussion of the myriad investment characteristics. The investment characteristics of different investments are analyzed by many types of investors, who continually seek to meet various investor objectives and combinations of investor objectives. Particular categories of investors have different needs and desires that must be fulfilled by the particular investment characteristics of a given investment or set of investments. The following list of investor objectives is provided to manifest the diversity of possible objectives and to allow the reader to compare these objectives with the investment characteristics presented in the first part of this chapter:

1. Positive cash flow
2. Tax shelter
3. Financial leverage
4. Appreciation
5. Inflation hedge
6. Diversification
7. Retirement fund
8. Estate building
9. Use investment
10. Psychological benefits

Positive Cash Flow

To many investors, cash flow is the name of the game. Even though rental income is subject to ordinary income tax rates, many investors' primary objective is cash flow, which can be spent on consumption or reinvested in other real estate projects or other investments to obtain a degree of portfolio diversification.

Many times the person seeking positive cash flow is a young investor just beginning an investment program. Such a person usually has not yet attained the dubious distinction of being in a high tax bracket, which in itself might cause one to avoid positive cash-flow investments. Such a person may be operating at the outset under the assumption that it takes money to make money. Hence, a positive cash flow is sought to be reinvested to make more money by purchasing more and/or larger investment properties. The relatively low tax bracket of such an individual, combined with allowable tax-shelter benefits, may result in a minimum of the investment returns going to the coffers of Uncle Sam, leaving sufficient cash flow for reinvestment and/or consumption.

Tax Shelter

The benefits of depreciation, accelerated depreciation, and mortgage interest deductibility for income tax purposes may be a major reason for purchasing income-producing real estate. Numerical examples in this chapter have demonstrated how an investor can have zero or even negative cash flow for tax purposes and yet at the same time have a positive cash flow from the property, as well as shelter income from other sources, such as salary income.

Investors in high tax brackets often name tax shelter as their primary investor objective. It is possible to shelter income not only because of depreciation write-offs: By lowering the amount of income subject to taxation, an investor may actually fall into a lower tax bracket. Qualifying for a lower tax bracket allows an investor to pay a lower percentage on taxable income. Some investors view this situation as an additional tax-savings benefit.

Finally, the tax benefit of capital gains is available, if a property is held for at least one year. The capital-gains tax rate paid on appreciation in value is much lower (about half) than the rate paid on ordinary income. These tax rates will be explained in Chapter 20.

Financial Leverage

Most of the books with titles like *How I Made a Million Dollars in My Sleep*, present stories about people who have successfully employed the benefits of financial leverage. Often such stories explain how an investor started with one rental single-family home and then expanded this investment into a multimillion-dollar real estate portfolio through financial leverage. Financial leverage is usually sought by all types of investors: high–tax bracket types and low–tax bracket types.

The numerous benefits of financial leverage are fully explained in Chapter 18 in the section on financial risk (p. 310). Most investors seek financial leverage despite the financial risk that comes with it. Most investors feel that the benefits of leverage far outweigh the risks.

Appreciation

The factors that cause appreciation in the value of real estate have been enumerated and explained in this chapter. It is often true that real estate investments which return appreciation to the investor do not also return positive cash flow. Hence, in such situations, those investors seeking positive cash flow may not be able to compete for some of the properties expected to have ample appreciation.

The typical set of reasons for this perhaps unusual state of affairs is as follows:

1. A property is expected to increase in value at a rapid rate.
2. Many investors wish to purchase this property, and therefore bid to purchase it.
3. Some bidders are in high tax brackets and are therefore seeking tax shelters, even if this means zero or negative cash flow.
4. Some bidders are foreign investors with huge amounts of capital to invest, much of which must be invested merely to protect the capital, with no great need for positive cash flow.

5. These investors bid the price up to the point where the costs of financing such a price cause there to be no positive cash flow or even a negative cash flow.

Another type of real estate investment that might meet the needs of investors seeking appreciation—but not those of investors seeking positive cash flow—is land purchased for future development. Such investments may endure many years of negative cash flow because of carrying charges for property taxes, insurance, and land loan debt service before returning a positive cash flow from resale at an appreciated price.

Inflation Hedge

Real estate investments are considered to be one of the best hedges against inflation, the loss of the dollar's purchasing power. Three basic characteristics common to real estate investments have proven this statement to be true:

1. Rising real values (refer to p. 295, "Appreciation of Capital")
2. Escalation clauses in real property leases
3. Variable interest rates and equity participations common to real estate mortgage investments

Diversification

Most investors are aware that it is risky to *keep all one's eggs in one basket*. To avoid the risk of having all one's capital tied up in only one investment, many investors seek to diversify their investment portfolios by purchasing real estate as well as stocks, bonds, and other investments. Investment portfolio diversification is also provided by buying different kinds of real estate (office buildings, shopping centers, apartment buildings, etc.) and by buying properties in different locations.

The whole purpose of diversification is to avoid having the poor performance of one or two investments totally wipe out an investor's capital investment. It is hoped that within a diversified portfolio, when one investment does poorly, another will do well. In other words, bad investments will be offset by good ones.

Retirement Fund

Some real estate investors buy properties which may not return any positive cash flow until the mortgage loans on such properties are totally paid off. Such investors time the payoff of mortgage loans to coincide with retirement. By structuring one's real estate investments in this manner, an investor is able to get the best of both worlds, as follows:

1. During the years when a person is working and earning income, the

real estate produces depreciation and mortgage interest deduction benefits to shelter that income.

2. During the years of retirement, when one's income is lower, a positive cash flow is provided by the real estate; the debt service payments are no longer required because the mortgage loan has been paid off.

Estate Building

Investors who wish to leave an estate of wealth to their children can use real estate investments to build such an estate. It is possible, through proper tax planning, to leave an estate to one's heirs and avoid capital-gains taxation altogether. However, estate tax, at both the state and federal levels, cannot be avoided.

Sometimes estate taxation causes problems to those who inherit real estate. Often, some or all of the real estate in an estate must be sold in order to pay the estate tax. If the real estate in the inherited estate is not very liquid or marketable, the heirs may be faced with a large tax obligation which they may not be able to pay.

Use Investment

Except for street vendors, perhaps no business exists that can operate without real estate. Businesses can own or rent. Sometimes the benefits of renting, such as flexibility regarding mobility or little or no capital investment, outweigh real estate ownership. However, many businesses find that the benefits of real estate ownership, such as depreciation, appreciation, and leverage, far outweigh renting. Furthermore, the costs of renting may be very high, the worry of being subject to a lease may be undesirable, and the absence of permanent location may be unsettling. Hence, investment for the use of the real estate itself is very attractive to many investors.

Psychological Benefits

It is often true that business real estate is purchased for the prestige and status that may be attached to an impressive building. The colossal Sears building in Chicago, the Transamerica Corporation's "pyramid" in San Francisco, and the Seagram Building in New York (constructed of the artistically more striking bronze, rather than the equally functional and less-expensive steel) are good examples of buildings that return psychological benefits to the owner-investors and to the high-rent-paying tenant-occupants. Banks and insurance companies are generally known for erecting "monuments" for their corporate headquarters in order to manifest a facade of stability.

It is doubtful that the prestige, pride of ownership, and consumer recognition sought to meet competition actually result in the added income that is sufficient to justify the increased cost of such real estate investments. However, prestige is a real factor in the marketplace. It is therefore an investor objective that must be recognized to have real value to many real estate investors.

SUMMARY AND CONCLUSIONS

This chapter has attempted to present a description of real estate investments from two points of view: the characteristics of the investments and the objectives of the investors. The competition for real estate investments involves a series of interactions whereby individual investors seek to maximize their objectives by purchasing investments that have the individual characteristics that best meet their needs and desires.

Only when such a match of investment characteristics and investor objectives can be made will real estate investors make a commitment or outlay of financial capital for the purpose of earning a financial return commensurate with the risks to which the outlay is subject during the time the commitment is maintained. The risks and returns of real estate investments are the subjects of the next two chapters.

CHAPTER 18

Real Estate Investment Risks

KEY TERMS

Locational risk The real estate investment risk associated with the physical location and economic location (situs) of a given investment property

Business risk An expression of the degree of uncertainty of the productivity analysis of a real estate investment; also called "earning power risk"

Purchasing power risk The possibility that the real or true value of an investment's dollar returns will decline because of inflation

Cost-push inflation An increase in prices caused by an increase in the costs of the factors of production

Demand-pull inflation An increase in prices caused by consumer demand increasing more rapidly than the supply of a good or service

Monetary inflation An increase in prices caused by the Fed's increasing the money supply and/or monetizing the debt

Real-cost inflation An increase in prices caused by the increased effort required to produce the same quantity and/or quality of a good or service

Interest rate risk The degree of uncertainty associated with the likelihood of changes in the future general level of interest rates and the impact such changes have on investment value

Management risk The extent to which an investment requires "care and feeding" over the investment holding period; also called "ownership burden" or "worry factors"

Financial risk The uncertainty about an investor's financial ability to meet debt-service requirements

Mortgage constant The ratio of annual debt-service payments over the original mortgage loan amount; represents the percentage per dollar borrowed that must be paid annually to the lender in order to both amortize the principal and pay the interest due

INVESTMENT RISKS

Most real estate investments are long term in nature. Because of the long-term nature of real estate investments, they are subject to a variety of risks. For example, business conditions tend to be cyclical, government programs and tax laws change over time, inflation and interest rates vary over time, local economic conditions change with developments in the economic base of a community, new transportation patterns cause locational values to change, and consumer preferences influence the desirability of neighborhoods and architectural designs. The potential for change, the difficulty of projecting estimates far into the future, and the nonliquidity of real estate call for a high level of expert analysis of the various risks to which real estate investments are subject. The following six investment risks will be defined and explained:

1. Locational risk
2. Business or earning power risk
3. Purchasing power risk
4. Interest rate risk
5. Management risk
6. Financial risk

Locational Risk

It is often said that the three most important considerations necessary for wise real estate investment are "location, location, and location." The property value of a real estate investment is a function of the property's ability to produce income. This income productivity is a function of the property's site, improvement, and locational characteristics. Site and improvements analyses were discussed in Chapter 15 under the general topic of "Background Analysis" (p. 255). The so-called Ratcliff model, "The Locational Basis of Real Estate Value," will be presented here to explain locational risk analysis. This applies to both physical location and economic location (situs).

The Ratcliff Model.[1] Ratcliff has identified the following three basic elements of locational value and locational risk:

1. *Convenience* is the ease (or freedom from discomfort) of movement of persons or goods from the subject property's location to other points to which movement is desirable or essential. Convenience is measured in the disutilities of time and cost involved in getting from the subject site to the other sites. This maze of so-called linked establishments or groups of related land uses forms what is called the tributary area. The greater the convenience factor of a given

1. Richard U. Ratcliff, *Real Estate Analysis* (New York: McGraw-Hill, 1961), pp. 62–80.

property within its tributary area, the greater its value. The greater the disutilities of time and cost, the greater the locational risk.

2. *Favorable exposure* refers to the esthetic satisfactions and/or prestige value of a given location. A mountain view or high ground may be esthetically pleasing; a Park Avenue or Wall Street address may provide social or business prestige. The greater the favorable exposure, the greater the protection from locational risk.
3. *Unfavorable Exposure* refers to objectionable, inharmonious, or incompatible conditions of a given location. Pollution, traffic congestion, poor access, and urban blight are factors that can cause a given property to suffer unfavorable exposure. Such conditions are detrimental to property values and increase the locational risk of such properties from an investment point of view.

Locational risk analysis must be extended into the future, since the three basic elements of location may change over time. Because of this dynamic nature of the three location factors, the evaluation of locational risk and returns must account for all potential changes. The greater the probabilities for change, the greater the locational risk. Finally, because of the fixity of location of real estate investments, such investments are more susceptible to locational risk than perhaps any other type of investment.

Business or Earning Power Risk

Business risk, also called earning power risk, is an expression of the degree of uncertainty of the property's productivity analysis. The analysis of the income which a property is expected to produce involves the determination of potential gross income, using market rentals at 100 percent occupancy, the estimation and deduction of vacancy and collection losses, and the estimation and addition of other income in order to arrive at the net operating income (NOI). The NOI estimate is a measure of a property's earning power. The reliability of this estimate is usually a function of the type of business that is operated within the real estate.

For example, the confidence level of predicting income for a budget motel might not approach the level of confidence of predicting income for either a well-located and well-maintained apartment building or an office building or warehouse leased to a blue-chip corporation. The greater the potential variability between projected and actual income produced by a real estate investment, the greater the business or earning power risk. Mortgage lenders, as noted in Chapter 14, attempt to protect themselves from business risk by requiring higher debt coverage ratios (NOI divided by debt service) for the more risky types of real estate investments. Lenders will loan less on more risky projects, causing a lower debt service requirement, which in turn produces a higher debt-coverage ratio.

Purchasing Power Risk

Purchasing power risk, also called price level risk or inflation risk, is the uncertainty that the real or true value of an investment's dollar returns will decline. A brief explanation of the four basic sources of inflation will amplify the implications and ramifications of inflation for real estate investments.

Cost-Push Inflation. When the factors of production increase in cost, the result is often an increase in the price of the product or service provided to the consumer. For example, if the costs of leather, rubber, and labor increase, it is likely that the price of shoes will be inflated.

Demand-Pull Inflation. When consumer demand increases more rapidly than the supply of a good or service, the result is often an increase in the price of the good or service. For example, if a new industry locates in a town, the sudden surge in housing demand caused by the additional employees will tend to pull up the price of homes in the town.

Monetary Inflation. The U.S. money supply is controlled by the Federal Reserve System. The Fed, through open-market purchases of government securities, at times pumps too much money into the economy, thereby causing monetary inflation. Federal government deficit spending that is financed by the direct purchase of government securities by the Fed is called monetization of the debt. Monetization is purely inflationary and is sometimes called the "printing press effect" because it pumps new money directly into the system.

Real Cost Inflation. Increases in prices caused by the increased effort required to produce the same quantity and/or quality of a good or service is called real cost inflation. For example, the costs of oil, gas, and mineral production may increase because of the additional effort required to discover and recover such depleting natural resources. Marginally developable land's costing more to develop than easy-to-develop land previously developed is another example of real cost inflation.

Real estate investments have traditionally been superior hedges against inflation risk. The rising costs of construction and financing have a tendency to increase the value of real estate already in place. It is also common for commercial real estate leases to contain escalation clauses calling for increased rents to offset inflationary rises in the cost of living. Some mortgage investors require equity participations as protection against inflation and interest rate risk.

Interest Rate Risk

Interest rate or money rate risk is the degree of uncertainty associated with the likelihood of changes in the future general level of interest rates and the impact such changes have on investment value. For example, as interest rates rise (either because of a shortage of the supply of loanable funds or an increase in the demand for loanable funds), prices of existing bonds and mortgages fall. When interest rates decline, bond and mortgage values rise. Even the values of the most secure bonds, such as United States government bonds, are highly subject to changes in interest rates.

Suppose an investor purchased a $1000 bond which paid interest at the rate of 7 percent, or $70 a year in dollar figures. Assume that the general level of interest rates subsequently rose to 9 percent because of an increase in the demand for loanable funds. The original investor's bond still only pays $70 a year, whereas new bonds pay $90 a year. Obviously the investor would like to sell the 7 percent bond and buy a 9-percent one. However, the person who would buy the 7 percent bond will not pay $1000 for it, since his return would be only 7 percent. He or she would rather buy a new 9-percent bond, unless the 7-percent bond were priced to return 9 percent. The $70 a year is 7 percent of $1000, but it is also 9 percent of $777.78 ($70 divided by .09 equals $777.78). Hence, if the old bond sold for a lower price, it would have a return equal to the going market rate. Actually, the years to maturity (the years remaining over which this bond will pay interest) will affect its resale price, since at the end of this term the bond will be redeemed for the full $1000.

In any case, an inverse relationship exists between the general level of interest rates and the price of fixed interest rate investments, such as bonds and mortgages. A variable rate mortgage, however, would not be subject to interest rate risk, since its investment rate of return varies with some index which is supposed to be representative of the going market rate.

Finally, to the degree that changes in the general level of interest rates affect capitalization rates, a small change in interest rates causes large variations in real estate investment values. For example, if an investment property produces an NOI of $12,000 and this income is capitalized at 10 percent, the investment value is $120,000 ($12,000 divided by .10 equals $120,000). If the general level of interest rates then rises and investors demand higher rates of return, the appropriate capitalization rate might be 12 percent. The value of the investment property producing a $12,000 NOI then drops from $120,000 to $100,000 ($12,000 divided by .12 equals $100,000). Thus interest rates affect capitalization rates, and capitalization rates materially affect the market values of real estate investments. However, if interest rates have risen because of inflation (see Chapter 14) it is possible that rent escalation clauses will take effect. If so, the income to be capitalized by a higher capitalization rate may increase proportionately to the capitalization rate increase, such that the property value will not decline. For example, income might rise to $14,400 as the capitalization rate rises to 12 percent, and the property value remains $120,000 ($14,400 divided by .12 equals $120,000).

Management Risk

Management risk or the manageability of an investment is the extent to which it requires "care and feeding" over the investment holding period. As a rule, real estate investments, as compared with most other investments, requires investors to look after their investments more closely, because of their complex nature. For example, investment in real estate requires the ability of investors to handle a variety of legal complications, such as acquiring clear title, dealing with zoning boards, meeting environmental protection standards, negotiating tenant actions, and complying with building, safety, health, and sanitation codes.

Other aspects of this management or ownership burden include the worries a property owner must bear regarding natural hazards such as fires, floods, hurricanes, mudslides, etc. Most of these hazards are insurable at some price. However, other worry factors, such as neighborhood transition, crime rates, vandalism, condemnation, changes in transportation routes, and changes in governmental policies regarding economic, political, and social issues, may not be insurable.

The impact upon value of these worry factors is not readily available. Real estate investors cannot simply read the *Wall Street Journal* to obtain an accurate estimate of their investment portfolios, the way stock and bond investors can. Instead, real estate investors must continually worry about the value and safety of their investments and bear the burden of the ownership of a very complex type of investment.

Financial Risk

The use of borrowed capital to obtain leverage of capital and leverage of the rate of return on equity is well suited to real estate investments because the real estate, which is hypothecated to the lender, provides the lender with excellent loan security. The uncertainty of the investor's financial ability to make his or her debt service (principal and interest) payments is called financial risk. The degree of financial risk for stock and bond investments is readily measured by national security rating firms, such as Moody's and Standard and Poor's, which grade securities in terms of the relationship between the amount of funds a company has to satisfy security holders and the amount of funds required to meet these demands.

The degree of this uncertainty or risk of debt repayment for real estate investments is a function of the relationship between the amount of NOI projected to be produced by the investment property and the amount of debt service required on the loan. The greater the NOI relative to the debt service, the lower the financial risk; the greater the debt service relative to the NOI, the greater the financial risk. In other words, the debt coverage ratio (NOI/Debt Service), employed in the analysis of business risk, may also be employed in the analysis of financial risk. If the debt coverage ratio is lower than the standard (perhaps 1.25), there is either not enough NOI, which indicates business risk, or too much debt service, which indicates financial risk in the form of either too large a loan or too high a mortgage constant.

It should be noted that the NOI or property productivity is a function of market demand and the competitive position of the property within the market. On the other hand, the debt service requirement is a function of investor-lender loan negotiations. Negotiations for commercial real estate loans revolve around bargaining over the interest rate and the term of the loan, which are represented by a single number or percentage called the *mortgage constant*.

Mortgage Constant. The ratio of annual debt service payments over the original loan amount is called the mortgage constant. This ratio represents the percent per dollar borrowed that must be paid annually to the lender in order to both amortize (pay off) the principal and pay the interest due. Since most real estate loans are paid on a monthly basis, the annual mortgage constant is the sum of the twelve monthly payments or the product of the monthly payment times twelve.

For example, the monthly payment (principal and interest) on a $100,000 loan at 9 percent interest for 25 years is $839.20. The sum of twelve of these payments or the product of this payment times twelve is $10,070.40, which is the annual debt service requirement. This debt service divided by the original loan amount ($100,000) computes a mortgage constant of 10.07 percent.

The study of a table of mortgage constants reveals certain interesting relationships which affect the loan negotiation process.

TABLE 18-1. Mortgage Constant Table

Interest Rate	*Loan Term in Years*			
	15	20	25	30
9 percent	12.17	10.80	10.07	9.66
9.25 percent	12.35	10.99	10.28	9.87
9.50 percent	12.53	11.19	10.48	10.09
9.75 percent	12.71	11.38	10.69	10.31

The following observations should be noted:

1. The greater the interest rate, the greater the mortgage constant
2. The longer the loan term, the smaller the mortgage constant
3. The mortgage constant times the original loan amount equals the annual debt service requirement

4. The mortgage constant is a function of the interest rate, the term to maturity, and the frequency of payments within the year.

Because of the relationships (1) and (2), it is possible to increase the interest rate, yet lower the mortgage constant, by extending the loan term. For example, the mortgage constant for 9 percent, 20 years is 10.80; for 9.75 percent, 25 years, the constant is lowered to 10.69, despite a .75 percent increase in the interest rate. Even though the interest rate is considerably higher, the mortgage constant and therefore the debt service payments are smaller, because the principal amortization is spread out over five more years.

Since debt service is subtracted from NOI to get cash throw-off to equity or before-tax cash flow, minimizing debt service by negotiating the lowest possible mortgage constant is very important to real estate investors. Such investors would even be willing to pay a higher interest rate, if in so doing the mortgage constant were lowered by the lender's extending the term of the loan. It is true that by extending the loan term a larger amount of total interest will be paid to the lender over the total loan term. However, since most real estate investments are sold or traded before the longer loan term is reached, cash-flow maximization through lower payments usually overrides this fact.

Benefits of Leverage. The main reason why investors are willing to incur and even seek financial risk is to reap the benefits of financial leverage. As stated in Chapter 17, if the return on the total capital investment (debt and equity positions) is greater than the cost of the borrowed capital, the excess return is added to the return on the investor's equity, thereby increasing or levering the rate of return to the investor's equity position. This phenomenon is called positive financial leverage.

However, leverage is a two-edged sword. If the return on the total capital investment is lower than the cost of the borrowed capital—or, put another way, if the cost of the borrowed capital is greater than the return on the total capital investment—the excess cost is subtracted from the return on the investor's equity, thereby lowering or reverse-levering the rate of return to the investor's equity position. This phenomenon is called negative financial leverage.

Some numerical examples will demonstrate exactly how the phenomena of positive and negative leverage work. Assume the following:

1. Value or price: $1 million
2. NOI: $120,000; $90,000
3. Return on investment: 12 percent; 9 percent (determined by dividing NOI by value or price; also called the overall rate of return or OAR)
4. Mortgage constant: 10 percent as calculated for a 28-year loan term at 9.25 percent interest rate

5. Loan-to-value ratios: 0 percent; 50 percent; 75 percent; 90 percent

To demonstrate the power of financial leverage, the calculation for the rate of return to equity will be calculated on a "cash-on-cash" basis for a variety of four different loan-to-value ratios (LTVRs), first with an NOI of $120,000 to demonstrate positive financial leverage, then with an NOI of $90,000 to demonstrate negative financial leverage. The cash-on-cash equity return is computed by substracting debt service (DS) from NOI to get cash throw-off to equity (CTOE), and then dividing CTOE by the amount of the equity position (E) as determined by the difference between the original loan amount and the value or price, $1 million. (Remember debt service is computed by multiplying the mortgage constant times the loan amount.)

The various relationships required for these examples may be summarized as follows:

1. Equity equals value minus loan
2. Loan equals LTVR times value
3. Debt service equals mortgage constant times loan
4. CTOE equals NOI minus debt service
5. "Cash on cash" equals CTOE divided by E equals return to equity

The example of positive financial leverage is presented in Table 18-2 and the example of negative leverage is presented in Table 18-3.

TABLE 18-2. Positive Financial Leverage

OAR 12 percent > Mortgage Constant 10 percent

LTVR	*NOI − DS = CTOE*	*CTOE ÷ E = Return to Equity*
0 percent	$120,000 − $ 0 = $120,000	$120,000 ÷ $1 million = 12 percent
50 percent	$120,000 − $50,000 = $ 70,000	$ 70,000 ÷ $ 500,000 = 14 percent
75 percent	$120,000 − $75,000 = $ 45,000	$ 45,000 ÷ $ 250,000 = 18 percent
90 percent	$120,000 − $90,000 = $ 30,000	$ 30,000 ÷ $ 100,000 = 30 percent

TABLE 18-3. Negative Financial Leverage

OAR 9 percent < Mortgage Constant 10 percent

LTVR	*NOI − DS = CTOE*	*CTOE ÷ E = Return to Equity*
0 percent	$90,000 − $ 0 = $90,000	$90,000 ÷ $1 million = 9 percent
50 percent	$90,000 − $50,000 = $40,000	$40,000 ÷ $ 500,000 = 8 percent
75 percent	$90,000 − $75,000 = $15,000	$15,000 ÷ $ 250,000 = 6 percent
90 percent	$90,000 − $90,000 = $ 0	$ 0 ÷ $ 100,000 = 0 percent

The following observations and generalizations can be made regarding financial leverage as portrayed in Tables 18-2 and 18-3.

1. Positive financial leverage exists when the OAR is greater than the cost of borrowing, as represented by the mortgage constant.
2. Negative financial leverage exists when the OAR is lower than the cost of borrowing, as represented by the mortgage constant.
3. Leverage is amplified by increasing the amount borrowed (LTVR); doing so moved the return to equity from 12 percent to 30 percent with positive leverage, and from 9 percent to 0 percent with negative leverage.
4. The impact of leverage on the return to equity is relatively more powerful or greater in the range of high LTVRs than in the range of low LTVRs. For example, in the 0 to 50 percent LTVR range, return to equity was levered only 2 percent (from 12 to 14 percent) in Table 18-2, and only 1 percent (from 9 to 8 percent) in Table 18-3. In the 50 to 90 percent LTVR range, return to equity was levered 16 percent (from 14 to 30 percent) in Table 18-2, and 8 percent (from 8 to 0 percent) in Table 18-3.
5. The interest rate (9.25 percent) was held constant as LTVRs increased. In practice, the interest rate usually increases as the LTVR increases. However, even if the interest rate increases, the cost of borrowing, as represented by the mortgage constant, does not necessarily increase, since the loan term might be extended as well.

Further Considerations of Leverage. Difficult though it may be to believe, what has been said thus far regarding financial leverage barely scratches the surface in explaining all the ramifications and benefits available to the investor who employs positive financial leverage. Furthermore, the numerical examples presented in Tables 18-2 and 18-3 are somewhat oversimplified. The examples do not consider the after-tax effects, investment strategy, portfolio diversification, or investor objectives. The following list of further considerations of leverage are offered as food for thought, since some of the explanations are beyond the scope of this text:

1. All appreciation in property value accrues to the equity position and can be realized as a cash flow upon resale or refinancing. If the refinancing is chosen, these dollars are tax free or tax deferred until the property is sold.
2. Since debt service is fixed, all increases in NOI are realized by the equity investor, further levering the return to equity. This phenomenon is called operating leverage.
3. The interest portion of the debt service is deductible for income

tax purposes, which enhances the after-tax cash-flow position of the equity investor. In fact, investors in very high tax brackets are sometimes better off paying a higher rate of interest.

4. Through leverage, the small investor can purchase larger investments.
5. Similarly, large investors can purchase and own more properties, thereby gaining a degree of investment portfolio diversification. For example, a large investor with $1 million could employ leverage and purchase ten $1 million properties like the one presented in Table 18-2.
6. By employing leverage, large investors can purchase the very largest investments, which are often priced better than small investment properties because there are fewer buyers competing for them.
7. By owning more properties through leverage of investment capital, investors obtain a higher degree of investment liquidity. For example, should a need for cash arise, it should be easier to sell one out of many properties than one out of one.
8. Also, by owning more properties through leverage of capital, investors can multiply their tax shelters available from depreciation, since the total investment (exclusive of land), not just the equity investment, is depreciable.
9. Chapter 17 covered the benefits of mortgaging out and walking money available to some mortgage borrowers.
10. Finally, Chapter 17 also explained the benefit of equity buildup through amortization available to investors whose property value is maintained and who may realize or cash in on this benefit by either selling or refinancing the property.

SUMMARY AND CONCLUSIONS

This chapter has discussed six very important investment risks to which all real estate investments are subject. The importance of any one of the six risks relative to a given investment may vary over time. The fact that real estate investments are often held for a relatively long time period makes such investments particularly vulnerable to the various risks. However, as with most types of investments, the greater the risk, the higher the return—usually.

The qualities of long economic life, durability, and the fixity of location characteristic of real estate investments may carry high risk over the long term, but also aid yielding relatively high rates of return. For example, the ownership of a real estate investment which is (1) occupied by financially stable tenants, (2) well located within the market area, (3) professionally managed, and (4) properly financed may be risky over the long term, but should also yield ample returns to the investor.

Regarding interest rate risk, fixed-rate investments such as mortgages, which are usually subject to this risk, may avoid it if a variable-rate mortgage is used. If capitalization rates rise because of inflation, income produced by the real estate might increase due to rent escalation clauses, so that property value remains unchanged. Proper investment planning greatly aids risk avoidance.

Finally, financial risk may not be avoided, but rather sought with great effort, by the well-informed real estate investor. The numerous benefits possible from the proper implementation of financial leverage may far outweigh the potentially disastrous ramifications of financial risk. Investors, therefore, may seek high risks in hopes of earning high returns. Measurement of investment returns is the subject of the next chapter.

CHAPTER 19

Measuring Real Estate Investment Returns

KEY TERMS

Required rate of return The rate of return necessary to attract investment capital in a market of competitive investments
Expected rate of return The rate of return estimated by the investment productivity analysis
Free and clear rate of return The ratio of a property's net operating income over the price or property value; also called the *broker's net rate*
Broker's equity rate of return The ratio of the cash throwoff to equity or before tax cash flow over the original equity investment; also called the *cash spendable rate*, the *cash-on-cash rate*, the *equity dividend rate*, and the *cash-flow rate*
Average rate of return An arithmetic average of the total returns to equity less the original equity investment; also called the *accounting return*
Payback period The number of years it will take for an investment proposal's cash flow to equity to totally return the original equity investment to the equity investor
Multiplier The reciprocal of a rate
Time value of money A concept that holds that a dollar received today (in the present) has *more value* than a dollar received tomorrow (in the future) or, conversely, a dollar received tomorrow (in the future) has *less value* than a dollar received today (in the present)
Present value discounted cash-flow analysis A method of investment analysis that recognizes the time value of money
Internal rate of return The rate of discount that equates the present value of negative cash flows of an investment with the positive cash flows of an investment, thereby reflecting the true or effective yield or rate of return of said investment

INTRODUCTION

Investors seek to offset the incurrence of investment risks with investment returns. The old maxim: "The greater the risk, the greater the return" usually holds true in the area of real estate investments. In fact, it is this general relationship that causes some investors to seek, rather than to avoid, high-risk investments, in hope of earning appropriately high returns. Furthermore, investors differ regarding the amount of risk they are willing to bear. However, within a given range of acceptable risk, all investors seek to maximize their return. Chapter 18 covered the various risks attached to investing in real estate. Six different types of investment risks were presented and explained. Chapter 19 will discuss the opposite side of the coin—investment returns.

Having established a set of specific real estate investment objectives, and having investigated, analyzed, and determined the inherent risks of various real estate investments, it now becomes the task of the potential real estate investor to allocate his or her available capital to possible real estate investment proposals. It is the purpose of this chapter to discuss how these decisions can be made based upon measurement of return analyses.

TRADITIONAL METHODS

Most investors would agree that it is very difficult to quantify and measure accurately the degree of risk inherent in specific investments. On the other hand, it is apparently very easy for investors to quantify and measure "accurately" the return inherent in specific investments. However, a serious problem exists with the return analyses employed by real estate investors in the evaluation of investment alternatives.

The basic problem is that a plethora of methods exists for determining investment return. Most investors must decide which method of return measurement is correct, accurate, efficient, and appropriate for any given type of investment. As will be shown in this chapter, most investors have traditionally taken the easy way out of the problem, by greatly oversimplifying the problem and using an inadequate measure of return. The sad thing about this typical state of affairs is that most of the investors have been totally unaware of the errors of their ways. Not unlike the professor of economic theory who, while stranded on a desert island with only a can of beans for survival, said, "First, assume a can opener . . . ," these investors have been "starving" for help.

Valuation Techniques

Over the years, the field of investment analysis has seen a rapid increase in the number of available measures of investment profitability. Much confusion has been caused by the existence of many methods for determining the relative desirability of alternative real estate investments, for the following reasons:

1. There is usually a trade-off between (a) the simplicity of calculation and degree of understanding and (b) the complexity of application and volume of information required.
2. There is often the dilemma that the different approaches or methods produce both different relative ranking and different indications of investment profitability.

Initially, emphasis was not necessarily placed on the ranking of proposals by rates of return, but on valuation. At first, emphasis was placed on estimating the investment value of a particular property and comparing the investment value with the sales price of the property. If investment value equaled or exceeded investment cost, the property was acceptable. Investment value was calculated by converting the projected income into value by the direct capitalization with an overall rate method explained in Chapter 16, (p. 279). This method makes the following assumptions:

1. An appropriate overall rate can be derived from the ratios of annual net operating incomes to sales prices of comparable properties.
2. The subject property's annual net operating income can be stabilized or averaged.
3. Value can be estimated with the formula V = I/R such that value equals the stabilized net operating income divided by the appropriate overall rate.

As stated in Chapter 16, this method makes no inherent estimates as to the behavior or variability of the income or capital recapture period, since there is no assumption about remaining economic life. Furthermore, this method of valuation does not differentiate land from building. Variations of this original direct capitalization approach were later provided by Frederick M. Babcock, who felt that different rates should be used for land and buildings. Hence, Babcock developed the so-called land, building, and property residual approaches to value. The assumptions and limitations of these and other valuation techniques were also presented in Chapter 16.

Rate of Return Techniques

The use of valuation methods to evaluate real estate investment opportunities is quite static in that only one proposal can be considered at a time. For this reason, the attention of real estate investors shifted to a more practical decision-making technique known as the *traditional rate of return* approach. This approach involves (1) determining the *required rate of return*, (2) estimating the *expected rate of return*, and (3) accepting only those investment proposals whose expected rate of return equals or exceeds the required rate of return.

Required Rate of Return. In Chapter 16, the distinction between return *of* investment and return *on* investment was explained: return of investment was called the *capital recapture rate*, and return *on* investment, for appraisal purposes, was labeled the *discount rate*, or rate of return necessary (in a market of competitive investments) to attract investment capital. For investment purposes, the discount rate and the required rate of return are synonymous.

It was also explained that the discount rate must be greater than the riskless or safe rate because the discount rate is the rate necessary (or required) to compensate the investor for all the various risks inherent in the particular investment. The summation or buildup method was presented as the theoretical justification and explanation of this phenomenon.

The determination of the required discount rate is the subject of much controversy. However, possible methods of determining this rate include the band of investment, abstraction, and market comparison approaches. The points of controversy regarding these approaches usually center around the fact that such calculations totally ignore such important market realities as income taxation, debt financing, investment holding periods, and property value appreciation (or depreciation).

Expected Rate of Return. Traditionally, the expected rate of return has received much more investor attention than the required rate of return. The expected rate has been formulated in a variety of ways, each of which relies upon the productivity analysis used to estimate the future income and expenses of each investment property proposal. Generally, either the gross income, net income, or some other income, which has been estimated in the productivity analysis, is divided by either the total property value or investor's equity to calculate the expected rate of return.

Free and Clear Rate of Return. The *free and clear rate of return*, also known as the *broker's net rate*, is calculated by dividing the net operating income by the total property value or purchase price. For example, if NOI is $120,000 and value or price is $1 million, the free and clear rate is 12 percent ($120,000 divided by $1 million equals .12 or 12 percent). This formulation is a basic productivity measure of the total capital invested and implies free and clear ownership with no mortgage debt. This rate is, in fact, the overall rate (OAR), which was discussed in Chapters 16, 17, and 18. This method of measuring return is fundamental to the direct capitalization method of appraisal discussed in Chapter 16. In Chapters 17 and 18 this rate of return technique was shown to be critical to financial leverage. One must borrow below this rate in order to employ positive financial leverage.

Broker's Equity Rate of Return. Real estate brokers usually will calculate a rate of return on equity to aid in the marketing of investment real estate.

Such a rate is calculated by dividing the return to the equity investor (after payment of debt service) by the original equity investment. Real estate brokers are often criticized for misleading and confusing potential investors through the misrepresentation of the rate of return which an equity investor could realize by owning the real property. The problem here is that the rate of return on an equity investment will vary greatly depending on how the return and equity are defined.

The return to the equity investment could be defined as any of the following:

1. Cash flow, also called cash throw-off to equity (CTOE), or before-tax cash flow (BTCF); calculated by subtracting debt service (DS) from net operating income (NOI)
2. Cash flow plus after-tax effects
3. Cash flow plus after-tax effects plus equity buildup
4. Cash flow plus after-tax effects plus equity buildup plus appreciation

Likewise, the equity investment could be defined as any of the following:

1. Original cash down payment
2. Original cash down payment plus prepaid interest, underwriting commissions, legal fees, and other closing costs
3. Original cash down payment plus prepaid interest, underwriting commissions, legal fees, and other closing costs adjusted for the tax effect of the deductible items

These two lists of possible definitions are neither complete nor exhaustive. Many definitions of return to equity and equity investment may be encountered in the real world of investment real estate. Hence, extreme caution should be taken in using these measures. It is essential for the broker and the investor to have a meeting of the minds as to what is included in the computations used by each party. One must also be sure that the figure is calculated in the same manner for every property when comparing alternative investment proposals.

It is most common for investors to use the first definition in each list to calculate the equity rate of return. This calculation is also called the cash spendable rate, the cash-on-cash rate, the equity dividend rate, and the cash-flow rate. If the after-tax effects are also figured in calculating this rate, one need only add the words *after-tax* in front of these four names. Finally, it should be noted that neither equity buildup nor appreciation can be *realized* until the investor sells or refinances the property. In other words, you cannot buy a loaf of bread with equity buildup or appreciation.

Average Rate of Return. The average rate of return calculation requires

(1) adding up all returns expected by the equity investor during the entire investment holding period, (2) subtracting the initial equity investment from the total expected returns, (3) dividing this remainder by the number of years in the projected investment holding period to obtain the annual average return in dollars, and (4) dividing the annual average return in dollars by the initial equity investment to obtain the annual average return per dollar of initial equity. This rate of return is also called the *accounting return*.

An example of this four-step calculation assuming (1) \$100,000 initial equity investment, (2) 10-year investment holding period, and (3) \$20,000 annual cash flow to equity would be as follows:

$$\text{Average rate} = \frac{10\ (\$20{,}000) - \$100{,}000}{10} \div \$100{,}000 = .10 = 10 \text{ percent}$$

Payback Period. The payback period is defined as the number of years it will take for an investment proposal's cash flow to equity to return totally the original equity investment to the equity investor. For example, the payback period for the above example is five years, since it pays \$20,000 a year and the initial equity investment is \$100,000. Investments with the shortest payback period are deemed the most desirable.

Income Multipliers. A multiplier is the reciprocal of a rate. For example, the multiplier for the rate 20 percent is 5, since 20 percent equals 1/5 and the reciprocal of 1/5 is 5. Real estate is often bought and sold on the basis of income multipliers, either gross or net. An income multiplier is calculated by dividing the property value or price by the gross or net income. For example, given a property value of \$1 million and a gross income of \$200,000, the gross income or gross rent multiplier (GRM) is 5.

Investors use the GRM to compare market values of investment properties where there are reasonable similarities of age, size, location, and operating experience. When multiplier analysis is applied to NOI, the process is more properly considered part of the income approach to value, since the net income multiplier of an investment property is simply the reciprocal of the overall rate (OAR = NOI divided by price). Finally, income multipliers can be expressed on either a monthly (single-family residences) or an annual (apartment buildings) basis.

Limitations of Traditional Methods

Generally speaking, the traditional methods of measuring investment returns fail to account for various realities of the real estate investment marketplace. The following list of limitations of the traditional methods discussed thus far should make the point that most of these measures of return are poorly equipped to provide a clear, concise, and unequivocal indication of investment profitability and desirability, considering the variety of investment characteristics that may meet the objectives of today's well-informed and competent real estate investor.

1. The timing and duration of cash flows are ignored. Money has a time value; that which is received sooner is more valuable than that which is received later. Hence, future cash flows and proceeds upon resale must be converted from future values into present values, considering investor-required rates of return.
2. No provision is made for uneven cash flows. Often only first-year income or at best average or stabilized income, is used. The realities of incomes changing because of variances in occupancy rates and expenses, declining amounts of mortgage interest and accelerated depreciation tax deductions, and increases in income from graduated-rent, escalation, and percentage-rent clauses in leases, are overlooked.
3. After-tax effects from depreciation, capital gains, depreciation recapture, and other less-known tax code benefits are usually not considered.
4. Since some methods assume free and clear ownership, no provision is made for debt-financing and refinancing. Consideration of financial leverage and all its amazing benefits is usually deleted.
5. Different possible investment holding periods usually are not considered. The fact that income tax laws typically encourage turnover of real estate investments within an 8 to ten-year period is ignored. Instead, the unrealistic assumption that the investment holding period equals the remaining economic life of the property is often made.
6. Some methods apparently imply that the overall rate is more significant to investors than the rate of return to the equity position.
7. Appreciation or depreciation in value upon resale is ignored. Appreciation might be an investor's primary objective.
8. The original project cost or amount of initial equity investment required is typically omitted.
9. Transaction costs at the front end or tail end of the investment holding period are not considered.
10. The impacts of inflation and risk upon a potential investment proposal are not considered.

These ten limitations of the traditional methods of measuring investment profitability and desirability and the demands by more sophisticated real estate investment decision makers for more precision in real estate investment analysis brought about the development of the so-called contemporary methods of measuring investment profitability and desirability.

CONTEMPORARY METHODS

Particularly because of the limitations which distort, partially disregard, or totally ignore the timing and duration of cash flows and the time value of money, a move developed to the more sophisticated measurement techniques which do account for these factors. It should be noted that not even these contemporary methods explicitly account for risk or inflation. Hence, when comparing present values and/or rates of return among alternative investment proposals, the proposals should represent cash flows of similar risk and duration. Additionally, since future cash flows are discounted to the present and compared with present dollar outlays, the comparisons are valid only when constant dollars are assumed.

Valuation Techniques

Contemporary methods for measuring value include the following:

1. Present value discounted cash-flow analysis
2. Mortgage-equity analysis
3. Profitability index

Present Value Discounted Cash-flow Analysis. The concept of the time value of money holds that a dollar received in the present has *more value* than a dollar received in the future, and conversely, a dollar received in the future, has *less value* than a dollar received in the present. The difference in value is a function of the rate of return required by the investor or paid or returned by the investment.

For example, a $100 savings account investment bearing an interest rate of return of 6 percent per year will accumulate in one year's time to a *future value* of $106, consisting of the original investment of $100 and the earned interest of $6. The *present value* of this future amount of $106 will be $100 if an investor's required rate of return is 6 percent. If an investor requires *more* than a 6 percent rate of return, this investment is worth, or has a *present value* of, *less* than $100. For example, if an investor requires a 10 percent rate of return, this investment with a future value of $106 has a present value of only $96.36, because 10 percent of $96.36 is $9.64, which added to $96.36 totals $106.

Conversely, if an investor requires *less* than a 6 percent rate of return, the investment projected to have a future value of $106 has a present value of more than $100. For example, if an investor requires only a 4 percent rate of return, this investment with a future value of $106 has a present value of $101.92, because 4 percent of $101.92 is $4.08, which added to $101.92 totals $106.

Tables and calculators containing present value factors, also called discount factors, for the conversion or discounting of future values to present values are used by contemporary real estate investors. These tables and calculators contain appropriate factors for many required rates of return, also called discount rates, for each year. For example, the discount or present value factors for the above examples are .943396, .909091, and .961538, respectively. These factors multiplied by the future value of $106 calculate the present value at a 6 percent, 10 percent, and 4 percent required rate of return, as shown below:

Required Rate of Return	*6 percent*	*10 percent*	*4 percent*
Future value	$106	$106	$106
Discount factor	× .943396	× .909091	× .961538
Present value	$100	$ 96.36	$101.92

Proper use of the tables or calculators allows an investor to calculate values which are accurate whatever the timing, variability, and duration of the cash flows. The sum of these discounted cash flows equals the present value of a given investment proposal. Furthermore, the cash flows can also be computed on an after-debt service, after-tax, and after-resale or refinancing basis in order to account for the myriad factors which are ignored by most of the traditional methods of valuation.

It should also be noted that the longer one has to wait for a cash flow, the less its value in the present. In other words, the further into the future a cash flow is to be received, the smaller its discount factor for a given required rate of return or discount rate, and therefore the smaller its value in the present.

For example, observe the following calculations where the present value of a $10,000 cash flow decreases the further into the future it is received:

Year	*Cash Flow*	*10 Percent Discount Factor*	*Present Value*
1	$10,000	.909091	$9,090.91
2	$10,000	.826446	8,264.46
3	$10,000	.751315	7,513.15
4	$10,000	.683013	6,830.13
5	$10,000	.620921	6,209.21

Also, for a given time period, the higher the discount rate, the lower the value in the present. For example, observe the following calculations where the present value of a single cash flow of $10,000 decreases as the required discount rate increases:

Required Discount Rate	*5 Percent*	*10 Percent*	*15 Percent*
Cash flow	$10,000	$10,000	$10,000
Five-year discount factor	× .783526	× .620921	× .497177
Present value	$7,835.26	$6,209.21	$4,971.77

The present value discounted cash flow analysis allows the value of an investment property to be expressed in terms of today's value as one number for a specific required rate of return or discount rate. Alternatively, the so-called net present value (NPV) may also be calculated by investors who wish to consider the time value of money and who set a minimum rate of return as an investment requirement. The NPV is defined as the difference between the present value of the positive cash flows and the present value sum of the initial cash outlay and the negative cash flows, if any, projected to be incurred during the investment holding period. If the NPV is positive, the investment's rate of return exceeds the minimum rate requirement, thereby making the investment proposal acceptable. If the NPV is zero, the investment's rate of return is equal to the minimum rate requirement, thereby also making the investment proposal acceptable. If the NPV is negative, the investment's rate of return is below the minimum rate requirement, thereby making the investment proposal unacceptable.

Another method of investment analysis which utilizes present value concepts and also calculates investment value as a function of a specified minimum rate of return requirement is the mortgage-equity analysis.

Mortgage-Equity Analysis. Some critics of the present value approaches presented thus far choose to emphasize the minimum rate of return requirement earned on equity capital, rather than that earned on total capital. Furthermore, these critics calculate two present values: one for the mortgage position and one for the equity position on an after-tax basis.

In mortgage-equity analysis the after-tax cash flow (ATCF) is calculated as NOI minus DS minus tax liability or plus tax savings (NOI − DS = CTOE ± Tax Liability or Tax Saving = ATCF. The positive cash flows of ATCF projected for the investment holding period are discounted at the required rate of return. This present value calculation is added to the present value of the net equity reversion (NER), which is the projected resale price net of commissions, costs of sale, capital-gains taxes, and the remaining balance of the mortgage loan at the time of sale.

In other words, the sum of the present value of the ATCF plus the present value of the NER equals the present value of the equity position. Finally, the sum of the present value of the equity position plus the present value of the mortgage position equals the investment value of the real estate (Figure 19-1). One possible weakness of this method is that it requires knowing the dollar amount of the available mortgage, which is seldom known (unless the loan is being assumed) without first knowing the property value.

Many investors find mortgage-equity analysis attractive because it allows consideration of the following real-world factors:

1. Short investment holding periods
2. Debt financing and leverage
3. Capital appreciation or depreciation

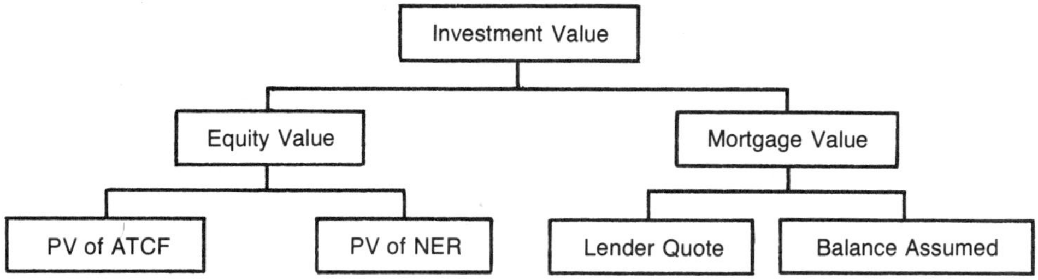

Figure 19-1 Mortgage-Equity Analysis

4. Rate of return to equity
5. After-tax effects

Others criticize the present value approaches, including mortgage-equity analysis, for not facilitating the comparison of different investment alternatives. The critics developed an index to measure the profitability or value of an investment in terms of a common denominator.

Profitability Index. The present value data—the present value of the positive cash flows and the present value sum of the initial cash outlay and the negative cash flows (if any)—can be translated into a benefit-cost ratio called the *profitability index* (PI), which can be employed to compare different investment proposals. The PI is calculated by dividing the present value of all the positive flows by the present value of all negative flows. The same discount rate is used for present values of both positive and negative flows.

If the PI is equal to or greater than one, then the minimum rate requirement has been met or surpassed. Furthermore, in comparing two or more investments, the one with the largest PI is deemed most desirable. In fact, a ranking of investment PIs can be used to rank alternative investment proposals, since the PI shows the relative profitability, or the dollar of return per dollar of cost.

Some investors shun the use of the PI because it runs into problems when comparing investments that have different initial cash-outlay requirements. The investment with the highest PI may also have the highest cost, a cost that may be prohibitive to certain investors. Finally, while the PI indicates if the minimum rate requirement has been met or surpassed, many investors want to know exactly what the rate of return is on any given investment proposal.

Rate of Return Techniques

Since investors desire a measure of the rate of return for a given investment, the following three variations of the profitability index are used to provide this very desirable information:

1. Internal rate of return
2. Adjusted or terminal rate of return
3. Financial management rate of return.

Internal Rate of Return. The internal rate of return (IRR) is a variation of the PI, since the IRR is defined as the rate of discount that makes the PI exactly equal to one. Thus, the IRR is the rate of discount which makes the present value of the positive cash flows of an investment exactly equal to the present value sum of the initial cash outlay and the negative cash flows, if any, of the same investment. The IRR is, therefore, also the rate of discount which makes the NPV exactly equal zero, since the NPV is the difference between the present values of the positive and negative cash flows. To summarize, the IRR is the rate of discount or rate of return that causes the following equations to be true:

1. $\text{PI} = \dfrac{\text{PV positive cash flows}}{\text{PV negative cash flows}} = 1$
2. $\text{NPV} = \text{PV positive cash flows} - \text{PV negative cash flows} = 0$
3. $\text{PV positive cash flows} = \text{PV negative cash flows}$

While what has been presented thus far in defining the IRR may be relatively straightforward, the actual calculation of the IRR is quite cumbersome. The process requires a series of repetitious trial-and-error estimates to find the rate of interest or rate of return whose discount factors multiplied by the cash flows will satisfy these three value equations. This process of selecting an interest rate and calculating the present value of all cash flows continues until the correct rate is chosen. Hence, the sheer number of calculations usually requires the use of a computer or at least a very sophisticated electronic calculator.

Once the IRR is found for a given investment, it may be compared to IRRs of other investments. It must be remembered, however, that the IRR does not account for risk. Therefore, in making investment comparisons one must compare investments within the same risk category. Incidentally, IRRs can be calculated for either the total capital investment position or the equity capital investment position only.

Unfortunately, there are a variety of potential problems associated with reliance on IRR as the exclusive method of measuring returns to derive investment desirability. For example, it is possible for there to be multiple IRRs or no IRR within the realm of real numbers for a given investment alternative. This is very rare, but possible. Discussion of this problems is beyond the scope of this text. Mention of these problems is made to introduce the adjusted or terminal value rate of return and the financial management rate of return, adaptations of the IRR which seek to avoid IRR's problems.

Adjusted or Terminal Value Rate of Return. The so-called adjusted or terminal value rate of return is used when the IRR and NPV methods produce conflicting results regarding two investment proposals. The solution to this situation is to adjust the IRR calculations by assuming that all cash flows are reinvested at some rate to accumulate or compound to a terminal value for each investment at the end of the projected investment holding period.

The result of such maneuvers is that each investment has one initial negative cash outflow and one terminal positive cash inflow. The IRR for each investment is then recalculated with these adjusted figures. The investment with the greater IRR is thereby determined to be the preferred investment choice.

Financial Management Rate of Return. The financial management rate of return (FMRR) is a specialized version of the adjusted or terminal value rate of return. The FMRR is described as specialized because its calculation has been modified to include as many of the unique characteristics of the real estate market as possible.[1] For example, FMRR makes the following assumptions:

1. Only cash flows after financing and taxes from the property under evaluation are considered.
2. Funds can be invested at any time in any amount at a safe after-tax rate and withdrawn when needed.
3. Funds can also be invested in "run of the mill" real estate projects of comparable risk at after-tax rates above the safe rate.

The reader is directed to the footnote for further study of the FMRR, for the author has already gone beyond the scope of the text with what little has already been said. It is important to recognize that very sophisticated techniques such as the FMRR are available to real estate investors.

SUMMARY AND CONCLUSIONS

Within a given range of acceptable risk, all investors seek to maximize their return. Investors differ regarding the amount of risk they are willing to bear. However, "the greater the risk, the greater the return" usually applies to real estate investments. Since return is so important in investment analysis, investors require tools to measure return.

Traditional methods of measuring return for real estate investments include both valuation techniques and rate of return techniques. Direct capitalization and the residual techniques are two traditional methods of

1. M. Chapman Findlay and Stephen D. Messner, "Real Estate Investment Analysis: IRR versus FMRR." *The Real Estate Appraiser* (July–August, 1975), pp. 5–20.

the valuation of real property. Since these methods are quite static, rate of return techniques, including the free and clear rate, broker's equity rate, average accounting rate, as well as the payback method and income multipliers, have traditionally been employed by unsophisticated and sophisticated investors alike.

Generally speaking, the traditional methods of measuring investment returns ignore or fail to consider various realities of the real estate marketplace, such as the timing and duration of cash flows, variability of uneven cash flows, after-tax effects on cash flow, mortgage financing, different investment holding periods, importance to investors of the return to equity, property value appreciation or depreciation, original project cost, transaction costs, inflation, and risk.

These limitations and the demand by sophisticated investors for more precise measurement of investment returns brought about the development of the so-called contemporary methods of measuring return. Contemporary valuation techniques include (1) present value discounted cash-flow analysis, (2) mortgage-equity analysis, and (3) profitability index. Contemporary rate of return techniques include: (1) internal rate of return, (2) adjusted or terminal value rate of return, and (3) financial management rate of return.

The calculation of these return measures and the assumptions of their methodologies are quite complex and sophisticated. Further study of these tools beyond what has been presented in this text is required of the serious real estate student or practitioner. The demands for accurate and precise tools of analysis for use in wise and intelligent real estate decision making will not abate in the future. The sophistication of computers and the development of better methods of analysis will continue.

CHAPTER 20

Tax Factors in Real Estate Investment

KEY TERMS

Gross income The income from all sources, including wages, salaries, tips, dividends, interest, pensions, annuities, rents, royalties, business income, farm income, and gains upon sale or exchange of property
Adjusted gross income Gross income minus adjustments
Adjustments Sick pay, certain moving expenses, business expenses, the $100 per person dividend exclusion, state and municipal bond interest, pension and annuity return-of-capital payments, depreciation, repairs, costs of farm and business operations, and basis upon sale or exchange of assets
Taxable income Adjusted gross income minus deductions and exemptions
Itemized deductions Certain medical expenses, charitable contributions, interest expense, taxes, casualty losses, and other costs
Standard personal deduction A flat amount of deduction allowed individuals who do not itemize deductions
Low-income-allowance deduction A deduction aimed at completely removing low-income people from the tax rolls
Exemption A set dollar amount allowed per taxpayer and for each of the taxpayer's dependents
Basis The original cost of acquiring a property or the original value of a property upon acquisition
Adjusted basis Basis *plus* the costs of capital improvements and capitalized carrying costs *minus* depreciation, casualty losses, and the basis attributed to a sale of a part of the real property

TAX LAW INVESTMENT IMPACT

As stated in Chapter 17, many investments have income tax benefit characteristics, and many investors have tax shelter as one of their prime objectives. Tax shelter is often one of the most attractive characteristics of many real estate investments: tax shelter is often the *most* important objective of many real estate investors. Investments analyzed on a before-tax basis may appear marginal, yet when analyzed on an after-tax basis these same investments may actually be very attractive to certain investors, especially those subject to high tax rates.

This investment attractiveness is usually purposefully provided for in the federal laws known as the Internal Revenue Code. The code is aimed at fulfilling the desires of Congress to induce certain types of economic activity within the system. Congress created the Internal Revenue Service (IRS) as the administrative agency charged with the responsibilities to collect income tax and interpret the code and its periodic congressional revisions. The IRS interprets the code by issuing general regulations and making specific rulings regarding individual situations. The federal courts also grant opinions and make decisions which further interpret and clarify the code, the regulations, and the rulings.

The power of Congress to change the tax laws virtually overnight creates an investment risk not specifically mentioned in Chapter 19. The risk of tax-law change is real and must be considered. A tax-law change can nearly instantaneously make a good investment a bad one. The wise real estate investor will not allow the tax factors of an investment property to override the basic economic considerations. An investment proposal must have a fundamental economic rationality of its own without considering the tax benefits. No amount of creative tax wheeling and dealing by itself can make an economically unsound project a viable investment venture. The preferred investment strategy is first to verify the basic economic viability of a project and then to employ proper tax planning merely to enhance the attractiveness of the project.

Proper tax planning can enhance investment returns in the following ways:

1. Tax deductibility of certain cash expenditures, such as operating expenses (including property taxes) and mortgage interest, reduces current tax liability, thereby lowering the effective initial and/or carrying costs of the real estate investment. For example, assuming an investor with a 50 percent effective tax rate, if the down payment required to purchase a property includes tax-deductible prepaid interest, the effective after-tax initial cost of buying the property is reduced by one half of the prepaid interest payments. Prepayment of interest, however, has a time-value-of-money penalty which somewhat offsets the benefit. Assuming the same investor, the costs of carrying a speculative land investment with property tax and mortgage interest payments is also reduced by one half of these payments.
2. Tax deductibility of depreciation, a noncash expenditure, reduces taxable investment income but not cash flow, thereby causing tax shelter of investment income. For example, assuming the same 50

percent tax rate investor, if a property produces $100,000 of income and $100,000 of depreciation is allowed, taxable income would be zero, thereby causing a tax shelter of $100,000 and a tax savings of $50,000, one half the tax shelter.

3. Tax deductibility of depreciation in amounts large enough not only to shelter income from the investment but also to shelter income from other sources, such as salary income, is also possible. For example, if the allowable depreciation in the previous example were $150,000, a tax loss of $50,000 would shelter salary income by $50,000, resulting in an additional tax savings of one half of the shelter, $25,000.
4. By owning many properties through the leverage of equity capital, real estate investors can multiply their tax shelters available from depreciation, since the total investment (exclusive of land), not just the equity investment, is depreciable.
5. The deferment of the taxability of current income to a future time, when the investor is likely to be in a lower tax bracket, will cause the tax liability to be calculated at a lower rate, thereby further enhancing investment return. Real estate investors do not avoid income taxes; they shift the time of payment of income taxes. This deferral of payment of the tax is valuable because the real estate investor has had the use of this money during all the time prior to the resale. For example, the depreciation deductions allowed in (2) and (3) above will eventually be taxed upon the sale of the property. The depreciation deductions lower the taxpayer's basis, which is subtracted from the net sales proceeds upon resale to determine the capital gain. This amount becomes taxable upon the sale. However, if the property has been held for at least 12 months, the capital gain will be taxed at the capital-gains rate, which is lower than the ordinary income rate. Furthermore, if the resale is delayed until the investor is retired and therefore most likely falls into a lower effective tax rate, additional tax savings will be realized through payment of tax at a lower rate.

INCOME DEFINITIONS

The IRS Code defines *gross income* as income from all sources, including wages, salaries, tips, dividends, interest, pensions, annuities, rents, royalties, business income, farm income, and gains upon sales or exchanges of property. Gross income is reduced to *adjusted gross income* by subtracting *adjustments* including sick pay, certain moving expenses, business expenses, the $100-per-person dividend exclusion, state and municipal bond interest (tax-exempt income), pension and annuity return-of-capital adjustments, depreciation, repairs, costs of farm and business operations, and basis (cost plus capital improvements and selling costs minus depreciation) upon sale or exchange.

Adjusted gross income is reduced to *taxable income* by subtracting *deductions* and *exemptions* for taxpayer dependents. *Itemized deductions* include certain medical expenses, charitable contributions, interest expenses, taxes, casualty losses, and other costs. A flat *standard* or *personal deduction* is available to individuals who do not itemize deductions. There is also a special *low income allowance*, which is aimed at completely removing low-income people from the tax rolls. Once a taxpayer has determined allowable itemized deductions, he or she deducts that total or the larger of the allowable standard deduction or low-income allowance from the adjusted gross income.

In addition, the taxpayer is allowed to lower adjusted gross income further by the total allowable *exemptions* to arrive at taxable income. Exemptions of a set dollar amount are allowed for the taxpayer himself or herself and for each of the taxpayer's dependents. A dependent is a person closely related to the taxpayer who relies on him or her for in excess of 50 percent of support and whose income is below some maximum annual amount set by the code. Extra exemptions are available for dependents who are blind or over 65 years of age.

A summary of these calculations is as follows:

> Gross income minus adjustments equals Adjusted gross income.
> Adjusted gross income minus Deductions (itemized, standard, low income allowance) minus Exemptions equals Taxable income.

Types of Taxable Income

Taxable income may be either ordinary income or capital gains income. *Ordinary income* usually consists of the salary, wages, commission, tips, or profits one earns from his or her gainful occupation. Interest, dividends, annuity and pension payments that are not a return of invested capital, royalties, rents, and business or farm profits are also considered ordinary income. The tax rate paid on ordinary income depends on the marital status of the taxpayer. Usually singles and married people filing separately pay a higher rate than widows, widowers, married people filing jointly, and people who qualify as heads of households.

Capital gains income results from the sale or exchange of capital assets or assets that, for tax purposes, are treated as capital assets. For tax purposes, in addition to the personal residence category, real estate is classified as follows:

1. *Property held for sale to customers.* May *not* deduct depreciation, may deduct interest and expenses, may *not* tax-defer exchange; treated as ordinary income or loss; is *not* a capital asset

2. *Property held for investment*. May *not* deduct depreciation, may deduct interest and expenses, may tax-defer exchange; is a capital asset
3. *Property held for use in a trade or business*. May deduct depreciation, may deduct interest and expenses, may tax-defer exchange; treated as a capital gain when sold at a gain, and as an ordinary loss when sold at a loss (Section 1231 asset)
4. *Property held for the production of income*. May deduct depreciation, may deduct interest and expenses, may tax-defer exchange; treated as a capital gain when sold at a gain, and as an ordinary loss when sold at a loss (Section 1231 asset)

Items (3) and (4) above are considered Section 1231 assets. The statement that they are given capital gains and ordinary loss treatment needs slight modification. All Section 1231 gains and losses are first netted. It is the *net* figure that is given capital gains or ordinary loss treatment.

Capital gains and losses are *long term* if the assets are held for one year or more (as of January 1, 1978); otherwise they are short term. The long-term gains and losses are netted; the short-term gains and losses are netted. If both the netted long and short positions are gains, the net short-term capital gains income is taxed at the ordinary income tax rates and the net long-term capital gains income is taxed at the more favorable capital gains income tax rates.

If both the netted long and short positions are *losses*, a set of special rules applies whereby such losses may *partially* offset ordinary income. These net losses (both long and short) may offset ordinary income up to $3,000 per year. If such losses exceed $3,000, they may be carried forward to future years indefinitely (for individuals). However, although short-term losses may offset ordinary income dollar for dollar, it takes two dollars of long-term loss to offset one dollar of ordinary income. If a taxpayer has both short- and long-term losses, the short-term losses are applied first.

If either the short or long position ends up with a net gain and the other ends up with a net loss, the two net positions must be netted again to obtain a "net net" short or long, gain or loss position. This "net net" position is then treated as in the last two paragraphs.

There are two methods for calculating the more favorable capital gains income tax. The taxpayer may compute the tax both ways and then elect the method with the lower tax. These methods are called the regular method and the alternative method.

Under the *regular method*, one half of the net long-term capital gain is added to ordinary income and taxed as such, resulting in a tax rate of one half the ordinary rate. Under the *alternative method* one simply pays 25 percent of the net long-term capital gain as the tax. This 25 percent rule applies only to an individual's first $50,000 of net long-term capital gain. Other rules apply to additional amounts of gain and to different taxable entities. These rules and many others are beyond the scope of this text. What has been presented thus far is aimed at giving the reader a rough idea of the complexity of tax law and inspiring a curiosity to pursue further study of tax law.

TAX RATES AND BRACKETS

Real estate investment brokers are sometimes criticized for making investment property presentations which always assume that the potential purchaser-investor is in the 50 percent tax bracket, when in fact this rate may not at all apply to the particular investor. The critics refer to this tenuous practice of investment presentation as the "myth of the 50 percent bracket." A potential purchaser-investor should determine the investment value of a property on an after-tax basis based upon the tax rates which actually apply to his or her own situation. Furthermore, some potential investors are misinformed regarding the differences between one's *marginal tax bracket*, *effective tax rate*, and *effective marginal tax rate*.

An investor's marginal tax bracket is the rate of tax paid on the last dollar earned. For example, a married taxpayer filing jointly for a 1977 income of $30,000 is in the 36 percent marginal tax bracket. This percentage can be found in IRS Schedule Y for 1977 (Figure 20-1) as follows: "For income over $27,200, but not over $31,200, pay $5,660 plus 36 percent of the amount over $27,200." Hence, the last dollar of income will increase the tax at the rate of $.36 per dollar earned. However, the *effective tax rate* of this person's total income would not be 36 percent. Adding $5,660 to 36 percent of $2,800 (the amount earned over $27,200) which is $1,008, yields a total tax of $6,668. The total tax of $6,668 divided by the total income of $30,000 calculates the *effective tax rate* to be 22.23 percent.

If this investor were to enjoy a $10,000 tax deduction due to the tax shelter of a potential real estate investment, a broker might state that such a deduction would offer a 36 percent or $3,600 tax savings. However, upon consulting the tax table once again, the tax saving can be computed to be 31.84 percent or $3,184. The $10,000 tax shelter lowers the taxable income to $20,000; "for income over $19,200, but not over $23,200, pay $3,260 plus 28 percent of the amount over $19,200." The total tax would therefore, be, $3,260 plus 28 percent of $800 (the amount earned over $19,200), which is $224, for a total tax of $3,484. The difference between $6,668 (the income tax payable without the real estate investment) and $3,484 (the income tax payable with the real estate) is a savings of $3,184 or 31.84 percent of the $10,000 tax shelter.

The investor's effective marginal rate for a $10,000 tax deduction from owning a real estate investment would be 31.84 percent, not 36 percent, as one might be led to believe. The true savings is still substantial; however,

1977 Tax Rate Schedules

If you cannot use one of the Tax Tables, figure your tax on the amount on Schedule TC, Part I, line 3, by using the appropriate Tax Rate Schedule on this page. Enter tax on Schedule TC, Part I, line 4.
Note: *Your zero bracket amount has been built into these Tax Rate Schedules.*

SCHEDULE X—Single Taxpayers Not Qualifying for Rates in Schedule Y or Z

Use this schedule if you checked **Box 1** on Form 1040—

If the amount on Schedule TC, Part I, line 3, is: / Enter on Schedule TC, Part I, line 4:

Not over $2,200 .... —0—

Over—	But not over—		of the amount over—
$2,200	$2,700	14%	$2,200
$2,700	$3,200	$70+15%	$2,700
$3,200	$3,700	$145+16%	$3,200
$3,700	$4,200	$225+17%	$3,700
$4,200	$6,200	$310+19%	$4,200
$6,200	$8,200	$690+21%	$6,200
$8,200	$10,200	$1,110+24%	$8,200
$10,200	$12,200	$1,590+25%	$10,200
$12,200	$14,200	$2,090+27%	$12,200
$14,200	$16,200	$2,630+29%	$14,200
$16,200	$18,200	$3,210+31%	$16,200
$18,200	$20,200	$3,830+34%	$18,200
$20,200	$22,200	$4,510+36%	$20,200
$22,200	$24,200	$5,230+38%	$22,200
$24,200	$28,200	$5,990+40%	$24,200
$28,200	$34,200	$7,590+45%	$28,200
$34,200	$40,200	$10,290+50%	$34,200
$40,200	$46,200	$13,290+55%	$40,200
$46,200	$52,200	$16,590+60%	$46,200
$52,200	$62,200	$20,190+62%	$52,200
$62,200	$72,200	$26,390+64%	$62,200
$72,200	$82,200	$32,790+66%	$72,200
$82,200	$92,200	$39,390+68%	$82,200
$92,200	$102,200	$46,190+69%	$92,200
$102,200	....	$53,090+70%	$102,200

SCHEDULE Y—Married Taxpayers and Qualifying Widows and Widowers

If you are a married person living apart from your spouse, see page 7 of the instructions to see if you can be considered to be "unmarried" for purposes of using Schedule X or Z.

Married Filing Joint Returns and Qualifying Widows and Widowers

Use this schedule if you checked **Box 2 or Box 5** on Form 1040—

If the amount on Schedule TC, Part I, line 3, is: / Enter on Schedule TC, Part I, line 4:

Not over $3,200 .... —0—

Over—	But not over—		of the amount over—
$3,200	$4,200	14%	$3,200
$4,200	$5,200	$140+15%	$4,200
$5,200	$6,200	$290+16%	$5,200
$6,200	$7,200	$450+17%	$6,200
$7,200	$11,200	$620+19%	$7,200
$11,200	$15,200	$1,380+22%	$11,200
$15,200	$19,200	$2,260+25%	$15,200
$19,200	$23,200	$3,260+28%	$19,200
$23,200	$27,200	$4,380+32%	$23,200
$27,200	$31,200	$5,660+36%	$27,200
$31,200	$35,200	$7,100+39%	$31,200
$35,200	$39,200	$8,660+42%	$35,200
$39,200	$43,200	$10,340+45%	$39,200
$43,200	$47,200	$12,140+48%	$43,200
$47,200	$55,200	$14,060+50%	$47,200
$55,200	$67,200	$18,060+53%	$55,200
$67,200	$79,200	$24,420+55%	$67,200
$79,200	$91,200	$31,020+58%	$79,200
$91,200	$103,200	$37,980+60%	$91,200
$103,200	$123,200	$45,180+62%	$103,200
$123,200	$143,200	$57,580+64%	$123,200
$143,200	$163,200	$70,380+66%	$143,200
$163,200	$183,200	$83,580+68%	$163,200
$183,200	$203,200	$97,180+69%	$183,200
$203,200	....	$110,980+70%	$203,200

Married Filing Separate Returns

Use this schedule if you checked **Box 3** on Form 1040—

If the amount on Schedule TC, Part I, line 3, is: / Enter on Schedule TC, Part I, line 4:

Not over $1,600 .... —0—

Over—	But not over—		of the amount over—
$1,600	$2,100	14%	$1,600
$2,100	$2,600	$70+15%	$2,100
$2,600	$3,100	$145+16%	$2,600
$3,100	$3,600	$225+17%	$3,100
$3,600	$5,600	$310+19%	$3,600
$5,600	$7,600	$690+22%	$5,600
$7,600	$9,600	$1,130+25%	$7,600
$9,600	$11,600	$1,630+28%	$9,600
$11,600	$13,600	$2,190+32%	$11,600
$13,600	$15,600	$2,830+36%	$13,600
$15,600	$17,600	$3,550+39%	$15,600
$17,600	$19,600	$4,330+42%	$17,600
$19,600	$21,600	$5,170+45%	$19,600
$21,600	$23,600	$6,070+48%	$21,600
$23,600	$27,600	$7,030+50%	$23,600
$27,600	$33,600	$9,030+53%	$27,600
$33,600	$39,600	$12,210+55%	$33,600
$39,600	$45,600	$15,510+58%	$39,600
$45,600	$51,600	$18,990+60%	$45,600
$51,600	$61,600	$22,590+62%	$51,600
$61,600	$71,600	$28,790+64%	$61,600
$71,600	$81,600	$35,190+66%	$71,600
$81,600	$91,600	$41,790+68%	$81,600
$91,600	$101,600	$48,590+69%	$91,600
$101,600	....	$55,490+70%	$101,600

SCHEDULE Z—Unmarried or legally separated taxpayers Who Qualify as Heads of Household

Use this schedule if you checked **Box 4** on Form 1040—

If the amount on Schedule TC, Part I, line 3, is: / Enter on Schedule TC, Part I, line 4:

Not over $2,200 .... —0—

Over—	But not over—		of the amount over—
$2,200	$3,200	14%	$2,200
$3,200	$4,200	$140+16%	$3,200
$4,200	$6,200	$300+18%	$4,200
$6,200	$8,200	$660+19%	$6,200
$8,200	$10,200	$1,040+22%	$8,200
$10,200	$12,200	$1,480+23%	$10,200
$12,200	$14,200	$1,940+25%	$12,200
$14,200	$16,200	$2,440+27%	$14,200
$16,200	$18,200	$2,980+28%	$16,200
$18,200	$20,200	$3,540+31%	$18,200
$20,200	$22,200	$4,160+32%	$20,200
$22,200	$24,200	$4,800+35%	$22,200
$24,200	$26,200	$5,500+36%	$24,200
$26,200	$28,200	$6,220+38%	$26,200
$28,200	$30,200	$6,980+41%	$28,200
$30,200	$34,200	$7,800+42%	$30,200
$34,200	$38,200	$9,480+45%	$34,200
$38,200	$40,200	$11,280+48%	$38,200
$40,200	$42,200	$12,240+51%	$40,200
$42,200	$46,200	$13,260+52%	$42,200
$46,200	$52,200	$15,340+55%	$46,200
$52,200	$54,200	$18,640+56%	$52,200
$54,200	$66,200	$19,760+58%	$54,200
$66,200	$72,200	$26,720+59%	$66,200
$72,200	$78,200	$30,260+61%	$72,200
$78,200	$82,200	$33,920+62%	$78,200
$82,200	$90,200	$36,400+63%	$82,200
$90,200	$102,200	$41,440+64%	$90,200
$102,200	$122,200	$49,120+66%	$102,200
$122,200	$142,200	$62,320+67%	$122,200
$142,200	$162,200	$75,720+68%	$142,200
$162,200	$182,200	$89,320+69%	$162,200
$182,200	....	$103,120+70%	$182,200

Figure 20-1 1977 Tax Rate Schedules

caution should be used not to overstate the tax benefits of investment. A broker might end up in court defending against a charge of misrepresentation. Finally, it should be evident once again from the presentation of this tax-rate calculation problem that the tax laws are quite complex and therefore require much study in order to understand fully their impact upon real estate investment analysis.

TAX BASIS

Basis is the original cost of acquiring a property or the original value of a property upon acquisition. The method of determining basis depends upon whether the property was purchased, exchanged, inherited, received as a gift, held in joint ownership or in a life estate, received for services rendered, acquired through foreclosure, repossession, involuntary conversion, or options, or converted from personal residence to income-producing property. Basis is an essential input for the determination of gain or loss upon sale or exchange. Basis is critical to the amount of depreciation deductions allowed by the IRS.

Basis may increase or decrease over time after acquisition. The result of these changes is called adjusted basis. Adjusted basis is the figure used in calculating gain or loss upon sale or exchange and in computing depreciation. Since land is not depreciable, an allocation of basis between land and improvements is often necessary.

Allocation of Basis

The three basic acceptable methods of making such an allocation of basis are the following:

1. The property tax assessor's ratio of land to improvements multiplied by the purchase price or value of the property
2. The price or value allocation stated in a sales or exchange contract between a buyer and a seller in a so-called arm's length transaction, where each is dealing from equal bargaining positions
3. The price or value allocation as determined by a competent real estate appraiser

Adjusted Basis

Once the original unadjusted basis is determined by the various rules (beyond the scope of this text) of the IRS Code, changes in the basis may take place in the form of additions or reductions. As stated above, the adjusted basis, which accounts for these additions and reductions, is the figure used in calculating gain or loss upon sale or exchange and in computing depreciation.

Additions to Basis. Capital improvements and capitalized carrying costs are the two allowable items which increase basis. Capital improvements must be distinguished from normal repairs and maintenance. Repairs and maintenance, including property improvements with a useful life of one year or less, are current deductions and do not affect basis. Capital improvements with a useful life of more than one year, or which prolong the useful life of the property, are allowed as additions to basis. Basis is increased by the amount of the cost of such improvements.

Capitalized carrying costs are permitted to be capitalized (at the taxpayer's election) for two types of property. A taxpayer may elect to capitalize and thereby increase the basis of unimproved and unproductive land by the amounts paid for annual property taxes and mortgage interest. A taxpayer may also capitalize carrying costs during construction even if the property is improved and/or productive.

Costs of purchasing a property, such as purchase commissions (if any) and legal fees or title insurance premiums for protection of title may be added to the basis of real property. Costs of selling a property may be added to the basis or subtracted from the sales price (to get adjusted sales price) with no difference in the result. The IRS, however, usually takes the position that the costs of sale are subtracted from the selling price for capital gain and loss purposes.

Reductions of Basis. Basis may be reduced in the following situations:

1. Partial divestiture of property by a taking because of condemnation by the power of eminent domain
2. Sale of an undivided interest in a property
3. Sale of parcels acquired at different times
4. Casualty loss
5. Sale of an easement (the amount received for the easement reduces basis)
6. Depreciation

DEPRECIATION

As previously stated, depreciation is a noncash expense. It lowers taxable income without lowering cash flow. The amount of depreciation allowed by the IRS to be deducted in any one year is a function of (1) adjusted basis, (2) useful life of the property, (3) method of depreciation, and (4) salvage value (if any).

Useful Life

The IRS regulations define *useful life* as the period over which an asset may reasonably be expected to be useful to the taxpayer in his or her trade or business or in the production of his or her income. The IRS has also issued useful life guidelines for various classes of assets. However, since it is the useful life to the taxpayer that matters, taxpayers often claim shorter lives than those suggested by the guidelines. The shorter lives are supported either by claiming inferior construction quality or stating that the *physical life* may be equal to that in the guidelines, but that the *economic life* is much shorter.

The shorter the life one claims, the greater the depreciation tax shelter. Another way to increase depreciation write-offs is to employ *component* (as opposed to composite) depreciation, whereby individual parts (or components) are depreciated separately. Since certain parts of buildings, such as carpets, drapes, roofs, and certain equipment wear out rapidly, their costs may be separated into several short-lived depreciation schedules. By so doing, the taxpayer effectively creates "accelerated" depreciation.

Depreciation Methods and Salvage Value

Once basis and useful life have been determined, a method of depreciation must be elected by the taxpayer. The available choices are diagrammed in Figure 20-2 and the allowable application to property types are listed below the diagram.

Salvage Value. At the end of the economic life of a building, it usually may be sold for something, even if what is left is to be used for some other purpose. The price estimated to be received upon the building sale at the end of its life is called *salvage value*. Salvage value is not depreciable; this fact must be accounted for in the various depreciation methods.

Both the straight-line and the sum of years digits methods of depreciation specifically account for the salvage value of a property by requiring that salvage value be subtracted from the basis before allocating the basis over the property's useful life. The declining balance methods ignore salvage value in calculating each year's depreciation. Yet these methods recognize salvage value by never permitting the declining basis to fall below the salvage value.

Straight-Line Method. The depreciable basis, less salvage value, is divided by the useful life to obtain the annual amount of straight-line depreciation. Alternatively, the so-called straight-line rate of depreciation can be calculated by dividing 100 percent by the useful life of the property. This rate is then multiplied by the depreciable basis less salvage value to obtain the annual dollar amount of depreciation. The straight-line rate is also employed in the application of the declining balance methods.

Assume a five-year useful life for demonstration and comparison purposes. Assume a property is purchased for $130,000 with the following allocations for depreciation purposes: (1) $10,000 land value and (2) $20,000 salvage value. The annual amount of depreciation would be

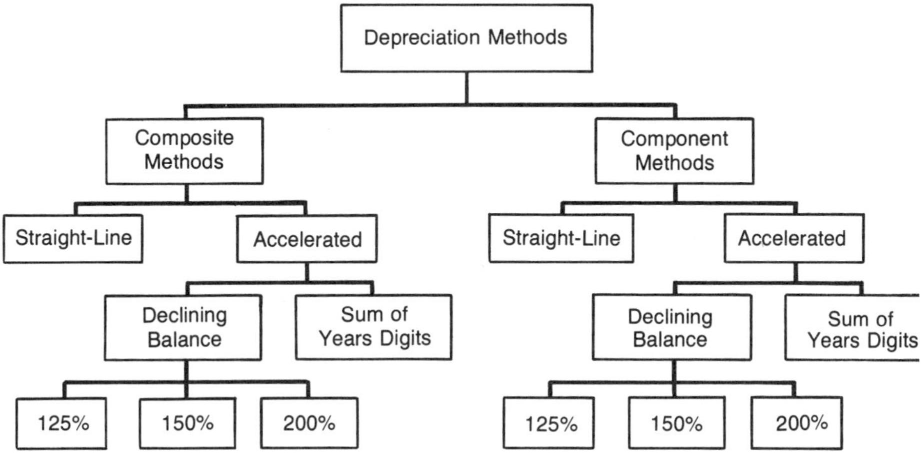

Allowable Application to Property Types

Depreciation Method	Property Type
Straight-line	All real properties
SOYD	New residential rental for first owner only
125% DB	Used residential with at least a 20-year life remainir
150% DB	New commercial properties
200% DB	New residential rental for first owner only

Figure 20-2 Depreciation Methods

$20,000 ($130,000 minus $10,000 minus $20,000 equals $100,000 and $100,000 divided by 5 years equals $20,000 per year). Alternatively, the straight-line rate would be 20 percent (100 percent divided by 5 years equals 20 percent per year).

Accelerated Methods. The accelerated methods of depreciation allow the taxpayer to take depreciation deductions that are larger than those allowed by the straight-line method. However, this statement holds true only in the early years of ownership. Since the total amount of depreciation is the same as under the straight-line method, larger amounts in earlier years mean smaller amounts in later years. At this point the taxpayer may elect to shift to the straight-line method for the remaining useful life.

Declining Balance Methods (DB). The three declining balance methods "accelerate" the straight-line depreciation rate by multiplying a percentage in excess of 100 percent by the straight-line rate to obtain an accelerated rate of depreciation. This rate is multiplied, ignoring salvage value, by the property basis, the balance of which is reduced each year by the prior year's depreciation.

Using the 125 percent declining balance method for the example above, the accelerated rate would be 25 percent (125 percent times 20 percent). The accelerated rate using the 150 percent declining balance method would be 30 percent; using the 200 percent method it would be 40 percent. Note that 25, 30, and 40 percent in the example are each multiplied by $120,000 (ignoring salvage value) to get the following first year's amounts of depreciation: $30,000, $36,000, and $48,000 respectively. Each of these is larger than the $20,000 available under the straight-line method.

Sum of Years Digits Method (SOYD). Under the sum of years digits method, the annual amount of depreciation is calculated by multiplying a factor or fraction by the basis less salvage value. This factor is a different fraction of one each year, calculated as follows: (1) the numerator is the number of years of useful life remaining and (2) the denominator is always the sum of the digits of the years of useful life.

In the example used above, the five numerators of the five factors or fractions would be 5, 4, 3, 2, and 1. While the denominator in each case would be 15, the sum of the digits one through five (1 + 2 + 3 + 4 + 5 = 15). Hence, the five factors in the example would be 5/15, 4/15, 3/15, 2/15, and 1/15.

Comparison of Methods. A comparison of the various methods of depreciation is presented below for the five-year example. Note that five years was chosen to keep the examples and comparison short and simple.

Comparison of Depreciation Methods

	Depreciation Method				
Year	*S − L*	*125% DB*	*150% DB*	*200% DB*	*SOYD*
1	$ 20,000	$30,000	$36,000	$ 48,000	$ 33,333
2	20,000	22,500	25,200	28,800	26,667
3	20,000	16,875	17,640	17,280	20,000
4	20,000	12,656	12,348	5,920	13,333
5	20,000	9,492	8,644	0	6,667
Total	$100,000	$91,523	$99,832	$100,000	$100,000

The following comments can be made regarding this comparison of depreciation methods:

1. The 200 percent DB, SOYD, 150 percent DB, and 125 percent DB methods grant accelerated depreciation in only the early years; the order in which these four methods are listed is also the order of maximum (200 percent DB) to minimum (125 percent DB) acceleration available.
2. Two of the accelerated methods (125 percent DB and 150 percent

DB) do not fully depreciate the tax basis over the five-year useful life.

3. A shift to the straight-line method should be made in year three for the 125 percent DB, 150 percent DB, and 200 percent DB methods and in year four for the SOYD method.
4. With a shift to straight-line, all the accelerated methods would be fully depreciated in four years.
5. For a useful life longer than five years, the numbers would be different, but the same general relationships that have been shown to exist would still exist.

Crossover Point

It has been pointed out previously that depreciation *does not require* a cash outlay but is deductible for tax purposes. It is also important to note that mortgage loan principal amortization *does require* a cash outlay but is not deductible for tax purposes. Note also that if accelerated depreciation is employed, depreciation deductions *decrease* over time while principal amortization payments simultaneously *increase* (assuming level-payment amortization) over time. The interaction of these two phenomena cause the *crossover point*.

The crossover point occurs when the nondeductible cash-outlay amortization payment equals or exceeds the deductible noncash depreciation expense. After this point, taxable income continues to exceed cash flow, causing most investors to dispose of such property. For example, using the $130,000 property from the comparison of depreciation methods, further assume a hypothetical five-year $100,000 loan with annual debt service of $26,000. Assume that the hypothetical amortization schedule for this loan is as follows:

Hypothetical Amortization Schedule*

Year	*Debt Service*	*Interest*	*Principal*
1	$ 26,000	$10,000	$ 16,000
2	26,000	8,000	18,000
3	26,000	6,000	20,000
4	26,000	4,000	22,000
5	26,000	2,000	24,000
Totals	$130,000	$30,000	$100,000

**The principal and interest payments are not accurate, but rather are rounded off for demonstration purposes.*

Comparing the principal amortization column with the depreciation column for 200 percent DB presented earlier, the crossover point can be demonstrated as follows:

Crossover Point Demonstration

Year	*200 Percent DB*	*Principal*	
1	$ 48,000	$ 16,000	
2	28,800	18,000	
3	17,280	20,000	← Crossover point
4	5,920	22,000	
5	0	24,000	
Totals	$100,000	$100,000	

If the net operating income is $36,000, the before-tax cash flow or cash throw-off to equity would be $10,000 each year, since debt service is $26,000 (NOI − D. S. = CTOE). However, the taxable income will eventually exceed the CTOE in the third year, as shown below.

Taxable Income Calculations

Year	1	2	3	4	5
NOI	$36,000	$36,000	$36,000	$36,000	$36,000
Depreciation	−48,000	−28,800	−17,280	−5,920	− 0
Mortgage interest	−10,000	−8,000	−6,000	−4,000	−2,000
Taxable income	−$22,000	−$ 800	$12,720 ↑ Crossover point	$26,080	$34,000

The first year's tax shelter of NOI and $22,000 of other income looks great. However, in the third year, the fact that the depreciation deduction has decreased $30,720 ($48,000 to $17,280) and the principal amortization payment has increased $4,000 ($16,000 to $20,000) has caused a $34,720 total difference in taxable income (−$22,000 to $12,720). In the third year, taxable income exceeds cash flow (CTOE) because the deduction for depreciation and interest of $23,280 ($17,280 plus $6,000) is less than the debt service payment of $26,000. Or put another way, in the third year, the nondeductible $20,000 cash-outlay amortization payment exceeds the $17,280 deductible noncash depreciation expense, which is the definition of the crossover point. After this point the taxable income continues to exceed the CTOE of $10,000, since taxable incomes in years four and five are $26,080 and $34,000, respectively.

When taxable income is greater than cash flow, the taxpayer's tax is increased beyond what would be payable if the tax were figured on cash flow without any tax shelter benefits. Thus beyond the crossover point, after-tax cash flow continues to decline and may even become negative when CTOE is still positive.

In the example, if the taxpayer has an effective tax rate of 50 percent, the tax liability in year four is $13,040 (50 percent times $26,080 taxable income), while CTOE is still $10,000, resulting in a negative after-tax cash flow of −$3,040 for the investor. It is possible for an investment to look attractive on a before-tax basis (CTOE = $10,000) and, at the same time, be disastrous on an after-tax basis (loss of −$3,040). Hence, investors should evaluate potential investments on both a before-tax and an after-tax basis.

The conclusions to be drawn from the explanation and demonstration of the crossover point are the following:

1. Principal payments have detrimental tax effects.
2. In the early years of an investment, the detrimental tax effects of principal amortization are more than offset by the favorable tax effects of depreciation deductions.
3. Since principal payments increase and accelerated methods depreciation deductions decrease, the detrimental effects will eventually offset the favorable effects.
4. Beyond this crossover point it is possible for an investment to simultaneously experience a positive before-tax cash flow and a negative after-tax cash flow.
5. Once the crossover point is reached, investors seek to dispose of the property and to acquire another with more favorable tax characteristics.

TAX EFFECTS OF PROPERTY DISPOSITION

Whenever a property is disposed of, whether by sale or exchange, a gain or loss is *realized*. The realized gain or loss may not, however, be *recognized* for tax purposes. It is possible to postpone or defer recognition for tax purposes. If and when recognized, such gain or loss may be treated as ordinary income or as capital gains income. The taxation of these two types of income was discussed earlier in this chapter.

Dealer versus Investor

A dealer's income from the sale of property is taxed at ordinary income tax rates; an investor's income from the sale of property held for a year or more is taxed at the more favorable capital gains rate. A *dealer* is defined as a person who sells and holds property for sale to customers in the ordinary course of business. For example, a builder with an inventory of properties for sale and a licensed real estate broker who frequently buys and sells (deals) properties, or does so as his or her primary business, are both considered dealers and are taxed as such.

On the other hand, an *investor* is defined as a person who either holds property for long-term investment purposes or uses property in a trade or business. A dealer may also, at times, be an investor. The determination of dealer or investor is based on the factual situation of each transaction.

Depreciation Recapture

Except for certain subsidized low-income housing properties, the portion of a gain upon sale of a property which is due to so-called excess depreciation is taxable (or recaptured) as ordinary income and not as capital gains income. *Excess depreciation* is the difference between depreciation figured on a straight-line basis and depreciation taken on an accelerated basis.

The rationale for this recapture of the excess depreciation is to prevent the conversion of an ordinary income deduction (depreciation) into a capital gain when the amount of the previous deducted depreciation is realized or recovered in the net sales price. Even though excess depreciation is recaptured upon sale, the deductions during ownership provide a time-value-of-money benefit to the investor, since the tax is deferred to a future time when perhaps the taxpayer is in a lower tax bracket.

Possible Cash Deficit

Upon sale, both the income tax and the mortgage balance must be paid off from the sales proceeds. It is possible for the after-tax proceeds or net reversion to be *negative*. The fact that accelerated depreciation deductions accumulate more quickly than principal amortization payments (especially if high-leverage financing is employed) causes this phenomenon to be possible.

For example, assume 200 percent DB in the hypothetical five-year depreciation problem used earlier, highly levered with an interest-only $120,000 loan, and a resale price of $138,000 at the end of year two. The net reversion would be calculated as follows:

Sales price	$138,000		
Adjusted basis	– 53,200	($130,000 Basis – $76,800 Depreciation)	
Total gain	$ 72,000		
Excess depreciation	– 24,000	× 50 percent (ordinary rate)	= $12,000
Capital gain	$ 48,000	× 25 percent (capital gains rate)	= $12,000
Total tax			$24,000

Sales price	$138,000
Mortgage balance	– 120,000
Total tax	– 24,000
Net reversion	–$ 6,000

The above example may not be typical, but real estate investors should be aware that it is possible, and they must plan for its occurrence.

Installment Sales

A taxpayer may delay the payment of tax if the transaction qualifies as an installment sale. By so doing, the payment of the tax is spread out over the installment period. If no more than 30 percent of the sales price is paid in the year of sale and the seller carries back a purchase-money mortgage for the remainder of the purchase price, the gain may be reported under the installment method.

The purchase-money mortgage must bear an interest rate of at least 6 percent or the IRS will impute a rate of 7 percent. The annual taxable income is figured as follows:

1. Calculate the *gain* in the usual manner.
2. Calculate the so-called *contract price* as the sales price minus loans (if any) assumed by the buyer and payable to third parties.
3. Divide the *gain* by the *contract price* to obtain the percentage or ratio. Multiply the ratio by the payments received each year to determine the amount of gain to be reported each year.

For example, assume a $200,000 sales price, $100,000 loan assumed, and adjusted basis of $150,000.

1. The sales price of $200,000 minus the adjusted basis of $150,000 equals a gain of $50,000.
2. The sales price of $200,000 minus the loan assumed of $100,000 equals a contract price of $100,000.
3. The gain of $50,000 divided by the contract price of $100,000 equals a ratio of reportable gain of 50 percent.

As long as no more than $60,000 (30 percent of $200,000) is received in the year of sale, only 50 percent of the installment payments would be reported as taxable.

Tax-Deferred Exchanges

Tax-deferred exchanges are a unique disposition technique. They are not "tax-free," as many real estate people incorrectly describe them. The tax on the gain, if any, will eventually be paid upon a sale sometime in the future. However, rather than sell a property for cash, pay tax on the gain, and buy another property, the payment of the tax may be deferred by exchanging the property for another property of *like kind*. Like-kind property has a broad definition which essentially includes all types of real property. Tax is payable on any *boot* received in the exchange. Boot includes cash, unlike property (personal exchanged for real), and net mortgage relief (obtained by trading a mortgaged property for one with no mortgage or a smaller mortgage).

The trading investors maintain the basis of their old property for their new property. However, one's basis is increased by any boot paid or any increase in mortgage indebtedness assumed and is reduced by any boot received or any gain recognized. Tax-deferred exchange is a very complicated subject, one beyond the scope of this text. However, a simplified example is provided to whet the reader's intellectual appetite.

Mr. Able owns an office building with a market value of $100,000, a loan of $70,000, and an equity position, therefore, of $30,000. He exchanges it for Ms. Baker's industrial warehouse building, which has a market value of $120,000, a loan of $80,000, and an equity position, therefore, of $40,000.

Since Ms. Baker's equity is greater than Mr. Able's equity by $10,000, Mr. Able will also pay Ms. Baker $10,000 cash. Since each will acquire the other's property subject to their respective mortgage loans, Ms. Baker, by the exchange, will be relieved of an $80,000 loan and acquire a property subject to a $70,000 loan. Therefore, Ms. Baker will enjoy net loan relief of $10,000 in addition to receiving the $10,000 cash. Hence, Ms. Baker will receive and be taxed on $20,000 of boot. Her basis will also be reduced by this $20,000 of boot.

Mr. Able will have paid $10,000 in cash and increased his mortgage indebtedness by $10,000. Hence, Mr. Able will not have received any boot and will not pay any tax. Mr. Able's basis will increase by the $20,000 represented by the cash paid and the increase in loan amount.

Sale of Personal Residence

Capital gains taxes on the sale of a personal residence can be deferred if another personal residence, the cost of which equals or exceeds the adjusted sales price of the original residence, is purchased and occupied within a statutory period as follows:

1. For *used* residences, a 36-month period beginning 18 months before and ending 18 months after the sale of the original residence is allowed
2. For *new* residences, a 42-month period beginning 18 months before and ending 24 months after the sale of the original residence is allowed

The *adjusted sales price* equals the actual sales price less selling expenses and/or fixing-up expenses. Real estate brokerage commissions, attorney's fees, title protection costs, and mortgage loan prepayment penalties are the usual allowable selling expenses. Noncapital improvement expenditures, such as painting, repairs, and minor landscaping, qualify as fixing-up expenses, if they are incurred within 90 days prior to the sale and are paid for within 30 days after the sale.

It is not necessary for all the *cash proceeds* from the sale of the original residence to be reinvested in the replacement residence, as long as the replacement residence has a purchase price equal to or greater than the adjusted sales price of the original residence. One can cash in on (realize) some of the gain without its being recognized for tax purposes.

The gain not recognized is, however, subtracted from the cost of the replacement residence, thereby lowering its basis. For example, if a residence which was purchased for $50,000 is sold for an adjusted sale price of $60,000 and a replacement residence is purchased for $70,000, the following items hold true:

1. No tax is payable on the $10,000 gain.
2. If the replacement residence is sold for more than the $60,000 basis ($70,000 minus $10,000) and not reinvested within either of the two statutory periods, the excess will be recognized as taxable gain. Note that the $60,000 basis could also be calculated as the $50,000 basis of the original residence plus the additional cash required to buy the replacement residence.

Hence, a taxpayer may continue deferring gains on the sales of personal residences indefinitely.

If the purchase price of the replacement residence is ever less than the adjusted sales price of the original residence, the gain taxed will be the difference between the cost of the replacement residence and the adjusted sales price of the original residence. For example, if the property in the last example, which was purchased for $50,000 and sold for $60,000, were replaced with a property costing $55,000, tax would be payable on $5,000 ($60,000 sales price of the original residence, minus $55,000, the cost of the replacement residence). Incidentally, condominiums and cooperatives are included in the definition of a residence.

Relief on Sale for Elderly. Elderly people often sell their residences to move to smaller and/or less expensive residences, or they move into apartments to be free from the maintenance and care required by homeownership. To lessen the tax burden of such a move, the IRS Code allows persons 65 years of age or over to take a once-in-a-lifetime exclusion from taxable gain, within certain limits, for the sale of personal residences.

As of 1978, if the adjusted sales price of the home is $35,000 no gain is recognized for tax purposes. If the adjusted sales price exceeds $35,000, a portion of the gain is exempted from taxation. The ratio of $35,000 to the adjusted sales price determines the portion of the gain that is tax exempt. For example, a home originally purchased for $50,000 and sold at age 65 for $70,000 shows a capital gain of $20,000. However, 50 percent ($10,000) would be exempt from taxation based on the ratio of $35,000 to $70,000:

$$\$20{,}000 \times \frac{\$35{,}000}{\$70{,}000} = \$20{,}000 \times .50 = \$10{,}000$$

Finally, in order to qualify for this special relief for the elderly, the property must have been owned by the taxpayer for the eight years immediately preceding the sale and must have been used as the taxpayer's personal residence for at least five of these eight years.

Conversion to Rental Property. A personal residence may be converted to rental property, and the taxpayer may begin to take deductions from income for depreciation, maintenance, and repairs. A signed lease and the collection of rent is prima-facie proof of such a conversion. A personal residence merely vacant and up for sale cannot be considered rental property. The taxpayer has the burden of proving the intent to convert. Once converted, the deferment of capital gains upon sale, discussed above, is no longer available to the taxpayer.

SUMMARY AND CONCLUSIONS

Tax shelter is often one of the most attractive characteristics of many real estate investments and often the most important objective of many real estate investors. After-tax investment analysis is critically important to wise investment decision making. Sometimes investments analyzed on a before-tax basis may appear to be marginal, yet when analyzed on an after-tax basis these same investments may actually be very attractive to certain investors subject to high tax rates. On the other hand, due to the depreciation-amortization crossover point, it is possible for a real estate investment to simultaneously experience positive before-tax cash flow and negative after-tax cash flow.

Congress passes the income tax laws and compiles them in the Internal Revenue Code. The various laws are aimed at stimulating certain types of economic activity within the system. The Internal Revenue Service collects the tax and interprets the code by regulations and rulings. The federal courts also grant opinions and make decisions regarding income tax law. The risk of tax-law change is real and must be considered. Tax-law changes can quickly make bad deals out of good. An investment proposal should have a fundamental economic rationale of its own without considering the tax effects.

Taxable income is calculated by subtracting adjustments, deductions, and exemptions from gross income. Taxable income is either ordinary income or capital gains income. Capital gains income is either short term and taxed at ordinary rates, or long term and taxed at more favorable capital gains rates, by either the regular or alternative method.

Marginal tax bracket, effective tax rate, and effective marginal tax rate are not the same; real estate investors should know the differences among them and be most cautious in the use of these terms.

Tax basis is the original cost of acquiring a property. Basis may increase or decrease and is then called adjusted basis, which is subtracted from the adjusted sale price of a property to determine gain or loss. Basis is also used in the computation of depreciation deductions. However, since land is not depreciable, basis must be allocated between land and improvements.

Depreciation is a noncash expense which lowers taxable income without lowering cash flow. The amount of allowable depreciation is a function of adjusted basis, useful life, salvage value, and method of depreciation. The various methods of depreciation include straight-line; 125 percent, 150 percent, and 200 percent declining balance; and sum of years digits.

While depreciation is a deductible noncash expense, mortgage loan principal amortization is a nondeductible cash outlay. Assuming accelerated depreciation and level-payment amortization, depreciation deductions decrease over time while principal amortization payments simultaneously increase over time, causing the phenomenon called the crossover point. Beyond the crossover point, taxable income exceeds cash flow, causing most investors to dispose of such property. It is even possible for the before-tax cash flow to be positive while the after-tax cash flow is negative. Investors should evaluate potential investments on both a before-tax basis and an after-tax basis.

When a property is sold or exchanged, a gain or loss is realized, yet it is possible to defer recognition of the gain or loss for tax purposes. Gains may be treated as ordinary income or capital gains income. A dealer's gain is taxed as ordinary income; an investor's gain (if the property was held for at least one year) is taxed at the more favorable capital gains rate.

Except for certain subsidized low-income housing properties, upon the sale of property, the portion of a gain due to excess depreciation is taxable as ordinary income by the depreciation recapture tax statute. Because depreciation recapture is taxed at ordinary rates and accelerated depreciation deductions accumulate more quickly than do principal amortization payments, it is possible, upon sale, for the after-tax proceeds or net reversion to be negative. Real estate investors should be aware of this possibility and must plan for its occurrence.

A taxpayer may delay payment of tax if a given transaction qualifies as an installment sale. If no more than 30 percent of the sales price is paid in the year of sale and the seller carries back a purchase-money mortgage bearing an interest rate of at least 6 percent, payment of the capital gains tax may be spread out proportionately over the installment period.

Although tax-deferred exchanges are not "tax-free," they do allow like-kind property to be exchanged so that capital gains tax payment can be delayed. Tax is recognized and payable for any boot received in the exchange. Boot includes cash, unlike property, and net mortgage relief. A trading investor keeps the basis of the old property as his or her basis for the new one. Basis in a trade may be increased by boot paid or by mortgage debt increases assumed; basis is reduced by boot received or gain recognized. A balance or equalization of all equity positions must be accomplished (usually by payment of cash) in order to complete an exchange.

Capital gains taxes on the sale of a personal residence can be deferred by purchasing and occupying (within a statutory time period) another residence, the cost of which equals or exceeds the adjusted sales price of the original residence. The adjusted sales price equals the actual sales price less selling and fixing-up expenses. A special exclusion of all or part of the gain on the sale of a personal residence is available if (1) the taxpayer is at least 65 years old and (2) the taxpayer owned the residence for the eight years immediately preceding the sale and occupied the property for five of these eight years.

A personal residence may be converted to rental property. The taxpayer has the burden of proving the intent to convert. Once the property is converted, the tax advantages of the sale of a personal residence are lost.

The tax factors of real estate investments constitute a very lengthy, very complex, and very important area of study. The success or failure of many investors hinges on their understanding of the tax laws and the investment and financial impact and ramifications thereof. One cannot afford to outguess Uncle Sam or to "sort of know" how tax law affects one's investments. Tax planning is a most important integral part of wise investment decision making. The best advice is to get advice. Competent legal and accounting counsel should always be sought through constant consultation with a reputable attorney and certified public accountant who specialize in real estate investment and tax matters.

Finally, this chapter has presented only the basics of the tax factors of real estate investments. Serious students and practitioners are hereby advised to pursue this complex area of study further in order to fully understand the impacts and ramifications of tax laws upon real estate investment analysis.[1]

1. See Mark Lee Levine, *Real Estate Transactions, Tax Planning and Consequences* (St. Paul, Minn.: West Publishing Company, 1976) and Mark Lee Levine, *Real Estate Tax Shelter Desk Book* (New York: Institute for Business Planning, 1978).

APPENDIX A

Legal Descriptions of Real Property

LEGAL DESCRIPTIONS[1]

While commonly the location of land is referred to by street numbers and city or by reference to the "Wheeler Farm," or the "Old Taylor Place," it is necessary to use the legal description in the preparation of those instruments relating to the title and use of real estate.

Numerous methods or types of description have been developed for the purpose of achieving greater accuracy and precision in identifying the land. The more common methods of land description are: (1) *The United States Governmental Survey System,* often referred to as the "rectangular survey system," (2) *metes and bounds,* (3) *recorded plat,* (4) *Colorado Coordinate System.*

The United States Governmental Survey System

Soon after the Revolutionary War ended and new areas were added to the public domain, it became apparent to our government leaders that a plan must be worked out for selling and locating lands in the western territory. Thomas Jefferson authored a plan which was adopted by Congress in modified form on May 20, 1785. Under this newly enacted law, the first surveys took place in the State of Ohio. Ohio was the testing ground for the rectangular survey system and some changes were made in the law as a result of experience gained in this original survey plan. The second of such surveys started in Indiana about 1810. By this time the system was well established and has since been extended westward to the Pacific Ocean. This system was not used within the area of the original colonies in America, where land locations were made in irregular form and without any orderly plan.

The object of the *government survey* was to create a checkerboard of identical squares covering a given area. The largest squares measure 24

1. Reprinted with the permission of the Colorado Real Estate Commission. *State of Colorado Real Estate Manual* (Denver: The Colorado Real Estate Commission, 1976), Chapter IX, pp. 1-14, Not Copyrighted.

miles on each side and are called "quadrangles." Each quadrangle is further divided into 16 squares called "townships" whose four bondaries each measure six miles and run north-south and east-west. A column of townships running north-south is called a "range" and is numbered numercially east and west according to its distance from the principal meridian. There are now 36 principal meridians located in different parts of the United States. In most of Colorado, ranges lie west and are numbered from the 6th principal meridian. The 6th principal meridian is located near Lincoln, Nebraska and is 402 miles due east of Colorado Boulevard in Denver. A row of townships running east and west is a "tier" or township and is numbered numerically according to its distance from the baseline. In most of Colorado, the main baseline follows a course approximating the 40 degrees line of latitude which is located just north of the city of Brighton in Adams County. (Forty degrees latitude is also the boundary line between Kansas and Nebraska.)

You will note in the above paragraph that most of Colorado was surveyed using the 6th principal meridian and 40 degrees latitude baseline as the starting point. However, there is a large section of Southwestern Colorado encompassing several counties which was surveyed using the New Mexico principal meridian and the New Mexico baseline as a starting point. Also, in an isolated instance certain portions of Mesa and Delta Counties in Western Colorado use the Ute Meridian (located just east of Grand Junction) as the main north-south survey line with an arbitrary baseline as the starting point. The historic reason for this is that a survey was thought to be needed when the plan was to settle the Ute Indians in and around what was later to become the city of Grand Junction. Because no surveys at that time had been extended west of the Continental Divide, it was necessary that a new meridian and a new baseline be established. This was done without any tie to anything such as an established meridian or a parallel.

Because of the curvature of the earth, the north-south lines or ranges converge as they extend toward the north pole. To keep the range lines as nearly six miles apart as possible, the lines are laid out for approximately 24 miles, and then jog so that they are again six miles apart, to preserve as nearly as may be the square shape of the township.

The north and west tiers of sections of the township are closing sections. Discrepancies of closure between the interior section line and exterior boundary line surveys are adjusted. These sections, usually contain more or less than the 640 acres in a normal section.

A township is six miles square or 36 square miles. Townships are numbered north and south from the base line. Each square mile which is equivalent to 640 acres is designated as a section. Sections within a township are numbered from the northeast corner, following a back and forth course, until the last section in the southeast corner is reached. For purposes of land description, sections are commonly divided into half-sections

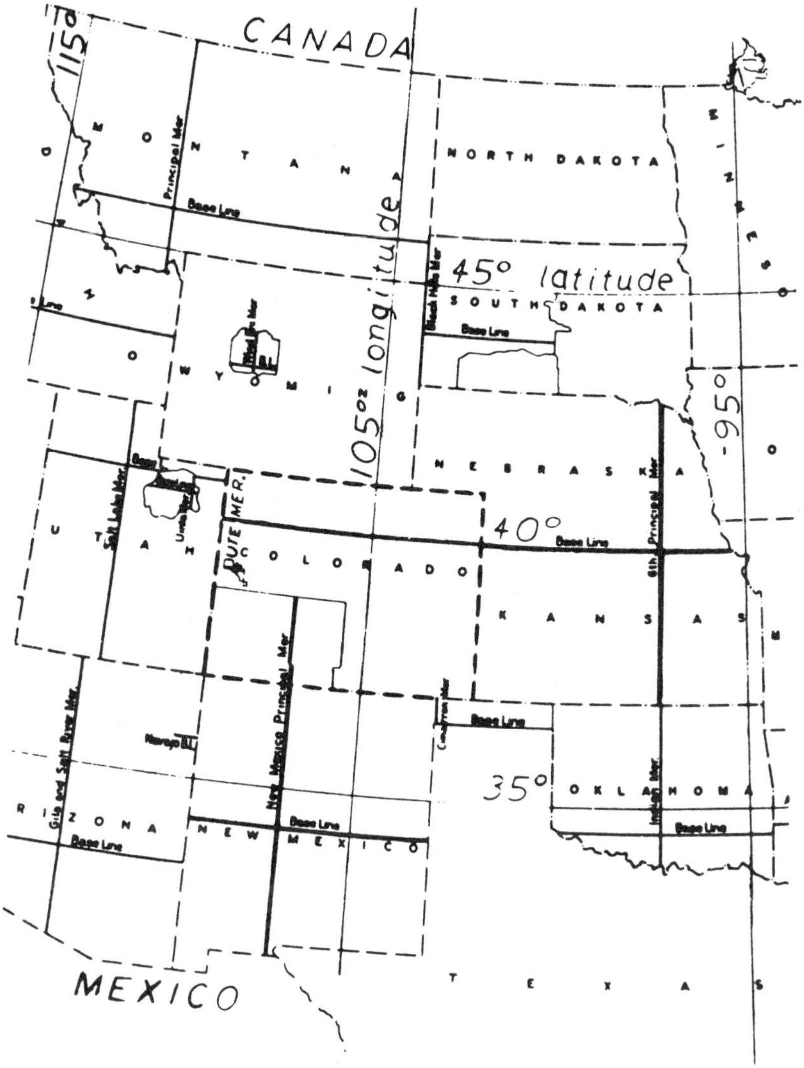

containing 320 acres, quarter sections containing 160 acres, etc. Land acreage descriptions are then generally made by referring to a particular quarter of a particular quarter of a particular section located within a particular township or tier either north or south of a particular base line, and either east or west of a particular meridian.

A section is the smallest subdivision usually surveyed by government surveyors, and at each section corner there is a marker known as "Survey Monument."

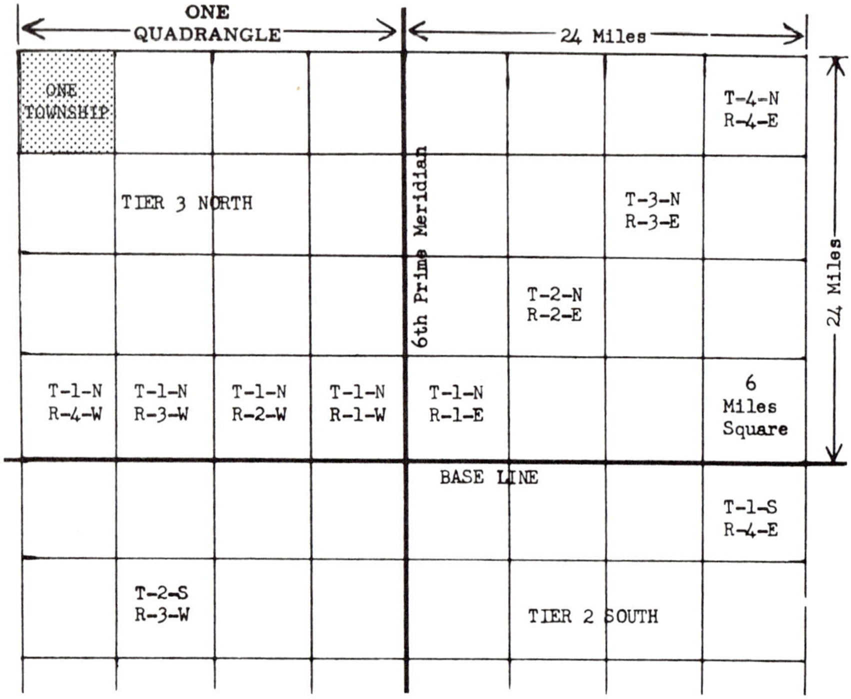

The above sketch shows the subdivision of **two** full **quadrangles** with the 6th Principal Meridian acting as the dividing line. Portion s of two additional quadrangles are shown below the base line.

36	31	32	33	34	35	36	31
1	6	5	4	3	2	1	6
12	7	8	9	10	11	12	7
13	18	17	16	15	14	13	18
24	19	20	21	22	23	24	19
25	30	29	28	27	26	25	30
36	31	32	33	34	35	36	31
1	6	5	4	3	2	1	6

Sectional map of Township showing adjoining Sections

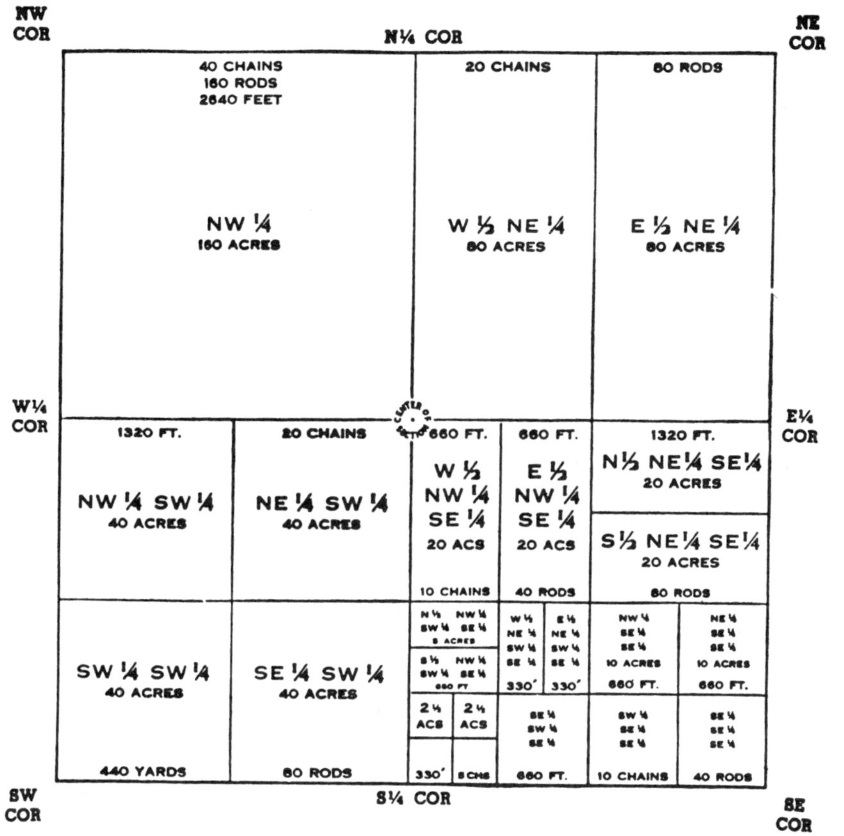
NW COR
N¼ COR
NE COR
40 CHAINS
160 RODS
2640 FEET
20 CHAINS
80 RODS
NW ¼
160 ACRES
W ½ NE ¼
80 ACRES
E ½ NE ¼
80 ACRES
W¼ COR
E¼ COR
1320 FT.
20 CHAINS
660 FT.
660 FT.
1320 FT.
NW ¼ SW ¼
40 ACRES
NE ¼ SW ¼
40 ACRES
W ½ NW ¼ SE ¼
20 ACS
E ½ NW ¼ SE ¼
20 ACS
N½ NE¼ SE¼
20 ACRES
S½ NE¼ SE¼
20 ACRES
10 CHAINS
40 RODS
80 RODS
SW ¼ SW ¼
40 ACRES
SE ¼ SW ¼
40 ACRES
2½ ACS
2½ ACS
330'
330'
330'
660 FT.
660 FT.
660 FT.
10 ACRES
10 ACRES
440 YARDS
80 RODS
660 FT.
10 CHAINS
40 RODS
SW COR
S¼ COR
SE COR

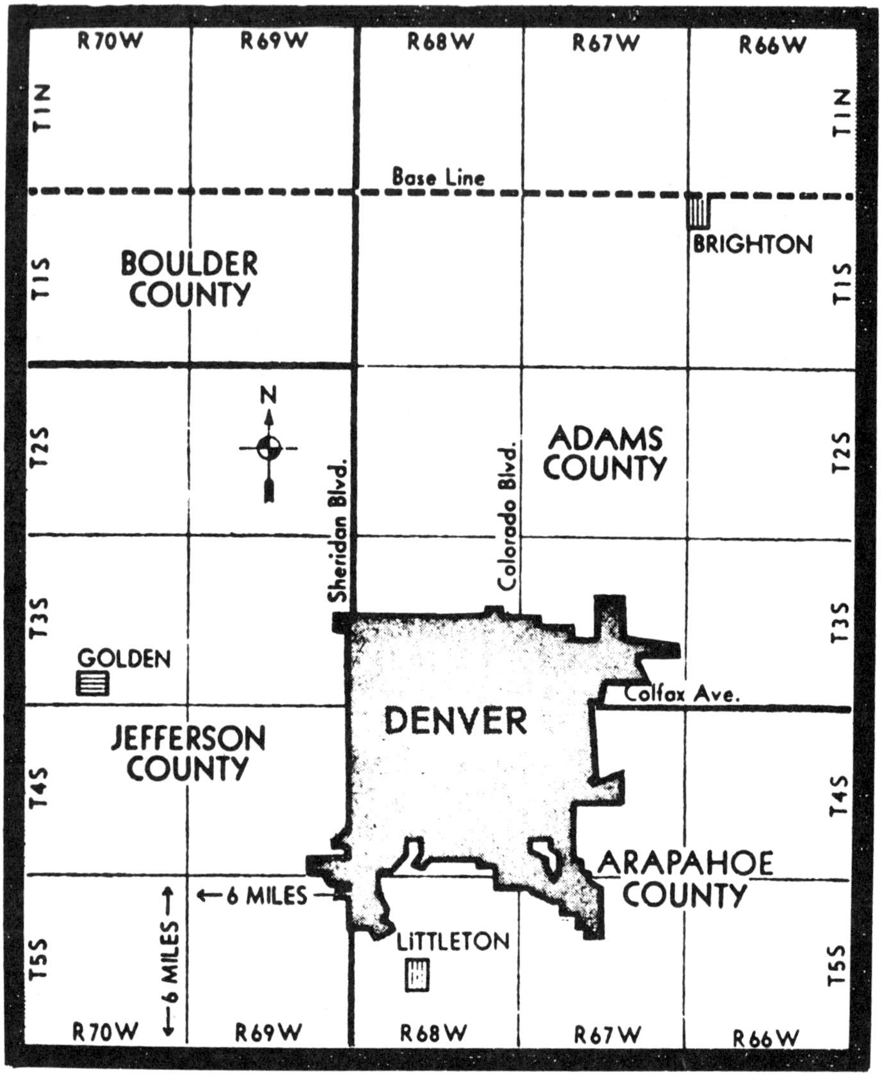

Map showing Denver and vicinity in terms of the actual Townships (tiers), and Ranges

Metes and Bounds Descriptions

Although the preferred method of land description is the public land rectangular survey system, when this cannot be accomplished the land is described by metes and bounds. Metes are measures of length and bounds are boundaries.

The United States and Canada are the only countries in the world using the rectangular system. In all the rest of the world, tracts of land are surveyed and described by metes and bounds—usually by identifying the Point of Beginning and the boundaries in relation to a recognized marker or monument or to natural features such as streams, bridges, piles of stones, trees, etc.

Metes and bounds are used in Colorado when it is necessary or desirable to describe a tract with irregular boundaries not conforming to the rectangular system. However, such a survey or description rarely or never relies on natural features only for location. As used in Colorado, metes and bounds surveys and descriptions are irregular parts of a section or some subdivision of a section. They always tie to some established corner or line of the public lands survey or to recognized corners or lines of a recorded plat. Metes and bounds should be established by a registered land surveyor. (Surveys do not have official status unless made by a registered surveyor.)

Bearing System

Metes and bounds are properly expressed in bearings and distances. The direction of a line—its bearing—is stated in terms of the angle it makes with the meridian, or north and south line, through the beginning point of the line. It is described in degrees and fraction of a degree (minutes and seconds) from the cardinal directions of north or south; never from the cardinal directions of east or west. Any cardinal direction of due north, south, east or west is expressed as such. All other measurements are described in degrees from these four cardinal positions (e.g., N. 70° 19′ E.; S. 24° 10′ W.).

In unsurveyed areas the meridian or cardinal direction was established by compass or astronomical observation and calculation. In almost all cases, now, bearings are determined from an already established line, such as a section line.

It is important when describing land by bearings and distances to state the source of information such as grant, survey, or deed records.

Degree numbering in the four quadrants

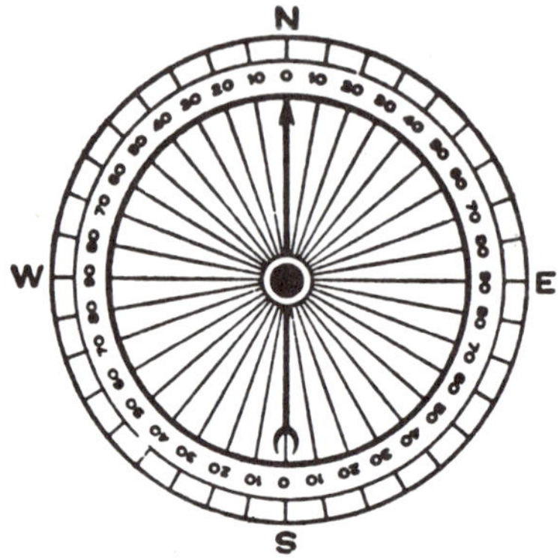

90 degrees in a right angle
360 degrees in a circle

Illustration of description using the bearing system for directions

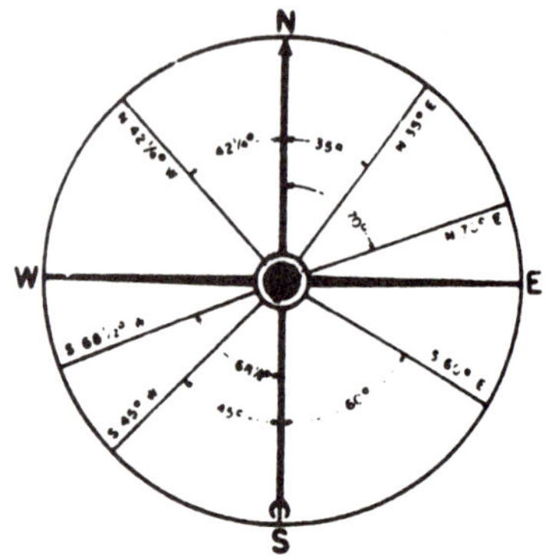

60 seconds equal one minute
60 minutes equal one degree

An example of metes and bounds description using the bearing system is as follows:

A tract of land in the Northwest one-quarter of the North-west one-quarter (NW ¼ NW ¼) of Section 30, Township 1 South, Range 60 West of the 6th P.M., described as follows: Commencing from the Northwest corner of said Section 30; thence South 20° 30′ East 140.60 feet to the Point of Beginning; thence North 88° 55′ East 200.00 feet; thence South 125.00 feet; thence South 88° 55′ West 200.00 feet; thence North 125.00 feet to the Point of Beginning, County of Adams, State of Colorado.

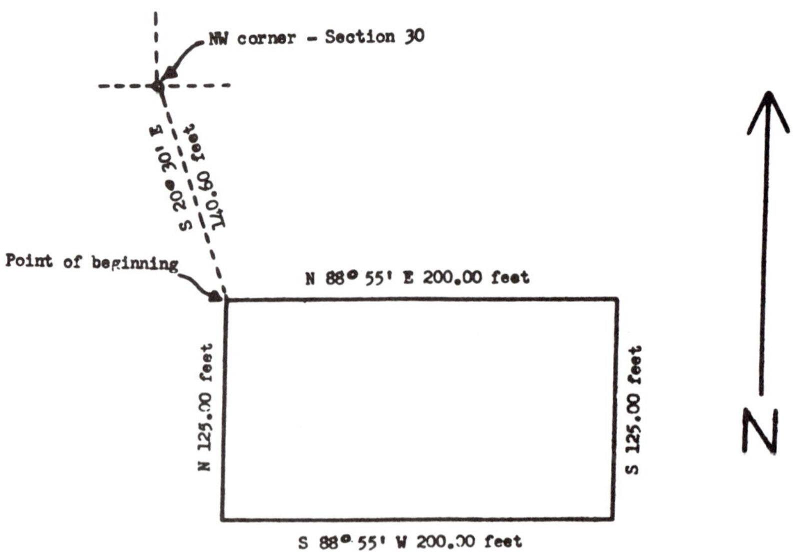

Azimuth System

The azimuth system is basically the same as bearings. It differs from bearings in that it expresses all directions in terms of the angle from one direction only through 360°, instead of being broken into four quadrants. Thus in order to indicate a direction, a surveyor would merely write for example, "290°", moving clockwise using North as the starting point, instead of "N 70° W." Surveyors often use it in their work but generally convert it to the usual bearing description. It is seldom used in descriptions.

Recorded Plat

A tract of land may be subdivided into blocks and lots, with proposed streets, alleys, public utility easements and such other information that the owner desires to include as part of the plan. A map is made, called a plat, identifying each lot by a number within a block and showing its boundaries and measurements. Generally, this map is then recorded in the office of the county clerk and recorder. A lot of a platted tract can thereafter be conveyed by a simple description referring to the plat, an example of which is shown.

The legal description of the shaded site would be written as follows:
Lot five (5), Block two (2), Capitol Hill Subdivision, an addition to the City and County of Denver, State of Colorado, according to the recorded plat in the office of the County Clerk and Recorder of said county.

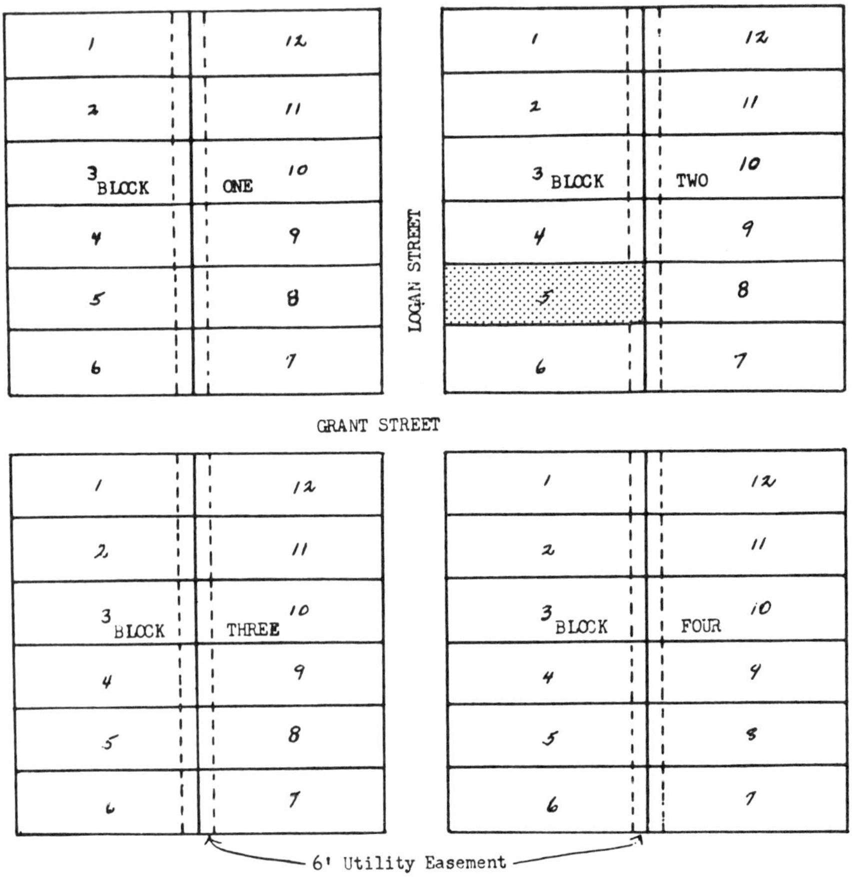

Colorado Coordinate System

Although various types of coordinate systems have been used by professional land surveyors and engineers for many decades, the application and use of state plane coordinates in Colorado legal descriptions on real estate documents is relatively new and may become commonplace in the future. The Colorado Coordinate System became effective July 1, 1967 under Title 38 Article 52 C.R.S. 1973. This statute is permissive in nature and shall not be construed as being mandatory at this time.

The plane coordinates of a point are the distances of that point from two defined baselines perpendicular to each other i.e. a north-south axis and an east-west axis, as measured in the plane of the baselines. The origin of such coordinate system is a Lambert conformal projection of the Clarke spheroid of 1866 (the earth's sphere) which projects the lines of latitude and longitude onto a plane surface (map)—the intersection of such defined lines in each Colorado coordinate zone being the beginning points.

The plane coordinates of a point on the earth's surface, to be used in expressing the position or location of such point in the appropriate zone of this system, consists of two distances, expressed in feet and decimals of a foot. An east-west direction is known as the "X-coordinate" and a north-south direction is known as the "Y-coordinate." These coordinates depend upon and conform to the coordinates on the "Colorado Coordinate System," of the triangulation and traverse stations of the United States Coast and Geodetic Survey within the State of Colorado, as those coordinates have been determined by that survey.

Colorado has been further divided into a North Zone, Central Zone and South Zone. Generally speaking, counties located in the northern one-third are designated "Colorado Coordinate System, North Zone" those counties in the Central one-third are designated "Colorado Coordinate System, Central Zone"; those counties in the southern one-third are designated "Colorado Coordinate System, South Zone." When any tract of land to be defined by a single description extends from one zone into another coordinate zone, the positions of all points on its boundaries may be described according to either of the two zones, the zone which is used being specifically named in the description.

Whenever the "Colorado Coordinate System" is used to describe a tract of land which in the same document is also described by reference to any subdivision, line or corner of the rectangular survey system, the description by coordinates shall be supplemental to the other. In event there is a conflict of the two descriptions used, the rectangular survey system shall prevail over the description by coordinates unless such coordinates are upheld by adjudication, at which time the coordinate description will prevail.

To the person who desires further information on this new concept of land description it is recommended that he [or she] study the statute or contact a registered land surveyor.

Example of a Metes and Bounds Description Using State Plane Coordinates as Supplemental Information

Commencing at the corner of Section 20, 21, 28 and 29, T 4 S, R 75 W, 6th P.M. and bearing North 22° 15′ West 202.50 feet to the Point of Beginning which is marked by a ⅝″ diameter iron rod set in concrete; then bearing North 79° 45′ West 155 feet to a brass marker set in a granite ledge and stamped "2928," said brass marker having grid coordinate X=1,916,572.14, and Y=624,697.82, on the Colorado Coordinate System, Central Zone; then South 22° 45′ West 106.50 feet; then South 70° 15′ East 145 feet; then North 25° 30′ E 133.50 feet to the Point of Beginning.

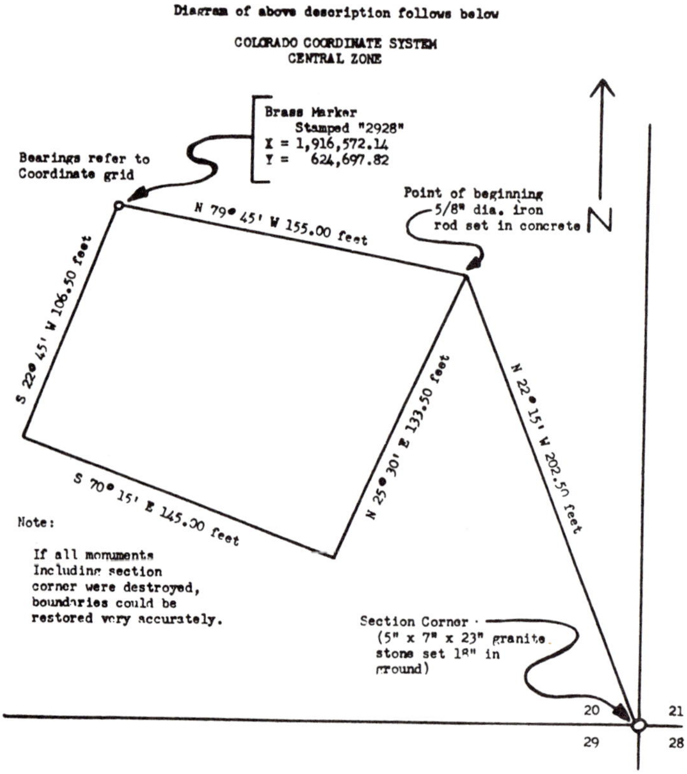

Any description is legal and valid if it unquestionably identifies the property. The phrase "legal description" refers to one of the types of land description explained in this [appendix]. These types of descriptions are more precise and accurate than informal descriptions such as street addresses.

Table of Land Measurement

Linear Measure	*Square Measure*
7.92 inches=1 link	144 sq. in.=1 sq. foot
12 inches=1 foot	9 sq. feet=1 sq yard
3 feet=1 yard	30¼ sq. yds.=1 sq. yd.
25 links=1 rod	16 sq. rds.=1 sq. chain
100 links=1 chain	1 sq. rd.=272¼ sq. ft.
16½ feet=1 rod	1 sq. chain=4356 sq. ft.
5½ yards=1 rod	10 sq. chains=1 acre
40 rods=1 furlong	160 sq. rods=1 acre
8 furlongs=1 mile	4,840 sq. yds.=1 acre
66 feet=1 chain	43,560 sq. ft.=1 acre
80 chains=1 mile	640 acres=1 sq. mile
320 rods=1 mile	1 sq. mile=1 section
8,000 links=1 mile	36 sq. miles=1 Twp.
5280 feet=1 mile	6 miles sq.=1 Twp.
1,760 yards=1 mile	1 sq. mi.=2.59 sq. kilm.

An Acre Is:

43,560 sq. feet.	660 feet × 66 feet.
165 feet × 264 feet.	160 square rods.
198 feet × 220 feet.	208.7 feet square (approx.)

or any rectangular tract, the product of the length and width of which totals 43,560 sq. feet.

Metric System

Most of the world does its measuring in meters. The United States is now moving toward the metric system. The metric system being used today is called the International System of Units, SI for short, and it has been accepted as the preferred system in nearly all countries of the world.

At some point in the future licensees will also have to be conversant with the metric system in order to handle legal descriptions and land descriptions. The metric system progresses logically in units of 10. In the metric system, prefixes have the same meanings whether measuring length, volume or mass, the most common being: micro = millionth; milli =thousandth; centi = hundredth; deci = tenth; mega = 1,000,000 times the base; kilo = 1,000 times the base; hecto = 100 times the base, deka = 10 times the base.

To convert between the units in the metric system, you need only move the decimal point to the right or left. The basic dimension of the metric system is the meter which equals approximately 3.3 feet. All dimensions of length can be expressed as variations of a meter: millimeter (mm), centimeter (cm), meter (m), or kilometer (km). Conversions between these measurements are simple decimal locations based on factors of 10.

The basic metric unit of land measurement is a square with each side 100 meters long, covering an area of 10,000 square meters. This unit of land is called the hectare (ha), and is equal to approximately 2.5 acres.

U.S. to Metric

Length
1 inch = 25.4 millimeters (mm)
1 foot = 0.3 meter (m)
1 yard = 0.9 meter
1 mile = 1.6 kilometer (km)

Area
1 sq. inch = 6.5 sq. centimeters (cm^2)
1 sq. foot = 0.09 sq. meter (m^2)
1 sq. yard = 0.8 sq. meter
1 acre = 0.4 hectare (ha)*
1 sq. mile = 2.6 sq. kilometers (km^2)

Metric to U.S.

Length
1 millimeter (mm) = 0.04 inch
1 meter (m) = 3.28 feet
1 meter = 1.09 yards
1 kilometer (km) = 0.62 mile

Area
1 sq. centimeter (cm^2) = 0.16 sq. inch
1 sq. meter (m^2) = 10.76 sq. feet
1 sq. meter = 1.20 sq. yards
1 hectare* = 2.47 acres
1 sq. kilometer = 0.39 sq. mile

Metric System

Unit	*Abbreviation*	*Number of Meters*	*Approximate U.S. Equivalent*
Length			
myriameter	mym	10,000	6.2 miles
kilometer	km	1,000	0.62 miles
hectometer	hm	100	109.36 yards
decameter	dkm	10	32.81 feet
decimeter	dm	0.1	3.94 inches
centimeter	cm	0.01	0.39 inches
millimeter	mm	0.001	0.04 inches
Area			
square kilometer	sq km or km^2	1,000,000	0.3861 square miles
hectare	ha	10,000	2.47 acres
are	a	100	119.60 square feet
centare	ca	1	10.76 square feet
square centimeter	sq cm or cm^2	0.0001	0.155 square inches

APPENDIX B

National Association of Realtors Code of Ethics

Preamble . . .

Under all is the land. Upon its wise utilization and widely allocated ownership depend the survival and growth of free institutions and of our civilization. The REALTOR® should recognize that the interests of the nation and its citizens require the highest and best use of the land and the widest distribution of land ownership. They require the creation of adequate housing, the building of functioning cities, the development of productive industries and farms, and the preservation of a healthful environment.

Such interests impose obligations beyond those of ordinary commerce. They impose grave social responsibility and a patriotic duty to which the REALTOR® should dedicate himself, and for which he should be diligent in preparing himself. The REALTOR®, therefore, is zealous to maintain and improve the standards of his calling and shares with his fellow-REALTORS® a common responsibility for its integrity and honor. The term REALTOR® has come to connote competency, fairness, and high integrity resulting from adherence to a lofty ideal of moral conduct in business relations. No inducement of profit and no instruction from clients ever can justify departure from this ideal.

In the interpretation of his obligation, a REALTOR® can take no safer guide than that which has been handed down through the centuries, embodied in the Golden Rule, "Whatsoever ye would that men should do to you, do ye even so to them."

Accepting this standard as his own, every REALTOR® pledges himself to observe its spirit in all of his activities and to conduct his business in accordance with the tenets set forth below.

Article 1. The REALTOR® should keep himself informed on matters affecting real estate in his community, the state, and nation so that he may be able to contribute responsibly to public thinking on such matters.

Article 2. In justice to those who place their interests in his care, the REALTOR®

Revised and approved by the Delegate Body of the Association at its 67th Annual Convention, November 14, 1974.

should endeavor always to be informed regarding laws, proposed legislation, governmental regulations, public policies, and current market conditions in order to be in a position to advise his clients properly.

Article 3. It is the duty of the REALTOR® to protect the public against fraud, misrepresentation, and unethical practices in real estate transactions. He should endeavor to eliminate in his community any practices which could be damaging to the public or bring discredit to the real estate profession. The REALTOR® should assist the governmental agency charged with regulating the practices of brokers and salesmen in his state.

Article 4. The REALTOR® should seek no unfair advantage over other REALtors® and should conduct his business so as to avoid controversies with other REALTORS®.

Article 5. In the best interests of society, of his associates, and his own business, the REALTOR® should willingly share with other REALTORS® the lessons of his experience and study for the benefit of the public, and should be loyal to the Board of REALTORS® of his community and active in its work.

Article 6. To prevent dissension and misunderstanding and to assure better service to the owner, the REALTOR® should urge the exclusive listing of property unless contrary to the best interest of the owner.

Article 7. In accepting employment as an agent, the REALTOR® pledges himself to protect and promote the interests of the client. This obligation of absolute fidelity to the client's interests is primary, but it does not relieve the REALTOR® of the obligation to treat fairly all parties to the transaction.

Article 8. The REALTOR® shall not accept compensation from more than one party, even if permitted by law, without the full knowledge of all parties to the transaction.

Article 9. The REALTOR® shall avoid exaggeration, misrepresentation, or concealment of pertinent facts. He has an affirmative obligation to discover adverse factors that a reasonably competent and diligent investigation would disclose.

Article 10. The REALTOR® shall not deny equal professional services to any person for reasons of race, creed, sex, or country of national origin. The REALTOR® shall not be a party to any plan or agreement to discriminate against a person or persons on the basis of race, creed, sex, or country of national origin.

Article 11. A REALTOR® is expected to provide a level of competent service in keeping with the Standards of Practice in those fields in which the REALTOR® customarily engages.

The REALTOR® shall not undertake to provide specialized professional services concerning a type of property or service that is outside his field of competence unless he engages the assistance of one who is competent on such types of property or service, or unless the facts are fully disclosed to the client. Any person engaged to provide such assistance shall be so identified to the client and his contribution to the assignment should be set forth.

The REALTOR® shall refer to the Standards of Practice of the National Association as to the degree of competence that a client has a right to expect the REALTOR® to possess, taking into consideration the complexity of the problem, the availability of expert assistance, and the opportunities for experience available to the REALTOR®.

Article 12. The REALTOR® shall not undertake to provide professional services concerning a property or its value where he has a present or contemplated interest unless such interest is specifically disclosed to all affected parties.

Article 13. The REALTOR® shall not acquire an interest in or buy for himself, any member of his immediate family, his firm or any member thereof, or any entity in which he has a substantial ownership interest, property listed with him, without making the true position known to the listing owner. In selling property owned by himself, or in which he has any interest, the REALTOR® shall reveal the facts of his ownership or interest to the purchaser.

Article 14. In this event of a controversy between REALTORS® associated with different firms, arising out of their relationship as REALTORS®, the REALTORS® shall submit the dispute to arbitration in accordance with the regulations of their board or boards rather than litigate the matter.

Article 15. If a REALTOR® is charged with unethical practice or is asked to present evidence in any disciplinary proceeding or investigation, he shall place all pertinent facts before the proper tribunal of the member board or affiliated institute, society, or council of which he is a member.

Article 16. When acting as agent, the REALTOR® shall not accept any commission, rebate, or profit on expenditures made for his principal-owner, without the principal's knowledge and consent.

Article 17. The REALTOR® shall not engage in activities that constitute the unauthorized practice of law and shall recommend that legal counsel be obtained when the interest of any party to the transaction requires it.

Article 18. The REALTOR® shall keep in a special account in an appropriate financial institution, separated from his own funds, monies coming into his possession in trust for other persons, such as escrows, trust funds, clients' monies, and other like items.

Article 19. The REALTOR® shall be careful at all times to present a true picture in his advertising and representations to the public. He shall neither advertise without disclosing his name nor permit any person associated with him to use individual names or telephone numbers, unless such person's connection with the REALTOR® is obvious in the advertisement.

Article 20. The REALTOR®, for the protection of all parties, shall see that financial obligations and commitments regarding real estate transactions are in writing, expressing the exact agreement of the parties. A copy of each agreement shall be furnished to each party upon his signing such agreement.

Article 21. The REALTOR® shall not engage in any practice or take any action inconsistent with the agency of another REALTOR®.

Article 22. In the sale of property which is exclusively listed with a REALTOR®, the REALTOR® shall utilize the services of other brokers upon mutually agreed upon terms when it is in the best interests of the client.

Negotiations concerning property which is listed exclusively shall be carried on with the listing broker, not with the owner, except with the consent of the listing broker.

Article 23. The REALTOR® shall not publicly disparage the business practice of a competitor nor volunteer an opinion of a competitor's transaction. If his opinion is sought and if the REALTOR® deems it appropriate to respond, such opinion shall be rendered with strict professional integrity and courtesy.

Article 24. The REALTOR® shall not directly or indirectly solicit the services or affiliation of an employee or independent contractor in the organization of another REALTOR® without prior notice to said REALTOR®.

Where the word REALTOR® is used in this Code and Preamble, it shall be deemed to include REALTOR-ASSOCIATE®. Pronouns shall be considered to include REALTORS® and REALTOR-ASSOCIATE®s of both genders.

The Code of Ethics was adopted in 1913. Amended at the Annual Convention in 1924, 1928, 1950, 1951, 1952, 1955, 1956, 1961, 1962, and 1974.

APPENDIX C

The Affiliates of the National Association of Realtors[1]

There are nine affiliated institutes, societies, and councils under the umbrella of the NATIONAL ASSOCIATION OF REALTORS®. These affiliates represent the major fields of activity in the real estate profession. One might draw an analogy to the medical profession: members of the National Association may be likened to general practitioners; members of the institutes, societies, and councils are specialists who practice in particular areas of the profession.

The affiliates of the National Association are:

- American Society of Real Estate Counselors (ASREC)
- Society of Industrial REALTORS® (SIR)
- American Institute of Real Estate Appraisers (AIREA)
- Farm and Land Institute (FLI)
- Institute of Real Estate Management (IREM)
- Real Estate Securities and Syndication Institute (RESSI®)
- REALTORS NATIONAL MARKETING INSTITUTE® (RNMI)
- Women's Council of REALTORS® (WCR)
- International Real Estate Federation (American Chapter) AC/IREF (FIABCI)

The need for the National Association's affiliates is evident. As stated in the 1977 *Operations Manual*: The National Association "recognizes the need to provide its members a greater opportunity for cooperation and discussion of administrative and business problems of the particular phases of the real estate business in which they are individually interested. Article XIII of the National Association Constitution provides that the Board of Directors may establish Societies, Institutes, or Councils of the National Association provided, however, that no Society, Institute or Council shall be established or maintained which has less than 100 members."

Each affiliate is supported by its own dues structure and has its own requirements for membership. These membership requirements vary within each separate or-

1. Reprinted with permission from *Realtor's® Review*, August 1977, pp. 10–14, 27.

ganization, but all affiliates are open to members of the National Association who satisfy the specific requirements for participation. Programs of the affiliates are designed to broaden the horizons of members and nonmembers in their quest for knowledge and information in the various specialties they represent. Through these programs, members and nonmembers will be better able to serve the many and varied real estate needs of the public with the highest degree of competence. Most of the programs lead to professional designations for demonstrated expertise in a specialized field of real estate.

To inform you of the options of specialized real estate activity available through the affiliates, we present an overview of each of the nine organizations, including a brief history of development and an outline of goals and objectives. For further information or details on membership requirements, contact the affiliates themselves. With the exception of the Society of Industrial REALTORS®, which is located in the National Association's Washington office at 925 15th St. N.W., Washington, D.C. 20005, each affiliate has a central office in the National Association's headquarters building at 430 N. Michigan, Chicago, Illinois 60611.

American Society of Real Estate Counselors

In 1953, a nucleus of REALTORS® with long and varied experience joined together to promote the growth and improve the quality of real estate counseling by adopting and enforcing standards of professional practice. The American Society of Real Estate Counselors (ASREC) was thus formed to help satisfy a need for competent, independent real estate advice and guidance rendered by qualified experts on a fee basis. Members use the professional designation C.R.E.—Counselor of Real Estate.

Estates, individuals, corporations, governments, municipalities, and institutions have come to recognize the necessity and value of objective advice from counselors with extensive and varied real estate experience. Members of ASREC advise clients of the effect of real estate economics upon their enterprises. The professional real estate advice rendered is fully correlated with but distinct and separate from legal, architectural, engineering, or tax services.

ASREC imposes professional obligations upon its member counselors through a Code of Professional Ethics. The Code is all embracing, setting out the counselor's responsibility to the public, his client, and his profession. It is subscribed to by every member and carefully enforced.

To become a member of ASREC and be entitled to use the C.R.E. designation, a REALTOR® must have had a varied background of experience as well as thorough knowledge of real property. He must be known for integrity and high standards of business and personal conduct. Invitation to membership is extended only to those individuals who offer their counseling services on a fee basis.

There are no educational requirements or courses of study leading to the Society's C.R.E. designation; however, ASREC offers occasional counseling workshops on classic problems of current real estate practices and seminars that are scheduled throughout the year. In addition, ASREC sends members two regular publications: *The Counselor*, a quarterly newsletter, and *Real Estate Issues*, a new professional journal containing articles written by scholars and practitioners in real estate.

Society of Industrial Realtors®

Established in 1941, the Society of Industrial REALTORS® (SIR) is the only one of the National Association's affiliates located in the Association's Washington offiice. *REALTORS® Review* featured an overview of SIR in the June 1977 article on our Washington office.

To reiterate, the Society's aims are: to encourage knowledge, education, integrity and quality workmanship in the industrial real estate field; to encourage the exchange of information among members; to provide certification and qualification of competent industrial property brokers; and to cooperate with governmental and civic organizations, public utilities, and financial institutions in matters relating to economic development and industrial real estate.

Members of the Society use the professional designation SIR. Among its services, SIR provides a monthly newsletter, *SIR Reports*, assistance with spot surveys to locate plants and sites, informational brochures, and a market letter.

American Institute of Real Estate Appraisers

The American Institute of Real Estate Appraisers (AIREA), often called the Appraisal Institute, is the oldest organization of professional appraisers in the United States and the only one affiliated with the National Association. Founded in 1932, the institute has, during its 45-year history, attained a national reputation for professional service to the public.

An appraisal is a solution to a real estate problem—what, in terms of dollars, is the value of a specific real property. The solution is arrived at through the gathering, analyzing, and interpreting of factual data, and the influence of economic, social, physical, and governmental forces on the particular problem. Five of the most common reasons for an appraisal are: (1) transfer of ownership; (2) financing or credit; (3) just compensation in condemnation proceedings; (4) a basis for taxation; and (5) rental payments or lease provisions.

The Appraisal Institute has an intensive program designed to test knowledge, experience, and judgment in the field of real estate appraising, and membership in the institute is awarded only to those who have demonstrated their ability to meet stringent requirements. These standards demand that a member have years of practical experience; pass extensive written tests; and submit numerous appraisal reports demonstrating the ability to render competent service to clients. Members meeting these standards are awarded either of two professional designations: MAI—Member, Appraisal Institute—awarded to those who have proven their ability to appraise all types of real property; and RM—Residential Member—the designation earned by those specialists who have demonstrated competence in the appraisal of single-family residences. All members of AIREA must subscribe to the institute's rigid Code of Ethics and Standards of Professional Conduct.

AIREA has been a pioneer in the field of continuing appraisal education. Its first case study course was presented in 1935. Today, the institute offers a series of nine intensive one- and two-week courses ranging from basic appraisal principles and techniques to more technical subjects.

AIREA is a major publisher of appraisal textbooks, monographs, and periodicals. Its current catalog includes approximately 40 different titles, one of the most popular being *The Appraisal of Real Estate*, a basic text. Regular publications for members include *The Appraisal Journal*, a quarterly, and *The Appraiser*, a monthly round-up of appraisal news and views.

Farm and Land Institute

The Farm and Land Institute (FLI) was organized in 1944 as the Institute of Farm Brokers. As the scope of its activities grew, the name was changed several times; the most recent change occurred in early 1975 when the present name was adopted.

FLI is open to members of the National Association and is devoted exclusively to advancing the interests of those who are involved in various phases of land development and proper land utilization.

FLI provides a forum to bring together members interested in improving their professional competence in all aspects of the land segment of the real estate business. This includes:

(1) identification of all phases of land activities, including brokerage, agribusiness, management, planning, appraising, acquisition, syndication, and development as recognized land specialities within the real estate profession;

(2) development and establishment of professional standards of practice;

(3) fostering professional expertise through educational activities and programs;

(4) identification of members to the public;

(5) designation of practitioners who have met rigid educational and experience requirements as Accredited Farm and Land Members (AFLM);

(6) formulation of recommendations for public policy affecting land use;

(7) advocacy of wise use of land and the reasonable rights and privileges of private ownership.

Membership in FLI is open to anyone who belongs to the National Association. The classes of membership in FLI are Active, Accredited, Affiliate, and Honorary Life. New members receive the *Farm and Land Real Estate Manual*, a 134-page softcover book covering a variety of subjects of concern to both rural and urban land specialists. In addition, the *Farm and Land REALTOR®* newsletter is published monthly. It reports on institute activities and carries articles helpful to professional growth and business proficiency.

Education is another key activity of the institute. Courses sponsored jointly with state chapters are held in strategically located cities.

Institute of Real Estate Management

Organized by property managers for the benefit of all individuals in the profession, the Institute of Real Estate Management (IREM) has been serving the professional needs of resident, supervisory, and executive property managers since its inception in 1934.

IREM serves the needs of property managers with dissemination of information, educational courses, research, and publications designed to increase their professionalism. Membership is made up of individuals who have demonstrated management knowledge and skills as established by rigid IREM standards. Upon successful completion of two written examinations and a management plan, a candidate who has also met the institute's standards of experience, and ethics is awarded the professional designation of CERTIFIED PROPERTY MANAGER®

(CPM®). A firm wishing to offer the public assurance of management proficiency may apply for special IREM certification; those firms qualifying in the areas of experience, integrity, financial stability, and insurance requirements receive the designation ACCREDITED MANAGEMENT ORGANIZATION® (AMO®). In addition, IREM has developed an education program for on-site managers of residential housing that leads to the recognition award ACCREDITED RESIDENT MANAGER® (ARM®). All members subscribe to the institute's Code of Ethics.

As its major method of disseminating information, IREM offers a thorough education in property management; its 10 courses, reorganized in structure and content in 1976, cover the major fields of property management.

The institute's second method of distributing information is through publication of books and periodicals.

IREM's regular publications include the *Journal of Property Management*, published six times a year, and the monthly newsletter, *CPM Aspects*.

Real Estate Securities and Syndication Institute

Established in 1972, the Real Estate Securities and Syndication Institute (RESSI®) is the newest affiliate of the Association.

Some of RESSI's basic objectives are: to provide an organization through the National Association in which those engaged in the creation, issuance, analysis, promotion, marketing, and management of real estate securities can participate and assemble; to confer and cooperate with governmental and business organizations and associations; to establish educational standards for its members; to develop and sponsor educational programs and publications; and to establish a certification and designation program. The origination, operation, and termination of various privately offered and publicly registered real estate securities offers a challenging and profitable opportunity to the creative real estate or securities licensee. RESSI assists members in learning the ncessary methods, skills, and regulations in an educational program offering two courses and several conferences in syndication techniques.

RESSI services include the opportunity to earn one of two professional designations, CRSM (Certified Real Estate Securities Marketer) or CRSS (Certified Real Estate Securities Sponsor), the only designations available in the real estate securities field. Members receive the newsletter, *RESSI® Review*, 10 times a year as well as other valuable services.

Realtors National Marketing Institute

Organized in 1923 as the National Institute of Real Estate Brokers, the REALTORS NATIONAL MARKETING INSTITUTE® took its present name in 1975 to reflect its growing responsibility in assisting Realtors, REALTOR-ASSOCIATES® and others in the profession to better and more profitably market not only properties but their professional services. Its primary functions are education and the upgrading of professional competence in the areas of residential sales, commercial-investment brokerage, and the administration of the real estate office. To that end, the Marketing Institute offers education courses and training materials, and access to professional designations for demonstrated expertise in specific fields: the Certified Real Estate Brokerage Manager (CRB) in real estate marketing management, the Certified Commercial-Investment Member (CCIM) in commercial-investment property marketing and, new in 1977, the Certified Residential Specialist (CRS) in residential sales.

As a clearinghouse for the latest successful techniques of practice, the institute provides several means for exchange of real estate ideas. The foremost is *real estate today®* magazine which is published and mailed 10 times each year. It is authored by the Realtors and Realtor-Associates whose creative approaches to the professional challenge will form the basis of future industry practice. Many of these same individuals have helped develop the institute courses which offer theory and practice on an ongoing basis for managers and salespeople.

Books, manuals, forms, sales aids, cassette tapes and films—all these, too, are developed by institute members. Some are designed for sales training; others are consumer- or client-oriented.

The Women's Council of Realtors®

A Women's Council was organized in 1939 within the National Association of Real Estate Boards. In later years, when the parent organization changed its name to the NATIONAL ASSOCIATION OF REALTORS®, so did its affiliate change its name to the Women's Council of REALTORS®.

The council's objectives are: (1) to provide a meaningful and continuing association of women in real estate, dedicated to the highest standards of professional performance and service; (2) to encourage its members continuously to expand their knowledge of the real estate profession by taking advantage of every educational opportunity; (3) to promote a greater knowledge and understanding of, and adherence to, the Realtor Code of Ethics: (4) to develop a greater capacity for leadership in its members through educational programs and training; (5) to encourage active participation in and contribution to the growth and progress of local boards, state associations, and the National Association; (6) to encourage recognition of women and their contributions to the real estate profession; and (7) to promote the growth of the council by assisting in the organization of local and state chapters.

The council's services include a monthly publication, *WRC Communiqué*; regional leadership and educational conferences; exchange of information on successful educational programs; educational programs offered at the three national meetings held each year; detailed guidelines for all national officers, plus state and local chapter presidents; an annually issued roster of the full membership; and local and state chapter program material.

International Real Estate Federation (American Chapter)

The American Chapter of the International Real Estate Federation was founded in 1956 as an affiliate of the National Association; members are required to hold some form of membership in their local board of Realtors. Through the American Chapter, members are eligible for membership in the International Real Estate Federation (FIABCI). In case you're wondering, FIABCI stands for *Federation Internationale des Administrateurs de Biens—Conseils Immobiliers* (translated International Federation of Real Estate Property Managers), the French name of the organization before it was changed in 1964 to International Real Estate Federation.

The promotion of high professional standards among individuals engaged in real estate in all nations of the world is the major objective of IREF. Each year, a World Congress is hosted by one of the 35-member countries of IREF. The World Congress brings together more than 2,000 national leaders from the 35 nations. They assemble to hear top authorities, to participate in work programs, and tc establish a friendly relationship with individuals dedicated to cooperation in real estate development, sales, management, and financing throughout the world.

Membership includes a roster listing of more than 6,000 names, addresses, and telephone numbers and specialties of real estate professionals in all the member countries. In addition, members keep abreast of the international real estate picture through the *FIABCI Reporter*.

APPENDIX D

Real Estate Contracts

The printed portions of this form approved by the Colorado Real Estate Commission (LC 10-10-75)

EXCLUSIVE RIGHT TO SELL LISTING CONTRACT
(RESIDENTIAL)

____________________, Colorado____________________, 19____

In consideration of the services of the hereinafter named real estate broker, I hereby list with said broker, from ____________________, 19____, to____________________, 19____, inclusive, the property described below and I hereby grant said broker the exclusive and irrevocable right to sell the same within said time at the price and on the terms herein stated, or at such other price and terms which may be accepted by me, and to accept deposits thereon and retain same until the closing of, or defeat of, the transaction. I further authorize said broker to list the property with any multiple listing service in which he is a participant, at the broker's expense, and to accept the assistance and cooperation of other brokers. I hereby agree to pay said broker____% of the selling price for his services (1) in case of any sale or exchange of same within said listing period by the undersigned owner, the said broker, or by any person, or (2) upon the said broker finding a purchaser who is ready, willing and able to complete the purchase as proposed by the owner, or (3) in case of any such sale or exchange of the said property within the 120 days subsequent to the expiration of this agreement to any party with whom the said broker negotiated and whose name was disclosed to the owner by the broker during the listing period.

In the event of forfeiture of payments made by a prospective purchaser, the sums received shall be divided between the broker and the owner, one-half thereof to said broker, but not to exceed the commission agreed upon herein, and the balance to the owner.

Address:____________________ ____________________
(Street) (City)

Legal Description:

Price $____________________ Terms:

Subject to general taxes and ______________________________

____

for year of closing, building and zoning regulations, easements and restrictive covenants of record, and the following encumbrances:

I authorize the holder of any note secured by the above listed encumbrances to disclose to the broker the amount owing on said encumbrances and the terms thereof.

Price to include any of the following items currently on the premises: Lighting, heating and plumbing fixtures; all outdoor plants, window and porch shades, venetian blinds, storm windows, storm doors, screens, curtain rods, drapery rods, central air conditioning, ventilating fixtures, attached TV antennas, attached mirrors, linoleum, awnings, water softener (if owned by seller), fireplace screen and grate, built-in kitchen appliances, wall-to-wall carpeting

____

all in their present condition, free and clear of all taxes, liens and encumbrances; provided, however, that the following fixtures of a permanent nature are to be excluded from the sale: ______________________________

____

In case of sale or exchange I agree to furnish, at my option and expense, an abstract of the title to said property, certified to date, or a current commitment for title insurance policy in an amount equal to the purchase price, showing merchantable title in the owner. If the title insurance commitment is selected, I agree to deliver the title insurance policy to purchaser after closing and pay the premium thereon.

In case of sale or exchange I agree to execute and deliver a good and sufficient__________warranty deed to the purchaser conveying said property free and clear of all taxes, liens, encumbrances and easements, except as listed above.

General taxes for year of closing, prepaid rents, water rents, sewer rents, FHA mortgage insurance premiums and interest on encumbrances, if any, and ______________________________

____

shall be apportioned to date of delivery of deed.

Taxes for all special improvements now installed, whether assessed or not, shall be paid by owners.

The printed portions of this form approved by the Colorado Real Estate Commission (LC 13-10-75)

EXCLUSIVE AGENCY LISTING CONTRACT

________________, Colorado ________________, 19____

In consideration of the services of the hereinafter named real estate broker, I hereby list with said broker, from ________________, 19____, to ________________, 19____, inclusive, the property described below and I hereby name said broker the exclusive agent to sell the same within said time at the price and on the terms herein stated, or at such other price and terms which may be accepted by me, and to accept deposits thereon and retain same until the closing of, or defeat of, the transaction. I further authorize said broker to list the property with any multiple listing service in which he is a participant, at the broker's expense, and to accept the assistance and cooperation of other brokers. I hereby agree to pay said broker ____% of the selling price for his services (1) in case of any sale or exchange of same within said listing period by said broker, or by any person, except sale or exchange to a purchaser procured by the owner without the assistance of said broker, or (2) upon the said broker finding a purchaser who is ready, willing and able to complete the purchase as proposed by the owner, unless the owner has previously executed a written contract for the sale of same to a purchaser who was procured by the owner without the assistance of the broker, or (3) in case of any such sale or exchange of the said property within the 120 days subsequent to the expiration of this agreement to any party with whom the said broker negotiated and whose name was disclosed to the owner by the broker during the listing period.

In the event of forfeiture of payments by a prospective purchaser on a contract obtained by or through the broker, the sums received shall be divided between the broker and the owner, one-half thereof to said broker, but not to exceed the commission agreed upon herein and the balance to the owner.

Address ________________ (Street) ________________ (City)

Legal Description:

Price $ ________________ Terms:

Subject to general taxes and ______________________________

____

for year of closing, building and zoning regulations, easements and restrictive covenants of record, and the following encumbrances:

I authorize the holder of any note secured by the above listed encumbrances to disclose to the broker the amount owing on said encumbrances and the terms thereof.

Price to include the following personal property:

to be conveyed by bill of sale at time of closing, in their present condition, free and clear of all personal property taxes, liens and encumbrances, except:

The following fixtures of a permanent nature are to be excluded from the sale:

No. LC 13-10-75. Exclusive Agency Listing Contract—Bradford Publishing Co., 1824-46 Stout Street, Denver, Colorado—(573-5011)—10-75

The printed portions of this form approved by the Colorado Real Estate Commission (LC 14-10-75)

OPEN LISTING CONTRACT

____________________, Colorado ____________________, 19____

In consideration of the services of the hereinafter named real estate broker, I hereby list with said broker, from ________________, 19____, to ________________, 19 ____, inclusive, the property described below, and I hereby grant said broker the right to sell the same within said time at the price and on the terms herein stated, or at such other price and terms which may be accepted by me, and to accept deposits thereon and retain same until the closing of, or defeat of, the transaction. I hereby agree to pay said broker ____% of the selling price for his services in case of any sale by the undersigned broker or upon the said broker finding a purchaser who is ready, willing and able to complete the purchase as proposed by the owner. In case of a sale made by any person other than the undersigned broker, this listing contract is void and of no effect.

In the event of forfeiture of payments by a prospective purchaser on a contract obtained by or through the broker, the sums received shall be divided between the broker and the owner, one-half thereof to said broker, but not to exceed the commission agreed upon herein and the balance to the owner.

Address: ____
(Street) (City)

Legal Description:

Price $____________________ Terms:

Subject to general taxes and ______________________________

for year of closing, building and zoning regulations, easements and restrictive covenants of record, and the following encumbrances:

I authorize the holder of any note secured by the above listed encumbrances to disclose to the broker the amount owing on said encumbrances and the terms thereof.

Price to include the following personal property:

to be conveyed by bill of sale at time of closing, in their present condition, free and clear of all personal property taxes, liens and encumbrances, except:

The following fixtures of a permanent nature are to be excluded from the sale:

In case of sale or exchange I agree to furnish, at my option and expense, an abstract of title to said property, certified to date, or a current commitment for title insurance policy in an amount equal to the purchase price, showing merchantable title in the owner. If the title insurance commitment is selected, I agree to deliver the title insurance policy to purchaser after closing and pay the premium thereon.

In case of sale or exchange I agree to execute and deliver a good and sufficient ______________ warranty deed to the purchaser conveying said property free and clear of all taxes, liens, encumbrances and easements, except as listed above.

No. LC 14-10-75. **Open Listing Contract —Bradford Publishing Co., 1824-46 Stout Street, Denver, Colorado —10-75**

The printed portions of this form approved by the Colorado Real Estate Commission (SC 21-10-75)

SPECIFIC PERFORMANCE CONTRACT
(RESIDENTIAL)

________________________, 19____

RECEIVED FROM ____,
Purchaser (as joint tenants), the sum of $________________, in the form of ________________
to be held by ________________________________, broker, in his escrow or trustee account,
as earnest money and part payment for the following described real estate situate in the ________________
County of ____________________, Colorado, to-wit:

with all improvements thereon and all fixtures of a permanent nature currently on the premises except as hereinafter provided,
in their present condition, ordinary wear and tear excepted, known as No. ________________________________
____which property
purchaser agrees to buy upon the following terms and conditions, for the purchase price of $________________,
payable as follows: $________________ hereby receipted for, $________________.

1. If a note and trust deed or mortgage is to be assumed, the purchaser agrees to pay a loan transfer fee not to exceed $________ and it is a condition of this contract that the purchaser may assume such encumbrance without change in its term or conditions except ____.

2. Price to include any of the following items currently on the premises: Lighting, heating and plumbing fixtures; all outdoor plants, window and porch shades, venetian blinds, storm windows, storm doors, screens, curtain rods, drapery rods, central air conditioning, ventilating fixtures, attached TV antennas, attached mirrors, linoleum, awnings, water softener (if owned by seller), fireplace screen and grate, built-in kitchen appliances, wall to wall carpeting ____, all in their present condition, free and clear of all taxes, liens and encumbrances; except as provided in paragraph 4; provided, however, that the following fixtures of a permanent nature are excluded from this sale: ____.

3. An abstract of title to said property, certified to date, or a current commitment for title insurance policy in an amount equal to the purchase price, at seller's option and expense, shall be furnished the purchaser on or before ____________________, 19____. If seller elects to furnish said title insurance commitment, seller will deliver the title insurance policy to purchaser after closing and pay the premium thereon.

4. Title shall be merchantable in the seller. Subject to payment or tender as above provided and compliance with the other terms and conditions hereunder by purchaser, the seller shall execute and deliver a good and sufficient ________________ warranty deed to said purchaser on ________________, 19____, or, by mutual agreement, at an earlier date, conveying said property free and clear of all taxes, except the general taxes for 19____, payable January 1, 19____, and except ____; free and clear of all liens for special improvements now installed, whether assessed or not; free and clear of all liens and encumbrances except easements for telephone, electricity, water and sanitary sewer, and except ____; and subject to building and zoning regulations, and restrictive covenants of record. Any encumbrance required to be paid may be paid from the proceeds of this transaction.

No. SC 21-10-75. Specific Performance Contract (Residential)—Bradford Publishing Co., 1824-46 Stout Street, Denver, Colorado—10-75

The printed portions of this form approved by the Colorado Real Estate Commission (SC 50-10-75)

RECEIPT AND OPTION FOR INSTALLMENT LAND CONTRACT
(RESIDENTIAL)

______________, 19____

RECEIVED FROM ______________________________
Purchaser (as joint tenants), the sum of $______________, in the form of ______________, to be held by ______________, broker, in his escrow account or trustee account, as earnest money and part payment for the following described real estate situate in the ______________ County of ______________, Colorado, to wit:

with all improvements thereon and all fixtures of a permanent nature currently on the premises except as hereinafter provided, in their present condition, ordinary wear and tear excepted, known as No. ______________

which property purchaser agrees to buy upon the following terms and conditions, for the purchase price of $______________, payable as follows: $______________ hereby receipted for, $______________.

Price to include:

1. Title shall be merchantable in the seller. An abstract of title to said property, certified to date, or a current commitment for a title insurance policy in an amount equal to the purchase price, at seller's option and expense, shall be furnished the purchaser on or before ______________, 19____. If seller elects to furnish said title insurance commitment, seller shall deliver the title insurance policy to purchaser after closing date specified in paragraph 2, and pay the premium thereon.

2. The closing date shall be ______________, 19____, unless the parties shall mutually agree upon an earlier date. On such date the seller and the purchaser agree to execute an installment land contract, for the sale of the above described property, wherein the seller agrees to execute a good and sufficient ______________ warranty deed to purchaser conveying said property free and clear of all taxes, except general taxes for 19____ payable January 1, 19____, and except ______________

______________;

free and clear of all liens for special improvements now installed whether assessed or not; free and clear of all liens and encumbrances except:

and, subject to building and zoning regulations and restrictive covenants of record, and easements for telephone, electricity, water and sanitary sewer and except ______________

____

______________.

Said deed shall be delivered to ______________

______________, a corporate escrow agent, pursuant to a written escrow agreement providing for delivery of deed to purchaser upon payment in full of the purchase price, or as follows:

The fee payable to the escrow agent shall not exceed $______________ and shall be shared equally by the purchaser and seller.

No. SC 50-10-75. **Receipt and Option for Installment Land Contract (Residential)**
—Bradford Publishing Co., 1824-46 Stout Street, Denver, Colorado —10-75

APPENDIX E

Replacement Cost Example

ONE STORY

GOOD QUALITY

Reprinted with the permission of Marshall and Swift Publication Company, Los Angeles.

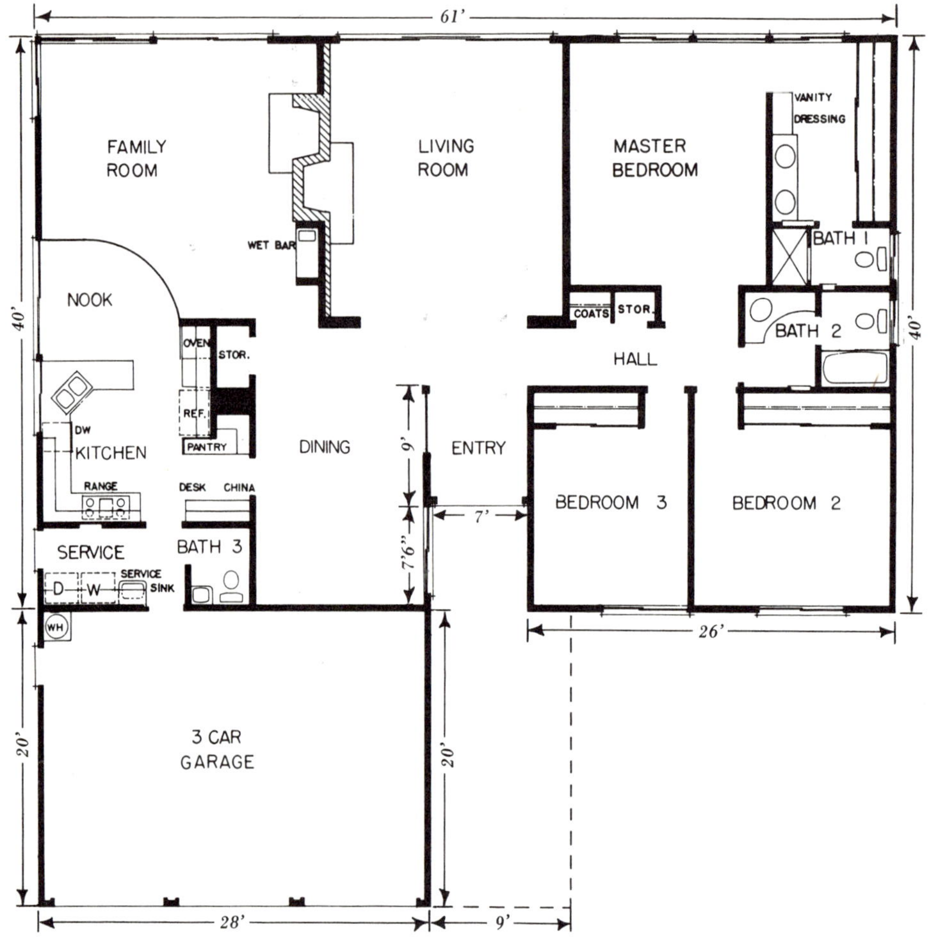
61'
FAMILY ROOM
LIVING ROOM
MASTER BEDROOM
VANITY
DRESSING
WET BAR
BATH 1
NOOK
COATS
STOR.
BATH 2
OVEN
STOR.
HALL
40'
40'
REF.
DW
KITCHEN
PANTRY
DINING
9'
ENTRY
RANGE
DESK
CHINA
7'
BEDROOM 3
BEDROOM 2
SERVICE
BATH 3
7'6"
D
W
SERVICE SINK
WH
26'
20'
3 CAR GARAGE
20'
28'
9'

SUBJECT RESIDENCE DESCRIPTION

FOUNDATION:	*Reinforced concrete perimeter footing and wall with continuous foundation under interior bearing walls. No abnormal soil conditions.*
STRUCTURAL FRAME:	*All frame members are wood. Quality of workmanship and materials is good.*
ROOF:	*Good quality wood shingles over 30 lb. felt on 1" x 6" spaced sheathing. Roof slope generally 4 in 12.*
INSULATION:	*4" rock wool batts placed between ceiling joists.*
INTERIOR FINISH:	*5/8" drywall, taped and spackled with paint, some wallpaper, and some hardwood paneling. Ceiling has drywall spray finish. Ceramic tile counter tops and splash in kitchen. Cultured marble wainscot at tub, stall shower and pullman tops.*
SASH AND DOORS:	*Painted hollow core doors throughout interior, sliding glass door in family room and living room, double door front entry and master bedroom, sliding aluminum sash with wood sills.*
FLOORS:	*Good quality shag carpeting on concrete slab. Kitchen, 1/2 bath and service porch floors are vinyl tile sheets. Ceramic tile in entry.*
PLUMBING:	*Thirteen good quality fixtures as follows: 1 glass enclosed tub with shower over, 1 stall shower with glass shower door, 4 lavatory sinks, 3 toilets, 1 kitchen sink, 1 wet bar, 1 laundry tray and washer dryer service, 1 water heater. Tub and sinks are cast iron.*
CABINETS AND CLOSETS:	*Adequate kitchen cabinets of good quality, natural hardwood with stain finish, large wardrobe type bedroom closets and shelved linen closet. Mirrored wardrobe doors in master dressing room.*
FIREPLACE:	*One stone veneered double fireplace of good quality, with ceramic tile hearths, and log lighters.*
HEATING AND COOLING:	*Gas fired forced air furnace. 5 ton refrigerated air conditioner utilizing forced air ducts with thermostat controls.*
ELECTRICAL:	*Flexible steel conduit, adequate outlets. Hanging light fixtures are of good quality. Recessed flourscent panel lighting in kitchen and master dressing room. Generous use of recessed fixtures throughout interior and exterior.*
BUILT-IN APPLIANCES:	*Good quality double electric oven and range, hood and fan, garbage disposer, and dishwasher.*
ATTACHED GARAGE:	*Wood frame with concrete slab floor and wood shingle roof. 3 overhead wood doors. Roof and exterior finish conform to that of the house.*
GENERAL QUALITY:	*Residence and garage reflect good quality workmanship and materials throughout.*

SQUARE FOOT APPRAISAL FORM

for use with the **RESIDENTIAL COST HANDBOOK**

Appraisal for ______ Property owner ______

Address ______

Appraiser ______ Date ______

TYPE		QUALITY		STYLE		EXTERIOR WALLS	
Conventional	☒	Low	☐	No. Stories ONE		Stucco	☒
Modern	☐	Fair	☐	Split level	☐	Siding or shingle	☐
Rustic	☐	Average	☐	1½ story - Fin.	☐	Brick veneer	☐
Apartment	☐	Good	☒	1½ story - Unfin.	☐	Common brick	☐
Town house	☐	Very good	☐	End row	☐	Face brick or stone	☐
Row house	☐			Inside row	☐	Concrete block	☐

Floor areas: 1st 2,388 2nd ______ 3rd ______ Total 2,388

Basement area: Unfinished NONE Finished ______ Garage area 560 Detached ☐ Attached ☒

Number multiple units ______ Total floor area ______ Built-in ☐ Carport ☐

Porches (a) 233 SQ. FT. (b) ______ Other ______ Number of plumbing fixtures THIRTEEN

APPRAISAL COMPUTATIONS

	Quan.	Cost	+	−	Extension
1. COMPUTE RESIDENCE BASIC COST: Floor area x selected sq. ft. cost	2,388	$17.61			$ 42,053
2. Basic residence cost adjustments Lines 3-13. Describe and indicate plus or minus			+	−	
3. Roofing WOOD SHINGLE (BASE)					
4. Flooring 1st floor CONCRETE SLAB @ -$.82 + CARPET @ $1.60	2,388	.78	+		1,863
5. Flooring upper floors NONE					
6. Heating - Cooling FORCED AIR, GAS (BASE) w/ REFRIG. A/C USING HTR DUCT	2,388	1.04	+		2,484
7. Ceiling insulation 4" ROCK WOOL BATTS	2,388	.18	+		430
8. Plumbing THIRTEEN FIXTURES (9 = BASE)	4	380	+		1,520
9. Built-in appliances BUILT-IN RANGE & OVEN, ELECTRIC @ $615;	1	615	+		615
10. RANGE HOOD & FAN @ $145; GARBAGE DISPOSER @ $135;	1	280	+		280
11. DISHWASHER @ $395	1	395	+		395
12. Fireplace DOUBLE, ONE STORY	1	1550	+		1,550
13. Miscellaneous					
14. SUBTOTAL ADJ. RESIDENCE COST: Line 1 plus or minus Lines 3-13					$ 51,190
15. BASEMENT, UNFINISHED					
16. Add for basement garage: Single ☐ Double ☐					
17. Add for basement outside entrance, below grade					
18. Add for basement interior finish					
19. Porches or balconies, describe OPEN SLAB @ $2.23 + ROOF @ $2.18 + CEIL. @ $.75	233	5.16	+		1,202
20.					
21. SUBTOTAL RESIDENCE COST: Total of Lines 14-20					$ 52,392
22. GARAGE OR CARPORT — sq. ft. area x selected sq. ft. cost	560	6.24	+		3,494
23. Attached garage — deduct for common wall	28	19.31		−	541
24. Garage roofing adjustment					
25. Garage miscellaneous					
26. SUBTOTAL GARAGE COST: Line 22 plus or minus Lines 23-25					2,953
27. SUBTOTAL OF ALL BUILDING IMPROVEMENTS: Sum of Lines 21 and 26					$ 55,345
28. Current local cost of buildings: Local multiplier 1.01 x Line 27					$ 55,898
29. Depreciation: Age ____ Condition ____ Deduction ____ % of Line 28					
30. Depreciated cost of building improvements: Line 28 less Line 29					
31. Yard improvements cost: List, total, apply local multiplier and depreciate on reverse side					
32. Landscaping cost: List and compute on reverse side					
33. Lot or land value					
34. **TOTAL INDICATED VALUE**: Total of Lines 30-33					

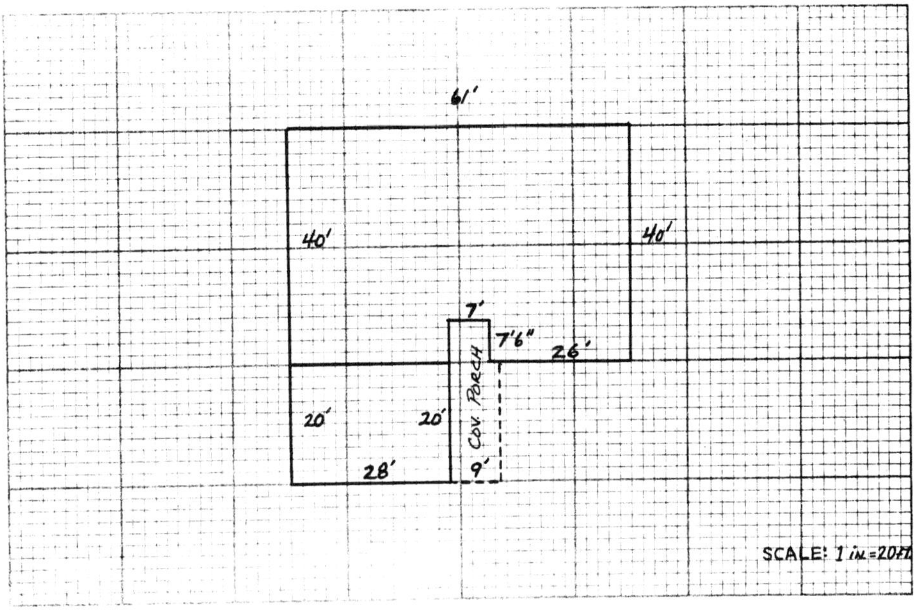

NOTES AND COMPUTATIONS

FLOOR AREA: 40.0' x 61.0' = 2,440 SQ FT.
LESS: 7.0' x 7.5' = − 52.5 SQ FT
TOTAL 2,387.5 OR 2,388 SQ FT

GARAGE AREA: 20.0' x 28.0' = 560 SQ FT

PORCH AREA: 20.0' x 9.0' = 180 SQ FT
7.0' x 7.5' = + 52.5 SQ FT
TOTAL 232.5 OR 233 SQ FT

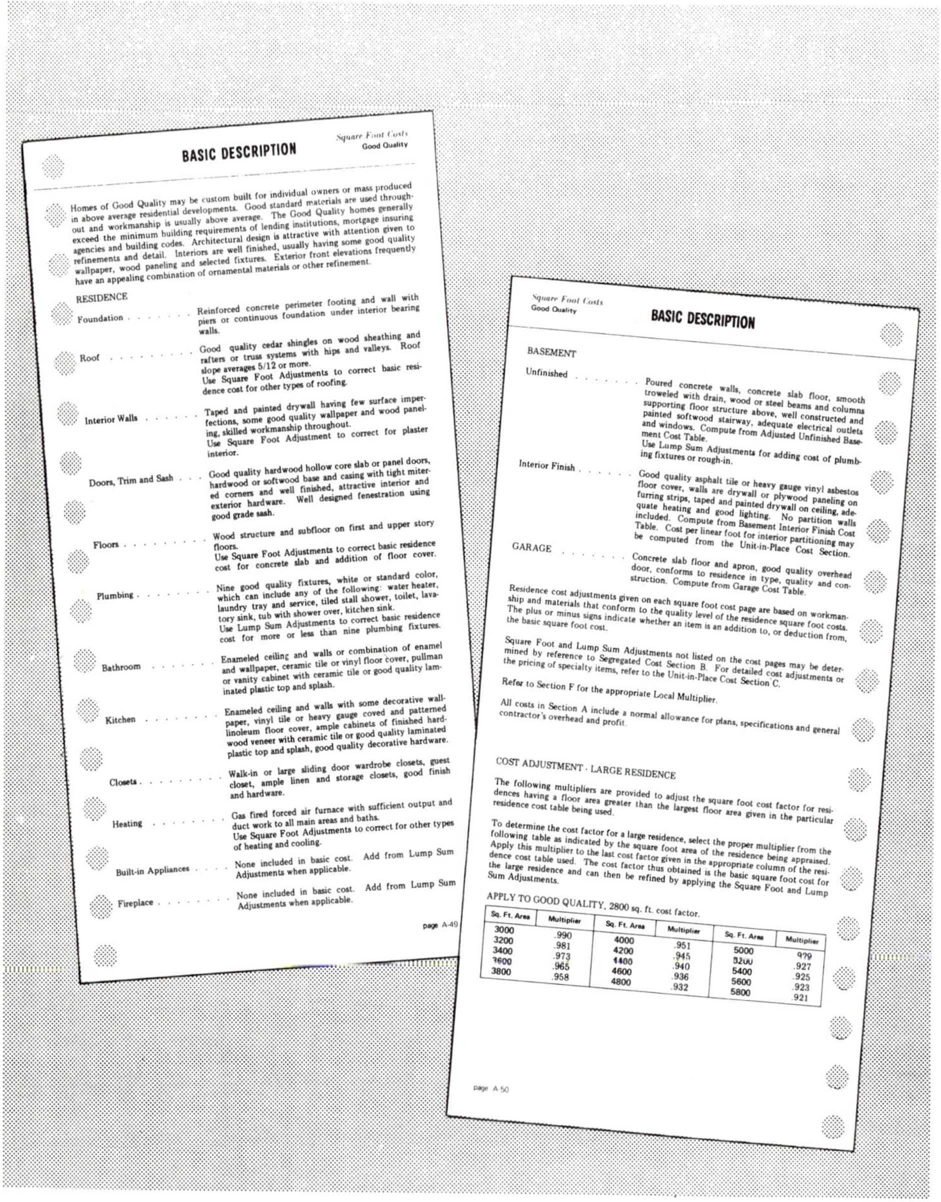

BASIC DESCRIPTION

Square Foot Costs
Good Quality

Homes of Good Quality may be custom built for individual owners or mass produced in above average residential developments. Good standard materials are used through-out and workmanship is usually above average. The Good Quality homes generally exceed the minimum building requirements of lending institutions, mortgage insuring agencies and building codes. Architectural design is attractive with attention given to refinements and detail. Interiors are well finished, usually having some good quality wallpaper, wood paneling and selected fixtures. Exterior front elevations frequently have an appealing combination of ornamental materials or other refinement.

RESIDENCE

Foundation . . . . Reinforced concrete perimeter footing and wall with piers or continuous foundation under interior bearing walls.

Roof . . . . Good quality cedar shingles on wood sheathing and rafters or truss systems with hips and valleys. Roof slope averages 5/12 or more.
Use Square Foot Adjustments to correct basic residence cost for other types of roofing.

Interior Walls . . . . Taped and painted drywall having few surface imperfections, some good quality wallpaper and wood paneling, skilled workmanship throughout.
Use Square Foot Adjustment to correct for plaster interior.

Doors, Trim and Sash . . . Good quality hardwood hollow core slab or panel doors, hardwood or softwood base and casing with tight mitered corners and well finished, attractive interior and exterior hardware. Well designed fenestration using good grade sash.

Floors . . . . Wood structure and subfloor on first and upper story floors.
Use Square Foot Adjustments to correct basic residence cost for concrete slab and addition of floor cover.

Plumbing . . . . Nine good quality fixtures, white or standard color, which can include any of the following: water heater, laundry tray and service, tiled stall shower, toilet, lavatory sink, tub with shower over, kitchen sink.
Use Lump Sum Adjustments to correct basic residence cost for more or less than nine plumbing fixtures.

Bathroom . . . . Enameled ceiling and walls or combination of enamel and wallpaper, ceramic tile or vinyl floor cover, pullman or vanity cabinet with ceramic tile or good quality laminated plastic top and splash.

Kitchen . . . . Enameled ceiling and walls with some decorative wallpaper, vinyl tile or heavy gauge coved and patterned linoleum floor cover, ample cabinets of finished hardwood veneer with ceramic tile or good quality laminated plastic top and splash, good quality decorative hardware.

Closets . . . . Walk-in or large sliding door wardrobe closets, guest closet, ample linen and storage closets, good finish and hardware.

Heating . . . . Gas fired forced air furnace with sufficient output and duct work to all main areas and baths.
Use Square Foot Adjustments to correct for other types of heating and cooling.

Built-in Appliances . . . . None included in basic cost. Add from Lump Sum Adjustments when applicable.

Fireplace . . . . None included in basic cost. Add from Lump Sum Adjustments when applicable.

page A-49

Square Foot Costs
Good Quality

BASIC DESCRIPTION

BASEMENT

Unfinished . . . . Poured concrete walls, concrete slab floor, smooth troweled with drain, wood or steel beams and columns supporting floor structure above, well constructed and painted softwood stairway, adequate electrical outlets and windows. Compute from Adjusted Unfinished Basement Cost Table.
Use Lump Sum Adjustments for adding cost of plumbing fixtures or rough-in.

Interior Finish . . . . . . Good quality asphalt tile or heavy gauge vinyl asbestos floor cover, walls are drywall or plywood paneling on furring strips, taped and painted drywall on ceiling, adequate heating and good lighting. No partition walls included. Compute from Basement Interior Finish Cost Table. Cost per linear foot for interior partitioning may be computed from the Unit-in-Place Cost Section.

GARAGE . . . . Concrete slab floor and apron, good quality overhead door, conforms to residence in type, quality and construction. Compute from Garage Cost Table.

Residence cost adjustments given on each square foot cost page are based on workmanship and materials that conform to the quality level of the residence square foot costs. The plus or minus signs indicate whether an item is an addition to, or deduction from, the basic square foot cost.

Square Foot and Lump Sum Adjustments not listed on the cost pages may be determined by reference to Segregated Cost Section B. For detailed cost adjustments or the pricing of specialty items, refer to the Unit-in-Place Cost Section C.

Refer to Section F for the appropriate Local Multiplier.

All costs in Section A include a normal allowance for plans, specifications and general contractor's overhead and profit.

COST ADJUSTMENT - LARGE RESIDENCE

The following multipliers are provided to adjust the square foot cost factor for residences having a floor area greater than the largest floor area given in the particular residence cost table being used.

To determine the cost factor for a large residence, select the proper multiplier from the following table as indicated by the square foot area of the residence being appraised. Apply this multiplier to the last cost factor given in the appropriate column of the residence cost table used. The cost factor thus obtained is the basic square foot cost for the large residence and can then be refined by applying the Square Foot and Lump Sum Adjustments.

APPLY TO GOOD QUALITY, 2800 sq. ft. cost factor.

Sq. Ft. Area	Multiplier	Sq. Ft. Area	Multiplier	Sq. Ft. Area	Multiplier
3000	.990	4000	.951	5000	.929
3200	.981	4200	.945	5200	.927
3400	.973	4400	.940	5400	.925
3600	.965	4600	.936	5600	.923
3800	.958	4800	.932	5800	.921

page A-50

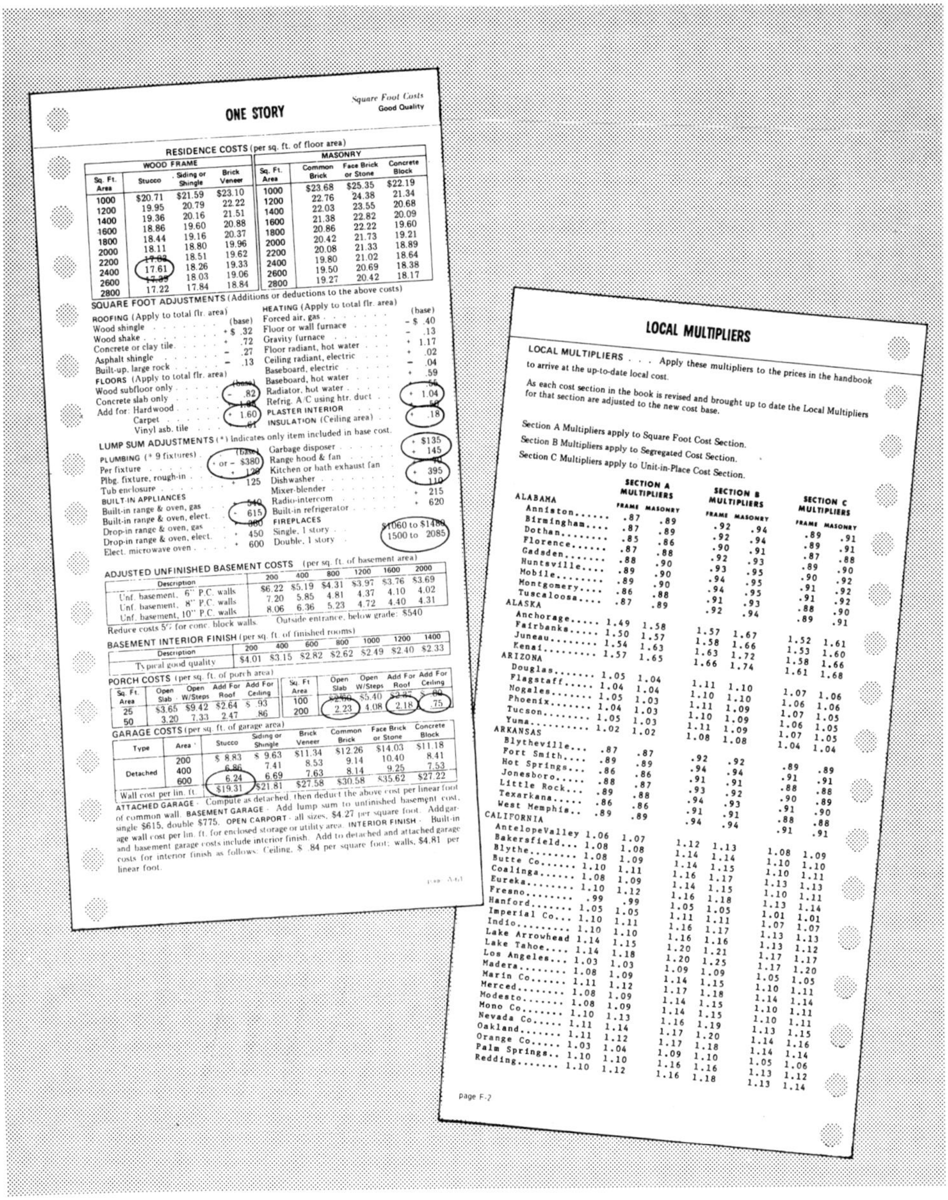

Square Foot Costs
Good Quality

ONE STORY

RESIDENCE COSTS (per sq. ft. of floor area)

WOOD FRAME				MASONRY			
Sq. Ft. Area	Stucco	Siding or Shingle	Brick Veneer	Sq. Ft. Area	Common Brick	Face Brick or Stone	Concrete Block
1000	$20.71	$21.59	$23.10	1000	$23.68	$25.35	$22.19
1200	19.95	20.79	22.22	1200	22.76	24.38	21.34
1400	19.36	20.16	21.51	1400	22.03	23.55	20.68
1600	18.86	19.60	20.88	1600	21.38	22.82	20.09
1800	18.44	19.16	20.37	1800	20.86	22.22	19.60
2000	18.11	18.80	19.96	2000	20.42	21.73	19.21
2200	[illegible]	18.51	19.62	2200	20.08	21.33	18.89
2400	17.61	18.26	19.33	2400	19.80	21.02	18.64
2600	[illegible]	18.03	19.06	2600	19.50	20.69	18.38
2800	17.22	17.84	18.84	2800	19.27	20.42	18.17

SQUARE FOOT ADJUSTMENTS (Additions or deductions to the above costs)

ROOFING (Apply to total flr. area)
Wood shingle (base)
Wood shake + $ .32
Concrete or clay tile + .72
Asphalt shingle − .27
Built-up, large rock − .13

FLOORS (Apply to total flr. area)
Wood subfloor only (base) − .82
Concrete slab only [illegible]
Add for: Hardwood + 1.60
Carpet .61
Vinyl asb. tile

HEATING (Apply to total flr. area)
Forced air, gas (base) − $ .40
Floor or wall furnace − .13
Gravity furnace + 1.17
Floor radiant, hot water + .02
Ceiling radiant, electric − .04
Baseboard, electric + .59
Baseboard, hot water .56
Radiator, hot water + 1.04
Refrig. A/C using htr. duct [illegible]
PLASTER INTERIOR + .18
INSULATION (Ceiling area)

LUMP SUM ADJUSTMENTS (*) Indicates only item included in base cost.

PLUMBING (* 9 fixtures) (base) + or − $380
Per fixture + 120
Plbg. fixture, rough-in + 125
Tub enclosure

BUILT-IN APPLIANCES
Built-in range & oven, gas 540 − 615
Built-in range & oven, elect. 880
Drop-in range & oven, gas + 450
Drop-in range & oven, elect. + 600
Elect. microwave oven

+ $135
Garbage disposer + 145
Range hood & fan 40
Kitchen or bath exhaust fan + 395
Dishwasher 110
Mixer-blender + 215
Radio-intercom + 620
Built-in refrigerator

FIREPLACES
Single, 1 story $1060 to $1480
Double, 1 story 1500 to 2085

ADJUSTED UNFINISHED BASEMENT COSTS (per sq. ft. of basement area)

Description	200	400	800	1200	1600	2000
Unf. basement, 6" P.C. walls	$6.22	$5.19	$4.31	$3.97	$3.76	$3.69
Unf. basement, 8" P.C. walls	7.20	5.85	4.81	4.37	4.10	4.02
Unf. basement, 10" P.C. walls	8.06	6.36	5.23	4.72	4.40	4.31

Reduce costs 5% for conc. block walls. Outside entrance, below grade: $540

BASEMENT INTERIOR FINISH (per sq. ft. of finished rooms)

Description	200	400	600	800	1000	1200	1400
Typical good quality	$4.01	$3.15	$2.82	$2.62	$2.49	$2.40	$2.33

PORCH COSTS (per sq. ft. of porch area)

Sq. Ft. Area	Open Slab	Open W/Steps	Add For Roof	Add For Ceiling
25	$3.65	$9.42	$2.64	$ .93
50	3.20	7.33	2.47	.86
100	[illegible]	$5.40	[illegible]	[illegible]
200	2.23	4.08	2.18	.75

GARAGE COSTS (per sq. ft. of garage area)

Type	Area	Stucco	Siding or Shingle	Brick Veneer	Common Brick	Face Brick or Stone	Concrete Block
Detached	200	$ 8.83	$ 9.63	$11.34	$12.26	$14.03	$11.18
	400	6.86	7.41	8.53	9.14	10.40	8.41
	600	6.24	6.69	7.63	8.14	9.25	7.53
Wall cost per lin. ft.		$19.31	$21.81	$27.58	$30.58	$35.62	$27.22

ATTACHED GARAGE - Compute as detached, then deduct the above cost per linear foot of common wall. BASEMENT GARAGE - Add lump sum to unfinished basement cost, single $615, double $775. OPEN CARPORT - all sizes, $4.27 per square foot. Add garage wall cost per lin. ft. for enclosed storage or utility area. INTERIOR FINISH - Built-in and basement garage costs include interior finish. Add to detached and attached garage costs for interior finish as follows: Ceiling, $ .84 per square foot; walls, $4.81 per linear foot.

page A-61

LOCAL MULTIPLIERS

LOCAL MULTIPLIERS . . . Apply these multipliers to the prices in the handbook to arrive at the up-to-date local cost.

As each cost section in the book is revised and brought up to date the Local Multipliers for that section are adjusted to the new cost base.

Section A Multipliers apply to Square Foot Cost Section.

Section B Multipliers apply to Segregated Cost Section.

Section C Multipliers apply to Unit-in-Place Cost Section.

	SECTION A MULTIPLIERS		SECTION B MULTIPLIERS		SECTION C MULTIPLIERS	
	FRAME	MASONRY	FRAME	MASONRY	FRAME	MASONRY
ALABAMA						
Anniston	.87	.89	.92	.94	.89	.91
Birmingham	.87	.89	.92	.94	.89	.91
Dothan	.85	.86	.90	.91	.87	.88
Florence	.87	.88	.92	.93	.89	.90
Gadsden	.88	.90	.93	.95	.90	.92
Huntsville	.89	.90	.94	.95	.91	.92
Mobile	.89	.90	.94	.95	.91	.92
Montgomery	.86	.88	.91	.93	.88	.90
Tuscaloosa	.87	.89	.92	.94	.89	.91
ALASKA						
Anchorage	1.49	1.58	1.57	1.67	1.52	1.61
Fairbanks	1.50	1.57	1.58	1.66	1.53	1.60
Juneau	1.54	1.63	1.63	1.72	1.58	1.66
Kenai	1.57	1.65	1.66	1.74	1.61	1.68
ARIZONA						
Douglas	1.05	1.04	1.11	1.10	1.07	1.06
Flagstaff	1.04	1.04	1.10	1.10	1.06	1.06
Nogales	1.05	1.03	1.11	1.09	1.07	1.05
Phoenix	1.04	1.03	1.10	1.09	1.06	1.05
Tucson	1.05	1.03	1.11	1.09	1.07	1.05
Yuma	1.02	1.02	1.08	1.08	1.04	1.04
ARKANSAS						
Blytheville	.87	.87	.92	.92	.89	.89
Fort Smith	.89	.89	.94	.94	.91	.91
Hot Springs	.86	.86	.91	.91	.88	.88
Jonesboro	.88	.87	.93	.92	.90	.89
Little Rock	.89	.88	.94	.93	.91	.90
Texarkana	.86	.86	.91	.91	.88	.88
West Memphis	.89	.89	.94	.94	.91	.91
CALIFORNIA						
AntelopeValley	1.06	1.07	1.12	1.13	1.08	1.09
Bakersfield	1.08	1.08	1.14	1.14	1.10	1.10
Blythe	1.08	1.09	1.14	1.15	1.10	1.11
Butte Co.	1.10	1.11	1.16	1.17	1.13	1.13
Coalinga	1.08	1.09	1.14	1.15	1.10	1.11
Eureka	1.10	1.12	1.16	1.18	1.13	1.14
Fresno	.99	.99	1.05	1.05	1.01	1.01
Hanford	1.05	1.05	1.11	1.11	1.07	1.07
Imperial Co.	1.10	1.11	1.16	1.17	1.13	1.13
Indio	1.10	1.10	1.16	1.16	1.13	1.12
Lake Arrowhead	1.14	1.15	1.20	1.21	1.17	1.17
Lake Tahoe	1.14	1.18	1.20	1.25	1.17	1.20
Los Angeles	1.03	1.03	1.09	1.09	1.05	1.05
Madera	1.08	1.09	1.14	1.15	1.10	1.11
Marin Co.	1.11	1.12	1.17	1.18	1.14	1.14
Merced	1.08	1.09	1.14	1.15	1.10	1.11
Modesto	1.08	1.09	1.14	1.15	1.10	1.11
Mono Co.	1.10	1.13	1.16	1.19	1.13	1.15
Nevada Co.	1.11	1.14	1.17	1.20	1.14	1.16
Oakland	1.11	1.12	1.17	1.18	1.14	1.14
Orange Co.	1.03	1.04	1.09	1.10	1.05	1.06
Palm Springs	1.10	1.10	1.16	1.16	1.13	1.12
Redding	1.10	1.12	1.16	1.18	1.13	1.14

page F-2

SEGREGATED COST APPRAISAL FORM

for use with the **RESIDENTIAL COST HANDBOOK**

1. Owner ______ Appraiser ______
2. Property Address ______
3. Quality GOOD Type CONVENTIONAL Number of Stories ONE Date ______

	UNITS	QUALITY	QUANTITY	UNIT COST	LUMP SUM EXTENSION
4. Foundation ONE STORY, FRAME & STUCCO	Square Ft. of Floor	GOOD	2,388	$.79	$ 1,887
5. Basement– Bulk Excavation	Cubic Ft. of Volume				
6. Wall	Square Ft. of Wall				
7. Floor/Ceiling	Square Ft. of Floor				
8. Stairway	Each				
9. Floors CONCRETE SLAB	Square Ft. of Floor	GOOD	2,388	1.08	2,579
10. CARPET (USE TOTAL FLR. AREA MINUS ENTRY FLR AREA)		GOOD	2,325	1.60	3,720
11. Exterior Wall STUCCO (PRIMARY)	Lineal Ft. of Wall	GOOD	217	32.37	7,024
12. Gable Wall NONE	Square Ft. of Wall				
13. Ceiling DRYWALL, SPRAY FIN. @ $.46 + CEIL. INSUL. @ $.17	Square Ft. of Floor	GOOD	2,388	.63	1,504
14. Roof WD. SHINGLE @ $2.25 x 1.06 (4 IN 12)	Square Ft. of 1st Floor	GOOD	2,388	2.39	5,707
15. Roof Dormers NONE	Lineal Ft. Across Face				
16. Interior Construction ONE STORY	Square Ft. of Floor	GOOD	2,388	4.64	11,080
17. Heating & Cooling COMBINED F.A. HEAT & REFRIG A/C	Square Ft. of Floor	AVG	2,388	1.73	4,131
18. Electrical FLEXIBLE STEEL CONDUIT	Square Ft. of Floor	GOOD	2,388	1.39	3,319
19. Plumbing THIRTEEN FIXTURES	Each	GOOD	13	370	4,810
20. Fireplace DBL-1 STY @ $1565 + 2 LOG LIGHTERS @ $50 EA.	Each	GOOD	1	1665	1,665
21. Built-in Appliances BUILT-IN RANGE & OVEN, ELEC @ $585	Each	GOOD	1	585	585
22. RANGE HOOD & FAN @ $140; GARBAGE DISPOSER @ $130		GOOD	1	270	270
23. DISHWASHER @ $380		GOOD	1	380	380
24. Stairways	Each				
25. Attic Finish	Square Ft. of Floor				
26. Porches SLAB @ $2.18 + ROOF @ $2.58 + CEIL. @ $.85	Square Ft. of Porch	GOOD	233	5.61	1,307
27. MISC: CERAMIC TILE @ $3.70 (PAGE C-6)		GOOD	63	3.70	233
28. Garage– Foundation FRAME - STUCCO	Lineal Ft. of Wall	GOOD	68	3.45	235
29. Exterior Wall STUCCO (PRIMARY)	Lineal Ft. of Wall	GOOD	68	15.86	1,078
30. Floor and Roof CONC. @ $.95 + SHING. @ $1.98 x 1.06 (4 IN 12) SLOPE MULT.	Square Ft. of Floor	GOOD	560	3.05	1,708
31. Subtotal of Building Improvements					$ 53,222
32. Current Local Cost of Building: Local Multiplier 1.06 X Line 31					$ 56,415
33. Depreciation: Age ______ Condition ______ Deduction ______ % of Line 32					
34. Depreciated Cost of Building Improvements: Line 32 Less Line 33					
35. Yard Improvements *(from back of form)*					
36. Lot or Land Value					
37. **TOTAL PROPERTY VALUE**					

FORM 1008

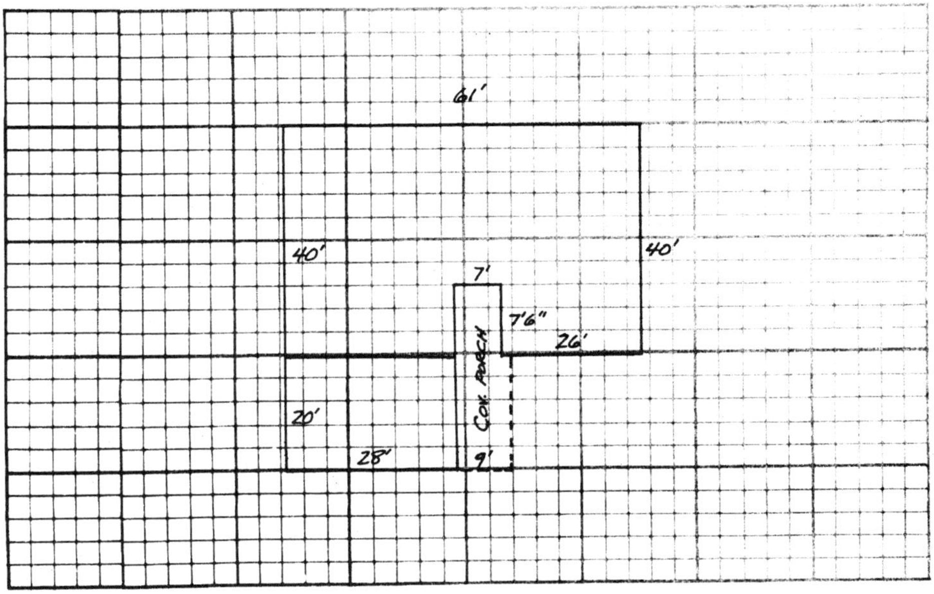

SKETCH AND PHOTOGRAPH

Yard Improvements	QUANTITY	UNIT COST	LUMP SUM EXTENSION
38. Fence			
39. Paving			
40. Landscaping			
41. Miscellaneous			
42.			
43.			
44.			
45. Total Yard Improvements			

COMPUTATIONS AND NOTES

RESIDENCE PERIMETER

REAR = 61 LINEAR FEET
RIGHT SIDE = 40 " "
FRONT = 28 + 7.5 + 7 + 7.5 + 26 = 76 " "
LEFT SIDE = 40 " "
TOTAL 217 LINEAR FEET

RESIDENCE FLOOR AREA

LIVING AREA: 40' x 61' = 2440 SQ. FT.
LESS 7' x 7.5' = 52.5 SQ. FT.
2,387.5 OR 2,388 SQ. FT.

GARAGE AREA: 20' x 28' = 560 SQ. FT.

PORCH AREA: 20' x 9' = 180 SQ. FT.
7.0' x 7.5' = 52.5 SQ. FT.
232.5 OR 233 SQ FT

FRONT ENTRY: 9' x 7' = 63 SQ. FT.

FORM 1008

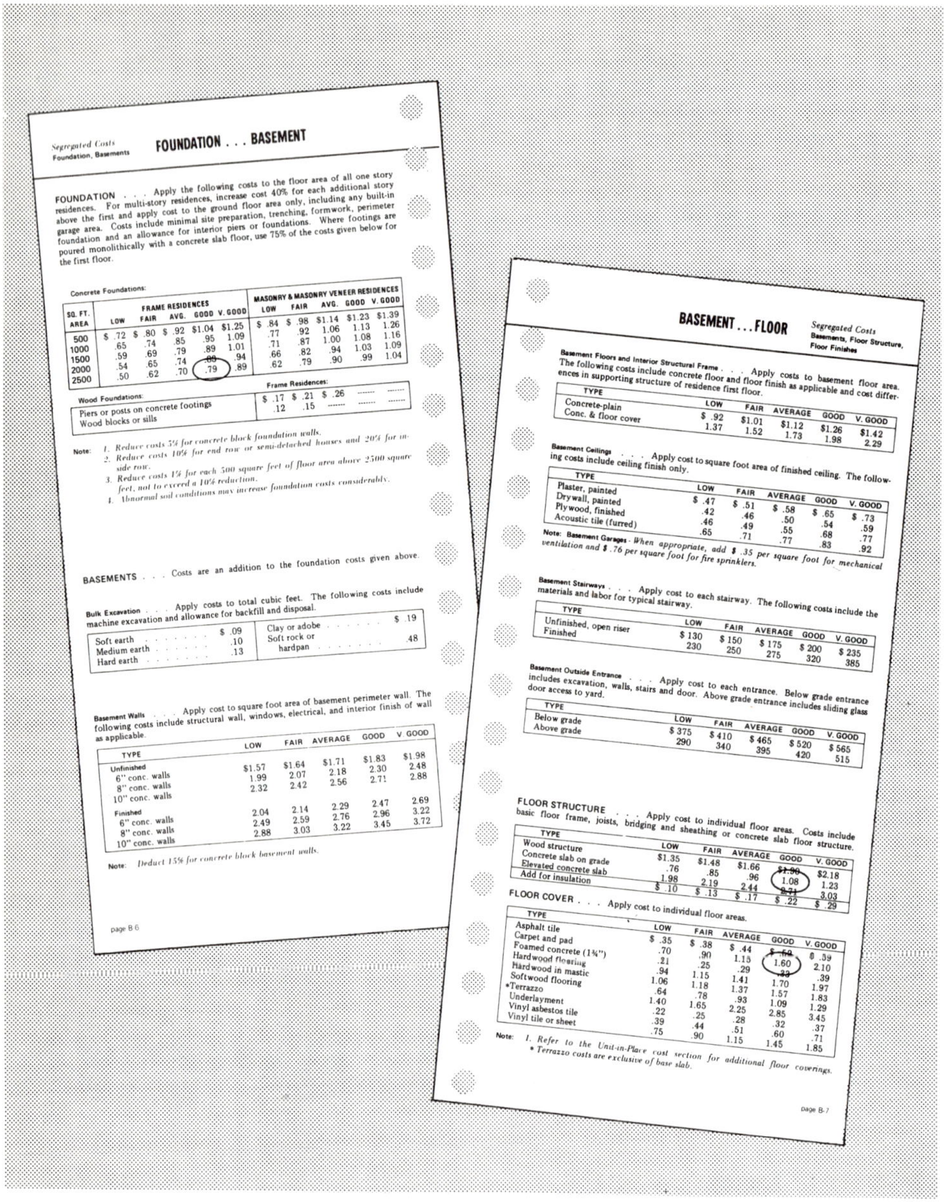

Segregated Costs
Foundation, Basements

FOUNDATION . . . BASEMENT

FOUNDATION . . . Apply the following costs to the floor area of all one story residences. For multi-story residences, increase cost 40% for each additional story above the first and apply cost to the ground floor area only, including any built-in garage area. Costs include minimal site preparation, trenching, formwork, perimeter foundation and an allowance for interior piers or foundations. Where footings are poured monolithically with a concrete slab floor, use 75% of the costs given below for the first floor.

Concrete Foundations:

SQ. FT. AREA	FRAME RESIDENCES LOW	FAIR	AVG.	GOOD	V. GOOD	MASONRY & MASONRY VENEER RESIDENCES LOW	FAIR	AVG.	GOOD	V. GOOD
500	$ .72	$ .80	$ .92	$1.04	$1.25	$ .84	$ .98	$1.14	$1.23	$1.39
1000	.65	.74	.85	.95	1.09	.77	.92	1.06	1.13	1.26
1500	.59	.69	.79	.89	1.01	.71	.87	1.00	1.08	1.16
2000	.54	.65	.74	[illegible]	.94	.66	.82	.94	1.03	1.09
2500	.50	.62	.70	.79	.89	.62	.79	.90	.99	1.04

Wood Foundations:

	Frame Residences:				
Piers or posts on concrete footings	$ .17	$ .21	$ .26	-------	-------
Wood blocks or sills	.12	.15	-------	-------	-------

Note:
1. *Reduce costs 5% for concrete block foundation walls.*
2. *Reduce costs 10% for end row or semi-detached houses and 20% for inside row.*
3. *Reduce costs 1% for each 500 square feet of floor area above 2500 square feet, not to exceed a 10% reduction.*
4. *Abnormal soil conditions may increase foundation costs considerably.*

BASEMENTS . . . Costs are an addition to the foundation costs given above.

Bulk Excavation . . . Apply costs to total cubic feet. The following costs include machine excavation and allowance for backfill and disposal.

Soft earth	$ .09	Clay or adobe	$ .19
Medium earth	.10	Soft rock or hardpan	.48
Hard earth	.13		

Basement Walls . . . Apply cost to square foot area of basement perimeter wall. The following costs include structural wall, windows, electrical, and interior finish of wall as applicable.

TYPE	LOW	FAIR	AVERAGE	GOOD	V. GOOD
Unfinished					
6" conc. walls	$1.57	$1.64	$1.71	$1.83	$1.98
8" conc. walls	1.99	2.07	2.18	2.30	2.48
10" conc. walls	2.32	2.42	2.56	2.71	2.88
Finished					
6" conc. walls	2.04	2.14	2.29	2.47	2.69
8" conc. walls	2.49	2.59	2.76	2.96	3.22
10" conc. walls	2.88	3.03	3.22	3.45	3.72

Note: *Deduct 15% for concrete block basement walls.*

page B-6

BASEMENT . . . FLOOR

Segregated Costs
Basements, Floor Structure, Floor Finishes

Basement Floors and Interior Structural Frame . . . Apply costs to basement floor area. The following costs include concrete floor and floor finish as applicable and cost differences in supporting structure of residence first floor.

TYPE	LOW	FAIR	AVERAGE	GOOD	V. GOOD
Concrete-plain	$ .92	$1.01	$1.12	$1.26	$1.42
Conc. & floor cover	1.37	1.52	1.73	1.98	2.29

Basement Ceilings . . . Apply cost to square foot area of finished ceiling. The following costs include ceiling finish only.

TYPE	LOW	FAIR	AVERAGE	GOOD	V. GOOD
Plaster, painted	$ .47	$ .51	$ .58	$ .65	$ .73
Drywall, painted	.42	.46	.50	.54	.59
Plywood, finished	.46	.49	.55	.68	.77
Acoustic tile (furred)	.65	.71	.77	.83	.92

Note: Basement Garages - *When appropriate, add $ .35 per square foot for mechanical ventilation and $ .76 per square foot for fire sprinklers.*

Basement Stairways . . . Apply cost to each stairway. The following costs include the materials and labor for typical stairway.

TYPE	LOW	FAIR	AVERAGE	GOOD	V. GOOD
Unfinished, open riser	$ 130	$ 150	$ 175	$ 200	$ 235
Finished	230	250	275	320	385

Basement Outside Entrance . . . Apply cost to each entrance. Below grade entrance includes excavation, walls, stairs and door. Above grade entrance includes sliding glass door access to yard.

TYPE	LOW	FAIR	AVERAGE	GOOD	V. GOOD
Below grade	$ 375	$ 410	$ 465	$ 520	$ 565
Above grade	290	340	395	420	515

FLOOR STRUCTURE . . . Apply cost to individual floor areas. Costs include basic floor frame, joists, bridging and sheathing or concrete slab floor structure.

TYPE	LOW	FAIR	AVERAGE	GOOD	V. GOOD
Wood structure	$1.35	$1.48	$1.66	$1.90	$2.18
Concrete slab on grade	.76	.85	.96	1.08	1.23
Elevated concrete slab	1.98	2.19	2.44	2.71	3.03
Add for insulation	$ .10	$ .13	$ .17	$ .22	$ .29

FLOOR COVER . . . Apply cost to individual floor areas.

TYPE	LOW	FAIR	AVERAGE	GOOD	V. GOOD
Asphalt tile	$ .35	$ .38	$ .44	$ .52	$ .59
Carpet and pad	.70	.90	1.15	1.60	2.10
Foamed concrete (1¾")	.21	.25	.29	.33	.39
Hardwood flooring	.94	1.15	1.41	1.70	1.97
Hardwood in mastic	1.06	1.18	1.37	1.57	1.83
Softwood flooring	.64	.78	.93	1.09	1.29
*Terrazzo	1.40	1.65	2.25	2.85	3.45
Underlayment	.22	.25	.28	.32	.37
Vinyl asbestos tile	.39	.44	.51	.60	.71
Vinyl tile or sheet	.75	.90	1.15	1.45	1.85

Note: *1. Refer to the Unit-in-Place cost section for additional floor coverings.*
** Terrazzo costs are exclusive of base slab.*

page B-7

Segregated Costs
Exterior Wall, Gable, Ceiling

EXTERIOR WALL . . . CEILING

EXTERIOR WALL . . . Apply costs to lineal feet of exterior wall. The following costs include exterior finish, wall structure, interior finish, sash and exterior doors. Ceiling height, eight feet.

First story wall costs per lineal foot of perimeter

TYPE	LOW	FAIR	AVERAGE	GOOD	V. GOOD
Aluminum siding	$22.51	$26.54	$31.42	~~$30.64~~	$41.81
Asbestos or stucco	19.80	23.49	27.70	32.37	37.81
Wood siding or shingle	20.36	24.80	29.94	~~35.02~~	42.66
Brick veneer	26.27	30.95	37.02	44.03	52.30
Common brick	$30.10	$35.01	$40.01	$47.30	$57.20
Face brick	36.64	40.47	46.06	54.15	64.61
Stone, rough or cut	43.23	49.37	57.58	66.06	76.24
Concrete block	24.26	29.20	34.94	41.27	49.69
Insulation per lineal foot	$ .80	$ .88	$ 1.04	$ 1.28	$ 1.60

Note: *1. Reduce costs 10% for common walls of attached dwellings.*
2. Refer to Unit-in-Place cost section for above grade basement wall exterior finish or additional ornamentation of exterior walls.

Multistory wall cost adjustment . . . For each foot of additional height above first story, add to the first story exterior wall costs as follows:

TYPE	LOW	FAIR	AVERAGE	GOOD	V. GOOD
Aluminum siding	$ 2.19	$ 2.58	$ 3.06	$ 3.56	$ 4.07
Asbestos or stucco	1.93	2.27	2.69	3.15	3.67
Wood siding or shingle	1.98	2.41	2.91	3.49	4.15
Brick veneer	2.55	3.01	3.61	4.28	5.08
Common brick	$ 2.99	$ 3.40	$ 3.90	$ 4.59	$ 5.56
Face brick	3.56	3.95	4.48	5.27	6.28
Stone, rough or cut	4.20	4.82	5.61	6.43	7.41
Concrete block	2.37	2.82	3.40	4.02	4.84
Insulation per square ft.	$ .10	$ .11	$ .13	$ .16	$ .20

Note: *Reduce costs 30% for common walls of attached dwellings.*

GABLE WALL . . . Cost per square foot of gable wall. The following costs include gable wall structure and exterior finish only.

TYPE	LOW	FAIR	AVERAGE	GOOD	V. GOOD
Aluminum siding	$ 1.32	$ 1.39	$ 1.55	$ 1.77	$ 1.99
Asbestos or stucco	1.08	1.21	1.41	1.64	1.95
Wood siding or shingle	1.19	1.30	1.48	1.74	2.04
Brick veneer	1.46	1.58	1.84	2.16	2.52
Common brick	$ 2.19	$ 2.39	$ 2.70	$ 3.15	$ 3.64
Face brick	2.65	2.81	3.18	3.62	4.20
Stone, rough or cut	3.13	3.43	3.98	4.42	4.96
Concrete block	1.80	1.99	2.32	2.73	3.24

CEILING . . . Apply cost to total floor area. The following costs include finished ceiling only. Joists are included with roof cost.

TYPE	LOW	FAIR	AVERAGE	GOOD	V. GOOD
Drywall, painted	$ .42	$ .45	$ .49	$ .54	$ .60
Plaster, painted	.47	.52	.57	~~.65~~	.76
Drywall, sprayed plaster	.35	.39	.42	.46	.51
Tile, acoustic (furred)	.66	.71	.77	~~.88~~	.92
Plywood, painted	.46	.50	.55	.65	.83
Exposed beam, paint only	.20	.22	.25	~~.29~~	.33
Add for insulation	$ .11	$ .12	$ .14	$ .17	$ .21

ROOF . . . INTERIOR

Segregated Costs
Roof, Dormers, Interior Construction

ROOF STRUCTURE AND COVER . . . Apply costs to first floor area.

With Ceiling Joists . . . The following costs include ceiling joists, roof frame, 1" sheathing and roofing. Adjust selected cost by roof slope multipliers given below.

TYPE	LOW	FAIR	AVERAGE	GOOD	V. GOOD
Asphalt shingle	$1.53	$1.67	$1.83	$1.99	$2.25
Built-up, rock	1.49	1.66	1.87	~~2.18~~	2.43
Wood shingle	1.68	1.85	2.04	2.25	2.50
Rigid asbestos shingle	1.84	2.01	2.19	~~2.40~~	2.74
Wood shakes	1.94	2.13	2.34	2.57	2.82
Clay (mission) tile	2.49	2.66	2.85	3.07	3.32
Concrete tile (light weight)	2.38	2.51	2.67	2.84	3.04
• Slate	2.88	3.06	3.26	3.55	3.96

With Exposed Beam Ceiling . . . The following costs include heavy roof frame, 2" sheathing, roofing and insulation.

TYPE	LOW	FAIR	AVERAGE	GOOD	V. GOOD
Asphalt shingle	$1.79	$1.95	$2.14	$2.32	$2.63
Built-up, rock	1.73	1.92	2.17	2.47	2.82
Wood shingle	1.97	2.16	2.39	2.63	2.93
Rigid asbestos shingle	2.15	2.35	2.56	2.81	3.21
Wood shakes	2.23	2.45	2.69	2.96	3.24
Clay (mission) tile	2.71	2.90	3.11	3.35	3.61
Concrete tile (light weight)	2.67	2.81	2.99	3.18	3.40
Slate	3.20	3.40	3.62	3.94	4.40

Roof slope multipliers:

	Rise	:	Run	Multiplier	Rise	:	Run	Multiplier
Less than	3	in	12	1.00	6	in	12	1.12
	3	in	12	~~1.03~~	8	in	12	1.20
	4	in	12	1.06	12	in	12	1.42
	5	in	12	~~1.08~~	18	in	12	1.80

ROOF DORMERS . . . Apply costs to lineal feet, measured across face of dormer. Do not include sides. Costs are for dormer frame, exterior finish and roof. Interior finish cost for dormers is automatically computed from floor, ceiling and other segregated cost tables if dormer floor area is included in total residence floor area.

TYPE	LOW	FAIR	AVERAGE	GOOD	V. GOOD
Hip or gable roof	$29.50	$34.00	$40.00	$46.00	$56.50
Shed roof	24.00	28.50	34.50	40.00	47.00

INTERIOR CONSTRUCTION . . . Apply cost to total floor area. The following costs include drywall interior partitions, finish, interior doors and cabinet work.

TYPE	LOW	FAIR	AVERAGE	GOOD	V. GOOD
One Story	$3.06	$3.39	$3.84	$4.64	$5.91
Split Level	2.88	3.16	3.51	~~4.22~~	5.32
Two Story	2.70	2.92	3.17	3.79	4.72
One & One-Half Story, finished	2.74	2.98	3.25	3.92	4.91
One & One-Half Story, unfin.	3.38	3.74	4.22	5.07	6.24
Multiple Residence	3.73	4.12	4.68	5.33	6.32
Town or Row House					
One Story	3.58	3.86	4.18	4.71	5.52
Multi-Story	3.37	3.57	3.80	4.19	4.81
Add for plaster walls	$ .39	$ .42	$ .45	$ .49	$ .56

Segregated Costs
Heating-Cooling, Electrical, Plumbing, Fireplaces

MECHANICAL . . . ELECTRICAL

HEATING AND COOLING . . . Apply costs to total floor area being heated and cooled. Costs include all equipment, convectors and controls.

TYPE: HEATING	LOW	FAIR	AVERAGE	GOOD	V. GOOD
Forced air furnace, electric	$ .76	$ .84	$ .93	$1.06	$1.17
Forced air furnace, gas	.67	.72	.81	.90	1.02
Gas outlets only	.15	.16	.18	.20	.24
Glass panel, electric	.62	.66	.73	.82	.91
Gravity furnace, gas	.55	.61	.69	.77	.88
Floor or wall furnace	.37	.40	.44	.50	.60
Baseboard, electric	.65	.70	.77	.87	.98
Baseboard, hot water, gas	1.09	1.20	1.34	1.49	1.73
Baseboard, steam, gas	1.04	1.12	1.22	1.40	1.56
Radiators, hot water, gas	1.08	1.15	1.26	1.45	1.67
Radiators, steam, gas	.82	.90	.99	1.13	1.31
Floor radiant, hot water, gas	1.60	1.72	1.87	2.07	2.28
Ceiling radiant, electric	.68	.74	.82	.91	1.02
Wall heaters, electric	.33	.36	.40	.45	.52
COOLING					
Evaporative, no ducts	$ .25	$ .27	$ .30	$ .36	$ .38
Evaporative, w/ducts	.49	.51	.54	.61	.68
Refrig. A/C, w/ducts	.98	1.05	1.21	1.41	1.67
COMBINED HEATING & COOLING					
F.A. heat & refrig. A/C	$1.49	$1.60	$1.73	$1.94	$2.31
Heat pump system	1.83	2.03	~~2.20~~	2.54	2.84
VENTILATION					
Blowers and ducts	$ .19	$ .21	$ .23	$ .26	$ .30

Note: *1. Add 10% to gas heating systems if oil fired.*
2. Window type refrigerated coolers range in cost from $325 to $450 per ton capacity, including installation, depending upon size, type and local sources of supply. In determining ton capacity, a one horsepower motor produces approximately one ton of cooling. Add wiring allowance of $70 for 220 volt units. For heat pumps (reverse cycle AC) add 25%.

ELECTRICAL . . . Apply cost to total floor area. Costs include house service, wiring and light fixtures commensurate with quality.

TYPE	LOW	FAIR	AVERAGE	GOOD	V. GOOD
Romex (non-metallic sheathing) or knob and tube	$ .59	$ .67	$ .76	$ .90	$1.08
B.X. (steel armored cable)	.68	.75	.87	~~1.12~~	1.37
Flex (flexible steel conduit)	.82	.92	1.13	1.39	1.76
Rigid conduit	.99	1.17	1.43	~~1.78~~	2.28

PLUMBING . . . Apply cost to each plumbing fixture, including water heater as one fixture. The following costs include all rough and finish plumbing.

UNIT	LOW	FAIR	AVERAGE	GOOD	V. GOOD
Avg. cost per fixture	$240	$280	$320	$370	$425
Avg. cost, rough-in only	80	90	100	~~115~~	140

FIREPLACES . . . Apply cost to each fireplace. The following costs include complete fireplace. Double fireplaces are back-to-back or one directly above the other, using a common chimney.

TYPE	LOW	FAIR	AVERAGE	GOOD	V. GOOD
Single, one story	$560	$ 775	$ 905	$1105	$1380
Single, two story	680	950	1120	~~1355~~	1680
Double, one story	740	1020	1260	1565	1895
Double, two story	850	1175	1450	~~1700~~	2145
Add for: Heatilator type	$ 85	$ 105	$ 135	$ 175	$ 230
Raised Hearth	55	75	95	~~120~~	165
Log Lighter	30	35	40	50	60

Note: *Free standing metal fireplace costs are located in the Unit-in-Place Section.*

page B-10

BUILT-INS . . . STAIRWAYS

Segregated Costs
Built-in Appliances, Stairways, Attics

BUILT-IN APPLIANCES . . . Apply cost to each built-in appliance. Costs include installation, extra utility outlets and cabinet work as applicable.

APPLIANCE	LOW	FAIR	AVERAGE	GOOD	V. GOOD
Range & oven, gas (built-in)	$ 370	$ 420	$ 465	$ 520	$ 585
Range & oven combination, gas	265	280	310	~~366~~	430
Range & oven, electric (built-in)	405	470	525	585	645
Range & oven combination, elec.	300	330	375	~~430~~	495
Oven, elect. microwave (built-in)	------	------	495	~~505~~	710
Range fan and hood	80	95	115	140	185
Exhaust fan	45	50	55	~~65~~	85
Refrigerator-freezer (built-in)	370	435	515	~~595~~	695
Dishwasher	265	310	340	380	430
Mixer-blender	70	80	90	~~108~~	125
Garbage disposer	85	95	110	130	155
Radio-intercom	140	160	185	~~210~~	240
Add per satellite	20	25	30	35	45
Gas incinerator	225	250	270	310	360
Vacuum cleaner system	475	505	555	610	675
Bathroom heater, electric	40	50	70	80	95
Trash compactor	250	265	285	320	370
FREE STANDING APPLIANCES					
Refrigerator	$ 190	$ 245	$ 330	$ 430	$ 635
Washer	155	200	260	340	415
Dryer	115	150	195	260	340

Note: *Free standing appliance costs do not include plumbing, electrical or cabinet work.*

STAIRWAYS . . . Apply cost to each full flight of stairs. The following costs include stair framing, finish and railings. For partial flights, use proportionate cost.

Interior Stairways

FRAME - FINISH	LOW	FAIR	AVERAGE	GOOD	V. GOOD
Wood-softwood	$ 275	$ 340	$ 425	$ 520	$ 635
Wood-hardwood	345	430	535	675	795

Exterior Stairways

FRAME - FINISH	LOW	FAIR	AVERAGE	GOOD	V. GOOD
Wood-softwood	$ 195	$ 245	$ 305	$ 375	$ 475
Wood-cement compo.	375	435	510	615	740
All steel	420	505	605	755	935

BALCONIES OR STAIR LANDINGS . . . Apply cost to floor area.

QUALITY	WOOD FLOOR		CEMENT COMPOSITION FLOOR	
	WOOD RAIL	ORN. IRON RAIL	WOOD RAIL	ORN. IRON RAIL
Low	$4.41	$5.69	$5.24	$6.58
Fair	4.80	6.23	5.76	7.19
Average	5.41	6.95	6.43	7.91
Good	6.14	7.80	7.20	8.83
Very Good	7.01	8.89	8.08	9.98

Note: *1. Add for balcony roofs from porch roof table. 2. Add for plastered balcony ceiling or soffit $ .70 to $ .95 per square foot commensurate with quality.*

ATTICS . . . Attic finish may be priced from the appropriate Segregated and Unit-in-Place Cost tables or the following cost range can be used: $3.45 to $4.75 per square foot of floor area. Costs include softwood floors and stairway, drywall ceiling and walls, wiring, and gable windows. Plumbing and partition walls are not included and may be added from the Unit-in-Place Cost tables.

Segregated Costs
Porches, Carports

PORCHES . . . CARPORTS

PORCHES . . . Apply all component costs to porch floor area.

Open Concrete Porches - Including Perimeter Foundation

QUALITY	25 SQ. FT. WITH STEPS	25 SQ. FT. SLAB	100 SQ. FT. WITH STEPS	100 SQ. FT. SLAB	200 SQ. FT. WITH STEPS	200 SQ. FT. SLAB
Low	$6.75	$2.59	$4.23	$1.90	$3.13	$1.72
Fair	7.79	2.99	4.80	2.14	3.57	1.94
Average	8.48	3.26	5.01	2.33	3.79	~~2.05~~
Good	9.19	3.56	5.27	2.54	3.98	(2.18)
Very Good	9.83	3.73	5.44	2.65	4.17	~~2.25~~

Note: *Use $.90 per square foot for slab porches or patios without perimeter foundation.*

Open Wood Porches or Decks - With Wood Steps

QUALITY	25 SQ. FT.	100 SQ. FT.	200 SQ. FT.	300 SQ. FT.
Low	$4.49	$3.51	$3.10	$2.76
Fair	4.98	4.04	3.60	3.15
Average	5.63	4.59	4.18	3.66
Good	6.56	5.38	4.80	4.24
Very Good	7.61	6.27	5.49	4.86

Note: *Increase cost 5% for each foot of height above 3 feet.*

Add For Porch Roof and Posts - (No Ceiling Included)

TYPE	LOW	FAIR	AVERAGE	GOOD	V. GOOD
Asphalt shingle	$1.76	$1.92	$2.10	$2.28	$2.58
Built-up, rock	1.71	1.91	2.14	~~2.45~~	2.79
Wood shingle	1.92	2.12	2.34	(2.58)	2.87
Rigid asbestos shingle	2.11	2.31	2.51	~~2.76~~	3.15
Wood shakes	2.23	2.45	2.69	2.95	3.24
Clay (mission) tile	2.86	3.05	3.27	3.52	3.81
Concrete tile (light weight)	2.73	2.88	3.06	3.26	3.49
Slate	3.31	3.51	3.74	4.08	4.55

Add For Porch Ceiling

TYPE	LOW	FAIR	AVERAGE	GOOD	V. GOOD
Plaster	$ .66	$ .71	$ .77	($ .85)	$ .95
Wood, painted	.59	.65	.74	~~.87~~	1.05
Hardboard, painted	.52	.56	.61	.68	.73

CARPORTS . . . Apply costs to floor area of carport. The following costs include roofing, roof frame, supporting posts and bracing, painting and concrete slab.

TYPE	LOW	FAIR	AVERAGE	GOOD	V. GOOD
Asphalt shingle	$2.89	$3.26	$3.99	$4.78	$6.06
Built-up, rock	2.80	3.25	4.07	5.15	6.56
Wood shingle	3.15	3.60	4.45	5.42	6.74
Rigid asbestos shingle	3.46	3.93	4.77	5.80	7.40
Wood shakes	3.66	4.17	5.11	6.20	7.61
Clay (mission) tile	4.69	5.19	6.21	7.39	8.95
Concrete tile (light weight)	4.48	4.90	5.81	6.85	8.21
Slate	5.43	5.97	7.11	8.57	10.69
Deduct for asphalt floor	.32	.36	.39	.45	.49

Note:
1. *For pitched roof, use residence roof slope multipliers.*
2. *Use appropriate garage foundation, wall and ceiling costs for enclosed storage and utility areas.*
3. *Porch ceiling costs may be added to the above costs when appropriate.*

page B-12

Unit-in-Place Costs
Concrete Slab, Floor Cover, Hardwood

UNIT-IN-PLACE COSTS

CONCRETE STEPS

Cost per linear foot $3.70

CONCRETE SLAB . . Cost per sq. ft.

4" slab	$ .77
Reinforcing mesh	.12
Gravel or sand base	.13
Vapor barrier	.07
Total	$1.09

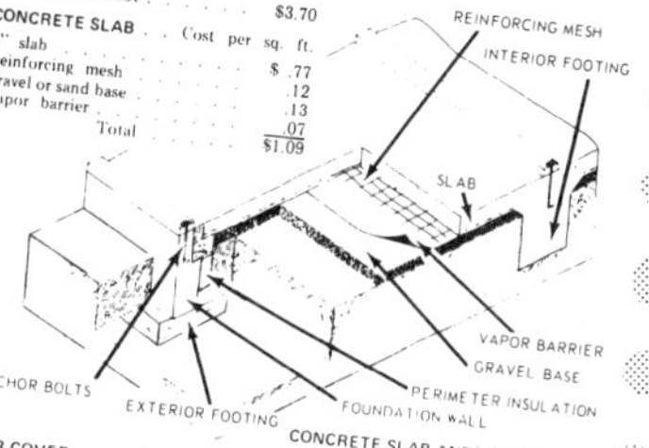

CONCRETE SLAB AND FOUNDATION

FLOOR COVER . . . Cost per square foot.

	FAIR	AVG	GOOD		FAIR	AVG	GOOD
Asphalt tile	$ .41	$ .49	$ .62	Quarry tile	$2.95	$3.20	$3.50
Brick, mortar	1.54	1.87	2.29	Rubber tile	1.03	1.17	1.53
Carpeting	.80	1.20	~~1.70~~	Slab color	.15	.22	.30
Ceramic tile	2.85	3.10	(3.70)	Slate	2.70	2.95	3.45
Cork tile	1.01	1.30	~~1.66~~	Softwood	.78	.93	1.09
Diato	1.13	1.34	1.65	*Terrazzo	1.65	2.40	3.60
Flagstone	2.19	2.61	3.25	Underlayment	.28	.30	.35
Foamed Conc.	.27	.35	.42	Vinyl tile	.96	1.29	1.69
Linoleum	.69	.91	1.17	Vin. asb. tile	.45	.54	.63
Marble	5.28	6.72	8.70	Vinyl sheet	.90	1.35	1.80

*Terrazzo costs are exclusive of base slab.

HARDWOOD . . . Cost per square foot.

	COMMON	SELECT	CLEAR
Strip, 2-1/4" x 1/2"	$1.35	$1.65	$1.95
Strip, 2-1/4" x 13/16"	1.65	2.00	2.35
Plank, imitation, 13/16"	1.85	2.25	2.65
Parquet, 13/16"	1.90	2.35	2.80
Parquet, 1/2" in mastic	1.65	1.95	2.35
Parquet, 13/16" in mastic	1.90	2.30	2.65
Pegged and grooved, 13/16"	2.15	2.65	3.05

COVE BASE . . . Cost per linear foot.

Ceramic tile	$2.80
Rubber topset	.74
Terrazzo	3.40
Vinyl topset	.72

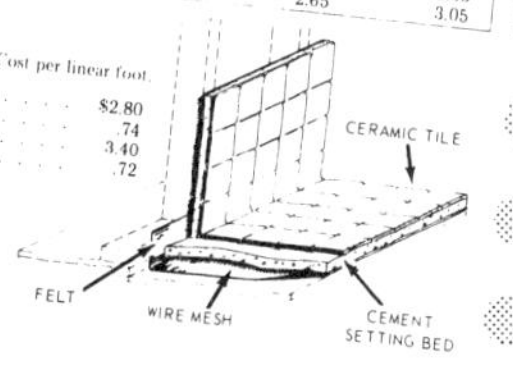

CERAMIC TILE FLOOR & WALL

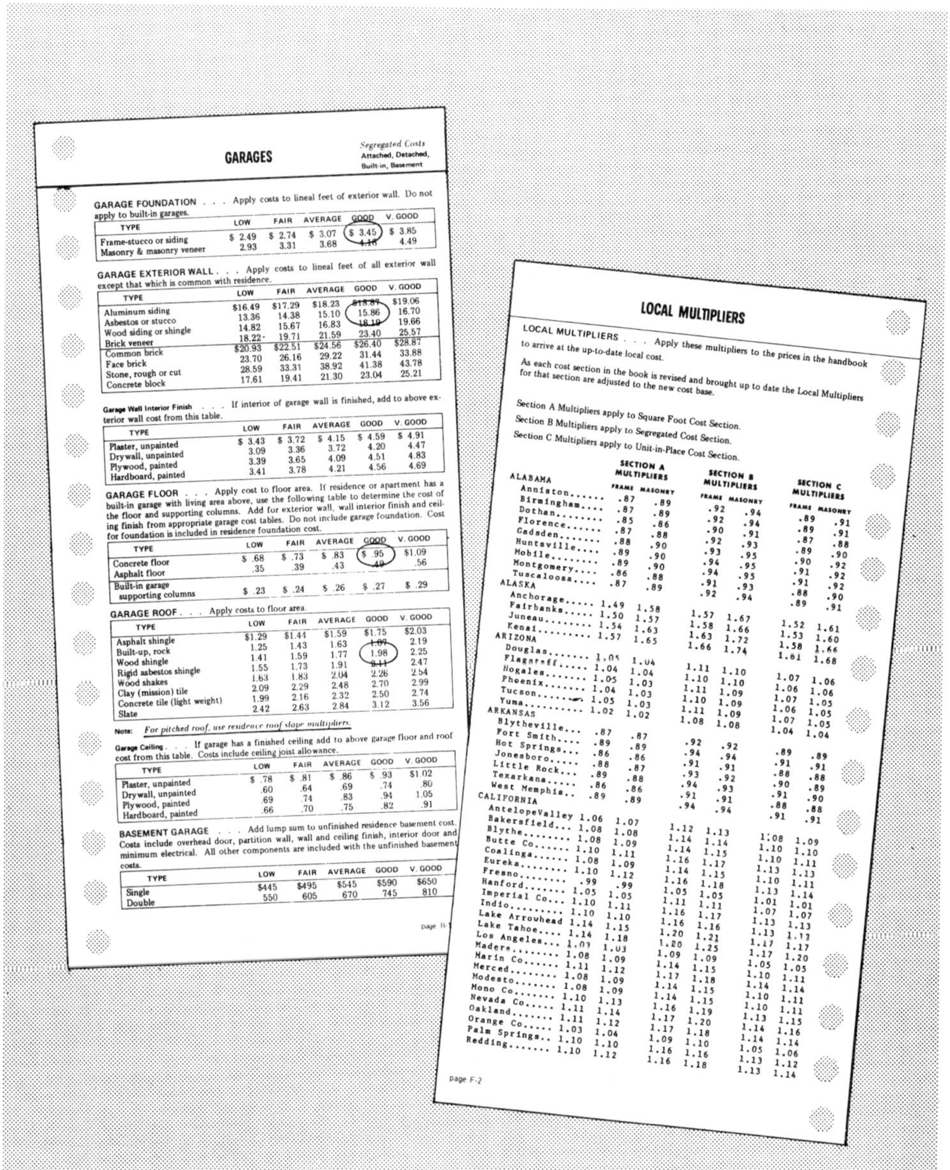

GARAGES

Segregated Costs
Attached, Detached, Built-in, Basement

GARAGE FOUNDATION . . . Apply costs to lineal feet of exterior wall. Do not apply to built-in garages.

TYPE	LOW	FAIR	AVERAGE	GOOD	V. GOOD
Frame-stucco or siding	$ 2.49	$ 2.74	$ 3.07	$ 3.45	$ 3.85
Masonry & masonry veneer	2.93	3.31	3.68	~~4.18~~	4.49

GARAGE EXTERIOR WALL . . . Apply costs to lineal feet of all exterior wall except that which is common with residence.

TYPE	LOW	FAIR	AVERAGE	GOOD	V. GOOD
Aluminum siding	$16.49	$17.29	$18.23	~~$18.87~~	$19.06
Asbestos or stucco	13.36	14.38	15.10	15.86	16.70
Wood siding or shingle	14.82	15.67	16.83	~~18.19~~	19.66
Brick veneer	18.22	19.71	21.59	23.40	25.57
Common brick	$20.93	$22.51	$24.56	$26.40	$28.87
Face brick	23.70	26.16	29.22	31.44	33.88
Stone, rough or cut	28.59	33.31	38.92	41.38	43.78
Concrete block	17.61	19.41	21.30	23.04	25.21

Garage Wall Interior Finish . . . If interior of garage wall is finished, add to above exterior wall cost from this table.

TYPE	LOW	FAIR	AVERAGE	GOOD	V. GOOD
Plaster, unpainted	$ 3.43	$ 3.72	$ 4.15	$ 4.59	$ 4.91
Drywall, unpainted	3.09	3.36	3.72	4.20	4.47
Plywood, painted	3.39	3.65	4.09	4.51	4.83
Hardboard, painted	3.41	3.78	4.21	4.56	4.69

GARAGE FLOOR . . . Apply cost to floor area. If residence or apartment has a built-in garage with living area above, use the following table to determine the cost of the floor and supporting columns. Add for exterior wall, wall interior finish and ceiling finish from appropriate garage cost tables. Do not include garage foundation. Cost for foundation is included in residence foundation cost.

TYPE	LOW	FAIR	AVERAGE	GOOD	V. GOOD
Concrete floor	$ .68	$ .73	$ .83	$ .95	$1.09
Asphalt floor	.35	.39	.43	~~.49~~	.56
Built-in garage supporting columns	$ .23	$ .24	$ .26	$ .27	$ .29

GARAGE ROOF . . . Apply costs to floor area.

TYPE	LOW	FAIR	AVERAGE	GOOD	V. GOOD
Asphalt shingle	$1.29	$1.44	$1.59	$1.75	$2.03
Built-up, rock	1.25	1.43	1.63	~~1.87~~	2.19
Wood shingle	1.41	1.59	1.77	1.98	2.25
Rigid asbestos shingle	1.55	1.73	1.91	~~2.11~~	2.47
Wood shakes	1.63	1.83	2.04	2.26	2.54
Clay (mission) tile	2.09	2.29	2.48	2.70	2.99
Concrete tile (light weight)	1.99	2.16	2.32	2.50	2.74
Slate	2.42	2.63	2.84	3.12	3.56

Note: *For pitched roof, use residence roof slope multipliers.*

Garage Ceiling . . . If garage has a finished ceiling add to above garage floor and roof cost from this table. Costs include ceiling joist allowance.

TYPE	LOW	FAIR	AVERAGE	GOOD	V. GOOD
Plaster, unpainted	$ .78	$ .81	$ .86	$ .93	$1.02
Drywall, unpainted	.60	.64	.69	.74	.80
Plywood, painted	.69	.74	.83	.94	1.05
Hardboard, painted	.66	.70	.75	.82	.91

BASEMENT GARAGE . . . Add lump sum to unfinished residence basement cost. Costs include overhead door, partition wall, wall and ceiling finish, interior door and minimum electrical. All other components are included with the unfinished basement costs.

TYPE	LOW	FAIR	AVERAGE	GOOD	V. GOOD
Single	$445	$495	$545	$590	$650
Double	550	605	670	745	810

page B-1

LOCAL MULTIPLIERS

LOCAL MULTIPLIERS . . . Apply these multipliers to the prices in the handbook to arrive at the up-to-date local cost.

As each cost section in the book is revised and brought up to date the Local Multipliers for that section are adjusted to the new cost base.

Section A Multipliers apply to Square Foot Cost Section.
Section B Multipliers apply to Segregated Cost Section.
Section C Multipliers apply to Unit-in-Place Cost Section.

	SECTION A MULTIPLIERS		SECTION B MULTIPLIERS		SECTION C MULTIPLIERS	
	FRAME	MASONRY	FRAME	MASONRY	FRAME	MASONRY
ALABAMA						
Anniston	.87	.89	.92	.94	.89	.91
Birmingham	.87	.89	.92	.94	.89	.91
Dothan	.85	.86	.90	.91	.87	.88
Florence	.87	.88	.92	.93	.89	.90
Gadsden	.88	.90	.93	.95	.90	.92
Huntsville	.89	.90	.94	.95	.91	.92
Mobile	.89	.90	.94	.95	.91	.92
Montgomery	.86	.88	.91	.93	.88	.90
Tuscaloosa	.87	.89	.92	.94	.89	.91
ALASKA						
Anchorage	1.49	1.58	1.57	1.67	1.52	1.61
Fairbanks	1.50	1.57	1.58	1.66	1.53	1.60
Juneau	1.54	1.63	1.63	1.72	1.58	1.66
Kenai	1.57	1.65	1.66	1.74	1.61	1.68
ARIZONA						
Douglas	1.05	1.04	1.11	1.10	1.07	1.06
Flagstaff	1.04	1.04	1.10	1.10	1.06	1.06
Nogales	1.05	1.03	1.11	1.09	1.07	1.05
Phoenix	1.04	1.03	1.10	1.09	1.06	1.05
Tucson	1.05	1.03	1.11	1.09	1.07	1.05
Yuma	1.02	1.02	1.08	1.08	1.04	1.04
ARKANSAS						
Blytheville	.87	.87	.92	.92	.89	.89
Fort Smith	.89	.89	.94	.94	.91	.91
Hot Springs	.86	.86	.91	.91	.88	.88
Jonesboro	.88	.87	.93	.92	.90	.89
Little Rock	.89	.88	.94	.93	.91	.90
Texarkana	.86	.86	.91	.91	.88	.88
West Memphis	.89	.89	.94	.94	.91	.91
CALIFORNIA						
AntelopeValley	1.06	1.07	1.12	1.13	1.08	1.09
Bakersfield	1.08	1.08	1.14	1.14	1.10	1.10
Blythe	1.08	1.09	1.14	1.15	1.10	1.11
Butte Co.	1.10	1.11	1.16	1.17	1.13	1.13
Coalinga	1.08	1.09	1.14	1.15	1.10	1.11
Eureka	1.10	1.12	1.16	1.18	1.13	1.14
Fresno	.99	.99	1.05	1.05	1.01	1.01
Hanford	1.05	1.05	1.11	1.11	1.07	1.07
Imperial Co.	1.10	1.11	1.16	1.17	1.13	1.13
Indio	1.10	1.10	1.16	1.16	1.13	1.12
Lake Arrowhead	1.14	1.15	1.20	1.21	1.17	1.17
Lake Tahoe	1.14	1.18	1.20	1.25	1.17	1.20
Los Angeles	1.03	1.03	1.09	1.09	1.05	1.05
Madera	1.08	1.09	1.14	1.15	1.10	1.11
Marin Co.	1.11	1.12	1.17	1.18	1.14	1.14
Merced	1.08	1.09	1.14	1.15	1.10	1.11
Modesto	1.08	1.09	1.14	1.15	1.10	1.11
Mono Co.	1.10	1.13	1.16	1.19	1.13	1.15
Nevada Co.	1.11	1.14	1.17	1.20	1.14	1.16
Oakland	1.11	1.12	1.17	1.18	1.14	1.14
Orange Co.	1.03	1.04	1.09	1.10	1.05	1.06
Palm Springs	1.10	1.10	1.16	1.16	1.13	1.12
Redding	1.10	1.12	1.16	1.18	1.13	1.14

page F-2

APPENDIX F

FNMA—FHLMC Form Guidelines

APPRAISAL REPORT—SINGLE FAMILY RESIDENCE*

Purpose:	This form is to be used by the appraiser who was previously nominated and recommended by the Seller to FNMA and determined to be acceptable by FNMA. This form is required for appraisals on all single family mortgages offered to FNMA for purchase.
Prepared by:	Seller and Appraiser (Typed or legibly printed.) The Seller is to give a copy of these instructions to each appraiser on the Seller's list of appraisers who are acceptable to FNMA.
Signed by:	Appraiser
Prepare:	Original and three copies.
Distribution:	Original and one copy (with original photographs) to be forwarded to FNMA with the Seller's Request for Approval of Property. Seller should retain third copy and appraiser should retain fourth copy.

INSTRUCTIONS

A. The Seller must complete the portion of the form entitled "to be completed by lender" prior to giving the form to the designated appraiser.

B. The appraiser may use carbon copies or make machine photo-copies of the original report, but, irrespective of the method of duplicating, the appraiser must place an original signature on the original and each copy of the report.

C. The appraisal form may be printed in either ink, ball point pen, pencil, or typewritten. When the report is prepared in pencil, the original of the report in pencil should be retained as the appraiser's file copy and photocopies should be used for the two copies sent to FNMA and the one copy retained by the Seller.

When the appraisal report is printed in either pen or pencil it must be done in a neat, orderly and legible manner. Evey effort should be made to insure that the completed form is neat and easy to read. An "X" should be used when checking the appropriate boxes on the form.

*Source: George F. Bloom and Henry S. Harrison, *Appraising the Single Family Residence* (Chicago: American Institute of Real Estate Appraisers, 1978). Reprinted with the permission of the publisher.

In addition to being neat, the form should be well documented. Any changes or corrections in the report, particularly the final value estimate, should be crossed out and initialed by the appraiser, rather than erased.

D. Since the appraisal report form is short, all blanks must be filled in and all boxes checked as appropriate. In addition, the appraiser is to use the space provided in each section of the report for explanatory comments.

The following instructions are arranged by sections in the order found in the form.

GUIDELINES

I. *Lender's (Seller's) Section*:

All of the information requested in the section at the top of page one is to be furnished by the Seller prior to giving the form to the appraiser for a particular assignment. The property rights appraised are to be indicated by checking the appropriate box and the sale price of the subject property, loan charges to be paid by the seller of the property, and other sales concessions, are to be entered in the spaces provided.

Instructions to the appraiser will generally consist of directions to the property and the means of gaining access thereto.

II. *Neighborhood Description and Analysis*

Nothing in the form or the attachments thereto is intended to preclude the appraiser from considering the social and economic characteristics of the neighborhood to the extent that they presently, or are likely to, affect the value of the subject property. However, the appraiser is to report detrimental neighborhood conditions in factual, specific terms by giving the addresses of the affected properties and an exact description of the nature of the conditions involved in each case. For example: "There are junked and abandoned cars (or refrigerators, etc.) in the front (or rear) yards of the properties at (addresses);" or, "the houses at (addresses) are vacant (or boarded up, or vandalized as evidenced by broken windows, etc.);" or, "a lack of maintenance is evident in the neighborhood by uncut grass (or peeling paint, or fallen gutters and downspouts, etc.) at (addresses)." Furthermore, if the value trend in the neighborhood is declining as a result of detrimental conditions, statements to that effect must be supported by reporting actual property sales which demonstrate the trend. Such information may be provided in the comment section or in an addendum to the report.

Major considerations in this section of the form which may require further explanation and instruction are:

1. *Present Land Use*—enter the estimated percentage of each type of property in the neighborhood. If the use is other than one of those indicated on the form, enter the percentage and state the type in the spaces provided. Use "O" where none of the listed uses are in evidence. The total of uses must equal 100%.
2. *Change in Present Land Use*—indicate by checking the appropriate box what your professional judgment indicates to be the trend of change in land uses in the neighborhood. Major factors to be considered in this category include present uses, market supply and demand, and zoning. If change is likely or is already taking place, state from what

use and give the use to which the neighborhood is in transition. Elaborate further on such changes in the comment section or in a separate addendum.

3. *Predominant Occupancy*—indicate the predominant type of occupancy by checking the appropriate box or giving the estimated percentage of vacancy. It should be emphasized that this question refers to occupancy rather than to building types. For example, if the neighborhood consists of two family properties of which 90% are owner-occupied, then the owner box should be checked. If there is only a relatively small preponderance of owners over tenants (e.g. 60% owners vs. 40% tenants), then this situation should be reported in the comment section since the long term stability of the neighborhood could be adversely affected for single family residential purposes.
4. *Single Family Price Range*—enter the lowest and highest typical prevailing prices of single family residential properties in the neighborhood. However, isolated extremes at either end of the range should not be reported. Also, state the predominant price most frequently found.
5. *Single Family Age*—give the typical age range of single family properties in the neighborhood together with the predominant age. Do not report occasional extremes at either end of the range.

Neighborhood Rating Grid—as part of the neighborhood analysis, the appraiser is also to rate the various characteristics of the neighborhood in terms of good, average, fair or poor. These ratings are to be based on comparison by the appraiser of the subject neighborhood with competing neighborhoods as to the present and probable future characteristics listed while recognizing the effect of these factors upon continued market appeal for residential purposes.

The quality ratings which the appraiser is being asked to provide are defined as follows:

Good—this rating is to be applied when the characteristics being considered are outstanding and superior to those found in competing neighborhoods.

Average—this indicates that the factors being rated are equal to the norm found to be acceptable in competing neighborhoods.

Fair—this rating is to be used where the factors concerned are below what is typical for comparable neighborhoods.

Poor—a rating of this nature is appropriate if the characteristics under consideration are either non-existent or in such small supply that single family residential values are, or may be, adversely affected.

In connection with these ratings, it should be noted that the appraiser must explain in the comment section the reasons for any ratings of "fair" or "poor." A separate addendum to the report should be used for this purpose if necessary.

Neighborhood Rating Factors—the following represent some of the considerations which should enter into rating the various aspects of the neighborhood. In this connection, the appraiser should remember that these ratings are based upon competitive locations and, therefore, should never rate a neighborhood in one price range against a non-competitive area. It should also be noted that different income and user groups may place more weight on some factors than others.

Employment Stability—consideration should be given to the number of employment opportunities and the variety and type of industries in the community. One-industry or cyclical industry areas would normally not be rated as favorably as those having a broader variety of employment with greater stability.

Convenience to Employment—the distance, both in terms of time and mileage, is to be considered here. This factor is particularly important in view of the increasing cost of gasoline. The availability, cost, and convenience of public transportation is also to be considered as an alternative to customary means of private transportation.

Convenience to Shopping—rate the neighborhood in terms of distance, time, and required means of transportation, to shopping for daily necessities.

Convenience to Schools—consider the time and distance to schools. If bus transportation is required, travel time is a factor.

Quality of Schools—the reputation of neighborhood schools and/or the school system as a whole for quality education to the extent that it affects real restate value is to be considered here.

Recreational Facilities—consider the number, type, and quality of such facilities available in the neighborhood as compared to competing neighborhoods. The extent to which such facilities are expected by the market for properties in the subject's price range is also a consideration.

Adequacy of Utilities—rate the extent to which the utility systems (water, sewer, electricity, and gas, if the latter is available) serving the neighborhood are adequate to serve the residents' needs as compared to similar neighborhoods. Consideration of utilities includes public, private (community or subdivision) and individual.

Property Compatibility—factors to be considered in this category include the types of land uses prevalent in the neighborhood, lot sizes, price ranges, and building ages and styles.

Protection from Detrimental Conditions—the appraiser is to consider here the extent to which present, or probable future, land uses or environmental conditions presently, or are likely to, adversely affect single family residential property values in the neighborhood.

Police and Fire Protection—this rating covers the extent to which these services are adequate and equivalent to those provided for competing neighborhoods.

General Appearance of Properties—consider the extent to which properties in the subject neighborhood are receiving proper maintenance (both buildings and yards) to preserve property values.

Appeal to Market—this is essentially an overall summary rating of the extent to which all aspects of the property and the neighborhood will appeal to the market—i.e. an indication of the marketability of the subject property and the neighborhood.

Comments—in addition to the factors already mentioned, about which further explanation is to be given, this section should be used to elaborate upon any favorable or unfavorable aspects of the neighborhood which have not been adequately covered in the preceding analysis and which are likely to affect the long term stability of property values in the neighborhood. In summary, the basis for any deductions for economic obsolescence in the Cost Approach should be made evident in this section.

III. *Site Description and Analysis*:

Detailed instructions are being given herein only for those items which may not be self-explanatory.

Zoning Classification—state the zoning category as designated by the local zoning code and the major permitted uses.

Highest and Best Use—this factor is critical and deserving of thorough analysis. Do not automatically check the box indicating the present use. If some other use would be more appropriate on the basis of zoning, market demand, and predominant land uses in the neighborhood, state the use specifically. Further explanation should then be provided in the comment section.

Electricity, Water, Sewer, etc.—"public" means governmentally supplied and regulated. It does not, therefore, include community systems sponsored, owned, or operated by the developer or a private company not subject to government regulation or financial assistance. If such systems are found, further explanation thereof must be given in the comment section or an addendum to the report.

Off-Site Improvements—if access to the subject property is by private street or other such right-of-way, describe the nature thereof and provision for maintenance in the comment section or attach an addendum giving details.

Topo, Size, Shape, etc.—provide a brief description of these features of the subject site and how they compare to other sites in the neighbrohood. Elaborate under comments if additional information is needed to clarify an item.

Comments—this space is for further explanation of favorable and unfavorable factors which affect the value of the site. The appraiser should also describe any easements, encroachments, or other detrimental conditions.

IV. *Description of Improvements*:

Detailed instructions are set forth herein only to the extent that the information desired in the form may need clarification.

Number of Units—this should be one unit in all cases since a different appraisal form is required for a greater number of units.

Number of Stories—this is the number of above-grade floors of finished living area and should be the same number used to calculate the gross living area in the Cost Approach.

Exterior Walls—specify the material used for the exterior wall covering, such as wood siding (e.g.—clapboard, board and batten, etc.), shingles, or brick. If the latter, specify whether veneer or solid masonry (either brick or brick on some form of masonry block).

Roof Material—state the material used for roof covering—e.g. wood shingles or shakes, asphalt or asbestos shingles, tile, etc.

Gutters and Downspouts—specify the material used for both. If none are present, the appraiser should state the width of the roof overhang and note the site grading around the foundation walls together with any evidence of dampness in the basement.

Windows—list the type of windows—e.g. casement (wood or metal), sliding, double hung (wood or metal), etc.

Insulation—the appraiser should make every effort to determine and report the extent and adequacy of insulation since this is likely to have an increasing effect upon the value of the property due to the high cost of energy.

Foundation Walls—specify the material used—e.g. poured concrete, cinder or concrete block, etc.

Basement—calculate and enter the percentage of basement area in relation to first floor area and indicate the various features requested on the form to the extent present. Also, indicate the existence of any adverse conditions by checking the boxes provided. If the basement is partially finished, estimate and state the percentage of finished area to total area. Also, state the materials used for ceiling, wall, and floor finish.

Comments—the appraiser should here describe any physical deterioration or functional inadequacy found in the basic structure. Such conditions should then be reflected in the estimate of depreciation in the Cost Approach.

Room List—enter the number of each type of room on every level. For this purpose, baths are calculated as follows: three plumbing fixtures (wash bowl, toilet, tub or shower) constitute one bathroom, two fixtures are a half bathroom, one fixture (toilet only) is a quarter bathroom, and one fixture (wash bowl only) is a wash room and is listed under "other." The total count of rooms, bedrooms, and baths is to be reported for the finished area above grade only. These totals will then be used for the subject in the Market Data Analysis.

Interior Finish and Equipment:

1. *Floors*—this is intended to describe the floor finish in the major portion of the house. If hardwood, so indicate by checking the box provided for this purpose. If wall-to-wall carpeting, state the material over which the carpet is installed. If some other type of floor covering prevails, check the third box on the line and state the material. Floor covering in the kitchen or other areas such as the foyer may be described under special features.
2. *Trim/Finish*—this question refers to the sufficiency of this item as well as the quality of materials and workmanship. The definitions of good, average, fair, and poor to be applied in rating this item are the same as set forth in the section on Neighborhood Description.
3. *Bath Floor and Wainscot*—if other than ceramic, check the appropriate box and state the material.
4. *Special Features*—describe any features not mentioned previously in the report such as other floor finish, fireplaces (including location thereof), and built-ins (e.g. cabinets, bookcases, etc.)

Property Rating Grid—the property ratings indicate how the subject property compares to competing properties as to quality and soundness of construction, convenience of living, and appeal to the market. All of these factors have a major effect upon the marketability of any single family property. The rating factors of good, average, fair and poor are the same as previously defined in the instructions for the Neighborhood Description.

Quality of Construction—consideration is to be given to the quality of workmanship throughout and the quality and durability of materials used in all components of the building.

Condition of Improvements—the appraiser is to rate the condition of the building and is to take note of all aspects of physical depreciation and report these in the comment section.

Room Sizes and Layout—this item includes consideration of the adequacy of room sizes as well as proportions of the rooms and sufficient wall area to permit appropriate furniture groupings. The layout is to be rated as to the extent to which it facilitates the proper flow of traffic, privacy of sleeping areas, and easy access to all rooms without interfering with the intended use of other rooms. Stairways, halls, and doors must also have adequate width. A rating below average should be reflected by an estimate for functional obsolescence in the Cost Approach. Conversely, if a deduction is made for functional obsolescence, it should be supported by appropriate ratings in this item and "Overall Livability."

Closets and Storage—rate the adequacy and convenience of closets and general storage as compared to competing properties. This is an important item which can have a substantial effect on liveability and marketability and should, therefore, not be ignored by the appraiser.

Plumbing—Adequacy and Condition—considerations affecting this item include the number, style, and condition of plumbing fixtures; the materials used for piping and the condition thereof; and the proper operation of any on-site water or septic systems. In the event that the evaluation of adequacy and condition does not permit a single rating, the appraiser should give two ratings and explain or indicate which rating applies to each factor.

Electrical—Adequacy and Condition—this rating includes the adequacy of electrical service available within the building, the number and location of outlets and switches, the quality and condition of the wiring, and the adequacy and style of lighting fixtures. Split ratings are to be handled in the manner described above.

Kitchen Cabinets—rate the adequacy of the amount of kitchen storage space provided in relation to the likely number of occupants of the house. The style, quality, and condition of the cabinets are also factors in the rating to be given.

Compatibility to Neighborhood—this rating is to indicate the extent to which the size, age, price, architectural design, and construction of the subject property conform to the neighborhood.

Overall Livability—this rating basically represents a composite of all of the above factors to the extent that they contribute to the sense of comfort and satisfaction likely to be experienced by an owner/occupant of the property.

Appeal and Marketability—consideration is to be given here to the overall appeal of the subject property to the market based on the above factors together with the architectural attractiveness of the property and, therefore, the demand which will probably be generated by the particular combination of these factors.

Effective Age—the appraiser is to report the estimated effective age of the subject property, as distinct from its chronological age, based on its utility and condition.

Remaining Economic Life—state here the estimated remaining number of years over which the improvements can still be expected to make a contribution to the value of the property.

Porches, Patios, Pools, Fences, etc.—describe all improvements which have not previously been mentioned and which will be included in the cost and market approaches.

Comments—the appraiser is to make specific, factual comments here on the reasons for any ratings of fair or poor. Furthermore, it is in this space that the appraiser must specifically describe all items of physical depreciation, whether curable or incurable, and provide an itemized listing of repairs needed to cure deferred maintenance together with the cost thereof.

If more space is required, a separate addendum sheet should be attached to the report. The appraiser should bear in mind at all times that the comments in this section will form the basis and support for the estimate of physical depreciation in the Cost Approach. If new construction, the appraiser is also to comment on whether the property is covered by the Home Owner's Warranty program.

V. *Required Attachments to Form*:

Photos—attach to the report on a separate sheet, quality (sharp and clear) photos of the front and rear of the subject property as well as at least one street scene which includes the subject property. It is not necessary or even desirable to attach the photos in the margin at the bottom of page one of the form as indicated on the form.

Location map—submit, as an attachment to the report, a sketch or copy of a map showing the location of the subject property, its relation to major traffic arteries, distance to the nearest intersection, and the location of any favorable factors or detrimental conditions as previously reported in the neighborhood description.

Exterior Building Sketch—submit, as an attachment to the report, a perimeter plan of the building (not necessarily to scale) showing the exterior building lines with dimensions which must correspond to those used in the gross building area calculations set forth in the Cost Approach. In both cases, inches should be converted to tenths of a foot. Dimensions must be shown for every exterior wall. An interior layout would be helpful to the reviewer and may be provided in conjunction with the sketch but is optional.

VI. *Cost Approach*:

Building Area Calculations—measurements must be exact and be the same as those shown in the exterior building sketch. The total gross building area thus calculated is to be entered on the line calling for "Total Gross Living Area." This is to include finished and habitable above-grade living area only. Finished basement or attic areas are to be calculated and shown separately for use in the cost estimate but are not to be included in the total gross living area.

Comment on Functional & Economic Obsolescence—use this space to fully describe the causes of these forms of obsolescence and support the estimate of the loss in value. No comment as to physical depreciation is needed here since it will already have been explained and estimated in the comment section of the building description.

Estimate of Reproduction Cost New—note that what is required here is reproduction cost—i.e., the cost of reproducing the subject structure using the same materials and workmanship as well as the same layout. It is, however, recognized that in some cases typically involving older buildings containing obsolete materials or unusual functional features, it will be difficult, if not impossible, to estimate reproduction cost new with any reasonable degree of accuracy. In such cases, therefore, replacement cost may be used but then this should be specifically stated along with a description of the materials and quality upon which the estimate of replacement cost is based as well as the functional deficiencies thereby eliminated.

Extras—these are to include such items as finished basement or attic areas and baths. Show square foot areas and cost factors.

Depreciation—this estimate is to reflect, and be supported by, the comments and calculations made previously on the form. In all instances, the depreciation estimate must be allocated to one of the three types shown on the form. A lump sum total estimate combining several forms of depreciation will not be acceptable.

Land Value—this will normally be estimated on the basis of comparison to sales of similar lots or, in the case of built-up neighborhoods, by extraction from sales of improved properties.

If the final value estimated by the appraiser is the value indicated by the Cost Approach, then the appraiser should also state on an attachment the source of data as to cost factors and recite comparable land sales.

VII. *Market Data Analysis and Approach to Value*:

It is expected that the appraiser will use comparables which have sold as recently as possible (usually no earlier than six months prior to the date of the appraisal), are located in the same neighborhood as the property being appraised and therefore subject to the same locational influences, and as similar as possible in size and physical features. If this is not possible, the appraiser shall attach an explanation as to the reasons for selecting comparables which do not meet the above criteria. Listings are not considered as indicative as actual sales, but in the absence of a sufficient number of truly comparable sales, no more than one listing may be used if accompanied by an explanation of the reason for the use of such listing and a complete analysis of the listing which shall include a supported estimate of the probable selling price.

Sales of properties with FHA or VA financing will not be acceptable unless an appropriate downward adjustment has been made to reflect the loan discount paid by the seller.

If the total adjustments for all factors exceed 25% of the sale price of the comparable, then the appraiser should reconsider whether the comparable is, in fact, truly comparable and should, therefore, be replaced by another more indicative sale.

The appropriate descriptive information (or a rating as to good, fair, etc. as defined in the neighborhood description) is to be entered in the subject property column for each property characteristic set forth in the "Item" column. This is to assist the appraiser and the reviewer in relating the comparables to the subject property. In view of the brevity of the form, it is mandatory that the appraiser complete the analysis of all items.

It is felt that further explanation would be beneficial as to the following specific items in the market data analysis:

Address—identify location of subject property and all comparables with exact street number and name as well as the name of the town or city in which the property is located.

Proximity to Subject—give the distance of the comparable from the subject property in terms of blocks, fractions of a mile or miles as the case may be, as well as the direction.

Sale Price—state the price for which the subject property and the comparables sold.

Price/Living Area—calculate the total sales price per square foot of gross above-grade building (living) area in order to provide this indicator of value.

Data Source—give the source from which the data pertaining to each comparable was obtained—e.g. deed records, recordation tax stamps, brokers, multiple listings, data bank, buyer or seller, etc.

Date of Sale and Time Adjustment—provide the month, day, and year of sale for the subject property and each comparable. Then proceed to make the appropriate adjustment indicated by the market for the time difference between the date of sale and the date of the appraisal. Of course, the comparables should be as current as possible in order to reduce the risk of error in making the adjustment.

Location—give an overall quality rating (e.g. good, average, etc.) for the subject and a comparison rating (e.g. superior, equal, inferior) for the comparables and make the adjustment indicated by the market for differences between the comparables and the subject property.

Site/View—an overall quality rating of good, average, fair or poor is to be given for the subject property and a comparison rating, as indicated under "location" above, should be provided for both site and view for each comparable. However, if an adjustment is being made for site features but not for view or vice-versa, enter the item in the box in lieu of the comparison rating so that the reviewer will know for what specific factor the adjustment was made. Factors to be considered by the appraiser under site include size, shape, topography, drainage, encroachments, easements or any detrimental site conditions.

Design and Appeal—this adjustment category considers such aspects of the property as appeal of exterior design, interior attractiveness and special features, and any other characteristics which would make the property attractive or unattractive to purchasers in general and otherwise enhance, or detract from, its marketability. The appraiser is to rate the subject property in accordance with the ratings given in the building description on page one of the form and is to give comparison ratings, as indicated for the preceding items above, for each of the comparables. The appropriate adjustments may then be made.

Quality of Construction—this item covers quality of materials and workmanship in all respects, including exterior walls, roof covering, framing (walls, floors, and roof), finish flooring, interior walls, trim, doors, hardware, plumbing and electrical systems, baths, kitchen, and mechanical equipment. The appraiser is to indicate an overall quality rating for the subject property commensurate with the rating on page one of the form and is to give comparison ratings, as indicated previously, for each of the comparables. The adjustments are to reflect the market's monetary reaction based on these comparisons.

Age—the appraiser is to report the effective age of the subject property as well as that of the comparables and make the necessary adjustments indicated by the market.

Condition—the appraiser's opinion of the condition of the subject property (whether good, average, fair or poor) is to be stated, whereas for the comparables, comparison ratings of superior, equal, or inferior are to be reported and adjustments are to be made as indicated by the market.

Living Area, Room Count, and Total Living Area—the appraiser is to report the total room count (number of finished, above-grade rooms as indicated on page one of the form), the number of bedrooms and baths, and the total square foot living area (above grade—as obtained from the calculations in the Cost Approach) for the subject property and for each comparable. Adjustments which are reflective of the market are to be made for each item as indicated.

Basement and Basement Finished Rooms—the appraiser is to report basement improvements such as finished rooms, recreation room, etc. found in the subject property and the comparables. If there is no basement (slab or crawl space) or a partial basement, this should also be indicated. Appropriate adjustments are to be made to reflect differences between the comparables and the subject property.

Functional utility—this item refers to room sizes and layout and, therefore, overall livability. A rating should be given for the subject property which will summarize the ratings for these factors found on page one of the form. Comparison ratings such as those indicated previously are to be given for the comparables and appropriate adjustments made to represent the market's reaction to any differences.

Air Conditioning—the presence or absence of this feature and the type thereof (central, sleeve or window units) are to be noted for the subject property as well as the comparables and adjustments made accordingly.

Garage/Carport—the appraiser is to report and make adjustments on the basis of whether the subject property and the comparables have garages or carports and, if so, the capacity in terms of the number of cars. The increase or decrease in value should not necessarily represent the cost of construction but should rather be based on the market's response.

Porches, Patio, Pools, etc.—the appraiser should indicate the presence or absence of these or similar exterior building or site improvements and make the necessary adjustments indicated by the market. Cost data may, at times, serve as a guide but are not necessarily indicative since improvements such as pools may not return their entire cost upon resale as added value.

Other—the items under this heading are to be reported for the subject property and the comparables whether or not adjustments are being made.

The items shown are simply intended to illustrate some of the more common features which may be found and for which adjustments may be appropriate. Therefore, the appraiser should not feel constrained to consider only the physical features shown.

Sales or Financing Concessions—the monetary value of concessions such as builder or seller price discounts, financing charges or benefits (e.g. loan points which are included in the sale price, "buy-downs" of the mortgage interest rate by the builder), gifts of merchandise (e.g. "a free new car in the garage with every purchase") must be reported for the subject property and the comparables and the value adjusted accordingly. It is not acceptable for the appraiser to simply ignore these items and say that they have no effect upon value.

The two blank lines following the above item are for such other adjustments as the appraiser feels are appropriate under the circumstances of the particular appraisal assignment and are intended to provide the appraiser with sufficient flexibility to do a professional job.

Net Adjustments (Total)—report the net total of the adjustments made for all the above items and indicate whether, on balance, the total is plus or minus. If the total adjustments appear excessive in relation to the sale price, the appraiser would be well advised to re-examine the comparable for comparability.

Indicated Value of Subject—add or subtract the net total adjustment from the sale price at the top of each column to arrive at the value of the subject property indicated by each of the comparables. It is expected that the indicated values will not be identical for all comparables.

Comments on Market Data—reconcile the values indicated by the comparables as adjusted in the market data analysis above and explain the reasons for giving more weight to one comparable over the others.

Indicated Value by Market Data Approach—the estimated value resulting from reconciliation.

VIII. *Indicated Value by the Income Approach*:

If the subject property is located in a neighborhood where rentals predominate and rental data is readily available together with sales, then this approach to value should be used prior to final reconciliation. If the final estimate of value is based upon the Income Approach, the supporting rental and sales data along with calculations of the indicated rent multipliers must be attached as an addendum to the report.

IX. *Requirements of the Appraisal, Comments, and Final Reconciliation*:

Indicate by checking the appropriate box whether the subject property was appraised in "as is" condition or whether the appraisal is based on certain repairs, alterations, or other conditions in order to achieve the estimated value. Also, if the property being appraised is proposed or under construction, indicate that the valuation is subject to satisfactory completion in accordance with plans and specifications.

Comments and Conditions of Appraisal—this space is to be used to itemize in detail the required repairs or other conditions as indicated above together with the estimated cost thereof. Comments on any portion of the report are also appropriate in this section if further explanation is needed to support the property analysis or the value estimate. If the space provided is not sufficient, attach an addendum to the report.

Final Reconciliation—the appraiser is to explain in this space the relevance and validity of each approach to value and present justification for the value selected as the final value estimate. It should be emphasized that final reconciliation is not an averaging process.

X. *Other Requirements for Completion of Form*:

The appraiser is to indicate, by checking the appropriate box, whether FNMA Form 1004B (Certification, Contingent and Limiting Conditions, and Market Value Definition) have previously been filed with the client (Seller) and, if so, on what date. This procedure may be followed only if these items are applicable to the appraisal at hand and do not vary from the previous appraisal for which Form 1004B was submitted. The date of such filing must then be given in every instance. Otherwise, since it is recognized that a particular appraisal assignment may require different or additional limiting conditions, the appraiser may add these to Form 1004B and file it with the report. However, if there are no such changes, the appraiser may prefer, as a matter of practice, to file Form 1004B with the client in connection with each report. This, of course, will also be acceptable.

The appraiser is expected to be familiar with these instructions for proper completion of the appraisal report and, by signing the report, certifies that it is in compliance with the instructions.

The estimated market value is to be reported as of a specific date and in numbers which have been rounded off to the nearest one hundred dollars.

The space for the signature of a review appraiser has been provided only in recognition of the fact that some appraisals will be performed by multi-appraiser firms which require that the principal of the firm co-sign each report. Only in such instances will a review appraiser's signature be applicable. In this event, it should be indicated whether the review appraiser co-signing the report has personally inspected the property.

RESIDENTIAL APPRAISAL REPORT

File No.

To be completed by Lender

Borrower/Client ______ Census Tract ______ Map Reference ______

Property Address ______

City ______ County ______ State ______ Zip Code ______

Legal Description ______

Sale Price $ ______ Date of Sale ______ Property Rights Appraised ☐ Fee ☐ Leasehold ☐ DeMinimis PUD(FNMA only ☐ Condo ☐ PUD)

Actual Real Estate Taxes $ ______ (yr) Loan charges to be paid by seller $ ______ Other sales concessions ______

Lender ______ Lender's Address ______

Occupant ______ Appraiser ______ Instructions to Appraiser ______

NEIGHBORHOOD

Location	☐ Urban	☐ Suburban	☐ Rural
Built Up	☐ Over 75%	☐ 25% to 75%	☐ Under 25%
Growth Rate ☐ Fully Dev.	☐ Rapid	☐ Steady	☐ Slow
Property Values	☐ Increasing	☐ Stable	☐ Declining
Demand/Supply	☐ Shortage	☐ In Balance	☐ Over Supply
Marketing Time	☐ Under 3 Mos.	☐ 4–6 Mos.	☐ Over 6 Mos.

Present Land Use ____% 1 Family ____% 2–4 Family ____% Apts. ____% Condo ____% Commercial

____% Industrial ____% Vacant ____% ______

Change in Present Land Use ☐ Not Likely ☐ Likely (*) ☐ Taking Place (*)

(*) From ______ To ______

Predominant Occupancy ☐ Owner ☐ Tenant ______ % Vacant

Single Family Price Range $ ______ to $ ______ Predominant Value $ ______

Single Family Age ______ yrs to ______ yrs Predominant Age ______ yrs

	Good	Avg.	Fair	Poor
Employment Stability	☐	☐	☐	☐
Convenience to Employment	☐	☐	☐	☐
Convenience to Shopping	☐	☐	☐	☐
Convenience to Schools	☐	☐	☐	☐
Adequacy of Public Transportation	☐	☐	☐	☐
Recreational Facilities	☐	☐	☐	☐
Adequacy of Utilities	☐	☐	☐	☐
Property Compatibility	☐	☐	☐	☐
Protection from Detrimental Conditions	☐	☐	☐	☐
Police and Fire Protection	☐	☐	☐	☐
General Appearance of Properties	☐	☐	☐	☐
Appeal to Market	☐	☐	☐	☐

Note: FHLMC/FNMA do not consider the racial composition of the neighborhood to be a relevant factor and it must not be considered in the appraisal.

Comments including those factors, favorable or unfavorable, affecting marketability (e.g. public parks, schools, view, noise) ______

SITE

Dimensions ______ = ______ Sq. Ft. or Acres ☐ Corner Lot

Zoning classification ______ Present improvements ☐ do ☐ do not conform to zoning regulations

Highest and best use: ☐ Present use ☐ Other (specify) ______

	Public	Other (Describe)
Elec.	☐	______
Gas	☐	______
Water	☐	______
San. Sewer	☐	______
	☐ Underground Elect. & Tel.	

OFF SITE IMPROVEMENTS

Street Access: ☐ Public ☐ Private

Surface ______

Maintenance: ☐ Public ☐ Private

☐ Storm Sewer ☐ Curb/Gutter

☐ Sidewalk ☐ Street Lights

Topo ______

Size ______

Shape ______

View ______

Drainage ______

Is the property located in a HUD Identified Special Flood Hazard Area? ☐ **No** ☐ **Yes**

Comments (favorable or unfavorable including any apparent adverse easements, encroachments or other adverse conditions) ______

IMPROVEMENTS

☐ Existing (approx. yr. blt.) 19 ____ ☐ Proposed ☐ Under Construction | No. Units ____ No. Stories ____ | Type (det, duplex, semi/det, etc.) | Design (rambler, split level, etc.) | Exterior Walls

Roof Material | Gutters & Downspouts ☐ None | Window (Type): ____ ☐ Storm Sash ☐ Screens ☐ Combination | Insulation ☐ None ☐ Floor ☐ Ceiling ☐ Roof ☐ Walls

Foundation Walls

BSMT. ____ % Basement ☐ Outside Entrance ☐ Concrete Floor ☐ Floor Drain ☐ Sump Pump ____ % Finished

Finished Ceiling ____
Finished Walls ____
Finished Floor ____

☐ Crawl Space
☐ Slab on Grade

Evidence of: ☐ Dampness ☐ Termites ☐ Settlement

Comments ____

ROOM LIST

Room List	Foyer	Living	Dining	Kitchen	Den	Family Rm.	Rec. Rm.	Bedrooms	No. Baths	Laundry	Other
Basement											
1st Level											
2nd Level											

Finished area above grade contains a total of ____ rooms ____ bedrooms ____ baths.

INTERIOR FINISH & EQUIPMENT

Kitchen Equipment: ☐ Refrigerator ☐ Range/Oven ☐ Disposal ☐ Dishwasher ☐ Fan/Hood ☐ Compactor ☐ Washer ☐ Dryer ☐ ____

HEAT: Type ____ Fuel ____ Cond. ____ AIR COND: ☐ Central ☐ Other ____ ☐ Adequate ☐ Inadequate

Floors ☐ Hardwood ☐ Carpet Over ____ ☐ ____
Walls ☐ Drywall ☐ Plaster ☐ ____
Trim/Finish ☐ Good ☐ Average ☐ Fair ☐ Poor
Bath Floor ☐ Ceramic ☐ ____
Bath Wainscot ☐ Ceramic ☐ ____
Special Features (including fireplaces): ____

ATTIC: ☐ Yes ☐ No ☐ Stairway ☐ Drop-stair ☐ Scuttle ☐ Floored
Finished (Describe) ____ ☐ Heated
CAR STORAGE: ☐ Garage ☐ Built-in ☐ Attached ☐ Detached ☐ Car Port
No. Cars ____ ☐ Adequate ☐ Inadequate Condition ____

PROPERTY RATING

	Good	Avg.	Fair	Poor
Quality of Construction (Materials & Finish)	☐	☐	☐	☐
Condition of Improvements	☐	☐	☐	☐
Rooms size and layout	☐	☐	☐	☐
Closets and Storage	☐	☐	☐	☐
Plumbing—adequacy and condition	☐	☐	☐	☐
Electrical—adequacy and condition	☐	☐	☐	☐
Kitchen Cabinets—adequacy and condition	☐	☐	☐	☐
Compatibility to Neighborhood	☐	☐	☐	☐
Overall Livability	☐	☐	☐	☐
Appeal and Marketability	☐	☐	☐	☐

Effective Age ____ Yrs. Est. Remaining Economic Life ____ Yrs.

PORCHES, PATIOS, POOL, FENCES, etc. (describe) ____

COMMENTS (including functional or physical inadequacies, repairs needed, modernization, etc.) ____

FHLMC Form 70 Rev. 7/77 ATTACH DESCRIPTIVE PHOTOGRAPHS OF SUBJECT PROPERTY AND STREET SCENE **FNMA Form 1004 Rev. 7/77**

CN-028 (Rev. 7-77)

VALUATION SECTION

COST APPROACH

Purpose of Appraisal is to estimate Market Value as defined in Certification & Statement of Limiting Conditions (FHLMC Form 439/FNMA Form 1004B). If submitted for FNMA, the appraiser must attach (1) sketch or map showing location of subject, street names, distance from nearest intersection, and any detrimental conditions and (2) exterior building sketch of improvements showing dimensions.

Measurements	No. Stories	Sq. Ft.
x	x	
x	x	
x	x	
x	x	
x	x	
x	x	

Total Gross Living Area (List in Market Data Analysis below) ______

Comment on functional and economic obsolescence: ______

ESTIMATED REPRODUCTION COST – NEW – OF IMPROVEMENTS:

Dwelling ______ Sq. Ft. @ $ ______ = $ ______

______ Sq. Ft. @ $ ______ = ______

Extras ______ = ______

______ = ______

______ = ______

Porches, Patios, etc. ______ = ______

Garage/Car Port ______ Sq. Ft. @ $ ______ = ______

Site Improvements (driveway, landscaping, etc.) = ______

Total Estimated Cost New . . . . = $ ______

Less	Physical	Functional	Economic		
Depreciation	$ ______	$ ______	$ ______	=	$ (______)

Depreciated value of improvements . . . . . . = $ ______

ESTIMATED LAND VALUE . . . . = $ ______
(If leasehold, show only leasehold value)

INDICATED VALUE BY COST APPROACH . . . $ ______

The undersigned has recited three recent sales of properties most similar and proximate to subject and has considered these in the market analysis. The description includes a dollar adjustment, reflecting market reaction to those items of significant variation between the subject and comparable properties. If a significant item in the comparable property is superior to, or more favorable than, the subject property, a minus (-) adjustment is made, thus reducing the indicated value of subject; if a significant item in the comparable is inferior to, or less favorable than, the subject property, a plus (+) adjustment is made, thus increasing the indicated value of the subject.

ITEM	Subject Property	COMPARABLE NO. 1		COMPARABLE NO. 2		COMPARABLE NO. 3	
Address							
Proximity to Subj.							
Sales Price	$		$		$		$
Price/Living area	$ ⌀		$ ⌀		$ ⌀		$ ⌀
Data Source							
Date of Sale and Time Adjustment	DESCRIPTION	DESCRIPTION	+(–)$ Adjustment	DESCRIPTION	+(–)$ Adjustment	DESCRIPTION	+(–)$ Adjustment
Location							
Site/View							
Design and Appeal							
Quality of Const.							
Age							
Condition							
Living Area Room Count and Total	Total / B-rms / Baths	Total / B-rms / Baths		Total / B-rms / Baths		Total / B-rms / Baths	

MARKET DATA ANALYSIS

Item	Subject	Comparable No. 1		Comparable No. 2		Comparable No. 3	
Gross Living Area	Sq.Ft.	Sq.Ft.		Sq.Ft.		Sq.Ft.	
Basement & Bsmt. Finished Rooms							
Functional Utility							
Air Conditioning							
Garage/Car Port							
Porches, Patio, Pools, etc.							
Other (e.g. fire-places, kitchen equip., heating, remodeling)							
Sales or Financing Concessions							
Net Adj. (Total)		☐ Plus; ☐ Minus	$	☐ Plus; ☐ Minus	$	☐ Plus; ☐ Minus	$
Indicated Value of Subject			$		$		$

Comments on Market Data ______

INDICATED VALUE BY MARKET DATA APPROACH . . . . $ ______

INDICATED VALUE BY INCOME APPROACH (If applicable) Economic Market Rent $ ______ /Mo. x Gross Rent Multiplier ______ = $ ______

This appraisal is made ☐ "as is" ☐ subject to the repairs, alterations, or conditions listed below ☐ completion per plans and specifications.

Comments and Conditions of Appraisal: ______

Final Reconciliation: ______

This appraisal is based upon the above requirements, the certification, contingent and limiting conditions, and Market Value definition that are stated in

☐ FHLMC Form 439 (Rev. 9/75)/FNMA Form 1004B filed with client ______ 19 ______ ☐ attached.

If submitted for FNMA, the report has been prepared in compliance with FNMA form instructions.

I ESTIMATE THE MARKET VALUE, AS DEFINED, OF SUBJECT PROPERTY AS OF ______ 19 ______ to be $ ______

Appraiser(s) ______ Review Appraiser (If applicable) ______

☐ Did ☐ Did Not Physically Inspect Property

FHLMC Form 70 Rev. 7/77 Forms and Worms 315 Whitney Ave., New Haven, CT. 06511 REVERSE FNMA Form 1004 Rev. 7/77

(Picture)	(Picture)
Elevation	Street Scene

EXTERIOR BUILDING SKETCH (Optional)

Drawing

Request Date: ________ Received: ________

Loan Counselor: ________

Loan Amount: ________

Loan Rate: ________

Type/Ratio: ________

Existing Loan: ________

Existing Rate: ________

COMMENTS

____

____

____

____

PROPERTY SUMMARY

Condition G A F Quality G A F

Location G A F

Appraised Value $________

CN-028b

Location Map

Date________

Reviewer________

Reviewer________

LOAN COMMITTEE RECOMMENDATIONS

________% Prime Recommendation

________% Secondary Recommendation

Or the same % of Sales Price if less

Prime Recommendation

$________ at Prime + ________% ________yrs.

Secondary Recommendation

$________ at Prime + ________% ________yrs.

VA Discount________ FHA Discount________

THESE RECOMMENDATIONS ARE SUBJECT TO:

Inside Inspection________ Final Inspection________

Proof of Legal Access________

Hold $________ for Repair/Completion/Street Imps.

Engineer's Certification________

Soil Report and Engineered Foundation________

Proof of Sufficient Water Supply________

Subject to Flood Insurance________

Septic System Approval by Co. Health Dept.________

____

____

____

____

DEFINITION OF MARKET VALUE: The highest price in terms of money which a property will bring in a competitive and open market under all conditions requisite to a fair sale, the buyer and seller, each acting prudently, knowledgeably and assuming the price is not affected by undue stimulus. Implicit in this definition is the consummation of a sale as of a specified date and the passing of title from seller to buyer under conditions whereby: (1) buyer and seller are typically motivated; (2) both parties are well informed or well advised, and each acting in what he considers his own best interest; (3) a reasonable time is allowed for exposure in the open market; (4) payment is made in cash or its equivalent; (5) financing, if any, is on terms generally available in the community at the specified date and typical for the property type in its locale; (6) the price represents a normal consideration for the property sold unaffected by special financing amounts and/or terms, services, fees, costs, or credits incurred in the transaction. ("Real Estate Appraisal Terminology," published 1975.)

CERTIFICATION AND STATEMENT OF LIMITING CONDITIONS

CERTIFICATION: The Appraiser certifies and agrees that:

1. The Appraiser has no present or contemplated future interest in the property appraised; and neither the employment to make the appraisal, nor the compensation for it, is contingent upon the appraised value of the property.

2. The Appraiser has no personal interest in or bias with respect to the subject matter of the appraisal report or the participants to the sale. The "Estimate of Market Value" in the appraisal report is not based in whole or in part upon the race, color, or national origin of the prospective owners or occupants of the property appraised, or upon the race, color or national origin of the present owners or occupants of the properties in the vicinity of the property appraised.

3. The Appraiser has personally inspected the property, both inside and out, and has made an exterior inspection of all comparable sales listed in the report. To the best of the Appraiser's knowledge and belief, all statements and information in this report are true and correct, and the Appraiser has not knowingly withheld any significant information.

4. All contingent and limiting conditions are contained herein (imposed by the terms of the assignment or by the undersigned affecting the analyses, opinions, and conclusions contained in the report).

5. This appraisal report has been made in conformity with and is subject to the requirements of the Code of Professional Ethics and Standards of Professional Conduct of the appraisal organizations with which the Appraiser is affiliated.

6. All conclusions and opinions concerning the real estate that are set forth in the appraisal report were prepared by the Appraiser whose signature appears on the appraisal report, unless indicated as "Review Appraiser." No change of any item in the appraisal report shall be made by anyone other than the Appraiser, and the Appraiser shall have no responsibility for any such unauthorized change.

CONTINGENT AND LIMITING CONDITIONS: The certification of the Appraiser appearing in the appraisal report is subject to the following conditions and to such other specific and limiting conditions as are set forth by the Appraiser in the report.

1. The Appraiser assumes no responsibility for matters of a legal nature affecting the property

appraised or the title thereto, nor does the Appraiser render any opinion as to the title, which is assumed to be good and marketable. The property is appraised as though under responsible ownership.

2. Any sketch in the report may show approximate dimensions and is included to assist the reader in visualizing the property. The Appraiser has made no survey of the property.

3. The Appraiser is not required to give testimony or appear in court because of having made the appraisal with reference to the property in question, unless arrangements have been previously made therefor.

4. Any distribution of the valuation in the report between land and improvements applies only under the existing program of utilization. The separate valuations for land and building must not be used in conjunction with any other appraisal and are invalid if so used.

5. The Appraiser assumes that there are no hidden or unapparent conditions of the property, subsoil, or structures, which would render it more or less valuable. The Appraiser assumes no responsibility for such conditions, or for engineering which might be required to discover such factors.

6. Information, estimates, and opinions furnished to the Appraiser, and contained in the report, were obtained from sources considered reliable and believed to be true and correct. However, no responsibility for accuracy of such items furnished the Appraiser can be assumed by the Appraiser.

7. Disclosure of the contents of the appraisal report is governed by the Bylaws and Regulations of the professional appraisal organizations with which the Appraiser is affiliated.

8. Neither all, nor any part of the content of the report, or copy thereof (including conclusions as to the property value, the identity of the Appraiser, professional designations, reference to any professional appraisal organizations, or the firm with which the Appraiser is connected), shall be used for any purposes by anyone but the client specified in the report, the mortgagee or its successors and assigns, mortgage insurers, consultants, professional appraisal organizations, any state or federally approved financial institution, any department, agency, or instrumentality of the United States or any state or the District of Columbia, without the previous written consent of the Appraiser; nor shall it be conveyed by anyone to the public through advertising, public relations, news, sales, or other media, without the written consent and approval of the Appraiser.

9. On all appraisals, subject to satisfactory completion, repairs, or alterations, the appraisal report and value conclusion are contingent upon completion of the improvements in a workmanlike manner.

Date:........................ **Appraiser(s)**...

FHLMC FORM 439 REV. 9/75 FNMA FORM 1004B

APPENDIX G

Ellwood Tables

Source: L. W. Ellwood. *Ellwood Tables for Real Estate Appraising and Financing*, 3rd edition (Chicago: American Institute of Real Estate Appraisers, 1974), pp. 81, 84, 97, 100, 113, 116, 129, 132, 145, 148. Reprinted with the permission of the publisher.

8% ANNUAL COMPOUND INTEREST TABLE 8%

EFFECTIVE RATE = 8% BASE = 1.08

YEARS	1 AMOUNT OF 1 AT COMPOUND INTEREST $S^n = (1+i)^n$	2 ACCUMULATION OF 1 PER PERIOD $S_{\overline{n}|} = \frac{S^n - 1}{i}$	3 SINKING FUND FACTOR $1/S_{\overline{n}|} = \frac{i}{S^n - 1}$	4 PRES. VALUE REVERSION OF 1 $V^n = \frac{1}{S^n}$	5 PRESENT VALUE ORD. ANNUITY 1 PER PERIOD $a_{\overline{n}|} = \frac{1-V^n}{i}$	6 INSTALMENT TO AMORTIZE 1 $1/a_{\overline{n}|} = \frac{i}{1-V^n}$	n YEARS
1	1.080000	1.000000	1.000000	.925926	.925926	1.080000	1
2	1.166400	2.080000	.480769	.857339	1.783265	.560769	2
3	1.259712	3.246400	.308034	.793832	2.577097	.388034	3
4	1.360489	4.506112	.221921	.735030	3.312127	.301921	4
5	1.469328	5.866601	.170456	.680583	3.992710	.250456	5
6	1.586874	7.335929	.136315	.630170	4.622880	.216315	6
7	1.713824	8.922803	.112072	.583490	5.206370	.192072	7
8	1.850930	10.636628	.094015	.540269	5.746639	.174015	8
9	1.999005	12.487558	.080080	.500249	6.246888	.160080	9
10	2.158925	14.486562	.069029	.463193	6.710081	.149029	10
11	2.331639	16.645487	.060076	.428883	7.138964	.140076	11
12	2.518170	18.977126	.052695	.397114	7.536078	.132695	12
13	2.719624	21.495297	.046522	.367698	7.903776	.126522	13
14	2.937194	24.214920	.041297	.340461	8.244237	.121297	14
15	3.172169	27.152114	.036830	.315242	8.559479	.116830	15
16	3.425943	30.324283	.032977	.291890	8.851369	.112977	16
17	3.700018	33.750226	.029629	.270269	9.121638	.109629	17
18	3.996019	37.450244	.026702	.250249	9.371887	.106702	18
19	4.315701	41.446263	.024128	.231712	9.603599	.104128	19
20	4.660957	45.761964	.021852	.214548	9.818147	.101852	20
21	5.033834	50.422921	.019832	.198656	10.016803	.099832	21
22	5.436540	55.456755	.018032	.183941	10.200744	.098032	22
23	5.871464	60.893296	.016422	.170315	10.371059	.096422	23
24	6.341181	66.764759	.014978	.157699	10.528758	.094978	24
25	6.848475	73.105940	.013679	.146018	10.674776	.093679	25
26	7.396353	79.954415	.012507	.135202	10.809978	.092507	26
27	7.988061	87.350768	.011448	.125187	10.935165	.091448	27
28	8.627106	95.338830	.010489	.115914	11.051078	.090489	28
29	9.317275	103.965936	.009619	.107328	11.158406	.089619	29
30	10.062657	113.283211	.008827	.099377	11.257783	.088827	30
31	10.867669	123.345868	.008107	.092016	11.349799	.088107	31
32	11.737083	134.213537	.007451	.085200	11.434999	.087451	32
33	12.676050	145.950620	.006852	.078889	11.513888	.086852	33
34	13.690134	158.626670	.006304	.073045	11.586934	.086304	34
35	14.785344	172.316804	.005803	.067635	11.654568	.085803	35
36	15.968172	187.102148	.005345	.062625	11.717193	.085345	36
37	17.245626	203.070320	.004924	.057986	11.775179	.084924	37
38	18.625276	220.315945	.004539	.053690	11.828869	.084539	38
39	20.115298	238.941221	.004185	.049713	11.878582	.084185	39
40	21.724521	259.056519	.003860	.046031	11.924613	.083860	40
41	23.462483	280.781040	.003561	.042621	11.967235	.083561	41
42	25.339482	304.243523	.003287	.039464	12.006699	.083287	42
43	27.366640	329.583005	.003034	.036541	12.043240	.083034	43
44	29.555972	356.949646	.002802	.033834	12.077074	.082802	44
45	31.920449	386.505617	.002587	.031328	12.108401	.082587	45
46	34.474085	418.426067	.002390	.029007	12.137409	.082390	46
47	37.232012	452.900152	.002208	.026859	12.164267	.082208	47
48	40.210573	490.132164	.002040	.024869	12.189136	.082040	48
49	43.427419	530.342737	.001886	.023027	12.212163	.081886	49
50	46.901613	573.770156	.001743	.021321	12.233485	.081743	50
51	50.653742	620.671769	.001611	.019742	12.253227	.081611	51
52	54.706041	671.325510	.001490	.018280	12.271506	.081490	52
53	59.082524	726.031551	.001377	.016925	12.288432	.081377	53
54	63.809126	785.114075	.001274	.015672	12.304103	.081274	54
55	68.913856	848.923201	.001178	.014511	12.318614	.081178	55
56	74.426965	917.837058	.001090	.013436	12.332050	.081090	56
57	80.381122	992.264022	.001008	.012441	12.344491	.081008	57
58	86.811612	1072.645144	.000932	.011519	12.356010	.080932	58
59	93.756540	1159.456755	.000862	.010666	12.366676	.080862	59
60	101.257064	1253.213296	.000798	.009876	12.376552	.080798	60

9% ANNUAL COMPOUND INTEREST TABLE 9%

EFFECTIVE RATE = 9% BASE = 1.09

YEARS	1 AMOUNT OF I AT COMPOUND INTEREST $S^n = (1+i)^n$	2 ACCUMULATION OF I PER PERIOD $S_{\overline{n}\rvert} = \frac{S^n - 1}{i}$	3 SINKING FUND FACTOR $1/S_{\overline{n}\rvert} = \frac{i}{S^n - 1}$	4 PRES. VALUE REVERSION OF I $V^n = \frac{1}{S^n}$	5 PRESENT VALUE ORD. ANNUITY 1 PER PERIOD $a_{\overline{n}\rvert} = \frac{1-V^n}{i}$	6 INSTALMENT TO AMORTIZE I $1/a_{\overline{n}\rvert} = \frac{i}{1-V^n}$	n YEARS
1	1.090000	1.000000	1.000000	.917431	.917431	1.090000	1
2	1.188100	2.090000	.478469	.841680	1.759111	.568469	2
3	1.295029	3.278100	.305055	.772183	2.531295	.395055	3
4	1.411582	4.573129	.218669	.708425	3.239720	.308669	4
5	1.538624	5.984711	.167092	.649931	3.889651	.257092	5
6	1.667100	7.523335	.132920	.596267	4.485919	.222920	6
7	1.828039	9.200435	.108691	.547034	5.032953	.198691	7
8	1.992563	11.028474	.090674	.501866	5.534819	.180674	8
9	2.171893	13.021036	.076799	.460428	5.995247	.166799	9
10	2.367364	15.192930	.065820	.422411	6.417658	.155820	10
11	2.580426	17.560293	.056947	.387533	6.805191	.146947	11
12	2.812665	20.140720	.049651	.355535	7.160725	.139651	12
13	3.065805	22.953385	.043567	.326179	7.486904	.133567	13
14	3.341727	26.019189	.038433	.299246	7.786150	.128433	14
15	3.642482	29.360916	.034059	.274538	8.060688	.124059	15
16	3.970306	33.003399	.030300	.251870	8.312558	.120300	16
17	4.327633	36.973705	.027046	.231073	8.543631	.117046	17
18	4.717120	41.301338	.024212	.211994	8.755625	.114212	18
19	5.141661	46.018458	.021730	.194490	8.950115	.111730	19
20	5.604411	51.160120	.019546	.178431	9.128546	.109546	20
21	6.108808	56.764530	.017617	.163698	9.292244	.107617	21
22	6.658600	62.873338	.015905	.150182	9.442425	.105905	22
23	7.257874	69.531939	.014382	.137781	9.580207	.104382	23
24	7.911083	76.789813	.013023	.126405	9.706612	.103023	24
25	8.623081	84.700896	.011806	.115968	9.822580	.101806	25
26	9.399158	93.323977	.010715	.106393	9.928972	.100715	26
27	10.245082	102.723135	.009735	.097608	10.026580	.099735	27
28	11.167140	112.968217	.008852	.089548	10.116128	.098852	28
29	12.172182	124.135356	.008056	.082155	10.198283	.098056	29
30	13.267678	136.307539	.007336	.075371	10.273654	.097336	30
31	14.461770	149.575217	.006686	.069148	10.342802	.096686	31
32	15.763329	164.036987	.006096	.063438	10.406240	.096096	32
33	17.182028	179.800315	.005562	.058200	10.464441	.095562	33
34	18.728411	196.982344	.005077	.053395	10.517835	.095077	34
35	20.413968	215.710755	.004636	.048986	10.566821	.094636	35
36	22.251225	236.124723	.004235	.044941	10.611763	.094235	36
37	24.253835	258.375948	.003870	.041231	10.652993	.093870	37
38	26.436680	282.629783	.003538	.037826	10.690820	.093538	38
39	28.815982	309.066463	.003236	.034703	10.725523	.093236	39
40	31.409420	337.882445	.002960	.031838	10.757360	.092960	40
41	34.236268	369.291865	.002708	.029209	10.786569	.092708	41
42	37.317532	403.528133	.002478	.026797	10.813366	.092478	42
43	40.676110	440.845665	.002268	.024584	10.837951	.092268	43
44	44.336960	481.521775	.002077	.022555	10.860505	.092077	44
45	48.327286	525.858735	.001902	.020692	10.881197	.091902	45
46	52.676742	574.186021	.001742	.018984	10.900181	.091742	46
47	57.417649	626.862762	.001595	.017416	10.917597	.091595	47
48	62.585237	684.280411	.001461	.015978	10.933575	.091461	48
49	68.217908	746.865648	.001339	.014659	10.948234	.091339	49
50	74.357520	815.083556	.001227	.013449	10.961683	.091227	50
51	81.049697	889.441077	.001124	.012338	10.974021	.091124	51
52	88.344170	970.490773	.001030	.011319	10.985340	.091030	52
53	96.295145	1058.834943	.000944	.010385	10.995725	.090944	53
54	104.961708	1155.130088	.000866	.009527	11.005252	.090866	54
55	114.408262	1260.091796	.000794	.008741	11.013993	.090794	55
56	124.705005	1374.500057	.000728	.008019	11.022012	.090728	56
57	135.928456	1499.205063	.000667	.007357	11.029369	.090667	57
58	148.162017	1635.133518	.000612	.006749	11.036118	.090612	58
59	161.496598	1783.295535	.000561	.006192	11.042310	.090561	59
60	176.031292	1944.792133	.000514	.005681	11.047991	.090514	60

10% ANNUAL COMPOUND INTEREST TABLE 10%

EFFECTIVE RATE = 10% BASE = 1.10

YEARS	1 AMOUNT OF 1 AT COMPOUND INTEREST $S^n = (1+i)^n$	2 ACCUMULATION OF 1 PER PERIOD $S_{\overline{n}\vert} = \frac{S^n - 1}{i}$	3 SINKING FUND FACTOR $1/S_{\overline{n}\vert} = \frac{i}{S^n - 1}$	4 PRES. VALUE REVERSION OF 1 $V^n = \frac{1}{S^n}$	5 PRESENT VALUE ORD. ANNUITY 1 PER PERIOD $a_{\overline{n}\vert} = \frac{1-V^n}{i}$	6 INSTALMENT TO AMORTIZE 1 $1/a_{\overline{n}\vert} = \frac{i}{1-V^n}$	n YEARS
1	1.100000	1.000000	1.000000	.909091	.909091	1.100000	1
2	1.210000	2.100000	.476190	.826446	1.735537	.576190	2
3	1.331000	3.310000	.302115	.751315	2.486852	.402115	3
4	1.464100	4.641000	.215471	.683013	3.169865	.315471	4
5	1.610510	6.105100	.163797	.620921	3.790787	.263797	5
6	1.771561	7.715610	.129607	.564474	4.355261	.229607	6
7	1.948717	9.487171	.105405	.513158	4.868419	.205405	7
8	2.143589	11.435888	.087444	.466507	5.334926	.187444	8
9	2.357948	13.579477	.073641	.424098	5.759024	.173641	9
10	2.593742	15.937425	.062745	.385543	6.144567	.162745	10
11	2.853117	18.531167	.053963	.350494	6.495061	.153963	11
12	3.138428	21.384284	.046763	.318631	6.813692	.146763	12
13	3.452271	24.522712	.040779	.289664	7.103356	.140779	13
14	3.797498	27.974983	.035746	.263331	7.366687	.135746	14
15	4.177248	31.772482	.031474	.239392	7.606080	.131474	15
16	4.594973	35.949730	.027817	.217629	7.823709	.127817	16
17	5.054470	40.544703	.024664	.197845	8.021553	.124664	17
18	5.559917	45.599173	.021930	.179859	8.201412	.121930	18
19	6.115909	51.159090	.019547	.163508	8.364920	.119547	19
20	6.727500	57.274999	.017460	.148644	8.513564	.117460	20
21	7.400250	64.002499	.015624	.135131	8.648694	.115624	21
22	8.140275	71.402749	.014005	.122846	8.771540	.114005	22
23	8.954302	79.543024	.012572	.111678	8.883218	.112572	23
24	9.849733	88.497327	.011300	.101526	8.984744	.111300	24
25	10.834706	98.347059	.010168	.092296	9.077040	.110168	25
26	11.918177	109.181765	.009159	.083905	9.160945	.109159	26
27	13.109994	121.099942	.008258	.076278	9.237223	.108258	27
28	14.420994	134.209936	.007451	.069343	9.306567	.107451	28
29	15.863093	148.630930	.006728	.063039	9.369606	.106728	29
30	17.449402	164.494023	.006079	.057309	9.426914	.106079	30
31	19.194342	181.943425	.005496	.052099	9.479013	.105496	31
32	21.113777	201.137767	.004972	.047362	9.526376	.104972	32
33	23.225154	222.251544	.004499	.043057	9.569432	.104499	33
34	25.547670	245.476699	.004074	.039143	9.608575	.104074	34
35	28.102437	271.024368	.003690	.035584	9.644159	.103690	35
36	30.912681	299.126805	.003343	.032349	9.676508	.103343	36
37	34.003949	330.039486	.003030	.029408	9.705917	.103030	37
38	37.404343	364.043434	.002747	.026735	9.732651	.102747	38
39	41.144778	401.447778	.002491	.024304	9.756956	.102491	39
40	45.259256	442.592556	.002259	.022095	9.779051	.102259	40
41	49.785181	487.851811	.002050	.020086	9.799137	.102050	41
42	54.763699	537.636992	.001860	.018260	9.817397	.101860	42
43	60.240069	592.400692	.001688	.016600	9.833998	.101688	43
44	66.264076	652.640761	.001532	.015091	9.849089	.101532	44
45	72.890484	718.904837	.001391	.013719	9.862808	.101391	45
46	80.179532	791.795321	.001263	.012472	9.875280	.101263	46
47	88.197485	871.974853	.001147	.011338	9.886618	.101147	47
48	97.017234	960.172338	.001041	.010307	9.896926	.101041	48
49	106.718957	1057.189572	.000946	.009370	9.906296	.100946	49
50	117.390853	1163.908529	.000859	.008519	9.914814	.100859	50
51	129.129938	1281.299382	.000780	.007744	9.922559	.100780	51
52	142.042932	1410.429320	.000709	.007040	9.929599	.100709	52
53	156.247225	1552.472252	.000644	.006400	9.935999	.100644	53
54	171.871948	1708.719477	.000585	.005818	9.941817	.100585	54
55	189.059142	1880.591425	.000532	.005289	9.947106	.100532	55
56	207.965057	2069.650567	.000483	.004809	9.951915	.100483	56
57	228.761562	2277.615624	.000439	.004371	9.956286	.100439	57
58	251.637719	2506.377186	.000399	.003974	9.960260	.100399	58
59	276.801490	2758.014905	.000363	.003613	9.963873	.100363	59
60	304.481640	3034.816395	.000330	.003284	9.967157	.100330	60

11% ANNUAL COMPOUND INTEREST TABLE 11%

EFFECTIVE RATE = 11% BASE = 1.11

YEARS	1 AMOUNT OF I AT COMPOUND INTEREST $S^n = (1+i)^n$	2 ACCUMULATION OF I PER PERIOD $S_{\overline{n}\vert} = \frac{S^n - 1}{i}$	3 SINKING FUND FACTOR $1/S_{\overline{n}\vert} = \frac{i}{S^n - 1}$	4 PRES. VALUE REVERSION OF I $V^n = \frac{1}{S^n}$	5 PRESENT VALUE ORD. ANNUITY 1 PER PERIOD $a_{\overline{n}\vert} = \frac{1 - V^n}{i}$	6 INSTALMENT TO AMORTIZE I $1/a_{\overline{n}\vert} = \frac{i}{1 - V^n}$	n YEARS
1	1.110000	1.000000	1.000000	.900901	.900901	1.110000	1
2	1.232100	2.110000	.473934	.811622	1.712523	.583934	2
3	1.367631	3.342100	.299213	.731191	2.443715	.409213	3
4	1.518070	4.709731	.212326	.658731	3.102446	.322326	4
5	1.685058	6.227801	.160570	.593451	3.695897	.270570	5
6	1.870415	7.912860	.126377	.534641	4.230538	.236377	6
7	2.076160	9.783274	.102215	.481658	4.712196	.212215	7
8	2.304538	11.859434	.084321	.433926	5.146123	.194321	8
9	2.558037	14.163972	.070602	.390925	5.537048	.180602	9
10	2.839421	16.722009	.059801	.352184	5.889232	.169801	10
11	3.151757	19.561430	.051121	.317283	6.206515	.161121	11
12	3.498451	22.713187	.044027	.285841	6.492356	.154027	12
13	3.883280	26.211638	.038151	.257514	6.749870	.148151	13
14	4.310441	30.094918	.033228	.231995	6.981865	.143228	14
15	4.784589	34.405359	.029065	.209004	7.190870	.139065	15
16	5.310894	39.189948	.025517	.188292	7.379162	.135517	16
17	5.895093	44.500843	.022471	.169633	7.548794	.132471	17
18	6.543553	50.395936	.019843	.152822	7.701617	.129843	18
19	7.263344	56.939488	.017563	.137678	7.839294	.127563	19
20	8.062312	64.202832	.015576	.124034	7.963328	.125576	20
21	8.949166	72.265144	.013838	.111742	8.075070	.123838	21
22	9.933574	81.214310	.012313	.100669	8.175739	.122313	22
23	11.026267	91.147884	.010971	.090693	8.266432	.120971	23
24	12.239157	102.174151	.009787	.081705	8.348137	.119787	24
25	13.585464	114.413307	.008740	.073608	8.421745	.118740	25
26	15.079865	127.998771	.007813	.066314	8.488058	.117813	26
27	16.738650	143.078636	.006989	.059742	8.547800	.116989	27
28	18.579901	159.817286	.006257	.053822	8.601622	.116257	28
29	20.623691	178.397187	.005605	.048488	8.650110	.115605	29
30	22.892297	199.020878	.005025	.043683	8.693793	.115025	30
31	25.410449	221.913175	.004506	.039354	8.733146	.114506	31
32	28.205599	247.323624	.004043	.035454	8.768600	.114043	32
33	31.308214	275.529222	.003629	.031940	8.800541	.113629	33
34	34.752118	306.837437	.003259	.028775	8.829316	.113259	34
35	38.574851	341.589555	.002927	.025924	8.855240	.112927	35
36	42.818085	380.164406	.002630	.023355	8.878594	.112630	36
37	47.528074	422.982490	.002364	.021040	8.899635	.112364	37
38	52.756162	470.510564	.002125	.018955	8.918590	.112125	38
39	58.559340	523.266726	.001911	.017077	8.935666	.111911	39
40	65.000867	581.826066	.001719	.015384	8.951051	.111719	40
41	72.150963	646.826934	.001546	.013860	8.964911	.111546	41
42	80.087569	718.977896	.001391	.012486	8.977397	.111391	42
43	88.897201	799.065465	.001251	.011249	8.988646	.111251	43
44	98.675893	887.962666	.001126	.010134	8.998780	.111126	44
45	109.530242	986.638559	.001014	.009130	9.007910	.111014	45
46	121.578568	1096.168801	.000912	.008225	9.016135	.110912	46
47	134.952211	1217.747369	.000821	.007410	9.023545	.110821	47
48	149.796954	1352.699580	.000739	.006676	9.030221	.110739	48
49	166.274619	1502.496534	.000666	.006014	9.036235	.110666	49
50	184.564827	1668.771153	.000599	.005418	9.041653	.110599	50
51	204.866958	1853.335979	.000540	.004881	9.046534	.110540	51
52	227.402323	2058.202936	.000486	.004397	9.050932	.110486	52
53	252.416579	2285.605259	.000438	.003962	9.054894	.110438	53
54	280.182402	2538.021837	.000394	.003569	9.058463	.110394	54
55	311.002466	2818.204239	.000355	.003215	9.061678	.110355	55
56	345.212738	3129.206705	.000320	.002897	9.064575	.110320	56
57	383.186139	3474.419443	.000288	.002610	9.067185	.110288	57
58	425.336614	3857.605581	.000259	.002351	9.069536	.110259	58
59	472.123641	4282.942195	.000233	.002118	9.071654	.110233	59
60	524.057242	4755.065835	.000210	.001908	9.073562	.110210	60

12% ANNUAL COMPOUND INTEREST TABLE 12%

EFFECTIVE RATE = 12% BASE = 1.1200

YEARS	1 AMOUNT OF I AT COMPOUND INTEREST $S^n = (1+i)^n$	2 ACCUMULATION OF I PER PERIOD $s_{\overline{n}\|} = \frac{S^n - 1}{i}$	3 SINKING FUND FACTOR $1/s_{\overline{n}\|} = \frac{i}{S^n - 1}$	4 PRES. VALUE REVERSION OF I $V^n = \frac{1}{S^n}$	5 PRESENT VALUE ORD.ANNUITY 1 PER PERIOD $a_{\overline{n}\|} = \frac{1 - V^n}{i}$	6 INSTALMENT TO AMORTIZE I $1/a_{\overline{n}\|} = \frac{i}{1 - V^n}$	n YEARS
1	1.120000	1.000000	1.000000	.892857	.892857	1.120000	1
2	1.254400	2.120000	.471698	.797194	1.690051	.591698	2
3	1.404928	3.374400	.296349	.711780	2.401831	.416349	3
4	1.573519	4.779328	.209234	.635518	3.037349	.329234	4
5	1.762342	6.352847	.157410	.567427	3.604776	.277410	5
6	1.973823	8.115189	.123226	.506631	4.111407	.243226	6
7	2.210681	10.089012	.099118	.452349	4.563757	.219118	7
8	2.475963	12.299693	.081303	.403883	4.967640	.201303	8
9	2.773079	14.775656	.067679	.360610	5.328250	.187679	9
10	3.105848	17.548735	.056984	.321973	5.650223	.176984	10
11	3.478550	20.654583	.048415	.287476	5.937699	.168415	11
12	3.895976	24.133133	.041437	.256675	6.194374	.161437	12
13	4.363493	28.029109	.035677	.229174	6.423548	.155677	13
14	4.887112	32.392602	.030871	.204620	6.628168	.150871	14
15	5.473566	37.279715	.026824	.182696	6.810864	.146824	15
16	6.130394	42.753280	.023390	.163122	6.973986	.143390	16
17	6.866041	48.883674	.020457	.145644	7.119630	.140457	17
18	7.689966	55.749715	.017937	.130040	7.249670	.137937	18
19	8.612762	63.439681	.015763	.116107	7.365777	.135763	19
20	9.646293	72.052442	.013879	.103667	7.469444	.133879	20
21	10.803848	81.698736	.012240	.092560	7.562003	.132240	21
22	12.100310	92.502584	.010811	.082643	7.644646	.130811	22
23	13.552347	104.602894	.009560	.073788	7.718434	.129560	23
24	15.178629	118.155241	.008463	.065882	7.784316	.128463	24
25	17.000064	133.333870	.007500	.058823	7.843139	.127500	25
26	19.040072	150.333934	.006652	.052521	7.895660	.126652	26
27	21.324881	169.374007	.005904	.046894	7.942554	.125904	27
28	23.883866	190.698887	.005244	.041869	7.984423	.125244	28
29	26.749930	214.582754	.004660	.037383	8.021806	.124660	29
30	29.959922	241.332684	.004144	.033378	8.055184	.124144	30
31	33.555113	271.292606	.003686	.029802	8.084986	.123686	31
32	37.581726	304.847719	.003280	.026609	8.111594	.123280	32
33	42.091533	342.429445	.002920	.023758	8.135352	.122920	33
34	47.142517	384.520979	.002601	.021212	8.156564	.122601	34
35	52.799620	431.663496	.002317	.018940	8.175504	.122317	35
36	59.135574	484.463116	.002064	.016910	8.192414	.122064	36
37	66.231843	543.598690	.001840	.015098	8.207513	.121840	37
38	74.179664	609.830532	.001640	.013481	8.220993	.121640	38
39	83.081224	684.010196	.001462	.012036	8.233030	.121462	39
40	93.050970	767.091420	.001304	.010747	8.243777	.121304	40
41	104.217087	860.142390	.001163	.009595	8.253372	.121163	41
42	116.723137	964.359477	.001037	.008567	8.261939	.121037	42
43	130.729914	1081.082614	.000925	.007649	8.269589	.120925	43
44	146.417503	1211.812527	.000825	.006830	8.276418	.120825	44
45	163.987604	1358.230031	.000736	.006098	8.282516	.120736	45
46	183.666116	1522.217634	.000657	.005445	8.287961	.120657	46
47	205.706050	1705.883750	.000586	.004861	8.292822	.120586	47
48	230.390776	1911.589800	.000523	.004340	8.297163	.120523	48
49	258.037669	2141.980576	.000467	.003875	8.301038	.120467	49
50	289.002189	2400.018245	.000417	.003460	8.304498	.120417	50
51	323.682452	2689.020434	.000372	.003089	8.307588	.120372	51
52	362.524346	3012.702886	.000332	.002758	8.310346	.120332	52
53	406.027268	3375.227233	.000296	.002463	8.312809	.120296	53
54	454.750540	3781.254500	.000264	.002199	8.315008	.120264	54
55	509.320605	4236.005040	.000236	.001963	8.316972	.120236	55
56	570.439077	4745.325645	.000211	.001753	8.318725	.120211	56
57	638.891767	5315.764723	.000188	.001565	8.320290	.120188	57
58	715.558779	5954.656489	.000168	.001398	8.321687	.120168	58
59	801.425832	6670.215267	.000150	.001248	8.322935	.120150	59
60	897.596932	7471.641099	.000134	.001114	8.324049	.120134	60

8% MONTHLY COMPOUND INTEREST TABLE 8%

EFFECTIVE RATE = 2/3% BASE = 1.00666666+

MONTHS	1 AMOUNT OF I AT COMPOUND INTEREST $S^n = (1+i)^n$	2 ACCUMULATION OF I PER PERIOD $S_{\overline{n}\rvert} = \frac{S^n - 1}{i}$	3 SINKING FUND FACTOR $1/S_{\overline{n}\rvert} = \frac{i}{S^n - 1}$	4 PRES. VALUE REVERSION OF I $V^n = \frac{1}{S^n}$	5 PRESENT VALUE ORD. ANNUITY 1 PER PERIOD $a_{\overline{n}\rvert} = \frac{1 - V^n}{i}$	6 INSTALMENT TO AMORTIZE I $1/a_{\overline{n}\rvert} = \frac{i}{1 - V^n}$	n MONTHS
1	1.006667	1.000000	1.000000	.993377	.993377	1.006667	1
2	1.013378	2.006667	.498339	.986799	1.980176	.505006	2
3	1.020134	3.020044	.331121	.980264	2.960440	.337788	3
4	1.026935	4.040178	.247514	.973772	3.934212	.254181	4
5	1.033781	5.067113	.197351	.967323	4.901535	.204018	5
6	1.040673	6.100893	.163910	.960917	5.862452	.170577	6
7	1.047610	7.141566	.140025	.954553	6.817005	.146692	7
8	1.054595	8.189176	.122112	.948232	7.765237	.128779	8
9	1.061625	9.243771	.108181	.941952	8.707189	.114848	9
10	1.068703	10.305396	.097037	.935714	9.642903	.103704	10
11	1.075827	11.374099	.087919	.929517	10.572420	.094586	11
YEARS							
1	1.083000	12.449926	.080322	.923361	11.495782	.086989	12
2	1.172888	25.933190	.038561	.852596	22.110544	.045228	24
3	1.270237	40.535558	.024670	.787255	31.911805	.031337	36
4	1.375666	56.349915	.017746	.726921	40.961913	.024413	48
5	1.489846	73.476856	.013610	.671210	49.318433	.020277	60
6	1.613502	92.025325	.010867	.619770	57.034522	.017534	72
7	1.747422	112.113308	.008920	.572272	64.159261	.015587	84
8	1.892457	133.868583	.007470	.528414	70.737970	.014137	96
9	2.049530	157.429536	.006352	.487917	76.812497	.013019	108
10	2.219640	182.946036	.005466	.450523	82.421481	.012133	120
11	2.403869	210.580392	.004749	.415996	87.600600	.011416	132
12	2.603389	240.508387	.004158	.384115	92.382799	.010825	144
13	2.819469	272.920391	.003664	.354677	96.798498	.010331	156
14	3.053484	308.022575	.003247	.327495	100.875783	.009914	168
15	3.306921	346.038223	.002890	.302396	104.640592	.009557	180
16	3.581394	387.209151	.002583	.279221	108.116871	.009250	192
17	3.878648	431.797246	.002316	.257822	111.326733	.008983	204
18	4.200574	480.086130	.002083	.238063	114.290596	.008750	216
19	4.549220	532.382969	.001878	.219818	117.027313	.008545	228
20	4.926803	589.020419	.001698	.202971	119.554291	.008365	240
21	5.335725	650.358749	.001538	.187416	121.887606	.008205	252
22	5.778588	716.788131	.001395	.173053	124.042099	.008062	264
23	6.258207	788.731119	.001268	.159790	126.031475	.007935	276
24	6.777636	866.645339	.001154	.147544	127.868388	.007821	288
25	7.340176	951.026401	.001051	.136237	129.564522	.007718	300
26	7.949407	1042.411050	.000959	.125796	131.130667	.007626	312
27	8.609204	1141.380579	.000876	.116155	132.576785	.007543	324
28	9.323764	1248.564531	.000801	.107253	133.912075	.007468	336
29	10.097631	1364.644698	.000733	.099033	135.145030	.007400	348
30	10.935730	1490.359462	.000671	.091443	136.283493	.007338	360
31	11.843390	1626.508488	.000615	.084435	137.334707	.007282	372
32	12.826386	1773.957818	.000564	.077964	138.305356	.007231	384
33	13.890969	1933.645368	.000517	.071989	139.201617	.007184	396
34	15.043913	2106.586907	.000475	.066472	140.029189	.007142	408
35	16.292550	2293.882508	.000436	.061378	140.793337	.007103	420
36	17.644824	2496.723552	.000401	.056674	141.498922	.007068	432
37	19.109335	2716.400303	.000368	.052330	142.150433	.007035	444
38	20.695401	2954.310116	.000338	.048320	142.752012	.007005	456
39	22.413109	3211.966325	.000311	.044617	143.307487	.006978	468
40	24.273386	3491.007874	.000286	.041197	143.820391	.006953	480
41	26.288065	3793.209733	.000264	.038040	144.293988	.006931	492
42	28.469961	4120.494198	.000243	.035125	144.731288	.006910	504
43	30.832954	4474.943112	.000223	.032433	145.135074	.006890	516
44	33.392074	4858.811111	.000206	.029947	145.507915	.006873	528
45	36.163600	5274.539965	.000190	.027652	145.852182	.006857	540
46	39.165161	5724.774109	.000175	.025533	146.170065	.006842	552
47	42.415850	6212.377465	.000161	.023576	146.463585	.006828	564
48	45.936345	6740.451660	.000148	.021769	146.734611	.006815	576
49	49.749039	7312.355752	.000137	.020101	146.984865	.006804	588
50	53.878184	7931.727602	.000126	.018560	147.215941	.006793	600

9% MONTHLY COMPOUND INTEREST TABLE 9%

EFFECTIVE RATE = 3/4% BASE = 1.0075

MONTHS	1 AMOUNT OF I AT COMPOUND INTEREST $S^n = (1+i)^n$	2 ACCUMULATION OF I PER PERIOD $S_{\overline{n}\vert} = \frac{S^n - 1}{i}$	3 SINKING FUND FACTOR $1/S_{\overline{n}\vert} = \frac{i}{S^n - 1}$	4 PRES. VALUE REVERSION OF I $V^n = \frac{1}{S^n}$	5 PRESENT VALUE ORD. ANNUITY 1 PER PERIOD $a_{\overline{n}\vert} = \frac{1 - V^n}{i}$	6 INSTALMENT TO AMORTIZE I $1/a_{\overline{n}\vert} = \frac{i}{1 - V^n}$	n MONTHS
1	1.007500	1.000000	1.000000	.992555	.992555	1.007500	1
2	1.015056	2.007500	.498132	.985167	1.977722	.505632	2
3	1.022669	3.022556	.330845	.977833	2.955556	.338345	3
4	1.030339	4.045225	.247205	.970554	3.926110	.254705	4
5	1.038066	5.075564	.197022	.963329	4.889439	.204522	5
6	1.045852	6.113631	.163568	.956158	5.845597	.171068	6
7	1.053696	7.159483	.139674	.949040	6.794637	.147174	7
8	1.061598	8.213179	.121755	.941975	7.736613	.129255	8
9	1.069560	9.274778	.107819	.934963	8.671576	.115319	9
10	1.077582	10.344339	.096671	.928003	9.599579	.104171	10
11	1.085664	11.421921	.087550	.921094	10.520674	.095050	11
YEARS							
1	1.093806	12.507586	.079951	.914238	11.434912	.087451	12
2	1.196413	26.188470	.038184	.835831	21.889146	.045684	24
3	1.308645	41.152716	.024299	.764148	31.446805	.031799	36
4	1.431405	57.520711	.017385	.698614	40.184781	.024885	48
5	1.565681	75.424136	.013258	.638699	48.173373	.020758	60
6	1.712552	95.007027	.010525	.583923	55.476848	.018025	72
7	1.873201	116.426928	.008589	.533845	62.153964	.016089	84
8	2.048921	139.856163	.007150	.488061	68.258438	.014650	96
9	2.241124	165.483222	.006042	.446204	73.839381	.013542	108
10	2.451357	193.514276	.005167	.407937	78.941692	.012667	120
11	2.681311	224.174837	.004460	.372951	83.606419	.011960	132
12	2.932836	257.711569	.003880	.340966	87.871091	.011380	144
13	3.207957	294.394278	.003396	.311724	91.770017	.010896	156
14	3.508885	334.518079	.002989	.284990	95.334563	.010489	168
15	3.838043	378.405768	.002642	.260549	98.593409	.010142	180
16	4.198078	426.410426	.002345	.238204	101.572769	.009845	192
17	4.591886	478.918251	.002088	.217775	104.296613	.009588	204
18	5.022637	536.351673	.001864	.199098	106.786855	.009364	216
19	5.493795	599.172746	.001668	.182023	109.063530	.009168	228
20	6.009151	667.886868	.001497	.166412	111.144953	.008997	240
21	6.572851	743.046850	.001345	.152140	113.047869	.008845	252
22	7.189430	825.257356	.001211	.139093	114.787589	.008711	264
23	7.863848	915.179775	.001092	.127164	116.378106	.008592	276
24	8.601531	1013.537537	.000986	.116258	117.832217	.008486	288
25	9.408414	1121.121935	.000891	.106287	119.161622	.008391	300
26	10.290988	1238.798492	.000807	.097172	120.377014	.008307	312
27	11.256354	1367.513922	.000731	.088838	121.488171	.008231	324
28	12.312278	1508.303747	.000662	.081219	122.504035	.008162	336
29	13.467254	1662.300628	.000601	.074254	123.432775	.008101	348
30	14.730576	1830.743479	.000546	.067886	124.281865	.008046	360
31	16.112405	2014.987432	.000496	.062063	125.058136	.007996	372
32	17.623860	2216.514738	.000451	.056741	125.767833	.007951	384
33	19.277100	2436.946695	.000410	.051875	126.416663	.007910	396
34	21.085425	2678.056691	.000373	.047426	127.009849	.007873	408
35	23.063383	2941.784467	.000339	.043358	127.552164	.007839	420
36	25.226887	3230.251727	.000309	.039640	128.047967	.007809	432
37	27.593344	3545.779207	.000282	.036240	128.501249	.007782	444
38	30.181790	3890.905340	.000257	.033132	128.915658	.007757	456
39	33.013050	4268.406685	.000234	.030291	129.294525	.007734	468
40	36.109901	4681.320260	.000213	.027693	129.640901	.007713	480
41	39.497259	5132.967977	.000194	.025318	129.957571	.007694	492
42	43.202375	5626.983364	.000177	.023146	130.247083	.007677	504
43	47.255056	6167.340803	.000162	.021161	130.511766	.007662	516
44	51.687906	6758.387497	.000147	.019346	130.753748	.007647	528
45	56.536588	7404.878447	.000135	.017687	130.974978	.007635	540
46	61.840110	8112.014707	.000123	.016170	131.177236	.007623	552
47	67.641139	8885.485227	.000112	.014783	131.362146	.007612	564
48	73.986344	9731.512616	.000102	.013516	131.531199	.007602	576
49	80.926774	10656.903210	.000093	.012356	131.685753	.007593	588
50	88.518263	11669.101820	.000085	.011297	131.827052	.007585	600

10% MONTHLY COMPOUND INTEREST TABLE 10%

EFFECTIVE RATE = 5/6% BASE = 1.00833333

MONTHS	1 AMOUNT OF I AT COMPOUND INTEREST $S^n = (1+i)^n$	2 ACCUMULATION OF I PER PERIOD $S_{\overline{n}\|} = \frac{S^n - 1}{i}$	3 SINKING FUND FACTOR $1/S_{\overline{n}\|} = \frac{i}{S^n - 1}$	4 PRES. VALUE REVERSION OF I $V^n = \frac{1}{S^n}$	5 PRESENT VALUE ORD. ANNUITY 1 PER PERIOD $a_{\overline{n}\|} = \frac{1 - V^n}{i}$	6 INSTALMENT TO AMORTIZE I $1/a_{\overline{n}\|} = \frac{i}{1 - V^n}$	n MONTHS
1	1.008333	1.000000	1.000000	.991735	.991735	1.008333	1
2	1.016736	2.008333	.497925	.983539	1.975274	.506258	2
3	1.025208	3.025069	.330570	.975410	2.950685	.338904	3
4	1.033752	4.050278	.246896	.967349	3.918035	.255229	4
5	1.042366	5.084030	.196694	.959355	4.877390	.205027	5
6	1.051053	6.126397	.163228	.951426	5.828817	.171561	6
7	1.059812	7.177450	.139325	.943563	6.772380	.147658	7
8	1.068643	8.237262	.121399	.935765	7.708146	.129732	8
9	1.077549	9.305906	.107458	.928031	8.636177	.115791	9
10	1.086528	10.383456	.096307	.920362	9.556540	.104640	10
11	1.095583	11.469984	.087184	.912755	10.469295	.095517	11
YEARS							
1	1.104713	12.565568	.079582	.905212	11.374508	.087915	12
2	1.220390	26.446915	.037811	.819409	21.670854	.046144	24
3	1.348181	41.781821	.023933	.741739	30.991235	.032267	36
4	1.489354	58.722491	.017029	.671432	39.428160	.025362	48
5	1.645308	77.437072	.012913	.607788	47.065369	.021247	60
6	1.817594	98.111313	.010192	.550177	53.978665	.018525	72
7	2.007920	120.950418	.008267	.498027	60.236667	.016601	84
8	2.218175	146.181075	.006840	.450820	65.901488	.015174	96
9	2.450447	174.053712	.005745	.408088	71.029355	.014078	108
10	2.707041	204.844978	.004881	.369406	75.671163	.013215	120
11	2.990504	238.860492	.004186	.334391	79.872985	.012519	132
12	3.303648	276.437875	.003617	.302695	83.676528	.011950	144
13	3.649584	317.950100	.003145	.274003	87.119542	.011478	156
14	4.031743	363.809198	.002748	.248031	90.236200	.011082	168
15	4.453919	414.470344	.002412	.224521	93.057438	.010746	180
16	4.920303	470.436373	.002125	.203239	95.611258	.010459	192
17	5.435523	532.262776	.001878	.183974	97.923008	.010212	204
18	6.004693	600.563212	.001665	.166536	100.015632	.009998	216
19	6.633463	676.015596	.001479	.150750	101.909902	.009812	228
20	7.328073	759.368830	.001316	.136461	103.624619	.009650	240
21	8.095418	851.450237	.001174	.123526	105.176801	.009507	252
22	8.943114	953.173772	.001049	.111817	106.581857	.009382	264
23	9.879575	1065.549089	.000938	.101218	107.853729	.009271	276
24	10.914096	1189.691570	.000840	.091624	109.005045	.009173	288
25	12.056944	1326.833392	.000753	.082939	110.047230	.009087	300
26	13.319464	1478.335753	.000676	.075078	110.990629	.009009	312
27	14.714186	1645.702391	.000607	.067961	111.844605	.008940	324
28	16.254954	1830.594505	.000546	.061519	112.617636	.008879	336
29	17.957060	2034.847238	.000491	.055688	113.317391	.008824	348
30	19.837399	2260.487900	.000442	.050409	113.950820	.008775	360
31	21.914633	2509.756088	.000398	.045631	114.524207	.008731	372
32	24.209382	2785.125915	.000359	.041306	115.043244	.008692	384
33	26.744421	3089.330559	.000323	.037390	115.513083	.008657	396
34	29.544911	3425.389403	.000291	.033846	115.938387	.008625	408
35	32.638649	3796.638004	.000263	.030638	116.323378	.008596	420
36	36.056343	4206.761180	.000237	.027734	116.671875	.008571	432
37	39.831913	4659.829611	.000214	.025105	116.987341	.008547	444
38	44.002835	5160.340233	.000193	.022725	117.272903	.008527	456
39	48.610506	5713.260852	.000175	.020571	117.531398	.008508	468
40	53.700662	6324.079483	.000158	.018621	117.765390	.008491	480
41	59.323823	6998.858807	.000142	.016856	117.977204	.008476	492
42	65.535802	7744.296352	.000129	.015258	118.168940	.008462	504
43	72.398257	8567.790939	.000116	.013812	118.342502	.008450	516
44	79.979301	9477.516170	.000105	.012503	118.499611	.008438	528
45	88.354179	10482.501530	.000095	.011318	118.641830	.008428	540
46	97.606016	11592.721980	.000086	.010245	118.770568	.008419	552
47	107.826641	12819.197020	.000078	.009274	118.887103	.008411	564
48	119.117499	14174.100030	.000070	.008395	118.992592	.008403	576
49	131.590658	15670.879080	.000063	.007599	119.088082	.008397	588
50	145.369919	17324.390450	.000057	.006879	119.174520	.008391	600

11% MONTHLY COMPOUND INTEREST TABLE 11%

EFFECTIVE RATE = 11/12% BASE = 1.00916667

MONTHS	1 AMOUNT OF I AT COMPOUND INTEREST $S^n = (1+i)^n$	2 ACCUMULATION OF I PER PERIOD $S_{\overline{n}\vert} = \frac{S^n - 1}{i}$	3 SINKING FUND FACTOR $1/S_{\overline{n}\vert} = \frac{i}{S^n - 1}$	4 PRES. VALUE REVERSION OF I $V^n = \frac{1}{S^n}$	5 PRESENT VALUE ORD. ANNUITY 1 PER PERIOD $a_{\overline{n}\vert} = \frac{1 - V^n}{i}$	6 INSTALMENT TO AMORTIZE I $1/a_{\overline{n}\vert} = \frac{i}{1 - V^n}$	n MONTHS
1	1.009166	1.000000	1.000000	.990916	.990916	1.009166	1
2	1.018417	2.009166	.497718	.981915	1.972832	.506885	2
3	1.027752	3.027584	.330296	.972996	2.945828	.339463	3
4	1.037173	4.055336	.246588	.964158	3.909987	.255755	4
5	1.046681	5.092510	.196366	.955400	4.865387	.205533	5
6	1.056275	6.139192	.162887	.946722	5.812110	.172054	6
7	1.065958	7.195468	.138976	.938122	6.750233	.148143	7
8	1.075729	8.261426	.121044	.929601	7.679834	.130211	8
9	1.085590	9.337156	.107098	.921157	8.600992	.116265	9
10	1.095541	10.422746	.095943	.912790	9.513782	.105110	10
11	1.105584	11.518288	.086818	.904499	10.418281	.095985	11
YEARS							
1	1.115718	12.623873	.079214	.896283	11.314564	.088381	12
2	1.244828	26.708565	.037441	.803323	21.455618	.046607	24
3	1.388878	42.423123	.023572	.720005	30.544874	.032738	36
4	1.549598	59.956150	.016678	.645328	38.691421	.025845	48
5	1.728915	79.518079	.012575	.578397	45.993033	.021742	60
6	1.928983	101.343692	.009867	.518407	52.537346	.019034	72
7	2.152203	125.694939	.007955	.464640	58.402903	.017122	84
8	2.401254	152.864084	.006541	.416449	63.660103	.015708	96
9	2.679124	183.177212	.005459	.373256	68.372043	.014625	108
10	2.989149	216.998138	.004608	.334543	72.595274	.013775	120
11	3.335050	254.732784	.003925	.299845	76.380486	.013092	132
12	3.720978	296.834038	.003368	.268746	79.773108	.012535	144
13	4.151566	343.807201	.002908	.240872	82.813858	.012075	156
14	4.631980	396.216043	.002523	.215890	85.539231	.011690	168
15	5.167987	454.689576	.002199	.193498	87.981936	.011365	180
16	5.766021	519.929598	.001923	.173429	90.171292	.011090	192
17	6.433258	592.719119	.001687	.155442	92.133575	.010853	204
18	7.177707	673.931759	.001483	.139320	93.892336	.010650	216
19	8.008303	764.542231	.001307	.124870	95.468684	.010474	228
20	8.935015	865.638042	.001155	.111919	96.881538	.010321	240
21	9.968965	978.432542	.001022	.100311	98.147855	.010188	252
22	11.122562	1104.279491	.000905	.089907	99.282835	.010072	264
23	12.409651	1244.689302	.000803	.080582	100.300097	.009970	276
24	13.845682	1401.347173	.000713	.072224	101.211853	.009880	288
25	15.447888	1576.133312	.000634	.064733	102.029043	.009801	300
26	17.235500	1771.145496	.000564	.058019	102.761477	.009731	312
27	19.229972	1988.724266	.000502	.052002	103.417946	.009669	324
28	21.455242	2231.480999	.000448	.046608	104.006327	.009614	336
29	23.938018	2502.329255	.000399	.041774	104.533684	.009566	348
30	26.708097	2804.519759	.000356	.037441	105.006345	.009523	360
31	29.798727	3141.679397	.000318	.033558	105.429983	.009484	372
32	33.247002	3517.854756	.000284	.030077	105.809682	.009450	384
33	37.094306	3937.560686	.000253	.026958	106.150002	.009420	396
34	41.386816	4405.834502	.000226	.024162	106.455022	.009393	408
35	46.176050	4928.296419	.000202	.021656	106.728408	.009369	420
36	51.519489	5511.217017	.000181	.019410	106.973440	.009348	432
37	57.481264	6161.592513	.000162	.017396	107.193057	.009328	444
38	64.132930	6887.228705	.000145	.015592	107.389896	.009311	456
39	71.554318	7696.834666	.000129	.013975	107.566320	.009296	468
40	79.834500	8600.127295	.000116	.012525	107.724446	.009282	480
41	89.072856	9607.947896	.000104	.011226	107.866170	.009270	492
42	99.380263	10732.392330	.000093	.010062	107.993196	.009259	504
43	110.880431	11986.956140	.000083	.009018	108.107048	.009250	516
44	123.711386	13386.696640	.000074	.008083	108.209091	.009241	528
45	138.027124	14948.413480	.000066	.007244	108.300550	.009233	540
46	153.999462	16690.850360	.000059	.006493	108.382523	.009226	552
47	171.820100	18634.920020	.000053	.005820	108.455995	.009220	564
48	191.702923	20803.955170	.000048	.005216	108.521846	.009214	576
49	213.886562	23223.988540	.000043	.004675	108.580868	.009209	588
50	238.637266	25924.065330	.000038	.004190	108.633767	.009205	600

12% MONTHLY COMPOUND INTEREST TABLE 12%

EFFECTIVE RATE = 1% BASE = 1.0100

MONTHS	1 AMOUNT OF I AT COMPOUND INTEREST $S^n = (1+i)^n$	2 ACCUMULATION OF I PER PERIOD $S_{\overline{n}\vert} = \frac{S^n - 1}{i}$	3 SINKING FUND FACTOR $1/S_{\overline{n}\vert} = \frac{i}{S^n - 1}$	4 PRES. VALUE REVERSION OF I $V^n = \frac{1}{S^n}$	5 PRESENT VALUE ORD. ANNUITY 1 PER PERIOD $a_{\overline{n}\vert} = \frac{1 - V^n}{i}$	6 INSTALMENT TO AMORTIZE I $1/a_{\overline{n}\vert} = \frac{i}{1 - V^n}$	n MONTHS
1	1.010000	1.000000	1.000000	.990099	.990099	1.010000	1
2	1.020099	2.009999	.497512	.980296	1.970395	.507512	2
3	1.030300	3.030099	.330022	.970590	2.940985	.340022	3
4	1.040604	4.060400	.246281	.960980	3.901965	.256281	4
5	1.051010	5.101005	.196039	.951465	4.853431	.206039	5
6	1.061520	6.152015	.162548	.942045	5.795476	.172548	6
7	1.072135	7.213535	.138628	.932718	6.728194	.148628	7
8	1.082856	8.285670	.120690	.923483	7.651677	.130690	8
9	1.093685	9.368527	.106740	.914339	8.566017	.116740	9
10	1.104622	10.462212	.095582	.905286	9.471304	.105582	10
11	1.115668	11.566834	.086454	.896323	10.367628	.096454	11
YEARS							
1	1.126825	12.682503	.078848	.887449	11.255077	.088848	12
2	1.269734	26.973464	.037073	.787566	21.243387	.047073	24
3	1.430768	43.076878	.023214	.698924	30.107505	.033214	36
4	1.612226	61.222607	.016333	.620260	37.973959	.026333	48
5	1.816696	81.669669	.012244	.550449	44.955038	.022244	60
6	2.047099	104.709931	.009550	.488496	51.150391	.019550	72
7	2.306722	130.672274	.007652	.433515	56.648452	.017652	84
8	2.599272	159.927292	.006252	.384722	61.527703	.016252	96
9	2.928925	192.892579	.005184	.341422	65.857789	.015184	108
10	3.300386	230.038689	.004347	.302994	69.700522	.014347	120
11	3.718958	271.895856	.003677	.268892	73.110751	.013677	132
12	4.190615	319.061559	.003134	.238628	76.137157	.013134	144
13	4.722090	372.209054	.002686	.211770	78.822938	.012686	156
14	5.320969	432.096981	.002314	.187935	81.206433	.012314	168
15	5.995801	499.580197	.002001	.166783	83.321664	.012001	180
16	6.756219	575.621973	.001737	.148011	85.198823	.011787	192
17	7.613077	661.307750	.001512	.131352	86.864707	.011512	204
18	8.578606	757.860629	.001319	.116569	88.343095	.011319	216
19	9.666588	866.658829	.001153	.103449	89.655088	.011153	228
20	10.892553	989.255364	.001010	.091805	90.819416	.011010	240
21	12.274002	1127.400209	.000886	.081473	91.852697	.010886	252
22	13.830652	1283.065277	.000779	.072303	92.769683	.010779	264
23	15.584725	1458.472573	.000685	.064165	93.583461	.010685	276
24	17.561259	1656.125904	.000603	.056943	94.305647	.010603	288
25	19.788466	1878.846624	.000532	.050534	94.946551	.010532	300
26	22.298139	2129.813907	.000469	.044846	95.515320	.010469	312
27	25.126101	2412.610122	.000414	.039799	96.020074	.010414	324
28	28.312719	2731.271978	.000366	.035319	96.468018	.010366	336
29	31.903481	3090.348132	.000323	.031344	96.865546	.010323	348
30	35.949641	3494.964129	.000286	.027816	97.218330	.010286	360
31	40.508955	3950.895562	.000253	.024685	97.531409	.010253	372
32	45.646505	4464.650512	.000223	.021907	97.809251	.010223	384
33	51.435624	5043.562455	.000198	.019441	98.055821	.010198	396
34	57.958949	5695.894917	.000175	.017253	98.274641	.010175	408
35	65.309594	6430.959463	.000155	.015311	98.468831	.010155	420
36	73.592485	7259.248592	.000137	.013588	98.641165	.010137	432
37	82.925855	8192.585514	.000122	.012058	98.794103	.010122	444
38	93.442929	9244.292929	.000108	.010701	98.929827	.010108	456
39	105.293831	10429.383160	.000095	.009497	99.050277	.010095	468
40	118.647724	11764.772490	.000084	.008428	99.157169	.010084	480
41	133.695226	13269.522620	.000075	.007479	99.252029	.010075	492
42	150.651127	14965.112740	.000066	.006637	99.336214	.010066	504
43	169.757461	16875.746110	.000059	.005890	99.410924	.010059	516
44	191.286956	19028.695620	.000052	.005227	99.477225	.010052	528
45	215.546930	21454.693010	.000046	.004639	99.536064	.010046	540
46	242.883675	24188.367600	.000041	.004117	99.588280	.010041	552
47	273.687405	27268.740570	.000036	.003653	99.634619	.010036	564
48	308.397819	30739.781910	.000032	.003242	99.675743	.010032	576
49	347.510381	34651.038170	.000028	.002877	99.712238	.010028	588
50	391.583396	39058.339630	.000025	.002553	99.744626	.010025	600

Glossary

Abandonment Legal term that states that a landlord may reacquire his or her property if the tenant permanently leaves the premises prior to the expiration of the lease.

Absolute Deed Legal writing that appears to sell and convey title, but may actually be only a hypothecation if it can be proven that the intention was to offer security for a loan.

Absolute Title Title acquired only after all rights of redemption have expired.

Abstract and Opinion Method of title protection that includes (1) a history of title as shown by a summary or abstract of all recorded instruments that have ever affected title and (2) an opinion of the condition of the title rendered by an attorney or professional abstractor upon examination of the abstract.

Accelerated Depreciation Methods of depreciation that allow greater deductions (at least in the early years of an investment holding period) than would straight-line depreciation.

Acceleration Clause Loan clause that allows the lender to demand full payment of the debt upon default or the occurrence of some other specified event.

Acceptance Indication by some word or act of the offeree that he or she is willing to be bound by the terms and conditions of an offer.

Accord and Satisfaction Situation that prevails when a new contract has been agreed upon (accord) to replace the original one and its terms and conditions are completed (satisfaction).

Accretion Gaining of property by the action of the water adjacent to the property. Accretion includes alluvion, reliction, and/or avulsion.

Accrued Depreciation Difference between reproduction cost new or replacement cost new and the present worth of the improvements; also called *diminished utility*.

Acknowledgment Formal declaration, before a duly authorized officer (usually a notary public), by a person who has executed an instrument that such execution is his or her own free and voluntary act.

Actual Authority Authority given to the agent by the principal in either an expressed or an implied manner.

Actual Fraud Fraud that includes causing or tending to cause injury to another by stating known or unknown falsehoods, suppressing truths, making promises with no intention to perform them, or acting with the intention to deceive.

Actual Notice Knowledge inside someone's head because of what he or she has seen, heard, read, or observed.

Addition of Fixtures A tenant's affixing of personal property to his or her landlord's property, *without permission* for later removal, such that it becomes a permanent fixture and the attached property is acquired by the landlord.

Adjusted Basis Basis *plus* the costs of capital improvements and capitalized carrying costs *minus* depreciation, casualty losses, and the basis attributed to a sale of a part of the real property.

Adjusted Gross Income Gross income minus adjustments.

Adjusted Sales Price Actual sales price less selling expenses and/or expenses for repairs.

Adjusted or Terminal Value Rate of Return Variation of the internal rate of return (IRR) that assumes all cash flows are reinvested at some rate to accumulate or compound to an ending value at the termination of the projected investment holding period.

Adjustment and Correlation Process Process in which the appraiser must adjust each of the comparable properties to an estimate of what the property would have sold for if it had possessed all the important characteristics of the subject property.

Adjustments Alterations in taxable income due to sick pay, certain moving expenses, business expenses, the $100 per person dividend exclusion, state and municipal bond interest, pension and annuity return-of-capital payments, depreciation, repairs, costs of farm and business operations, and basis upon sale or exchange of assets.

Administrator Person appointed by the probate court to administer the estate of a deceased person who dies without a will.

Administratrix Female administrator.

Ad Valorem Legal term derived from Latin, meaning "according to value" and used to describe real estate property taxes—which are usually assessed according to value.

Adverse Possession Acquisition of title to the real property of another by the hostile, actual, exclusive, open, notorious, and continuous possession and occupation under an evident claim of right or title for the appropriate statutory time period.

Affiliates Suborganizations or specialized trade groups within the National Association of Realtors®.

After-Tax Cash Flow Cash throwoff to equity minus any tax liability or plus any tax savings.

Agency by Estoppel (Ostensible Agency) Agency created when one leads others (by action or words) to believe one is a party's agent or when a third party acts in belief that one is another's agent. In either case the parties are estopped from denying the supposed agency relationship.

Agency by Operation of Law (by Necessity) Agency created by an unusual or unforeseen set of circumstances, such as an emergency, and in which the agent acts outside the scope of his or her authority but in the best interests of his or her principal.

Agency by Ratification Agency relationship created by the principal's consent to the act.

Agent Person who is employed by, acts for or on behalf of, or acts in the place of another person (principal) in dealing with yet another person (third party).

Agricultural Fixtures Articles added to real estate by a tenant which are necessary for the cultivation of a crop.

Alienation Transfer of property ownership from one person to another.

Alienation Clause Loan clause that stipulates the rights of the lender upon sale and transfer of title of the hypothecated property.

Allodial System of "total" ownership of property in absolute independence by individuals which exists in the United States; the word is derived from the Old German *al* ("all") and *od* ("property")

Alteration Change in a material portion of a contract (such as date or price) made with fraudulent intent.

Alluvion Soil that has been washed up and deposited on the banks of the water, producing additional firm ground.

Ambulatory Instrument Any legal instrument that can be revoked before death.

Amenities Satisfaction of possession and use derived from a property; conditions of agreeable living or a beneficial influence arising from the location or improvements.

Amortization Liquidation of a financial obligation; payment of principal during the loan term.

Annual Percentage Rate (APR) Effective rate of interest paid on a real estate loan considering, in addition to the stated interest rate, all the financing charges.

Anticipation Principle of valuation that

holds that the value of a property is determined by the present worth of all present and future benefits expected to be derived from the ownership and/or use of the real estate.

Apparent Authority Authority created when the words or conduct of the principal have led third parties to believe that an agency relationship exists; also called *ostensible authority*.

Appraisal Process Orderly program or set of procedures followed to arrive at the solution to an appraisal problem.

Appraised Value Estimate by an appraiser of the amount of a particular value, such as assessed value, insurance value, or market value, based upon the data the appraiser has collected and interpreted.

Appreciation of Capital Increase or growth in the value of an investment.

Appurtenance Incidental right, privilege, or improvement that has been permanently added to and belongs to another right in real property and is transferred along with that other right when it is conveyed or sold.

Appurtenance Clause Clause in a deed that defines all the additional rights that are necessary to the proper use and enjoyment of the property and all improvements (buildings, fences, etc.) that exist on the property.

Assessed Value Value placed on land and buildings by a government unit as a basis for taxation.

Assignment Transfer of one's rights in a contract to another person.

Assume and Agree to Pay Arrangement whereby the buyer agrees to be primarily liable for the debt assumed from the seller.

Assumption Clause Loan clause stipulating the rights of the lender upon the taking over of the debt by another person (buyer).

Assumption Fee or Loan Transfer Fee Charge, usually paid by the buyer, that covers the processing of the paperwork involved in a loan assumption.

Attachments Involuntary, statutory, specific liens filed by plaintiffs in a lawsuit to prevent defendants from disposing of their real property prior to a judgment being decreed by the court.

Attorney-in-Fact Agent indicated in a power-of-attorney instrument.

Average Rate of Return Arithmetic average of the total returns to equity less the original equity investment; also called the *accounting return*.

Axial Theory Theory of land-use development which concludes that land uses tend to develop along and relative to time-cost functions of transportation axes that radiate out from a central business district.

Balance Condition in which all the factors of production are present in proper proportions so that value is maximized.

Bankruptcy Situation in which one's liabilities exceed one's assets.

Bargain and Sale Deed Deed that recites the consideration given and conveys the present and "after-acquired" title to real property without giving any warranties of title; also called a *deed without covenants*.

Basis Original cost of acquiring a property or original value of a property upon acquisition.

Beneficiary Lender in a deed of trust loan transaction.

Bequest Gift by will of personal property.

Bequestee Recipient of a gift by will of personal property.

Bilateral Contract in which the promise of one party is given in exchange for the promise of another party. Both parties must act.

Bill of Sale Receipt for the purchase of personal property.

Binder Preliminary informal contract that says that the purchaser and seller agree to contract in a formal manner within a short period of time in the future and, until such time, the informal contract will *bind* the two parties to contract with one another.

Blanket Mortgage (Trust Deed) Single mortgage or trust deed that covers more than one piece of real estate.

Boot Cash, net mortgage relief transferred in an exchange of property; tax is paid on any boot received in an exchange.

Broad Market Situation prevailing when there are many buyers and sellers in the market at the same time such that a sudden, but temporary, surge in number of buyers and sellers can be handled without extreme price variations.

Broker's Equity Rate of Return Ratio of the cash throwoff to equity or before-tax cash flow to the original equity investment; also called the *cash spendable rate*, the *Cash-on-Cash Rate**, the *equity dividend rate*, and the *cash-flow rate*.

Budget Mortgage Loan that provides that the monthly payment to the lender include, in addition to principal and interest, one-twelfth of the annual property taxes and annual hazard insurance.

*Terms spelled with capital letters are defined elsewhere in the Glossary.

Business Risk Expression of the degree of uncertainty of the productivity analysis of a real estate investment; also called "earning-power risk."

Capital Gains Treatment Preferential tax treatment available to profits made from the sale of certain assets.

Capitalization Conversion of income to value.

Capitalization Rate Sum of the discount rate and the capital recapture (recovery) rate, used to convert net operating income to value.

Capital Market Market for long-term borrowing and lending.

Capital Recapture (Recovery) Rate Return "of" total invested capital, expressed as an annual rate.

Cash-on-Cash Rate Cash throwoff to equity divided by original equity; a rate of return to equity.

Cash Throwoff to Equity Net operating income less debt service.

Certificate of Reduction Document that indicates the unpaid loan balance, annual interest rate (which may escalate upon assumption), and periodic payment size and schedule.

Certificate of Title Opinion of the condition of title made from the examination of the "original" records affecting title rather than from an examination of an abstract.

Certified Listing Variation of the exclusive right to sell listing which requires the seller to pay a deposit ($75 to $150) to cover the cost of a market data appraisal of the listed property: if the seller lists at the appraised value, the deposit is deducted from the commission at closing; if the seller does not list, the deposit is forfeited.

Chattel Fixtures Articles added to real estate by a tenant which are considered personal property and include trade, agricultural, and domestic fixtures.

Chattel Mortgage Loan on personal property, such as a car loan.

Closed Mortgage Opposite of an open mortgage; is either not due, in default, or, as with a construction loan, fully funded.

Closing Meeting of all parties to a real estate transaction to complete the title transfer process and to monetarily conclude or settle the transaction.

Closing or Settlement Statement Document that provides a full accounting for both buyer and seller of all the operations and costs of closing the transaction.

Codicil Supplement to a will made subsequent to the making of the will. It must be signed and witnessed, like the will itself.

Collateral Property that is hypothecated or pledged as security for payment of the loan.

Color of Title Situation that exists when a person takes possession under a defective or void instrument.

Commercial Easement in Gross Easement in gross held by a corporation, such as a utility company; such an easement may be sold and/or mortgaged.

Common Law Dedication Gift to the public that results when an owner wishes to give some of his or her land for public use, such as for a road in a subdivision. The owner must execute a deed, and the public may accept the property by local ordinance or by public use.

Common Law Lien Lien based upon a legal precedent set by a previous court decision, such as the right of a hotel to retain the luggage of a guest until his or her bill is paid.

Community Property Concurrent estate that confers ownership to husband and wife of equal shares of all real and personal property that was acquired through their joint efforts during their marriage.

Competent Party Individual who is of legal age (not an infant or a minor), not insane, not drunk, not a convict, not a spendthrift, or not an aged person with an appointed guardian; one of the four essentials of a valid contract.

Competition Principle that holds that profit breeds competition and excess profits breed potentially ruinous competition.

Component Depreciation Method of depreciation in which individual parts of a building are depreciated separately based on the life of each part.

Concentric-Circle Theory Theory of land-use development patterns which concludes that land uses tend to develop in concentric circles out from the central business district, circled by a mixed commercial and industrial area, circled by a low-income housing area, circled by a middle-income housing area, circled by a commuters' suburban area.

Concurrent Estates Interests in real property held simultaneously by more than one person.

Condemnation Clause Loan clause that states that any condemnation awards must be applied first to the debt outstanding.

Conditional Fee Estate having the limitation that, upon death of the grantee, it descends to "the heirs of his or her body" (not to be confused with a fee simple subject to a condition subsequent or the conditional fee of early English law).

Confiscation Right of a country to take the property of its enemies in time of war.

Conformity Condition of a reasonable degree of social, economic, and architectural homogeneity within a neighborhood area, maximizing property value.

Connie Mac Market for mortgage bonds backed by conventional mortgages.

Constant-Payment Loan Loan that calls for equal amounts of the principal plus the accrued interest to be paid each period.

Construction Loan Generally, interim, short-term loans used to finance the building of a structure.

Constructive Fraud Fraud that includes taking advantage of another to his or her detriment without actually deceiving him or her.

Constructive Notice Notice given by the public records; often called "legal notice."

Contingent Interest Loan Type of loan commonly used in commercial income property lending. The lender, in addition to collecting interest on the loan, participates in the benefits that normally accrue only to the equity position.

Contingent Remainderman A person who is not known ("inchoate") to be the recipient of the remainder at the time a life estate is granted.

Contract Deliberate agreement made between two or more legally competent persons, upon some legal (good or valuable) consideration, to do or not to do some legal act.

Contract Price Sales price minus loans, assumed or payable to third parties in an installment contract sale.

Contribution Value of any individual factor of production. It is a function of how much this factor enhances the property value by its presence or how it detracts from the property value by its absence.

Convenience Ease or freedom from discomfort of persons or goods in movement from the location of the subject property to other points on the urban landscape to which movement is desirable or essential; one of three basic elements of the Ratcliff model.

Conventional Life Estate Life estate created through the acts of the parties with a deed or will.

Conventional Loan Non-government-sponsored residential real estate loan.

Conveyance Document, such as a deed, used to transfer title to property from one person to another.

Conveyancer Person who examines the original records and prepares a certificate of title.

Corporation Legal entity or artificial person formed, under state law, by individual shareholders to own and operate a business.

Corporeal Term that refers to items of real property.

Cost Historical price once paid in the past.

Cost Approach Analysis in which a value estimate of a property is derived by estimating the reproduction cost or the replacement cost of the improvements, deducting the estimated accrued depreciation, then adding the market value of the land.

Cost-Push Inflation Increase in prices caused by an increase in the costs of the factors of production.

Counteroffer Rejection of the original offer by proposing a new offer, thus terminating the original offer.

Covenant against Encumbrances Deed warranty that guarantees there exist no claims or encumbrances against the property other than the ones specifically named in the under and subject clause of the deed.

Covenant of Further Assurance Deed warranty that guarantees the grantor will voluntarily execute, procure, and deliver to the grantee or to any future grantee any instruments or conveyances that subsequently become necessary to vest good title in the grantee. This covenant is real and does run with the land.

Covenant of Quiet Enjoyment Deed warranty that guarantees the grantee will not be disturbed in his or her possession or be evicted by someone holding a superior title. The covenant is real and therefore runs with the land.

Covenant of Right to Convey Deed warranty that guarantees that the grantor, due to his or her seisin, has full rights to sell property. This covenant does not run with the land.

Covenant of Seisin Deed warranty that guarantees that the grantor has absolute, perfect, full, and indefeasible title subject only to named encumbrances. This covenant is personal to the grantee and, therefore, does not run with the land.

Covenant of Warranty Agreement in a deed whereby certain guarantees are made by the grantor to the grantee.

Covenant of Warranty Forever Deed warranty that guarantees title and possession to be absolute and guarantees that the grantor will protect and defend the grantee against anyone who may attack the title. This covenant runs with the land.

Credit Deal Real estate loan that has the borrower's income and/or credit rating as the prime security.

Crop Mortgage Type of chattel mortgage.

Crossover Point Mathematical point where the nondeductible cash-outlay amortization payment equals or exceeds the deductible noncash depreciation expense.

Crowding-Out Effect Situation in which demand for loanable funds is high because of deficit budget financing and an expansionary economy, so the mortgage borrower is often outbid or "crowded-out" by the federal government and corporations for the available loanable funds in tight-money and capital markets.

Curtesy Legal life estate in all of the real estate of a deceased wife given by law to her surviving husband provided a live child was born from their marriage.

Dealer Person who sells and holds property for sale to customers in the ordinary course of business.

Debt-Coverage Factor Ratio of the net operating income over the debt service which gives a lender an indication of the cushion for error allowed for overoptimistic income projections.

Debt Service Periodic payment of principal and interest on a real estate loan.

Decedent One who has died.

Dedication Gift (grant) of land to the public; includes common law dedication, statutory dedication, and dedication by deed.

Dedication by Deed Gift to the public that results when a land developer specifically wishes to grant fee simple title in land that might otherwise be considered to be an easement for public use.

Deed Formally written *legal instrument* that conveys and evidences title.

Deed Covenants or Restrictions Limitations of property use contained in or amended to a deed.

Deed in Lieu of Foreclosure Alternative to foreclosure and a voluntary transfer of title to the lender.

Deed Restrictions or Covenants Limitations of property use contained in or amended to a deed.

Deed of Trust Three-party hypothecation instrument that pledges property as security for a loan, thereby creating a lien or title interest against the property, which may be foreclosed (in some states) without court action; also called a *trust deed*.

Default Clause Loan clause that stipulates all the rights of the lender (acceleration, foreclosure, etc.) upon any default or breaking of any of the covenants; this clause may also impose financial penalties for late payments.

Default Ratio Ratio of operating expenses plus debt service over effective gross income, which indicates the cushion for error in projecting income, vacancies, and expenses.

Defeasance Clause Loan clause that gives the borrower the right to redeem a property upon payment of the obligation to the lender.

Deferred-Interest Mortgage Proposal that lenders should charge below-market interest rates and the federal government would pay the difference; in return, the homeowner would repay the government out of any capital gain or profit realized when the home was sold.

Deficiency Judgment Legal provision that when in a foreclosure through public sale, a property sells for less than the debt outstanding, the lender may sue for the deficit.

Deficit Budget Phenomenon that exists when the federal government spends more than it collects through taxes.

Delivery Final and absolute transfer of a deed from seller to buyer in such a manner that it cannot be recalled by the seller. A necessary requisite to the transfer of title.

Demand Deposits Checking account deposits at commercial banks.

Demand-Pull Inflation Increase in prices that occurs when consumer demand increases more rapidly than the supply of goods and services.

Demographics Statistics on human population, especially with reference to size and density of population, distribution of age and marital status, educational levels, and other vital information.

Depreciation Noncash expense allowed as an expense in calculating federal income tax liability.

Depreciation Recapture Part of a capital gain earned due to having taken excess depreciation.

Developer One who organizes, coordinates, and supervises the land acquisition, construction of improvements, financing, sales, and management of a complete real estate project.

Devise Gift of real property by will.

Devisee Recipient of a gift of real property by will.

Disclosed Principal Principal whose identity and the existence of the agency relationship are made known to third persons.

Discount Loss incurred from the sale of a package of mortgages.

Discount Rate Annual competitive rate of return "on" total invested capital, necessary to compensate the investor for all the various risks inherent in a particular investment.

Discount Rate Interest rate charged by the Federal Reserve Board (the Fed) when commercial banks borrow from it.

Disintermediation Situation in which the supply of loanable funds at financial intermediaries declines because savings are being withdrawn to be directly invested in government securities, which offer high yields in order to attract the loanable funds required to finance deficit federal budgets.

Distributees Heirs and/or next of kin.

Doctrine of Estates Concept that defined "how long" (timewise as opposed to tenancywise) the relationship between the *person and the land* would last under the allodial system of property ownership.

Doctrine of Promissory Estoppel Concept that a written contract supersedes and bars all prior negotiations and conversations where it is intended that the contract be reduced to writing or be an integration of all prior discussions.

Doctrine of Tenures Concept that defined "how" land was *held* within the *person-to-person* relationships under the feudal system of property ownership.

Documentary Fee Name for the real estate transfer tax in some states.

Domestic Fixtures Articles added to real estate by a tenant which are necessary for additional comfort or ornamentation within his or her domicile.

Dominant Tenement Interest held by the owner of an easement.

Dower Legal life estate in part of the real estate of a deceased husband given by law to his surviving wife.

Down Payment Money the buyer pays the seller when first purchasing a property; original purchase price less all original loan amounts.

Duress Use of force or restraint to compel someone to do something against his or her free will.

Earnest Money Down payment made by the purchaser of real estate upon signing a contract as evidence of good faith.

Easement Nonpossessory right or interest held by one person in the land of another person such that the nonpossessing person is allowed partial use of the land for a specific purpose.

Easement Appurtenant Easement that exists for the benefit of the usually adjoining parcel of real estate; such an easement is irrevocable and is regarded as being so closely connected to the dominant tenement that, upon the sale of the dominant parcel, the easement is also conveyed even though the deed may not mention it.

Easement in Gross Easement that exists for the benefit of a person who usually does not own the adjoining parcel of real estate; such an easement is irrevocable but is extinguished at the death of the person who owns the easement.

Economic-Base Theory Urban analysis theory that divides the economic activities of a community into basic or primary activities and service or secondary activities.

Economic Life Estimated time period during which a building will produce a competitive return.

Economic Obsolescence Loss in value due to environmental forces existing outside the property itself; also called "locational diminished utility."

Economic Value Value of a real estate project as determined by the capitalization of the projected income rather than by the costs of development; economic value usually exceeds cost.

Effective Gross Income Potential gross income, less allowance for vacancy and rent loss, plus other income.

Effective Income Income that is regular, stable, calculable, and legal and therefore is counted in qualifying a person for a loan.

Effective Marginal Tax Rate Rate of tax paid on the last dollar earned after allowance for tax shelters.

Effective Tax Rate Percentage derived from dividing total annual tax by total annual income.

Ellwood Method Refinement of the investor's cash-flow method of income capitalization which employs a specialized formula to derive the capitalization rate, which is then divided into income to estimate value.

Emblements Rights to the "fruits of the soil by man," or crops that are planted annually and cultivated; such crops are called *Fructus Industriales*.

Eminent Domain Government power to condemn private property and acquire it by paying just compensation at fair market value; the property acquired can then be transferred into public use or even private use as long as the public benefits from such use.

Encroachment A trespass upon the property of another, such as the eave of a building that invades the airspace of a contiguous property.

Encumbrance Any right or interest in real property which affects or limits the fee simple title by either impairing the property's marketability or diminishing its value; includes easements, encroachments, deed restrictions, and liens.

Enforceable Characteristic of a contract which determines that courts can order performance of the contract.

Equal Credit Opportunity Act Regulation B of the Federal Reserve Board; outlines procedures lenders must follow in judging mortgage loan applicants and avoiding discrimination with respect to marital status, sex, age, race, color, religion (creed), national origin, or public assistance income or welfare support.

Equal Dignities Rule Rule stating that, since the Statute of Frauds requires contracts for the sale of real property to be in writing, so, too, should listing contracts, which grant the authority to act as agent in such transactions, be in writing.

Equitable Lien Lien declared by a court to prevent injustice, especially in situations not encompassed by common law precedent, statute, or civil code, such as vendors' and vendees' liens.

Equitable Mortgage Mortgage whose *intent* is to hypothecate real property to secure a loan.

Equitable Right of Redemption Legal common law right of a borrower to redeem property after a loan default and avoid foreclosure.

Equitable Title A person's right to obtain absolute ownership of property to which another has title under the law. A present right, created at the time of signing the sales agreement, which may ripen into ownership upon performance of conditions subsequent.

Equity Difference between a property's market value and the balance of any loans on the property.

Equity Buildup Method by which amortization, or paying off of principal of a loan, increases the investor's equity position, assuming property value does not decline.

Equity Kicker Real estate loan that, in addition to the interest rate, returns to the lender "a piece of the action," such as a percentage of the gross or net income, a portion of any resale or refinancing proceeds, or simply a share in the equity ownership of the project.

Escalation Clause Clause in a contract that allows the lender to raise the interest rate if the loan is assumed.

Escheat Transfer to the state, upon the passing of any required statutory period, of the property rights of one who dies with no heirs and with no last will and testament (intestate).

Escrow Legal instrument (deed or grant) deposited by the grantor (seller) with and held by a disinterested third party (escrowee) until the occurrence of a contingency or performance of a condition and then delivered by him or her to the grantee (buyer).

Escrow Agent, Escrow Holder, Escrow Officer, Escrowee A person, bank, title insurance company, or independent licensed and bonded escrow corporation.

Escrow, Closing In Arrangement whereby either or both purchaser and seller are not present to complete the title transfer process and a disinterested third party agent is hired and instructed to handle the closing and conclude the transaction.

Estate in Land Degree, nature, or extent of interest that a person has in the land or real estate or real property.

Estate Pur Autre Vie Conventional life estate measured by the life or lives other than that of the grantee.

Estate in Severalty Interest in property held by only one person to the exclusion or "severence" of all other persons.

Estoppel Certificate Statement from the real estate borrower which attests to the unpaid loan balance, the annual interest rate, and the date to which interest is current.

Excess Depreciation Depreciation taken via an accelerated method less straight-line depreciation.

Exclusive Agency Listing Listing for a set price, at a set commission percentage, for a specified time period, with only one broker, with the reservation that the owner may sell the property himself and pay no commission.

Exclusive Right to Sell Listing Listing for a set price, at a set commission percentage, for a specified time period, with only one broker, with *no* reservation that the owner himself or herself may sell the property to save paying the commission.

Executed Contract Contract that has been completed; all parties have fully performed their respective contractual obligations.

Execution The signing, sealing (if necessary), and delivering of the deed.

Executor Male person who has been

charged with the responsibility of carrying out the provisions of a will.

Executory Contract Contract that has not been completed; there still remains something to be done by one or more of the parties.

Executrix Female person who has been charged with the responsibility of carrying out the provisions of a will.

Exemption Set dollar amount allowed per taxpayer and for each of the taxpayer's dependents.

Expected Rate of Return Rate of return estimated by the investment productivity analysis.

Expense Ratio Ratio of operating expenses over effective gross income; used by lenders to check for underestimation of expenses.

Expressed Authority Authority given the agent by the principal either in writing, or orally, or by the conduct of the principal.

Factor Generally a commission merchant who usually sells personal property.

Fair Credit Opportunity Act Law giving an individual the right to examine (free of charge) a summary of the information on file with any credit reporting agency or bureau making reports on that individual.

Farmers Home Administration Federal government agency established to facilitate real estate lending in rural areas where the population does not exceed 10,000 persons, for people unable to secure credit elsewhere.

Favorable Exposure Aesthetic satisfactions and/or prestige value of a given location; one of three basic elements of the Ratcliff model.

Federal Home Loan Bank (FHLB) System Agency of the federal government created by Congress to regulate and supervise the savings and loan industry.

Federal Home Loan Mortgage Corporation Agency created by the Federal Home Loan Bank Board as a wholly owned subsidiary of the Federal Home Loan Bank System. Its primary purpose is to create a secondary mortgage market for lender members of the FHLB system to enable them to obtain conventional mortgage loans insured by private mortgage insurance.

Federal Housing Administration Agency created to insure mortgage loans against loss upon default and foreclosure.

Federal Land Bank System Federal agency established by Congress to make loans through the 500 federal land bank associations that own the 12 Federal Land Banks.

Federal National Mortgage Association Agency created by the Reconstruction Finance Corporation to give relief by buying FHA-insured and, since 1948, VA loans in the secondary mortgage market.

Fee Inheritable estate in real property.

Fee Simple Estate that has no limitations as to any particular class of heirs and is not subject to any restrictions other than the usual public and private land use restrictions.

Fee Simple Absolute Largest and most complete estate known to the law; contains the total "bundle of rights."

Fee Simple Determinable Fee simple qualified estate that *automatically reverts* to the grantor or the grantor's heirs upon the occurrence or nonoccurrence of a specified event.

Fee Simple Qualified Fee simple estate that can be terminated by the occurrence or nonoccurrence of some event specified in the written document creating the estate (also called *defeasible fee* or *base fee*).

Fee Simple Subject to a Condition Subsequent Fee simple qualified estate that *can* revert to the grantor or the grantor's heirs upon the occurrence or nonoccurrence of a specified event only if they *reenter* and exercise their *power of termination* or *right of entry for condition broken*.

Fee Simple Subject to an Executory Limitation Fee simple qualified estate that *automatically* passes to a *third person and that person's heirs* (not to the grantor or the grantor's heirs) upon the occurrence or nonoccurrence of a specified event.

Fee Tail Estate that, in England, abolished the conditional fee. It was created in 1285 by the Statute De Donis Conditionaibus; this estate never ripened to fee simple, and therefore its landed-gentry intent could not be foiled.

Feoffment Clump of earth handed by seller to buyer to symbolize the transfer of real property prior to the passing of the Statute of Frauds in 1677.

Fiduciary One charged with a relationship of particular trust and confidence, as between trustee and beneficiary, attorney and client, or principal and agent.

Finance Charge Total of certain costs incurred by the borrower in obtaining a real estate loan, such as loan origination fee, discount points, finder's fees, mortgage insurance, and credit life insurance.

Financial Management Rate of Return (FMRR) Specialized version of the adjusted or terminal-value rate of return.

Financial Risk Uncertainty of an investor's financial ability to meet debt service requirements.

Fiscal Policy Actions of the federal government with respect to the economy; fiscal policy includes the collection of funds by taxation and the spending of funds through the federal budget.

Fixed Expenses Expenses, such as property taxes and insurance, which change periodically but do not vary with occupancy.

Fixture Article that was once personal property but has been installed in or attached to real estate such that it is now regarded as part of the real estate.

Floor-to-Ceiling Loan Two-stage takeout loan: the "floor" amount is funded when the project is completed; the remainder of the loan, or "ceiling" amount, is funded when a given percentage (70 to 80 percent) of the project has been leased (rental achievement clause).

Foreclosure Action Judicial proceeding used by a lien holder to satisfy a debt through a forced sale of the property that has been offered as security for the debt of the property owner.

Foreclosure through Public Sale Foreclosure involving the sale of property to the highest bidder.

Fraudulent Misrepresentations Material statements made at a time when the agent knows the statements to be false and thus are clearly fraudulent, subjecting the real estate agent to civil, disciplinary, and possibly criminal actions against him or her.

Free and Clear Rate of Return Ratio of a property's net operating income over the price or property value; also called the *broker's net rate*.

Freehold Estates Interests in property for an indeterminable period of time or duration, "free" of a tenancy or lease.

Fructus Industriales Crops that are dependent on human effort or industry for their annual growth.

Fructus Naturales "Fruits of the soil by nature," which do not require annual planting and cultivation.

Fully Amortized Mortgage Type of loan whose payment schedule provides for the complete or total payment of the principal, or amount borrowed, during the term of the loan.

Functional Obsolescence Loss in value arising from decreased utility, inadequacy, superadequacy, or changes of taste in architectural style or design inherent in the structure itself.

General Lien Lien that encumbers all of a person's property, both real and personal; general liens include liens *in personam*, federal and state tax liens, and decedent's debt liens.

General Warranty Deed Deed that conveys present and after-acquired title and contains three present and three future covenants or warranties of title, with the warranties applying during and *before* the grantor's tenure of ownership.

Gift Grant to a private person, identical to a private grant, with the exception that no money or consideration is tendered by the purchaser.

Good Consideration Consideration that is love, affection, or friendship; also called *moral or meritorious consideration*.

Government National Mortgage Association (GNMA) Federal agency that subsidizes the financing of over 20 special assistance programs for military housing, low- and middle-income housing, housing for the elderly, and other housing programs that have little appeal to private investors because of poor borrowing credit, high mortgage risk locations, and/or the presence of adverse economic conditions.

Graduated Payment Mortgage Loan that provides for a divided amortization schedule with low monthly payments in early years and is aimed at making it possible for more consumers to qualify for the financing and ownership of a home. Also known as *flexible-payment mortgage*.

Grant Deed Deed used in California and other states in lieu of general or special warranty deeds; contains *only* the three present covenants applying *only* to the grantor's tenure of ownership.

Grantee Purchaser to whom a deed conveys title.

Granting Clause Operating words of a deed which manifest the intention of the grantor to convey title to the grantee, also known as *words of conveyance*.

Grantor Seller who conveys title by deed.

Gross Income Income from all sources, including wages, salaries, tips, dividends, interest, pensions, annuities, rents, royalties, business income, farm income, and gains upon sale or exchange of property.

Gross Rent Multiplier Ratio of sales prices or values over effective gross incomes which are representative of a given market and can be multiplied by income to obtain an estimate of value.

Ground Lease Lease that allows the developer control of the land with only a minimal financial commitment, paying rent rather than purchasing the property.

Guaranteed Trade-in Program Plan in which the broker agrees to offer the property for sale for a specified time period at the end of which, at the seller's option, the broker will purchase the property at a price less than the listed price by an amount equal to the commission plus estimated carrying and closing costs to be incurred by the broker.

Habendum One of the three major parts of a deed; defines the quantity of interest or the duration of ownership being conveyed to the grantee.

Heir One who acquires title to real property through descent.

Highest and Best Use Land use that is most likely to return the greatest net present value in income or amenities.

Holdback Final 5 to 10 percent of monies owed a contractor which is not paid until after the period for filing mechanic's liens has passed.

Holder in Due Course One who has taken a note, check, or bill of exchange in due course, before it is overdue, in good faith, for value, without knowledge that it has been previously dishonored, without notice of any defect at the time it was negotiated to him or her.

Homestead Legal life estate that provides for an exemption of a property, occupied by the surviving spouse, from attachment by the creditors of the deceased spouse or from forced sale of the property to satisfy the general debts of the deceased.

Hypothecation Pledge of property as security or collateral for a debt without delivery of title or possession of said property to the lender.

Implied Authority That authority which the agent reasonably needs to perform the expressed authority.

Improvements on the Land Structures, such as buildings, fences, and walls, which have been permanently affixed on a site for its use.

Improvements to the Land Include such things as curbs, sidewalks, streets, and utility lines, which have been added to make the land and structures more usable.

Income Approach Process of estimating the value of an income-producing property by capitalizing the annual net income expected to be produced by the property during its remaining useful life.

Incorporeal Legal term that refers to rights or relationships of real property.

Increasing and Decreasing Returns (Principle of) Principle according to which increasing the amounts of one or more factors of production will increase value up to a certain point, known as the "point of diminishing returns." Once this point is reached, any further increase in the factor(s) of production will have a negative effect.

Indenture Synonym for "deed"; originally indentures were made by tearing a sheepskin deed in half to provide both grantor and grantee with a copy of the deed instrument.

Independent Contractor One who agrees to perform work for an employer, but whose time and efforts are not regulated by the employer, who is responsible to the employer only for the results of the work, and who has no authority to deal with third parties for the employer.

Inflation Increase in the volume of money and credit without a comparable increase in productivity and/or output, resulting in a rise in the general level of prices.

Inheritable Fee Estate Freehold estate that may descend to one's heirs.

Innocent Misrepresentations Statements that are not known to be false but, in fact, are so and usually permit recision of the contract without liability against the real estate agent.

In Personam Legal term that pertains to suing for the monetary value of a thing rather than suing for the thing itself.

In Rem Legal term that pertains to suing for the thing itself rather than suing for its monetary value.

Installment Contract for Deed Financing technique employed to purchase real estate wherein the price plus interest are paid in installments with the seller or third-party trustee holding title until a set percentage of the price has been tendered. Also known as an *installment land sales contract or Land Contract for Deed.*

Installment Sale Treatment Arrangement by which, if no more than 30 percent of the sale price is paid in the year of sale and the seller carries back the remainder of the price, the seller may delay payment of tax on the gain by spreading tax payments over the installment period.

Instrument Formal legal document.

Intangible Term that refers to rights or relationships of personal property.

Integration Initial state of the life cycle of property value; its development stage.

Interest-Rate Risk Degree of uncertainty associated with the likelihood of changes in the future general level of interest rates and the impact such changes have on investment value.

Interim Financing Any and all types of real estate loans required during the time interval between "front-end" equity financing and long-term permanent financing; also used synonymously with *construction financing*.

Internal Rate of Return Rate of discount that equates the present value of negative cash flows of an investment with the positive cash flows of an investment, thereby reflecting the true or effective yield or rate of return of said investment.

Intestate Condition of one who dies without leaving a will and last testament.

Investor Person who either holds property for long-term investment purposes or uses property in a trade or business.

Involuntary Alienation Transfer of title whether the owner wishes it or not (against his or her will or volition) by operation of law or court action; includes partition action; quiet title action, foreclosure, declaratory relief action, execution or sheriff's sale, forfeiture, bankruptcy, marriage, escheat, eminent domain and condemnation, confiscation, equitable estoppel, probate, or estate sale.

Involuntary Liens Liens that arise out of the operation of the law, including common law, statutory, and equitable liens.

Inwood Factor Present value of an annuity factor.

Itemized Deductions Certain medical expenses, charitable contributions, interest expense, taxes, casualty losses, and other costs that may be itemized for deduction when figuring one's income tax.

Joint Tenancy Concurrent estate owned by two or more persons (excluding corporations) that confers ownership of the entire property, the right of survivorship, and an *equal* and *indivisible* portion to each person.

Joint Venture Pooling of resources in a specific business venture; joint ventures are treated as partnerships for tax purposes; also called a *one-shot-deal* partnership since there is no intent of a continuing relationship. If a developer does not own the required land, he or she may go in as a partner on the entire project with the owner of the land required.

Junior Lien Lien that is subordinate in right and claim to another lien.

Junior Mortgage Lien lower in priority than some other mortgage by virtue of date and time of recording or of a subordination clause.

Land The surface of the earth; the minerals, natural resources, and substances below the earth's surface; and the airspace, natural resources, and herbage above the earth's surface.

Land Contract for Deed Installment contract to purchase real estate in which the deed is to be delivered to the purchaser upon payment of all or a certain percentage of the purchase price.

Lease Contract that suspends the owner's (landlord's) rights of ownership during the term of the agreement in return for an income stream called "rent."

Leasehold Estates Interests in property for a determinable period of time or duration, as determined by and "not free" of a tenancy or lease, usually considered personal property.

Leasehold Mortgage Loan that is obtained for a building located on leased land.

Legacy Gift of money by will.

Legal Consideration Act or promise of one party bargained and exchanged for the act or promise of another party whereby each party is obligated to the other to do or not to do something not otherwise obligated to do or not to do; one of the four essentials of a valid contract.

Legal Life Estate Life estate created legally through the operation of law or statute (also known as *Marital Property*).

Legal Purpose One of the four essentials of a valid contract, holding that a contract's purpose and means of performance must not violate any laws or public policy.

Legal Title Technical title under the law, also called "naked title," usually held by a seller-vendor in an installment contract or by the trustee in a deed of trust lending arrangement.

Legatee Recipient of a gift of money by will.

Leverage of Capital Borrowing of other people's money by an investor (1) to raise or to increase (lever) the total amount of capital committed to an investment and (2) to increase (lever) the rate of return to equity.

License Right or privilege granted to an individual person giving permission to enter and use the land of another for a particular purpose.

Lien Encumbrance that gives the right to one person or legal entity to satisfy a debt, claim, or charge out of the property of another person or legal entity by selling the debtor's property.

Lien Theory Legal position that a mortgage is considered to create a charge against property and not to convey any title.

Life Estate Estate in real property that is not inheritable and is held for the duration of the life of some specified person.

Like-Kind Property All types of real (not personal) property; term applies to "tax-free" exchange deals.

Limited Agent Person who, as escrowee, cannot act as a mediator and is limited specifically to the duties prescribed in the escrow instructions.

Linked Establishments Related land uses as defined in the Ratcliff model.

Liquidated Damages Sum agreed upon by the parties to be full damages if default occurs.

Liquidity of Capital A measure of how quickly an investment can be converted into cash without a loss.

Lis Pendens Although technically not a lien, a *lis pendens* is a public notice, filed against specific real property, that an action at law is pending which may affect the title to the specific real property.

Listing Contract Employment agreement that establishes the agency relationship between the real estate agent and the principal, who is usually the owner of a property to be sold, leased, or exchanged.

Livery of Seisin From the French words meaning "to deliver legal possession," a term used to describe the symbolic transfer of real property prior to the passing of the Statute of Frauds in 1677.

Loan Discount Fee (Points) One-time interest charge paid by sellers and used to increase the lenders' yield on below-market-interest-rate, government-sponsored loans.

Loan Origination or Service Fee Fee paid by borrowers purportedly to cover the lender's administrative cost in processing the loan, but that merely increases the effective yield or rate of return earned on the loan.

Loan Servicing Activities of an investor's agent, which include collecting monthly principal, interest, taxes, and insurance payments for the secondary mortgage market investor; maintaining records for each loan; and handling any payment problems, even to the extent of handling a foreclosure.

Loan Underwriting Investigation, analysis, and determination of the risks involved in the making of a loan.

Loan-to-Value Ratio (LTVR) Percentage of a property's value that a lender can or may loan to a borrower.

Locational Risk Real estate investment risk associated with the physical location and economic location (*situs*) of a given investment property.

Low-Income-Allowance Deduction Deduction aimed at completely removing low-income people from the tax rolls.

Management Risk Extent to which an investment requires "care and feeding" over the investment holding period; also called *ownership burden* or *worry factors*.

Marginal Tax Bracket Rate of tax paid on the last dollar earned in a year.

Marital Property Any non-separately owned property acquired during marriage in community property states. In non–community property states, marital property may be acquired through dower, curtesy, or homestead rights.

Market Approach Process of estimating the value of property through the examination and comparison of actual sales of comparable properties.

Market Value Price at which a willing seller would sell and a willing buyer would buy, neither being under abnormal pressure; it is the highest price estimated in terms of money which a property will bring if exposed for sale in the open market, allowing a reasonable time to find a purchaser with knowledge of the property's use and capabilities for use.

Marketability of Capital Measure of how quickly an investment can be converted into cash regardless of any loss due to the conversion.

Maturity Date Ending date of a loan.

Mechanic's Lien Involuntary, statutory, specific lien against a property to satisfy a debt created by the work, labor, or service of a tradesman, laborer, or professional or by the purchase and delivery of materials and supplies to improve a parcel of real estate.

Menace Threat to commit duress or to inflict personal injury to the body or character of an individual to induce some certain behavior by the individual.

Merchantable or Marketable Title Title that is free of any major defects or clouds or color of title such that it is readily transferrable to a prudent purchaser and/or is quite capable of being pledged as collateral to a lender.

Mill Levy Real estate property tax rate, expressed in mills ($.001) and multiplied by a property's assessed value to calculate the property tax.

Misrepresentation Fraud that includes an unknowing or innocent misstatement of fact with no intention to deceive or injure the other party.

Mistake of Fact Error that misstates the conditions of a contract and, if curable and not caused by neglect of a legal duty or by ignorance of the law, causes a contract to be voidable.

Mistake of Law Error made with full knowledge of the facts but with ignorance of the legal effects of these facts.

Modification Improvement to or on a parcel of real estate.

Monetary Inflation Increase in prices caused by the Fed increasing the money supply and/or monetizing the federal debt.

Monetary Policy Actions of the Board of Governors of the Federal Reserve Bank to control, monitor, and change the supply and price of money and credit within the economy.

Monetization of the Debt Financing of deficit budgets by the sale of government securities to the Federal Reserve Bank, which "pays" for the securities with "new money" created by increasing the checking account balance of the Treasury Department at the Federal Reserve Bank.

Money Market The market for short-term borrowing and lending.

Moral Suasion Influence or persuasion powers the Fed has over bankers, politicians, economists, and consumers.

Mortgage Two-party hypothecation instrument that pledges property as security for a loan, thereby creating a lien or title interest against the property which must be foreclosed through court action.

Mortgage-Backed Securities Program Method of attracting capital to the mortgage market from institutional and individual investors by selling them securities backed or secured by blocks or pools of mortgage portfolios.

Mortgage Banker Mortgage company that (1) originates or underwrites mortgage loans with its own funds or, more likely, with a warehousing line of credit; (2) sells these loans in packages to secondary mortgage market investors; and (3) maintains a servicing arrangement for said investors.

Mortgage Broker Mortgage company that merely arranges (rather than originates) mortgage loans for a fee or commission by bringing together borrower and lender.

Mortgage Constant Ratio of annual debt service payments to the original mortgage loan amount; represents the percent per dollar borrowed that must be paid annually to the lender in order to both amortize the principal and pay the interest due.

Mortgage Disability Insurance Insurance that makes the mortgage payments while a borrower is physically disabled.

Mortgage Equity Method Means of calculating the so-called cash throwoff to equity as net operating income less debt service on the available mortgage; the cash throwoff to equity is capitalized to an equity value that, when added to the amount of the available mortgage, equals property value.

Mortgage Guarantee Mortgage Corporation The first private mortgage corporation; its purpose is to attract into the mortgage market investors who might not otherwise participate.

Mortgage Insurance Insurance that protects the lender against loss due to default and foreclosure.

Mortgage Life Insurance Insurance that pays off the mortgage balance upon death.

Mortgage-Out To borrow 100 percent of the costs to develop and build a real estate project.

Mortgage Warehouse Loan Short-term line of credit obtained by a mortgage banker and used to originate loans prior to their sale in the secondary mortgage market; such loans are the security or collateral for the warehouse loan prior to sale.

Mortgagee Lender in a mortgage loan transaction.

Mortgagee's Title Policy Title insurance policy that protects the lender from loss due to title problems or defects.

Mortgagor Borrower in a mortgage loan transaction.

Multiple-Listing Service Cooperative sales arrangement whereby brokers agree to pool their listings in a multiple list of a central listing bureau; when a broker works on the listing of another broker, he or she works as a subagent and the commission is shared when a sale is consummated.

Multiple-Nuclei Theory Theory of land-use development patterns that concludes that the automobile has allowed land uses to tend to develop around a variety of economic focal points and that the type of land-use patterns that evolve are a function of the type of land use contained in each economic focal point.

Multiplier The reciprocal of a rate.

Mutual Assent Also called the *meeting of the minds*, the *reality of consent, mutual consent*, or the *offer and acceptance*; exists when the parties to a contract agree on all the terms and conditions; one of the four essentials of a valid contract.

Mutual Mistake Mistake made by both parties to a contract and causing that contract to be void.

Mutual Mortgage Insurance FHA insurance premium of ½ percent (.005) of the annual loan balance paid by the borrower, collected by the lender, and paid to the FHA. This fund insures the lender against loss and provides enough funds for the full operation of the FHA.

National Association of Realtors® Oldest and largest trade organization in the real estate industry, formed in 1908.

National Flood Insurance Act Law requiring property owners in HUD-designated flood plains to obtain flood damage insurance on properties financed with loans obtained from federal agencies and federally insured or regulated lending institutions. Without such insurance the loans will not be made.

Nascent Title Title coming into being, as during foreclosure proceedings.

Negative Financial Leverage Borrowing at an interest rate greater than the overall rate, thereby decreasing the rate of return to equity.

Negligent Misrepresentations Statements believed to be true but made without reasonable grounds for such belief and, in fact, false and usually considered a form of deceit, with the real estate agent being liable for both a civil action for damages, initiated by the injured party, and a disciplinary action to suspend or revoke the agent's license, initiated by the state real estate commission.

Net Equity Reversion Projected resale price of a property less commissions, costs of sale, capital gains tax, and the mortgage loan balance at time of sale.

Net Listing Listing agreement in which a "net" price acceptable to the seller is specified, and the commission (if any) is the difference between the net price and the actual, or gross, price at which the broker is able to sell or lease the property.

Net Mortgage Relief Result of obtaining a property with no mortgage or a smaller mortgage debt while exchanging a property with a mortgage or a larger mortgage debt.

Net Operating Income (NOI) Effective gross income minus all expenses chargeable to the operation of the property.

Net Present Value (NPV) Difference between the present value of positive cash flows and the present value sum of the initial cash outlay and the negative cash flows, if any, projected to be incurred during the investment holding period.

Next of Kin Nearest relative as determined by law; acquires personal property through descent.

Nonliquidity Difficulty in quickly turning an investment into cash without a loss.

Nonownership States States in which no person owns oil and gas while it is still in the ground but each landowner has the exclusive right to drill on his or her property and to extract all oil and gas that may be drained from beneath this property or adjacent lands.

No-Recourse Clause Loan contract clause that effectively transfers the note or bond and mortgage without any further obligation on the part of the assignor.

Novation Kind of assignment involving the transfer of rights in property coupled with the release from obligation to the assignor, wherein the assignee's agreement to assume such obligations is accepted in discharge of the assignor's promises. A novation is, in effect, a substitution of parties resulting in a new contract.

Offer Proposal by one party (offeror) to act in a certain manner on the condition that the other party (offeree) act in a certain requested manner.

Open-End Mortgage Home loan that allows the borrower at any time to reborrow part or all of the equity buildup obtained by paying off or amortizing the loan.

Open Listing Listing for a set sale price, at a set commission percentage, for an unspecified time period, made with (open to) several brokers, each of whom has an equal opportunity to earn a commission with the reservation that, if the property owner sells the property, no one earns a commission; also called a *general, simple, pocket*, or *nonexclusive listing*.

Open Market Operations The buying of government securities by the Fed to inject money into the economy or the selling of government securities to eject money out of the economy.

Open Mortgage Mortgage that is due but not yet paid or, as with a construction loan, is not yet fully funded.

Operating Expenses Costs of maintaining the production of income by the property, usually varying with occupancy.

Option Right given by the owner (optionor) to another (optionee) to purchase or lease a property at a specific price within a set time, for which right a consideration is paid.

Option Listing Variation of the exclusive right to sell listing which gives the broker an option to purchase the property at the listed or some lower price.

Ordinary Income Salary, wages, commissions, tips,or profits one earns from gainful occupation; also includes interest, dividends, annuity, and pension payments that are not a return of capital, royalties, rents, and business or farm profits.

Ordinary Life Estate Conventional life estate measured by the life of the grantee.

Owner's Title Policy Title insurance policy that protects the purchaser from loss due to title problems or defects.

Ownership States States in which oil and gas can be absolutely owned as real property by a landowner, subject to the right of capture by adjacent landowners.

Package Mortgage Loan that includes personal property as security.

Parol Evidence Rule Rule that makes inadmissible all oral or other extrinsic (outside the contract) information or evidence that would change the terms, conditions, or wording of a written contract.

Partially Disclosed Principal Unidentified person who authorizes someone else to act in his or her behalf; however, the existence of the agency relationship is made known.

Participation or Trust Mortgage Arrangement in which two or more lenders pool funds to make a loan that is too large for any one lender to fund.

Partition Action Judicial proceeding in which a co-owner sues his or her other co-owner(s) in order to have his or her property interests severed or partitioned from the other co-owner(s).

Partnership Co-ownership of a business by two or more persons; the partnership itself does not receive income or pay taxes, but rather the partners individually receive the income and pay the taxes.

Passing of Papers or Day to Pass papers In Massachusetts, a closing or the day of closing is often referred to as passing of papers or day to pass papers.

Patent Acquisition of title to real property from the United States government.

Payback Period Number of years it will take for an investment proposal's cash flow to equity to totally return the original equity investment to the equity investor.

Percolating Waters Underground waters that are unconfined.

Permanent Financing A loan that is long-term and will usually carry very stiff penalties for payment prior to the maturity date or during a fairly lengthy period of at least the first 5 to 10 years of the loan.

Permanent Takeout Commitment Written contractual agreement that guarantees that the construction lender will be fully paid off upon completion of construction according to plans and specifications.

Perpetual Liens Liens that always take precedence over the recording of any other lien; property taxes and special assessments are types of perpetual liens.

Personal Property Anything that is not real property.

Physical Deterioration Loss in value due to wear and tear, decay, dry rot, cracks, encrustations, or structural defects.

Physical Life Time period estimated for a building to be in existence.

Piggyback Mortgage Type of mortgage used in residential financing, involving two lenders sharing a single loan so that the homeowner obtains a bigger loan.

PITI Principal, interest, taxes, and insurance payments made periodically, usually monthly, to the lender, who escrows the taxes and insurance amounts; also referred to as a *Budget Mortgage*.

Police Power Right of government to limit property rights, without compensation, in order to protect the health, welfare, safety, and morals of the public.

Positive Financial Leverage Borrowing at an interest rate that is lower than the overall rate, thereby increasing the rate of return to equity.

Potential Gross Income Income a property will produce with 100 percent occupancy at the market rent.

Power of Attorney Written instrument authorizing a person, the attorney-in-fact, to act as the agent of another to the extent indicated in the instrument.

Power of Termination See *Fee Simple Subject to a Condition Subsequent*.

Premises One of the three major parts of a deed; contains the terms and propositions upon which the transfer of title is to be made.

Premium Profit made from the sale of a package of mortgages.

Prepayment Penalty Clause in a note which provides for a penalty in the event of early payoff of the note.

Prescription Creation of an *easement* by a person who openly, visibly, notoriously, continually, and adversely uses part of another's land for the proper statutory period of time (not to be confused with the *acquisition of title* through adverse possession).

Present Value Discounted Cash-Flow Analysis Method of investment analysis that recognizes the time value of money.

Price Amount of money paid, offered, or asked in a sale.

Primary Mortgage Market Marketplace in which lenders deal face-to-face with mortgage borrowers in originating or underwriting loans, thereby serving as a direct source of mortgage funds.

Principal Employer of an agent.

Principle of Substitution The maximum value of a property tends to be set by the cost of acquiring an equally desirable and valuable substitute property, assuming no costly delay is encountered in making the substitution.

"Printing Press Effect" Inflation due to the creation of "new money" by monetization of the debt by the Fed.

Prior Appropriation Rights Doctrine stating that the person who first diverts water to his or her own use has the right to continue that use even if the person uses all the water available from the entire watercourse.

Private Grant Sale of real property between a purchaser and a buyer, with the purchaser paying a sales price for the property.

Private Mortgage Corporation A privately owned company created to buy and sell mortgages in the secondary mortgage market, adding yet another dimension of liquidity to this market.

Private Mortgage Insurance Non-government insurance that insures only the top 15 to 20 percent rather than all or 100 percent of a loan.

Procuring Cause Effective cause of a certain result. A broker is said to be the procuring cause of a sale when he or she is instrumental in securing the buyer. Required as a condition for earning a commission by a broker with an open listing.

Profit Personal right to remove soil or minerals from the land of another.

Profitability Index (PI) Benefit-cost ratio calculated by dividing the present value of all positive cash flows by the present value of all negative cash flows.

Progression Principle that among unlike properties, where a worse or less valuable property is in the minority the value of the worse property will be favorably affected by the properties of greater value.

Promissory Note (Bond) Legal instrument that creates and evidences the debt between borrower and lender and establishes an unconditional written promise of the borrower to repay the loan according to the stated terms.

Property Taxation Perpetual claim (lien) on real estate property for the collection of *ad valorem* (according to value) taxes that are used to pay for the costs of government administration and services.

Public Grant Gift of land by the United States government.

Puffing Praise of a property by the seller or his or her agent couched in more or less general terms. Such unwarranted praise does not constitute an illegal misrepresentation.

Purchase-Money Mortgage Type of mortgage used when a purchaser executes a promissory note and mortgage (deed of trust) in favor of the seller in lieu of cash or purchase money and the seller executes a deed to the purchaser.

Purchasing-Power Risk Uncertainty that the real or true value of an investment's dollar return will decline due to inflation.

Quiet Title Action Judicial proceeding used to clear a title from a disputed claim or color of title to make it marketable or insurable.

Quitclaim Deed Deed that does not imply that the grantor has good title or even any title at all; it conveys the grantor's present interest in the property, such that if he or she has title everything is conveyed and if he or she has no title nothing is conveyed.

Ratcliff Model A theoretical explanation of the locational basis of real estate values.

Real-Cost Inflation Increase in prices caused by the increased effort required to produce the same quantity and/or quality of a good or service.

Real Estate or Realty Tangible commodity or physical product consisting of land and improvements on and to the land.

Real Estate Appraiser One who estimates the value of real property for a fee.

Real Estate Boards Early trade organizations of the real estate brokerage business.

Real Estate Broker Intermediary who earns a fee or commission for negotiating sales, exchanges, and/or leases of real property between two or more parties.

Real Estate Deal Real estate loan that has the income from the property itself as the prime security.

Real Estate Investment Trust Specialized business trust that is exempt from federal corporate taxation if it distributes 90 percent or more of its income to its shareholders and meets a variety of other stipulations regarding its real estate and other investments portfolio.

Real Estate Salesperson Subagent of and working for a real estate broker.

Real Estate Settlement Procedures Act (RESPA) Congressional act that imposed requirements on lenders in regard to the closing of real estate transactions and other related matters involving real estate brokers.

Real Estate Transfer Tax State tax levied upon the sale of real estate, computed as a percentage of value or equity and used in some states to aid county assessors in their determination of property values for ad valorem taxation purposes.

Real Property Intangible interests, benefits, and rights inherent in the ownership of the tangible commodity or physical product of real estate or realty.

Real Property Manager Agent of a real property owner hired to maintain the physical features, investment, and income of the owner's real estate assets.

Realization Incurring of a profit or loss.

Realtor® Copyright trade name that can be used only by members of the National Association of Realtors®, formerly the National Association of Real Estate Boards.

Realty Tax Service Means of keeping a lender informed of property tax assessments and billings so that the lender can keep tax payments current in order to protect a mortgage lien claim.

Receipt and Option Contract Contract that is both a receipt by the broker for the earnest money he or she has collected from the purchaser and a contract granting the purchaser an option to buy the seller's property.

Recital Clause Clause in a deed that states all or part of the chain of title to show how the grantor had originally acquired title.

Recognition Acknowledgment of a profit or loss by the Internal Revenue Service for taxation purposes.

Redlining Designation by lenders and/or appraisers of certain neighborhoods as high-risk loan areas because of the racial or ethnic makeup, crime rate, and/or age of properties in the area.

Reg Z Federal Reserve Board regulation issued to implement the Truth In Lending Act and enforced by the Federal Trade Commission.

Regression Principle that among unlike properties, where a better or more valuable property is in the minority the value of the better property will be adversely affected by the properties of lower value.

Release Mutual agreement that all obligations of an unperformed executory contract may be made at any time.

Release Mechanism Arrangement that allows part of the secured property (such as one lot in a subdivision) to be removed from hypothecation under a blanket mortgage (covering more than one property).

Reliction Increase in land caused when water recedes permanently below the normal water level, also called *dereliction*.

Remainder Fee simple estate (absolute or qualified) conveyed to either a third person or the third person's heirs upon the death of the person specified in a life estate.

Replacement Cost Cost of construction, at current prices, of a building having utility equivalent to the building being appraised but built with modern construction materials and methods according to current standards, design, and layout.

Reproduction Cost Cost of construction, at current prices, of an exact duplicate or replica using the same materials, construction standards, design, layout, and quality of workmanship and embodying all the deficiencies, superadequacies, and obsolescence of the subject building.

Required Rate of Return Rate of return necessary to attract investment capital in a market of competitive investments.

Reserve, Impound, or Escrow Account Money accumulated and held by a lender from which the lender pays property taxes, hazard insurance, mortgage insurance, etc., when these liabilities fall due.

Reserve Requirement Requirement determining what percentage of bank deposits can be lent and what percentage must be held as a reserve.

Return "of" Investment Rate of return required to recover or recapture any capital loss projected for a property during the investment holding period.

Return "on" Investment Rate of return necessary to attract investment capital; the *Discount Rate*.

Reverse-Annuity Mortgage Loan arrangement that reverses the flow of payments from borrower-to-lender to lender-to-borrower, intended for retired people. Upon retirement the lender would agree to reverse the cash flow, in effect buying the homeowner's equity in the home and paying for it by sending a monthly check to the retiree.

Reversion Fee simple estate (absolute or qualified) conveyed to either the original grantor of a life estate or the grantor's heirs upon the death of the person specified in the life estate.

Reversion Factor Present value of a dollar factor.

Revocation Recall, nullification, or voiding of a particular power, authority, or thing previously granted.

Right of Capture Right of landowners to drill on their property and drain (capture) oil and gas from beneath the adjacent property.

Right of Entry for Condition Broken See *Fee Simple Subject to a Condition Subsequent*.

Right of Survivorship Right of a concurrent estate owner to automatically acquire the interest of a deceased concurrent estate owner.

Riparian Rights Equal rights of landowners to use the water of defined streams or watercourses upon which their lands border.

Rollover Mortgage Short-term real estate loan renegotiated every three to five years.

Running the Chain of Title Searching the recorded history of all documents affecting a title.

Salvage Value Price estimated to be received upon the building sale at the end of its life; is not depreciable.

Seal Impression made to attest to the signing of an instrument. Under the old common law, instruments under seal were enforceable without consideration. This is no longer true.

Second Mortgage Mortgage loan subordinate (second in line) to a first mortgage.

Secondary Morgage Market Marketplace in which investors deal through intermediaries in making mortgage investments, thereby serving as an indirect source of mortgage funds.

Sector Theory Theory of land-use development patterns which concludes that land uses tend to develop along transportation corridors in a pie shape, with those uses that can pay the highest price (high-income housing) developing along the most preferred transportation corridor.

Servient Tenement Interest held by the fee owner of land restricted by the rights of the holder of an easement.

Settlement of Title Completion of the title transfer process.

Shared-Equity Mortgage Loan arrangement wherein the lender would charge a below-market interest rate; the borrower in return would promise the lender part of any capital gain or profit realized when the home was sold.

Situs Economic location of a parcel of real estate.

Sole Proprietorship Ownership of an entire business by one person.

Special Agent Agent with limited authority to conduct a single transaction or a specified set of transactions for or on behalf of the principal.

Special Assessments Taxes levied on real property owners to pay for local improvements or services that benefit only particular parcels of real estate; levied as perpetual liens according to the benefit received and not according to value.

Special Warranty Deed Deed that conveys present and after-acquired title and contains fewer than the six usual present and future covenants or warranties of title; said warranties apply *only* to the grantor's tenure of ownership.

Specific Lien Lien that encumbers only a particular piece or pieces of a person's property; specific liens include judgment liens *in rem*, mortgages, deeds of trust, property taxes, special assessments, mechanics' liens, vendor's and vendee's liens, attachments, and surety bail bond liens.

Specific Performance Remedy for breach of contract in which the court orders the party in default to perform the contract according to its terms. It is an equitable remedy available only where damages are inadequate, as in the case of contracts for the sale of land, and only if adequate consideration is required to be paid by the contract.

Specific Performance Contract Type of contract that compels both parties to perform according to the specific terms and conditions of the contract.

Spreading Agreement Arrangement that spreads a mortgage lien over additional property or collateral.

Standard Personal Deduction A flat amount allowed individuals who do not itemize deductions on their tax returns.

Standby Takeout Commitments Loans usually paid off in a short period of time, typically made by short-term lenders. This type of loan is used when money is so tight that no lenders will make a permanent takeout commitment and when interest rates are high, and the developer thinks they will fall by the time construction is completed, but the developer needs a commitment in order to have the construction loan funded.

Statute of Frauds Law that holds that certain contracts are unenforceable unless they, or a note or memorandum thereof, are in writing and are signed by the party to be charged or by a duly authorized agent.

Statute of Limitations Law that sets a maximum time limit within which a lawsuit must be filed after either the contract is consummated or the reason for the lawsuit arises.

Statutory Dedication Gift to the public that results when a recorded map that expressly indicates dedicated areas, such as streets and parks, is approved by local governmental officials.

Statutory Lien Lien created or defined by a statute or civil code of law, such as a mechanic's lien, attachment, judgment, property tax, special assessment, federal or state tax lien, or decedent's debts lien.

Statutory Right of Redemption Right of a borrower under civil law in some states to redeem property *after* foreclosure.

Straight-Line Depreciation Calculation of annual depreciation as depreciable basis minus salvage value divided by useful life.

Strict Foreclosure Method of foreclosure that exists in Connecticut, Vermont, and to some extent Illinois.

Subagent Person appointed by an agent to perform some duty, in whole or in part, relating to his or her agency. A person employed by an agent to assist in transacting the affairs of the principal.

Subdivider One who legally separates land into parcels for disposition or development.

Subordination Agreement Clause in a mortgage or trust deed by which the lender relinquishes priority in a subsequent mortgage or trust deed. It benefits the borrower. Also, a clause in any security instrument providing that such a lien will be subordinate in priority to any specified existing or anticipated lien. It converts an original security instrument into a junior instrument.

Subordination Clause Clause in a mortgage or trust deed that reorders the priority of liens such that the mortgage or deed of trust first recorded becomes a junior lien.

Subrogation Substitution of another person in place of the creditor, to whose rights he or she succeeds in relation to the debt. The doctrine is used very often where one person agrees to stand surety for the performance of a contract by another person.

Substitution Principle of valuation that holds that a property is not worth any more than the cost of a comparable property with the same utility and desirability.

Surety Bail Bond Lien Lien created when a person arrested on criminal charges offers equity in real property as bail in lieu of cash or bonds. The bail is posted by professional bail bonds persons, who file notice of such actions in the proper public offices.

Syndicate Term used to describe multiple ownership of an investment; also may be any legal form of ownership.

Tacking Regarding adverse possession, practice whereby continuous occupancy for the required statutory period may involve more than a single occupancy by one adverse possessor, such that successive time periods of adverse possession are "tacked on" to one another to total the required time period.

Takeout Commitment Formal commitment by either a permanent or a standby lender to pay off (take out) a construction loan when a real estate project is "completed according to plans and specifications."

Takes Back The financing by a seller of a sale by a purchase-money mortgage or deed of trust; also called *owner will carry*.

Tangible Term that refers to things of personal property.

Tax Bracket Percentage paid in income taxes on the last dollar earned in a given year.

Tax-Deferred Exchange Transfer of like-kind properties for one another.

Tax Saving Amount of income taxes not paid because of tax shelters.

Tax Shelter Amount of write-off against income allowed by the Internal Revenue Service.

Taxable Income Adjusted gross income minus deductions and exemptions.

Tenancy in Common Concurrent estate that confers indivisible interests (that need not be equal) in the entire property without the right of survivorship.

Tenancy by the Entirety Concurrent estate based on the concept that husband and wife are one person, or entirety, and that collectively as spouses they own the *entire* property interest, which neither as an *individual* owns separately.

Tenancy from Period to Period Leasehold with a definite rental period but no definite termination date; proper notice, as required by state law, must be given in order to terminate such an agreement (also called a *periodic tenancy*).

Tenancy at Sufferance Leasehold that arises when a tenant holds over beyond the termination of a lease; the landlord has a choice of eviction of the tenant or renewal of the lease.

Tenancy at Will Leasehold for an indefinite time period that is terminable at the will of either party.

Tenancy for Years Leasehold, for a definite period of time, which automatically terminates at the end of the stated time period (also called *estate for years*).

Tenure A medieval property interest whereby one did not own land but rather *held* it of the king; the word *tenure* is derived from the Latin "to hold."

Term Mortgage Mortgage that matures at the end of a term, with the total loan amount due and payable. Also known as *straight mortgage* and *nonamortized mortgage loan*.

Testate Condition of one who dies leaving a will and last testament.

Testator *Male* person who has made a will or last will and testament.

Testatrix *Female* person who has made a will or last will and testament.

Testimonium One of the three major parts of the deed; includes the covenants of warranty (if any), the execution, and the acknowledgment.

Thin Market Market in which there are few buyers and sellers and slow turnover, resulting in difficulty in obtaining comparable sales and in determining prices that are not highly vulnerable to change if just a few more buyers and/or sellers enter the market.

Third Party Person an agent deals with for a principal.

Time-is-of-the-Essence Clause Contract clause meaning that if closing does not take place on the designated date, the party causing the delay is in default and is usually subject to a monetary adjustment to compensate for the delay.

Time Value of Money Concept that holds that a dollar received today (in the present) has *more value* than a dollar received tomorrow (in the future); or conversely, a dollar received tomorrow (in the future) has *less value* than a dollar received today (in the present).

Title *Legal concept* that confers the rights of ownership.

Title by Accession Right of a property owner to any increase in property he or she owns caused by nature or by human actions.

Title by Descent or Succession Distribution of a decedent's property by descent, through an action called "intestate succession," when the decedent leaves no will; this is according to provisions of state statutes called "statutes of descent and distribution."

Title by Occupancy Adverse possession, prescription, and abandonment.

Title by Transfer Conveyance of title from one person to another, either by acts of the parties or by operation of law.

Title Insurance Contract that guarantees title and indemnifies the insured (subject to certain exceptions) against financial loss resulting from claims arising out of defects in title to real property which were existent but undisclosed at the time the policy was issued.

Title Theory Legal position in which a lender is deemed to hold legal title to property conveyed by the mortgage, subject to defeat by payment of the debt by the borrower, who holds equitable title.

Torrens System System of real property title registration used to verify the ownership and establish the status of title without the necessity of recurrent title searches and/or title insurance premiums.

Tort A private or civil wrong, not arising out of contract. Torts may be deliberate or negligent. Torts are actionable only if damage to specific individuals results from the wrongful acts.

Trade Fixtures Articles added to real estate by a tenant which are necessary for the conduct of the tenant's business, trade, or manufacturing.

Trading on the Equity Financial device of using other people's money to increase the rate of return on the investor's equity position.

Trespass Use of another's land without permission.

Trustee Disinterested third party (public or private) who holds and usually records legal title of hypothecated property for the benefit and protection of a lender in a deed of trust loan transaction.

Trustor Borrower in a deed of trust loan transaction.

Truth In Lending Act (TIL) Title I of the National Consumer Credit Protection Act, which makes lenders responsible to disclose to certain consumer borrowers certain information regarding the financing of real property.

Under and Subject Clause Clause in a deed

that contains any deed restrictions or restrictive covenants created by a previous grantor or developer.

Undisclosed Principal Unidentified person who authorizes someone else to act on his or her behalf. The existence of the agency relationship is *not* made known to third persons; hence the agent appears to be working for himself or herself.

Undue Influence Use of a confidential fiduciary relationship or a position of authority to induce some behavior by the other party to the relationship.

Unenforceable Contract Contract that was valid when made but cannot be proved or, for some legal reason, cannot be enforced by the court.

Unfavorable Exposure Objectionable, inharmonious, or incompatible conditions of a given location; one of three basic elements of the Ratcliff model.

Uniform Consumer Credit Code (UCCC) Law that makes lenders responsible for certain disclosures similar to those required by Reg Z of the Truth In Lending Act.

Uniform Settlement Statement Settlement sheet required by the Real Estate Settlement Procedures Act.

Unilateral Contract Contract whereby the promise of one party is given to another party to induce that person to act.

Units of Comparison Measurements such as price per square foot or per acre, used to account for differences in size between a certain property and comparable properties.

Useful Life Time period over which an asset may reasonably be expected to be useful to the taxpayer in trade or business or in the production of income and to earn any rate of return.

Usury Act of charging any interest rate above the maximum rate of interest that can legally be charged to a borrower.

Valid Contract Contract that contains the four essential elements and is without defects, is legally sufficient and authorized by law, and therefore is legally binding and enforceable in court.

Valuable Consideration Consideration that is money, property, or a right or benefit with value.

Value Quantity of one thing which can be obtained in exchange for another thing; the ratio of exchange of one commodity for another commodity.

Variable-Rate Mortgage Loan whose interest rate is tied to some market index, such as the prime rate or the rate of long-term government bonds.

Vendee's Lien An involuntary, equitable, specific lien filed by a buyer against a seller in default.

Vendor's Lien Involuntary, equitable, specific lien filed by a seller against a buyer in default.

Vested Remainderman Person known ("choate"), at the time a life estate is granted, to be the recipient of the remainder.

Veterans Administration Loan Program Government program created to guarantee loans against loss upon default and foreclosure.

Void Contract Contract that lacks one or more of the four essential elements and therefore is *not* legally binding and enforceable in court.

Voidable Contract Contract that is valid and enforceable in court but can be made void and unenforceable at the option of one or more of the parties.

Voluntary Alienation Transfer of title by private grant or sale, public grant, or gift.

Voluntary Lien Lien that arises out of agreements made between two or more parties, such as a mortgage or deed of trust agreement; also called a *contractual lien*.

Walking Money Money borrowed in *excess* of 100 percent of the costs of developing and building a real estate project.

Waste Destruction, abuse, or improper use of property such that the value of the property is impaired.

Water Rights Title to water; in some states, title to water is appurtenant to and is transferred with the land, while in other states title to water must be transferred separately from the land.

Will A will or last will and testament is a gift (usually a written instrument) by which a person may dispose of his or her property to others *upon and only upon* death.

Will, Formally Witnessed Will that is a written legal instrument drawn by a lawyer and signed by the testator and one or more witnesses in the presence of one another.

Will, Holographic Will that is totally written, dated, and signed in the handwriting of the testator *without* the presence or signatures of witnesses.

Will, Noncupative *Oral* will made by a person wounded in the armed forces or injured in an accident and in a state of the contemplation of death. Such wills can convey personal property only up to a certain value and must be made in the presence of witnesses, one of whom must reduce the will to writing and offer it to probate court within a stated time period (usually six months).

Wrap-Around Mortgage Loan subordinate to but acknowledging and encompassing one or more senior loans, such that the wrap-around lender makes the payments on the senior liens out of the payments received on the wrap-around loan.

Writ of Execution Court order that directs the sheriff or other proper public official to seize and sell the property of a judgment debtor to satisfy the payment of the judgment lien.

Yield Effective or actual rate of return earned on an investment.

Index